Norma Ims
202 F Roosevelt

D1609035

Basic Foods

Basic Foods

SECOND EDITION

JUNE C. GATES

Western Washington University

Holt, Rinehart and Winston

New York   Chicago   San Francisco   Dallas
Montreal   Toronto   London   Sydney

The professional career of June C. Gates has combined teaching and research in the areas of foods and nutrition. She has served on the faculties of San Jose State University, West Valley Community College, and other colleges, in addition to working on research and development projects for several food industries.

Mrs. Gates holds Master and Doctor of Public Health degrees in Public Health Nutrition, and Bachelor and Master of Science degrees in Nutritional Science—all from the University of California at Berkeley. As a registered dietitian, she is a member of the American Dietetic Association and served for four years as an officer in the San Jose–Peninsula District of the California Dietetic Association. Her other professional memberships include the honor societies Omicron Nu and Iota Sigma Pi.

Library of Congress Cataloging in Publication Data

Gates, June C, date
  Basic Foods.

  Includes bibliographical references and index.
  1. Food 2. Nutrition. 3. Cookery.
I. Title.
TX353.G33 1981   641.3   80-26409
ISBN 0-03-049846-5

PRINTED IN THE UNITED STATES OF AMERICA

Published simultaneously in Canada

  2 3 4   144   10 9 8 7 6 5 4 3 2

Project Editor:	Karen Mugler
Production Manager:	Lula Schwartz
Design Supervisor:	Renée Davis
Design:	Ben Kann
Illustrator:	Vernon Koski
Cover design and photography:	Ben Kann

Preface

This second edition of *Basic Foods*, like its predecessor, is intended for beginning foods classes. My years of study and experience in nutritional science and public health nutrition have resulted in the basic philosophy of this text, which emphasizes nutrition in food preparation. Food science and nutrition are often regarded as two different disciplines. In this text I have attempted to produce a compatible marriage between them. The practical application of theories and concepts of nutrition and food preparation have been thoroughly tested with my students and family, as well as in the laboratory.

It is important today, when food, money, time, and often good health as well are at a premium, to learn to conserve these precious commodities. Human nature is such that it tends to be unwilling to change, regardless of the clear dangers of staying the same. We tend to follow the old ways in food preparation even though the result may be a food that is high in calories, low in nutrients, expensive, and time-consuming to make. This text supplies the long-accepted methods of preparing food, pinpoints their deficiencies, and suggests ways of overcoming these deficiencies. It shows the student how to choose and prepare foods quickly, how to reduce calories, cholesterol, or fat, how to increase nutrient retention, and how to save money.

Time is a resource in short supply for many people, a circumstance that helps make convenience foods popular. If students are not taught to work efficiently in preparing foods, they will naturally choose to use convenience foods over their own food preparation at home. Such a choice may yield less nutrition for the food dollar than preparing foods on one's own. If students learn to produce satisfactory products quickly, they are more likely to make wise choices.

Although many convenience foods are more expensive than their homemade counterparts, such is not always the case. The text explains the costs of foods in their various forms and directs the student in cost comparison. Lack of space has limited comparisons between convenience foods and their counterparts prepared from basic ingredients, but many exercises that give the student experience in this kind of comparison are included in the second edition of *Basic Foods: A Laboratory Manual for Food Preparation*. In addition, exercises in the laboratory manual provide opportunities for utilizing nutrient labeling in comparing products. Because food costs have increased in proportion to limited incomes, it is exceedingly important for every person preparing food to learn how to spend food dollars wisely to get the maximum nutrition and satisfaction.

Sadly, many of us put too much emphasis on the gustatory delights of rich foods. In our mechanized and sedentary society, where physical labor is the exception rather than the rule, we still follow food consumption patterns common in the days when work lasted from dawn to dusk. No wonder, then, that obesity is now a major health problem in the United States. There is a great need to apply our knowledge of nutrition to preparing our foods. If we are indeed to reduce fat consumption in the United States, we must not continue to teach our students to prepare foods loaded with fat in the traditional way. The text provides many alternatives to foods with a large amount of saturated fat or cholesterol, such as substituting nonfat milk for whole milk or cream and using herbs and low-fat seasonings to replace cream sauces and butter commonly used for vegetables. It should be noted that chapters on candy and other traditional desserts contain important concepts of food chemistry as well as tips on nutritional enrichment.

Chapter 1 takes up the subject of nutrition for

two reasons. Some schools present nutrition and food preparation within the framework of a single course, particularly for students with minors in nutrition and foods. The overview of nutrition presented here gives such students the background they need. Chapter 1 also sets the tone for the rest of the text by emphasizing nutrient retention in preparing foods and the importance of choosing and preparing foods that provide the best possible nutrition.

This second edition of the text includes two new chapters—one on food foams and the other on plant proteins. Much of the information in these two chapters was drawn from various chapters in the first edition, but combining these sections gives coherence and emphasis to their subject matter. The chapter on food foams stresses the chemical and physical properties that various foams have in common. In line with the growing emphasis on increased intake of plant proteins and a reduced intake of meat, the chapter on plant proteins discusses the various sources of these proteins and their preparation.

Meal planning and preparation, difficult subjects to teach, are explored in Chapter 32, which presents organized steps to follow, from initial planning to final evaluation of the meal.

Some areas of food preparation demand a knowledge of chemistry and physics. This text presents the needed background information in these areas for students who have little or no scientific training. Acidity and alkalinity, leavenings, saturated and unsaturated fatty acids, and many other concepts are presented in simple terms to enable the student to make use of them in preparing food.

The text contains sufficient material for a full one-year course. It is also adaptable for shorter courses if chapters or parts of chapters are omitted, with the additional information available for the student to pursue independently. Using a complete text such as this one allows the course content to be adapted to the needs of both student and instructor.

Recipes *per se* are not included in this text. Proportions of ingredients, however, are given along with explanations of how a varying ratio of ingredients affects the food product. The principles that underlie methods of food preparation are explained to enable the student to apply these principles independently in developing recipes for creative cookery.

Enrollment of male students in college foods classes has increased in recent years. This text consequently refrains both from using the feminine gender and from referring to the female homemaker. It is written without the implication that food preparation is a female domain.

Peparing food is, finally, both a science and an art. Mastery of the concepts and techniques of food preparation allows the production of foods that are nutritious and esthetically pleasing, both in palatability and in appearance. Producing such results remains the goal of this text.

Acknowledgment must be made of the generous help of many people in preparing both the first edition of *Basic Foods* and this revision. The following teachers read the manuscript and offered many useful suggestions: Mary A. Dickey of the University of North Carolina at Greensboro; Jacqueline Karch of Illinois State University; Joyce Kliewer of the University of Northern Colorado; Ralph Lane of the University of Kentucky; Florine Rasch of the University of North Alabama; and Clarice Shank of South Dakota State University. I would like to thank Olivia Gates for assistance with photography; the staff at Holt, Rinehart and Winston for advice, direction, and editing; the many food producers and manufacturers who contributed photographs; colleagues who provided advice and information; and, finally, my family, who once again put up with my neglect of them and our home while I was working on this revision.

J. C. G.

Contents

Appendix

Basic Foods

Nutrients in Foods

Nutrition is the science of food—its nutrients, or life-sustaining substances, and how the body uses these substances. The nutrients required by living organisms include water, protein, carbohydrates, fats, vitamins, and minerals.

Many people in the world today live to eat, when the emphasis should be on eating to live. As Figure 1.1 implies, people are made of the foods they eat; the nutrients obtained from foods are required for optimal development of the body and for maintaining its health. This chapter briefly discusses the known nutrients and how they are used in the body. Because food preparation is our primary concern, foods are emphasized throughout as sources of nutrients.

Protein
PROTEINS IN THE BODY

Every cell in the body contains protein. Many hormones and all enzymes and antibodies are made up of protein. Protein is necessary for bone and muscle formation and maintenance. The need for protein in the body is a need for amino acids, which are used for synthesizing body protein tissues.

Figure 1.1

We are what we eat. Foods supply the body with nutrients for growth and maintenance. A wide variety of foods from all the food groups supply the nutrients the body needs. *(Wheat Flour Institute)*

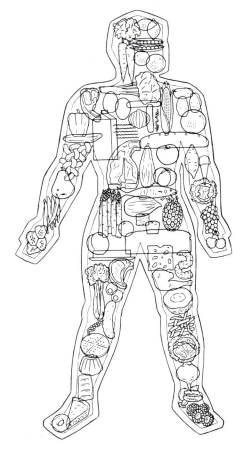

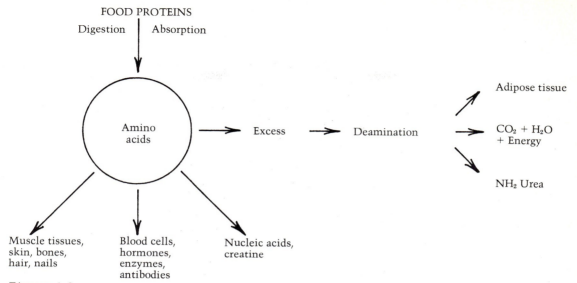

Figure 1.2

The body uses amino acids from foods for synthesizing body tissues; excess
protein intake becomes energy or is stored as body fat after deamination of
amino acids. The amino group removed by deamination is excreted as urea in
the urine. (*After George M. Briggs and Doris H. Calloway*, Bogert's Nutrition
and Physical Fitness [*Philadelphia: Saunders, 1979*])

Amino acids are the building blocks of protein. Twenty-two **AMINO ACIDS**
amino acids are common to foods and body tissues. When foods
are eaten, proteins are changed into amino acids in the process of
digestion. The amino acids are absorbed into the blood and are
carried to all the cells of the body, where synthesis, or formation,
of new body protein tissues occurs. Figure 1.2 diagrams how
amino acids function in the body. Amino acids that are not incorporated into body protein tissues are *deaminated*, that is, the
amino group NH_2 is removed, and the remaining organic acid is
converted into fat in the adipose tissues—the connective tissue
that contains stored fat—or is oxidized and used for energy.

Amino acids that can be synthesized from other amino acids
or from organic acids are called *nonessential amino acids*,
because they can be made in the body. Amino acids, that cannot
be made in the body are called *essential* amino acids. Food must
supply the nine essential amino acids. New protein tissues may
be synthesized in the body only when all the amino acids com-
posing that protein are present in the cell at the same time.

Amino acids are not stored in the body. If even one amino acid
is missing, the new protein tissue cannot be synthesized. A failure to synthesize protein would only happen in the case of a missing essential amino acid, for the body easily obtains the nonessential ones if protein and caloric intake are adequate.

COMPLETE AND INCOMPLETE PROTEINS

Some foods are better sources of essential amino acids than others. A food that contains all nine essential amino acids in amounts large enough to support the growth of animals is considered a complete protein food. If a food lacks, or is deficient in, one or more of the essential amino acids, so that it is incapable of supporting growth, it is considered an incomplete protein. Animal foods, including meats, milk, and eggs, are the main sources of complete proteins. In some cultures insects, rodents, and reptiles are used as sources of complete proteins.

Plants are the primary source of incomplete proteins in the human diet. Incomplete proteins vary in protein quality. Some plant foods, such as soybeans and peanuts, come very close to being complete proteins, while others, such as grains, other nuts, legumes, and gelatin, are not nearly adequate. The amino acids that are deficient or lacking altogether in plant proteins are described as *limiting amino acids* because these amino acids limit the food as a source of complete protein.

SUPPLEMENTARY PROTEINS

Animal proteins, which are expensive to produce, are very scarce in some parts of the world. As the world population continues to increase, people will very likely have to depend more on plant sources of protein than they now do. To rely on plant protein means that incomplete protein foods with limiting amino acids must be supplemented to make them complete. Table 1.1 lists some plant sources of protein and their limiting amino acids. The cereal proteins, which are low in lysine, are a good source of the amino acids tryptophan and methionine. Legume proteins are low in methionine and tryptophan but are good sources of the amino acid lysine. Consumed together, cereal proteins and legume proteins supply each other's limiting amino acids.

Animal proteins are good sources of the amino acids that plant proteins lack and thus can also supplement incomplete proteins. Drinking or combining milk with cereals and bread; filling sandwiches with meat, cheese, or egg spreads; and adding meat and

Table 1.1   Some common plant proteins, their most limiting and more abundant amino acids

Food source of incomplete protein	Limiting amino acids	Amino acids in good supply
Wheat, oats, rice, rye	Lysine	Methionine, tryptophan
Soybeans, legumes	Methionine, tryptophan	Lysine, threonine
Sesame, sunflower seeds	Lysine	Methionine, tryptophan
Peanuts	Lysine, methionine	Tryptophan
Gelatin	Tryptophan	
Corn	Tryptophan, lysine	Methionine

Table 1.2   Protein content of some common food sources of protein, for 100-gram amounts and for average servings

Food sources of protein	100 grams		Kilocalories per gram protein	Usual serving		
	Protein (grams)	Kilocalories		Amount	Protein (grams)	Kilocalories
Beef round, broiled	28.6	261	9.1	3 ounces	24.3	222
Ground beef, cooked	27.4	219	8.0	3 ounces	23.3	186
Bread, whole wheat	10.5	243	23.1	1 slice	2.6	61
Egg, boiled	12.9	163	12.6	1 large	6.5	82
Milk, nonfat	3.6	36	10.0	1 cup (8 fl oz)	8.8	88
Peanuts, roasted	26.0	585	22.5	½ cup	18.7	421
Redbeans, cooked	7.8	118	15.1	1 cup	14.4	218
Soybeans, cooked	11.0	130	11.8	1 cup	19.8	234

SOURCE: U.S. Department of Agriculture, *Composition of Foods,* Agriculture Handbook No. 8, by Bernice K. Watts and Annabel L. Merrill (Washington, D.C.: Government Printing Office, 1975); U.S. Department of Agriculture, *Nutritive Value of American Foods in Common Units,* Agriculture Handbook No. 456, by Catherine F. Adams (Washington, D.C.: Government Printing Office, 1975).

cheese to grains, pastas, and legumes are all examples of how animal proteins can supplement incomplete plant proteins.

To supplement incomplete proteins, however, the food furnishing the limiting amino acid must be eaten at the same meal with the incomplete protein. All the amino acids must be available simultaneously in the cells for protein synthesis to occur.

Textured Vegetable Proteins   Textured vegetable proteins are made from soybeans; they are equivalent to soybeans in protein content and are, therefore, incomplete proteins. This soybean product has been promoted as a meat extender, but it should not be depended upon exclusively as a replacement for meat or other proteins. Animal proteins are sources of vitamin B_{12}, zinc, and chromium. Plant foods lack this vitamin and are very low in these minerals. To rely only on plant proteins can sometimes result in deficiencies of these three nutrients, and possibly others, after a period of time.

About 0.8 gram of protein per kilogram of body weight, or 0.36 gram per pound of body weight, is needed by adults for the best possible health; growing children need more. An adult male weighing 150 pounds requires about 54 grams of protein daily; an adult female weighing 125 pounds needs about 45 grams.

PROTEIN REQUIREMENTS

Food sources of protein are not composed solely of protein; they contain water, fat, and sometimes carbohydrates as well. Thus, foods vary in their protein content. Table 1.2 lists the protein content of common food sources of proteins. For purposes of comparison, the food is analyzed in portions of 100 grams. As can be seen in Table 1.2 the 54 grams of protein needed by the adult male can be obtained from one egg, two slices of bread, 2 cups of milk, and 2.7 ounces of cooked round steak (about 4 ounces raw). Table 1.2 also lists the kilocalories per gram of protein in the various foods.

PROTEIN DEFICIENCY Most Americans consume ample amounts of protein, except in cases of extreme poverty or an inadequate vegetarian diet. Recent research indicates that a child who obtains insufficient protein during fetal life and the first year after birth is not only likely to experience retarded growth but also may have a reduced number of brain cells and, consequently, impaired mental capacity and development. Low protein intake during pregnancy is associated with such complications of pregnancy as eclampsia and toxemia and endangers the mother as well as the infant.

Severe protein deficiency in adults can cause malabsorption of foods, diarrhea, liver failure, wasting of muscle tissues, and edema or fluid retention. In children, severe protein deficiency causes the disease known as *kwashiorkor*. Extremely large intakes of protein, on the other hand, are not harmful, but neither are they of any particular benefit.

Fat in Nutrition Fats furnish energy and are desirable in foods for the flavor and richness they impart. Most Americans, however, probably consume too much fat, and the wrong kinds as well.

COMPOSITION OF FATS Most of the fat in food occurs as triglycerides, with small amounts of di- and monoglycerides as well as some sterols. A *glyceride* is made up of glycerol, which is the same as glycerin, and fatty acids. A triglyceride contains three fatty acids attached to glycerol, whereas di- and monoglycerides have, respectively, only two and one fatty acid attached to glycerol.

Fatty Acids A *fatty acid* is a chain of carbon atoms to which hydrogen atoms are attached. The chains may have as few as two or as many as 26 carbons in fatty acids that occur in foods. Except for the first and last carbons in the chain, each carbon can attach a maximum of two hydrogens. If each carbon in a chain has two hydrogens attached, the fatty acid they compose is *saturated*, because it contains all the hydrogen it is capable of carrying. However, if two adjacent carbons in a chain have only one hydrogen atom apiece, a double bond forms between them, making the fatty acid *unsaturated* because it is capable of adding more hydrogen. If a fatty acid contains more than one double bond, it is *polyunsaturated;* "poly" means many.

Essential and Nonessential Fatty Acids Polyunsaturated fatty acids are considered the essential fatty acids because the human body cannot synthesize them. Saturated fatty acids and fatty acids with only one double bond are nonessential fatty acids because they can be synthesized in the body.

Oils from plants, with the exception of coconut, olive, peanut, and palm oils, are the best sources of essential fatty acids. Fats from animal sources contain mostly nonessential fatty acids. It seems a paradox that meats, cheese, and eggs lack essential fatty acids when they supply the best available protein. In fact, the high content of saturated fatty acids in foods from animal sources has been used as an argument for vegetarianism. However, it is possible to consume animal protein with a minimal intake of animal fat if the following suggestions are heeded:

1. Choose lean cuts of meat, such as round instead of rib.
2. Consume more chicken, fish, and turkey than red meat.
3. Trim all visible fat from meats, including chicken and chicken skin.
4. Do not buy turkeys or other meats that contain added fat.
5. Substitute nonfat milk for full-fat or low-fat milk.
6. Eliminate or reduce intake of cream, butter, sour cream, rich ice cream, and cream substitutes made with coconut oil.
7. Eliminate or reduce intake of bacon, sausage, sandwich meats, wieners, and other similar meats of high fat content.
8. Use oils and polyunsaturated margarines for cooking and table fat.
9. Do not use fats rendered from meat for cooking; discard them.

FUNCTION OF FAT

Fat adds flavor to a diet and satisfies the appetite. Because fats are more slowly digested than protein and carbohydrates, their presence in the digestive tract delays feelings of hunger.

Fats in the body have several functions. They carry fat-soluble vitamins; in adipose tissue they serve as a reserve fuel; and the outer layer of fat under the skin helps prevent loss of heat from the body. The most important bodily function of fat, however, is to provide a source of essential fatty acids. Infants on diets deficient in essential fatty acids may fail to grow and also may develop skin eczema. Essential fatty acids seem to be necessary in mobilizing cholesterol and preventing it from being deposited in the arteries, a condition known as *atherosclerosis.*

LIPIDS

Lipid is a general term that includes glycerides as well as such other kinds of fatty substances as cholesterol, phospholipids, lecithoproteins, and prostaglandins. All these fatty substances have important functions in the body. *Cholesterol* is needed to synthesize vitamin D in the skin when it is exposed to ultraviolet rays from the sun and to synthesize adrenal and sex hormones and bile acids. *Prostaglandins* help regulate gastric secretion, pancreatic function, release of pituitary hormones, and smooth muscle metabolism. *Lecithin,* a phospholipid, is an excellent emulsifier. Fat is also a very important structural part of cell membranes, the sheath covering of many nerves, and blood vessels.

ATHEROSCLEROSIS   Atherosclerosis is a disease in which cholesterol and other substances accumulate inside the arteries, causing blood vessels to narrow and impeding the flow of blood. Narrowed arteries are more likely than healthy arteries to become blocked by blood clots. *Thrombosis,* the formation of a blood clot or *thrombus* that blocks an artery, can occur in the heart, brain, lungs, or legs. Atherosclerosis has been linked with high blood levels of cholesterol and triglycerides. A number of other health factors besides the intake of too much saturated fat and cholesterol are now associated with this disease, such as genetic tendencies, obesity, diabetes, smoking, sedentary life-style and lack of exercise, tension and pressures in day-to-day living, and high sugar intakes.

Many attempts have been made to reduce the incidence of atherosclerosis by educating people to increase their physical activity and exercise, to reduce their body weight to normal, to stop smoking, and so forth. Nutritionists have proposed reducing fat intake from 45 percent, the current level in this country, to 30 percent of a person's total caloric intake. They have also suggested that the intake of animal fats be reduced and polyunsaturated plant oils be substituted whenever possible. All these preventive steps are sound, and should be observed from birth through maturity. Good health habits developed at an early age are more likely to persist in adulthood.

Nutritionists have debated the wisdom of serving eggs, which are high in cholesterol, to infants, children, and people with low blood cholesterol levels. Some believe that egg yolks should be banned entirely; others take a more moderate view, recognizing that eggs are an excellent low-calorie source of important nutrients. One or two eggs a day is not excessive either for children during their growing years or for adults who appear to have no health problems to contraindicate their use.

This text emphasizes the preparation of foods with a minimum of fat and substitution of oils and polyunsaturated margarine for common animal fats.

MINERAL OIL   Mineral oil is not a food fat; it is a by-product of petroleum that resembles plant oils in appearance. It cannot be digested and is excreted unchanged in the feces. Because mineral oil is neither digested nor absorbed into the body, it has no caloric value and for this reason was formerly used in low-calorie salad dressings. Mineral oil is no longer permitted in commercial dressings, however, because it dissolves fat-soluble substances. In salad dressings, mineral oil picks up the fat-soluble carotene or vitamin A from foods in the digestive tract causing these vitamins to be excreted along with it in the feces. Mineral oil as a laxative has the same faults and should therefore be used for this purpose with moderation.

Carbohydrates are obtained in pure form from sugars, syrups, and starches. Food high in carbohydrates include cereals, baked products, legumes, fruits, vegetables, and nuts. These foods also contain cellulose and other nondigestible carbohydrates. Milk is the only source of the sugar lactose; however, lactose is added to many processed foods. Meat and eggs are devoid of carbohydrate, with the exception of a few shellfish and liver that contain glycogen, or animal starch.

Carbohydrates in Nutrition

The basic units of all carbohydrates are *monosaccharides,* or simple sugars. Two monosaccharides joined together form a *disaccharide;* many monosaccharides linked together form a *polysaccharide.* Mono- and disaccharides are often called *simple carbohydrates,* while polysaccharides are *complex carbohydrates;* these designations are related to the speed of digestion and absorption. The composition and sources of common food carbohydrates are shown in Table 1.3.

CARBOHYDRATE COMPOSITION

Table sugar and brown sugar are composed of sucrose. Sucrose is obtained commercially both from sugar beets and sugar cane; sugar from these sources is identical and can be used interchangeably. The differences in nutritional benefits are insignificant in all types of sugar. More vitamins and minerals are obtained from an apple than from 1 tablespoon of brown sugar or ½ cup of honey. Different kinds of sugar should be chosen for their flavor, not for their nutrient composition, which is negligible.

When food carbohydrates are eaten, monosaccharides are immediately absorbed; disaccharides and polysaccharides are digested into their component monosaccharides for absorption into the blood, which requires a slightly longer time. All kinds of

Table 1.3   Classification, composition, and sources of common food carbohydrates

Carbohydrate	Composition	Source
Monosaccharides		
Glucose (dextrose)		Corn syrup, honey, fruits
Fructose (levulose)		Honey, fruits
Galactose		Milk sugar
Disaccharides		
Maltose	Glucose + glucose	Corn syrup, malt
Sucrose	Glucose + fructose	Table sugar, honey, fruits
Lactose	Glucose + galactose	Milk sugar
Polysaccharides		
Starch	Glucose units	All plants
Cellulose	Glucose units	All plants
Glycogen	Glucose units	All living animals

starch are equally digestible, but some persons show variations in their ability to digest these and other food components.

FUNCTIONS OF CARBOHYDRATES The primary function of carbohydrate in the body is to supply energy. Glucose is the only source of energy used by the brain; muscles are able to use fatty acids as well as glucose for energy. Glucose is required for the complete oxidation of fats for energy. If the diet lacks carbohydrate, glucose can be formed from protein obtained from food or, in the case of starvation, from protein in body tissues, but it is preferable to provide sufficient carbohydrate in the diet. Sugars contribute sweetness to foods; both sugar and starch have specific functions in food preparation.

Nondigestible Carbohydrates Even though cellulose, like starch, is composed of glucose units, the body is unable to digest cellulose into monosaccharides because the glucose units of cellulose are linked together differently. Cellulose is thus excreted and has no caloric value. For many years, cellulose was thought to be unnecessary in the diet, but recent research has revealed that it and other nondigestible carbohydrates, such as lignin and pectin, are important sources of bulk or fiber. Diets high in fiber have long been recognized for their value in promoting normal and regular elimination, and now they also appear to be useful in the prevention and treatment of diseases of the digestive tract, such as diverticulosis, colitis, and hemorrhoids. The long-term use of high-fiber diets has been proposed as a way to prevent cancers of the colon and to reduce blood cholesterol levels.

Nondigestible carbohydrates have been variously called fiber, bulk, and roughage. The fibers, or threadlike substances, in fruits and vegetables are composed mostly of nondigestible carbohydrates. Besides being nondigestible, these carbohydrates absorb water and result in an increase in the volume or bulk of the stool (feces); hence the term *bulk*. The term *roughage*, which is not generally used today, was formerly used when fibrous foods were erroneously thought to irritate the gastrointestinal tract. *Fiber* is the more generally accepted term today.

Cooking neither increases nor decreases the nondigestible carbohydrate content of foods. Cooking does decrease the bulk of some vegetables so that a cup of raw spinach, for example, will equal about ¼ cup when cooked. This needs to be considered when comparing the content of nondigestible carbohydrate in cooked and raw foods. The peelings on fruits and vegetables usually have a higher content of nondigestible carbohydrates than does the interior of the food.

CARBOHYDRATE REQUIREMENTS No dietary requirement exists for carbohydrate. As a rule, nutritionists recommend that the diet contain a minimum of 60 to 100 grams. Because carbohydrate is the most economical form of energy, it is practical to choose first those foods that supply needed protein, vitamins, and minerals, and then select the balance of calories from high-carbohydrate foods, preferably from complex carbohydrates and vegetables to increase the nondigestible carbohydrate intake.

Many foods that supply carbohydrate, such as candy, cakes, soft drinks, and other sweets, are considered desirable by Americans, and the excessive intake of these high-carbohydrate, low-nutrient foods, commonly known as "empty calorie" foods, has become a real nutritional problem. Americans consume over 100 pounds of sugar per capita each year. Nutritionists would like to see this high sugar intake drastically reduced, because it has been implicated as a factor in dental caries as well as in heart disease. Carbohydrate is best obtained from foods that also supply vitamins and minerals—fruits, vegetables, and whole-grain or enriched cereal products.

CARBOHYDRATE INTOLERANCE

The body needs enzymes to digest disaccharides and starch. Persons who lack certain enzymes cannot digest carbohydrate for absorption into the blood, and the undigested disaccharide is then excreted. The presence of sugar causes water to be drawn into the intestines by osmosis, a process that equalizes concentrations of solute on either side of a semipermeable membrane. This added water in turn causes abdominal cramps and diarrhea.

A deficiency or lack of the enzyme lactase, which is required for the digestion of lactose, is the most common type of carbohydrate intolerance. Persons with no lactase must avoid milk in all forms, even milk added in baking and cooking. Most people with this deficiency, however, have enough of the enzyme to handle small amounts of milk, but cannot consume it in unlimited quantities. Those with some enzyme present can often tolerate cultured milk products, such as buttermilk, yogurt, sour cream, and cheeses, because much of the lactose in these foods has been converted into lactic acid or removed in the whey.

Energy in the Diet

Fats, carbohydrates, and proteins can all furnish energy for the body, but they differ in the amount they furnish. Table 1.4 shows the caloric values of these nutrients.

People who are obese, or overweight, have accumulated excess body fat, a condition that can lead to a number of health problems, including heart disease, diabetes, gall bladder disease, arthritis, lung disability, and a shortened life span. Such consequences of obesity place it near the top of public health problems in the United States, but all bad effects can be reversed if body weight is reduced to normal.

Obesity develops when the intake of calories exceeds the expenditure of calories, as depicted in Figure 1.3. Obesity in infants and children is often a result of faulty eating patterns, as

Table 1.4	Physiological values of fuel nutrients	
Fuel nutrient	Physiological fuel value	
	(kcal/g)	(kjoules/g)
Carbohydrate	4	17
Protein	4	17
Fat	9	38

well as possibly a lack of physical activity. Adult obesity often results from following the same eating patterns of younger and more active years; older adults need to adjust their food intake to their reduced activity, or better, increase their physical activity so that they can continue to eat the foods they enjoy.

SUGGESTIONS FOR REDUCING BODY WEIGHT

Regardless of when and how obesity begins, an overweight person must change his or her habits both in eating and activity to lose weight. This is not an easy task to accomplish. The food preparer, therefore, must be conscious of obesity as a potential or actual problem and take preventive measures by preparing foods that do not contribute excess calories. Such a program entails the reduction of fat and concentrated sugars in foods by decreasing the amounts of cream, table fat, fried foods, fatty meats, nuts, rich desserts, and such snacks as chips and crackers. People often do not realize that their choice of food contributes to their overweight state because they are not familiar with the caloric value of different foods.

Vitamins and Minerals

The animal organism seems to require about 14 vitamins and 20 minerals. Most of the nutrients needed by humans have probably been identified, but this is not known for a fact. Much has yet to be learned about these nutrients, the amounts needed, and their functions in the body.

Figure 1.3

Energy obtained from food should balance expenditure of energy for activities and body maintenance, if normal body weight is to be maintained. *(Wheat Flour Institute)*

Vitamins are organic compounds that must be obtained from food because they cannot be synthesized in the body. The body needs only very small amounts of vitamins, as can be seen from Table 10, Recommended Dietary Allowances, in the appendix. Vitamins, which have widely different functions in the body, are measured by weight in milligrams or micrograms. Some vitamins are present in such small amounts that they must be measured by a decimal fraction of a microgram; other vitamins occur in several active forms that differ in biological value. These vitamins are measured in International Units (I.U.). One I.U. of vitamin D equals 0.025 microgram; 400 I.U. equals 10 micrograms. One I.U. of vitamin A equals 0.344 microgram of vitamin A acetate, 0.300 microgram of vitamin A alcohol, or 0.60 microgram of beta carotene, which are the active forms of this vitamin.

Vitamin A activity eventually will be expressed as retinol equivalents (RE), based on the source of vitamin A activity. The term will not become widely used until the RE of foods is shown in food composition tables. One I.U. equals 1 milligram of synthetic vitamin E (DL-alpha-tocopherol acetate) and 1.36 I.U. of vitamin E equals 1 milligram of natural vitamin E (D-alpha-tocopherol acetate).

Minerals, or elements, are inorganic substances required in small amounts that also cannot be synthesized in the body but must be obtained from food. Some minerals are important constituents of bones; others are required to activate specific enzymes involved in chemical reactions, to maintain acid-base balance and water balance, and to promote normal nerve and muscle functioning. Table 1.5 lists all known vitamins and minerals, their functions in the body, their food sources, and their stability during food preparation.

Recommended Dietary Allowances

Recommended Dietary Allowances (RDA), determined by the Food and Nutrition Board of the National Academy of Sciences, are based on current research findings that establish the nutritional needs of humans, at various ages and for both sexes. The 1980 revised version of the RDA is included in Table 10 in the appendix. The levels of nutrients given in the RDA are those amounts considered adequate to meet the known nutritional needs of practically all healthy persons in the United States.

Dietary Goals for the United States

In 1977 the Senate Select Committee on Nutrition and Human Needs published their "Dietary Goals" with the aim of promoting better health and reducing heart disease. These recommendations encouraged Americans to reduce total caloric intake to maintain ideal body weight; to reduce total fat intake, especially saturated fat; to reduce sugar and salt intake; and to increase intake of vegetables, fruits, whole grains, legumes, low-fat milk products, poultry, and fish. Many nutritionists agree that these

Table 1.5   Vitamins and minerals needed in nutrition, their function in the body, their sources in foods, and their stability in food preparation

Nutrients	Functions	Best food sources	Stability
FAT-SOLUBLE VITAMINS			
Vitamin A activity	Promotes health of epithelial tissues, eyes, teeth	Liver, butter, cream, egg yolks, leafy green vegetables, deep yellow and orange fruits and vegetables	Easily oxidized
Vitamin D	Regulates absorption and utilization of calcium and phosphorus	Fish liver oils, fortified milks; very small amounts in egg yolks, butter, liver, salmon, sardines	Very stable
Vitamin E	Serves as an antioxidant in the body and in foods	Oils and germs of grains, green leafy vegetables, nuts, legumes	Oxidized in rancid fats; destroyed by ultraviolet light
Vitamin K	Required for synthesis of prothrombin needed in normal blood clotting	Leafy green vegetables, liver	Easily oxidized and destroyed by light
WATER-SOLUBLE VITAMINS			
Ascorbic acid (Vitamin C)	Required for formation of collagen in connective tissues; cell wall integrity	Citrus fruits, strawberries, tomatoes, cantaloupes, broccoli, cabbage, green peppers, leafy greens	Easily oxidized, destroyed by heat and by alkaline medium
Biotin	Required in enzyme systems involving carbon dioxide	Liver, yeast, cauliflower, nuts, chocolate, legumes	Easily oxidized, destroyed by alkaline medium
Choline	Component of phospholipids, acetylcholine	Egg yolks, whole grains, legumes, wheat germ, meat, milk, vegetables	Stable
Folic acid	Required for blood cell formation, coenzyme for use of carbon and hydrogen	Liver, yeast, leafy green vegetables, legumes, whole grains, fruits and other vegetables	Destroyed by heat in acid medium; also destroyed by alkaline medium
Niacin	Coenzyme for tissue oxidations, hydrogen transport	Liver, lean meat, whole grains, nuts, yeast, legumes	Stable
Pantothenic acid	Component of coenzyme A, which metabolizes two carbon fragments, lipids	Liver, kidney, yeast, egg yolks, peanuts, whole grains, lean beef, nonfat milk, potatoes, tomatoes, broccoli, salmon	Destroyed by heat and by alkaline and acid media; stable in neutral media

Nutrients	Functions	Best food sources	Stability
Pyridoxine (Vitamin B_6)	Required for metabolism of amino acids and use of carbon dioxide, amino, and sulphur groups	Wheat germ, meat, liver, whole grains, peanuts, soybeans, corn	Destroyed by light and by heat
Riboflavin (Vitamin B_2)	Required for oxidation-reduction reactions in tissues	Liver, milk, cheese, eggs, leafy green vegetables, lean meat, whole grains, yeast	Destroyed by light and by heat in alkaline medium
Thiamin (Vitamin B_1)	A coenzyme required for energy production	Whole grains, legumes, nuts, liver, pork, leafy green vegetables	Destroyed by dry heat and by alkaline medium
Vitamin B_{12}	Required for red blood cell maturation, use of carbon	Liver, eggs, meat, milk, cheese	Destroyed by alkaline medium and by light

MINERALS

Nutrients	Functions	Best food sources	Stability
Calcium	Strengthens structure of bones and teeth; promotes clotting of blood, water balance, muscle contraction, nerve response	Milk, cheese, leafy green vegetables, clams, oysters, almonds, legumes, water	
Chlorine	Provides hydrochloric acid of gastric juice, acid-base balance, activity of muscles and nerves, water balance	Table salt, many foods, water	
Chromium	Required for metabolism of blood glucose, fatty acid synthesis, insulin metabolism	Corn oil, meat, whole grains	
Copper	Required for utilization of iron, enzymes in energy metabolism	Liver, shellfish, nuts, legumes, water	
Fluorine	Provides resistance to development of dental caries	Water, naturally occurring or fluoridated	
Iodine	Needed for synthesis of thyroxine hormone	Iodized table salt, water, variable amounts in foods	
Iron	Part of hemoglobin, carries oxygen in blood, oxidative enzymes	Liver, meat, oysters, leafy green vegetables, dried apricots, prunes, peaches, raisins, egg yolks, legumes, nuts, whole grains	

(continued)

Table 1.5   (continued)

Nutrients	Functions	Best food sources	Stability
Magnesium	Activates enzymes, temperature regulation, nerve and muscle activity, protein synthesis	Whole grains, legumes, nuts, leafy green vegetables, water	
Manganese	Required for enzyme activity, many metabolic functions	Whole grains, legumes, nuts, leafy green vegetables, meat	
Phosphorus	Aids structure of teeth and bones, acid-base balance, energy metabolism	Liver, meat, eggs, milk, cheese, nuts, legumes, whole grains, refined cereals	
Potassium	Promotes water balance, nerve and muscle activity	Meat, milk, leafy green vegetables, dates, bananas, cantaloupes, apricots, citrus fruits, bamboo shoots, prunes	
Selenium	Component of enzyme, glutathione peroxidase	Seafoods, meats, grains	
Sodium	Promotes acid-base balance, water balance, nerve and muscle activity	Table salt, leavenings, MSG, soy sauce, condiments, milk, cheese, eggs, meat, fish, water	
Sulfur	Component of protein, thiamin, and biotin; involved in oxidation-reduction reactions	Meat, eggs, milk, cheese, all foods containing protein	
Zinc	Constituent of hormone, insulin; promotes enzyme activity in metabolism	Oysters, liver, wheat germ, yeast, seafood, many foods	

Molybdenum, nickel, tin, vanadium, and silicon have roles in many animal organisms, but their need by humans has not yet been verified. Cobalt is part of the vitamin B_{12} molecule that cannot be synthesized in the human body; there is thus no need for this element.

recommendations offer sound guidelines for achieving good nutrition, and all of them are emphasized in this textbook.

Food Composition Tables   Many publications provide information about the nutrient content of common foods. The Department of Agriculture has two publications that are standards, Home and Garden Bulletin No. 72, *Nutritive Value of Foods*, which lists nutrients in average servings of food, and Agricultural Handbook No. 8, *Composition of Foods*, which lists nutrients for 100-gram amounts and for the edible portion of 1 pound as purchased. Knowledge of nutrients in 100-gram amounts of foods is helpful in comparing one food with another. Knowledge of the nutrient composition of 1 pound of food as purchased is useful for working with large quantities of food and for determining the refuse or waste that can be expected from various foods.

In these nutrient composition tables, the amounts of nutrients listed are average figures for a number of samples of each food, taken from different varieties and different parts of the country; because an equal portion of the same food can vary considerably in nutrient content. Food composition tables, however, do not account for lack of absorption or utilization of nutrients in the body. For instance, spinach, which contains a fair amount of calcium, also contains oxalic acid that binds the calcium and prevents its absorption. Phytic acid in the bran of cereal grains also binds calcium and some other minerals, thus limiting their absorption. Spinach and whole-grain cereals contain many other nutrients that make them worth including in the diet, but they cannot be depended upon for calcium, even though the food composition table lists it as a nutrient in these foods.

Food composition tables, furthermore, include only a few of the nutrients in foods. Thiamin, riboflavin, and niacin are no more important in the diet than folic acid, pyridoxine, and vitamin B_{12}, but the U.S.D.A. tables list only the first three vitamins, and not the last three. Thus, a diet selected according to these tables will be adequate in the first three vitamins but may not be in all of the last three.

Even though food composition tables cannot be considered exact sources of the amount of nutrients in foods, they do provide some guides as to the nutrient content of various foods. When better chemical methods are developed for nutrient analysis and more knowledge of nutrient utilization is gained, nutrient composition tables will become more reliable indicators of food content.

Nutrient Fortification of Foods

Three terms are used to indicate the addition of nutrients to foods. *Restoration* is the addition of a nutrient to replace that lost in processing so that the food contains the same level of the nutrient found in the unprocessed food. Such nutrient additions must be declared on the label. An example of restoration is the addition of ascorbic acid to dehydrated potatoes.

Enrichment is similar to restoration but entails compliance with precise federal guidelines for the amount and kinds of nutrients added to specific products. Flours and cereals are enriched; in fact, many are required to be enriched, and are so labeled.

Fortification refers to the addition of nutrients that do not naturally occur in the food. The addition of such nutrients is intended to prevent nutrient deficiencies. Examples are the forti-

Figure 1.4

Many foods have been enriched
or fortified with vitamins and
minerals. *(Wheat Flour
Institute)*

fication of salt with iodine and of milk with vitamin D, as shown
in Figure 1.4. When cream is removed from milk, the fat-soluble
vitamin A is also removed; nonfat milk may be restored by the
addition of the vitamin.

Manufactured Foods

Many years ago, oleomargarine was created as a substitute for
butter. Margarine and hydrogenated shortening, a substitute for
lard, were among the earliest of manufactured foods. Since that
time, a multitude of products have been created to replace natural
foods, for improved flavor or usability, longer storage life, reduced
cost, or replacement of a natural food that is difficult to procure.
In Hawaii, imitation milk is plentiful because real milk is less
available. Imitation sour cream, ice cream, and whipping cream
are less expensive than their natural counterparts, but the coconut oil used in most of these imitation products has more saturated fat than the butterfat it replaces, with no reduction in
calories.

Many manufactured foods are poor substitutes for the natural
food they attempt to replace. Imitation juices, whether powdered,
canned, or frozen, may contain as much or more vitamin C as the
real juice, but lack all the other vitamins and minerals found in
real juices. Many imitation products are high in sugar or water,
and if they contain natural juices at all, the amount is likely to be
small.

Meat analogs, known as imitation meat products, and textured vegetable protein are both soybean products. The quality of the protein in these products does not equal that of animal proteins, and they also lack some of the vitamins and minerals found in meats; thus they are best used as meat extenders rather than meat substitutes. Pregnant women and growing children should not depend on these products to provide an adequate intake of complete protein.

Nutrient Retention in Food Preparation

Much has been said about food as the source of nutrients, but the preparation of foods so that their nutrients are retained is just as important a process as proper food selection. Two main types of nutrient loss occur during food preparation: solution loss, in which nutrients dissolve from food, and destruction of nutrients.

SOLUTION LOSSES

Solution loss occurs mainly with the water-soluble nutrients: minerals, vitamin C, and the B-complex vitamins. Nutrients are not destroyed just because they are dissolved out of foods, unless the solution into which the nutrients dissolve is discarded. The nutrient, which is still biologically active, merely changes its location.

When foods are soaked in water to be cleaned, freshened, or softened, their nutrients have an opportunity to dissolve into the water. Nutrient solution losses increase as the proportion of water increases and with longer soaking. In the past, it was customary to soak certain fresh vegetables to remove insects. However, such vegetables do not need to be soaked if they are already free of insects. Dried beans are usually soaked to reduce their cooking time, but they should always be cooked in the water in which they were soaked to retain their maximum nutrient value. Vegetables should never be soaked to freshen them. Instead, rinse them briefly in water, shake off the excess, and place the vegetables in a plastic bag in the refrigerator.

Cooking foods in water can result in even greater solution losses than soaking, because heat causes cell membranes to be more permeable and nutrients pass into the cooking solution more readily. This also applies to canned foods. The juices in a can of food contain about one-third of the water-soluble nutrients that were once in the food itself.

Reducing Solution Losses   Some solution losses are unavoidable in food preparation. Unnecessary losses, however, can be reduced in the following ways:

1. Avoid soaking foods unless it is absolutely necessary; use the soaking liquid as a medium in which to cook the food.
2. Cook vegetables in the least possible amount of water by using stir-fry, waterless, steaming, and pressure cooker methods.
3. Shorten cooking time three ways:

> *a.* Cook vegetables only to the tender-crisp stage, never until they are mushy.
> *b.* Cover the pan to retain heat. Nutrients do not evaporate from foods; this is not a reason to use a cover.
> *c.* Start foods in boiling water, in a hot pan, or on a hot heating element, to speed the heating time.
>
> 4. Use cooking liquids whenever possible for soups, gravies, and sauces; save meat drippings from pan frying and broiling meats, after discarding the fat, and use when meat flavor is desired.

NUTRIENT DESTRUCTION

Only vitamins are destroyed; minerals are never destroyed. Vitamins can be destroyed by heat, oxidation, light, and acidic or alkaline media. Some vitamins are subject to one type of destruction but not to another; this information is included in Table 1.5.

Heat Destruction Heat alters the structure of some vitamins and causes them to lose their special properties. Vitamins affected in this way include thiamin, vitamin C, pyridoxine, folic acid, vitamin B_{12}, and riboflavin. Thiamin is especially subject to destruction by dry heat, as in toasting and baking. Toasting or browning dry rice before steaming it can destroy half or more of its thiamin content and some of its protein quality.

The destruction of nutrients by heat can be minimized by reduced cooking time, as previously described. Braised and stewed meats should be cooked at simmering temperatures only long enough to become tender. Meats should be oven roasted only to the rare or medium stage, with a thermometer being used to indicate the desired degree of doneness. Although pressure cooking produces very high temperatures, it also greatly reduces cooking time and so balances out the resulting nutrient loss.

Light Destruction Vitamins that are destroyed by light include folic acid, riboflavin, pyridoxine, vitamin B_{12}, vitamin E, vitamin A, and vitamin K.

Milk is an excellent source of riboflavin, but if it is allowed to stand in the light, considerable destruction of riboflavin can occur. Cartons and brown glass bottles help prevent such destruction. No light destruction of other vitamins appears likely in food preparation.

Effect of pH Folic acid, thiamin, and ascorbic acid are destroyed in alkaline media. Because baking soda produces an alkaline medium, excess soda should not be used to leaven baked products, nor should any soda be added to green vegetables during cooking.

Oxidation Vitamins subject to destruction by oxidation include vitamin A, carotene, vitamin C, vitamin E, vitamin K, thiamin, pyridoxine, biotin, and folic acid. The mechanism that results in the oxidative browning of fruits and vegetables, which is discussed in detail in Chapter 6, is also responsible for the oxidation of vitamins; procedures that prevent browning also prevent oxidation of vitamins. Rancidity in fats and wilting in fresh vegetables both produce oxidation of vitamins. Oxidation of vitamins can be reduced by taking these effective measures:

1. Leave foods in large pieces so that less surface area is exposed for oxidation, but keep in mind that small pieces of food cook more quickly, thus reducing the heat destruction of vitamins.
2. Add food, especially vegetables, to boiling water, or have the pan or heating element already hot to inactivate quickly the enzymes that cause oxidation.
3. Keep foods refrigerated or frozen to slow enzyme activity.
4. Inactivate enzymes with an acidic medium, especially in salads.
5. Do not chop foods too far in advance of serving or cooking.
6. Do not buy wilted produce; keep purchased produce crisp and fresh by storing it properly.

Nutrient Labeling of Processed Foods

The Food and Drug Administration has established standards for labeling processed foods that give the consumer a better knowledge of food choices. If a processor adds nutrients to foods or makes claims about the nutrients in a product, the product must show the standard nutrient label. The nutrient standard for labeling is the U.S. Recommended Daily Allowance (U.S. RDA), which should not be confused with the Recommended Dietary Allowances (RDA) established by the National Research Council. The U.S. Recommended Daily Allowance is based on the RDA, but is not as detailed for needs based on sex and age. Table 11 in the appendix lists the U.S. RDA used for labeling purposes.

The information now required on such food labels includes:

1. size of serving
2. number of servings in the container
3. calories per serving
4. grams of protein, carbohydrate, and fat per serving
5. percentage of the U.S. RDA for protein, vitamin A, vitamin C, thiamin, riboflavin, niacin, calcium, and iron per serving

Nutrient labeling may additionally provide information concerning the cholesterol and saturated and polyunsaturated fatty acid content per serving.

One of the benefits of nutrient labeling is the establishment of guidelines for the contents of frozen dinners. Frozen dinners must contain one or more sources of animal protein that contribute at least 70 percent of the total protein. In addition, these dinners must contain potatoes, rice, or a cereal-based product, as well as one or more vegetables other than potatoes or rice. Finally, the nutrients in frozen dinners must be listed as percent of the U.S. RDA per 100 calories.

Figure 1.5

Nutrient labeling lets the consumer compare the nutrient values of processed foods. *(Del Monte Corporation)*

Figure 1.5 is an example of a nutrient label for a specific product. Other specifications in the labeling law cover special products and circumstances not included here. Such excellent sources of nutrients as fresh fruits, vegetables, meats, nuts, and legumes, are not labeled for their nutritional content. Nutritional labeling may help increase general knowledge of nutrition so that consumers can make better choices in feeding themselves and their families.

Choosing Foods for Their Nutrients

The nutrient content of foods in a meal can be calculated and the choice of foods changed until the revised nutrient content equals the RDA amounts, but this is a very tedious and time-consuming process. A simpler method, which comes close to providing the RDA level of nutrients (depending on specific food choices), is to use a food group plan. The Basic Four Food Groups is a plan that has been widely used during the last two decades. Its four groups are (1) milk and cheese, (2) meats and meat substitutes, (3) fruits and vegetables, and (4) breads and cereals. This food group plan is easy to use but has its drawbacks. Its most serious flaw is that it includes all fruits and vegetables in one group when they vary greatly in nutrient content and are not always interchangeable.

Dr. Jean Mayer, formerly professor of Nutrition at Harvard University, and Dr. Phillip L. White, secretary of the American Medical Association Council of Nutrition, would like to see a return to the Basic Seven Food Groups, a plan used before the adoption of the Basic Four Food Groups plan. They believe that the Basic Seven plan puts more emphasis on the consumption of fruits and vegetables. Table 1.6 lists the Basic Seven groups, the number of servings recommended from each group, and the foods that belong to each group. As the table shows, fruits and vegetables

BASIC SEVEN FOOD GROUPS

Table 1.6   Basic Seven Food Groups

Group	Number and size of daily servings	Important sources
1. Pro-vitamin A sources	One serving ½ cup or more	Apricots, purple plums, prunes, carrots, beet greens, chard, endive, dandelion greens, pumpkin, winter squash, sweet potatoes, peaches, persimmons, nectarines
These foods are good sources of both pro-vitamin A and ascorbic acid		Cantaloupes, mangoes, papayas, broccoli, kale, collard greens, watercress, mustard greens, red and green sweet peppers, spinach, turnip greens, tomatoes and juice, romaine, green asparagus
2. Ascorbic acid sources	One serving ½ cup or more	Grapefruit and juice, oranges and juice, lemons and juice, tangerines and juice, guavas, kumquats, strawberries, brussels sprouts, cauliflower, kohlrabi, cabbage
3. Other fruits and vegetables	Two servings ½ cup or more	Potatoes and other vegetables and fruits not mentioned in the above groups
4. Milk products	Two servings 1 cup	Whole, low-fat, and nonfat milk, buttermilk, yogurt, cheese, ice cream, cream soups and sauces made with milk, custard and puddings made with milk
5. Meats and meat substitutes	Two servings 3 ounces 1 cup	Meat, fish, poultry, cheese, eggs, legumes, nuts, textured protein
6. Bread and cereals	Four servings 1 slice; ½ cup	Whole grain or enriched breads, cereals, and pastas
7. Fats	1 tablespoon	Butter, margarine, polyunsaturated oils

are divided into three groups according to their nutrient contribution. Between Groups 1 and 2 are fruits and vegetables that are good sources of both vitamin A and vitamin C; they can therefore be used in either group.

This plan is scaled to meet adult nutritional needs; children and teenagers have different food requirements. Younger children require smaller servings than adults, but they still need the variety of foods indicated. Because children are growing and forming bones, their need for calcium is greater than an adult's. Children need three or more servings of milk each day, while teenagers may need four or more servings.

The number of servings from each group is only suggested; it is not a minimum or maximum requirement. Two cups of milk daily supplies adequate calcium and riboflavin for an adult, but these nutrients can also be obtained by eating more leafy green vegetables (ones without oxalic acid) and legumes. Two servings from the meat group ensure an adequate protein intake, but milk and cheese can also supply protein. The bread and cereal group supplies some B vitamins and minerals that are also available in the meat and produce groups. The oils in the fat group supply essential fatty acids and the table fats supply vitamin A. Essential fatty acids may also be obtained from seeds and nuts; vitamin A is available in milk products; and provitamin A, or carotene, may be obtained from extra servings from Group 1 produce. The intake of fats and cereals can be increased or decreased to meet caloric needs. Most people eat a great deal from these two groups of foods. Better nutrition and less obesity might result if an overweight person limited his or her intake of fats and cereals to not more than four servings daily, with a corresponding increase in the intake of low-calorie vegetables.

> Methuselah ate what he found on his plate,
> And never as people do now,
> Did he note the amount of the calorie count;
> He ate it because it was chow.
> He wasn't disturbed as at dinner he sat,
> Devouring a roast or a pie,
> To think it was lacking in granular fat
> Or a couple of vitamins shy.
> He cheerfully chewed each species of food,
> Unmindful of trouble or fears,
> Lest his health might be hurt by some fancy dessert;
> And he lived for over nine hundred years.[1]
>
> —Anonymous

[1]Olaf Mickelsen, *Nutrition, Science, and You* (New York: Scholastic Book Services, 1964), p.121.

1. What six kinds of nutrients are required by animals and humans?
2. What are the building blocks of protein?
3. Name some ways proteins are used in the body.
4. Distinguish between essential and nonessential amino acids.
5. Distinguish between complete and incomplete proteins.
6. What types of foods are sources of complete protein? Of incomplete protein?
7. What is a limiting amino acid?
8. Why and how are some proteins supplemented? Give examples.
9. What is a triglyceride?
10. Distinguish between saturated and unsaturated fatty acids.
11. What is a polyunsaturated fatty acid? An essential fatty acid?
12. What is the best source of essential fatty acids? Of nonessential fatty acids?
13. Describe some ways to decrease the intake of saturated fatty acids.
14. What is atherosclerosis?
15. Name some foods that are good sources of carbohydrate.
16. What criteria should be used in choosing carbohydrate foods besides their carbohydrate content?
17. How does cellulose differ from starch and sugars?
18. Why is fiber important in the diet?
19. How can the caloric content of foods be reduced during food preparation?
20. Give the physiological energy value of protein, fat, and carbohydrate.
21. What is a vitamin?
22. What is nutrient fortification of foods?
23. What is a manufactured food?
24. Describe briefly how and why solution losses of nutrients occur in food preparation.
25. Name some procedures that can be used to reduce solution losses of nutrients.
26. Name four ways in which vitamins are destroyed in food preparation.

References

Bieri, John G. "An Overview of the RDAs for Vitamins." *Journal of the American Dietetic Association* 76, no. 2 (February 1980): 134.

Briggs, George M., and Calloway, Doris H. *Bogert's Nutrition and Physical Fitness.* Philadelphia: Saunders, 1979.

Dunning, H. Neal, and Johnson, O. C. "Nutrient Labeling and Guidelines." In U.S. Department of Agriculture, *Shopper's Guide,* Yearbook of Agriculture. Washington, D.C.: Government Printing Office, 1974.

Goodhart, Robert S., and Shils, M. E., eds. *Modern Nutrition in Health and Disease*, 6th ed. Philadelphia: Lea & Febiger, 1980.

Hofmann, Lieselotte, ed. *The Great American Nutrition Hassle.* Palo Alto, Calif.: Mayfield, 1978.

Labuza, Theodore P., and Sloan, A. E., eds. *Contemporary Nutrition Controversies.* St. Paul, Minn.: West, 1979.

Leverton, Ruth. "Organic, Inorganic: What They Mean." In U.S. Department of Agriculture, *Shopper's Guide,* Yearbook of Agriculture. Washington, D.C.: Government Printing Office, 1974.

Mertz, Walter. "The New RDAs: Estimated Adequate and Safe Intake and Calculation of Available Iron." *Journal of the American Dietetic Association* 76, no. 2 (February 1980): 128.

Munro, Hamish N. "Major Gaps in Nutrient Allowances." *Journal of the American Dietetic Association* 76, no. 2 (February 1980): 137.

Nutrition Reviews. *Present Knowledge in Nutrition,* 4th ed. New York: Nutrition Foundation, 1976.

Schneider, Howard A., Anderson, C. E., and Coursin, D. B., eds. *Nutritional Support of Medical Practice.* New York: Harper & Row, 1977.

U.S. Department of Agriculture. *Nutrition Labeling—Tools for Its Use.* Agriculture Information Bulletin No. 382, by Betty Peterkin, Jennie Nichols, and Cynthia Cromwell. Washington, D.C.: Government Printing Office, 1975.

——. Dietary Goals for the United States. Washington, D.C.: Government Printing Office, 1977.

Preserving the Safety of Foods

The foods we eat should be wholesome, nutritious, and pleasing. Occasionally, however, foods can cause illness. This chapter examines the causes and prevention of foodborne illnesses, the use of chemicals and food additives in processed food, and the governmental controls used to maintain safe levels of these additives in our foods.

A *foodborne illness* is an illness caused by eating contaminated food. Food may be contaminated by any of the five following substances:

1. naturally occurring toxic substances
2. toxic chemicals
3. pathogenic microorganisms
4. toxins produced by microorganisms
5. animal parasites or their eggs

Foodborne Illness

FOODS WITH NATURAL TOXINS

Some plants develop *toxins,* or poisons, as they grow. Over the centuries, people have learned not to use poisonous plants for food or have learned how to process some poisonous plants to remove their toxic substance. The same plant may contain both toxic and nontoxic parts. For example, the leaves of the tomato plant are highly toxic, but the fruit is not. Some plants may contain a toxic substance but in such small amounts that normal servings of these plants may be safely eaten. For example, oxalic acid, which occurs in spinach, chard, beet greens, and rhubarb, is toxic. When these foods are eaten, most of their oxalic acid combines with calcium in the digestive tract and is excreted in the feces; the rest is detoxified in the liver. The amount of oxalic acid in such cases is small enough for the body to handle. The same is not true of the leaves of the rhubarb, however, for their oxalic acid content is great enough to produce illness when they are consumed.

Solanin is a compound formed just under the skin of white potatoes when they are stored in a warm, lighted area. The presence of solanin causes a green discoloration of the skin that is usually removed when the potatoes are peeled. Even when the potatoes are not peeled, the amount of solanin consumed in a normal serving is not sufficient to cause illness. *Goitrin,* a substance that interferes with the formation of thyroid hormone, occurs naturally in vegetables of the cabbage family, but it does not cause illness in the amounts that are normally consumed.

Eating wild mushrooms frequently causes illness or death because people cannot distinguish between edible and toxic varieties. Some seafoods have been known to cause toxicity and death during certain seasons when feeding on toxic plants. Other fish have been observed to absorb toxic chemicals from seawater. The level of mercury in seafood, for example, is monitored by the federal government to prevent the marketing of toxic fish.

The body is able to detoxify many harmful substances, especially when it is well nourished and healthy. Problems are likely to develop only when excessively large amounts of toxic substances are consumed in a short period of time. Salt (sodium chloride) and water are essential for life. Yet both these substances can be toxic if too much is consumed in too short a time.

Most of the plants that people have eaten over the centuries are safe to eat, even though some may contain small amounts of toxic substances. Not all substances promoted as foods, however, may be equally safe. Apricot pits, which have recently grown in popularity, contain a substance that is changed in the body into cyanide, a potent poison. Wild vegetables have also been suggested as a source of food, but these should be eaten with caution unless their freedom from toxicity is assured.

CHEMICALS IN FOODS Toxic chemical contaminants of foods should be distinguished from nontoxic chemical additives. Poisoning from toxic chemicals that get into foods inadvertently is not a common occurrence, although some cases have been reported. Chemicals known to be toxic when ingested in excessive amounts include antimony, arsenic, cadmium, copper, lead, mercury, and zinc. Zinc and copper are trace elements required by the body for proper functioning, but they are toxic when ingested in large amounts.

Utensils as a Source of Chemical Contamination Foods can become contaminated when they are prepared or stored in utensils made of, or containing, toxic chemicals. Acids in foods increase the solubility of metals from the containers. The longer the food sits in the container, the more metal dissolves into the food. Some types of containers that can contaminate food include:

1. *Improperly glazed pottery* is hazardous because the lead in the glaze is not completely volatilized during the firing process, remaining on the pottery to dissolve in the food placed in it. Pottery manufactured commercially in the United States is safe for food; homemade pottery may not be. Foreign pottery may also be unsafe if it was purchased in this country before 1974, when the U.S. government established standards for imported pottery. Foreign pottery purchased abroad remains an unknown factor.
2. *Copper utensils* are unsafe only where food is in direct contact with the copper. Copper used on the bottom of stainless steel pots is safe because the food is not in direct contact with the copper.
3. *Galvanized containers* contain zinc used in the galvanizing process. It will dissolve into food placed in the container.
4. *Chipped enameled pans* expose the base metal antimony on the interior surface of the pan, causing contamination of foods.
5. *Brass and cadmium containers* are unsafe because these metals are

easily dissolved by foods. Some metal ice cube trays and beverage pitchers have been plated with cadmium.

Aluminum, stainless steel, iron, unchipped enamelware, glass, and properly glazed pottery are all safe materials for fabricating food utensils. Some iron from iron pots dissolves into food, but does not cause toxicity; in fact, it can be nutritionally beneficial, for iron is a nutrient in short supply in the diets of many Americans.

Agricultural Chemicals and the Food Supply   Pesticides, herbicides, and fertilizers are the main chemicals used on or around growing plants. Herbicides eliminate undesirable vegetation. Pesticides destroy insects that reduce the yield of crops; Figure 2.1

Figure 2.1
Extreme damage and loss of crops can be caused by insect infestation. *(U.S. Department of Agriculture)*

shows an extreme case of destruction of corn by insects. Fertilizers supply nutrients to the plant.

Insects destroy food intended for people and animals; they also carry diseases to people and animals as well as to plants. Thus, pesticides are necessary to ensure a continuing food supply and to prevent outbreaks of such diseases as yellow fever and malaria. However, research continues to seek ways of preventing insect attacks without having recourse to toxic pesticides. Scientists have developed strains of crops that are genetically resistant to certain insects. They have developed biological controls for some insects, and they have tested the ways in which chemical insecticides are formulated, diluted, and applied to determine the methods that are most effective in destroying insects and least harmful to people and the environment.

State and county agents carry on specialized educational programs to inform farmers of new developments in this field and to monitor the use of pesticides. Regulations control which pesticide or herbicide may be sprayed on a particular crop, how and in what dilution it is to be applied, the timing of its application, and

Figure 2.2

Pesticide residues in the environment are monitored by this federal worker collecting soil samples for analysis. *(U.S. Department of Agriculture)*

Figure 2.3

Environmental samples are analyzed for pesticide and herbicide residues. *(U.S. Department of Agriculture)*

other factors as well, to ensure that harvested foods will not be contaminated. The federal government monitors pesticide and herbicide residues in soils, water, sediment, crops, livestock, and some species of aquatic and land animals. Figure 2.2 shows a federal worker obtaining a soil sample for analysis of chemical residues; Figure 2.3 shows a federal laboratory where such samples are analyzed.

Such techniques for obtaining and analyzing representative samples of toxic residues from the environment continue to improve. Both federal and state controls attempt to ensure that the food supply, in addition to being adequate, is safe, unadulterated, and wholesome.

Organic fertilizer, or *humus,* is composed of animal excrement and partially or wholly decayed plant matter. In order for plants to absorb nutrients, bacteria in the soil must break down the fertilizer into its composite mineral matter, including nitrogen, phosphorus, calcium, and magnesium. A plant can only absorb mineral ions through its roots; it cannot utilize organic molecules in the fertilizer.

Chemical fertilizers are mixtures scientifically formulated to contain the correct ratios of various chemicals needed by the plant for growth. Soils in different areas of the country vary in their composition and, therefore, in their ability to supply the minerals needed by plants. In the western states, adding iron to the soil increases crop yield; in the southeastern states, adding phosphorus to the soil increases crop production. Organic fertilizers loosen the soil and cause it to absorb water and hold it better, permitting easier penetration by plant roots. But organic fertilizer is not available in large enough quantities, nor is it properly balanced in mineral content, to meet total crop production needs. Chemical fertilizers can supply the nitrogen a plant needs just as effectively as an organic fertilizer can, and thus greatly improve the yield per acre of crops. The use of chemical fertilizers has made possible the plentiful food supply of recent years.

Food Additives   Not all chemicals in foods are toxic; some are added to perform a function in foods. These chemicals are known as *food additives,* and their use is under government control. Food additives are added in minute amounts to some foods during processing to achieve a specific effect. Manufacturers, however, are required to prove that any chemical substance they propose to add to a food will not cause toxicity under conditions defined by the regulations. Additives that meet these criteria are listed in the GRAS ("generally regarded as safe") list. Once a substance has been placed on this list, it is not forever approved; all GRAS additives are subject to reevaluation.

Substances that have been used as additives for centuries

include common table salt (sodium chloride), vinegar (acetic acid solution), table sugar (sucrose), and baking soda (sodium bicarbonate). In recent years, the long-term effects of chemical food additives have become a focus of scientific concern. Although an additive may not cause toxicity in a single serving or even in many servings, it still may become over many years a cause of

Table 2.1   *Additives in foods*

Function of additive	Typical additives	Products containing additives
Acid-base control	Hydrogen chloride Citric acid Sulfuric acid Sodium citrate Sodium hydroxide Acetic acid Phosphoric acid Calcium oxide Tartaric acid	Baked products of all kinds—fresh, frozen and mixes—crackers, chocolate, butter, cheese, soft drinks, pickles, jams, jellies, preserves, candies
Anticaking agents	Calcium stearate Calcium silicate	Table salt Baking powder
Antioxidants	Sodium bisulfite Sulfur dioxide Ascorbic acid Tocopherols Butylated hydroxy anisole (BHA) Butylated hydroxy toluene (BHT)	Mixes of all kinds Dehydrated foods Frozen fruits Vegetable oils, margarine Chips and crackers Dips and cheese products Bakery products—fresh, frozen, Ready-to-eat-cereals
Bleaching agents	Chlorine dioxide Potassium bromate Potassium iodate	Wheat flour, cheeses
Color	Artificial colors Caramel Beta carotene	Beverages, candy, cheeses, ice cream, syrup, margarine, dessert powders, baked products, and mixes
Effervescent agent	Carbon dioxide	Carbonated beverages
Emulsifiers	Lecithin Monoglyceride Diglyceride Vegetable gums Methyl cellulose	Mayonnaise, salad dressings, shortenings, margarine, imitation creams and milks, ice cream, candy, beer, baked products—fresh, frozen, and mixes of all kinds
Firming agents	Calcium chloride Aluminum potassium sulfate (alum)	Pickles, canned tomatoes, maraschino cherries, canned apples
Flavor	Artificial flavors Spices, herbs Monosodium glutamate	Beverages, dessert powders, baked products—fresh, frozen, and mixes of all kinds—frozen desserts, margarine, candy, gum, syrup, jams,

cancer. Cyclamates were banned temporarily because they were found to cause bladder tumors when injected in rats. Recent research suggests that excessive consumption of table salt may be related to high blood pressure, and excessive consumption of sugar may be related to heart disease, in some persons. These two popular food additives have not been banned, but nutritionists

Function of additive	Typical additives	Products containing additives
	Diacetyl Hydrolyzed vegetable protein Sodium chloride	jellies, preserves, frozen dinners, canned soups, meats
Fumigants	Methyl bromide Ethylene oxide	Fresh fruits, grains, nuts
Leavening	Sodium carbonate Calcium carbonate Monocalcium phosphate Sodium aluminum sulfate Dicalcium phosphate Disodium phosphate Potassium acid tartrate Yeast	Leavening of all baked products—fresh, frozen and mixes
Nutritional enrichment	Potassium iodide Vitamins Minerals	Table salt, milk, margarine, cereal products, flours
Moisture retention	Propylene glycol Sorbitol Glycerine	Coconut, candy
Preservatives	Calcium proprionate Benzoic acid Sodium benzoate Sodium nitrite Sodium nitrate Sodium chloride	Cheese products, margarine, cured meats, bakery products—fresh, frozen and mixes—dietetic jellies
Stabilizers and thickeners	Sodium caseinate Modified starch Methyl cellulose Vegetable gums: pectin, agar, carageenan, sodium alginate, etc.	Dessert powders, canned soups, canned sauces, syrups, beverages, ice cream and other frozen desserts, jams, jellies, preserves, mixes of all kinds, salad dressings
Sweeteners	Saccharin Corn Syrup Glucose Dextrose Lactose Sucrose	Dietetic foods, all kinds of baked products, mixes, dessert powders, candies, syrups

recommend moderate intake until more definitive answers are available.

Almost 2,000 additives have been placed on the GRAS list, too many to include here in their entirety. Table 2.1 lists some common additives, their functions, and the foods in which they are found. These additives and many others are considered safe in their usual amounts and are necessary to obtain high quality in processed foods. If a person wishes to limit chemical additives in the diet, he or she must reduce the intake of processed foods. Even with additives, chemical pesticides, and fertilizers, our food supply is probably safer now than it was a century ago when bacterial and insect infestations produced a constant risk of food-borne disease. Food additives make possible convenience foods, as well as a wide variety of foods throughout the year.

The presence of additives in food products is declared in the food's ingredient list, with the ingredient present in the greatest concentration by weight being listed first. Because most additives are present in very small amounts, they are found at the bottom of the list.

Acids are needed to form pectin gels, to neutralize baking soda in leavening, and to pickle fruits and vegetables. *Anticaking agents* keep salt, and garlic and onion powder, free-flowing. *Antioxidants* retard rancidity in products containing fats and prevent enzymatic browning of dehydrated and frozen fruits. *Bleaching agents* whiten flour and strengthen its gluten. *Emulsifiers* form a stable emulsion between two liquids that ordinarily do not mix, such as oil and water. *Firming agents* make pickles crisp and prevent canned tomatoes and apples from disintegrating. *Leavening agents* give structure and porosity to baked products.

Artificial flavors are found in a wide number of foods. Many are natural flavors isolated from their food source. For instance, amyl acetate is the typical flavor of bananas; benzaldehyde, of almonds; and allyl isothiocyanate, of mustard. Monosodium glutamate (MSG), a very common flavor enhancer, is the sodium salt of glutamic acid, an amino acid found in all proteins. Glutamic acid is a by-product of sugar refining.

Nutritional enrichment has reduced the incidence of several nutritional deficiency diseases in the United States. The addition of potassium iodide to table salt, for example, has reduced the incidence of goiter, and vitamin D added to milk has reduced the incidence of rickets.

Preservatives serve a wide variety of functions. Sugar and salt have been used as preservatives for centuries; when they are present in high concentration, they withdraw water from the cells of microorganisms. Because many foods are not amenable to preservation with large concentrations of salt or sugar, other substances have been developed.

Fumigants are used on fruit containers to retard mold during shipping and on grains and nuts in storage to retard spoilage.

Stabilizers and *thickeners* make foods more viscous, delay the melting of ice cream, and prevent *syneresis*, or "weeping" in starch pastes. They are present in frozen and canned sauces and puddings. Saccharin is a nonnutritive sweetener with no caloric value. Other sweeteners listed in Table 2.1 are naturally occurring sugars. *Artificial colors* make food look attractive.

Despite improved technology in refrigeration, freezing, and other preservation techniques, a high incidence of foodborne illness, either from bacterial contamination of foods or from production of toxins in foods by bacteria, still occurs. Bacterial contamination is a far greater public health problem than chemical contamination.

Any disease caused by bacteria or a virus may be contracted from food, milk, or water contaminated with its microorganisms. Diseases that may be transmitted through contaminated food or drink include tuberculosis, diphtheria, typhoid fever, dysentery, pneumonia, meningitis, whooping cough, infectious hepatitis, scarlet fever, brucellosis, streptococcal sore throat, colds, and flu. Additionally, gastrointestinal illness may be caused by bacteria producing such symptoms as fever, nausea, vomiting, abdominal cramps, diarrhea, and headache. Gastrointestinal symptoms last from a few hours to several days and may be mild or severe, depending on the type of bacteria, how many are ingested, and the physical health of the infected person.

Bacteria are one-celled microscopic plants capable of a rapid rate of multiplication under ideal conditions. Bacteria that are *pathogenic*, or capable of causing disease, grow best at temperatures between 60–115°F (16–46°C), that is, room and body temperatures. These bacteria are destroyed by high heat, and the higher the temperature, the more rapid their destruction. Figure 2.4 shows the temperatures that control the bacteria commonly involved in foodborne illnesses. Neither refrigeration nor freezing destroys bacteria. Lowered temperatures slow or may even stop their multiplication, destroying some of the less viable bacteria, but when the contaminated food returns to room temperature, the growth and multiplication of the bacteria resumes.

Bacterial growth also requires moisture and food. Bacteria thrive and multiply on food if moisture is present. They can exist in a dormant state on dry foods—crackers, for example—but are unable to multiply because of lack of moisture. Thus, dry foods are not likely to cause foodborne illness because the number of bacteria present is too small to be harmful. Many bacteria, such as *Staphylococcus aureus*, will survive in dust in a dormant state; when moisture and food become available, they resume their multiplication. Bacteria need time to reproduce and produce tox-

PATHOGENIC MICROORGANISMS AND THEIR TOXINS

Figure 2.4

The growth of bacteria in foods can be controlled by temperature.

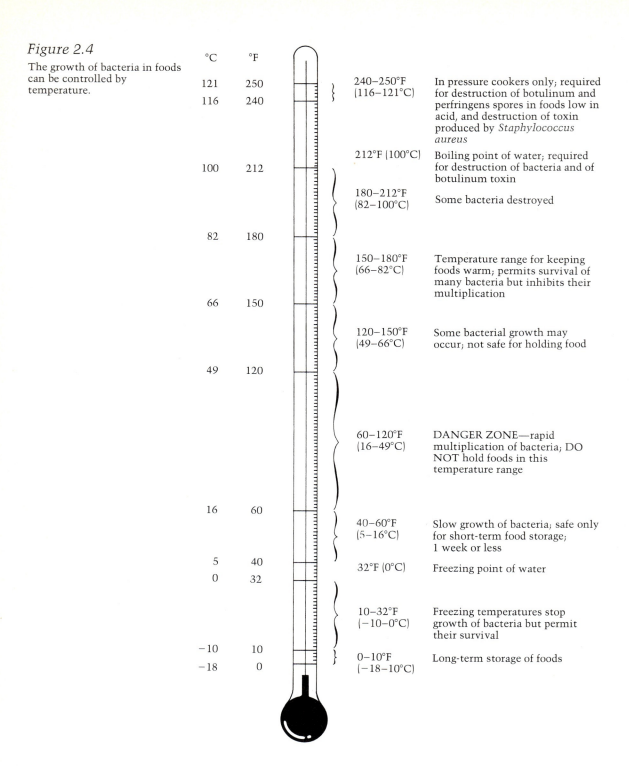

°C	°F		
121	250	240–250°F (116–121°C)	In pressure cookers only; required for destruction of botulinum and perfringens spores in foods low in acid, and destruction of toxin produced by *Staphylococcus aureus*
116	240		
100	212	212°F (100°C)	Boiling point of water; required for destruction of bacteria and of botulinum toxin
		180–212°F (82–100°C)	Some bacteria destroyed
82	180		
		150–180°F (66–82°C)	Temperature range for keeping foods warm; permits survival of many bacteria but inhibits their multiplication
66	150		
		120–150°F (49–66°C)	Some bacterial growth may occur; not safe for holding food
49	120		
		60–120°F (16–49°C)	DANGER ZONE—rapid multiplication of bacteria; DO NOT hold foods in this temperature range
16	60		
		40–60°F (5–16°C)	Slow growth of bacteria; safe only for short-term food storage; 1 week or less
5	40		
0	32	32°F (0°C)	Freezing point of water
		10–32°F (−10–0°C)	Freezing temperatures stop growth of bacteria but permit their survival
−10	10		
−18	0	0–10°F (−18–10°C)	Long-term storage of foods

ins; reducing the time during which foods sit in a condition favorable to bacterial growth helps control contamination.

Salmonella and Streptococci Bacteria *Salmonella* and *streptococci* bacteria do not produce spores or toxins as do perfringens, staphylococci, and botulinum. Both are easily destroyed by heating foods to the boiling point, and growth is prevented at refrigerator or freezer temperatures below 40°F (4.5°C).

Table 2.2 summarizes the causes, symptoms, and control of these and other bacterial foodborne illnesses. Both salmonella and streptococci bacteria are quite widespread and, in small amounts, do not cause illness. Illness results only when large numbers of these bacteria are allowed to develop in food. Therefore, foods susceptible to bacterial contamination must be heated to destroy the bacteria or cooled to prevent their multiplication. Particularly susceptible are all types of protein and starchy foods—meats, custards, puddings, potato and macaroni salads, dry and evaporated milk, and eggs. A common error in food preparation that can cause contamination is to use the same cutting board and knife for cooked foods and for cutting up or trimming raw meats. The next greatest source of food contamination is a lack of hygiene in food handlers. Figure 2.5 shows the many possible routes and vectors by which pathogenic organisms are spread.

Persons may be carriers of disease organisms without exhibiting symptoms of the disease; therefore, food workers need to observe good hygiene when they are preparing foods. Human carriers of *Salmonella typhi,* the organism that produces typhoid fever, have caused widespread epidemics. Many communities require food workers in public eating places to undergo health examinations. Pasteurization of milk and sanitary control of public water supplies have also reduced the incidence of foodborne illnesses.

Spore- and Toxin-Forming Bacteria *Clostridium botulinum* forms both spores and toxin; *Clostridium perfringens* also forms spores, but the toxins are produced in the intestine after the bacteria are ingested. *Staphylococcus aureus* produces toxin only. With all three, the toxin alone causes illness. Staph and botulinum bacteria may be ingested without causing illness so long as the bacteria do not produce toxin.

Table 2.2 shows that such bacteria can be destroyed by heating food to at least 140°F (60°C) for 30 minutes, or to higher temperatures for shorter periods of time. The botulinum and perfringen spores and the staph toxin can only be destroyed by heating food to 240°F (116°C) or higher. Foods should not be held initially at temperatures that permit the growth of the bacteria, for it is during this growth that spores and toxins are produced. Perfringens

Table 2.2   Bacterial foodborne illness: Causes, symptoms, and control

Name of illness	Cause	Symptoms
Salmonellosis	Salmonellae bacteria are widespread in nature (about 1,200 known species); live and grow in intestinal tracts of humans and animals; multiply at temperatures between 44–115°F (7–46°C)	Severe headache, vomiting, diarrhea, abdominal cramps, fever, chills; severe infections can lead to death
Streptococcal poisoning ("strep")	*Streptococcus faecalis* survive at temperatures up to 140°F (60°C) for 30 minutes; present in feces of humans and animals	Nausea, sometimes vomiting, abdominal cramps, diarrhea; relatively mild
Perfringens poisoning	*Clostridium perfringens* are spore-forming bacteria that grow without oxygen; spores withstand boiling temperatures and will germinate and grow in foods	Nausea without vomiting, diarrhea, abdominal cramps, gas
Staphylococcal poisoning ("staph")	*Staphylococcus aureus* grow and produce toxins at temperatures up to 120°F (49°C); toxin requires temperature of 240°F (116°C) for destruction in low-acid foods	Vomiting, diarrhea, abdominal cramps, sweating; generally mild and mistaken for stomach flu
Botulism	*Clostridium botulinum* are spore-forming bacteria that grow and produce toxin without oxygen. Spores require temperature above 240°F (116°C) for destruction; toxin in low-acid food destroyed by boiling 20 mins.	Double vision, inability to swallow, speech difficulty, respiratory paralysis; nausea, vomiting, abdominal cramps appear early. Fatality rate = 65% in U.S.

and staph poisoning resemble salmonella and strep in their mode of transmission, symptoms, control, and carrier foods. Staph poisoning is a particular risk in cream-filled pastries as well as in meats and starchy foods. All of these bacteria exist in soil, water, and dust and thereby contaminate animal and plant foods.

Botulinum and perfringens bacteria are *anaerobes*—they grow best in the absence of oxygen. Botulinum is usually not contracted by eating fresh meats and vegetables. Rather, it is contracted from eating processed foods that have been sealed in cans, bottles, or vacuum-packed packages. These bacteria also do not grow in acidic foods that have a pH below 4.5. At this pH level the bacterial spores are easily destroyed by boiling. Thus, canned fruits can be processed in boiling water baths because they are sufficiently acidic for the spores to be destroyed at boiling temperature. Low-acid meats and vegetables must be processed under pressure in order to obtain the 240°F (115°C) temperature needed

Characteristics	Control
Transmitted by eating infected food, or by contact with infected persons or carriers; also by insects, rodents, pets, animals Onset: 5–72 hours, usually 12–36 Duration: 2–7 days	Heat food to 140°F (60°C) or higher for 10 minutes to destroy bacteria; chill to 40°F (4.5°C) or less to prevent multiplication; practice good hygiene in food preparation
Transmitted by eating infected food or by contact with infected persons or carriers Onset: 2–36 hours, usually 6–12 Duration: 1 day	Same as for salmonella
Transmitted by eating food contaminated with abnormally large numbers of the bacteria Onset: 8–24 hours, usually 12 hours Duration: 1 day	Prevent growth by keeping foods refrigerated to 40°F (4.5°C) or below
Transmitted by consumption of foods containing the toxin Onset: 1–8 hours, usually 2–4 Duration: 1 to 2 days	Keep foods above 140°F (60°C) or below 40°F (4.5°C) to prevent production of toxin by bacteria; destroy toxin by heating at 240°F (116°C) for 30 minutes
Transmitted by eating food containing the toxin. Onset: 2 hours to 6 days, usually 12–36 hours Duration: 3–6 days; paralysis may last for 6–8 months	Process home canned low-acid foods in pressure cooker for proper time; boil home canned vegetables and meats for 20 minutes before eating

to destroy the spores. If the temperature during processing is too low or the time of processing at the higher temperature is too short, all of the spores will not be destroyed and will grow and produce toxin.

In commercial canning, careful controls are maintained to assure the proper heat destruction of the botulinum spore. Although occasional slips occur, the incidence of botulinum poisoning from commercially canned foods is low in relation to the amount of canned foods produced in this country; the Food and Drug Administration seeks to reduce it still further. Most cases of botulism result from improperly processed home-canned foods. For this reason, all meats and vegetables canned at home must be boiled for 20 minutes before tasting or eating; this will destroy botulinum toxin, if it is present. One incident of botulism occurred when a person ate washed raw mushrooms that had been placed in a jar and covered to the top with a pickling solu-

Figure 2.5

Disease organisms can be transmitted in many ways.

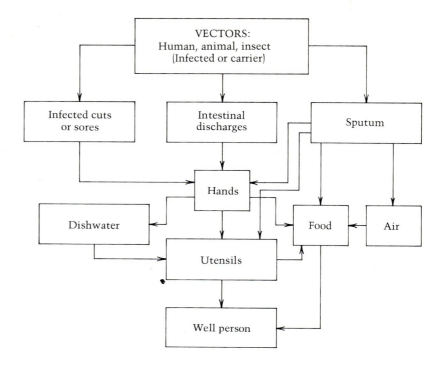

tion; the sealed jar had been allowed to sit on a cupboard shelf at room temperature without heat processing for about 2 weeks. A government publication has also reported botulism in low-acid foods held in refrigerators for 2 weeks or longer, probably in airtight containers.

Botulinum spores have also been identified in honey. This has been linked to sudden infant death syndrome in some infants who were fed formula that had been sweetened with honey. The spores produced the toxin in the intestinal tract of the infants who had not matured enough to produce sufficient gastric acidity to inactivate the spores.

USEFUL BACTERIA

Not all bacteria causes illness; in fact, some are useful in food preparation. *Lactic acid* bacteria convert the sugar lactose, from milk, into lactic acid. Lactic acid fermentation is used in the production of buttermilk, butter, yogurt, sour cream, and cheese. Different strains of lactic acid bacteria yield products with different flavors.

ANIMAL PARASITES

Parasites in foods include roundworms, tapeworms, and a variety of protozoa. *Trichinella spiralis,* a roundworm, is the most common food parasite in the United States. It is found in pork and occurs when pigs are fed raw garbage infested with the parasite or its eggs. Many states now require that garbage be sterilized before it is fed to pigs. Trichinellae are destroyed at temperatures above 140°F (60°C), although all pork should be cooked to an internal temperature of 150°F (65.5°C) as a safety factor. Storage at 5°F (−15°C) for 30 days, or at −10°F (−23°C) for 20 days, or at −20°F (−29°C) for 12 days will also make the meat safe to eat.

Immature trichinellae worms are *encysted*, enclosed in a capsulelike membrane, in the muscle of infected pork. If these worms are not destroyed by cooking or freezing, they are freed, when eaten, by the action of digestive juices in the human host. The worm matures and reproduces in the human intestinal tract. This is the first stage of the illness, and symptoms of nausea, vomiting, diarrhea, and abdominal pain are evident. In the second stage, the new generation of worms migrate to various areas of the body and form cysts in the muscles. The infected person experiences irregular fever, chills, edema around the eyes, profuse sweating, thirst, muscle pain, weakness, and labored breathing. In the third stage, as the disease abates, some tissue repair may occur, but generalized toxemia and *myocarditis*, inflammation of the muscle tissue of the heart, may also be present.

Once the parasites leave the intestinal tract, there is no cure for trichinosis. The severity of the disease is proportional to the number of organisms ingested. The life span of the parasite is about 5 years.

MOLDS AND YEASTS

For many years it was assumed that molds were harmless, but recently it was discovered that the mold *aspergillus flavus* produced a mycotoxin, aflatoxin, which is known to cause liver damage and possibly cancer when it is consumed. The toxicity of other molds is not known. All moldy foods should be discarded except mold-ripened cheeses—such as Roquefort, blue, Camembert, and Brie—which have been eaten for many years. Molds are also used in the production of the Oriental condiments soy sauce and miso.

Molds are *fungi*, or tiny plants, that require oxygen for growth. They also require moisture, but less than that required by yeast and bacteria, and will grow at refrigerator temperatures, but more slowly than at higher temperatures.

Yeasts are microscopic one-celled plants used for the fermentation of glucose and the production of carbon dioxide for leavening yeast breads. Fermentation of sugars by yeast also occurs in the production of alcoholic beverages and vinegar. Wild yeasts in the air, however, can result in the undesirable fermentation of fruits and juices. For many centuries wild yeasts were a problem in wine making, producing undesirable flavors in wine and at times rendering it undrinkable. Louis Pasteur discovered that grape juice must be sterilized and inoculated with a pure strain of yeast to produce desirable ferments.

INSECT AND RODENT INFESTATIONS

Many kinds of foods are attractive to insects and rodents. Flies, roaches, ants, and rodents contaminate the foods they touch with microorganisms, which can cause a variety of foodborne illnesses. The problem is twofold: (1) to keep food areas clean of food debris and foods properly stored to prevent the attraction of pests, and (2) to prevent the entrance of pests into food preparation and storage areas.

Grains, flours, nuts, cereals, bread mixes, and dried fruits are all subject to insect infestation; they often contain eggs and larvae at the time of purchase that later hatch out. The hatching of larvae can be prevented by storing such products for several weeks in the freezer, after which they can be kept at room temperature without problems.

Infested food products should be discarded. If an infested product is located in a cupboard, all products in the cupboard should be removed and checked for infestation. The cupboard should be thoroughly washed with hot soapy water and ammonia or chlorine bleach. The cupboard should then be sprayed with a pesticide specific for crawling insects and allowed to dry for 24 hours before the noninfested products are returned to the cupboard. The area should be checked carefully every week for a month to be sure that no more insects have hatched. Each time insects are discovered, the washing and spraying procedures should be repeated.

The proper storage of food products can prevent infestation. Use glass jars with screw-on lids, cannisters with tightly fitting lids, or rigid plastic containers, such as those used for freezer storage. Many insects are able to penetrate paper and plastic bags and cardboard cartons. If the food product is purchased in one of these containers, it should be transferred to a safe container for storage.

The entrance of flying insects can be prevented by screening windows and doors and by the use of air conditioning for ventilation. The entrance of rodents and crawling insects can be prevented by filling in cracks and openings where they might enter. It may be necessary to spray insecticides around the exterior of the building and in the attic and crawl spaces or basement to obtain better control. Traps can be used to catch rodents.

Garbage should be stored in closed metal cans off the ground to prevent access to food wastes by insects and rodents and to prevent breeding of insects. Containers may need to be washed and sprayed at intervals.

Preventing Foodborne Illnesses

The prevention of foodborne illness requires utmost cleanliness of facilities, equipment, utensils, and persons working with the food. Because foodborne illness is such an important health problem, it is profitable to be specific on this point. People often do not recognize that certain of their habits may contribute to health problems.

You must wash your hands before washing dishes to reduce

the bacterial contamination of the dishwater. Furthermore, your hands should be clean before you put away clean dishes. Do not dry dishes on the same towel you have used for your hands. Dish towels should not be draped around your neck, held under your arm, or placed on a dirty counter. Use only clean towels for drying dishes. Avoid touching the food surfaces of dishes with your hands. Carry flatware by the handles only.

Those who prepare foods for others should be healthy. At times, however, a person must work with foods even though he or she may have a respiratory infection. If you must sneeze, cough, or blow your nose, leave the food preparation area and wash your hands well before returning. Always wash your hands and clean your nails before preparing food. Avoid touching your hands to your face, hair, or other parts of the body when preparing foods; this contaminates your hands with bacteria. Infected wounds, sores, and pimples harbor staph bacteria; either avoid working with foods when such infections are present or do so with extreme attention to hygiene, for pus from cuts and sores has been responsible for more than one outbreak of staph food poisoning. Clothing should be clean. Those preparing food for the public should wear aprons or uniforms and enclose their hair in a cap or net, for hair carries a very high bacterial count.

In preparing foods, use utensils wherever possible instead of hands. Bowls and pots should be scraped with a rubber scraper, not with a finger or the side of the hand. Avoid licking fingers; doing this contaminates them with bacteria. To taste foods, transfer a small amount to the tasting spoon from the cooking spoon without touching one to the other. Never taste food with the cooking or stirring spoon and then return it to the food. Never taste ground raw meat; if it is important to check seasonings in a raw meat mixture such as meat loaf, remove a small sample and heat in a small utensil on the surface unit or in the oven until cooked before tasting it. Raw meat dishes such as steak *tartare* should be made from fresh meat, preferably cut into pieces shortly before serving, and refrigerated until served.

Floors, countertops, and the insides of cupboards and drawers should be free of dust and food debris that attract or harbor bacteria, insects, and rodents. Infestation of insects and rodents should be eliminated with approved nontoxic methods. Pesticides and cleaning supplies should not be stored in the same cupboard with food, nor should they be placed in empty food containers. Screen windows to keep out winged insects; vacuum floors to avoid stirring up dust. Mops, sponges, dish towels and cloths should all be kept clean and sanitized with chlorine bleach or other disinfectants and with boiling or hot soapy water. Food equipment should be cleaned after each use, with mixers, grinders, blenders, and food processors disassembled for cleaning, because particles of food left in crevices can permit the growth of pathogenic bacteria. Counters, chopping boards, and knives used for preparing raw meats should be sanitized before they are used for other foods.

Seafoods from polluted waters should never be eaten. It is advisable to cook all seafoods; infectious hepatitis and other illnesses have been contracted by eating raw seafoods. The surfaces of all meats are contaminated with bacteria, some pathogenic and some *putrefactive*.

Putrefactive bacteria produce odors, and meat on which such bacteria have developed is referred to as "ripe" or "high." Although many putrefactive bacteria are harmless, their presence indicates that pathogenic bacteria have had an equal opportunity to multiply. Growth of putrefactive bacteria can occur even though the meat is refrigerated. Such meat should be very well cooked; it is better to use meats before such putrefaction occurs. Ground meats will be contaminated with bacteria not just on the surface but throughout. Ground meat should be cooked to the medium or well-done stage to destroy the bacteria.

Wash fruits and vegetables thoroughly to remove soil, microorganisms, and spray residues. In the United States, commercial produce may be safely eaten raw. In some parts of the world, human wastes are used for fertilizing plants, causing a high risk of bacterial infections. All plant foods grown in such areas must be thoroughly cooked before they are safe to eat.

All food should be stored or held at its proper temperature, as described in the next chapter. Large amounts of food should be divided into smaller portions to permit both faster chilling and reheating. Loss or gain of heat occurs much more rapidly in a smaller mass than in a larger mass; thus, food is allowed to remain in the dangerous temperature zone for a shorter period of time if it is divided into smaller portions. Frozen foods should be cooked from the frozen state or thawed in the refrigerator, but should not be allowed to warm to room temperature. Hot cooked foods can be placed directly in the refrigerator or freezer; they should never be cooled at room temperature for more than a half hour.

Study Questions

1. Name four or five causes of foodborne illnesses.
2. Name three foods that contain oxalic acid.
3. Why are rhubarb stalks edible and rhubarb leaves inedible?
4. What mechanism does the body have for the elimination of oxalic acid?
5. Many foods that are eaten daily contain toxic substances, but people who eat these foods suffer no apparent ill effect. Explain.
6. Name two chemical elements required by the body as nutrients that can also cause toxicity. Explain.
7. Why are chemical pesticides, fertilizers, and herbicides used in agricultural production?
8. What types of substances do plants require as nutrients?
9. Why are insects a problem in agricultural production?

10. Name three ways of controlling insect infestations.
11. Name ways of controlling chemical pesticides and herbicides to prevent residues on foods.
12. What is a food additive?
13. What is the GRAS list?
14. Sugar and salt are food additives. Under what circumstances might they be harmful to the body?
15. Why are food additives used and what are some possible advantages of using them?
16. Choose a packaged food and list the names of additives that appear in the list of ingredients; try to locate each additive in Table 2.1 and write down its function.
17. Name some diseases that can be contracted by eating foods contaminated by their bacteria.
18. Name two bacteria whose presence in food causes gastrointestinal symptoms when eaten.
19. What are "gastrointestinal" symptoms?
20. What are bacteria?
21. What is the ideal temperature range for the growth of bacteria that cause foodborne illnesses?
22. Do boiling and freezing temperatures destroy bacteria? Spores? Toxins?
23. What is the effect of refrigerator temperatures on bacteria?
24. Name three bacteria that produce toxins that cause illness when they are consumed.
25. Describe some possible routes of transmission of disease-causing microorganisms in food preparation.
26. Explain briefly the cause of botulism.
27. List two ways to destroy trichinellae.
28. Make a list of ways to prevent foodborne illnesses in food preparation.
29. Name three useful microorganisms and give an example of how each is used in foods.
30. What foods are susceptible to growth of: (a) staphylococcus; (b) salmonella; (c) streptococcus; (d) perfringens; (e) botulinum?

References

Committee on Food Protection, Food and Nutrition Board, National Research Council. *Toxicants Occurring Naturally in Foods.* Washington, D.C.: National Academy of Sciences, 1973.

Davis, Carole A. "Safe Handling of Food and Home Storage." In U.S. Department of Agriculture, *Handbook for the Home,* Yearbook of Agriculture. Washington, D.C.: Government Printing Office, 1973.

Food and Drug Administration. "Focus on Food Safety." *FDA Consumer* 13, no. 3 (April 1979): 2–16.

Hall, Richard L. "Food Additives." *Nutrition Today* 8, no. 4 (July/August 1973): 20.

Jay, James W. *Modern Food Microbiology,* 2d ed. New York: Van Nostrand, 1978.

Longree, Karla, and Blaker, G. G. *Sanitary Techniques in Foodservice.* New York: Wiley, 1976. (Reprint of 1971 edition.)

National Institute for Foodservice Industries. *Applied Foodservice Sanitation,* 2d ed. Lexington, Mass.: Heath, 1978.

Tannenbaum, Steven R., ed. *Nutritional and Safety Aspects of Food Processing.* New York: Marcel Dekker, 1979.

U.S. Department of Agriculture. *Controlling Household Pests,* Home and Garden Bulletin No. 96. Washington, D.C.: Government Printing Office, 1977.

U.S. Department of Health, Education and Welfare; Public Health Service. *Diseases Transmitted by Foods,* by Frank L. Bryan. Washington, D.C.: Government Printing Office, 1971.

General Principles of Food Preparation

A knowledge of the general principles of food preparation lays a firm foundation for learning more specific procedures. Understanding equipment and utensils, measurements, the effect of food composition on its preparation, and the principles involved in heating foods helps provide this foundation; safe and efficient working habits make food preparation a satisfying experience.

Efficiency allows a task to be accomplished with the least expenditure of time and energy. This is a commodity that is often taken for granted; time wasted or misused, however, can have undesirable consequences. Fatigue and motivation are two human elements that must be reckoned with before maximum efficiency can be achieved. Fatigue can have psychological roots; studies have shown that unpleasant or disliked tasks produce fatigue more quickly than do enjoyable tasks. Fatigue often occurs with no physiological basis and has been shown to reduce work capacity.

However, motivation can offset fatigue, whether or not it has a physical basis. Motivation is the incentive to action, the desire to achieve a goal, and can be increased by setting goals. Having a goal is a challenge to accomplish a task in a given amount of time and helps decrease the monotony of a job. Intermediate goals for large tasks are also useful. Accomplishing each part of the task is an impetus for completing the next step, until the final goal is reached.

Efficiency in food preparation means identifying those ways in which specific jobs can be performed most quickly with the least expenditure of energy. Knowing how to use equipment increases efficiency. For instance, it is faster to crumble bread or cheese in a blender than it is to grate the cheese or put the bread through a grinder. Storage and work areas should be organized so that working materials are within easy reach; keeping implements needed for stirring and turning foods close by the range can save walking across the kitchen each time one of them is needed.

One of the greatest enemies of efficiency is procrastination. Procrastination in cleanup operations is a common vice in food preparation. You save much time by cleaning as you work. Such habits also provide more clutter-free work space. Used utensils and equipment can be immediately put to soak or placed in the dishwasher; dried-on foods are difficult to remove from utensils. Cleanup seems less arduous if it is done at each step and not allowed to accumulate into a single mountainous task.

Organizing the steps needed to accomplish a job can also save time and improve efficiency. Time estimates for preparing each item in a meal determine the order in which they must be prepared. Smaller jobs should be performed while waiting for other foods to bake or boil. Using the same equipment for several jobs decreases the time required for cleaning up. Using assembly line techniques, perform all tasks of one kind at one time. Do all trimming and peeling before starting to chop; measure all dry ingredients before measuring wet ingredients.

Each task should be approached with a questioning attitude. Be aware that it is possible to increase your efficiency in performing almost any task. Efficiency improves routine tasks and adds to the skill and knowledge you need to handle new jobs.

Safety in Food Preparation

Safety, like efficiency, might be called "enlightened self-interest." Safety in food preparation includes a wide range of factors, from wiring and grounding of electrical appliances to kitchen construction and ventilation, but all cannot be enumerated here. Rather, we will emphasize the actions of the person preparing food, with some simple do's and don'ts to help prevent accidents and injuries:

1. Avoid wearing long, flowing scarves or ties that might get caught in machinery and cause injury; keep hair pinned up; hair and hats should not impair vision.
2. Do not work barefoot or in sandals in food preparation areas; your feet are not adequately protected from falling objects, hot spilled liquids, or slipping on wet floors.
3. Clean up spills on floors as soon as they occur.
4. Do not leave drawers, cupboard doors, and oven doors open; these can become obstacles in passageways and cause falls.
5. Use safe ladders and stools to reach objects on high shelves.
6. Do not leave the range surface unit turned on when it is unattended; often it is impossible to tell that an electric unit is turned on until you have been burned.
7. Handles of pots on the stove should be turned in so that they do not extend out into the passageway.
8. Do not use damp towels for handling hot containers; the moisture in the towel heats up rapidly and can result in burns.
9. When removing a lid from a hot pot, tilt the lid away from your face. Steam can cause more severe burns than boiling water because steam releases heat when it condenses to water on the skin.
10. Fat used for frying causes more severe burns than boiling water because foods are fried at temperatures of 350–400°F (177–205°C), while water boils at only 212°F (100°C).
11. Fat is highly flammable and burns readily. Do not allow fat to become overheated or spatter during cooking. If a fat fire does occur, place a lid on the pot to exclude oxygen, or smother the flames with salt or baking soda. Do not put sugar or flour on a fat fire; these substances are flammable and will feed the fire. Do not put water on a fat fire; water causes the fat to spatter and will spread the fire.
12. Ice or cold water is the best first-aid treatment for burns and bruises.
13. Knives should be carried by their handles and kept sharp. Dull knives are more likely to cause cuts than sharp ones.
14. Do not put your hands or any utensils in grinding or mixing equipment while it is in operation; turn off the motor to add, remove, or stir substances in the mixer, grinder, or garbage disposal.

15. Use equipment for its intended purpose. For example, do not use knives to punch holes in cans or to pry lids off jars and bottles.

The success of many cooking operations depends on appliances. This section compares various appliances and discusses their safe and efficient use. For help in selecting brands of appliances, the reader should consult the consumer organizations that evaluate these and other products. A partial list of such organizations is provided at the end of the chapter.

GAS AND ELECTRIC RANGES

Cooking with electricity requires different techniques than cooking with gas. Gas surface units give instantaneous heat and can change quickly back and forth from low to high heat; electric surface units heat and cool more slowly. To compensate for this delay in cooking with electricity, turn on the surface unit a few minutes before it is needed, so that it will have time to heat up; turn it off a few minutes before the food is finished cooking to utilize the residual heat. If the temperature needs to be reduced during a cooking operation because a food is boiling over or burning, the pot can be placed partly on the heating element or removed entirely until the element cools. Experience in using an electric range soon minimizes these problems, for a person can quickly learn which setting on the control knob achieves the desired results.

Both gas and electric ranges differ widely in their control knobs or switches, which can allow either infinite settings for heat control or only a few. Push-button controls usually permit five heat settings for a surface unit, which may prove a limitation in a few cooking procedures. If a given setting, for example, is too low to maintain the desired pressure in a pressure cooker or the fat temperature for deep-fat frying, the next higher setting may cause too high a pressure or too hot a temperature. Sometimes it is possible to maintain the desired pressure in a pressure cooker by placing the pan over only a part of the surface unit while it is on the higher setting. A pot of fat, however, might tip over under these circumstances. Controls with infinite settings for surface units eliminate such problems.

Gas flames sometimes cause problems because they envelop the sides of a small saucepan, causing foods to burn around the sides of the pan. In situations where rapid evaporation requires high heat, as in some types of candy making, it is not practical to lower the heat when burning starts. Some gas ranges, however, are designed to prevent this problem.

Smooth-top electric ranges are a recent innovation. They are attractive and easier to clean than conventional surface units. Since heating on smooth-top ranges is by conduction only, it is slower. Also, utensils used on these range tops must have absolutely flat bottoms to make complete contact with the surface heating unit. Because few ordinary pots have absolutely flat bottoms, specially constructed utensils must be purchased for use on smooth-top ranges.

Both gas and electric ovens tend to have inaccurate thermostats. Oven thermostats should be checked with a reliable oven thermometer after the oven has been heated for at least 15 minutes. If the thermometer shows a difference of 25°F or more, set the oven thermostat higher or lower than the desired temperature according to the deviation shown.

Some ranges have self-cleaning and continuous-cleaning ovens. Self-cleaning ovens burn or carbonize food splatters and spills by the use of special cleaning cycles. Some ranges are easier to clean by hand than others. Similarly, some cleaning agents are easier to use than others. Oven sprays, for example, are simple to apply, but they are no more effective than pastes and jellies and are expensive to use. The thermostat sensor in the oven should never be touched with cleaners; they will corrode it and impair its accuracy. Cleaners should likewise never contact the heating elements on range tops or in an electric oven. Cleaners may be safely used to clean stainless steel, baked enamel, and chrome-plated surfaces in the oven and on the range top. They should not be used to clean aluminum because they corrode it, nor should they be used in continuous-cleaning ovens. Aluminum should be soaked in a baking soda solution or scoured with a steel wool soap pad. When selecting a gas or electric stove, remember that cooking with electricity costs two or three times as much as cooking with gas. However, the availability of either form of energy can be as much a deciding factor as the cost.

MICROWAVE OVENS

Microwave ovens use *microwaves* to cook foods. Microwaves are electromagnetic waves of high frequency and short wavelength that travel at the speed of light. If they hit substances that block them or offer resistance, the microwaves cause the molecules in the resisting substance to speed up their motion; this increased speed of the molecules produces heat.

A magnetron in the microwave oven produces the microwaves that enter the food and meet resistance from the molecules in the food. The microwaves penetrate the food to a depth of 1 inch; the heat produced is then conducted into the interior of the food. This method of heating permits faster heat penetration of foods than conventional methods, which involve conduction of heat by air, water, and other materials. Figure 3.1 demonstrates the cooking action of a typical microwave oven.

Microwave cooking procedures differ from conventional ones. A microwave oven has no temperature control; cooking is regulated by time alone. The time required to cook food by microwaves depends on the type and amount of food. Two potatoes take longer to cook than one, but not twice as long; a large squash takes longer to cook than a small one. Foods with a high fat or

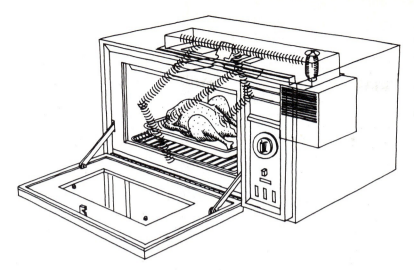

Figure 3.1

Cooking action in a microwave oven: microwaves produced by the magnetron are deflected by stirrer blades (fan) and oven walls into the food being cooked. *(John R. Free, "The Facts About Microwave Ovens,"* Popular Science *202* [1973]: 79)

sugar content heat more rapidly in a microwave oven than foods with a high water content. Foods cooked in microwave ovens do not brown unless the oven is equipped with special browning facilities.

Brands and models of microwave ovens vary in the time they require to cook a given food because the magnetrons vary in microwave output; thus, recipes and times must be developed accordingly for each oven. In addition, some microwave ovens have variable power settings that alternate the microwaves on and off for 1 second out of 10 to 10 seconds out of 10. The lower setting increases cooking time, but allows the food to cook more slowly. Some trial and error is necessary to obtain satisfactory results with microwave cookery, and for some cooking procedures the conventional cooking methods remain superior.

Metal containers and materials should not be used in microwave ovens because the metal ions block microwaves and prevent them from entering the food. Some microwave ovens can heat frozen dinners in their aluminum trays, but the waves penetrate the top surface only. Glass, china, some plastics, paper, plastic wrap, and wax paper are satisfactory materials to use in cooking foods in a microwave oven. The paper and plastic wraps do not heat during cooking; glass and china may heat by conduction from the food.

Some concern has been expressed about radiation leakage from microwave ovens. No radiation occurs in the foods cooked in these ovens, but it can come from the oven directly into the air. Federal standards have been established to limit the leakage of radiation to a maximum permissible level of 5 milliwatts per square centimeter when measured 2 inches (5 centimeters) from the oven with the door closed. Newer models of microwave ovens have doors designed to meet these standards. Additionally, safety interlocks on the doors turn off the magnetron when the door is opened. Damage to the door or seal, or food particles and grease that collect around the seal, can interfere with the seal's operation and cause radiation leakage. Heavy objects should not be placed on the door so that it does not warp. The oven should be cleaned, especially around the seal, after each use. A microwave oven should never be operated when it is empty; the magnetron could be damaged.

DISHWASHERS AND GARBAGE DISPOSERS

Dishwashers save time. Dishes cleaned in them are more sanitary than hand-washed dishes, so long as they are not contaminated by dirty hands when they are removed from the dishwasher. Similarly, a garbage disposer that pulverizes wastes and disperses them into the sewage system is a convenient and sanitary way of handling food wastes. A disposer can eliminate the need to clean refuse containers, since there will be no garbage residue to attract insects and rodents.

REFRIGERATORS AND FREEZERS

Refrigerators are essential in food preparation, but their value is greatly reduced if proper temperature is not maintained. The storage temperature of both refrigerators and freezers should be checked with appropriate thermometers. Table 3.1 shows the preferred temperature of storage for various foods in a refrigerator. Foods can be placed in the refrigerator in such a way as to take advantage of the different temperatures in the various areas. Most refrigerators are coldest at the bottom and warmest on the top shelves. The back part of the shelves is likely to be colder than the front, especially if the refrigerator door is opened frequently. A temperature of 40°F (4.5°C) is desirable for most refrigerator storage; 50°F (10°C) is the maximum temperature allowable for refrigerator storage.

Freezers should maintain a temperature of 0°F (−18°C) or less, but many do not. Higher temperatures shorten the storage life of food stored in a freezer and reduce the quality of the food stored.

Refrigerators, like other appliances, require periodic cleaning.

Table 3.1   Temperatures for storage of various foods in the refrigerator

Temperature		Food
(°F)	(°C)	
23–30	−5−−1	Fish and shellfish
33–38	0.5–3	Meat and fowl
38–46	3–8	Dairy products
44–50	7–10	Fruits and vegetables

Some bacteria and molds multiply slowly at refrigerator temperatures. Spills inside the refrigerator should be cleaned up when they occur; containers should be wiped off before storage, and many fruits and vegetables should be washed and placed in plastic bags to reduce soil accumulation in the refrigerator. Neither freezers nor refrigerators should be allowed to build up excessive amounts of frost, which reduces their efficiency.

Food preparation frequently involves mixing, beating, whipping, and creaming ingredients. Using an electric mixer for these tasks not only saves time and physical energy but often obtains better results than hand mixing. Electric mixers come in three types, each with varying capabilities. Hand mixers, which do not have stands, are equipped with two small metal beaters suitable for small mixing tasks, such as beating eggs, cream, and batters. A second, larger mixer has twin metal beaters and a stand as well. This mixer can be adjusted to accommodate two sizes of bowls that rotate to help mix the contents. The sides of the bowl can be scraped down with a rubber scraper while the mixer is operating, but care must be exercised not to catch the scraper in the beaters. The third type of mixer has a stationary bowl and only one beater. This beater simultaneously rotates and moves around the bowl, a beating action termed *hypocycloidal* or *planetary*. This mixer must be stopped before the sides of the bowl can be scraped down. Many beaters providing different kinds of mixing action are available for this mixer.

Unlike mixers, food blenders are suitable for some mixing operations but not for others. Most importantly, blenders can be used to chop, grind, and liquefy many kinds of foods. Some blenders have removable blades; these are easiest to clean and also allow food to be removed conveniently. The blades can also be detached and used on regular Mason canning jars. A blender should always be disassembled for cleaning. Food particles left in the blender can promote bacterial growth that could contaminate food placed in the blender at a later date.

Food processors can be used for slicing, shredding, grating, and chopping foods; they also have limited mixing capability. Slicing with a food processor is not as uniform as when done by hand, no matter how carefully foods are placed in the processor's feed tube. Processors can take over many of the jobs formerly done in the blender, often with better results. Blenders are more useful for small quantities of food that need to be finely chopped or pureed.

A *pressure cooker* is an airtight utensil that can be used for cooking and canning foods. When water is placed in the pan, the cover closed, and heat applied, some of the water in the pan is converted to steam. Since steam is a gas, the more molecules of steam that form in the space above the water in the pan, the greater the pres-

FOOD MIXERS, BLENDERS, AND PROCESSORS

PRESSURE SAUCEPANS

Table 3.2 Relationship of pressure to temperature in a pressure cooker		
Pressure (pounds)	Temperature	
	(°F)	(°C)
5	228	109
10	239	115
15	250	121

sure is on the surface of the water. More heat converts more of the water to steam, and the temperature increases until an equilibrium is reached. Thus, a pressure cooker is able to cook foods at a higher temperature and more quickly than is possible at atmospheric pressure. Table 3.2 shows the relationship between pounds of pressure in a pressure cooker or canner and the temperature inside the pressure pan. Some of the newer pressure saucepans provide only one pressure setting, 15 pounds.

Because of the great pressure produced inside the pan during cooking, a pressure cooker can be a hazard if it is used incorrectly. A pressure cooker should never be heated without water or other liquid in the pan, nor should it be filled too full. Instructions supplied with various pressure pans explain their limitations; most pans have safety valves that permit the release of excessive pressure. Pressure pans should also be vented to remove air, because air molecules in the pressure pan produce a lower temperature for any given pressure than an airless environment does. Venting is accomplished by leaving the air vent open while the contents boil a few minutes, thus driving out the air. This procedure is not necessary for cooking meats and vegetables, but it is essential in pressure canning low-acid foods.

Foods continue to cook in a pressure pan as long as the pressure is up inside the pan, even though heat is no longer being applied. In cooking vegetables, which require only a very short cooking time, it is often necessary to reduce the pressure quickly to prevent overcooking. This is done by placing the pan in the sink and running cold water over it. Electric pressure pans should be unplugged before being cooled in this manner.

Pressure saucepans use a weight for maintaining the pressure inside the pan. Occasionally, this weight becomes dislodged while the pressure is up, and the contents of the pan start to spray out. If the pressure weight cannot be replaced, the vent should be covered with an inverted pot and the pressure pan quickly cooled under cold water to reduce the pressure.

Utensils for Food Preparation
POTS AND PANS

Cooking pots should be made of materials that conduct heat rapidly; iron and aluminum are better conductors of heat than glass and stainless steel. Although copper is an excellent heat conductor, it is not recommended for utensils because toxic amounts of copper can contaminate food. Copper is used instead on the bottom of stainless steel pots to improve their conductivity. A pot with a thick bottom—cast iron, heavy aluminum, and stainless steel pans with copper bottoms—provide even heat conduction. The pan should have straight sides and a tight-fitting cover; handles should remain cool when the pot is heated.

Both pans and mixing bowls should be made of materials that do not cause discoloration of foods prepared in them. Iron pots are excellent for cooking meats but cause discoloration of some light-colored vegetables, milk, and egg mixtures. The iron from the pot dissolves and reacts with tannins in potatoes and other vegetables, producing a gray or black discoloration. The iron combines with sulfur in eggs to produce a green discoloration. Discolored foods are not harmful to eat, but they are unattractive in appearance.

Minerals dissolved out of foods and water tend to accumulate inside aluminum pans and, to a lesser extent, in stainless steel pans. Mineral deposits can cause a gray or greenish discoloration in egg and milk mixtures cooked in these pans. Aluminum mixing bowls can also cause discoloration in egg mixtures. Stainless steel, and sometimes aluminum, pans can be cleaned by boiling a vinegar solution in the pan to dissolve the mineral deposits. Glass is usually free of such mineral deposits.

Burned food is easier to remove from stainless steel and glass pans than from other pans, because stainless steel and glass can be coated with an oven cleaner to dissolve the carbonized food. Aluminum and iron require scouring; an oven cleaner would corrode these metals.

Glass utensils, when hot, break if they are placed on a damp or cold surface. The difference in temperature between the hot glass utensil and the cold or damp surface produces an uneven contraction of the glass, causing it to crack. Similarly, hot objects should not be placed on glass refrigerator shelves.

BAKING PANS

Conduction is the principal mode of heat transfer on the surface unit of a range; radiation is equally, if not more, important in the oven. Dull, dark surfaces absorb radiant energy and bright, shiny surfaces reflect it. This principle can be applied in baking to regulate browning, which occurs through heat absorption. Foods with a high sugar and fat content—cakes, cookies, and sweetbreads—brown more readily than such sugarless foods as pie crust or pizza dough. Thus, pie crust browns better when baked in a glass pan that permits maximum transmission of radiant energy or in a dark pie pan that absorbs heat well. Sweet doughs and cookies are best baked in shiny aluminum or stainless steel pans that reflect some of the heat and thus prevent excessive browning; sweet doughs baked in dark pans tend to burn.

Teflon-coated pans have been in use for a number of years because foods baked in them show less tendency to stick to the pan. Removal of some foods, however, is easier if the Teflon pan is lightly greased. Two-piece pans, in which the sides and bottom separate, are a necessity for baking sponge cakes and a great convenience for baking shortened cakes; the separation makes removal of the cake from the pan an easy process.

When a recipe calls for a pan size that is not available, substitutions should be based as closely as possible on the surface area of the pan. Using a pan with a larger surface area than specified, for example, means that the dough or batter lies in a thinner layer and bakes more quickly, which may affect its texture. Table 2 in the appendix lists the surface area of some common baking pans.

COOKING TOOLS A wide variety of tools is available for food preparation, but many are gadgets with only limited application. Tools with multiple functions are better investments than tools with only one use; a strainer, for example, can be used to sift flour as well as to remove lumps or seeds from foods, thus dispensing with the need for a sifter. The flour can be sifted through the strainer by tapping the rim of the strainer with one hand. The choice of tools depends both on the kind of food preparation involved and the resources available for purchasing equipment.

Cutlery Many kinds of knives are needed for specific jobs in food preparation. Knives that hold a sharp cutting edge are best for all jobs; blades of hammer-forged, high-carbon steel are highly recommended. Cutlery requires proper care if it is to remain sharp. It should be stored so that the cutting edges do not strike hard objects, to prevent dulling or nicking. Good-quality knives should be sharpened on an oiled whetstone and feathered on an iron. The iron will not sharpen a dull knife, but it does help keep a smooth, fine edge on a knife that has been sharpened on a stone.

MEASURING EQUIPMENT Measuring equipment of good quality is essential for successful food preparation. The American Standards Association has defined the capacities of various measures, but not all measuring equipment has been standardized to meet these specifications. To determine the accuracy of a measuring utensil, fill it with water and then measure the water in a graduated metric cylinder of appropriate size. Variations of 5 percent more or less than the standard are allowable; a 1-cup measure may hold 12 milliliters more or less than 237 milliliters, or a variation of slightly less than 1 tablespoon. Tables 1, 2, and 3 in the appendix list the abbreviations, capacities, and equivalents of various measures.

Nested sets of cups, sometimes called Mary Ann cups, include measures for 1 cup, ½ cup, ⅓ cup, and ¼ cup, when measurements are level with the top of the cup; these are preferred for measuring dry ingredients and solid fats. Liquids should be measured in transparent graduated cups with spouts. Measuring spoons should be used for amounts of less than ¼ cup, either of liquid or of dry ingredients. These spoons are available in sets that include a tablespoon, teaspoon, ½ teaspoon, and ¼ teaspoon. Measuring tablespoons and teaspoons are not the same capacity as those used for eating and table service. It is important in food preparation to know the equivalents for the various measuring utensils, such as teaspoons per tablespoon or tablespoons per cup.

Figure 3.2

The 250-milliliter liquid
measure is divided into fifths of
50-milliliter graduations.

Metric Measures The National Bureau of Standards has added
to its existing regulation on cooking and baking utensils (Z61.1)
information defining the capacity of metric measures. To avoid
confusion, these measures are not called "cups" or "spoons" but
are identified only by their metric volume in liters or milliliters.

The liquid measures include liter and half-liter measures graduated by 50 milliliter divisions and a 250 milliliter measure with
25 milliliter graduations as shown in Figure 3.2. Single-capacity
dry level measures contain 250, 125, and 50 milliliters each.
These are equivalent to the nested or Mary Ann cups long in use.
Small measures have capacities of 25, 15, 5, 2, and 1 milliliter
each. All these measures are being produced commercially in the
United States and are the accepted metric measures in use in
Canada.

New cookbooks are being published using only metric measures, and volumes of food ingredients are expressed in liters and
milliliters. For instance, a recipe may list 710 ml of flour (about
3 cups in the English system). One preparing the food must decide
which measures to use to obtain the desired volume: $(2 \times 250 \text{ ml})$
$+ (1 \times 125 \text{ ml}) + (1 \times 50 \text{ ml}) + (1 \times 25 \text{ ml}) + (1 \times 10 \text{ ml})$. Recipes
using cups and spoons can easily be converted into the corre-
sponding metric volume by referring to a table of equivalent measures, such as Table 3.3 and Table 2 of the appendix.

Food ingredients can be measured either by volume or by
weight (mass). Weighing yields more accurate results than volume measures, with accurate scales and correct techniques. Large
quantities of foods can be weighed faster than they can be measured. The United States now uses the English system of weights,
whose basic unit is the avoirdupois pound containing 16 ounces.
Conversion to the metric system will mean the use of kilograms,

Table 3.3   Equivalent volumes of standard measuring utensils in the English and metric systems of measurement

Teaspoon	Tablespoon	Cup	Pint	Quart	Fluid ounce	Milliliter	Deciliter	Liter
1.0	—	—	—	—	—	4.97	0.05	—
3.0	1.0	—	—	—	0.5	14.9	0.15	—
48.0	16.0	1.0	0.5	0.25	8.0	236.6	2.37	0.237
96.0	32.0	2.0	1.0	0.5	16.0	473.2	4.73	0.473
192.0	64.0	4.0	2.0	1.0	32.0	946.4	9.46	0.946
6.0	2.0	—	—	—	1.0	29.6	0.296	—
—	—	—	—	—	—	1.0	0.01	0.001
—	—	—	—	—	—	100.0	1.0	0.1
—	—	—	—	—	—	1000.0	10.0	1.0

Table 3.4   Equivalent weights in the English and metric systems

English system (avoirdupois)		Metric system			
Pounds	Ounces	Kilograms	Grams	Milligrams	Micrograms
1.0	16.0	0.454	453.59	—	—
0.0625	1.0	0.028	28.35	—	—
2.2	35.3	1.0	1000.0	—	—
—	0.035	0.0001	1.0	1000	100,000
			.1	1	1000

grams, and milligrams as units of weight. Table 3.4 shows the English and metric weight equivalents. Table 3 in the appendix provides the factors and method for conversion from one system to the other. A common error in weighing is to obtain an incorrect *tare*—that is, the weight of the container the material is contained in—for the weighing vessel.

Confusion often results in distinguishing fluid (fl.) ounces, a measure of volume, from avoirdupois (avdp.) ounces, a measure of weight or mass. When the term "ounce" is used alone without a modifier, it is an avoirdupois ounce and refers to the weight of the material. The term "fluid ounce" is used to indicate volume measure. These two kinds of ounces are equal only when measuring water; 1 fluid ounce of water weighs 1 ounce (avdp.). The same is true in the metric system, in which 1 milliliter of water weighs 1 gram and 1 liter of water weighs 1 kilogram. A fluid ounce of oil, however, weighs less than 1 ounce (avdp.), and a fluid ounce of milk weighs more than 1 ounce. Table 9 in the appendix lists the weight/volume relationships of many foods, along with the yield from their various market forms.

With conversion to the metric system, this table will need to be completely revised so that only metric weights are used, probably as grams per 100 or 500 milliliters, depending on the ingredient or food and how it is sold and used. Once the change to metric is universal, the purchasing of foods and ingredients will be greatly simplified.

Thermometers   Thermometers are important measuring utensils. Many kinds are available for specific uses, varying in the upper and lower limits of the scale and in the degree intervals used. Table 3.5 lists the types of thermometers and their lower and upper temperature limits. Scale divisions on candy and jelly thermometers must be clearly marked in 1 degree Fahrenheit units, for exact temperatures are critical to the success of these cooking processes.

Thermometers are not always accurate. A thermometer can be checked in boiling water if its scale goes to the boiling point, or it can be compared with another thermometer that has been tested in boiling water. Some oven thermometers cannot be tested in boiling water because they should not get wet. They can be checked against a tested thermometer in a warm oven.

Most household thermometers use the Fahrenheit scale. Within a few years, however, the United States will probably change to the metric system of measurements, in which case the Celsius scale will become standard. Fahrenheit-Celsius conversions and formulas for calculating conversions are given in Tables 3 and 4 in the appendix.

Even the most accurate measuring equipment does not reproduce specifications of a recipe unless measuring techniques are also accurate. Ingredients vary in their tendency to pack down or lump, and in their tendency to resist measurement entirely. Consequently, methods of measurement vary according to individual ingredients and recipes. For example, food ingredients that tend to cling to measuring utensils should be scraped out of the utensil with a rubber scraper to ensure that they are completely transferred. As much as 2 or 3 tablespoons of honey or oil can be left in a measure if it is not scraped out, producing a short measure.

Measurements in Food Preparation
MEASURING FOOD MATERIALS

Table 3.5   Temperature range for thermometers used in food preparation

Type of thermometer	Temperature range	
	(°F)	(°C)
Refrigerator/freezer	−40–60	−40–16
Oven	150–500	66–288
Meat	140–200	60–93
Candy/jelly	200–400	93–204
Deep fat	200–450	93–232

Furthermore, ingredients measured in single-capacity measures should be level at the brim.

Flours and Powdered Sugar   Refined flours and powdered sugar tend to pack down, and the sugar tends to lump; measuring these ingredients when they are packed down produces considerable variation. Two methods of measurement have been developed to overcome this problem. The first is sifting. Flour can be sifted to incorporate air and separate granules; sifting also removes lumps from powdered sugar. Cake flour should be sifted when it is used in sponge and butter cakes. Figure 3.3 shows how flour may be sifted directly into a measure. Flour can also be sifted separately and spooned lightly into the measure. Either way, the measure should be filled to overflowing and leveled off. Do not jar the measure during measurement; this causes the flour to become packed down.

Sifting flour before measuring it is not always necessary, because the ratio of ingredients in most quick breads and yeast breads is less critical than it is in many cakes. For most breads, a second adequate form of measurement is to stir the flour well until it is light, spoon it lightly into the measure until it overflows, and then level it off. Flour measured by weighing does not need to be sifted. The air incorporated in the flour by sifting is of little consequence once liquid is added; such air has little or no effect on the finished product. Sifting is not an efficient way to mix dry ingredients, either. Dry mixing is accomplished more quickly and thoroughly if the ingredients are stirred well with a French or flat whip or a fork.

Whole wheat flour contains bran, which keeps it from packing down. Stir whole wheat flour before filling the cup lightly and leveling it. Most other dry granulated materials, such as soy flour, wheat germ, cornmeal, and fine bread crumbs, need only to be stirred before the measure is filled.

Granulated Sugars   White granulated sugar is one of the easiest ingredients to measure because it does not pack. A measure can be dipped into the sugar, filled, and leveled. Brown sugar contains 2 percent water, which causes it to lump, especially if it is allowed to dry out. Brown sugar should be packed into the measure, with no air pockets, for an accurate measurement. Turned out of the measure, brown sugar should hold its mold, as shown in Figure 3.4.

Sometimes brown sugar develops firm lumps that can be broken up by blending the sugar in an electric blender. Lumps do not form if the waxed paper liner in the package is closed and the box is stored in the refrigerator or in a tightly closed jar after it has been opened.

Figure 3.3

One way to measure flour: sift it directly into the measure until it overflows, then level it off with a straightedge.

Figure 3.4

When either solid fat or brown sugar is measured, it should be pressed into a single-capacity measure to eliminate air pockets. Properly measured brown sugar retains the mold of the measure when turned out.

Solid Fats   Solid fats include hydrogenated shortening, lard, margarine, and butter. These solids resist molding in a measure and often leave air spaces. The solid fat should be packed into the single-capacity measure of the desired size, pressing the fat firmly down so that no air pockets remain, as shown in Figure 3.4. When regular margarine and butter are sold four cubes or sticks to a pound, whole cubes or parts of cubes can be used to measure these fats. Table 3.6 shows the approximate relationships of weight to volume for table fats. Many brands of margarine carry markings on the wrappers as guides to measurement. Margarine sold five cubes to a pound and whipped and diet margarines and spreads cannot be measured in this way; these table fats are not recommended for baking.

Liquids   Oil, honey, milk, molasses, juices, water, melted fat, and other liquid ingredients should be measured in a graduated transparent liquid measure with a pour spout. Fill the measure to the desired graduation and check it by holding the measure at eye level so that the *meniscus,* the curved upper surface of the transparent liquid, matches the desired line on both sides of the measure. Opaque liquids that do not show a meniscus are measured by aligning the top of the liquid with the line. The liquid measure can also be placed on a level countertop to make the measurement, but the reading should be made at eye level.

Measuring Small Amounts   Baking powder, baking soda, salt, and spices are used in such small amounts that they must be measured in the small capacity measures of 15 milliliters or less. These ingredients should be stirred and free of lumps; then the measure should be dipped into the ingredient and leveled off. If less than 1 milliliter is required, the 1 milliliter measure can be filled, leveled, and half or more of its contents removed. Still smaller amounts are often described as a pinch, a sprinkle, or, in the case of seasonings, ''to taste.''

Coarse Foods   Chopped nuts, vegetables, fruits, raisins, coconut, and grated cheese are coarse foods. They can be measured in any kind of measure lightly filled, not packed.

MEASURING APPROXIMATIONS   Many foods are measured by approximation. One recipe may require a large egg, but the sizes of a dozen large eggs vary somewhat. Another recipe may call for two stalks of celery or half a medium onion, but onions and celery bunches come in different sizes; furthermore, inside celery stalks are smaller than outside ones. A size that one person calls medium, another calls small or large. As a rule, the amount of such ingredients can vary and still produce a satisfactory result. If the amount of celery, onion, or some other ingredient is critical, a definite measure—125 milli-

Table 3.6   *Approximate weights and volumes for margarine and butter*

Pounds	Cubes	Cups	Tablespoons	Milliliters
1	4	2	32	500
1/2	2	1	16	250
1/4	1	1/2	8	125
1/8	1/2	1/4	4	60
1/16	1/4	1/8	2	30

The smallest possible measuring utensil should be used to measure ingredients; 50 milliliters of milk should not be measured in a 500-milliliter measure. Also, a single measure rather than multiples of a smaller measure should be used—a 15-milliliter measure instead of three 5-milliliter measures or one 250-milliliter measure instead of two 125-milliliter measures. liters, for example—should be specified in the recipe.

Heat in Food Preparation

Heat is a form of energy. Heating food ingredients can produce complex chemical changes in the food. In food preparation, heat is measured in temperature with a thermometer, as described earlier in this chapter. In nutrition, heat is measured in *kilocalories* or *joules.* Foods are classified according to their caloric value, which is the amount of heat or energy they produce in the body when they are eaten.

A *small calorie,* abbreviated cal., is the amount of heat required to raise the temperature of 1 gram of water from 14.5°C to 15.5°C at normal atmospheric pressure. A *large calorie,* also called a kilocalorie and abbreviated Cal. (or kcal.), is the amount of heat required to raise the temperature of 1 kilogram of water from 14.5°C to 15.5°C at normal atmospheric pressure. Currently, food tables use kilocalories. However, joules will replace calories when the metric system is introduced. One small calorie equals 4.184 joules, and 1 kilocalorie equals 4.184 kilojoules. Conversion formulas for calories and joules are given in the appendix.

COOKING

The word *cook* has several connotations. Its broadest meaning suggests the preparation of food for eating, and such preparation may not involve the use of heat. Here, however, cooking is considered in its narrower sense, as the application of heat to foods.

Advantages of Heating Foods   Heating foods provides the following benefits:

1. Heat destroys bacteria, their spores and toxins, and parasites in foods.

2. Different cooking procedures, such as frying, roasting, and boiling, produce variety in the flavors of foods.
3. Heat improves the texture of foods by softening cellulose in plants and connective tissues in meat and solidifying baked products.
4. Heat reduces the bulk of some foods.
5. Heat improves the digestibility of some foods.

Disadvantages of Heating Foods   Heating foods can also have the following undesirable effects:

1. Heat destroys some vitamins.
2. The texture of some foods becomes excessively soft.
3. Some foods show undesirable color and flavor changes.

These disadvantages are brought on only by improper cooking techniques. Chapter 1 includes a section on nutrient retention in food preparation; these principles are emphasized throughout the text. This text also stresses attaining the best possible texture in cooked foods. The correct preparation of food eliminates any potential disadvantage of heat.

COOKING MEDIA   Foods are heated in four media: air, water, steam, and fat. The temperatures reached in each medium affect both the cooking procedures and the nature of the cooked food.

Air   Air is the cooking medium for baking, roasting, and broiling foods. In roasting and baking, heat is transferred to the food by the hot air surrounding it. Radiant energy is involved also in broiling. Roasting, baking, and broiling are known as *dry heat cookery methods* and give foods a different flavor than moist heat does.

Water   Water is the medium for boiling, simmering, stewing, braising, or poaching foods; these are the *moist heat cookery methods*. Water boils at 212°F (100°C) at sea level. The boiling point of water is the temperature at which vapor (steam) pressure within the liquid is equal to, or just exceeds, the atmospheric pressure on its surface. Water boils when the bubbles of steam break vigorously on its top surface.

Heating a pot more than necessary for a full rolling boil does not increase the temperature of the water, but it does increase the rate of evaporation. Food cooked at highest heat is more likely to burn as a result of rapid water evaporation. At higher elevations, the boiling point of water decreases; for each 960 feet of elevation, it is 1 degree Celsius lower. At an elevation of 5,000 feet, water boils at about 95°C, causing foods to take longer to cook.

Many foods taste better if they are cooked at temperatures of less than boiling. *Simmering* is cooking at less than the boiling point, where bubbles only occasionally break through the top surface of the water. *Stewing* and *braising* are the same as simmering, but refer to meat, not liquids. *Poaching* is cooking at even lower temperatures, where no bubbles at all break the surface of the water.

WATER PURITY Dissolved in water are such minerals as calcium, magnesium, iron, chlorine, carbonates, and sulfates. The presence of these minerals makes water "hard." The amount of minerals present in water depends on its source. The higher the mineral content, the harder the water is; if the mineral content is low, the water is considered naturally "soft." Hard water is more alkaline than soft water.

Artificially softened water has been passed through a resin that absorbs calcium, magnesium, and iron and replaces these ions with the more soluble sodium. This treated water remains alkaline, however. Although artificially softened water is better for washing clothes and cleaning, nutritionists do not recommend it for regular cooking and drinking because its high sodium content may contribute to the development of high blood pressure. Recent studies indicate that death from heart disease occurs less frequently in areas with naturally hard water. Artificially softened water may be used for washing fruits and vegetables, but a hard water tap should be available to supply water for cooking and drinking in households with water softeners. Purified water is water from which all minerals have been artificially removed. This water is prepared by a process of reverse osmosis and deionization. Two resins are used for the deionization process. One replaces the cations of calcium, magnesium, and iron with hydrogen ions, and the other replaces the anions of sulfate, carbonate, and chlorine with hydroxyl ions. The hydrogen ion (H^+) and hydroxyl ion (OH^-) combine to form water (H_2O).

The hardness of water affects food preparation because both the minerals in hard water and its alkaline composition can alter foods.

Steam Another method of moist heat cookery is steam, which is produced at the same temperature as boiling water. If steam is compressed, as in a pressure cooker, the temperature of both water and steam increases, as previously described. Using steam to cook foods reduces the dissolution of nutrients from food. However, such a gain may also result in greater heat destruction of nutrients, because foods may take longer to cook in steam than in boiling water.

Methods of steam cookery include:

1. cooking foods on a rack above boiling water
2. cooking foods in their own water, as in stir-fry and waterless vegetable cookery, and baking meat in a covered pan in the oven
3. wrapping foods in aluminum foil, either to bake in the oven or to

cook over wood coals or charcoal, so that they cook in their own juices

Fat Fat is the cooking medium for sautéing, pan frying, and deep-fat frying foods. Pan frying and sautéing are two names for the same process, cooking food in a small amount of fat, although sautéing is sometimes thought to use less fat than pan frying. In deep-fat cookery, foods are completely submerged in fat. Fats can reach much higher temperatures than water or steam; most foods are fried at temperatures between 325 and 400°F. Foods cook more quickly when they are deep-fat fried because of these higher temperatures, and they take on a distinct texture and flavor.

ENERGY TRANSFER   For food to be cooked, heat must be transferred from its source to the food. In conventional ranges and in wood and charcoal fires, heat is transferred by *conduction, radiation,* and *convection.* Microwaves are also a method of energy transfer.

Microwaves The cooking action of microwave ovens has already been described. Microwave cookery needs no medium, because microwaves can be transmitted in a vacuum as well as in air and water. Microwaves cause agitation of the molecules in food, thereby producing heat. They are the fastest mode of energy transfer.

Conduction Heat is carried from one molecule to another in conduction. An electric surface unit or gas flame touches a pot and conducts heat to it, though some radiation is also involved. Heat is then transferred from the pot to its contents. In pan broiling, heat is conducted directly from the pot to the food, for no cooking medium is present. When foods are cooked in fat or water, however, heat is first conducted to the liquid medium and then from the fat or water to the food.

The speed of heating by conduction depends on the conductivity of the material in the pot and also on the nature of the food being cooked. Fluid food mixtures heat more rapidly than viscous ones. Thus, water heats faster than a thick sauce or pudding. Conduction also occurs in roasting and baking, but the medium in these cases is air. Air is not as good a conductor as water; thus, a potato takes longer to bake than to boil.

Radiation Radiant energy transfer, like microwaves, requires no medium. The heat source gives off infrared light rays, which are longer than light waves but travel at the speed of light, to transfer heat. Radiant energy transfer is thus a rapid one. Sources of radiation include the glowing red heating elements of electric ranges and appliances, gas flames, and the glowing coals and flames of charcoal and wood. Heat transmission by radiation is also affected by food containers. Clear glass is the best transmitter of radiant energy. Oven temperature should be reduced by 25° when cakes are baked in glass containers because of rapid radiant energy transfer. As previously noted, bright shiny pans reflect radiant energy and therefore delay cooking; dark, dull surfaces absorb radiant energy and speed cooking.

Convection   Heat transfer by convection is based on the principle that hot air or liquid rises and cold air or liquid sinks. Heat increases the speed of molecules and causes them to occupy more space and be less dense than the closely packed cold molecules. When heat is applied at the bottom of a pot, the liquid at the bottom heats first. As the heated liquid becomes less dense, it rises above the unheated portions, which flow, in turn, to the bottom of the pan.

The same phenomenon occurs inside an oven. The top of a cake browns more rapidly when it is placed on the top shelf of the oven for this reason. Pans must therefore be placed in the oven in such a way that convection currents are not impeded. Figure 3.5 illustrates pan placement in an oven.

Mixtures of Energy Transfer   Foods are usually cooked by more than one of these methods of heat transfer. Even in microwave cookery conduction of heat, from the outside of the food to the interior, occurs. The effects of each method of heat transfer need to be considered in selecting the proper pan for cooking a particular food, the temperature, and the cooking time.

Foods are composed of water, protein, fat, carbohydrate, acids, enzymes, pigments, flavoring substances, vitamins, and minerals. Not all foods have all these components; some contain only one. Specific components affect the method of food preparation and the nutritive value of foods; in addition they provide a basis for grouping foods both by method of preparation and by nutrient contribution.

All of these food components, with the exception of minerals, are composed of the elements carbon, hydrogen, and oxygen. Some also contain nitrogen, and others have small amounts of sulfur, phosphorus, and other elements. The main chemical difference between fats and carbohydrates, for instance, lies in their different ratios of carbon, hydrogen, and oxygen and the way these elements are combined or linked together. In a way, all foods are simply different combinations of the same chemical elements. Table 3.7 shows the approximate range of the basic components of typical groups of foods.

Almost all foods contain water, but in widely varying amounts. The water content of a food, for example, may change when the

Figure 3.5

When only one pan is baked at a time, it should be placed near the center of the oven. When two or more pans are baked, they should be placed so that they are not directly over each other; they should not touch each other or the oven walls, and each should be surrounded by 2 inches of space, if possible.

2 cake layers

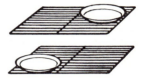

4 cake layers

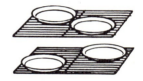

Food Composition

WATER

Table 3.7   Approximate range of basic components of typical groups of foods

Type of food	Water (%)	Protein (%)	Fat (%)	Carbohydrate (%)
Cooked cereals, pastas, grains, bread	35–85	2–9	0–3	10–50
Legumes, cooked	69–71	7–8	<1	20–21
Nuts	3–5	15–26	46–64	16–29
Fruits and vegetables	70–95	<1–2	0–(26)	3–25
Milk, whole	87	3.5	3.5	5
Cheese	35–80	9–36	1–32	0–3
Meats, cooked	40–70	11–32	2–55	0–5

food is cooked. Meats lose water during cooking; dry cereals and legumes absorb water. Table 3.8 shows the water content of a few representative foods before and after cooking.

PROTEIN   Meats and cheese are the best sources of protein, while vegetables and fruits have very little, as can be seen in Table 3.7. Foods with a high protein content, such as meats, eggs, cheese, and milk, require special attention when they are cooked.

FAT   Most fats used in food preparation, such as oils, shortening, and lard, contain 100 percent fat. The common table fats, butter and margarine, however, are only 81 percent fat because they contain water and milk solids as well. Fats occur in many foods in a form that is not readily apparent. A lean piece of meat with all visible fat removed can contain as much as 6 percent fat. Most fruits and vegetables, however, contain little or no fat, with the exception of coconuts, olives, and avocados. Nuts (except chestnuts) have a very high fat content.

CARBOHYDRATES   Sugar and starch are pure carbohydrate; thus, foods with a high sugar or starch content are high-carbohydrate foods. Cellulose, a nondigestible carbohydrate, is plentiful in fruits, vegetables, and whole grains.

ACIDS   Foods vary considerably in their acid content, a circumstance that affects their preparation and processing. Active acidity is of prime importance in food preparation and processing. Active acidity is measured in terms of the concentration of *hydrogen ions* (H^+).

The hydrogen ion is the positively charged atom that results when water and other compounds ionize. Water (H_2O) can ionize or separate into its component ions, H^+ and OH^-. The hydrogen ion contributes acidity and the *hydroxyl ion* (OH^-) contributes alkalinity. When water ionizes, equal numbers of hydrogen and hydroxyl ions are produced; therefore, pure water is neither acidic nor alkaline but neutral.

Most foods, however, have such a small amount of hydrogen ion that large decimal fractions are required to express acidity. A system has been devised for expressing the hydrogen ion concentration in pH units. The *pH* of a substance is the negative log of its hydrogen ion concentration. Thus, a food with a hydrogen ion concentration of 0.0001 mole per liter has a pH of 4; a food with a hydrogen ion concentration of 0.0000001 mole per liter has a pH of 7.

Using pH to indicate the acidity of substances is a less cumbersome procedure than using the actual hydrogen ion concentration. As the pH number decreases, the acidity increases. Substances with a pH of less than 7 are acidic. Substances with a pH greater than 7 are alkaline. At pH 7, substances are neutral; this is the pH of pure water. A substance of pH 3 is ten times more acidic than a substance of pH 4. The pH of some common foods is given in Table 13 in the appendix. Cream of tartar, vinegar, and citric acid (sour salt), having low pHs, are used to increase the acidity of food mixtures. Baking soda, or too much baking powder, produces alkalinity.

Enzymes are produced inside the cells of all plants and animals. They are proteins and, unlike bacteria, are not capable of self-multiplication. Enzymes function in cells as catalysts to speed up chemical reactions. Most enzymes are specific in their activity, so that a different enzyme is needed for each chemical reaction. For instance, one group of enzymes helps change starch into sugar in ripening fruit; another group of enzymes changes sugar to starch as corn and peas mature.

The enzymes in cells remain active even when the tissue they are a part of is no longer alive. After fruit has been picked or an animal has been slaughtered, their enzymes continue to function; a tomato or pear ripens after it has been picked green.

Enzymes also have specific temperatures at which they are active. Because they are protein, enzymes are inactivated by high heat, such as that found in cooking. At refrigerator and freezer temperatures, enzyme activity is slowed down, but it resumes when the temperature is raised again. Most enzymes involved in food preparation are active at body and room temperatures, although some are active at slightly higher temperatures. Enzymes are also active within a specific pH range and can often be inactivated by altering the pH.

Oxidative enzymes, which catalyze the addition of oxygen to various substances, cause the greatest problem in food preparation. They produce rancidity in fats, browning in some fruits and vegetables when the cell structure is cut or damaged, destruction

ENZYMES

Table 3.8
Comparison of the water content of typical foods, before and after cooking

Food	Percent water	
	Raw	Cooked
Turkey	68	61
Oats	9	84
Legumes, dry	11	69
Spinach	91	92
Peas, green	83	87

of some vitamins, and a change in flavor in some milk products. These undesirable effects can be avoided by controlling enzyme activity.

PIGMENTS Pigments produce color in foods and thus contribute to a food's esthetic appearance. Food color is a subjective quality; people accept a color in one food that they abhor in another. Green vegetables are acceptable, but green scrambled eggs are not. Color is also an indication of freshness in many foods. A bright yellow banana is likely to be fresh, but a black one may be past its prime or totally inedible. Bright red indicates freshness in meat; a brownish-red color indicates lack of freshness.

The method of preparation can also affect the color of foods, especially that of fruits and vegetables, whose pigments are strongly affected by the pH of the medium in which they are cooked. Acidity and alkalinity must be controlled in cooking fruits and vegetables.

FLAVORING SUBSTANCES Flavor is a combination of taste and smell. Like color, a flavor that is acceptable in one food may not be in another. Bitterness is acceptable in coffee, but not in milk. Flavor also contributes to the esthetic quality of foods. A food with an unacceptable flavor is not likely to be eaten.

Four Basic Taste Sensations People are able to distinguish only four taste sensations—sweet, sour, salty, and bitter—because the tongue has receptors only for these four tastes. However, these taste sensations interact so that the presence of one substance alters the taste perception of another. Sugar reduces acidity and bitterness and is added to coffee for this purpose. Acid also reduces bitterness but increases saltiness; a vinaigrette sauce on cooked greens reduces their bitterness. Salt reduces acidity and increases sweetness, which may be why many people like to salt apples, cantaloupe, watermelon, and grapefruit.

Contribution of Odor to Flavor The odor of foods is the other component affecting flavor. *Aromatic compounds* in foods, or in herbs and spices added to foods, are responsible for the odor of food. Aromatic compounds are *volatile* oils, that is, oils that will evaporate or vaporize. Freshly picked apples, for example, have a distinctive odor that is lost after they are kept several months in storage. Aromatic compounds are sensed by receptors in the upper part of the nose and may not be stimulated by ordinary breathing. Sniffing and breathing through the mouth, however, allow the aromatic compounds to stimulate these olfactory receptors. When a person eats, the taste buds on the tongue perceive the tastes at the same time that the aromatic compounds are released to stimulate the olfactory receptors in the nose.

Nasal congestion interferes with the ability to taste foods for this reason.

Acceptance of Flavor and Flavor Intensity   Each food has its own distinctive package of flavors that combines the four taste sensations with specific aromatic oils. Flavor acceptability is a learned characteristic that depends partly upon a person's childhood exposure to various flavors in foods. Many persons have pronounced likes and dislikes based on their previous experiences and learned behavior.

The flavor of foods can vary in intensity according to the person tasting them. Children have a large number of taste receptors and frequently refuse highly seasoned foods, accepting them only if the seasoning is diluted. Because taste receptors decrease in number with increasing age, older people are better able to tolerate highly seasoned foods. Smoking, too, dulls a person's sensitivity to flavors.

Heat brings out the flavor of foods, possibly by increasing the volatility of aromatic substances. Conversely, cold temperatures decrease flavor. An ice cream mixture that tastes sweet and flavorful at room temperature may be less flavorful and sweet after it is frozen.

Seasonings and Condiments   The natural flavors of foods can be altered by various seasonings and condiments. Catsup, barbecue sauces, meat sauces, salad dressings, and marinades are typical condiments and seasonings that are used to change the flavors of foods, sometimes to the point of masking completely the natural flavor of the food. Some people saturate everything they eat with catsup, salt, or hot peppers. The discriminating gourmet, however, appreciates the natural flavor of each food and uses seasonings to enhance and enrich the natural flavors, not to extinguish them. It takes experience to choose the most desirable seasoning for a particular food, to blend the flavors, and to add the correct amount of seasoning to achieve the desired effects. Table 14 in the appendix lists seasonings and their suggested uses.

SALT   Many foods taste flat without salt, which is one of the most important flavoring substances. Common table salt is a compound of sodium and chlorine, essential nutrients that are, however, already amply supplied in food. Excessive salt intake may pose a nutritional problem, because large amounts of sodium in the diet are thought to contribute to the development of high blood pressure. The best solution to the problem is to learn to like foods with minimal amounts of salt added and to refrain from salting foods, such as fruits, that do not absolutely need it. Undersalting a food is preferable to oversalting it, for more salt can always be added, but too much salt cannot be removed. Table 3.9

Table 3.9   Recommended ratio of salt for various foods and ingredients

Food or ingredient	Amount	Salt (teaspoon)
Dry cereal, pasta, rice	1 cup	1
Flour	1 cup	¼
Dry legumes	1 pound	2
Ground meat, stew	1 pound	¾
Soup, sauce, gravy	1 cup	¼
Vegetables, fresh	1 pound	¾

lists some approximate ratios for adding salt to various foods. The amount of salt added to foods that already contain sizable amounts of such salted fats as butter or margarine or that contain salted stock, meat stock base, or soy sauce may need to be reduced.

EXTRACTS   Extracts are obtained by the separation of aromatic oils from their natural source. In instances where extracting these natural flavors is impossible or impracticable, imitation or synthetic extracts are prepared. Some flavors available in natural or synthetic extracts include vanilla, peppermint, mint, lemon, orange, anise, cherry, wintergreen, banana, maple, butter, raspberry, brandy, rum, black walnut, root beer, cherry, pineapple, strawberry, and many others. Flavored gelatin desserts, soft drinks, candies, cake mixes, and ice cream are a few of many products that contain these flavoring extracts.

Bouillon and meat stock bases are also flavoring extracts. They provide additional meat flavor in gravies, soups, sauces, and casseroles, and can also be used to season legumes and vegetables. Different brands of extracts have different flavors, so brands should be compared to locate a desired flavor.

SPICES, HERBS, AROMATIC SEEDS   *Spices* are obtained from the bark, roots, fruits, or berries of perennial plants; *herbs* are the leaves of shrubs or trees; and *aromatic seeds* are the seeds of certain plants. The aromatic oils in spices, herbs, and seeds produce the flavors they contribute to foods. These oils are volatile and easily lost when they are stored in open containers or at warm temperatures. Ground and crushed dried leaves lose most of their flavor bouquet after they are stored for about a year.

One-fourth teaspoon of crushed dried herbs, or 1½ teaspoons of freshly minced herbs, is the recommended seasoning for four servings of a given food. Herbs and spices should be added to cooked foods during the cooking process so that their flavors may be extracted and blended, but they should not be cooked so long that their flavor is excessively volatilized. Flavor extraction is a far slower process in cold mixtures, such as salad dressings, so in these instances herbs and spices should be added as far in advance of serving time as possible.

The presence of too many different spices and herbs in a single dish can have a cloying effect and should be avoided. A better practice is to use one herb at a time in cooking until you are thoroughly familiar with their individual flavors. Seasoning the same food with different herbs on different occasions can also provide variety. For instance, season spinach one time with a mustard sauce, and another time with sesame seeds or nutmeg. Try dill weed, rosemary, sesame seed, or almonds with green beans. In this way you will acquire a preference for certain flavors imparted by herbs and spices. The first time you try a new seasoning, limit the amount; as the flavor becomes more familiar, increase the amount accordingly.

SPICE AND HERB BLENDS   Many spice companies prepare blends of spices and herbs that are particularly helpful to the novice who is not familiar with traditional combinations. Blends are available for poultry, seafood, lamb, Italian dishes, salads, and pickling and barbecuing. Chili and curry powders are blends in themselves; blends are also made for seasoning apple and pumpkin pies. Using a blend means not having to measure each spice separately. A particular blend, such as apple pie spice, does not need to be limited only to apple pie but can also be used to season cakes, cookies, puddings or other appropriate dishes. Curry powder can be added to soups, salads, casseroles, sandwich fillings, and dips as well as curries. As with extracts, the blends produced by different companies vary in flavor, and their effects should be compared.

VEGETABLE SPICES AND ADJUNCTS   Many plants that do not qualify either as herbs, spices, or aromatic seeds are used for seasoning. They are often available in dried form, which is more convenient but less potent in flavor. When garlic is dried, for example, it becomes slightly bitter and loses some of its pungency. Other dried plant products include onion, horseradish, mushrooms, chives, parsley, mint, lemon peel, and orange peel. Freshly grated orange and lemon peels are more flavorful than their dried forms because their aromatic oils are very volatile. However, dried mushrooms, which are widely used in Oriental cookery, are considered more flavorful than fresh ones. Substitutions of dried onions and garlic for their fresh counterparts are included in Table 8 in the appendix.

Salts of onion, garlic, celery, and seasoning blends are also available on the market. When such flavored salts are used, the amount of table salt used should be reduced correspondingly. These salts may not be acceptable as flavoring where saltiness is not desired, as in a dip or a spread for bread.

FLAVOR ENHANCERS

Flavor enhancers do not themselves contribute flavor to a food; they bring out the flavor the food already possesses. In commercially processed food products, flavor enhancers include vegetable protein hydrolysates, certain nucleotides, and monosodium glutamate (MSG). Of these substances, only monosodium glutamate is available for noncommercial use.

Monosodium glutamate is obtained by the fermentation of the molasses residue left after sugar is refined from sugar beets. It is a sodium salt of glutamic acid, an amino acid, and occurs naturally in many foods. The presence of MSG as a flavor enhancer increases the level of sodium in foods, and for this reason the Food and Drug Administration has recommended that it not be added to baby foods.

MSG can be added to meats, soups, sauces, and casseroles. For best effect, ½ teaspoon should be used per six servings of food. The salt appears to have its greatest effect in protein dishes, although it can be also added to vegetables and salads. Mushrooms and soy sauce are two foods that have a high natural content of MSG.

Consumer Awareness

In the last 15 years or so, "Consumer, beware!" has become almost a byword. Certainly, a knowledge of pitfalls in the marketplace can help a consumer obtain better products for less money. All aspects of consumerism cannot be discussed here, but a few that pertain to purchase and consumption of food products will be mentioned.

REGULATORY AGENCIES

Federal and state agencies have been established to regulate and control much of the commerical food supply in the United States. Many chapters in this text refer to government agencies that inspect foods for wholesomeness and grade them for quality. In addition, regulations and controls govern the planting, growing, harvesting, marketing, processing, packaging, storing, and transporting of many foods and food products.

New regulations for nutritional labeling are mentioned in Chapter 1. More regulations are being considered to control nutritional advertising claims. Political considerations occasionally place governmental agencies on the side of the producer rather than the consumer. Regulations sometimes limit both the producer and the consumer and occasionally are a distinct disadvantage to the consumer. Moreover, governmental agencies are often limited in budget and manpower, a circumstance that limits their effectiveness in creating and enforcing regulations. The regulation of food supply is a costly and involved process in which many political, sociological, and economic forces are brought to bear that are not always equitably resolved. With or without the help of regulations, however, a consumer must still be knowledgeable and learn to make wise choices.

More of a family's income is spent for food than for any other item in its budget. Later chapters provide suggestions for economical purchase of specific foods, such as meat, eggs, milk, and cereal, but other factors must be considered as well: the content of packages, the composition of products, and the comparative costs of various brands, forms, and sizes of food products.

Packaging is often deceptive. Two boxes of cereal may be the same size, yet one contains twice the weight of the other. Some containers, such as those for dips and cheese spreads, have an indented bottom that gives them the appearance of containing more than they actually do. A consumer must therefore always consider the weights of products, not the size of their containers.

A consumer can also be misled about the composition of food products. Chapter 31 shows the wide variation in water and juice content of commercial juice drinks. Juice drinks that contain large amounts of water and sugar often have the same price but less nutritional value than pure fruit juice. Sugared cereals often contain more sugar than they do cereal, and they are more expensive than unsugared cereals.

Consumers need to learn to read ingredient listings on food products so that they can choose according to best value, noting that ingredients are listed in order of decreasing content. Some ready-to-eat cereals advertise that one serving supplies a certain percentage of the day's total nutrient needs, but this information is misleading. Many of these nutrients do not occur naturally in cereals; they are added so that eating the cereal is somewhat like taking a vitamin pill. Neither the cereal nor the vitamin pill, however, contain all nutrients, in the amounts needed, that humans require. Scientists do not yet know our exact nutritional needs for optimal health and longevity, and such needs may vary from one person to another. Nutrients listed on cereal boxes should be compared with those in Table 10, "Recommended Dietary Allowances," in the appendix; cereals do not contain all the nutrients listed. Such fortified cereals are usually more expensive than regular cereals.

Canned foods vary not only in quality but also in quantity for a given size of can. Any food packed in liquid, such as green beans, green peas, peaches, cherries, or tomatoes, varies in its proportion of solid food to liquid from brand to brand. The net weight on the can is the combined weight of the solid food and the liquid. Figure 3.6 shows the amounts of fruit in two brands of fruit cocktail after the juice has been drained from the fruit. Attempts to obtain legislation requiring that the drained weight of food be listed on cans have failed because producers claim that foods absorb some liquid in the can during storage and thus the weight of solid foods cannot be controlled. Some canners have agreed to show the weight of solid food placed in the can before liquid is added. However, this voluntary labeling apparently does not

Figure 3.6

The can of fruit cocktail on the left costs 8 cents more than the one on the right. Although the can on the left has only slightly more liquid than the can on the right, the quality of the fruits differs. The fruits are arranged with peaches at center top, then, clockwise, grapes, cherries, pineapple, and pears. In the center are pear stems (on the right) and pieces of peach with small pieces of pit (on the left). The grapes from the can on the right are of very poor quality.

apply to products such as applesauce and tomato sauce, which can vary considerably in the proportions of solids and added water but cannot be strained for comparison. In this case, consistency and flavor are the only guides.

Unit Pricing   Some food stores have a unit-pricing policy. The unit price is the price per unit of measure; the unit of measure may be either fluid or avoirdupois ounces. Thus, a 10-ounce box of cereal that costs 50 cents a box has a unit price of 5 cents per ounce. This example of unit pricing is easy to calculate, but calculation for many products is more difficult, because sizes carry fractions of ounces as well as odd weights and measures. For easier comparison of prices, the retail store places a sticker on the edge of the shelf under each product giving the name of the product, its size, cost, and unit price. With the rapid changes in prices of products, however, stores do not always keep unit price stickers up-to-date; therefore, stickers must always be checked against the price stamped on the package. Because the "large economy size" of a product is not always more economical than smaller sizes, unit prices of various sizes of a product, as well as of different brands, should be compared. Computer grocery checkout systems, already installed in some stores, may eliminate unit pricing.

The following suggestions for the wise use of food money are only a beginning. Practice and alertness allow a consumer to find many other ways to stretch a food dollar:

GOOD SHOPPING HABITS

1. Plan meals and make a list of foods that are needed to make the meals. Avoid impulse buying. Check newspaper advertisements for food specials and plan meals around them.
2. Learn to use low-priced foods, such as ground meat, whole chickens, and legumes in meals. Prepare these economy foods in as many attractive ways as possible.
3. Choose grades of quality according to the food's intended use; small potatoes that cost less per pound than big ones are satisfactory for mashing and braising.
4. Gauge total food consumption as accurately as possible. Avoid buying excessive amounts of perishable items that will deteriorate before they can be eaten. Make use of leftovers.
5. Prepare foods from the beginning instead of relying constantly on more expensive convenience foods.
6. Buy foods in season.
7. Compare the prices of staple foods among local markets; shop at the store that is most economical and stocks the widest variety of products needed.
8. Compare store brands with advertised name brands for quality, cost, and yield; choose the best buy.

Study Questions

1. Name two factors that affect efficiency in food preparation.
2. Many safety practices required in food preparation concern the food preparers themselves; list some do's and don'ts that will help prevent accidents and injury.
3. Briefly describe the differences between gas and electric stoves.
4. What is the principal advantage of microwave cookery?
5. How does the control on a microwave oven differ from that on a conventional oven?
6. What types of utensils should be used for cooking in a microwave oven?
7. What factor should be considered in substituting one baking pan for another?
8. What advantage does a pressure pan have over a regular saucepan?
9. What is the difference between a fluid ounce and an avoirdupois ounce?
10. What are the two basic methods of measuring foods? Indicate which is likely to be more accurate.
11. Describe briefly two methods of measuring flour. Which method produces less flour in the cup? Why?
12. How should brown sugar and fat be measured? Why?
13. Name some advantages of heating foods.
14. Name the four media for heating foods and give an example of a food preparation method in each medium.
15. Name three dry-heat cookery methods and three moist-heat cookery methods.
16. What is the highest temperature possible for foods cooked in water at normal atmospheric pressure?
17. How is simmering different from boiling? From poaching?
18. What is hard water? How is it different

from naturally soft water?

19. How is hard water changed when it is artificially softened?
20. How does purified water differ from hard water?
21. Is steam hotter than boiling water? Explain.
22. Give two methods of cooking foods in which the temperature is higher than that of boiling water. What is an advantage of such methods?
23. How do microwaves cook food?
24. Describe three factors that affect the speed of heat transfer by conduction.
25. What materials are the best heat conductors for cooking utensils?
26. What is the fastest method of heat transfer? Why is it the fastest?
27. What material in baking pans and cooking pots permits the greatest transmission of radiant energy?

28. Compare the heat absorption characteristics of shiny and dull surfaces; of light and dark colors.
29. Give some reasons why it is difficult to give exact times for oven baking.
30. At what pH are substances considered neutral—neither acid nor alkaline?
31. Name three substances that are sources of acid in food preparation.
32. Name two substances that can make foods alkaline.
33. What is an enzyme?
34. What are the four taste sensations perceived by tastebuds in the mouth?
35. What are the two components of flavor?
36. What kinds of substances in foods are primarily responsible for the odors of foods?
37. How do heat and cold affect the perception of flavor?

References

Carlisle, Helen, and Hall, R. L. "Be an Artful Seasoner with Spices and Herbs." In U.S. Department of Agriculture, *Food for Us All*, Yearbook of Agriculture. Washington, D.C.: Government Printing Office, 1969.

Consumer Reports. "Built-in Dishwashers." April 1976, p.280. Mount Vernon, N.Y.: Consumers Union of the United States.

——. "Microwave Ovens." April 1976, p.314.

——. "Blenders." May 1977, p.350.

——. "Ceramic Cooktops." October 1977, p.586.

——. "Refrigerator-Freezers." January 1978, p.23; October 1978, p.624.

——. "Food Processors." August 1978, p.495.

——. "Gas and Electric Ranges." August 1979, p.461.

Fetterman, E., and Klamkin, C. *Consumer Education in Practice*. New York: Wiley, 1976.

Harris, Barbara. *Let's Cook Microwave!* 1975. Microwave Cooking Consulting Service, P.O. Box 2992, Portland, OR 97208.

Kramer, Amihud. *Food and the Consumer*. Westport, Conn.: AVI Publishing, 1973.

National Nutrition Consortium, Inc. *Nutrition Labeling: How It Can Work for You* (1975). The National Nutrition Consortium, Inc., 9650 Rockville Pike, Bethesda, MD 20014.

Peet, L. J.; Pickett, M. S.; and Arnold, M. G. *Household Equipment*, 8th ed. New York: Wiley, 1979.

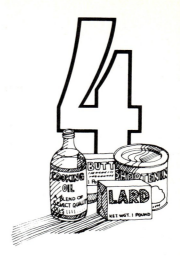

Fats in Foods

Naturally occurring food fats are composed mostly of triglycerides, with small amounts of mono- and diglycerides, cholesterol, and other lipids. Glycerides are composed of glycerol and fatty acids, as described in Chapter 1.

Chemical and Physical Characteristics of Fats

Fats are greasy substances that do not mix with water. They are lighter in weight than water; thus, cream rises to the top of milk and oil rises to the top of oil and vinegar salad dressings.

SOLID AND LIQUID FATS

Fat, like water, has both solid and liquid states. Liquid oil crystallizes when its temperature is lowered, just as water does when it freezes. Oil solidifies when it is refrigerated or frozen. The temperature at which a fat changes from a liquid to a solid varies according to the type of fat. Furthermore, this change itself occurs over a range of temperatures, not at any single point. *Oil* is a fat that is normally liquid at room temperature, while *solid* or *plastic fats* are solid at room temperature. Some solid fats are brittle and hard at room temperature; others are soft and pliable. The hardness of a solid fat depends on its ratio of fat crystals to liquid oil. The more crystals a fat has, the firmer it is.

The length of the carbon chains in fatty acids—that is, the number of carbons in a fatty acid—and the number of double bonds a fat has are two major factors that determine both its melting point and whether it is an oil or a solid fat at room temperature. Solid fats have longer carbon chains and fewer double bonds; oils have more double bonds and/or shorter carbon chains. Fats from animal sources are usually solid; fats from plant sources are mostly oils. Most plant fats are consequently good sources of essential fatty acids, because the large number of double bonds that causes them to be liquids also provides essential fatty acids. Exceptions to this rule are coconut, olive, palm, and peanut oils, which lack essential fatty acids but are oils because they contain fatty acids with short carbon chains and only one double bond.

Table 4.1 shows the composition of some common food oils, solid fats, nuts, and seeds; water, protein, and carbohydrate content are included for purposes of comparison. Saturated fat and oleic acid represent the nonessential fatty acid content. Oleic and linoleic acids are fatty acids, but oleic acid contains only one double bond. The essential fatty acid is the linoleic acid content. Linoleic acid contains only two double bonds, but when it is present in food, the body can use it to synthesize fatty acids with three and four double bonds as they are needed.

HYDROGENATION

Liquid oils can be changed into solid fats by a process called *hydrogenation*, in which hydrogen is added to the carbons joined by double bonds, thus saturating them. Hydrogenation reduces the content of essential fatty acids in the fat.

Table 4.1   Composition of edible oils, solid fats, nuts, seeds, and chocolate, edible portion of 100 grams

Food	Water (g)	Protein (g)	Carbohydrate (g)	Fat (g)	Fatty acids Saturated (g)	Oleic (g)	Linoleic (g)	Weight per cup (g)	Calories per 100 grams
Oils									
Coconut	0	0	0	100	86	6	2	210	884
Corn	0	0	0	100	10	28	53	210	884
Cottonseed	0	0	0	100	25	21	50	210	884
Olive	0	0	0	100	11	76	7	210	884
Peanut	0	0	0	100	18	47	29	210	884
Safflower	0	0	0	100	8	15	72	210	884
Sesame	0	0	0	100	14	38	42	210	884
Soybean	0	0	0	100	15	20	52	210	884
Sunflower	0	0	0	100	10	21	64	210	884
Solid fats									
Lard	0	0	0	100	40	44	12	220	902
Shortening, all vegetable	0	0	0	100	25	44	26	188	884
Shortening, vegetable + animal	0	0	0	100	43	41	11	188	884
Table fats									
Butter	15	0.6	0.4	81	46	27	2	224	716
Margarine, first ingredient on label:									
Corn oil, liquid, stick	16	0.6	0.4	80	15	36	24	224	720
Corn oil, liquid, tub	16	0.6	0.4	80	14	30	32	224	720
Cottonseed or soybean, partially hydrogenated	16	0.6	0.4	80	15	46	14	224	720
Safflower oil, liquid, tub	16	0.6	0.4	80	13	16	48	224	720
Soybean oil, liquid, stick	16	0.6	0.4	80	15	40	25	224	720
Soybean oil, liquid, tub	16	0.6	0.4	80	15	31	33	224	720
Animal fats									
Poultry	0	0		100	32	45	18	—	—
Beef, lamb, pork	0	0		100	48	42	4	—	—
Nuts									
Almond	4.7	18.6	19.5	54	4	36	11	152	627
Brazil	4.6	14.3	10.9	68	17	22	25	130	654
Cashew	5.2	17.2	29.3	46	8	32	3	140	561
Chestnut, dried	8.4	6.7	78.6	4	—	—	—	150	377
Coconut, fresh	50.9	3.5	9.4	35	30	2	trace	130	346
Filbert	5.8	12.6	16.7	62	3	34	10	134	634
Hickory	3.3	13.2	12.8	69	6	47	12	—	673
Macadamia	3.0	7.8	15.9	72	—	—	—	132	691
Peanuts, roasted	1.8	26.2	20.6	48	9	24	13	144	582
Peanut butter	1.8	27.8	17.2	52	10	24	15	227	581
Pecan	3.4	9.2	14.6	71	6	43	18	108	687
Pine nuts (piñon)	3.1	13.0	20.5	61	—	—	—	136	635
Pistachio	5.3	19.3	19.0	54	5	35	10	120	594
Walnut, black	3.1	20.5	14.8	60	5	11	41	120	628
Walnut, English	3.5	14.8	15.8	63	7	10	42	120	651
Seeds									
Pumpkin	4.4	29.0	15.0	47	8	17	20	128	553
Safflower	5.0	19.1	12.4	60	5	9	43	—	615
Sesame	5.5	18.2	17.6	53	7	20	22	128	582
Sunflower	4.8	24.0	19.9	47	6	9	30	130	560
Chocolate									
Chocolate, bitter	2.3	10.7	28.9	53	30	20	1	—	505
Cocoa powder, medium fat	4.1	17.3	51.0	19	11	7	trace	112	265

SOURCE: U.S. Department of Agriculture, *Fats in Food and Diet*; U.S. Department of Agriculture, *Composition of Foods.*

Hydrogenated fats were developed as economical substitutes for lard and butter. Newer methods of preparing margarine subject only a small part of the oil to hydrogenation, with liquid oil being added to produce the desired consistency. The result is a compound margarine with a higher content of essential fatty acids than regular margarine. Compound margarine can be identified on its package because "liquid oil" is listed as the first ingredient. Partially hydrogenated or partially hardened oil is the first ingredient listed on packages of regular margarine.

Characteristics of Food Fats
HYDROGENATED SHORTENING

Shortenings are prepared from hydrogenated oils or from mixtures of oils and animal fats. Different brands of shortening vary in their characteristics; some are soft and pliable, others are brittle and hard. Most shortenings contain 10 to 12 percent air. A cup of shortening weighs only 188 grams compared to lard, which weighs 220 grams. Mono- and diglycerides have been added to many shortenings to improve their emulsifying properties in cakes. The presence of emulsifiers, which cause one liquid to be dispersed in another with which it cannot be mixed, makes shortening a less desirable medium for frying, because the emulsifiers cause fat to smoke at lower temperatures.

LARD

Lard is fat rendered from the fatty tissues of pork. Various grades of lard are available that differ in texture, color, flavor, and odor, depending on the processing treatment. Lard has a high content of saturated fat.

TABLE FAT

Butter and margarine are *table fats.* As shown in Table 4.1, butter and margarine are alike in water, fat, and milk solid content, but they differ in their ratios of essential and nonessential fatty acids; butter is low in linoleic acid. Although 1 cup of table fat weighs about the same as 1 cup of lard (224 grams), the table fat contains only 181 grams of fat (81 percent of 224). The rest is water, milk solids, and salt. If table fat is substituted for other fats in baking, adjustments must be made to arrive at the same amount of fat, water, and salt.

Clarified butter, known as *ghee* in India, is pure butterfat with all the water and milk solids removed. It is made from melted butter that is allowed to resolidify. When the fat hardens, the fat that rises to the top may be easily separated from the water portion. Because milk solids and water in table fat tend to brown readily, clarified fat used in pan frying eliminates excessive browning. Butter and margarine are often preferred over oils for their flavors.

Margarines contain artificial flavors and colors, and some contain sodium benzoate as a preservative. *Sodium benzoate* is the sodium salt of benzoic acid, which occurs naturally in cherries and cranberries. Most margarines are fortified with vitamin A so that they will contain the same amount of this vitamin that butter does.

This text uses the term "margarine" to refer to the product just described, which resembles butter in composition. Three other types of products exist that differ from regular margarine in their composition; whipped margarine, diet margarine, and spreads. Whipped margarine, as the name implies, has air whipped into it; 1 cup of whipped margarine weighs only 150 grams. Diet margarine contains about 50 percent water, a much higher water content than regular margarine. Spreads contain about 35 percent water and 60 percent fat. The purpose of adding air and water to these special margarines is to reduce the fat content, and thus to reduce the calories in a given amount. However, the same effect can be obtained for less money simply by using less regular margarine. The reduced fat and increased water content of diet and whipped margarine make them impossible to use as substitutes for regular margarine or butter in most baked products, because the incorrect ratios of fat and water produce an inferior result.

OILS

Oils are extracted from a number of different plant seeds and, with a few exceptions, can be used interchangeably. Salad oils are oils that have been *winterized*, that is, they have been chilled with the resulting crystals filtered out. Winterized oil remains liquid at refrigerator temperatures and is thus more suitable for salads than for frying. Some salad oils and olive oil smoke at the temperatures required for deep-fat frying.

Corn, cottonseed, sesame, and soy oils are similar in their linoleic acid content; whichever is least expensive is satisfactory for most purposes. For special fat-controlled diets, doctors may recommend the use of safflower or sunflower oils, which have a higher linoleic acid content. Supply and demand affect the price of oil, with manufacturers of margarine, shortening, and mayonnaise often using whichever oil is the least expensive at any given time for their product.

Rancidity of Fats

Rancidity is a form of deterioration in fats that affects the flavor, odor, and usability of the fat and of the foods that contain the fat. Two types of rancidity are recognized—*hydrolytic* and *oxidative.*

HYDROLYTIC RANCIDITY

Hydrolytic rancidity converts the glycerides in fats to glycerol and fatty acids, essentially the same chemical process that occurs when fats are digested in the body. This rancidity does not affect the flavor, odor, or nutritive value of a fat; it does, however, affect its use in frying, for the presence of free fatty acids lowers the temperature at which fat smokes. For hydrolytic rancidity to occur, the glyceride must be hydrolyzed. In the process of *hydrolysis,* a molecule of water is added to break the bond between the glycerol and the fatty acid. Obviously, then, the presence of water in fat promotes hydrolysis, as do high temperatures. When a food is fried in fat, water in the food is changed into steam, which bubbles up through the fat. The more the fat is used for frying, the more hydrolysis occurs, and the lower is the smoking point of the fat.

The enzyme *lipase,* which is present in natural, unheated fats, such as butter, also promotes hydrolysis. This is a primary cause of rancidity in butter. Hydrolytic rancidity does produce a change in the flavor and odor of butter, because butter contains a high proportion of *butyric acid,* a four-carbon fatty acid. A small amount of butyric acid is partly responsible for the unique flavor of butter, but a large amount of this acid causes butter to develop a goaty odor and flavor. By the same principle, hydrolysis can also cause bitterness in cream.

OXIDATIVE RANCIDITY

Oxidative rancidity is a process of oxidation of the double bonds in unsaturated fatty acids. Oxygen is added to the double bond, causing the fatty acids to form such chemical compounds as peroxides, ketones, and aldehydes, which produce noxious odors and flavors in fat.

Oxidative rancidity is promoted by high temperatures, light, and some metals, such as copper and iron. The pigments in meat and salts also promote oxidative rancidity. Evidence suggests that the compounds formed by oxidation of fatty acids may be toxic when they are fed in large amounts to laboratory animals; their effects on humans, however, need further study. The compounds do cause oxidation of vitamins A, C, and E, as well as of other fatty acids. Oxidative rancidity, like hydrolytic rancidity, lowers the smoking point of fat. Once oxidative rancidity starts, it rapidly accelerates, because the products formed act as catalysts for further oxidation. Saturated fats, such as hydrogenated shortening, are less subject to oxidative rancidity than such unsaturated fats as oils and some margarines.

RANCIDITY IN FOODS

Both hydrolytic and oxidative rancidity can occur in any food that contains fat, even if only small amounts of fat are present in the food. A representative, but not exhaustive, list of foods that are susceptible to rancidity includes cheese, cheese products, all kinds of cream, salad dressings, mayonnaise, bacon and other smoked meats, nuts, nut butter, bread crumbs, cookies, ready-to-eat cereals, whole-grain flours and meals, crackers, frozen baked products, frozen fish, pie crust and cake mixes, chocolate, dehydrated entrées, dried soups, dried meats, dried eggs, potato chips, snack chips of all kinds, and all oils and fats.

PREVENTING RANCIDITY

Once a food has become rancid, it cannot be reclaimed. Therefore, strict measures must be taken to prevent rancidity from occurring. Reuse of fats for frying is a common cause of rancidity. The

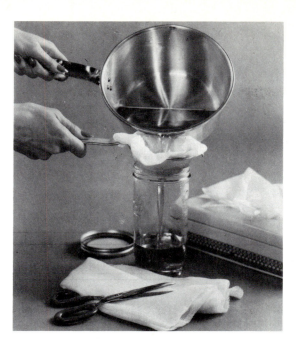

Figure 4.1

To reduce the development of rancidity in fats, strain used fat through several thicknesses of cheesecloth to remove solid food particles and store in airtight containers in a cool, dark location. *(Best Foods, Division of CPC International, Inc.)*

following measures can minimize the development of rancidity in fats:

1. Avoid overheating fats; do not heat fats to the smoking point or allow fats to heat indefinitely when they are not being used.
2. Fats that are to be reused for frying should be strained through several thicknesses of cheesecloth to remove all food particles before they are stored (Figure 4.1).
3. Store all fats in a cool place, refrigerator, or freezer.
4. Store fats in closed containers to exclude air and moisture.
5. Store fats in opaque containers—dark-colored bottles or dark cupboards.
6. Do not use iron and copper kettles for deep-fat cookery; these metals accelerate oxidation.
7. Add fresh fat to used fat for frying.
8. Use fats that contain antioxidants.

ANTIOXIDANTS

Antioxidants are substances that prevent or inhibit *oxidation,* the combination of a substance with oxygen. Many antioxidants are effective because oxygen combines with the antioxidant more easily than with the substances that the antioxidants are protecting, thereby binding the available oxygen and preventing oxidation. Naturally occurring antioxidants include vitamins C and E, the mineral selenium, and the phospholipid lecithin. Some spices, particularly sage and rosemary, as well as oatmeal flour, have antioxidant properties.

Manufactured antioxidants include butylated hydroxy anisole (BHA), butylated hydroxy toluene (BHT), propyl gallate, and gallic acid. All manufactured antioxidants are on the GRAS list. Synergists are often used with antioxidants to make them more effective. Common synergists include vitamin C, citric acid, phosphoric acid, sulfuric acid, ethylenediaminetetraacetate (EDTA), and some amino acids.

Fats in Food Preparation

The fact that consumption of fat per capita in the United States is about 40 percent of the total caloric intake shows how important a role fat occupies in food preparation. Fat seasons foods and provides lubrication. It is used to form such emulsions as mayonnaise and hollandaise sauce. The name *shortening* was given to some fats because of their use in baked products to interfere with the development of gluten, by shortening the gluten strands and increasing the tenderness of the product.

FAT AS A COOKING MEDIUM

Fat is also a cooking medium. Foods cook quickly in fat because of the high temperatures it allows, and many persons enjoy the flavor and texture of fried foods. However, fried foods are more expensive and higher in calories than foods cooked by water or other methods. Cooking foods in deep fat also requires more cleaning up than most other methods of cooking.

Effect of Heat on Fat   When fat is heated, its chemical and physical characteristics are changed, and these changes can affect the fat's usability. If correct procedures are not used, foods can absorb excessive amounts of fat during cooking. Temperatures for baking and for cooking foods in water are not high enough to alter fats in the foods or fats added to food mixtures. Only when fats themselves are heated to frying temperatures does heat affect fat. As discussed, high heat can cause hydrolysis of triglycerides. High heat can also cause the free fatty acids formed by hydrolysis to link together to form large *polymers,* or chains of fatty acids, that make the fat more viscous. Fatty acid polymers cause the gummy residue that is often seen on cookie sheets after baking cookies. Fatty acid polymers in the fat darken its color, lower its smoking point, and cause the fat to foam when foods are cooked in it. Foods cooked in such fats also tend to absorb more fat during cooking than if they are cooked in fats that are free of hydrolysis products and fatty acid polymers.

Smoking Points of Fats   The smoking point of a fat is the temperature at which smoke rises from heated fat. The smoke results from the conversion of glycerol to acrolein. Acrolein has an acrid odor and is quite irritating to the mucous membranes of the nose and eyes. The greater the concentration of mono- and diglycerides and free fatty acids a fat has, the lower is the temperature at which the fat smokes when it is heated. Solid fats with added mono- and diglycerides are not as suitable for frying, therefore, as fats without these added emulsifiers. Proper care of the fat prevents hydrolytic decomposition and helps keep the smoking point high.

Fat Absorption in Frying Foods Fried foods should be heated enough to cook them all the way through; they should have a good brown color and a minimum of fat absorption. The most important factor influencing these characteristics is the temperature of the fat medium. If it is too low, the food must remain in the fat longer to brown properly; the longer the food is in the fat, the more fat will be absorbed. If the temperature is too high, the food browns too quickly and may not be heated enough on the inside to destroy bacteria and to completely cook it.

The cooking temperature of the fat is determined by the size and shape of a food and whether it is precooked or completely raw. A food that is already cooked needs only heating, while raw foods require a longer time to cook. A potato chip, because it is smaller, can be cooked at a higher temperature than a French fry. Large pieces of food have less surface area, and so absorb less fat, than the same amount of food cut or shaped into smaller pieces; however, the smaller pieces cook more quickly, so that these two factors partly counteract each other. Comparing the fat content, in dry weight, of French-fried potatoes with potato chips shows that the larger pieces of French fries contain about 24 percent fat, while the smaller pieces of potato chips contain 40 percent fat. Croquettes shaped into perfectly round balls have less surface area than finger-shaped croquettes, but heat penetration is faster in the elongated finger shape, so that the elongated croquette can be fried at a higher temperature for a shorter time than the round shape. Heating of the interior occurs by conduction; a ball-shaped croquette has a wider diameter and heat must be conducted a greater distance than in the elongated croquette.

The composition of batters and doughs also affects fat absorption. A lean batter, with a low proportion of sugar, eggs, and fat, absorbs less fat during frying than a rich dough with a high proportion of these ingredients. As previously mentioned, foods cooked in fats with a high content of fatty acid polymers absorb more fat than food cooked in fats that are less viscous.

Cooking Equipment for Frying A deep-fat fryer with a thermostat control is desirable for frequent frying. The thermostat should be checked for accuracy, and the fryer should be easy to clean. Fat used in such pots should be strained and cleaned after each use, and other precautions taken to prevent rancidity; gummy residues should not be allowed to build up in the fat container.

For occasional frying, any deep pot with straight sides is suitable. Stainless steel and aluminum pots are inert and thus will not cause the fat to oxidize. Stainless steel is easiest to clean; an oven cleaner can dissolve gummy residues. A deep-fat thermometer should be clipped to the side of the pan so that the bulb is immersed in the fat and the scale is in a handy position for reading during frying. A wire basket is helpful for cooking small pieces of food. Large pieces of food can be removed from the fat with a long-handled fork, a Foley fork, a slotted spoon, or tongs. A rack covered with several layers of absorbent paper towels can be placed on a baking sheet to drain fried foods.

Techniques in Deep-Fat Cookery   The pot used for deep-fat frying should be filled no more than half full with oil. Fat expands when heated and frequently boils up or foams when foods are added to it. The fat should be heated to the correct temperature for the food being fried, as indicated in Table 4.2. When a temperature range is known, heat the fat to the highest temperature, because adding the food to the fat cools it down. The foods added should be room temperature (with a few exceptions) to avoid excessive cooling of the fat. The amount of food fried at one time depends on the size of the pot. Avoid adding so much food at one time that the temperature of the fat drops lower than the lowest limit of the frying range for that food (see Figure 4.2).

While the food is frying, keep the temperature within the correct range by increasing or decreasing the heat under the pot. If an electric heating element is used and the temperature climbs too high, the pot should be removed from the element until the temperature of the fat decreases to the correct level.

Foods should be dry when they are placed in the hot fat so that they do not spatter and foam. Recipes for tempura and fritters call for foods dipped into batter with a high water content. These foods should be added cautiously to the hot fat to keep the fat from foaming and spattering excessively. Batter-dipped foods and foods coated in crumbs or flour tend to lose some of their coating materials in the fat; such pieces of coating materials should be removed as they form to prevent them from burning and darken-

Table 4.2	Temperatures for deep-fat frying	
Temperature range		**Foods**
(°F)	(°C)	
325–360	163–182	Uncooked chicken, fish, doughnuts
375–385	191–196	Precooked shrimp, croquettes, tempura, fritters
385–395	196–201	French-fried potatoes, onion rings
395–400	201–205	Potato and tortilla chips, rosettes

Figure 4.2

Potatoes for French frying should be dry before being submerged in hot fat. Use a thermometer to control the temperature so that fat absorption is minimal. *(Best Foods, Division of CPC International, Inc.)*

Figure 4.3

Seafoods are especially suitable for batter dipping and deep-fat frying. Shown here are shrimp, scallops, and small fish, whole and in pieces, that have been batter-dipped and fried. *(Best Foods, Division of CPC International, Inc.)*

ing the fat. To reduce this loss, dip or coat the pieces and allow them to set in single layers for a short time before frying; in this way, the excess coating falls off before the food is placed in the hot fat (Figure 4.3). If a thin coating of batter is desired, use a thin batter. A breadier covering requires a thick batter with a high ratio of flour to liquid.

Soft mixtures, such as corn fritters, tend to disintegrate into crumbs when they are placed in hot fat. To keep the fritter intact, dip about 1 tablespoon of the fritter mixture into a spoon, then hold the spoon just above the surface of the hot fat. With a rubber scraper, transfer the fritter mixture gently from the spoon to the hot fat. The same tool should not be used both to place batter-dipped foods in the hot fat and to remove them, for this causes extra drops of batter to fall into the fat from the uncooked batter on the tool.

Small pieces of food, such as French-fried potatoes and onion rings, need to be stirred occasionally during cooking so that they brown evenly and do not stick together. Large pieces of food, such as chicken or doughnuts, need to be turned over as soon as they are browned on the underside. When a food is completely fried, it should be drained over the pot of fat for a few seconds, then drained on absorbent paper. If a great deal of frying is being done at one time, fresh paper should be substituted occasionally, because fat-soaked paper is not very effective in absorbing excess fat from fried food.

Fat is a highly flammable cooking medium. Never overheat the fat, not only to prevent excessive hydrolysis but also to reduce the likelihood of fire. Fat should never be heated to the smoking point, even in pan frying; do not use fat that smokes at the temperature required for frying. The fumes from smoking fat accumulate on, and darken, kitchen walls and ceilings. Do not allow fat to drip on a hot heating element or flame when foods are removed from hot fat. Be prepared to handle a fire.

Nutritional Value of Food Fats

Fat is a source of energy and carries fat-soluble vitamins. Animal fats are high in saturated fatty acids; plant oils are the best source of essential fatty acids. Nutritionists recommend that fat supply no more than 30 percent of a person's total caloric intake; the amount of essential fatty acid required is so small that a minimal fat intake easily meets this need. Vitamins A, E, and K are plentiful in leafy green vegetables, and vitamins A and D are available in fortified, fat-free milk; thus, it is not necessary to eat fatty foods to obtain these nutrients. Fat intake can be reduced, and essential fatty acid intake increased, in the following ways:

1. Reduce the consumption of fried foods—broil, bake, or cook foods in water.
2. Use correct temperatures and techniques in frying to prevent excessive fat absorption.
3. Use oils, not animal fats, for food preparation; discard all fats rendered from meats during cooking.
4. Store and care properly for oils to prevent rancidity.
5. Limit the consumption of such high-fat foods as nuts and seeds to a level that does not exceed caloric needs.

Study Questions

1. What are the constituents of naturally occurring fats?
2. What is a glyceride?
3. Why does oil rise to the top when it is mixed with water?
4. What is an oil?
5. Which melts at a lower temperature, a solid fat or an oil?
6. What is the primary source of oils? Of solid fats?
7. What are two factors that determine whether a fat is an oil or a solid fat?
8. Which is a better source of essential fatty acids, an oil or a solid fat?
9. Why are coconut, peanut, olive, and palm oils not good sources of essential fatty acids, even though they are oils?
10. What happens to an oil when it is hydrogenated?
11. Is hydrogenation of oil a harmful process? Explain.
12. What effect does hydrogenation have on the essential fatty acid content of an oil?
13. Hydrogenation of compound margarine

differs from the original process for manufacturing regular margarine. What effect does the newer process have on the margarine's essential fatty acid content?

14. How can one determine if a margarine has been manufactured by the newer compound process?
15. Why does 1 cup of hydrogenated shortening weigh less than 1 cup of lard?
16. Why are some hydrogenated shortenings not recommended for deep-fat frying?
17. Why does 1 cup of table fat contain less fat than 1 cup of lard?
18. Can regular margarine be substituted for hydrogenated shortening in cookie, cake, and other recipes? Why?
19. What is ghee?
20. How are table fats clarified?
21. Can whipped or diet margarine be substituted for regular or compound margarine in cookie, cake, and other recipes? Why?
22. How is oil winterized, and for what reason?
23. What factor determines the suitability of a fat for deep-fat frying?
24. What oils are considered good sources of essential fatty acids?
25. Name two types of rancidity that affect fats and foods containing fat.
26. In what ways are fats affected when they become rancid?
27. What is hydrolytic rancidity?
28. What are two causes of hydrolytic rancidity?
29. What is oxidative rancidity?
30. What factors promote oxidative rancidity?
31. What types of fatty acids are most susceptible to oxidative rancidity?
32. Is rancidity a problem in food processing and food preparation? Why?
33. Can the products of rancidity be removed from foods and fats that have turned rancid?
34. Name some ways to minimize the development of rancidity in fat.
35. What is an antioxidant?
36. Name some substances used as antioxidants.
37. Name some ways fats are used in food preparation.
38. What are some advantages of fat as a cooking medium? Disadvantages?
39. What changes occur in fats that are heated to high temperatures?
40. What is the smoking point of a fat?
41. What is acrolein?
42. What factors cause a decrease in the smoking points of fats?
43. How can a high smoking point in a fat be maintained?
44. Describe the desirable characteristics of fried foods.
45. What happens to foods fried at too low a temperature? At too high a temperature?
46. What factors determine the correct temperature in frying foods?
47. What factors affect the amount of fat absorbed by foods fried in deep fat?
48. What factors affect the amount of food that should be added to the fat at one time for frying?

References

Bennion, Marion. "Fats as Cooking Media, Shortening Agents, and Components of Pastry." In *Food Theory and Applications*, edited by Pauline C. Paul and Helen H. Palmer. New York: Wiley, 1972.

——, and Park, R. L. "Changes in Frying Fats with Different Foods." *Journal of the American Dietetic Association* 52, no. 4 (April 1968): 308.

Brown, Helen B. *Current Focus on Fat in the Diet* (White Paper). Chicago: The American Dietetic Association, 1977.

Fleischman, A. I., Florin, A., Fitzgerald, J., Caldwell, A. B., and Eastwood, G. "Studies on Cooking Fats and Oils." *Journal of the American Dietetic Association* 42, no. 5 (October 1963): 394.

Kilgore, Lois T. "How to Avoid Confusion in Fats and Oils Buying or Use." In U.S. Department of Agriculture, *Food for Us All*, Yearbook of Agriculture. Washington, D.C.: Government Printing Office, 1969.

——. *Composition of Foods*, Agriculture Handbook No. 8, by Bernice K. Watts and Annabel L. Merrill. Washington, D.C.: Government Printing Office, 1975.

——. *Fats in Food and Diet*, Agriculture Information Bulletin No. 361. Washington, D.C.: Government Printing Office, 1977.

5

Emulsions and Salad Dressings

Most food emulsions are mixtures of fat and water. Common emulsions are homogenized milk and cream, cheese, ice cream, butter, margarine, mayonnaise, and salad dressings. Emulsion formation is an important process in the preparation of cream puffs, shortened cakes, soups, sauces, frostings, and desserts.

Emulsions

An *emulsion* is a mixture of two *immiscible* liquids, that is, liquids that do not mix with each other, such as oil and water. An oil-and-vinegar dressing is an emulsion. When these two liquids are shaken together, they remain dispersed or distributed, one in the other, only for a few minutes, and then separate, with the oil rising to the top. An oil-and-vinegar dressing is an *unstable* emulsion, because the emulsion is only temporary. A *stable* emulsion that lasts indefinitely requires an emulsifying agent.

EMULSIFYING AGENTS

An *emulsifying agent* is a substance that is soluble in, or has an affinity for, both liquids that make up the emulsion. Mayonnaise is a stable emulsion; it, too, contains oil and vinegar. The emulsifying agent in mayonnaise is egg. Lecithin, a phospholipid found in egg yolks, is an excellent emulsifier; egg proteins also have emulsifying properties. Egg yolk, egg white, or the whole egg may be the emulsifier in mayonnaise. The emulsifier coats the droplets of oil and keeps them from combining. The oil droplets then remain dispersed in the vinegar, or water, phase.

Lecithin is prepared commercially from soybeans for addition to many products, such as candy, that need an emulsifying agent. Mono- and diglycerides, which are also effective emulsifiers, are added to hydrogenated shortening used in cakes. Many vegetable gums are also used as emulsifiers; these are naturally occurring, nondigestible polysaccharides of sugars, such as galactose and mannose, that are similar to cellulose, a polysaccharide of the sugar glucose. Vegetable gums are extracted from seaweed, legumes, and other plants; they include acacia, agar, algin, guar, carageenan, karaya, locust bean, tragacanth, and xanthan, to name only a few. Vegetable gums are used in commercial salad dressings, ice cream, cream cheese, and many other products. Synthetic gums are also used.

PREPARING MAYONNAISE

To obtain the stable emulsion mayonnaise, the two immiscible liquids must be considerably agitated with the emulsifier. An electric blender forms the emulsion most rapidly; an electric mixer requires a slightly different technique. A rotary hand beater can also be used, but takes a much longer time to form the emulsion.

Mayonnaise is prepared in a blender with egg, vinegar, seasonings, and one fourth of the oil blended at high speed for 1 minute; the remaining oil is added slowly while the blender is still running. With an electric mixer or rotary beater, only ½ teaspoon of

Figure 5.1

Only ½ teaspoon of oil should be combined initially with egg, vinegar, and seasonings. the mixture should be beaten well before more oil is added, a small amount at a time, to form a stable mayonnaise emulsion.

oil is combined initially with the egg, vinegar, and seasonings; the remaining oil is added ½ teaspoon at a time with rapid beating until the emulsion is well formed (Figure 5.1), at which point the oil can be added more rapidly. Never add more oil at one time than has already been emulsified.

Better results are obtained from the mixer and rotary-beater methods if the bowl is small enough to permit the ingredients to be caught up completely in the beaters for satisfactory agitation. Also, oil at room temperature emulsifies more rapidly than cold oil. The amount of oil that can be emulsified by a given amount of emulsifying agent is limited; the usual ratio is about 1 cup of oil per egg. Adding too much oil or adding the oil too rapidly causes the emulsion to break. Using the maximum amount of oil per egg produces a more viscous emulsion.

BROKEN EMULSIONS   A broken emulsion appears curdled and oily and has a fluid consistency. Besides the two ways already mentioned, emulsions can be broken by freezing, drying, or excessive jarring. Melting margarine and butter breaks them as emulsions and causes them to separate into their two phases. Mayonnaise in mixed dishes and sandwiches that have been frozen becomes oily when it is thawed because the emulsion has been broken. If the emulsion breaks while mayonnaise is being made, it can be formed again by starting over with more egg, vinegar, and seasonings, adding the broken emulsion in place of oil. Add the broken emulsion slowly enough, and with sufficient agitation, to ensure formation of a stable emulsion.

Hollandaise is an emulsion of egg yolk, lemon juice, and hot melted table fat. The easiest way to prepare hollandaise is in a blender. Bubbling hot melted table fat is added slowly to the egg yolk and lemon juice while all the ingredients are blended at high speed. Hollandaise may be served hot and can be kept warm over hot water until it is needed. If the emulsion should separate, it can usually be formed again with blending. Hollandaise sauce may be refrigerated and used cold on vegetables, such as artichokes.

HOLLANDAISE SAUCE

"Salad dressing" is a confusing term, because it can refer to a specific product as well as to a general category for any type of seasoned dressing used for salads.

Types of Salad Dressings

The preparation of mayonnaise has already been described. Commercial mayonnaise is required by federal law to contain a minimum of 65 percent oil, but most contain about 80 percent oil. The flavor of commercial dressings varies according to seasonings and to the kind and amount of acid ingredient used. Imitation mayonnaise, as its list of ingredients shows, contains more water than oil; this is the reason it is labeled "imitation." Imitation mayonnaise also contains vegetable gum to provide viscosity. Comparing by labels, real mayonnaise contains 100 kilocalories and imitation mayonnaise contains 50 kilocalories per tablespoon.

MAYONNAISE

Starch-based salad dressings are often called "cooked" salad dressings because starch, egg, and water must be cooked together, forming a pudding-like mixture to which oil, vinegar, and seasonings are added. Commercial salad dressing is required by law to contain a minimum of 30 percent oil; it has about 65 kilocalories per tablespoon. Most salad dressings tend to be more tart in flavor than mayonnaise. Cooked salad dressing can be prepared with the ratios of fat, acid, and seasonings altered to produce the desired flavor.

STARCH-BASED SALAD DRESSINGS

Liquid salad dressings, ones that pour, are available in a multitude of flavor combinations based on traditional French or Italian dressing. These commercial products are stabilized with vegetable gums and emulsifiers to provide homogeneous stable emulsions. They are required by law to contain a minimum of 35 percent oil and have approximately the same caloric value as starch-based salad dressing.

LIQUID SALAD DRESSINGS

LOW-CALORIE SALAD DRESSINGS

A number of low-calorie commercial salad dressings are available; all carry nutrition labeling and contain from 16 to 50 calories per tablespoon. They are seasoned acidic mixtures, thickened with vegetable gums and xanthan with varying amounts of oil. Homemade low-calorie dressings can be prepared from canned condensed tomato soup or evaporated milk; dilute gelatin solutions have been added to some low-calorie dressings for viscosity.

Preparing French Dressings

Homemade French dressings are mixtures of vinegar and oil with a variety of different seasonings. Any type of oil may be used; olive oil is often preferred for its flavor, but it is more expensive than other oils and lacks essential fatty acids. Combining olive oil with another vegetable oil is often a good compromise. Mineral oil should not be used for dressings (see Chapter 1).

VINEGARS

Vinegar provides tartness or acidity in French dressing. The acetic acid in vinegar is produced by yeast fermentation of the sugars in the foods from which vinegar is made. Table 5.1 shows the food sources for various types of vinegar.

Even though most vinegars are standardized to contain about 5 percent acetic acid, some contain 4.5 and others contain 6 percent acid. The strength of the vinegar affects its tartness; thus the amount used must be adjusted to the acidity level. Besides tartness, vinegars vary in flavor depending on their food source, because other acids and alcohol produced during the fermentation react to provide the flavors and aromas typical of each kind of vinegar.

Not only do different kinds and flavors of vinegar exist but each vinegar can be seasoned separately to yield a variety of flavors. Tarragon and garlic vinegar are two commercial products. However, it is easy to prepare herbed or spiced vinegar simply by placing desired herbs or spices in the vinegar for a few weeks, after which the vinegar is strained. Possible additions to vinegar include whole allspice, cloves, ginger, nutmeg, cinnamon bark, or chili peppers.

Table 5.1   Sources of various types of vinegar

Type of vinegar	Source
Wine	Grapes
Cider	Apples
Malt	Malted grain
Distilled	Alcohol

OTHER ACIDS IN FRENCH DRESSINGS

True French dressing contains vinegar, but a variety of flavors can be obtained by substituting different acid ingredients. Lemon juice is a popular alternative. Orange and pineapple juice make delightful sweet-tart marinades or dressings for fruit salads when they are mixed with a little oil and sugar. Tomato juice can be combined with vinegar or lemon juice, or the juice from sweet and dill pickles can be used in place of vinegar.

RATIOS OF OIL AND VINEGAR

The amounts of oil and vinegar in French dressings also produce different flavors; the ratios chosen depend on personal preference. The more oil and less vinegar is used, the less tart the salad dressing and salad will be. Three or four parts of oil to one part of vinegar produce a dressing that is only slightly tart. A very tart salad dressing, on the other hand, would contain one part of oil to three or four parts of vinegar. Equal parts of oil and vinegar make a happy compromise for most tastes. If caloric intake must be limited, reduce the amount of oil, for oil contains 125 kilocalories per tablespoon.

SEASONINGS

The final touch of creativity in French dressings is seasoning. Seasoning can be very simple—only salt, or salt and sugar. Sugar reduces acidity and is often desirable in dressings with a high proportion of vinegar. Artifical sweeteners can be used for the same effect where calories and/or sugar intake must be curtailed. Fresh or dry herbs add variety to the dressings. Some spice companies offer special blends of herbs and seasonings for salads. However, a better flavor blend is obtained if dry herbs are ground in the palm of the hand or in a mortar just before they are added to the dressing.

Variations of Salad Dressings

Mayonnaise, imitation mayonnaise, and salad dressings can all be a base to which other ingredients are added to achieve different flavors. These dressings can be varied with the addition of finely minced vegetables (onions, parsley, chives, pickles, olives), fruits (crushed pineapple, chopped maraschino cherries), grated cheeses of all kinds, and condiments (chili sauce, horseradish, prepared mustard, pickle relish) (Figure 5.2). Some of these ingredients can also be added to French dressings. A blender can be a useful tool in the preparation of these dressings.

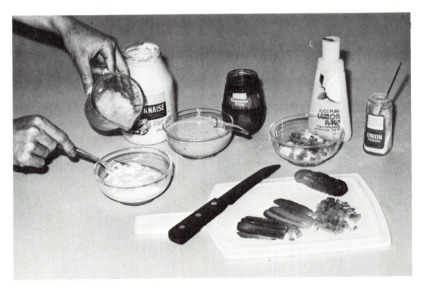

Figure 5.2

A variety of ingredients can be added to mayonnaise or salad dressing. Left, crushed pineapple is added to mayonnaise to make a fruit salad dressing; center, Thousand Island dressing is prepared from equal parts of mayonnaise and hamburger relish; right, the ingredients for tartar sauce are mayonnaise, chopped dill pickles, lemon juice, and onion powder or juice.

SANITARY QUALITY AND STORAGE OF SALAD DRESSINGS

Mayonnaise, salad dressing, and some types of French dressings are good media for growth of staph bacteria that cause foodborne illness, as discussed in Chapter 2. These products and foods that contain them should be refrigerated. Because many contain high proportions of oil, they are subject to rancidity, which is also slowed by refrigeration.

Study Questions

1. What is an emulsion?
2. Distinguish between, and give examples of, stable and temporary emulsions.
3. What is the function of the emulsifying agent in an emulsion?
4. Describe the technique required to obtain a stable emulsion.
5. What factors cause an emulsion to break?
6. Name and briefly describe several types of dressings for salads.
7. Why are some commercial French dressings stable emulsions?
8. What is the most common acid ingredient in French dressings? What acid ingredients can replace it?
9. How can the ratios of oil and vinegar in French dressings be changed to produce different flavors?
10. How does sugar affect the acidity of French dressings?

References

Campbell, Ada Marie, Penfield, Marjorie P., and Griswold, Ruth M. *The Experimental Study of Food*, 2d ed. Boston: Houghton Mifflin, 1979.

Desrosier, Norman W., ed. *Elements of Food Technology*. Westport, Conn.: AVI Publishing, 1977.

Kilgore, Lois T. "How to Avoid Confusion in Fats and Oils Buying and Use." In U.S. Department of Agriculture, *Food for Us All*, Yearbook of Agriculture. Washington, D.C.: Government Printing Office, 1969.

Paul, Pauline C., and Palmer, Helen H. "Colloidal Systems and Emulsions." In *Food Theory and Applications*, edited by Pauline C. Paul and Helen H. Palmer. New York: Wiley, 1972.

Petrowski, Gary E. "Emulsion Stability and Its Relation to Foods." *Advances in Food Research* 22 (1976): 309.

Fruits

Custom mostly determines whether a plant food is classified either as a fruit or a vegetable. According to botanical classification, a *fruit* is the seed-bearing part of a plant, which means that squashes, cucumbers, green beans, peas in the pod, okra, and tomatoes are actually fruits, though these plants are usually regarded as vegetables. Furthermore, sweetness cannot be used as a factor to distinguish between fruits and vegetables, because not all fruits are sweet, and some vegetables are. It suffices that all plant foods now classified as fruits, except rhubarb stalks, are the seed-bearing part of a plant, but some vegetables are also seed bearers.

Technological developments in recent years have made fruits available in a more plentiful supply and a wider variety than ever before. Seasonal availability of such common fruits as apples, cantaloupes, and watermelons has been extended to the point where these and other fresh fruits can be purchased most of the year. Breeding and agricultural practices have produced fruits that are heartier, more resistant to plant diseases and insects, more flavorful, and more prolific than was ever possible in the past. Harvesting and storage procedures have also been developed to keep fruits in good edible quality for much longer periods of time than formerly. When the fresh product is unavailable or too expensive, processing technology makes available frozen, canned, and dehydrated fruits. Finally, transportation and marketing technology provides for a wide distribution of fruits from all over the world, so that today these fruits are familiar to more Americans than ever before. Exotic imported fruits, such as fresh pineapples, papayas, mangoes, guavas, and kiwi, are increasingly easy to locate in large metropolitan markets.

Composition and Structure of Fruits

The walls of plant cells contain varying amounts of cellulose, hemicellulose, lignin, and minute amounts of protein. Inside the cells is the protoplasm containing the cell nucleus, sugars, minerals, acids, enzymes, tannins, pigments, vitamins, and starch. The cells are joined together by pectic substances. Where the cells do not meet exactly, air spaces form.

WATER AND PROTEIN CONTENT OF FRUITS

Most fruits have a high water content that is located mainly inside the cells. With the exception of avocados, coconuts, and olives, fruits contain relatively little fat. The protein content of fruits is also limited, with only that needed for the fruit's life processes present. Most protein in fruits is found in the enzymes, which are necessary for the synthesis of plant substances and for changes in the plants as they grow. Some enzymes in fruits change pectic substances so that fruits soften as they ripen. Other enzymes change acids so that fruits become less tart, and still other enzymes change starch in the fruit to sugar and promote oxidation.

Fruits have a high carbohydrate content that includes sugars, starch, and nondigestible carbohydrates. Many immature fruits have a high starch content, which is hydrolyzed as the plant ripens to form sugar; a green apple has a starchy flavor for this reason. Nondigestible carbohydrates include cellulose, hemicellulose, lignin, and pectic substances that serve as structural components in the fruits in the same way as bones do in animals. These structural components change as the fruit ripens and are also affected by cooking. Descriptions of carbohydrates are given in Chapter 1.

A high content of organic acids exists in fruits. Some acids occur in larger amounts in some fruits than in others—for instance, benzoic acid in cherries and cranberries, malic acid in apples and peaches, citric acid in citrus fruits, and tartaric acid in grapes.

The cell walls of plants are semipermeable membranes when plants are raw or uncooked and therefore permit the passage of water into and out of the cell. However, they block the passage of *solute,* or dissolved, substances, such as sugars, minerals, and other components of the cell protoplasm. This is the process of *osmosis*—the passage of solvent (water), but not of solute, through a semipermeable membrane. Water tends to pass from a region of low solute concentration to one of high solute concentration until the solute concentrations are equal on each side of the membrane.

If a slice of raw apple is placed in water, the water enters some of the cells of the apple because the concentration of solutes is greater inside the cells. The additional water causes the cells to expand, producing what is known as *turgor,* or crispness. Of course, raw fruit left in water for too long starts to decay or disintegrate. An example of the opposite process is when raw fruits, such as strawberries, are sprinkled with sugar. The concentration of solute on the outside of the cell is then greater than inside the cell, and water passes out of the cells. The fruit soon becomes covered with syrup.

Diffusion When plants are heated, their cell walls lose their semipermeable characteristics, so that both solute and solvent pass in or out of the cells until the concentrations are equal on each side of the permeable membrane. This process is known as *diffusion.* If fruit is cooked in water, osmosis occurs until the cell walls become completely permeable. This is the point at which diffusion occurs. During the initial stages of cooking, water enters the cells through osmosis, but in the later stages, the concentrations of solute and solvent equalize.

Diffusion affects the appearance of a fruit only when it is cooked in heavy syrup. In this case the high concentration of sugar causes water to pass out of the cells, shriveling the fruit and thinning the surrounding syrup with water from the fruit. To make a compote, where plump pieces of fruit are desired, cook the fruit in a syrup that has the same concentration of solutes as the protoplasm inside the fruit cells, which is about one volume of sugar to two volumes of water. More sugar can be added after cooking is completed to make a sweeter preserve. For applesauce and other fruit sauces, cook the fruit in water first, then add the sugar at the end of the cooking period. These effects of sugars on fruit vary according to the variety of fruit and its stage of maturity.

Preparing Raw Fruits

Fresh fruits must always be washed to remove dust and contamination from the hands that have touched them during harvesting and marketing. Many fruits must be pared, cored, pitted, or trimmed in other ways before they are ready for eating. Some fruits are subject to *enzymatic browning* when their cell structure is cut or broken, which results in browning of the cut surface of the fruit.

ENZYMATIC BROWNING

Oxidative enzymes in the cells of fruit catalyze a chemical reaction between tannins inside the cells and oxygen. When the tannins are oxidized, they turn brown. Oxidized tannins are not harmful to eat, but brown color on fruits is considered unappetizing. Browning can be prevented by inactivating the enzymes and excluding oxygen. Excluding oxygen, however, is not always possible because it is present in the air spaces between the cells in the fruit. Many fruits turn brown when they are bruised for this reason. The pressure that caused the bruise ruptures cell walls and allows the enzymes in the cells to use the oxygen in the air spaces outside the cells to oxidize the tannins inside the cells.

Enzymes can be inactivated by changing pH, by heat, and by high salt concentrations. The application of heat is obviously not desirable when the fruit is to be served raw. The pH can be lowered, making the fruit more acidic, by sprinkling acidic juices from citrus fruits and pineapple over the fruit subject to enzymatic browning, or by dipping the fruit in these juices. This process lowers the pH sufficiently to inactivate the enzymes (Figure 6.1). Citric and acetic acids and cream of tartar also lower the pH. The choice of acid depends on how the fruit is served; a very acidic flavor would not be acceptable in some dishes.

Submerging fruit in a salt solution prevents browning for a short time, but the resulting saltiness does not agree with the flavors of most fruits. It is, however, a practical measure for such vegetables as potatoes and eggplant. In any case, preventing enzymatic browning should not require extensive soaking of foods in a solution that will later be discarded, for doing this increases the solution losses of nutrients.

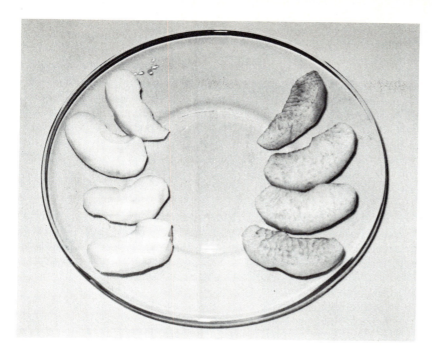

Figure 6.1
These apple slices were exposed to air for 1 hour. The slices on the left retain their natural color because they were dipped in pineapple juice; the slices on the right, untreated, show enzymatic browning.

Certain antioxidants are also effective in preventing enzymatic browning. Ascorbic acid and a substance in pineapple juice have antioxidant properties. Antioxidants are effective because they are more readily oxidized than the tannin that they protect. Sulfur dioxide and sodium bisulfite are used to prevent browning during fruit processing for canning and dehydration. Ascorbic acid is frequently used to prevent browning in frozen fruits.

The enzymatic browning reaction is actually made use of in the preparation of apple butter. Part of the brown color in this product is caused by oxidation of the tannins.

Fruits that are subject to enzymatic browning include apples, apricots, avocados, bananas, cherries, nectarines, papayas, peaches, persimmons, and pears.

Cooking Fruits

Cooked fruits may be served many ways, but heat and other cooking procedures affect their texture and flavor.

EFFECT OF HEAT ON FRUIT

Heat softens cellulose and hemicellulose in the cell walls of fruits so that they lose their crisp texture. The pectic substances between the cells become more soluble, causing the cells to separate from one another. Starch in the cells becomes gelatinized. Water is lost from inside the cells, and air is lost from the spaces between the cells. All of these changes cause a fruit to become softer in texture, less crisp, and more translucent. Even though raw fruits are considered tender, cooking increases their tenderness until they can be easily pierced, mashed, or crushed.

FLAVOR IN COOKED FRUIT

The flavoring substances of fruits can be lost into the liquid in which the fruits are cooked. As in cooking other foods in water, the more water used for cooking, the greater is the loss of sugars, flavoring components, and nutrients to the surrounding liquid. If fruits are cooked in a minimum of water, the fruit retains more of its natural sugars and flavors and is more likely to be acceptable with little or no added sugar. The less sugar added, the lower both the calories and the cost. Fruits can be cooked by microwave without adding water, thus reducing the need for sugar.

EFFECT OF SUGAR IN COOKING FRUIT

The diffusion of water from cells when fruits are cooked in concentrated sugar solutions has already been described. Sugar also retards the softening of cellulose and hemicellulose and inhibits solution of the pectic substances. These effects slow the fruit's tenderization during cooking, which is one reason why fruits used in sauce are cooked without sugar. However, the use of sugar is an advantage with fruits that tend to disintegrate when they are cooked, such as berries and freestone peaches. Adding sugar at the beginning of the cooking period helps these soft fruits retain their shape, but too much sugar may toughen some apples and pears when they are cooked. Fruits cooked in sugar are more translucent than ones cooked without sugar.

Exercise caution when adding sugar to sweetened canned and frozen fruits in pies and cobblers. Excessive amounts can cause the fruit to shrivel, and the water drawn from the fruit will thin the surrounding sauce and make it watery.

Fruit Purées

Many fruits can be made into purées or juices by blending the fruit in a blender with a small amount of water or fruit juice. Some require little or no added sugar. Apricots, berries, peaches, persimmons, and nectarines are some fruits that can be used to make purées. Purées are delicious on pancakes, waffles, quick breads, cakes, puddings, cottage cheese, yogurt, and ice cream.

If a purée is served as soon as it is prepared, it need only be sweetened to taste. About ¼ teaspoon of ascorbic acid powder should be added to each blender batch of fruits that are subject to enzymatic browning. Can purées by filling jars, sealing them, and processing them in a hot water bath. To freeze a purée, heat it to the boiling point first to completely inactivate the enzymes; a microwave is ideal for this.

Selecting, Storing, and Serving Fresh Fruits

Grade standards have been established for many raw fruits by the Agricultural Marketing Service of the U.S. Department of Agriculture; however, the use of these grades by packers is voluntary. The quality standard for each grade is individually determined by fruit. If a packer chooses to label fruits with a given grade, the fruit must meet the quality standards for that grade and fruit. The top grade for raw fruits is U.S. Fancy or U.S. No. 1.

Fruits are more fragile than many vegetables and need gentle handling to prevent bruising that leads to rapid spoilage. Some fruits are picked green and allowed to ripen during marketing, sometimes even after purchase. Bananas, pears, avocados, papayas, persimmons, and many other fruits would probably be inedible if they were picked ripe, because of the time needed for shipping and marketing. The ripeness at which a fruit is picked that still results in good flavor varies according to the fruit. Some fruits are much more flavorful if they are allowed to ripen fully before they are harvested, but this is not always possible unless the fruits are grown at home.

Qualities to look for in selecting a fruit and care in handling vary according to fruit. Some desirable characteristics of individual fruits are indicated in the following descriptions.

KINDS OF FRUITS

Apples One dozen varieties of apples account for 90 percent of all apples grown in the United States. Different varieties are more available in some areas than in others, and they also vary in their suitability for different purposes.

In selecting apples for any purpose, look for firm, crisp, and well-colored fruits; avoid those with shriveled skins, bruises, worm holes, and decayed spots. Irregular brown spots on the skin surface do not affect eating quality, although such areas are usually removed before serving for reasons of appearance. Overly mature apples yield when they are pressed and have a dry, mealy texture. Apples stored at freezing temperatures turn brown around the core, caused by enzymatic browning that occurs when expansion of water in the cells during freezing causes the cells to rupture.

Raw apples may be kept in commercial storage for many months if they are properly treated and held. The apples are coated with a thin wax or oil that seals the pores in the skin, preventing loss of water and carbon dioxide. A storage temperature just above freezing and a controlled atmosphere that is low in oxygen, high in carbon dioxide, and properly humid can hold apples from the fall harvest season until early summer. At home, apples keep longer when they are refrigerated.

Apricots Apricots have a very short season and, because of the distance they have to be transported, are often picked green, a practice that results in very poor flavor. Select firm, golden-colored fruits; avoid apricots that are green, or overly ripe, or that have a wilted or shriveled appearance. This fruit is very fragile and deteriorates rapidly, and moisture accelerates the process.

Apricots should be refrigerated and left unwashed until they are to be served.

Avocados Because of their fragility, avocados are picked green and are often green when purchased. They ripen well at room temperature; the process can be retarded by refrigeration, and the avocados then ripened later at room temperature. To test for ripeness, insert a toothpick into the avocado near the stem. The fruit is ripe if the pick moves freely in and out. An avocado does not ripen well after it has been cut. Many varieties are available that differ in shape, color, and skin texture.

Bananas Bananas are picked green because they have a better flavor than if allowed to tree ripen and because they keep better over the great distances they must be shipped. Bananas ripen best at temperatures between 60–70°F (16–20°C). If they are stored below 55°F (13°C) while they are still green, they will not ripen properly, even when they are held at the ideal temperature later. Storage at temperatures below 55°F gives banana skins a dull, gray, aged appearance. Once ripe, however, bananas can be refrigerated; refrigeration causes their skin to turn brown or black but permits holding for a longer time.

During the ripening process, the starch in bananas turns to sugar and the skin color changes from green to yellow, then becomes flecked with brown. Babies and young children tolerate fully ripe bananas best; some people, however, prefer to eat slightly green bananas. Very ripe bananas are often available at bargain prices and are excellent for cooking (Figure 6.2). A bluish-green chalky substance that is sometimes seen on banana skins is a copper-sulfate insecticide spray. This should be rinsed off before the fruit is eaten to avoid contaminating the edible part.

Berries Berries come in many kinds, but because they are selected and handled in similar ways, they can be considered as a group. Berries should show a uniform color according to species; avoid berries that are green and underripe, or containers with decayed berries. Blackberries, dewberries, loganberries, raspberries, and youngberries should not have their stem caps attached. Strawberries, however, should have their stem caps attached, and the cap should appear fresh, not wilted.

Refrigerate berries without washing them until shortly before serving time, because wet fruit decays more rapidly. Several hours before serving, the berries can be washed, stemmed, and sugared. Many fully ripe berries are sweet enough not to need additional sugar.

Cantaloupes Cantaloupes have a better flavor when they are vine-ripened. Those picked too green for good flavor still have

Figure 6.2
Fried bananas have a delicate flavor; served any way, bananas are a popular fruit. *(United Fresh Fruit and Vegetable Association)*

part of the stem attached or show a torn and jagged stem scar. If the fruit has ripened on the vine, the stem separates easily from the melon, leaving a smooth, clean scar. The surface netting should be coarse and corky and should stand out in bold relief on some parts of the melon. The skin color under the netting should be a yellowish buff or pale yellow, never green. Good odor is another indication of ripeness. Avoid choosing overripe melons, which are indicated by a pronounced yellow rind and a soft texture.

Firm melons sometimes benefit by being held at room temperature for a few days to soften the flesh, but such treatment does not increase sweetness. Melons keep best at refrigerator temperatures, but the atmosphere should not be humid. A humid atmosphere encourages decay, usually beginning in the stem area. Cantaloupes in season are an economical, low-calorie source of nutrients.

Casaba Melons Casaba melons are pumpkin-shaped but slightly pointed at the stem end. They have no netting, but shallow, irregular furrows run from the stem end to the blossom end. The hard rind is light green or yellow in color. The stem does not separate from a ripe melon and must be cut when the melon is harvested. A golden yellow rind indicates ripeness. If casaba melons are purchased green, they may be held at room temperature until they are ripe. A ripe melon should be slightly soft in the stem but should show no dark, sunken, or water-soaked spots, for these indicate decay.

Cherries   The best cherries for raw eating are dark red or almost black—Bing, Black Tartarian, Schmidt, Chapman, Republican, and Lambert. Lighter red cherries are tart, and are suitable for cooking and baking in pies; many are commercially processed and canned for this purpose. Light-colored Royal Ann cherries are used to make maraschino and candied cherries.

Decay in cherries is indicated by leaking flesh and brown discoloration and mold on the surface. Choose plump, ripe cherries with fresh-looking stems. Store fresh cherries in the refrigerator unwashed, but wash them before eating.

Crenshaw Melons   Ripe crenshaw melons have a pleasant aroma and a deep golden-colored rind that yields slightly to pressure at the blossom end. Like other melons, they keep best when refrigerated.

Figs   Black figs are best for raw eating. Ripeness is indicated by a dark color, with a loss of green and a soft texture. Kadota figs are good for cooking and canning; black figs are used in making fig newtons. Figs are usually harvested when they are ripe, and they do not keep long. Figs should be refrigerated unwashed for a longer storage life. Discard the skin of black figs before eating, but not the skin of green figs, which is edible.

Grapefruits   Grapefruits with white flesh and pink flesh are available; pink grapefruits are often considered sweeter. Thick-skinned fruit is likely to be pointed, not flat, at the stem end, with a skin surface that is rough, ridged, or wrinkled; such fruit has a rather spongy feel. Thin-skinned fruit is firm, smooth-textured, and well-rounded, except in the stem area, which is flat. A thin-skinned fruit heavy for its size produces the most juice. Grapefruit can be held for long periods in cool areas and even longer when refrigerated.

Grapes   Grapes are grown for table, wine, raisins, juice, and canning. Some table grape varieties for raw eating include Thompson Seedless, Perlette, Lady Finger, Tokay, Cardinal, Emperor, Concord, Delaware, and Catawba. Grapes should be vine-ripened; they do not improve in color, sweetness, or flavor after they have been harvested. The red and purple varieties of grapes should be free of any green coloration; white grapes should have an amber cast. Grapes keep best at temperatures just above freezing and at high humidity.

Honeydew and Honeyball Melons   The honeydew melon weighs between 4 and 8 pounds and has a flavor highly prized for desserts. It is smooth with only traces of netting and is creamy white or creamy yellow in color. The honeyball melon is very similar to the honeydew melon except that it is very round, much smaller, and irregularly netted over the surface. For best flavor, choose melons that are not green and are slightly soft at the stem end. Avoid melons with a dead white or greenish-white color; these are immature and lacking in flavor. Melons keep best when refrigerated; place them in plastic bags to prevent their strong odors from permeating other foods in the refrigerator.

Kiwi   The kiwi, or Chinese gooseberry, Figure 6.3 is likely to become better known as its cultivation in California increases. The kiwi is the size and shape of a large lemon and has a brown, fuzzy skin. For best eating, it should be as soft as a ripe pear. Peel a kiwi with a floating-blade peeler or paring knife, as you would an apple, and discard the thin, brown skin. The outer circumference of the peeled fruit is a deep, translucent green that fades to a creamy white in the center, where rows of tiny black edible seeds are found. Its texture resembles a cucumber's, but it is more fragile. The flavor of a kiwi has been described as a composite of strawberry, rhubarb, peach, and gooseberry. Low in calories, the kiwi is a richer source of ascorbic acid than even citrus fruits.

Lemons   Completely yellow lemons are likely to be less acidic than lemons with some green color. Like grapefruit, thin-skinned lemons have a greater yield of juice than ones with thick skins; thick-skinned lemons also show the same characteristics as thick-skinned grapefruits. Dark yellow, hard-skinned, or leathery-skinned lemons are overly mature and should not be pur-

Figure 6.3

Some tropical fruits are, top center and clockwise: papaya, kiwi, kumquat, and mango.

Figure 6.4

Lemons cut in fancy shapes
make garnishes for many foods.
(Sunkist Growers, Inc.)

chased. Lemons keep best when refrigerated. Lemons are a popular garnish for other foods; Figure 6.4 shows ways to slice lemons.

Limes   Good limes have glossy skins and a bright color, and are heavy for their size. They may be used almost interchangeably with lemons and can provide a delightful difference in a meringue pie or a salad dressing. Limes are usually harvested and consumed when they are green and slightly more acidic than lemons. Fully ripe, limes have a light orange-yellow or lemon-yellow color.

Mandarins   Mandarins are a variety of orange that includes tangerines and tangelos, both of which have the characteristic of being easily peeled and sectioned. Good mandarins have a fresh, shiny appearance. Avoid shriveled or dry-looking fruit.

Mangoes   Mangoes are harvested green for marketing and should be ripened at room temperature. Green mangoes are often used in chutney but should not be eaten raw. Ripe mangoes have a yellow-orange color with a rosy spot at one end. Mangoes may have a turpentine flavor if they are eaten unchilled or green. It is often difficult to separate the flesh of this fragile fruit from its large, almond-shaped pit. The washed fruit can be peeled with a floating-blade peeler and wedges of flesh cut lenghtwise from the pit. These slices are delicious marinated in pineapple juice, orange juice, or lemonade; the marinade also acts to protect the fruit from browning. Ripe mangoes should be refrigerated.

Nectarines   Nectarines, which are hybrid fruits, have the shared characteristics of peaches and plums. Ripe fruit has a rich orange-yellow color flecked with red. Nectarines are usually marketed while they are still slightly green and should be ripened at room temperature; the sugar content will not increase after harvesting. Avoid hard or shriveled fruit, which may indicate premature harvesting. Refrigerate ripe fruit unwashed, but wash it before eating. A nectarine browns when it is cut.

Figure 6.5

(Left) To make an orange peel cup: the hook on the plastic tool makes a slit around the circumference of the orange; then the curved plastic blade is inserted between the rind and the flesh to remove the peel in two pieces. Alternatively, a knife can be used to make the slit and a flat spoon handle to separate the peel from the flesh. The edges of the two cups can be shaped into points or scallops with scissors. *(Sunkist Growers, Inc.)*

Oranges   Navel oranges are easiest to peel and are best for eating out of hand. The Valencia, which is harder to peel, is good for juice and slicing. State laws require that oranges be fully mature before harvesting. Skin color, however, is not a reliable index of maturity, because oranges from Texas and Florida may have color added to their skins and are so labeled. The color is approved for such use and is a harmless vegetable dye. Thin-skinned oranges yield more juice; characteristics for distinguishing between thin and thick skins in oranges are the same as for grapefruit. Orange rinds shaped into attractive baskets are shown in Figures 6.5 and 6.6.

Figure 6.6

(Right) Fruit salad served in orange cups makes a pleasing arrangement. *(Sunkist Growers, Inc.)*

Papayas A good papaya should have a deep yellow color with a minimal amount of green at the stem end only; it should be plump and free of decay spots. Green fruit can be ripened at room temperature but has a poor flavor; ripe fruit should be refrigerated unwashed.

Peaches Two major types of peaches are clingstone and freestone. Freestone peaches have a softer flesh that falls apart easily and are preferred for their flavor for raw eating and freezing. Cling peaches are best for canning because they hold their shape better, but both types are available canned. Ripe peaches of either kind are a rich yellow-orange color with areas of red. Avoid hard peaches or ones with a distinctly green color. Also avoid soft, overly ripe, or bruised peaches. Refrigerate unwashed fruit; wash just before serving. To peel a peach, submerge it in boiling water for 30 seconds, then in cold water. Peaches are subject to enzymatic browning.

Pears Bartlett pears, the most popular variety, are available in late summer and can be held until late fall under controlled storage conditions. Winter varieties—Anjou, Bosc, Winter Nellis, and Comice—hold up well in storage and stay available even through spring. Pears are harvested when they are still slightly green to protect their quality, and they ripen readily at room temperature. Avoid shriveled pears or pears whose flesh is weakened near the stem. Pears are subject to enzymatic browning.

Persian Melons These melons resemble cantaloupes in their color and netted skin, but they are larger, about the size of honeydew melons. Persian melons have orange-colored flesh and finer netting on their skin than cantaloupes, but otherwise the characteristics of quality are the same. Refrigerate for longer storage.

Persimmons A ripe persimmon has a delicate, fragrant, sweet flavor, but the high tannin content of even slightly green fruit is astringent and causes the mouth to pucker. A fully ripe persimmon is somewhat translucent in color. A way to hasten the ripening process is to place an almost ripe persimmon in a closed container with an apple. The ethylene gas given off by the apple hastens maturation in the persimmon. Persimmons ripened in this way can be refrigerated for a short time until they are to be served. Immature fruit can also be ripened, though more slowly, at room temperature. Buy persimmons that are fully orange in color with no green coloration, and hold at room temperature until they turn translucent; avoid overly soft or bruised fruit.

Pineapples Pineapples should be ripened before harvesting, but most pineapples available in the market have been cut green.

Although the green color changes to yellow after the fruit is picked, this does not increase either the sweetness or the flavor of the pineapple. Fresh green leaves on a fully yellowed fruit indicate that it has ripened before harvesting. If the leaves are brown, the fruit was harvested while immature. Pineapple that was picked green softens and loses some of its acid as its color changes to yellow, but it lacks the full flavor and sweetness of a fruit ripened before harvest. Avoid pineapple with brown areas on the skin; this indicates decay. Methods of paring and cutting fresh pineapple are shown in Figure 6.7.

Plums Plums are of two major types—Japanese and European. Japanese plums are juicy, are never blue or purple, and come in a variety of shapes. European plums, which are always blue or purple, have a milder flavor and firmer flesh. A prune is a type of plum that is especially suited to drying. It is blue-black in color, with a pit that is easily separated from the flesh. Fresh plums are best stored just above freezing temperature and at high humidity.

Pomegranates Ripe pomegranates are ruby red and have a leathery-textured skin filled with pulp-covered seeds. Membranes between the kernel sections are white and bitter. All pomegranates have the same number of seeds, but larger fruit has more pulp and juice around each seed. The kernels, or seeds surrounded by pulp capsules, are easily removed from the membranes; they may be swallowed with the pulp or discarded. The kernels provide a bright red sparkle as a garnish for salads and desserts. Separate the juice from the seeds by crushing the kernels in a food mill or by grinding them in a blender, then straining out the seeds. This juice, which can be frozen, can be added as a red color to punch, jelly, and gelatin, or it can be used to make syrup.

Rhubarb Rhubarb, which is the stem of a plant, is not a fruit but is used like a fruit. Large rhubarb stems may be tough and require removal of tough strings to make them more edible. Young stems or rhubarb grown in hothouses do not have tough strings. Only the stems of the rhubarb plant should be eaten; the leaves contain toxic levels of oxalic acid.

Watermelons The best indication of ripeness in watermelons, though not always infallible, is color. Ripeness is indicated not by the melon's predominant green but by its yellowish underside. Avoid melons that are white or pale green on the underside. An even better indication of eating quality is the appearance of a cut melon. A mature, full-flavored watermelon has dark brown or black seeds and a rich red flesh. Immature melons have pale red or pink flesh and light-colored seeds. Melons with a grainy dry flesh are overly mature and lack juiciness. Melons with a hard

Figure 6.7

Some methods of preparing, cutting, and serving fresh pineapple. *(Castle and Cooke Foods)*

To serve pineapple quarters, cut the pineapple from bottom through the crown, first in half, then in quarters.

Cut away the hard fibrous core leaving the crown on.

Loosen fruit by cutting close to the rind with a sharp straight, or curved serrated, knife.

Cut crosswise through loosened fruit, then cut lengthwise once or twice to make bite-size pieces.

To make a *Pineapple Ruby* cut top and bottom of pineapple away with a sharp knife. Save top and crown.

Insert long, sharp knife close to the rind, and cut with saw-like motion completely around the pineapple.

Remove the cylinder of pineapple and slice into spears. Then arrange again in cylinder shape.

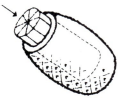

Set the rind on a serving dish and put the cylinder of spears back in. Place the top back on the pineapple so that it looks "uncut."

To make the *Outrigger* cut the pineapple in quarters, leaving crown on.

Loosen fruit by cutting under the core, but without removing it. Insert knife again and cut close to rind.

Remove the fruit and make several crosswise cuts.

Slip the pieces of fruit back into the shell in a staggered arrangement.

To remove rind from pineapple, cut top and bottom away with a sharp kitchen knife. Using the same knife cut strips of rind away.

Then remove "eyes" of fruit. Use sharp knife to cut diagonal strips away.

Pineapple can then be cut in spears, as shown, and served. Or, the spears can be cut crosswise to make wedges.

white streak running their length are also undesirable. Although cut melons cost slightly more than whole melons, it is often worth the extra cost to be able to check the interior quality, which cannot be determined from an uncut melon.

Tropical Fruits Improved transportation and marketing techniques have made exotic fruits more available, but supply is highly variable. Some tropical fruits less available in the United States include akee, breadfruit, carambola, cherimoya, granadilla, guava, kumquat, loquat, lychee, mangosteen, papaw, plantain, plumcot, quince, sapodilla, tamarind, white sapota, and several varieties of apples. Further information on these and other fruits and vegetables is available in Moyer's *Buying Guide* (see references for this chapter).

Processed Fruits

Processing makes available many fragile fruits that would otherwise be eaten only a few weeks or months during the year. Certain types of processing, however, are better suited to some kinds of fruits than to others. Procedures for commercial and home processing of fruits and vegetables are described in Chapter 30.

FROZEN FRUITS

Many fruits are available frozen. Because frozen fruits are processed without cooking, they retain most of the characteristics of freshness except texture, which is softened by freezing. Frozen fruits are packed sugared, unsugared, or with syrup added. Read the package label to select the product that best meets your specific needs. Sometimes frozen fruit is more economical than the fresh; this is especially true of frozen orange or lemon juice. Make price comparisons by comparing the yields from each form of the fruit as shown in Table 9 of the appendix.

Frozen fruits may or may not be graded; as with other food products, grading is voluntary. Grade A is the top grade and Grade C is the lowest, but all grades contain fully edible, unspoiled fruit. The lowest grade usually contains pieces of fruit that are somewhat frayed and pieces that do not hold their shape as well as those of a higher grade. If no grades are used, compare brands to determine which is most suitable for your specific needs and provides the most quality for cost. For some purposes, the lower grade or quality of fruit may be a more economical choice.

Avoid purchasing frozen fruits that are not completely frozen or that show evidence of having been thawed and refrozen. Signs of previous thawing include juice stains on the package and accumulation of heavy frost on the outside of the package. Frozen foods should be held at 0°F (−8°C) or lower for long-term storage; higher temperatures shorten the length of time that the frozen fruit retains its original quality. Improperly stored frozen fruits may have large amounts of frost inside the package, may have lost color or turned brown, may be excessively soft or flabby, and may show loss of flavor. Many of these changes are caused by oxidative reactions.

CANNED FRUITS

Many more fruits are available canned than frozen. The size of the can and the form the fruit is in—sliced, crushed, chunks, halves, or sauce—add to the variety. Fruits may be packed in water, light syrup, or heavy syrup; they may also be artificially sweetened or pickled. Canned foods may carry grades like frozen fruits that indicate the same standard. Grade A canned fruit is supposed to be full-flavored, free of defects, uniform in shape, with good texture (not mushy or frayed) and excellent color. Many food processors pay to have a full-time U.S.D.A. inspector at their plant to certify the quality of their products. Most processors also maintain a quality control staff to check on such specific characteristics as acidity, color, texture, microbiological safety, and overall eating quality. As with frozen fruits, canned fruits that do not carry a grade on their labels must be compared by brand.

Because canned fruits lose about a third of their water-soluble nutrients into the surrounding liquid, it is advisable to use the juice. Juice from canned fruit may be used to sweeten punch or lemonade, a good substitute for soft drinks. The juice can also be flavored and used as syrup, used in place of sugar to sweeten cereals, and added to gelatin mixtures.

A recently developed waterless process for canning fruits, vegetables, and meats, known as the steril-vac process, should soon be available commercially. In this process, the food is blanched to expel air and reduce bulk. It is then packed into one-piece molded cans with 1 to 2 tablespoons of liquid. The lid is loosely attached and a flame is applied to the bottom of the can to produce steam, which expels air and forms a vacuum in the can when it is sealed. The sealed can is processed at a high temperature for a short time. Foods can be processed with or without salt and sugar. A fresher flavor, about 25 percent more food in the can, increased energy efficiency, and increased nutrient retention are all benefits of this new process.

DEHYDRATED FRUITS

When fruits are dehydrated, or dried, part of their natural water is removed. They are preserved because insufficient water remains to support the growth of microorganisms. Removal of water from the plant tissue makes a dried fruit less tender, and it will usually not be able to reabsorb its original water content if it is rehydrated.

Regular dried fruit contains about 25 percent water and usually requires soaking and cooking for maximum rehydration. Excessive amounts of water should not be used for rehydration, for this causes solution of flavor, sugars, and nutrients. Vacuum-dehydrated fruits contain only 1 to 3 percent water. Apples dried by this process are crisp like a cracker or chip; other fruits, such as peaches and prunes, are hard; but all have the advantage of rehydrating more rapidly and more completely than regular dried fruit. With less water, they are lighter in weight and less expensive to transport. Because normal atmospheric humidity is greater than the amount of water in vacuum-dehydrated fruits, they must be stored in airtight containers.

Tenderized dehydrated fruits are regular dehydrated fruits that have been partially rehydrated to give the fruit a water content of 50 percent. Many persons enjoy eating them uncooked or unsoaked, as one would eat candy. These fruits rehydrate more readily than regular dehydrated fruits and no soaking is necessary. One way to rehydrate tenderized fruit is to allow it to stand overnight in water in a covered container; it will hydrate by the next day. Dehydrated fruit should not be allowed to stand at room temperature too long after rehydrating, for it will eventually ferment.

Dehydrated apricots, peaches, apples, and pears darken if they are stored at high temperatures exposed to light. Their quality is best maintained if they are frozen or at least stored in a cool, dark location. Dehydrated fruits do not need to be rehydrated. They can be chopped or ground and added to confections, cookies, cakes, muffins, breads, and meat dishes. Combinations of dried fruits can be used in compotes or in fruit soup, a Scandinavian specialty.

Nutritional Value of Fruits

Along with vegetables, fruits are the major dietary source of vitamins A and C, as well as some minerals and B vitamins. As Table 6.1 demonstrates, the nutrient content of fruits is highly variable. Vitamin A content can vary from as little as 10 I.U. per 100 grams in limes to 4800 I.U. in mangoes; vitamin C content can vary from 2 milligrams per 100 grams in figs to 242 milligrams in guavas. A variety of fruits in the diet is most likely to provide adequate amounts of all nutrients. Nutrient contribution, along with cost, is an important consideration in making choices. Some ways of serving fresh fruits—both alone and with other foods—are shown in Figure 6.8.

Fresh fruits are fairly low in calories because they contain much water and little fat. However, fruits canned or frozen in a heavy syrup are considerably higher in calories. Light syrup has fewer calories than heavy syrup; water-packed, canned fruits have about the same calories as fresh fruit. Juice-packed fruits have about the same caloric value as fruits packed in light syrup, but they may be slightly higher in some nutrients, depending on the type of juice used. Most canned fruits carry nutritional labeling, so they are easily compared.

Table 6.1 Nutrient contributions of fresh and dried fruits for 100-gram amounts, edible portion

Fruit	Approximate measure	Water (g)	Calories	Protein (g)	Fat (g)	Carbohydrate Total (g)	Carbohydrate Fiber (g)	Vitamin A (I.U.)	Ascorbic acid (mg)	Niacin (mg)	Pantothenic acid (mg)	Riboflavin (mg)	Thiamin (mg)	Pyridoxine (mg)	Calcium (mg)	Phosphorus (mg)	Iron (mg)	Potassium (mg)
Apples, unpared	1 small	84.4	58	0.2	0.6	14.5	1.0	90	4	0.1	0.10	0.02	0.03	0.03	7	10	0.3	110
Apricots	3	85.3	51	1.0	0.2	12.8	0.6	2700	10	0.6	0.24	0.04	0.03	0.07	17	23	0.5	281
Avocados	½ medium	74.0	167	2.1	16.4	6.3	1.6	290	14	1.6	1.07	0.2	0.11	0.42	10	42	0.6	604
Bananas	1 small	75.7	85	1.1	0.2	22.2	0.5	190	10	0.7	0.26	0.06	0.05	0.51	8	26	0.7	370
Blueberries	⅔ cup	83.2	62	0.7	0.5	15.3	1.5	100	14	0.5	0.16	0.06	0.03	0.07	15	13	1.0	81
Cantaloupes	¼ small	91.2	30	0.7	0.1	7.5	0.3	3400	33	0.6	0.25	0.03	0.04	0.09	14	16	0.4	251
Casaba melons	1/20	91.5	27	1.2	trace	6.5	0.5	30	13	0.6	—[a]	0.03	0.04	—	14	16	0.4	251
Cherries, sour red	15 large	83.7	58	1.2	0.3	14.3	0.2	1000	10	0.4	0.14	0.06	0.05	0.06	22	19	0.4	191
Cherries, sweet	15 large	80.4	70	1.3	0.3	17.4	0.4	110	10	0.4	0.26	0.06	0.05	0.03	22	19	0.4	191
Cranberries	1 cup	87.9	46	0.4	0.7	10.8	1.4	40	11	0.1	0.22	0.02	0.03	0.03	14	10	0.5	82
Currants, black	¾ cup	84.2	54	1.7	0.1	13.1	2.4	230	200	0.3	0.40	0.05	0.05	0.07	60	40	1.1	372
Currants, red	¾ cup	85.7	50	1.4	0.2	12.1	3.4	120	41	0.1	0.06	0.05	0.04	0.04	32	23	1.0	257
Elderberries		79.8	72	2.6	0.5	16.4	7.0	600	36	0.5	0.14	0.06	0.07	0.23	38	28	1.6	300
Figs	2 large	77.5	80	1.2	0.3	20.3	1.2	80	2	0.4	0.30	0.05	0.06	0.11	35	22	0.6	194
Grapefruits	½ medium	88.4	41	0.5	0.1	10.6	0.2	80	38	0.2	0.28	0.02	0.04	0.03	16	16	0.4	135
Grapes	⅔ cup	81.5	68	1.0	0.6	16.5	0.5	100	4	0.3	0.07	0.03	0.05	0.08	14	16	0.4	165
Guavas	1 medium	83.0	62	0.8	0.6	15.0	5.6	280	242	1.2	0.15	0.05	0.05	—	23	42	0.9	289
Honeydew melons	¼ small	90.6	33	0.8	0.3	7.7	0.6	40	23	0.6	0.21	0.03	0.04	0.06	14	16	0.4	251
Kiwis		85.6	36	0.8	trace	7.3	—	—	56	—	—	—	—	—	—	—	—	—
Kumquats	5	81.3	65	0.9	0.1	17.1	3.7	600	36	—	—	0.10	0.08	—	63	23	0.4	236
Lemons, peeled	1 medium	90.1	27	1.1	0.3	8.2	0.4	20	53	0.1	0.19	0.02	0.04	0.08	26	16	0.6	138
Lemons, with peel	1 medium	87.4	20	1.2	0.3	10.7	—	30	77	0.2	—	0.04	0.05	—	61	15	0.7	145
Limes, peeled	1 large	89.3	28	0.7	0.2	9.5	0.5	10	37	0.2	0.83	0.02	0.03	—	33	18	0.6	102
Loganberries	⅔ cup	83.0	62	1.0	0.6	14.9	3.0	200	24	0.4	—	0.04	0.03	—	35	17	1.2	170
Loquats	6	86.5	48	0.4	0.2	12.4	0.5	670	1	—	—	—	—	—	20	36	0.4	348
Lychees	7	81.9	64	0.9	0.3	16.4	0.3	170	42	—	—	0.05	0.05	—	8	42	0.4	170
Mangoes	1 small	81.7	66	0.7	0.4	16.8	0.9	4800	35	1.1	0.16	0.05	0.05	—	10	13	0.4	189
Nectarines	2 medium	81.8	64	0.6	trace	17.1	0.4	1650	13	—	—	—	—	0.02	4	24	0.5	294
Oranges	1 small	86.0	49	1.0	0.2	12.2	0.5	200	50	0.4	0.25	0.04	0.10	0.06	41	20	0.4	200
Papaws	⅔	76.6	85	5.2	0.9	16.8	—	—	—	—	—	—	—	—	—	—	—	—
Papayas	⅓ medium	88.7	39	0.6	0.1	10.0	0.9	1750	56	0.3	0.22	0.04	0.04	—	20	16	0.3	234
Peaches	1 medium	89.1	38	0.6	0.1	9.7	0.6	1330	7	1.0	0.17	0.05	0.02	0.02	9	19	0.5	202
Pears	½ large	83.2	61	0.7	0.4	15.3	1.4	20	4	0.1	0.07	0.04	0.02	0.02	8	11	0.3	130
Persimmons, Japanese	1	78.6	77	0.7	0.4	19.7	1.6	2710	11	0.1	—	0.02	0.03	—	6	26	0.3	174
Persimmons, Native	1	64.4	127	0.8	0.4	33.5	1.5	—	66	—	—	—	—	—	27	26	2.5	310
Pineapples	⅔ cup	85.3	52	0.4	0.2	13.7	0.4	70	17	0.2	0.16	0.03	0.09	0.09	17	8	0.5	146
Plums	1½	82.1	63	0.6	0.2	16.6	0.5	283	5	0.5	0.19	0.03	0.05	0.05	14	18	0.5	213
Pomegranates	1 medium	82.3	63	0.5	0.3	16.4	0.2	trace	4	0.3	1.51	0.03	0.03	—	3	8	0.3	259
Pricklypears		88.0	42	0.5	0.1	10.9	1.6	60	22	0.4	—	0.3	0.1	—	20	28	0.3	166
Quince		83.8	57	0.4	0.1	15.3	1.7	40	15	0.2	0.08	0.03	0.02	0.04	11	17	0.7	197
Raspberries, red	⅔ cup	84.2	57	1.2	0.5	13.6	3.0	130	25	0.9	0.24	0.09	0.03	0.06	22	22	0.9	168
Rhubarb	¾ cup	94.8	16	0.6	0.1	3.7	0.7	100	9	0.3	0.08	0.07	0.03	0.03	(96)[b]	18	0.8	251
Sapodillas	½ cup	76.1	89	0.5	1.1	21.8	1.4	60	14	0.2	—	0.02	trace	—	21	12	0.8	193
Strawberries	⅔ cup	89.9	37	0.7	0.5	8.4	1.3	60	59	0.6	0.34	0.07	0.03	0.05	21	21	1.0	164
Tangerines	1 large	87.0	46	0.8	0.2	11.6	0.5	420	31	0.1	0.20	0.02	0.06	0.07	40	18	0.4	126
Watermelons	½ cup	92.6	26	0.5	0.2	6.4	0.3	590	7	0.2	0.30	0.03	0.03	0.07	7	10	0.5	100
Dried Fruits																		
Apples	⅔ cup	24.0	275	1.0	1.6	71.8	3.1	—	10	0.5	—	0.12	0.06	0.13	31	52	1.6	569
Apricots	⅔ cup	25.0	260	5.0	0.5	66.5	3.0	10900	12	3.3	0.75	0.16	0.01	0.17	67	108	5.5	979
Dates	⅔ cup	22.5	274	2.2	0.5	72.9	2.3	50	0	2.2	0.78	0.10	0.09	0.15	59	63	3.0	648
Figs	5	23.0	274	4.3	1.3	69.1	5.6	80	0	0.7	0.43	0.10	0.10	0.17	126	77	3.0	640
Peaches	⅔ cup	25.0	262	3.1	0.7	68.3	3.1	3900	18	5.3	—	0.19	0.01	0.10	48	117	6.0	950
Pears	⅔ cup	26.0	268	3.1	1.8	67.3	6.2	70	7	0.6	—	0.18	0.01	—	35	48	1.3	573
Prunes, tenderized	12	28.0	255	2.1	0.6	67.4	1.6	1600	3	1.6	0.46	0.17	0.09	0.24	51	79	3.9	694
Raisins	⅝ cup	18.0	289	2.5	0.2	77.4	0.9	20	1	0.5	0.04	0.08	0.11	0.24	62	101	3.5	763

SOURCE: U.S. Department of Agriculture, *Composition of Foods; Nutritive Value of Foods;* and *Pantothenic Acid, Vitamin B_6 and Vitamin B_1 Foods,* Home Economic Research Report No. 36, by M. L. Orr (Washington, D.C.: Government Printing Office, 1969).

[a] Dash indicates value is unknown.

[b] Calcium in rhubarb combines with oxalic acid and cannot be absorbed by the human body.

Figure 6.8

Many kinds of fruits make nutritious, low-calorie treats as salads, desserts, or snacks. *(United Fresh Fruit and Vegetable Association)*

Study Questions

1. What is the botanical definition of a fruit?
2. What are the components of a cell wall?
3. What substances are found in the protoplasm of plant cells?
4. What is osmosis? Does osmosis occur in cooked fruits? Why?
5. What happens if raw fruit, such as apple, is placed in water? If it is sprinkled with sugar? Why do such changes occur?
6. How does cooking affect the permeability of plant cell walls?
7. What is diffusion?
8. What happens when fruit is cooked in heavy syrup? Why do such changes occur?
9. What method should be used to prepare a fruit compote to ensure that the fruit neither disintegrates nor shrivels but remains intact and plump?
10. What is enzymatic browning?
11. Explain why fruits turn brown when bruised.
12. Why does changing the pH of a fruit prevent enzymatic browning? How is the pH changed? What other methods will prevent enzymatic browning?
13. Describe several ways that heat affects

Fruits   119

fruits when they are cooked.

14. What effect does the amount of water used in cooking fruits have on their flavor?
15. Name two fruits that ripen best after they are picked green.
16. Why is it preferable to allow most fruits to ripen before they are picked?
17. What is controlled-atmosphere storage?
18. Should green bananas be refrigerated? Why?
19. When some fruits ripen, what changes occur?
20. Why should some fruits, such as berries, not be washed until they are ready to eat?
21. How can thick-skinned and thin-skinned citrus fruits be distinguished?
22. How does the highest grade of canned or frozen fruits differ from the lowest grade?
23. What are some indications that a frozen fruit may have been thawed and refrozen, or improperly held in frozen storage?
24. What is the approximate distribution of water-soluble nutrients in the liquid and solids of canned fruits?
25. Compare the water content of regular dehydrated fruit, vacuum-dehydrated fruit, and tenderized dehydrated fruit.
26. What causes darkening of dehydrated fruits during storage, and how can this effect be prevented?
27. What are the principal nutritional contributions of fruits?
28. How does the type of liquid used in canning fruit affect its caloric content?

References

Camp, Susan C., and Williams, Izola F. "New Ways with Fruits." In U.S. Department of Agriculture, *Food for Us All*, Yearbook of Agriculture. Washington, D.C.: Government Printing Office, 1965.

Charley, Helen. "Fruits and Vegetables." In *Food Theory and Applications*, edited by Pauline C. Paul and Helen H. Palmer. New York: Wiley, 1972.

Fogle, Harold W. "New Stone Fruit Varieties Add Zest to Our Diets." In U.S. Department of Agriculture, *Science for Better Living*, Yearbook of Agriculture. Washington, D.C.: Government Printing Office, 1968.

Gilpin, Gladys L., Greeley, E. T., and Rose, E. W. "Fruit—Buy It with Care, Serve It with Flair." In U.S. Department of Agriculture, *Food for Us All*, Yearbook of Agriculture. Washington, D.C.: Government Printing Office, 1969.

Hoffman, M. B. "Making A Better Apple, or Puzzles and Pomology." In U.S. Department of Agriculture, *Contours of Change*, Yearbook of Agriculture. Washington, D.C.: Government Printing Office, 1970.

Leonard, Sherman; Carroad, P. A.; Merson, R. L.; Heil, J. R.; and Wolcott, T. K. *Steril-Vac Peach Study* (Progress Report). 1978. (Department of Food Science and Technology, University of California, Davis, CA 95616.)

Moyer, William C. *The Buying Guide for Fresh Fruits, Vegetables, Herbs and Nuts.* Fullerton, Calif.: Blue Goose, 1974.

Seelig, R. A. *Selection and Care of Fresh Fruits and Vegetables* (1971). United Fresh Fruit and Vegetable Association, 777 14th Street, NW, Washington, DC 20005.

Stadtman, E. R. "Nonenzymatic Browning in Fruit Products." *Advances in Food Research* 1 (1948): 325.

U.S. Department of Agriculture. *How to Buy Fresh Fruits*, Home and Garden Bulletin No. 141. Washington, D.C.: Government Printing Office, 1967.

——. *Fruits in Family Meals*, Home and Garden Bulletin No. 125, 1971.

——. *How to Buy Canned and Frozen Fruits*, Home and Garden Bulletin No. 191, 1971.

Vegetables

Vegetables add color, flavor, and texture to the diet; they are also good sources of many nutrients that are not plentiful in other foods. Preparing vegetables properly is important to maintain desirable colors, flavors, and textures as well as to retain as many nutrients as possible. This chapter deals with the effects of heat on vegetables and the preparation of cooked vegetables. The preparation of raw vegetables is described in Chapter 8.

Composition and Structure of Vegetables

Vegetables have a cellular structure similar to that of fruits as described in Chapter 6, but vegetables have a slightly different nutritive composition. Table 7.1 lists the composition and nutrients of commonly served cooked vegetables. If they are compared as a group with the fruits listed in Table 6.1, it will be seen that vegetables have a higher protein, water, and starch content and a lower sugar content than fruits; their fat content is about the same. Because of these differences, fruits tend to have slightly more calories than cooked vegetables. Vegetables also have a higher content of cellulose and lignin than fruits. In some vegetables, the lignin content increases noticeably as the vegetable matures, producing a woody or hard texture in overly mature vegetables. Woody cores in carrots and excessive stringiness in sweet potatoes, yams, okra, snow peas, green beans, and asparagus are all caused by an increase in lignin.

Like fruits, vegetables contain both starch and sugars. In some vegetables, however, sugar turns to starch during maturation. Corn and peas are sweet and juicy when they are young and immature, but as they mature, they become more starchy and less sweet. Vegetables also contain some organic acids, though not in as great quantity as fruits. Organic acids can cause problems when vegetables are cooked, particularly in their effect on some pigments. Oxalic acid occurs in spinach, chard, beet greens, and rhubarb as explained in Chapter 1. Vegetables also tend to have more minerals than fruits.

PIGMENTS IN VEGETABLES

The four main pigments that occur in plants are *anthocyanin, anthoxanthin, carotenoid,* and *chlorophyll.* These pigments occur both in fruits and vegetables but in fruits are only a problem in juices. The pigments in juices are discussed in Chapter 31. Most problems with pigments occur when vegetables are cooked, because various cooking media can cause undesirable color changes. Table 7.2 lists the color of these four pigments in their natural state and how acidic and alkaline media affect them. Anthocyanin and anthoxanthin pigments dissolve in water; carotenoid and chlorophyll pigments dissolve in fat. The water-soluble pigments may be leached from the vegetables if they are cooked in too much water, but not the fat-soluble pigments.

Table 7.1 Nutrient composition of vegetables and legumes for 100-gram amounts, edible portion cooked

Vegetable	Approximate measure	Water (g)	Calories (g)	Protein (g)	Fat (g)	Carbohydrate Total (g)	Carbohydrate Fiber (g)	Vitamin A (I.U.)	Ascorbic acid (mg)	Niacin (mg)	Pantothenic acid (mg)	Riboflavin (mg)	Thiamin (mg)	Pyridoxine (mg)	Calcium (mg)	Phosphorus (mg)	Iron (mg)	Potassium (mg)
Artichoke	1 large	86.5	8–44	2.8	0.2	9.9	2.4	150	8	0.7	0.29[a]	0.04	0.07	0.1	51	69	1.1	301
Asparagus	6 spears	93.6	20	2.2	0.2	3.6	0.7	900	26	1.4	0.62[a]	0.18	0.16	0.15	21	50	0.6	183
Beans, green snap	¾ cup	92.4	25	1.6	0.2	5.4	1.0	540	12	0.5	0.19[a]	0.09	0.07	0.08[a]	50	37	0.6	151
Beans, yellow wax	¾ cup	93.4	22	1.4	0.2	4.6	1.0	230	13	0.5	0.25[a]	0.09	0.07	—[b]	50	37	0.6	151
Beans, lima green	⅔ cup	71.1	111	7.6	0.5	19.8	1.8	280	17	1.3	0.47[a]	0.10	0.18	—	47	121	[illegible]	422
Beets, root only	⅔ cup	90.9	32	1.1	0.1	7.2	0.8	20	6	0.3	0.15[a]	0.04	0.03	0.05[a]	14	23	0.5	208
Beet greens	½ cup	93.6	18	1.7	0.2	3.3	1.1	5100	15	0.3	0.25[a]	0.15	0.07	0.10[a]	(99)[d]	25	1.9	332
Broccoli	⅔ cup	91.3	26	3.1	0.3	4.5	1.5	2500	90	0.8	1.17[a]	0.20	0.09	0.19[a]	88	62	0.8	267
Brussels sprouts	¾ cup	88.2	36	4.2	0.4	6.4	1.6	520	87	0.8	0.72[a]	0.14	0.08	0.23[a]	32	72	1.1	273
Cabbage, green	⅔ cup	93.9	20	1.1	0.2	4.3	0.8	130	33	0.3	0.20	0.04	0.04	0.16[a]	44	20	0.3	163
Cabbage, spoon	⅔ cup	95.2	14	1.4	0.2	2.4	0.6	3100	15	0.7	—	0.08	0.04	—	148	33	0.6	214
Carrots	¾ cup	91.2	31	0.9	0.2	7.1	1.0	10500	6	0.5	0.28[a]	0.05	0.05	0.15[a]	33	31	0.6	222
Cauliflower	1 cup	92.8	22	2.3	0.2	4.1	1.0	60	55	0.6	1.00[a]	0.08	0.09	0.21[a]	21	42	0.7	206
Celeriac, raw	4–6 roots	88.4	40	1.8	0.3	8.5	1.3	—	8	0.7	—	0.06	0.05	0.16	43	115	0.6	300
Chard, Swiss	¾ cup	93.7	18	1.8	0.2	3.3	0.7	5400	16	0.4	0.17	0.11	0.04	—	(73)[d]	24	1.8	321
Collard greens	½ cup +	89.6	33	3.6	0.7	5.1	1.0	7800	76	1.2	0.45[c]	0.20	0.11	0.19[c]	188	52	0.8	262
Corn on cob	1 medium ear	74.1	91	3.3	1.0	21.0	0.7	400	9	1.4	0.41[c]	0.10	0.12	0.28[c]	3	89	0.6	196
Cowpeas, green	⅔ cup	71.8	108	8.1	0.8	18.1	1.8	350	17	1.4	0.40[c]	0.11	0.30	0.11[c]	24	146	2.1	379
Dandelion greens	⅔ cup	89.8	33	2.0	0.6	6.4	1.3	11700	18	—	—	0.16	0.13	—	140	42	1.8	232
Eggplant	1 cup	94.3	19	1.0	0.2	4.1	0.9	10	3	0.5	0.08[a]	0.04	0.05	0.22[a]	11	21	0.6	150
Jerusalem artichokes, raw		79.8	7–75	2.3	0.1	16.7	0.8	20	4	1.3	—	0.06	0.20	0.07[a]	14	78	3.4	—
Kale	1 cup	91.2	28	3.2	0.7	4.0	1.1	7400	62	—	0.10[a]	—	—	0.30[a]	134	46	1.2	221
Kohlrabi	¾ cup	92.2	24	1.7	0.1	5.3	1.0	20	43	0.2	0.16[a]	0.03	0.06	0.15[a]	33	41	0.3	260
Lambsquarters	½ cup	88.9	32	3.2	0.7	5.0	1.8	9700	37	0.9	—	0.26	0.10	—	258	45	0.7	—
Mustard greens	½ cup	92.6	23	2.2	0.4	4.0	0.9	5800	48	0.6	0.21[a]	0.14	0.08	—	138	32	1.8	220
Mustard spinach	½ cup	94.5	16	1.7	0.2	2.8	0.8	8200	65	—	—	—	—	—	158	18	0.8	—
New Zealand spinach		94.8	13	1.7	0.2	2.1	0.6	3600	14	0.5	0.31[a]	0.10	0.03	—	(48)[d]	28	1.5	463
Okra	8–9 pods	91.1	29	2.0	0.3	6.0	1.0	490	20	0.9	0.26[a]	0.18	0.13	0.07[a]	92	41	0.5	174
Onions, mature	½ cup	91.8	29	1.2	0.1	6.5	0.6	40	7	0.2	0.13[a]	0.03	0.03	0.13[a]	24	29	0.4	110
Parsnips	¾ cup	82.2	66	1.5	0.5	14.9	2.0	30	10	0.1	0.60	0.08	0.07	0.09	45	62	0.6	379
Peas, green	½ cup +	81.5	71	5.4	0.4	12.1	2.0	540	20	2.3	0.75[a]	0.11	0.28	0.16[a]	23	99	1.8	196
Peas, edible pod	¾ cup	86.6	43	2.9	0.2	9.5	1.2	610	14	—	—	0.11	0.22	—	56	76	0.5	119
Potatoes, raw	1 medium	79.8	76	2.1	0.1	17.1	0.5	trace	20	1.5	0.38	0.04	0.10	0.25	7	53	0.6	407
baked in skin	1 medium	75.1	93	2.6	0.1	21.1	0.6	trace	20	1.7	—	0.04	0.10	—	9	65	0.7	503
boiled in skin	1 medium	79.8	76	2.1	0.1	17.1	0.5	trace	16	1.5	—	0.04	0.09	—	7	53	0.6	407
peeled, boiled	1 medium	82.8	65	1.9	0.1	14.5	0.5	trace	16	1.2	—	0.03	0.09	—	6	42	0.5	285
French fried	18 pieces	44.7	274	4.3	13.2	36.0	1.0	trace	21	3.1	0.54[a]	0.08	0.13	0.18[a]	15	111	1.3	853
Potato chips	50 chips	1.8	568	5.3	39.8	50.0	1.6	trace	16	4.8	—	0.07	0.21	0.18	40	139	1.8	1130
Pumpkin, canned	½ cup	90.2	33	1.0	0.3	7.9	1.3	6400	5	0.6	0.40	0.05	0.03	0.06	25	26	0.4	240
Rutabagas	½ cup	90.2	35	0.9	0.1	8.2	1.1	550	26	0.8	0.16	0.06	0.06	0.10	59	31	0.3	167
Salsify	⅔ cup	81.0	12–70	2.6	0.6	15.1	1.8	10	7	0.2	—	0.04	0.03	—	42	53	1.3	266
Spinach	½ cup	92.0	23	3.0	0.3	3.6	0.6	8100	28	0.5	0.30[a]	0.14	0.07	0.28[a]	(93)[d]	38	2.2	324
Squash, summer	½ cup	95.5	14	0.9	0.1	3.1	0.6	390	10	0.8	0.36[a]	0.08	0.05	0.08[a]	25	25	0.4	141
Squash, winter	½ cup	81.4	63	1.8	0.4	15.4	1.8	4200	13	0.7	0.40[a]	0.13	0.05	0.15[a]	28	48	0.8	461
Sweet potatoes	1 small	63.7	141	2.1	0.5	32.5	0.9	8100	22	0.7	0.82[a]	0.07	0.09	0.22[a]	40	58	0.9	300
Taro (Dasheen), raw	1⅓ corms	73.0	98	1.9	0.2	23.7	0.8	20	4	1.1	—	0.04	0.13	—	28	61	1.0	514
Tomatoes, boiled	½ cup	92.4	26	1.3	0.2	5.5	0.6	1000	24	0.8	0.33[a]	0.05	0.07	0.10[a]	15	32	0.6	287
Turnips, boiled	⅔ cup	93.6	23	0.8	0.2	4.9	0.9	trace	22	0.3	0.20[a]	0.05	0.04	0.09[a]	35	24	0.4	188
Turnip greens	⅔ cup	93.2	20	2.2	0.2	3.6	0.7	6300	69	0.6	0.38[a]	0.24	0.15	0.26[a]	184	37	1.1	—

SOURCE: U.S. Department of Agriculture, *Composition of Foods; Nutritive Value of Foods; Pantothenic Acid, Vitamin B_6, and Vitamin B_{12} in Foods.* All values are for cooked vegetables unless otherwise specified.

[a]Value for raw food.
[b]Dash indicates value is unknown
[c]Value for frozen food, uncooked.
[d]Calcium combines with oxalic acid and cannot be absorbed by the human body.

Table 7.2   *Vegetable pigments, their natural colors, and the effect of acidic and alkaline media on color*

Pigments	Natural color	Acidic medium	Alkaline medium
Anthocyanin	Red to purple	Red	Blue to blue-green
Anthoxanthin	Colorless, white	White	Creamy white, yellow
Carotenoid	Orange, yellow, red-orange, red	Retains natural color	Natural color with brownish tint
Chlorophyll	Green	Brownish green, yellowish green	Bright green

Anthocyanin   Red cabbage is the only vegetable that contains anthocyanin pigment. Beets and beet greens contain derivatives, betacyanins and betaxanthins, which are more stable. Many kinds of cherries, berries, and plums contain anthocyanin pigment, which is stable in raw food. If red cabbage is cooked in tap water, it turns blue or bluish-green because most tap water is alkaline. The red color of cabbage is more likely to be retained if the cabbage is cooked by a waterless method or if some acidic juice, such as lemon, is added. Some older cookbooks recommend cooking red cabbage with apple, which can also be a source of acid. The color reaction of this pigment to changes in pH is reversible; if the cabbage should start to turn blue during cooking, the color can be changed back to red by the addition of acid.

Beet pigments are not affected by alkaline media, but if peeled, cut beets are cooked in water, much of their pigment dissolves into the water, leaving their color very pale and washed out. This condition can be prevented by leaving 1 inch of stem and root on whole, unpeeled beets for cooking in water. The beets can be peeled and cut up after they are cooked and will have a much better color. If peeled beets are steamed or cooked by waterless methods, their color is retained.

Ions from metals—iron, tin, and, to a lesser extent, aluminum—react with anthocyanin pigment to form complexes of various shades of blue. For this reason, tin cans are lacquered on the inside to prevent contact between the tin and the contents of the can. Vegetables containing this pigment should not be cooked in iron pots, nor should they be left standing in aluminum pots. Stainless steel and glass pots, however, are inert. A clean aluminum pot is satisfactory if the vegetable is cooked quickly, but some aluminum pots may have a buildup of mineral deposits from water and foods that can cause discoloration.

Anthoxanthin   Anthoxanthin pigments are colorless or white and are often masked by other pigments in plants. Vegetables in which anthoxanthin is not masked include white potatoes, onions, cauliflower, turnips, salsify, and parsnips. (White flour also contains this pigment, which can cause a yellowish color in baked products if the medium is excessively alkaline.) Many people are accustomed to the creamy white color of these vegetables when they are cooked in alkaline tap water, so normal cooking procedures should cause no problem. However, if these vegetables are cooked in far too much water, excess alkalinity could produce a distinctly yellow color that would be unacceptable. To obtain a bright white color, a small amount of acid may be added during the last half of the cooking period.

Anthoxanthin pigment is chemically similar to anthocyanin pigment. If white vegetables containing anthoxanthin pigment are cooked for a long time, the pigment changes into anthocyanin pigment and the vegetable develops a pinkish color. For this reason cabbage that has been cooked for a long time and overprocessed home-canned pears appear slightly pink in color.

Carotenoid Several chemical compounds belong to the carotenoid group of pigments. These include *alpha* and *beta carotenes, lycopene,* and *xanthophylls.* The orange color of winter squashes and carrots is produced by carotene pigment. Lycopene is responsible for the red color of tomatoes. A xanthophyll pigment in corn produces its yellow color.

Because these pigments are not soluble in water, they do not dissolve out of foods that are cooked in water. Additionally, these pigments are fairly stable in both acidic and alkaline media of normal cooking procedures. Overlong heating or extremely alkaline media can produce a slight brown discoloration, but this result is not likely under ordinary cooking conditions. Foods containing carotenoid pigments do not present problems in normal food preparation.

Chlorophyll Green chlorophyll pigment is responsible for the color of every green vegetable. Chlorophyll in leaves is the food factory of the plant, for chlorophyll converts carbon dioxide from the air, in the presence of light, into carbohydrate in the plant. Retaining color in green vegetables is probably the greatest problem in cooking vegetables because so many vegetables contain this pigment, which is unstable in acidic media. As shown in Table 7.2, chlorophyll is stable in an alkaline medium but turns brownish-green or yellow-green in acidic media.

Green vegetables cooked in water tend to keep their green color because tap water is usually alkaline. If the tap water is naturally soft and, therefore, nearly neutral, or if green vegetables are cooked by a waterless method, acids released from the vegetables themselves can produce an acidic medium; heating them an excessively long time accentuates the problem. It is important to remember that a short cooking time helps prevent undesirable color change. Since some acids in vegetables are volatile, uncover the pot for a minute when the vegetables start to boil, and stir them to dissipate the volatile acids, and then recover the pot. Baking soda should *never* be added to green vegetables to help retain their color. Not only does the alkalinity produced by baking soda destroy ascorbic acid and some B vitamins, it also has a deleterious effect on both texture and flavor.

Vegetables vary in acidity, as can be seen in the table in the appendix that shows the pH of foods. Cabbage at pH 5.2 contains 10 times more acid than peas at pH 6.2. Peas thus retain their color much better than cabbage in normal cooking. However, the long heat needed to process canned peas does produce a color change. Green vegetables should not be cooked in large amounts of water to aid in color retention because this procedure increases solution loss of nutrients. A pressure cooker, because it is a closed system that does not allow for volatilization of plant acids, can produce poorly colored green vegetables, especially if they are overcooked even for a few seconds. Short cooking times and allowance for volatilization of acids from the vegetables best preserve the nutrients of vegetables as well as their natural colors.

Frozen vegetables often retain their color better than the same vegetable prepared fresh, probably because the plant acids were volatilized during the blanching process carried out before the vegetables were frozen.

ENZYMATIC BROWNING OF VEGETABLES

Only a few vegetables show enzymatic browning when they are pared or cut; these include white and sweet potatoes, salsify, and eggplant. The use of acidic fruit juices or other acidic media to prevent browning, as recommended in Chapter 6, is not appropriate with vegetables, because the flavors of the acids are not compatible either with the vegetables themselves or with their preparation. A little browning is reversible with cooking, if the vegetable is quickly pared and started to cook. Eggplant and sweet potatoes, however, turn brown so quickly that some treatment is necessary, and preparing white potatoes for French frying also requires some preventive measures. Placing these vegetables in a salt solution is an effective measure to prevent browning and also provides a slight, desirably salty flavor.

TEXTURE OF COOKED VEGETABLES

Heat, pH, cooking media, and the characteristics of the vegetables themselves all affect the texture of vegetables when they are cooked.

Heat Heat affects vegetable tissues in the same way that it affects fruits, reducing their bulk (Figure 7.1) and increasing their tenderness. Vegetables contain much more lignin than fruits, and it is not softened by cooking. The woody centers of overly mature carrots remain stringy and tough even after they are cooked. The parts of vegetables that have a high lignin content, such as the lower section of asparagus stalks, the stems of some greens, and

Figure 7.1

A 1-pound bunch of spinach, as purchased, yields a basketful of trimmed washed leaves, 5 to 6 cups chopped leaves, and 1 cup cooked greens, enough for two 1/2-cup servings.

the strings on green beans, are best removed before cooking. Extended cooking of the stems of some greens to make them tender is a futile effort that often overcooks the leaves and causes a loss of nutrients.

The pH of the Cooking Medium At pH 4 to 4.5, softening of vegetables during cooking is retarded. Either increased or decreased acidity causes vegetables to become softer, because the pectic substances cementing the plant cells together are least soluble at pH 4 to 4.5. The substances become more soluble with increased alkalinity, or higher pH, and also with increased acidity, or decreased pH. The limited acidity of pickling solutions (pH 3 to 4) along with other factors helps produce firmness in pickled vegetables. Adding baking soda to vegetables during cooking is not recommended because it produces mushiness. If acids are used with vegetables for flavor or for promoting the natural colors of the anthocyanin or anthoxanthin pigments, they should be added near the end of the cooking period.

Hard Water High concentrations of calcium in the cooking medium can also affect the texture of cooked vegetables. Hard water can contain many calcium and magnesium ions that form insoluble complexes with the pectins in vegetables and interfere with softening during cooking. Calcium pectate increases the firmness of plants when they are cooked; calcium chloride is added to pickles during processing to increase their firmness, and to whole tomatoes and apple slices during canning to prevent them from disintegrating. However, normal cooking in hard water presents no problems for most fruits and vegetables. The effect of hard water on legumes is discussed in Chapter 24.

Cooking Time   The length of time a vegetable is cooked affects its texture. Longer cooking causes greater solution of the pectic substances and softening of the cellulose, thereby increasing the tenderness of the cooked vegetable. The desirable degree of tenderness in cooked vegetables is an individual preference. Some persons like vegetables soft and mushy; others prefer them crunchy. Although the size of pieces and the nature of the vegetable itself determine the cooking time necessary for a vegetable to reach a given texture, the tender-crisp stage can usually be reached more quickly than the soft, mushy stage. Vegetables cooked only until they are tender and crisp are more likely to retain their flavor, color, and nutrients.

Individual Characteristics of Vegetables   A final factor affecting the texture of cooked vegetables is the nature of the vegetable itself. Potatoes as a group become tender more quickly than carrots. However, the same vegetable can show individual differences because of variety, growing conditions, or even storage conditions. Thus, some potatoes may become mealy when they are cooked, while others become waxy or soggy.

FLAVOR OF COOKED VEGETABLES   The flavor of cooked vegetables is produced by the interaction of aromatic compounds, organic acids, sugars, and other substances as described in Chapter 3. Most flavoring components in vegetables are desirable; a few are not. Some flavoring components are soluble in water, and some are volatile; thus, flavors can be lost from the vegetables both by solution and by evaporation.

Loss of Flavors   Loss of flavors is caused by long cooking times and by using too much water as a cooking medium. Both of these procedures have deleterious effects on texture and color, as well as on nutrient retention as described in Chapter 1. Solution losses in water of sugars and other flavoring substances, as well as of nutrients, leave the vegetable with a weak, watery flavor.

Strong Flavors   Onions possess a strong flavor that can be made milder when the onions are cooked in a large amount of water, because the sulfur compounds that contribute to the flavor of onions dissolve readily in water. Because onions are not a particularly good source of any nutrients, they obviously have nothing to lose in any amount of water. This method has also been used in cooking spinach and chard to eliminate oxalic acid and in cooking leafy greens, such as dandelion and turnip greens, to eliminate bitter flavor, but it is not recommended. These green vegetables are excellent sources of ascorbic acid, iron, and other minerals and B vitamins, which are lost if the vegetables are cooked in large amounts of water.

The sulfur compounds in vegetables of the cabbage, or Brassica, family are different from those found in onions. Sulfur compounds in cabbage become obnoxious with prolonged cooking; raw cabbage is milder in flavor than cooked cabbage. To keep mild flavors, cabbage, broccoli, cauliflower, turnips, kale, and kohlrabi should be cooked just until they are tender.

Seasoning Cooked Vegetables   Most of the cooked vegetables listed in Table 7.1 are very low in calories, with the exception of starchy vegetables like corn, beans, and peas. But the caloric content of vegetables can be doubled and quadrupled with the addition of such common seasonings as table fat, bacon fat, oily dressings, sour cream, and cream sauces. Many of these seasonings, furthermore, completely mask the natural flavors of the vegetables. Cultivate a taste for the natural flavor of vegetables, and use seasonings only to enhance and preserve these natural flavors without overly increasing the caloric content. Herbs, acidic sauces that are low in fat, and mixtures of vegetables and condiments can produce tasty vegetable dishes (Figure 7.2); Table 7.3 lists some spices and herbs that are compatible with specific vegetables. The suggested herbs are not intended to be used all at once but interchangeably.

Figure 7.2

The strong flavor of collard greens can be masked with such seasonings as chopped green chiles and catsup. Seeds should be removed from the chiles before they are chopped to reduce pepperiness; chopped chiles and catsup are stirred into the cooked greens.

Table 7.3   Suggested use of spices and herbs with vegetables

Vegetable	Spice or herb[a]
Asparagus	Mustard seed, seasame seed, tarragon
Lima beans	Marjoram, oregano, sage, savory, tarragon, thyme
Snap beans	Basil, dill, marjoram, mint, mustard seed, oregano, savory, tarragon, thyme
Beets	Allspice, bay leaves, caraway seed, cloves, dill, ginger, mustard seed, savory, thyme
Broccoli	Caraway seed, dill, mustard seed, tarragon
Brussels sprouts	Basil, caraway seed, dill, mustard seed, sage, thyme
Cabbage	Caraway seed, celery seed, dill, mint, mustard seed, nutmeg, savory, tarragon
Carrots	Allspice, bay leaves, caraway seed, dill, fennel, ginger, mace, marjoram, mint, nutmeg, thyme
Cauliflower	Caraway seed, celery salt, dill, mace, tarragon
Cucumbers	Basil, dill, mint, tarragon
Eggplant	Marjoram, oregano
Onions	Caraway seed, mustard seed, nutmeg, oregano, sage, thyme
Peas	Basil, dill, marjoram, mint, oregano, poppy seed, rosemary, sage, savory
Potatoes, white	Basil, bay leaves, caraway seed, celery seed, dill, chives, mustard seed, oregano, poppy seed, thyme
Spinach	Basil, mace, marjoram, nutmeg, oregano
Squash	Allspice, basil, cinnamon, cloves, fennel, ginger, mustard seed, nutmeg, rosemary
Sweet potatoes	Allspice, cardamom, cinnamon, cloves, nutmeg
Tomatoes	Basil, bay leaves, celery seed, oregano, sage, sesame seed, tarragon, thyme
Green salads	Basil, chives, dill, tarragon
Creamed vegetables	Curry powder

SOURCE: U.S. Department of Agriculture, *Vegetables in Family Meals*, Home and Garden Bulletin No. 105 (Washington, D.C.: Government Printing Office, September 1965).

[a]Add about ¼ teaspoon of dried herb, or 1 teaspoon of fresh herb, for 2 cups of cooked vegetable. Add dried herbs during cooking; add fresh herbs just before serving.

Selecting and Caring for Fresh Vegetables

Fresh vegetables of good quality should have a bright, natural color and be free, or nearly free, of such defects as decay or discolorations that indicate tissue destruction. They should be crisp and not be wilted or shriveled.

TRIMMING VEGETABLES AND WASTE

Trimming and cleaning vegetables before refrigerating them means that space is conserved; if the inedible parts are removed, the edible parts occupy less space in the refrigerator.

The amount of waste produced by trimming vegetables depends both on the quality of the vegetable and how much of it is considered inedible. Some people remove the stems of leafy greens at the base of the leaf; others leave the stems on unless they are excessively stringy or tough. Some prefer to use only the flowers of broccoli or the tips of asparagus; others use much of the stalks. If a bunch of greens has a large amount of yellowed or decayed leaves, the waste from trimming is greater than it is when most of the leaves are green. Remember that the leaves of plants are richest, the flowers intermediate, and the stems lowest in nutrient content. Also, stems have a high content of lignin that is not softened by cooking. Consider all these factors before deciding how to trim vegetables.

Take waste into account in calculating what quantities of fresh vegetables to buy and also in comparing the costs of fresh with frozen and canned forms of a vegetable. The Department of Agriculture's Handbook No. 8, *Composition of Foods*, gives the nutrients for 1 pound of food as purchased (A.P.) together with the percent of refuse. Multiplying the A.P. weight by the percent of refuse gives the nonedible portion of the food, which must be subtracted from the original amount to determine the edible portion (E.P.). The Department of Agriculture has produced two other booklets for determining yields and costs of various foods: Home and Garden Bulletin No. 183, *Your Money's Worth in Foods*, and Home Economics Research Report No. 37, *Family Food Buying*, which can be ordered by mail for a small fee. The figures for percentages of waste in these publications are based on averages that can vary considerably for some vegetables.

CLEANING VEGETABLES

Properly cleaning vegetables before refrigeration means less dirt in the refrigerator and reduces the time required for last-minute meal preparation. Vegetables to be eaten raw must be carefully cleaned, because no heat will be provided to destroy microorganisms. Warm water is better than cold water for cleaning vegetables; hot water wilts vegetables and should not be used.

The kind and amount of washing necessary depends on the type of vegetable and the kind and amount of soil. Many vegetables can be washed by immersion in water. After agitating them, remove the vegetables from the water; do not allow the soiled water to drain off the vegetables. If the water appears dirty after the first immersion, immerse the vegetables again in fresh water until the water appears fairly clean. A short soak in warm, salted water may be needed to remove aphids or other insects. Such soaking should be minimal and used only when necessary.

Large leafy vegetables, such as Swiss chard, are often difficult to immerse in water for cleaning. Clean these large leaves by running tap water over each side of the leaf while unfolding the leaf and brushing it lightly to remove the soil. Using running water to wash vegetables is more expensive than immersion washing because it takes more water, but the cost is not appreciable. Some vegetables may need to be lightly brushed with a vegetable brush to remove all the soil.

STORING FRESH VEGETABLES

Most vegetables keep best when refrigerated. Decay in white potatoes can be delayed in this way, but storage at refrigerator temperatures increases the sugar content of potatoes and makes them unsatisfactory for frying and mashing. Most refrigerators have drawers for storing fruits and vegetables; these are often called *hydrators* because they have a higher humidity than the rest of the refrigerator. Foods tend to dry out when they are stored in some types of refrigerators; such drying causes fresh vegetables to wilt. If vegetables kept in hydrator drawers still wilt, the vegetables should be placed in plastic bags inside the drawers. Fresh produce stored in plastic bags should not be in contact with excessive amounts of water, for this can cause decay. Washed vegetables should be fairly dry before they are placed in plastic bags. Absorbent paper towels can also be placed in the bags along with the vegetables to absorb excess moisture and prevent decay.

How long vegetables can be refrigerated before they begin to deteriorate depends on the type of vegetable, its quality, and the temperature and humidity of storage. Under ideal conditions, carrots can be kept for several months, celery for several weeks, and leafy greens for about a week.

Table 7.4   Vegetables classified as parts of a plant system

Bulbs	Flowers	Fruits	Fungi	Leaves
Chives	Artichoke	Avocado	Mushroom	Beet greens
Garlic	Broccoli	Cucumber		Bok choy
Leek	Brussels	Eggplant		(Chinese chard)
Onion	sprouts	Olive		Cabbage:
Scallion	Cauliflower	Pepper:		green
Shallot		green		red
		red		savoy
		Pumpkin		spoon
		Squash:		(Chinese)
		acorn		Celtuce
		banana		Chard, Swiss
		butternut		Chicory
		chayote		Collard greens
		crookneck		Dandelion greens
		hubbard		Endive
		straightneck		Escarole
		white bush		Kale
		scallop		Lettuce:
		zucchini		bibb
		Tomato		butterhead
		Topepo		iceberg
		Water chestnut		red leaf
				romaine(cos)
				Mint
				Mustard greens
				Nasturtium leaves
				Parsley
				Sorrel
				Spinach
				Spinach, New Zealand
				Turnip greens
				Watercress

Vegetables represent various parts of the plant system: leaves, roots, tubers, seeds, bulbs, flowers, and stems. Table 7.4 classifies vegetables according to the part of the plant they represent. Like fruits, vegetables vary in their characteristics; some of these differences are discussed in the following individual descriptions of vegetables.

Artichokes   The globe, or French, artichoke is the unopened flower bud of a plant belonging to the thistle family. The leaves of the artichoke are actually scales, and the artichoke is at its best when these scales are closed tightly together. Size is not an indication of quality. The scales of overly mature artichokes show browning and spreading. Most commercially grown artichokes are free of insects, but if insects are present, soak the artichokes in warm salt water. To wash an artichoke, cut off the top, spread the scales apart, and direct briskly running water between them. Clipping off the thorns on the tips of the lower leaves is optional.

Roots	Seeds	Stems	Tubers
Bean sprouts:	Corn	Asparagus	Sunchoke
alfalfa			
mung	Beans:	Bamboo shoots	Taro (dasheen)
soy	green	Cardoon	White potato
Beets	lima	Celery	
Carrots	soy	Fennel (anise)	
Celeriac	wax		
(celery root)	Peas:		
Horseradish	chickpeas		
Kohlrabi	(garbanzo)		
Parsnip	cow peas		
Radish	(blackeye)		
Rutabaga	green		
Salsify	snow		
Sweet potato	(edible		
Turnip	pods)		

Figure 7.3

A diagram of the parts of the artichoke. When cooked, the soft tissue at the base of the leaf is eaten. The remainder of the leaf and the choke are discarded.

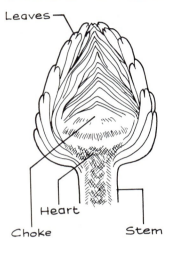

Washed and drained artichokes can be stored for several days in the refrigerator. Figure 7.3 is a diagram of the artichoke.

Asparagus Select green, crisp asparagus stalks with tightly closed tips. Avoid ridged asparagus stalks with open scales that show signs of decay. Remove the tough lower stems, wash the remainder in running water, and check for sand trapped between the scales and the stalk. Dry well and store in a plastic bag, with the bottoms of stalks wrapped in a damp paper towel, in the coldest part of the refrigerator. Asparagus can be steamed or boiled whole, or spears can be sliced and cooked by a waterless method (Figure 7.4). Do not overcook asparagus.

Beans, Snap Snap or green beans were formerly called string beans because the strings along the sides of the pod had to be removed to make them edible. But selective breeding has developed varieties that make stringing beans a lost art. Snap beans, when mature, are the familiar dried red bean. Fresh snap beans are at their best when the pods are young, tender, and crisp, and free of blemishes and decay. Fresh pods should be washed, dried, and stored in a plastic bag in the refrigerator; the tips are usually removed just before cooking. Green beans can be cooked whole or cut, by steaming or boiling (Figure 7.5). If they are "frenched," or sliced diagonally into thin strips, green beans can be cooked by a waterless method.

Figure 7.4

Asparagus and celery sliced diagonally are stir-fried with canned sliced water chestnuts just until tender; chopped green onions are stirred into the vegetables just before they are served.

Figure 7.5

Green beans and slices of fresh onion are simmered in a small amount of water just until tender; a dash of black pepper adds the finishing touch. *(United Fresh Fruit and Vegetable Association)*

Beans, Other Varieties   Yellow wax beans, lima beans, soybeans, garbanzo beans, and fava beans are other beans available fresh in the pod. They, too, should be crisp, fresh, and free of visible defects. Only the yellow wax bean has an edible pod; the seeds of the other beans are edible.

Beets   Look for globular-shaped beets that are free of decay. Large roots sometimes contain lignified strings that do not soften with cooking. For most purposes, cook the beets whole and unpeeled, with several inches of stems and root left on. The skins slip off easily after they are cooked. Beets can also be cooked by a waterless method if they are first peeled and grated.

Broccoli   Select bunches of broccoli of a good green color with tightly closed buds. Visible yellow flowers indicate overmaturity and poor quality; when cooked, this broccoli will be likely to lose its green color. Trim off the parts of the stalks that will not be used. If the large stalks seem fairly tender, they can be chopped and added to soups or stews. Wash broccoli flowers by immersion, drain well, and store in plastic bags in the refrigerator. For the best color and flavor, cook only to the tender-crisp stage by steaming or boiling. Broccoli leaves are rich in nutrients.

Brussels Sprouts   Select compact, firm sprouts that are bright green in color and unwilted. Remove any damaged or discolored outer leaves, wash by immersion, drain well, and store in a plastic bag in the refrigerator. Small sprouts can be cooked whole by steaming or boiling; larger sprouts cook more quickly if they are first cut into halves or quarters. Like other vegetables of the cabbage family, brussels sprouts should be cooked only until they are tender and crisp.

Cabbages   Types of cabbage include the familiar green and red heads, Savoy cabbage, and celery cabbage, also known as Napa or Chinese cabbage. Select firm, fresh, and well-colored heads. The more green color the head has, the better is its nutrient content and flavor. Overly mature heads are more yellow than green in color (except for red cabbage). Remove the outer damaged leaves, rinse the head under running water, drain, and store in the refrigerator in a plastic bag. Cabbage keeps several weeks under these conditions. Sliced cabbage is delicious cooked by a waterless method to the tender-crisp stage and seasoned with caraway or celery seed.

Carrots   Contrary to popular belief, carrots remain fresh longer if their tops are removed. Left on the carrot, the tops withdraw moisture from the root. Topless carrots are usually a better buy because they are easier to hold and market. Choose carrots that are firm and stiff, not flexible. Very large carrots occasionally have woody centers; the flavor of smaller carrots is sometimes preferred.

Trim the tops and roots from carrots, wash by immersion and brush if necessary, drain, and store in a plastic bag in the refrigerator. Carrots can be cooked by a waterless method if they are grated, shredded, or thinly sliced. Use moderate heat and stir frequently to cook carrots, because they have a high sugar content, but keep the pot covered so that the moisture from the carrots will not all be lost in the steam. Season with a little butter and finely minced parsley or green onion tops. Other ways of serving carrots are shown in Figure 7.6.

Cauliflower   Most cauliflower today is wrapped in plastic with the leaves removed to save shipping costs. Choose heads with a good white color and tightly packed flowers, free of brown spots and decay. Cauliflower can be left in its plastic wrap when it is stored in the refrigerator. To prepare the head, cut or break the flowers apart and wash them quickly under running water. Do

Figure 7.6

The versatile carrot can be mashed, sliced, or seasoned with tarragon and served with a cream soup. *(United Fresh Fruit and Vegetable Association)*

not soak them unless there is evidence of insect infestation. Steam or boil the flowers only until they are tender and crisp; do not overcook. If the flowers start to turn yellow during cooking, add 1 teaspoon of lemon juice or ½ teaspoon of cream of tartar.

Celeriac Celeriac, also known as celery root (Figure 7.12), is the root of a type of celery that resembles the turnip; this root is the only edible part of the plant. The unpeeled root keeps well in the refrigerator in a plastic bag. The knobby outer covering of the root should be removed before cooking; after paring, the root can be cubed and cooked in a small amount of water. Celeriac has a pronounced flavor; it can be used as a substitute for potatoes.

Corn Freshly picked corn is moist and sweet if it is not overly mature, but if corn is left unrefrigerated, the sugars rapidly turn to starch. For this reason, corn is usually chilled as soon as it is harvested. Fresh ears have green husks, a fresh cut at the stalk end of the ear, and corn silk that is not wilted or decayed. Ears left on the plant for too long have very large kernels with tough *pericarp*, or skin, covering the kernels. Corn ears can be stored in the refrigerator in their husks, or the husk and silk can be removed and the ears stored in plastic bags, but they must be refrigerated to maintain best quality.

Cowpeas   Also known as black-eyed peas, cowpeas can be dried and used as legumes; they have a different flavor and texture when they are eaten fresh. Shelled peas keep well in plastic bags in the refrigerator.

Eggplant   Choose pear-shaped eggplants that are heavy for their size, free of decay spots, and 3 to 6 inches in diameter at the large end. Eggplants can be stored in the refrigerator for a week or two. Cut eggplants brown quickly; to avoid this effect, place the cut vegetable in a solution of 1 teaspoon of salt per pint of water. Remove one slice at a time from the whole eggplant, peel, cut into strips or cubes, and place in the salt solution while preparing the next slice.

Kohlrabi   Kohlrabi is the German name for cabbage turnip. Kohlrabi is a root vegetable, a member of the cabbage or *Brassica* family. The flavor of kohlrabi resembles that of turnips, but it loses its sweetness and becomes bitter if it is allowed to remain in the ground until it is overly mature. Choose small, young roots. Follow the same preparation and cooking procedures as for celeriac.

Leafy Green Vegetables   Many kinds of green leaves are cooked and eaten as vegetables, including beet greens, bok choy or Chinese chard, Swiss chard, chicory, collard greens, dandelion greens, kale, mustard greens, Chinese mustard greens, sorrel, spinach, New Zealand spinach, and turnip greens. Some of these leafy greens are shown in Figure 7.7; all are high in nutrients and low in calories and should be served frequently. Because their selection, care, and preparation are similar, leafy greens are considered here as a group.

Choose fresh young leaves that are free from decay, yellow discoloration, and other blemishes. Avoid greens that are wilted, infested with insects, or overly mature. Many greens become tough, stringy, strong flavored, and bitter when they are too mature. Trim off inedible parts, wash, dry, and store in plastic bags in the refrigerator. Tender greens, such as spinach, can be cooked by waterless methods. Greens that are less tender, such as turnips, mustard, kale, and collards must be simmered in water for a short time; they tend to be stringy unless they are chopped crosswise in about 1-inch strips before cooking.

Because some greens tend to be slightly bitter, it is desirable to add seasonings that help modify the bitterness. The tartness of vinaigrette sauce has this effect. The pronounced flavor of bacon fat is also effective, because the fat coats the taste buds in the mouth and interferes with the perception of bitterness when the greens are eaten. An egg-mustard dressing or mustard sauce is still another alternative. Season Swiss chard with grated Swiss

Figure 7.7

A variety of leafy green vegetables. One way to season them is with sliced wieners and onions. *(United Fresh Fruit and Vegetable Association)*

cheese, spinach with sesame seed, nutmeg, or mace. Catsup, chili sauce, hot sauce, or sweet-sour sauce are other possible seasonings for greens, and chopped green chilis, pimientos, chives, onions, and garlic can be added for variety. Because people's tastes vary greatly, experiment with various combinations to discover personal preferences.

Okra   Okra is often disliked because it becomes mucilaginous, or ropy, when it is cooked, especially if the pods are cut or overcooked. Okra is frequently used in soups and gumbos. Select tender, young, crisp pods, since large pods may be stringy because of too much lignin. The pod should feel soft and velvety and should be no more than 2 to 3 inches long. Okra pods keep best when stored unwashed in a plastic bag in the refrigerator. Steam or fry whole pods until they are just barely cooked. Okra can be sliced, sprinkled with yellow cornmeal, and sautéed until it is crisp and lightly brown.

Onions Mature onions come in three types—white, yellow, and red (or purple) (Figure 7.8). Choose hard, firm, mature onions with small necks. Avoid onions with signs of decay or wet or soft necks. Mature onions should be kept in a cool, dry, dark place; they do not need to be refrigerated.

Parsnips Choose small or medium parsnips that are free of blemishes; avoid large ones, which are often woody. Store them in a plastic bag in the refrigerator. Parsnips can be peeled and cooked like carrots. If they are cooked in their skins, the skins can be easily slipped off afterwards. Parsnips can serve as a substitute for potatoes.

Figure 7.8

Various kinds of onions. Green spring onions are delicious steamed just until tender and served on toast with hollandaise sauce. *(United Fresh Fruit and Vegetable Association)*

Figure 7.9
Sweet potatoes boiled in their skins are used to make candied sweet potatoes. *(United Fresh Fruit and Vegetable Association)*

Peas, Green Green peas, like corn, lose their sweetness and become starchy if they are not properly chilled after they are harvested, and small peas have a sweeter, juicier flavor than large ones. Peas keep best if they are stored in their pods in plastic bags in the refrigerator.

Potatoes, Sweet (Yams) Two varieties of sweet potatoes are found in the United States, one yellow with a dry flesh, the other deep orange with a moist flesh. The orange sweet potato is erroneously called a yam; the true yam is not available in the United States. Select sweet potatoes that are free of worm holes and decay, for even if decayed areas are cut out, the rest of the potato will have a poor flavor. Sweet potatoes should not be refrigerated; store them in a cool, dry, dark location. Baking or boiling sweet potatoes in their skins avoids problems with enzymatic browning. If they are peeled before cooking, handle them in the manner described for eggplant. Glazed or candied sweet potatoes are a popular dish (Figure 7.9).

Potatoes, White Potatoes are a staple dinner food in the United States, which is perhaps a limiting role for this vegetable. Substituting other root vegetables and grains for potatoes can add variety in nutrients as well as in flavor.

New potatoes are freshly dug and immature. They are usually small, with thin skins that feather or separate from the potato. New potatoes are most suitable for boiling and creaming.

Choose mature potatoes without cuts, bruises, decayed spots, sprouts, or green discolorations. The green color is solanin, which forms in potatoes when they are stored in the light at too high a temperature. Solanin causes bitterness and may be toxic if it is consumed in large amounts; it should be removed when the potatoes are peeled.

In potatoes stored below 45°F (7°C) starch is hydrolyzed to sugar, which makes them unsatisfactory for frying because they become excessively brown; they cannot be used for mashing and baking either, because they lack mealiness and are gummy in texture. For this reason, potatoes should not be refrigerated. However, if cold-storage potatoes are held at room temperature for several weeks, the sugar changes back to starch and the potatoes may then be used for all these purposes.

Potatoes are thought to be high in calories, but this reputation is not entirely deserved. They do have more calories than many other vegetables, but no more than many fruits, as can be seen in Table 6.1 by comparison. It is the way that potatoes are seasoned and cooked that causes them to be high in calories. The table fat or sour cream used on a baked potato, for instance, may contain many more calories than the potato itself. The caloric content of mashed potatoes can be reduced by using nonfat milk or dry milk and by omitting table fat. Because mashed potatoes are often served with gravy, the flavors in the gravy can mask the absence of table fat.

A new variety of potato, the Butte, has been developed by the U.S. Department of Agriculture. It has an improved flavor, more nutrients, greater yield and resistance to disease, and improved storage stability over the commonly used Russet potato, which it is expected to replace.

Pumpkin   Pumpkin, a form of squash, is more often served in cakes and pies as a dessert than as a vegetable. Most pumpkin consumed in this country is purchased in cans. However, fresh pumpkin is not difficult to prepare. Remove the seeds, peel the skin, and cook it in a small amount of water; then mash the cooked pumpkin. Pumpkin is a low-acid food, and it must be processed as other vegetables in a pressure canner when it is preserved by canning.

Rutabagas and Turnips   These two root vegetables are members of the cabbage family. The roots should be firm, heavy for their size, free of blemishes or decay, and medium to small in size. They keep well in plastic bags in the refrigerator. Rutabagas and turnips may be boiled either in their skins or peeled and chopped.

They are often used in soups and stews, but also are good substitutes for potatoes.

Salsify Salsify, a root vegetable that resembles parsnips in apppearance, is often called "oyster plant" because its flavor is reminiscent of oysters. It is not a widely served vegetable, which may be a result of its rather exacting growing requirements. The flavor of salsify is improved by cold storage. Because the root turns brown quickly when it is cut, it should be handled in the manner described for eggplant. Like cauliflower, the bright white color of salsify is best retained if a small amount of lemon juice or cream of tartar is added during cooking.

Summer Squash "Summer squash" are squashes harvested while they are still immature. Poor quality in summer squash can be caused by overmaturity. If they are allowed to grow too large, their seeds become hard and their skins tough, and they have poor flavor and texture. Bitterness develops in squash that matures too long on the vine. Select small, firm squashes, free of blemishes and decay. Some common summer squashes are yellow straightneck and crookneck, zucchini, chayote, white bush scallop, and cocozelle (Figure 7.10).

Summer squash keeps well stored in plastic bags in the refrigerator; it may be washed before storage, but should be dried well to prevent decay. Trim off the stem ends, and cut as desired to cook by waterless methods, by steaming, baking (Figure 7.11), or by simmering in a small amount of water.

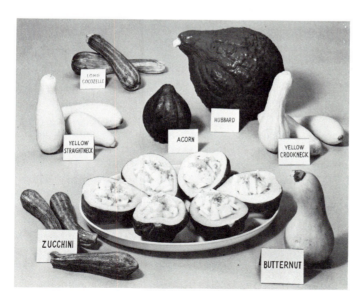

Figure 7.10

Different varieties of squash. In the center, acorn squash halves are stuffed with chopped apple and pineapple and topped with brown sugar before baking. *(United Fresh Fruit and Vegetable Association)*

Figure 7.11

Zucchini squash is delicious and economical baked in a lasagna casserole. *(United Fresh Fruit and Vegetable Association)*

Figure 7.12

Unusual root vegetables include, center top and clockwise: jicama, celery root, sunchokes, daikon, and ginger root.

Winter Squash   Winter squash is larger and more mature than summer squash; types include butternut, buttercup, banana, acorn, hubbard, turks turban, and others not so well known. Because they have hard shells, winter squash keep for several months uncut and stored in a cool, dry, dark place. Some of the larger varieties, such as banana squash, are cut into pieces of 1 to 2 pounds for marketing. The seeds and skin of winter squash are not eaten. Small squash, such as acorn, can be baked whole or cut in half and baked in the skin. The cooked flesh is removed from its skin and seasoned. A peeled, chopped squash can be cooked in a small amount of water and seasoned.

Sunchokes In the past, sunchokes have been called Jerusalem artichokes, but this name is misleading because they are not related to the artichoke or thistle family. Sunchokes are in fact the roots of a type of sunflower plant. Cooked, their flavor resembles that of the globe artichoke. Raw, they have a crisp, crunchy texture and a delicate nutty flavor. The raw tuber can be used in salads or as a chip with dips. Sunchokes make a good potato substitute when cooked. Sunchokes and some other unusual roots are shown in Figure 7.12.

Taro or Dasheen Both the leaves and roots of this tropical plant are food. The leaves have the flavor of spinach but must be cooked much longer, sometimes for an hour, to make them tender. In Polynesian countries, the root is fermented and mashed to make *poi*. The root may also be baked in its skin after it has been parboiled for 15 minutes; it may then be eaten like a baked potato. Roots colored deep violet have a better flavor than light- or cream-colored ones.

Tomatoes The tomato is almost as versatile a vegetable as the potato. The flavor of tomatoes is best when they are allowed to ripen before they are harvested, but in modern marketing practice, this means that the tomatoes would spoil by the time they reached the consumer. Most market tomatoes have been picked green or partially green. Select firm fruit that is free of blemishes and decay. Allow tomatoes to ripen at room temperature before refrigeration. Tomatoes keep fresh for a longer time if their stems are left on. Fresh tomatoes, as opposed to canned varieties, are most often used raw in salads, not cooked. However, they can be broiled, baked, or stewed.

The way vegetables are prepared for cooking affects their retention of nutrients as well as their flavor, texture, and appearance.

Preparing Vegetables for Cooking

TO PEEL OR NOT TO PEEL

Whether or not vegetables should be peeled before they are cooked, and the effect of peeling on nutrient retention, are topics that have been much debated by nutritionists. However, some vegetables are unattractive cooked in their skins; carrots, for example, turn a mottled brown color. Some peels left on foods during cooking affect the flavor and texture of the vegetable; celery root cooked unpeeled is extremely bitter. If a vegetable cooked in its skin turns an undesirable flavor or color, it will not be eaten and nothing is gained by such preparation, even though nutrient retention may be improved.

Solution loss of nutrients is reduced if potatoes are boiled in their skins, but potatoes boiled in their skins have a different flavor and texture than they do if they are peeled before they are cooked. A highly seasoned salad or casserole can effectively mask the flavor produced by the skins. Potatoes boiled in their skins are too gummy for satisfactory mashing.

Contrary to popular opinion, nutrients are not concentrated in the skins of fruits and vegetables. Studies of tomatoes have found less pesticide residues in peeled tomatoes than in unpeeled tomatoes. Peeling also reduces the bacterial count of vegetables. On the other hand, the skins of fruits and vegetables are good sources of fiber and should be consumed when feasible.

If the parings are thin, vegetables may either be pared or scraped with no difference in nutrient retention. Floating-blade peelers are designed to remove minimal amounts of edible food along with the skin so long as the pressure exerted in peeling is light. A worn blade may remove excessively thick peelings and should be replaced.

SIZE OF PIECES The question of nutrient loss when vegetables are chopped or subdivided before cooking has been another matter for debate. When a vegetable is cut into small pieces, more surface area is exposed for solution loss and for oxidation of nutrients. However, small pieces cook more rapidly than large pieces, thus reducing the destruction of nutrients by heat. Often, cutting vegetables into small pieces permits the use of waterless cooking methods that are not possible for whole vegetables. Sliced asparagus, thinly sliced or coarsely grated carrots, sliced celery, and many thinly sliced squashes can be cooked in their own juices with no added water, but these same vegetables require added water when they are cooked whole or in large pieces.

Vegetables cooked by waterless methods show minimal solution loss of nutrients because there is no solution into which the nutrients can dissolve. Cooking a finely chopped vegetable in a large amount of water is pointless unless one is making soup. Not only nutrients, but flavor and color, are lost through such methods. However, cut or chopped vegetables may be cooked in small amounts of water to the tender-crisp stage with little or no loss of flavor or nutrients. Because chopped vegetables cook more quickly than whole ones, the cooking time should be shortened accordingly.

Cooking Methods for Vegetables The choice of cooking method may depend not only on the flavor desired but also on the color, texture, and intended use of a vegetable. Time and available equipment are also influencing factors. Regardless of the method used, the cooking time should last only long enough for the vegetable to reach a tender and crisp texture.

BOILING Boiling has been a basic method of vegetable cookery for centuries. Methods of boiling vegetables vary greatly, however. Many people still cover vegetables with water and boil them for a long time, causing loss of nutrients and flavor. Only potatoes, beets, and other roots boiled in their skins should be covered with water, becasue the skins prevent excessive solution of nutrients. The cooking time, however, should be no longer than is needed to tenderize the roots.

For all other vegetables, boil a small amount of water with a little salt, add the prepared vegetable, and cover the pot. When boiling resumes, remove the cover and stir the vegetable or turn it over and reduce the heat. Replace the cover and let the vegetable simmer until it is tender. The heating element of an electric unit can be turned off when the vegetable returns to a boil, for enough residual heat is left in the element to finish cooking many vegetables. With green vegetables, remove the cover several times during cooking and stir the vegetable to volatilize the acids that are released from the vegetables during cooking. This procedure ensures the retention of green color.

Amount of Water   It is hard to say how much water to cook vegetables in; the quantity depends on the size of the pot, the vegetable, the size of the pieces, how long the vegetable needs to be cooked, and how well the cover fits the pot. For cooking most vegetables, water should cover the bottom of the pot to a depth of about ⅛ inch. If the vegetable requires a long cooking time (kale) or has a low water content (peas, beans, or potatoes), or if a loose-fitting cover allows steam to escape, more water is needed to prevent burning.

When peeled white potatoes are cooked for mashing, the amount of water for cooking can be adjusted so that very little remains when the potatoes are tender enough for mashing. The remaining water should not be discarded; it should be drained off and added back to the potatoes in place of milk after they are mashed. Nonfat dry milk powder can be used in the mashed potatoes in place of liquid milk, and extra milk powder can also be added to enrich them.

Cooking Time   The time required for cooking a vegetable depends on its stage of maturity, what parts of it are included, and the size of the pieces being cooked. The tender young leaves of spinach cook more quickly than thicker leaves of kale, finely chopped or grated vegetables cook more quickly than the whole vegetable, the flowers of broccoli and the tips of asparagus cook more quickly than lower stems and stalks, and tender young peas cook more rapidly than mature peas.

A steamed vegetable does not come into contact with the water that provides the steam, causing less solution loss of nutrients. Only the water that condenses on the vegetables from the steam contacts the vegetable surfaces. Special steamers can be purchased, or makeshift steamers can be constructed either by plac-

STEAMING

ing a colander in a pot or by fashioning cups or bowls from aluminum foil to hold the vegetables out of the surrounding water.

Even though steaming reduces solution loss of nutrients, it can result in increased heat destruction, because steaming takes longer than boiling to cook vegetables. An advantage of steaming, however, is that two or more vegetables can be cooked at the same time in separate compartments of the steamer with the same amount of heat.

PRESSURE COOKER   A pressure cooker combines boiling and steam cooking, but the steam is superheated. Vegetables cooked on a rack in a pressure cooker are steamed. The temperature in a pressure cooker at 15 pounds pressure is 250°F (121°C), which causes vegetables to cook much more quickly. This can be a disadvantage because vegetables can be overcooked in a matter of seconds. Carefully observe all cooking times for pressure cookers and cool the cooker quickly. (See Chapter 3 for information on pressure saucepans.)

WATERLESS COOKING   Waterless cooking of vegetables, also called stir-frying or panning, makes use of the water in food as the cooking medium. This method is suitable only for vegetables with a high water content that do not require a long cooking time to become tender. Oil or table fat should be added to the pan to keep the vegetables from sticking until heat produces water from the vegetables, but only enough barely to coat the bottom of the pan. Pan spray is sometimes effective without any other added fat.

Use moderate heat under the pan, enough to cook the vegetables fairly quickly but not to burn them. Cover the pan to retain heat and steam, but stir the vegetables occasionally to distribute the heat for even cooking. Vegetables must be cut in small enough pieces for the heat to penetrate rapidly to cook the food quickly. As with other methods, avoid overcooking. Two types of waterless cooking methods are shown in Figures 7.13 and 7.14.

BAKING   Potatoes and a few other vegetables, such as acorn squash, can be baked in their skins, but other vegetables must be pared, chopped, and placed in a covered oven dish to prevent dehydration if they are baked. Because convection of heat by air currents is a slow form of heat transfer, baking is one of the slowest of cooking methods. The advantages of baking for cooking vegetables are that very little water is needed and that different foods can be cooked at the same time.

MICROWAVE COOKERY   Microwave cookery is an ideal cookery method for vegetables. They can be cooked quickly in little or no added water, thereby reducing solution, heat, and oxidative losses of nutrients. As a rule of thumb, allow about 7 minutes per pound of food to be cooked in a microwave oven. Except when baking potatoes, cover

Figure 7.13

(Left) Spinach is cooked in a wok in a small amount of hot oil. This is an example of a type of waterless cookery known as stir-fry cooking. *(Best Foods, Division of CPC International, Inc.)*

Figure 7.14

(Right) Sliced celery and onion are stir-fried with cooked chicken in an electric fry pan and garnished with toasted slivered almonds. *(United Fresh Fruit and Vegetable Association)*

the vegetables during cooking and stir the food halfway through the cooking period to equalize the penetration of microwaves through the food mass. (See Chapter 3 for information on microwave ovens.)

Processed Vegetables

Vegetables are canned, frozen, and dehydrated both for convenience and for greater availability. Additionally, some kinds of processing provide unique products that cannot be duplicated under other conditions.

CANNED VEGETABLES

Canned foods are one of the most stable forms of processed foods. Storing them in the period between one crop and the next makes many foods available throughout the year with no deterioration in quality. However, destructive changes in canned foods can occur if they are stored at high temperatures. Canned vegetables are graded voluntarily, in the same manner as canned fruits.

The liquid in canned vegetables contains about one third of the water-soluble nutrients originally in the vegetables and should be used whenever possible. Canned vegetable liquids can be used in soups and gravies or can be thickened with starch and nonfat dry milk to make a white sauce to serve with the vegetable. Beef or chicken stock base can be added to the sauce or the vegetable juice to change the flavor. These liquids can also be frozen for later use. Avoid using juices from strong-flavored vegetables in ways that impair the flavor of other foods; for instance, do not use the juice from canned mustard greens to cook potatoes for mashing. Canned vegetables may be seasoned in many of the same ways as fresh vegetables.

The new steril-vac process described in Chapter 6 will also be used for vegetables. This type of processing will increase the solids content and reduce the liquid in canned vegetables, as well as improve flavor and nutrient retention.

Do not buy vegetables in cans that leak or are swollen or bulging, for these are signs of spoilage. Small dents in cans do not harm the contents, but badly dented cans may develop leaks and cause spoilage.

FROZEN VEGETABLES

Frozen vegetables closely resemble fresh vegetables in flavor, color, texture, and nutrient content. Select packages that do not show evidence of improper storage, as described under frozen fruits. For long-term storage, frozen vegetables should be kept at 0°F (−8°C); otherwise, they should be used within a few weeks or a loss in eating quality will result.

Frozen vegetables cook more quickly than their fresh counterparts, because they have been blanched before freezing, as described in Chapter 30. To cook a frozen vegetable, add it to boiling water without first thawing it. Many packages of frozen vegetables recommend using twice as much water as is actually needed, so reduce the amount accordingly. Avoid overcooking, to achieve the best flavor, texture, and color. Some frozen vegetables can be cooked by waterless methods and by microwave cookery. Frozen vegetables in pouches can be cooked in a microwave oven if a slit is first made in the pouch.

Special combinations of vegetables and seasonings are available frozen but are usually more expensive than plain frozen or fresh vegetables. They are intended for buyers who want and can afford an expensive convenience item. Many frozen vegetables are better bargains than their fresh counterparts, especially when the fresh vegetable is out of season. The different forms of frozen potatoes are almost always more economical than the fresh potato, and are also more convenient.

DEHYDRATED VEGETABLES

The development of freeze-drying has caused a boom in popularity for dehydrated vegetables. Fruits, nuts, legumes, and seeds have been dried for centuries, but attempts to dry vegetables were not successful; dehydrated vegetables would not rehydrate properly and lacked tenderness. Although freeze-drying has produced dried vegetables of better quality, their quality is still not equal to that of canned and frozen vegetables, and the process is expensive. Most dehydrated vegetables are used for special purposes where light weight is an advantage, such as in backpacking, rather than for everyday use. Dehydrated potatoes and onions, as well as dried herbs, are exceptions to the previous statement, for their use has greatly expanded in the last decade.

The process of dehydration calls for foods in small pieces or thin layers from which to produce dehydrated flakes or granules. This is suitable for preparing mashed potatoes or for adding dried onions or herbs to foods as seasonings, but so far, dehydrated potato sticks for French fries have not been developed. Dehydrated foods must be stored in airtight containers to prevent undesirable absorption of moisture.

A recent innovation is the production of "restructured" potato chips from rehydrated dried potatoes. The chopped potato mass can be shaped into a uniform size and shape, partially dried, and then fried in the same way as sliced fresh potatoes to produce potato chips.

Nutritional Quality of Cooked Vegetables

Fruits and vegetables (not legumes) are the major source of vitamins A and C in the diet; they also supply some minerals and B vitamins (except vitamin B_{12}). Individual vegetables vary greatly in nutrient content as shown in Table 7.1. For this reason, consuming a wide variety of vegetables is the best way to provide a complete assortment of nutrients. Most Americans could probably profit nutritionally from an increased intake of vegetables.

Nutrient losses in vegetables begin when the vegetables are harvested. Physical loss of nutrients occurs when the outer leaves from broccoli, cauliflower, lettuce, cabbage, and the like are discarded at harvest, in the market, or in the kitchen. Shipping and storing vegetables without refrigeration and allowing vegetables to wilt cause heat and oxidative losses of nutrients as described in Chapter 1. Wilted vegetables can be freshened with water and cooling, but this does not restore the lost nutrients.

Some destruction of vitamins by heat and oxidation does occur when vegetables are cooked and processed, but this disadvantage is counterbalanced by improved digestibility. Nutrients are located inside the cells, which are enclosed by indigestible cellulose cell walls. Cooking softens the cellulose, causing some of the cells to rupture so that the nutrients within are more available for absorption. Starch in vegetables is hydrolyzed more efficiently in the digestive tract if it has first been gelatinized by cooking. Cooking techniques that minimize nutrient destruction result in more nutritious cooked vegetables. Waterless cooking, boiling in small amounts of water, and microwave cookery result in about equal retention of nutrients. Refrigeration of vegetables before and after cooking also decreases nutrient loss.

A place exists in the diet for both cooked and raw vegetables. Cooked and raw vegetables alike are good sources of fiber and are ideal in plentiful amounts in low-calorie weight reduction diets, so long as they are not seasoned with high-calorie fats.

Study Questions

1. What is the cause of woodiness and strings in vegetables? Can woodiness and stringy fibers be softened by cooking? Explain why.
2. As vegetables mature, what changes occur in their starch and sugar content?
3. What are the four principal pigments in vegetables, and what is the natural color of each?
4. Which pigment is stable at any pH encountered in cooking?
5. What effect does an alkaline pH have on anthocyanin and anthoxanthin pigments?
6. Why does red cabbage tend to turn blue when it is cooked in tap water? Once red cabbage has started to turn blue, how can it be changed back to its normal red color?
7. If peeled beets are cooked in large amounts of water, how is their color affected?
8. How can a bright white color be retained when potatoes and cauliflower are cooked?
9. What effect does an acidic pH have on chlorophyll pigment?
10. Why do some green vegetables tend to turn an olive-green color when they are cooked by the waterless method in a covered pot?
11. How can green vegetables be cooked by waterless methods so that their natural green color is retained?
12. Name some vegetables that require special handling during paring and cutting for cooking to prevent enzymatic browning.
13. What effect does the pH of the cooking medium have on the texture of vegetables? Explain why.
14. If an acidic medium is desired for color or flavor in cooked vegetables, when should the acid be added?
15. How does hard water affect the texture of vegetables cooked in it?
16. Why is calcium chloride added to some vegetables when they are canned or pickled?
17. How is the flavor of a vegetable affected when it is cooked in a large amount of water?
18. How can onions be prepared so that they will have a mild flavor?
19. What techniques should be used in cooking vegetables in the cabbage family to keep their flavors mild?
20. What kinds of seasonings commonly added to vegetables considerably increase their caloric content?
21. Why should some vegetables be trimmed and washed before refrigeration?
22. What factors affect the amount of waste in vegetable preparation?
23. How does the amount of waste influence the cost and number of servings obtained from a given amount of a vegetable?
24. What are some advantages and disadvantages of cooking vegetables in their skins?
25. What are some advantages and disadvantages of chopping or subdividing vegetables before cooking them?
26. Name several factors that affect the time necessary to cook a vegetable.
27. What are some advantages and disadvantages of steaming vegetables?
28. Why is a waterless cooking method not satisfactory for some vegetables?
29. Why is it usually necessary to use a small amount of fat when cooking vegetables by waterless methods?
30. Why should vegetables be stirred occasionally when they are cooked by a waterless method?
31. What are some advantages and disadvantages of baking vegetables?
32. What are some advantages and disadvantages of cooking vegetables by microwave cookery?
33. Which of the following cooking methods would be expected to show the least and the greatest solution loss of nutrients from vegetables? Why?
    a. boiling in a large amount of water
    b. boiling in a small amount of water
    c. waterless cookery methods
    d. microwave cookery
34. What are some ways to use the liquid from canned vegetables?
35. Why do frozen vegetables cook more quickly than fresh ones?
36. Why should many kinds of vegetables be eaten?

Berke, Karen L. "Vegetables." In U.S. Department of Agriculture, *Consumers All,* Yearbook of Agriculture. Washington, D.C.: Government Printing Office, 1965.

Boswell, Victor R. "Our Vegetable Travelers." *National Geographic* XCVI (1949): 145.

Castille, Michael A.; Dawson, Elsie H.; and Thompson, Edward R. "The Vegetable Roundup—From Buying to Cooking." In U.S. Department of Agriculture, *Food for Us All,* Yearbook of Agriculture, Washington, D.C.: Government Printing Office, 1969.

Charley, Helen. "Fruits and Vegetables." In *Food Theory and Applications,* edited by Pauline C. Paul and Helen H. Palmer. New York: Wiley, 1972.

Harris, Barbara. *Let's Cook Microwave!* 1975. Microwave Cooking Consulting Service, P.O. Box 2992, Portland, OR 97208.

Moyer, William C. *The Buying Guide for Fresh Fruits, Vegetables, Herbs, and Nuts.* Fullerton, Calif.: Blue Goose, 1974.

U.S. Department of Agriculture. *Conserving the Nutritive Value of Foods,* Home and Garden Bulletin No. 90. Washington, D.C.: Government Printing Office, 1965.

——. *How to Buy Fresh Vegetables,* Home and Garden Bulletin No. 143, 1967.

——. *How to Buy Canned and Frozen Vegetables,* Home and Garden Bulletin No. 167, 1969.

——. *Vegetables in Family Meals,* Home and Garden Bulletin No. 105, 1971.

——. *How to Buy Potatoes,* Home and Garden Bulletin No. 198, 1972.

Salads

Salads serve many purposes—some are simple accompaniments to the main course, others are a separate course, and still others are a meal in themselves. Eating salads is an excellent way to ensure an adequate intake of raw fruits and vegetables, although many salads also use cooked vegetables and other foods. The word "salad" is derived from Latin *sal* and French *salar*, both words meaning "salt" or "to salt." Early salads were nothing more than raw vegetables and herbs dipped in salt. Salt was later replaced by combinations of vinegar, oil, and other seasonings. Today, salad simply means foods seasoned with a salad dressing.

Many people tend to think of salads only as iceberg lettuce and sliced tomatoes with French dressing. However, salads can possess an almost infinite variety of ingredients.

Salad Ingredients

SALAD GREENS

Salad greens are the foundation of most salads. The main ingredient of tossed green salads, they are also used as the base or shell for other types of salad; their rich green color makes them a pleasing background for the colors and textures of other ingredients. Table 8.1 gives the nutrient composition of raw vegetables suitable for salads; notice the wide variation in nutrient content of the different kinds of lettuce and other greens. As a general rule, deep green leaves have a higher nutrient content than light green leaves, although their caloric content is similar. The outer dark green leaves of iceberg lettuce have more vitamins A and C than the inner bleached leaves. The same is true of all other kinds of lettuce, as well as cabbage, celery, and other vegetables. An assortment of salad vegetables is shown in Figure 8.1.

Figure 8.1

These leafy green vegetables are suitable for salads. *(United Fresh Fruit and Vegetable Association)*

Table 8.1 Nutrient composition of vegetables that are eaten raw or added to salads for 100-gram amounts, edible portion

Vegetable	Approximate measure	Water (g)	Calories	Protein (g)	Fat (g)	Carbohydrate Total (g)	Carbohydrate Fiber (g)	Vitamin A (I.U.)	Ascorbic Acid (mg)	Niacin (mg)	Pantothenic acid (mg)	Riboflavin (mg)	Thiamin (mg)	Pyridoxine (mg)	Calcium (mg)	Phosphorus (mg)	Iron (mg)	Potassium (mg)
Bean sprouts, mung	¾ cup	88.8	35	3.8	0.2	6.6	0.7	20	19	0.8	—[a]	0.13	0.13	—	19	64	1.3	223
Bean sprouts, soy	¾ cup	86.3	46	6.2	1.4	5.3	0.8	80	13	0.8	—	0.20	0.23	—	48	67	1.0	—
Broccoli		89.1	32	3.6	0.3	5.9	1.5	2500	113	0.9	1.17	0.23	0.10	0.19	103	78	1.1	382
Cabbage, green	1¼ cup	92.4	24	1.3	0.2	5.4	0.8	130	47	0.3	0.20	0.05	0.05	0.16	49	29	0.4	233
Cabbage, red	1¼ cup	90.2	31	2.0	0.2	6.9	1.0	40	61	0.4	0.32	0.06	0.09	0.20	42	35	0.8	268
Cabbage, Savoy	1¼ cup	92.0	24	2.4	0.1	4.6	0.8	200	55	0.3	—	0.08	0.05	0.19	67	54	0.9	269
Cabbage, Chinese		95.0	14	1.2	0.2	3.0	0.6	150	25	0.6	—	0.04	0.05	—	43	40	0.6	253
Carrots	2 small	88.2	42	1.1	0.2	9.7	1.0	11000	8	0.6	0.28	0.05	0.06	0.16	37	36	0.7	341
Cauliflower	1 cup	91.0	27	2.7	0.2	5.2	1.0	60	78	0.7	1.0	0.10	0.11	0.21	25	56	1.1	295
Celery	2–3 stalks	94.1	17	0.9	0.1	3.9	0.6	240	9	0.3	0.43	0.03	0.03	0.6	39	28	0.3	341
Chervil		80.7	57	3.4	0.9	11.5	—	trace	9		—	—	—	0.03				
Chicory		95.1	15	1.0	0.1	3.2					—	—	—	—	18	21	0.5	182
Chives		91.3	28	1.8	0.5	5.8	1.1	5800	56	0.5	0.04	0.13	0.08	—	69	44	1.7	250
Cress, garden		89.4	32	2.6	0.7	5.5	1.1	9300	69	1.0	0.18	0.26	0.08	—	81	76	1.3	606
Cucumber, pared	1 medium	95.7	14	0.6	0.1	3.2	0.3	trace	11	0.2	0.24	0.04	0.03	0.04	17	18	0.3	160
Endive; escarole		93.1	20	1.7	0.1	4.1	0.9	3300	10	0.5	—	0.14	0.07	—	81	54	1.7	294
Lettuce, butterhead, Bibb		95.1	14	1.2	0.2	2.5	0.5	970	8	0.3	—	0.06	0.06	—	35	26	2.0	264
cos, romaine, dark green		94.0	18	1.3	0.3	3.5	0.7	1900	18	0.4	0.2	0.08	0.05	0.06	68	25	1.4	264
Lettuce, iceberg	¼ head	95.5	13	0.9	0.1	2.9	0.5	330	6	0.3	0.2	0.06	0.06	0.05	20	22	0.5	175
Mushrooms		90.4	28	2.7	0.3	4.4	0.8	trace	3	4.2	2.2	0.46	0.10	0.12	6	116	0.8	414
Onions, mature	1 medium	89.1	38	1.5	0.1	8.7	0.6	40	10	0.2	0.13	0.04	0.03	0.13	27	36	0.5	157
Green onions + top	6 onions	89.4	36	1.5	0.2	8.2	1.2	2000	32	0.4	0.14	0.05	0.05	—	51	39	1.0	231
Parsley	90 sprigs	85.1	44	3.6	0.6	8.5	1.5	8500	172	1.2	0.30	0.26	0.12	0.16	203	63	6.2	727
Sweet pepper, green	1 medium	93.4	22	1.2	0.2	4.8	1.4	420	128	0.5	0.23	0.08	0.08	0.26	9	22	0.7	213
Sweet pepper, red	1 medium	90.7	31	1.4	0.3	7.1	1.7	4450	204	0.5	0.27	0.08	0.08	—	13	30	0.6	—
Radishes	9 small	94.5	17	1.0	0.1	3.6	0.7	10	26	0.3	0.18	0.03	0.03	0.08	30	31	1.0	322
Spinach	2 cups	90.7	26	3.2	0.3	4.3	0.6	8100	51	0.6	0.30	0.20	0.10	0.28	(93)[b]	51	3.1	470
Summer squash		94.0	19	1.1	0.1	4.2	0.6	410	22	1.0	0.36	0.09	0.05	0.08	28	29	0.4	202
Tomato, ripe	¾ medium	93.5	22	1.1	0.2	4.7	0.5	900	23	0.7	0.33	0.04	0.06	0.10	13	27	0.5	244
Water chestnut	16 nuts	78.3	79	1.4	0.2	19.0	0.8	0	4	1.0	—	0.20	0.14	—	4	65	0.6	500
Watercress	90 sprigs	93.3	19	2.2	0.3	3.0	0.7	4900	79	0.9	0.31	0.16	0.08	0.13	151	54	1.7	282

[a] Dash indicates value is unknown.
[b] Calcium combines with oxalic acid and cannot be absorbed by the human body.

SOURCE: U.S. Department of Agriculture, *Composition of Foods; Nutritive Value of Foods; Pantothenic Acid, Vitamin B₆, and Vitamin B₁₂ in Foods.*

Figure 8.2

Steps in preparing head lettuce: loosen the core either by firmly rapping the base of the head on the counter or by cutting it out with a knife. To wash the leaves, direct cool tap water into the hole left by the core. Remove excess water by shaking the head, core area down, and allowing it to drain for a short time. Lettuce keeps fresh and crisp stored in a plastic bag in the refrigerator. *(Western Iceberg Lettuce, Inc.)*

Selecting and Cleaning Salad Greens   Select salad greens carefully for their color, texture, flavor, and nutrients. The principles described in Chapter 7 for selecting, cleaning, and storing leafy green vegetables for cooking apply equally to salad greens.

Crispness is a very important characteristic in salad greens. If the greens are washed before they are refrigerated, they will be crisp and clean when they are needed. Use plastic bags for refrigerator storage if the hydrator drawer does not maintain sufficient humidity to prevent wilting. Salad greens should never be placed in containers of water for crisping, for this causes solution losses of nutrients. Purchase leafy greens from markets where the produce is sprayed with water at intervals to prevent wilting. Such spraying does not cause solution losses of nutrients.

All lettuce tends to turn brown where its cells are cut, broken, or crushed. Although browning does not occur in lettuce as rapidly as in some other vegetables and fruits, it is caused by the same enzymatic oxidation of tannin-like compounds. Tearing lettuce greens is sometimes thought to produce less browning than cutting, because tearing causes the cells to separate from each other without breaking open, while cutting breaks open the cells. For the same reason, remove the core of iceberg head lettuce by grasping the head firmly in both hands and rapping its base sharply once on the counter top. The rapping shoves the stalk up into the head and breaks it off from the leaves. The core can then be easily twisted out with the fingers (Figure 8.2). As far as nutrient retention is concerned, whether lettuce is cut with a knife or broken into pieces is unimportant as long as the knife is not made of copper. When preparing lettuce some time in advance of serving, breaking it into pieces rather than cutting might prevent browning; otherwise, cut the lettuce or break it as desired.

Browned lettuce is not harmful to eat but does spoil the appearance of dishes in which it is used, and for this reason brown areas should be removed. Salad greens should be clean, dry, crisp, and free of discoloration. Except for cabbages and head lettuce, salad greens are best cleaned by separating them from the bunch and washing each leaf individually by immersion or with a spray of water.

Following are descriptions of some greens suitable for salads, with special pointers about preparing and serving them.

Cabbages All four cabbages mentioned in Chapter 7 can be eaten raw in salads. Cabbage is not as tender as lettuce; it should not be used as an underlining leaf for salads, therefore, and it is usually shredded to make chewing easier. Cabbage mixed with other greens adds crunchiness and a nippy flavor. Red cabbage also adds color contrast. Chinese cabbage is more tender and has a milder flavor than the others.

Cabbage is the principal green in coleslaw. Coarsely grated or finely shredded cabbage can be combined with grated carrots, chopped apples, and chopped pineapple for a sweet coleslaw, or with thinly sliced green and red pepper, green onions, and celery for a tart coleslaw. Instead of mayonnaise, the usual coleslaw dressing, substitute the juices from canned pineapple, sweet pickles, or dill pickles, depending on the flavor desired. The ascorbic acid in shredded cabbage is quite stable; this salad can be prepared ahead of time without loss of nutrients.

Endive, Escarole, and Chicory Often confused with one another, these are three different plants. The true endive, often called curly endive, grows in a bunchy head of loose, narrow, ragged-edged leaves. Escarole is an endive that also forms a loose head, but the leaves are slightly wider, a darker green, and do not curl at the tips. Chicory, also known as witloof chicory and French or Belgian endive, forms a bunch rather than a head, for it grows upright with an elongated head. Chicory is usually bleached white while it is growing, so it has a lower nutrient content than the other two endives.

Endives are hardier in salads and do not wilt as readily as most kinds of lettuce, but they have a slightly bitter flavor that some find unpleasant; it can be masked with an acidic dressing.

Butterhead, Bibb, Boston Lettuce These names all refer to the same plant, a head lettuce that is smaller than the more familiar iceberg lettuce. The leaves are darker green and have a softer, more velvety texture than those of iceberg lettuce, and the interior leaves are more yellow than green. The cuplike shape of the leaves makes them an ideal base for salads.

Cos, Romaine, Dark Green Lettuce This lettuce has an elongated head. The leaf texture is coarser and less crisp and the flavor is stronger than iceberg lettuce. Romaine has a higher nutrient content than iceberg lettuce.

New York, Imperial, Iceberg Lettuce   The lettuce commonly known as iceberg is not true iceberg lettuce, which has red tinged leaves and is of little commercial importance. The most widely eaten lettuce in the United States is actually the New York or Imperial strains, labeled iceberg commercially. The Imperial strains have been developed to resist mildew and brown blight, for head lettuce has rather exacting growth requirements and requires a relatively cool climate for good leaf and head development. Choose heads that are firm, well-greened, unwilted, and free from decay. Head lettuce is easier to prepare if the core is removed and water is directed into the core area to separate and wash the leaves. Allow the head to drain well and store it in a plastic bag in the refrigerator.

Leaf Lettuces   Loose-leaf lettuces are popular in home gardens but only the more hearty are sold commercially because they are highly perishable after harvesting. They wilt more rapidly in salads than commercial lettuces.

Red Leaf Lettuce   This lettuce forms a loose, bunching type of head. It is probably a variety of romaine but has more fragile, red-tipped leaves. Red leaf lettuce has a mild flavor but wilts more rapidly than romaine. It is attractive in tossed salads because of its color and is often used as a leaf base for salads.

Spinach   Many people overlook raw spinach as a leafy green, but its tender leaf makes a delightful addition to tossed salads. Shredded spinach also makes a good bed for other types of salads. The deep green color of spinach is attractive, and it resists wilting.

Mustard, Kale, Collard, and Turnip Greens   Raw, these vegetables add a sharp, biting flavor in tossed salads mixed with other greens. Use only the tender young leaves.

Watercress   Watercress, an aquatic plant cultivated in large ponds, has a sharp, peppery flavor. Its leaves are dime- or quarter-sized and grow in groups on sprigs from a main stem. Select fresh, green watercress; avoid yellowed, mottled leaves or leaves that have started to decay.

Many other vegetables may be used in salads either as accents or combined with greens to form a pleasing mixture.

OTHER SALAD VEGETABLES

Bean Sprouts   Soybean, mung bean, and alfalfa sprouts are all used in salads. They add a crunchy texture and a tangy flavor.

Broccoli, Cauliflower   Raw broccoli and cauliflower can be broken into small flowerets and added to tossed salads or mixed vegetable salads; these vegetables have a sharp, biting flavor and are crisp and tender. Try marinating them in a tangy dressing.

Carrots   Either coarsely grated or thinly sliced, raw carrots add color accents to green salads. Because carrots are less tender than some other vegetables, the pieces should not be too large. Select medium-sized carrots with a deep orange color for salads.

Celery   The two types of celery available are Pascal, which has narrow, dark green ribs, and Golden Hart, which has wide, bleached white ribs. To clean celery, slice off the base to separate the leaf stems and wash each stem under running water, brushing to remove soil from between the ribs. Whole celery is a *bunch*; one branch or stem is a *stalk*. The tender inside branches are best to use as celery sticks. The strings should be removed from the outer stalks first if they are used as celery sticks. It is not necessary to string celery stalks that are to be sliced crosswise or diagonally, because the strings are not a problem to eat in short lengths.

Cucumbers   Cucumbers, like celery, add texture and crunchiness to salads. Select firm cucumbers with a fresh green color; overly mature cucumbers are dull green or sometimes yellow and are often bitter. Most cucumbers are waxed to prevent loss of moisture; the wax, the same as that used on apples, is safe and edible, but cucumbers should be peeled because microorganisms can exist on the peel under the wax coating.

Green Beans, Green Peas, Asparagus   These vegetables are customarily cooked, but tender young green beans, peas and asparagus tips are delightful additions to salad either raw or cooked. Beans and asparagus are attractive sliced diagonally. All may be marinated for flavor before being added to the salad.

Green Onions, Scallions   "Green onion" and "scallion" are different names for the same plant, the immature onion, which if allowed to grow and mature would later be harvested as dry onion. Choose green onions with crisp green tops and 2 to 3 inches of blanched white root sections. The bulbs are most tender when they are less than ½ inch in diameter. The green tops are edible; they add color and a mild onion flavor, and they have a good nutrient content. Green onions can be trimmed by removing the root threads and any of the top that is wilted. They should then be rinsed, drained, and stored in a plastic bag in the refrigerator, where they will keep for several weeks.

Mushrooms   These edible fungi are a well-known garnish for beefsteak and many other meats and sauces, but they are also

delightful served raw in salads (Figure 8.3). The wide portion at the top of the mushroom is the cap; the thin tissues on the underside of the cap are the gills, which are not visible until the cap opens. Attached to the cap is the stem. Choose mushrooms with closed caps; avoid ones with open caps and dark, discolored gills, or mushrooms that are withered or show signs of decay.

To wash mushrooms, hold them one at a time under a gentle stream of running water and gently rub off any clinging soil with the fingers or a soft brush; a stiff brush should not be used because it damages the surface and causes the mushrooms to discolor. Mushrooms should not be washed until just before they are ready to use. Store dry, unwashed mushrooms in a plastic bag in the refrigerator to prevent withering; dampness causes them to mold and decay. Do not slice mushrooms until the last moment to prevent discoloration. Dip mushrooms in a lemon juice solution or marinate them in an acidic dressing in order to prevent browning as well as to add flavor. Both the stems and caps of mushrooms are edible.

Radishes Radishes add texture, color, and a sharp, peppery flavor to salads. The most popular variety is a small, marble-sized red radish. Large, carrot-sized red radishes are also common, and both are found white as well. The large white radishes, known as *daikon*, are popular in Japan for pickling. When choosing the marble-sized red radishes, avoid larger ones, because they are likely to be stringy or woody in texture and strong in flavor. Like carrots, these roots keep better with their tops removed and are often marketed now without tops in small plastic bags. Fresh radish tops, when available, can serve as leafy greens in tossed salads. Wash radishes by rubbing off the soil with the fingers while holding them under water. Drain and store in a plastic bag in the refrigerator.

Summer Squash Zucchini squash, in particular, is delicious served raw in tossed salads. It can be served in many of the same ways that cucumbers are served, as can white scallop squash.

Sweet Peppers Sweet peppers are often called bell peppers because of their shape. They may be harvested green or allowed to mature until they are red. Red peppers have a sweeter flavor and a higher nutrient content than green peppers, but the flesh of the red pepper is not as crisp as that of the green pepper. Select firm, fleshy peppers; flimsy peppers usually have thin walls and are not as meaty. Avoid peppers with spots of decay, for these spots enlarge rapidly. Peppers decay quickly when they are cut or when the humidity is high. Pepper shells can be stuffed with salad mixtures or the peppers can be sliced and added to many kinds of salads for color, texture, and flavor accents.

Tomatoes Tomatoes are a vital salad ingredient. Lettuce and tomato salad is probably the most common salad eaten in the United States; most tossed salads also include tomatoes. The small cherry tomato, which is popular both in salads and as a garnish, can be used whole or cut into halves or quarters. If full-sized tomatoes are chopped for salads, they do not need to be peeled. For those occasions when a tomato is served in slices, wedges, quarters, or whole—requiring cutting into bite-sized pieces at the table,—the tomato should be peeled, because the skin is difficult to cut with a fork.

A tomato may be peeled by rotating it over a gas flame, immersing it in boiling water for a minute, or heating it in a microwave oven for 30 seconds and then dipping it into ice water to loosen the skin. Figure 8.4 illustrates ways to cut tomatoes for stuffing.

OTHER SALAD INGREDIENTS Many other foods are added to salads for interest and variety. Following are brief descriptions of some of these foods.

Cooked Vegetables Even though salads are beneficial for incorporating raw vegetables into the diet, cooked vegetables may also be used with each other or in combination with some raw vegetables. Often a cooked vegetable that is rejected when it is served

Figure 8.4

Three ways to stuff a tomato.
Fillings can be potato, fish,
poultry, or vegetable salad
mixtures. *(United Fresh Fruit
and Vegetable Association)*

as a vegetable will be eaten when it is part of a salad mixture.
Potato salad is a favorite cooked vegetable salad. Macaroni, rice,
and bulgur wheat are also used in salad mixtures.

Water Chestnuts, Bamboo Shoots   These two foods are widely
used in Oriental cookery. Fresh water chestnuts are available in
some areas and need only be peeled and sliced to be added raw to
salads. Canned water chestnuts and bamboo shoots are just as
crisp as fresh ones. Both are very mild in flavor; their main purpose is to add crunchiness to mixtures that might otherwise be
soft and uninteresting.

Fresh Herbs   Salads may be seasoned with a variety of fresh
herbs, such as chives, chervil, garden cress, parsley, basil, rosemary, tarragon, and thyme. Table 8.2 suggests some possible
herbs and spices for salads. Most of these fresh herbs are easily

Table 8.2	Herbs for various types of salad
Salad	**Herbs and spices**
Aspic	Basil, savory, tarragon, thyme, oregano
Bean	Savory, curry, cumin, chili, dill
Cabbage	Caraway seed, celery seed, dill, mint
Chicken	Curry, marjoram
Fish	Basil, curry, dill
Fruit	Basil, mint, rosemary, cardamom
Tomato	Basil, savory, tarragon, thyme
Tossed green	Basil, chervil, chives, marjoram, savory, tarragon, oregano
Vegetable	Dill, caraway seed, celery seed, marjoram, savory, thyme

Figure 8.5

Fresh melons, strawberries, and bananas may be served with a small amount of whipped cream and mayonnaise dressing on top. *(Best Foods, Division of CPC International, Inc.)*

minced with kitchen shears: hold the sprigs of herbs tightly bunched together in one hand while snipping off pieces of the desired size with the shears in the other hand.

Fruits Both fresh and canned fruits are often used in salads; dried fruits are used less often. Many combinations of fruits are possible; Figure 8.5 illustrates one possibility. Fruits also combine well with vegetables, as shown in Figure 8.6.

Figure 8.6

Spicy fresh fruits are a good salad accompaniment for a vegetable-cheese casserole. *(United Fresh Fruit and Vegetable Association)*

Nuts, Seeds Nuts and seeds are not as widely used in salads as they might be. Walnuts in Waldorf salad is an old standby, but otherwise nuts are neglected in salads. Both salted and unsalted, they can add texture and flavor to salads. Herb seeds, such as mustard, dill, and caraway, have long been used, but adventurous salad makers are finding that salted and toasted sunflower, pumpkin, and sesame seeds are a gourmet treat in salads.

Cheeses Parmesan, Romano, Roquefort, and blue cheese have long been used in salad dressings. Cubes and julienne strips of processed cheese are often added to chef's salads, and cottage cheese is a favorite in fruit salads. More unusual is coarsely grated or cubed flavorful cheeses added to tossed salads or sprinkled over fruit and vegetable salads as a garnish.

Meats, Seafoods Small pieces of flavorful meats and seafoods not only add flavor to a salad, they also contribute protein. Crisply fried bacon bits, sausage crumbles, or chopped ham, as well as smoked and canned meats and fish and a variety of seafoods, are all good ingredients. Some of these meats improve tossed salads as well as potato, macaroni, and rice salads. One way to use cooked poultry in a salad is illustrated in Figure 8.7. Because the protein in meat is an excellent medium for bacterial growth, the utmost cleanliness must be observed in preparing such salads. Only clean utensils and equipment should be used, and the salad and salad ingredients should be kept well chilled until they are eaten.

Croutons Croutons are toasted bread cubes, usually flavored with butter, that add color, flavor, and texture to salads. Croutons may be prepared in the oven or in a frying pan and can be given

Figure 8.7

A scooped-out watermelon holds this salad mixture of melon balls, celery, grapes, and diced cooked turkey or chicken. *(United Fresh Fruit and Vegetable Association)*

special flavors or colors if they are shaken warm in a bag with garlic salt, onion salt, paprika, Parmesan or Romano cheese, or freshly minced herbs. Prepared croutons can be frozen in a plastic bag. When they are ready to use, spread them without thawing on a baking sheet and heat them in a moderate oven until they are crisp. To prevent croutons from becoming soggy in a salad, toss the salad with the dressing first, then add the crisp croutons and toss lightly just before serving.

Olives, Pickles, Pimientos, Relishes   These tangy ingredients are often added to starchy salads such as potato and macaroni, but they add zip to cooked vegetable salads and tossed salads as well. Pimiento is the canned form of sweet red pepper, packed in oil. Unused portions can be frozen for later use. Both the oil from pimientos and the liquid from pickles can replace all or part of the vinegar in oil-and-vinegar dressings.

Salad Preparation   Salads are not difficult to prepare, but some advice can make the task an easier and more satisfying experience.

SALAD INGREDIENTS   **Size of Pieces of Ingredients**   Most ingredients must be cut or subdivided for salads, because a salad is easier to eat if the pieces are small enough to be put into the mouth uncut. Soft ingredients, such as avocado or canned fruit, which are easily cut with a fork, are exceptions. The size of ingredients depends on the ingredients themselves and the type of salad. A carrot-and-raisin salad must contain grated carrots; it could not be easily chewed if the carrots were sliced or cubed. By the same token, a cabbage slaw contains only thinly shredded cabbage. If the ingredients in a tossed salad were all finely shredded and minced, on the other hand, the result would be unappetizing. In a tossed salad, the pieces must be large enough to be identifiable, although a tossed salad with pieces of lettuce and tomato so large they must be cut with a knife and fork is not satisfactory, either. In preparing ingredients for salads, therefore, keep in mind how they are to be eaten.

Fragile Ingredients   Some ingredients in salads, such as avocados, citrus fruit sections, and bananas, are easily crushed and lose their identities in salads if they are stirred too much. Mix the heartier ingredients with the dressing first, then gently add fragile ingredients, or arrange them over the top or around the side of the salad as a garnish. If several fragile ingredients are used together, they are best placed in an arranged salad with the dressing poured over them, so that no mixing is required.

Preventing Enzymatic Browning   The cause and prevention of enzymatic browning is discussed in Chapter 6. Raw fruits and vegetables that are subject to browning should be marinated or dipped in acidic juices. If acid fruits are already in the salad, separate treatment is not necessary. For instance, the apples in an apple salad that also contains pineapple or oranges will not turn brown once the two fruits are mixed together. If avocado or papaya slices are arranged on lettuce, marinate or dip them in a citrus fruit juice dressing beforehand.

Accents and Garnishes In planning and preparing salads, anticipate the total visual effect of the combined ingredients. Color is a vital feature. A tossed salad with green lettuce, green onions, and green peppers is rather monotonous in color. Red tomato, red and white radish slices, red cabbage, or pieces of orange carrots add color accents that enhance the salad. Bright red or green peel left on apples can do the same for a Waldorf salad.

Garnishes embellish or decorate a salad. Sometimes the same ingredients used as color accents can also serve as garnishes, such as slices of tomato or avocado arranged on the top of a tossed salad. A sprig of parsley or watercress can be placed beside a scoop of potato salad or, finely minced, sprinkled over the top. Other salad garnishes include slices of pickle, radish roses, sliced hard-cooked eggs, deviled eggs, stuffed green olives, pieces of pimiento, and carrot curls (Figure 8.8). Elaborate garnishes can be created by carving vegetables into a variety of shapes. Obviously, garnishes must be edible. Never garnish food with, for instance, a flower that might be poisonous.

Figure 8.8
Orange sections are an equally effective garnish for the gelatin salad mold or the avocado salad. *(United Fresh Fruit and Vegetable Association)*

Figure 8.9

Scooped-out pineapple halves hold a fruit mixture of pineapple and strawberries. *(United Fresh Fruit and Vegetable Association)*

Figure 8.10

Partially scooped-out avocado halves make containers for individual salads; here they are filled with apple, orange, and avocado slices served with a tangy lime dressing. *(United Fresh Fruit and Vegetable Association)*

SERVING SALADS

Containers for Salads Salads are often served in bowls, inside a lettuce leaf on a plate, or in other similar ways. The same salad can be more artfully served in a variety of novel containers. The container can be edible, as green pepper, tomato, and avocado halves, or orange, grapefruit, cantaloupe, pineapple, and watermelon boats or cups (Figures 8.9 and 8.10). A ring of cantaloupe can provide a base for a variety of salad mixtures.

A colorful mixture of ingredients in a glass bowl is always attractive, although salads are sometimes more attractive served in individual bowls and plates. After being briefly marinated to add flavor and prevent browning, sliced summer or tropical fruits can be attractively arranged on a platter.

Arrangement of Salads Salad arrangements should not look stiff or rigid, nor should flavor be sacrificed for appearance. Careful preparation can ensure the best of both worlds. When slices or pieces of ingredients are arranged on a platter for service to several people, it is sometimes difficult to obtain equal portions of the various ingredients, or the dressing may not be equally distributed over the various parts; marinating the ingredients beforehand helps eliminate one of the problems.

Dressings for Salads.   Most fruits and vegetables for salads are low in calories, but dressings usually are not. However, a simple, low-calorie dressing can often taste better than a rich, high-calorie dressing. For instance, a fruit salad is more refreshing dressed with a fruit juice marinade than with a whipped-cream or mayonnaise dressing.

The dressing should be appropriate for the salad and blend with the total meal and should also complement and enhance the flavors of the salad ingredients. Sweet-tart dressings go with fruit combinations, and tart dressings are preferred for tossed green and vegetable salads. Mayonnaise dressings blend with potato and macaroni salads and bind together ingredients in tuna and egg salads. The amount of dressing should be sufficient to flavor the ingredients, not drown them; too much dressing is perhaps a greater fault than too little. Tossed salads can be varied by changing the dressing and seasonings.

USE OF SALADS IN MEALS

The way a salad is to be used in a meal, as well as the other foods in the meal, influence the choice of salad. A light salad should be served with a heavy meal, and vice versa. Tart salads often go with fish and beef; sweeter fruit and gelatin salads complement ham, pork, veal, chicken, and turkey. Salads also contribute a needed contrast in texture, color, and flavor to meals. Appetizer salads served at the beginning of the meal should stimulate the appetite. A tossed salad with a light oil-and-vinegar dressing or a fruit salad with a sweet-tart dressing are suitable appetizer salads, but a potato or macaroni salad would not be satisfactory for this purpose.

Salads are often served with the main course, either on the dinner plate or separately. If the salad is served on the dinner plate, limit the amount of dressing used on it so that other foods on the plate will not become soaked in the dressing. A starchy potato or rice salad could be substituted for a starchy vegetable. If the entrée is low in protein, the salad might contain some meat or legume to fill this need.

When salad is served after the main course, a piquant and refreshing salad is appropriate. At this point in the meal, it can act both as dessert and as salad; fruits are ideal for this purpose. Such a dessert-salad is especially suitable after a heavy meal.

TYPES OF SALADS

Salads are classified by ingredients as well as by purpose: tossed green salads, vegetable salads, fruit salads, and gelatin salads. Any one of these may be an entrée and a buffet salad, a separate course, or a part of the main course.

Tossed Green Salad Green salads are composed mainly of leafy greens. An assortment of different greens provides variety in flavors, textures, colors, and nutrients (Figure 8.11). Raw or cooked vegetables of other kinds, and other foods outlined earlier in this chapter, also provide good accents. The greens should not be dressed until just before the salad is served, because salt and vinegar, or other acid ingredients, draw water out of the greens and cause them to wilt. Different flavors can be obtained by varying the herbs and seasoning in the dressing. Hardier ingredients, such as broccoli, cauliflower, or carrots, can be marinated in the dressing before they are added to the greens to produce a more flavorful salad. Leafy greens can be broken into pieces of the desired size up to 24 hours before serving time and held in a plastic bag in the refrigerator. Do not bruise the greens, avoid getting surplus water on them, and expel as much air as possible from the bag without crushing them.

Vegetable Salad Vegetable salads contain many of the same ingredients green salads do, except in different proportions (Figure 8.12). Raw and cooked vegetables other then leafy greens are the major components of a vegetable salad; they are often served on a lettuce leaf or a bed of greens. A vegetable salad should be prepared well in advance of serving time. The vegetables should be cooked only to the tender-crisp stage; they should never be soft and mushy. Most of the vegetables in such salads benefit by a long marination in the dressing, because it cannot penetrate and flavor these chunkier ingredients rapidly. The vegetables should be refrigerated while they are marinating. Leftover cooked vegetables, such as green peas, beans, carrots, and asparagus, are ideal

Figure 8.11

Curly endive and spinach leaves are combined in a tossed green salad; romaine leaves line the bowl. Carrot slices, radish roses, tomato wedges, and onion rings add color and flavor. *(United Fresh Fruit and Vegetable Association)*

Figure 8.12
A variety of fresh vegetables are combined in a salad bowl lined with escarole leaves; stuffed eggs provide a different and attractive garnish. *(United Fresh Fruit and Vegetable Association)*

for this type of salad because they do not require reheating when used in this way. If the vegetable was previously seasoned with table fat, remove the fat by placing the vegetable in a strainer or colander and briefly rinsing it with warm tap water. A variety of dressings can be used with these salads to provide different flavors.

Fruit Salad   Fresh and canned fruits keep their shape better than most frozen fruits and thus are generally preferred for use in salads. Fruits as a rule are juicier than vegetables and should be well drained before they are added to salads. Fragile fruits require special handling to prevent them from disintegrating. Nuts and seeds can provide texture as well as flavor to fruit salads.

Preparing fresh fruits in advance for salads presents some problems. In a fruit salad mixture containing such ingredients as pineapples, apples, cantaloupes, strawberries, pears, and bananas, some fruits can be prepared the day before and others cannot. The first three can be pared, cut, and combined. Pineapple helps keep the apples from browning; all three maintain good texture and

Figure 8.13

Figure 8.13

Fresh pineapple, cherries, strawberries, bananas, and oranges are combined and garnished with leaves of iceberg lettuce to make a fruit salad bowl. A whipped cream and mayonnaise dressing can be added if desired. *(Best Foods, Division of CPC International, Inc.)*

appearance. Strawberries can be washed, drained, and capped. They must be stored separately without added sugar, however, because they will discolor the other fruits and might themselves be crushed. Both bananas and pears tend to brown and also to disintegrate or become frayed; these should not be pared and cut until the last hour before they are served (Figure 8.13). The bananas, pears, and strawberries may be combined with the other fruits shortly before they are served.

Gelatin Salad The preparation of gelatin mixtures is described in Chapter 17. Many delightful salads can be prepared with unflavored gelatin added to a variety of fruit and vegetable juices to form a base for the incorporation of a variety of fresh or cooked fruits and vegetables, meats, cheeses, and other ingredients (Figure 8.14).

Main-Dish Salad Main-dish salads are hearty salads that comprise a whole meal, except for bread and dessert; they are often called *entrée salads*. Usually, raw or cooked fruits or vegetables are arranged on a bed of salad greens along with some source of protein. The protein often distinguishes the type of salad and can be any type of meat, seafood, cheese, egg, legume, or combination of these ingredients. The dressing is often ladled over, not mixed into, ingredients that have been artistically arranged.

Main-dish salads include the well-known crab or shrimp Louis and chef's salad; stuffed tomatoes and avocados; and potato, macaroni, rice, and bean salads containing meat or cheese. Several salad mixtures can be grouped together on one plate in their separate leafy green or shell. For example, a tomato stuffed with tuna or shell fish can accompany tangy coleslaw or marinated cooked or raw vegetables; potato, macaroni, or bean salad; and a dessert salad of fruits with a sweet dressing. For those who like salads, the main-dish salad can be a delightful treat.

Buffet Salad   A buffet salad can be a tossed salad, a vegetable salad, a gelatin salad, or a fruit salad, but all need special care when they are served in a buffet. They must be able to hold up well without refrigeration for a half hour or more; otherwise, the salad container should be placed in another container of chipped ice. Gelatin salads must contain a higher concentration of gelatin than normal to prevent excessive softening during service.

Buffet salads are usually attractively arranged, but artistry should not detract from the eating quality of the salad. Salads should be arranged so that servings are easy to remove. A buffet salad bar or smorgasbord is an excellent idea for serving buffet salads. An assortment of salad greens broken into eatable pieces, a range of other ingredients, and a choice of dressings are provided

Figure 8.14
A layered cheese-tomato aspic gelatin mold, attractively garnished with shrimp, makes a nutritious luncheon entrée.
(Knox of Thomas J. Lipton, Inc.)

so that each diner can create the salad he or she desires. People will often experiment with new foods and food combinations they might not otherwise try when the makings are presented in this way.

Nutritional Value of Salads

The nutrients obtained from salads depend entirely upon the nutrient content of the salad ingredients. Dark green leafy vegetables supply more nutrients than light green, bleached vegetables. Table 8.1 lists the nutrient content of many of the vegetables used in salads, and Table 6.1 lists the nutrients of fruits. Familiarity with the nutrient contents of these foods helps in planning salads that are nutritious as well as attractive and good-tasting.

Most salads also supply fiber. Recent studies indicate that fiber is probably much more important in the diet than was formerly realized. If the diet includes ample amounts of fiber, there will be less likelihood of ailments of the lower bowel developing, because fiber helps maintain normal elimination, as discussed in Chapter 1.

Study Questions

1. What is a salad?
2. How is the greenness of salad greens related, as a general rule, to their nutrient content?
3. Why is raw cabbage shredded, and tomatoes peeled, for salads?
4. What sanitary factors need to be considered when protein foods, especially meats, are served in salads?
5. How and when should croutons be added to a tossed salad? Why must they be added in this way?
6. What factors determine the size of pieces in preparing ingredients for salads?
7. Why do fragile ingredients in salads need special handling? How should they be handled?
8. What purpose do accents and garnishes serve in salads?
9. What are some factors to consider in choosing a dressing for a salad, in deciding how much dressing to use, and in deciding when the dressing should be mixed with the other ingredients?
10. What factors determine the kind of salad to serve with a meal?
11. Why are some vegetables marinated in the dressing before they are added to a salad?
12. Because fruits are often juicier than vegetables, how should they be handled before they are added to a salad?
13. What is a main-dish salad?
14. What factors need to be considered in preparing salads for a buffet?

References

Boswell, Victor R. "Our Vegetable Travelers." *National Geographic* XCVI (1949): 145.

Presper, Mary. "Spring Soups and Salads." *Family Health,* May 1974.

U.S. Department of Agriculture. *Tips on Selecting Fruits and Vegetables,* Marketing Bulletin No. 13. Washington, D.C.: Government Printing Office, 1961.

——. *Vegetables in Family Meals,* Home and Garden Bulletin No. 105, 1965.

——. *How to Buy Fresh Vegetables,* Home and Garden Bulletin No. 143, 1967.

Cereal Grains and Pastas

Figure 9.1

Four grains commonly found in breakfast cereals are: top left, oats; top right, rice; bottom left, wheat; bottom right, corn. *(Cereal Institute, Inc.)*

Cereals are the seeds of grasses. Nomad populations in past centuries probably gathered the seeds of wild grasses, but as populations became more stable, they cultivated the grasses instead. Today's domesticated cereal grains have been developed from centuries of cultivation and selective breeding. All cereal grains are not equally consumed in all parts of the world; this fact may be related to favorable growing conditions for a cereal in one area but not in others. Some cereal grains grow in cold climates; others require temperate or hot climates. Some will flourish in a dry region, but others require a wet climate. The four cereal grains that are most widely used in the United States are shown in Figure 9.1.

Even primitive peoples processed their cereal grains into various forms—whole, broken, coarsely ground, or finely ground—or other types of treatment that affect their flavor, edibility, and nutrient content. Cereal grains are similarly processed today. Whole or broken kernels of the grains are used in their natural state or they are processed into meal, flour, and starch, most of which are additionally processed into a multitude of other products.

Cereal grains are a primary source of protein in some countries.

As protein from animal sources becomes more limited with the expanding world population, cereals will probably become even more important in everyone's diet. Therefore, it is important to recognize the nutritional contributions and deficiencies of this group of foods and to understand how processing and cooking procedures affect the nutrients in grains.

Composition of Cereal Grains

All cereal grains have a large center area, high in starch, known as the *endosperm*. At one end is the *germ*, the area of the kernel that sprouts when allowed to germinate. The *bran*, or pericarp, is the outer covering of the kernel. The structure of the wheat kernel is shown in Figure 9.2.

The endosperm makes up about 83 percent of the grain. Besides having a high starch content, it also contains a small amount of protein, but very little cellulose. Fourteen percent of the kernel is bran with a high cellulose content, and a small amount of protein, minerals, and vitamins. The *aleurone* layers between the bran and endosperm are intermediate in nutrient content. The germ, which makes up about 3 percent of the grain, is a rich source of essential fatty acids, vitamin E, protein, the B vitamins, and minerals.

CEREAL GRAIN PROCESSING

Whenever the bran and germ are left on the endosperm, the grain is considered *whole grain* or *whole wheat*, even though it may be very finely subdivided, as whole wheat flour is. If the bran and germ are separated from the endosperm, the remaining endosperm is known as "milled" or "refined" wheat or cereal; refined wheat flour is called either "white" flour or simply "wheat flour." Milling cereals extends their storage life. When the germ of the grain is removed, most of its fat is also removed; therefore, refined grain is less likely to become rancid. Most products using whole grain are darker in color and have a coarser texture than the refined product. Many people prefer the lighter color and finer texture of the refined wheat products.

Enrichment In the United States, federal law requires that some refined cereal products be enriched. Because the bran and germ are the principal sources of nutrients in cereal grain, their removal leaves a refined product with greatly reduced nutrient content. Three vitamins—thiamin, riboflavin, and niacin—and iron are added to refined products in amounts that equal their content in whole grain to enrich the product to federal standards. Whole grain contains modest amounts of other vitamins, minerals, and protein that are not added in enrichment, but enriched refined products are far more nutritious than unenriched ones.

Ready-to-Eat Cereals Ready-to-eat cereals do not require cooking before they are eaten; they have been processed in such a way

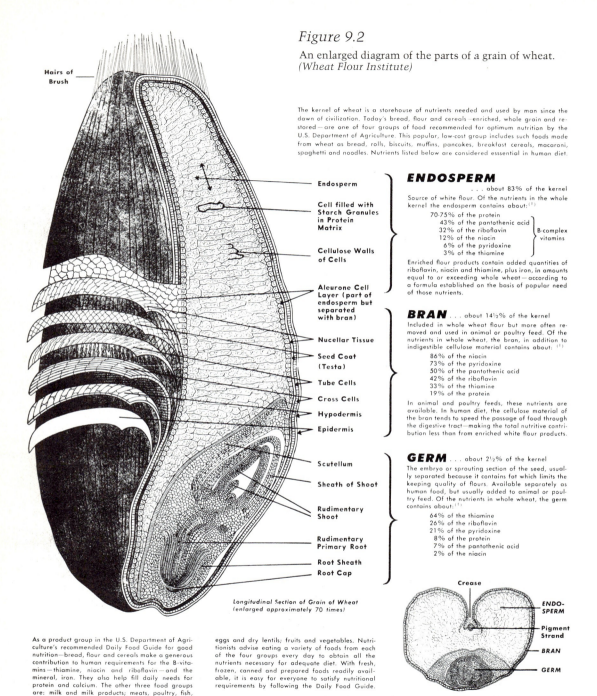

Figure 9.2

An enlarged diagram of the parts of a grain of wheat.
(Wheat Flour Institute)

Hairs of Brush

The kernel of wheat is a storehouse of nutrients needed and used by man since the dawn of civilization. Today's bread, flour and cereals —enriched, whole grain and restored — are one of four groups of food recommended for optimum nutrition by the U.S. Department of Agriculture. This popular, low-cost group includes such foods made from wheat as bread, rolls, biscuits, muffins, pancakes, breakfast cereals, macaroni, spaghetti and noodles. Nutrients listed below are considered esssential in human diet.

Endosperm

Cell filled with Starch Granules in Protein Matrix

Cellulose Walls of Cells

Aleurone Cell Layer (part of endosperm but separated with bran)

Nucellar Tissue

Seed Coat (Testa)

Tube Cells

Cross Cells

Hypodermis

Epidermis

Scutellum

Sheath of Shoot

Rudimentary Shoot

Rudimentary Primary Root

Root Sheath

Root Cap

Longitudinal Section of Grain of Wheat (enlarged approximately 70 times)

ENDOSPERM

. . . about 83% of the kernel

Source of white flour. Of the nutrients in the whole kernel the endosperm contains about:[1]

70-75% of the protein
43% of the pantothenic acid
32% of the riboflavin   } B-complex
12% of the niacin   vitamins
6% of the pyridoxine
3% of the thiamine

Enriched flour products contain added quantities of riboflavin, niacin and thiamine, plus iron, in amounts equal to or exceeding whole wheat — according to a formula established on the basis of popular need of those nutrients.

BRAN

. . . about 14½% of the kernel

Included in whole wheat flour but more often removed and used in animal or poultry feed. Of the nutrients in whole wheat, the bran, in addition to indigestible cellulose material contains about:[1]

86% of the niacin
73% of the pyridoxine
50% of the pantothenic acid
42% of the riboflavin
33% of the thiamine
19% of the protein

In animal and poultry feeds, these nutrients are available. In human diet, the cellulose material of the bran tends to speed the passage of food through the digestive tract—making the total nutritive contribution less than from enriched white flour products.

GERM

. . . about 2½% of the kernel

The embryo or sprouting section of the seed, usually separated because it contains fat which limits the keeping quality of flours. Available separately as human food, but usually added to animal or poultry feed. Of the nutrients in whole wheat, the germ contains about:[1]

64% of the thiamine
26% of the riboflavin
21% of the pyridoxine
8% of the protein
7% of the pantothenic acid
2% of the niacin

Crease

ENDO-SPERM

Pigment Strand

BRAN

GERM

Cross Section View

As a product group in the U.S. Department of Agriculture's recommended Daily Food Guide for good nutrition—bread, flour and cereals make a generous contribution to human requirements for the B-vitamins—thiamine, niacin and riboflavin—and the mineral, iron. They also help fill daily needs for protein and calcium. The other three food groups are: milk and milk products; meats, poultry, fish, eggs and dry lentils; fruits and vegetables. Nutritionists advise eating a variety of foods from each of the four groups every day to obtain all the nutrients necessary for adequate diet. With fresh, frozen, canned and prepared foods readily available, it is easy for everyone to satisfy nutritional requirements by following the Daily Food Guide.

[1]Research Association of British Flour Millers, Cereals Research Station, St. Albans, England, 1960.

that cooking has already taken place or is not required. During processing, either a single grain or a combination of grains is combined with other ingredients and, as a rule, ground to a paste. This mixture is formed into desired shapes and toasted; in this way, flakes, crumbles, crinkles, and puffs are produced (Figure 9.3). Today more than 92 percent of ready-to-eat cereals—except granola types—are fortified. Most of these cereals are fortified with 25 percent of the U.S. Recommended Daily Allowances of at least seven vitamins and iron per 1 ounce of cereal. A few cereals are fortified with 100 percent of these nutrients plus others not normally found in cereal products, such as vitamins A, C, and D. Nutrition labeling now includes the amount of added sugar in these products.

Cooked Cereals Several grains have been processed into products that can be served as a hot breakfast cereal after they are cooked in water. Both refined and whole grains are used in this way, either finely or coarsely ground, cracked, or in whole kernels. Instant cereals require only the addition of boiling water.

Wheat, corn, rice, oats, and rye are the major cereal grains consumed in the United States; a number of other grains have limited usage. Processing and individual characteristics of the grains influence the way they are used. Some of these differences are discussed in the following descriptions of individual grains.

CEREAL VARIETIES

Barley Barley is grown in many parts of the world, but in no region is it the primary grain for human consumption. Barley enjoyed greater popularity in the past than it does today, when it is used mainly for animal feed and for fermentation in making malt beer. Malt is prepared when barley is soaked in water until it starts to sprout, which develops an enzyme that changes the starch in the grain to *maltose,* a sugar. The malt is dried and roasted to develop flavor, then fermented to produce beer or ale. Barley has a limited use in soups and as a cooked cereal; it can also be prepared as a pilaf or used as the starchy ingredient in casseroles. Flour produced from barley is being tested for use in baked products.

Corn or Maize Corn, also called *maize,* may have originated in the Americas. Over the centuries, hybrids of corn have been developed that grow in almost any climate and are suitable for special purposes. Corn is used for animal feed as well as for human consumption, but different varieties are used for each purpose. Freshly harvested, corn may be eaten on the cob; it may also be frozen on or off the cob and the kernels may be canned. Corn is an excellent substitute for potatoes in meals.

The bran layer on a corn kernel is called the *pericarp.* If only

GRAINS FOR BREAKFAST CEREALS

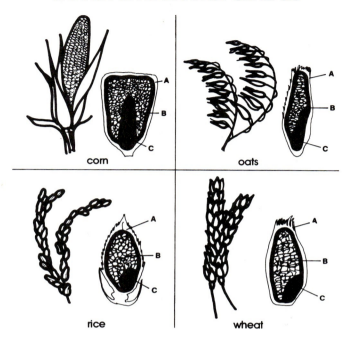

corn

oats

rice

wheat

A *BRAN consists of several thin outer layers of the grain kernel and is its protective coat.*
B *ENDOSPERM is the stored food supply for the new plant which develops as the kernel germinates. It comprises about 85% of the kernel.*

C *EMBRYO or GERM is the miniature plant which enlarges and develops after the kernel germinates.*

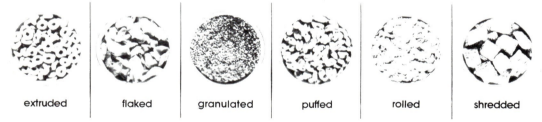

extruded   flaked   granulated   puffed   rolled   shredded

Figure 9.3

The structure of the four major grains in breakfast cereals and the forms into which they are processed. *(Cereal Institute, Inc.)*

the pericarp is removed in milling, the remaining germ and endosperm are ground into *decorticated cornmeal.* Removal of both germ and pericarp results in *degerminated cornmeal.* Ground, whole-kernel cornmeal is often cooked in water and served as a porridge. Various ethnic groups have different names for this dish. In Italy, "polenta" is a cornmeal porridge containing cheese and lard. Jamaicans mix the porridge with a small amount of meat or fish, pepper, and other spices and call the result "stamp and go." In the southern United States, plain porridge is known as "cornmeal mush."

Whole corn kernels, with germ and pericarp removed, are soaked to produce *hominy*, also known as *samp*. Dried, ground hominy is called *grits*. In the southern United States and in Central America, it is customary to soak or boil whole-kernel corn in dilute alkalis, such as lime (calcium hydroxide), wood ashes (potassium hydroxide), or lye (sodium hydroxide) for 20 to 30 minutes. The alkaline solution is discarded, and the kernels are washed and then ground into a paste called *masa*. Masa is used to make *tortillas*, a flat, pancakelike bread. Dried corn, which keeps well, is usually given this alkaline treatment, the purpose being to soften it and make it more usable. The corn is dried to improve its keeping quality between harvests.

Alkaline treatment of corn causes significant losses of some B vitamins, but it improves the availability of niacin, a B vitamin present in corn in limited amounts. Cultures that do not treat corn with alkali, but depend on it for 80 percent or more of their calorie intake, have a high incidence of *pellagra*, a disease caused by niacin deficiency. Pellagra is less common in cultures that treat corn with alkali.

A special variety of corn is needed to make popcorn, an American favorite. The endosperm in this corn must be hard and must possess 11 to 15 percent moisture. When these corn kernels are heated, the water in the kernel expands, and the corn "pops." Corn for popping that is stored in an open container loses moisture and does not pop satisfactorily; it should be stored in an airtight container.

Corn is processed into many products, including starch, corn syrup, high-fructose corn syrup, glucose, alcohol, and oil. It is also popular in ready-to-eat and cooked cereals.

The protein in corn is *zein*, which is deficient in the amino acids lysine and tryptophan. Growing children in countries that depend on corn as a major source of food often develop protein malnutrition. In recent years a hybrid corn has been developed with a protein quality that supports growth, but it has not been widely accepted because the soft endosperm of the hybrid corn does not keep or process as well as regular corn. Research continues to improve the processing characteristics of high-lysine and -tryptophan hybrid corn.

Millet Millet is often confused with sorghum. These two similar grains come from two distinctly different grasses. Millet is not widely eaten in the United States; it is mainly used as bird seed and poultry feed. It grows more readily than other grasses under such unfavorable growing conditions as drought, poor soil, and cold climates. Millet has a stronger flavor than most other cereals, a fact that may explain why it is not as popular for human consumption.

Millet can be eaten as *groats*, or whole grain. Sometimes it is husked, soaked, boiled, and ground into a meal, and it is also combined with wheat for making bread in some areas.

Oats The pericarp of oats is removed before milling. The grains are then flattened between heated rollers to produce the familiar "rolled oats." The grain is either subdivided into smaller pieces before rolling or is rolled into thinner pieces to produce quick-cooking or instant oats.

Oats are used for animal feed as well as for ready-to-eat and cooked cereals. In recent years rolled oats have been used as the major ingredient in granola; they are combined with other grains, seeds, nuts, and dried fruit; mixed with oil and sugar; and toasted. The high oil and sugar content of all granola makes it a high-calorie food. The high-protein content of oats makes it an ideal breakfast cereal. Oat flour is finding increased usage in a number of products and is recognized for its antioxidant properties, as mentioned in Chapter 4.

Rice Almost half of the world's population depends on rice as the principal food in their diet. White rice, or refined rice, is rice from which the bran and germ have been removed; brown rice contains the bran and germ. White rice is often polished with glucose and talc to improve its luster; hence its name, polished rice. Most people prefer the color and bland flavor of white rice; however, widespread *beriberi*, a disease caused by thiamin deficiency, has occurred in areas where it is a major part of the diet.

Converted rice is a compromise between polished rice and brown rice. Brown rice is parboiled, causing some of the nutrients in the bran to penetrate the endosperm. When it is dried and the bran is removed, the resulting product, converted rice, contains a higher content of nutrients than white rice, but not so much as brown rice. Converted rice has a creamy color and is not as fluffy when it is cooked as regular white rice. The thiamin content of converted rice is sufficient to prevent beriberi even when rice is a major part of the diet.

Other attempts have been made to enrich rice, but often without success. Coating raw rice kernels with nutrient solution has not been effective because the nutrients are easily washed off or discarded when the rice is cooked in too much water. Nutrient pellets, or rice grains impregnated with nutrients, have been mixed in with white rice, but users unknowingly remove and discard these pellets because they are a different color than the rest of the rice. Furthermore, the riboflavin in the pellets produces a blotchy yellow discoloration of the rice during cooking.

The genetic characteristics of rice grain determine its shape and texture when cooked. The three types of rice grains are classified according to the length and the shape of their kernel (Figure 9.4). Short grains are soft and chalky and tend to become slightly

sticky when they are cooked. Long grains are more slender and translucent and are fluffy, with each grain separate, when they are cooked. Both milled and brown rice are available in these three types of grains.

Instant rice is rice that has been precooked and dried; it only needs to be rehydrated by a short period of steaming. Quick-cooking rice is made of very small, partially cooked rice kernels. Cracked and broken rice kernels are used to make rice grits, which must be enriched by law because they are often eaten as a breakfast cereal.

Preseasoned mixes containing rice are usually costly convenience foods. Other products produced from rice include rice flour, starch, polish, bran, hulls, oil, and wine.

Wild rice, also known as Indian rice, grows wild in swamps and mud flats in the northeastern United States, but it is not a true rice. Mature grains are harvested from flat-bottomed boats and canoes, dried for several days, and then parched, or heated, to remove the husks. Wild rice is eaten as a whole grain; it is not milled. Its nutrient content resembles that of whole wheat. Wild rice is expensive and is considered an exotic food.

Rye   Because rye grows readily in cold climates where other grains do not, at one time it was a major cereal of northern Europe. Today it is found mostly in breads and crackers and is rarely eaten as a breakfast cereal.

Sorghum   Like rye and millet, sorghum grows in less than ideal climates, especially in arid regions. Not widely used in this country, it is a major grain in Africa and the Orient. Sorghum has an unusual flavor, somewhat foreign to American tastes which can be made more tolerable by steaming or dry-heat processing. Small amounts of sorghum are sometimes added to crackers and snack foods.

Some varieties of sorghum have a high sugar content and are used in making syrup; sorghum is also used by the brewing industry and for animal feed, and has a number of nonfood purposes as well. In Africa the grain is ground into meal for making porridge and bread; cakes made from it are called "mealies."

Triticale   *Triticale* is a hybrid grain obtained by crossbreeding rye and wheat. This hybrid was developed to obtain a higher protein quality than the grains from which it was bred. Some nutritionists believe that triticale may someday replace a good portion of both wheat and rye crops. Triticale can be cooked as a whole grain as a substitute for rice; it has been ground into flour for use in baked products and processed into cereal flakes.

Wheat   Most wheat produced in the United States is used as flour in baked products. Wheat is also used in ready-to-eat cereals and cooked cereals, often in combination with other grains.

Durum wheat is a very hard variety of wheat with a high protein content. Refined flour from durum wheat is used to make pastas. In this process, the endosperm of durum wheat is ground to form a product called "semolina." Semolina is mixed with water to form a dough that is shaped into various pasta forms and dried. Noodles are made with egg substituted for part or all of the water in the dough. High-quality durum pastas keep their shape well when they are cooked in water. Sometimes, however, semolina is diluted with regular wheat flour. This produces a poor-quality pasta that tends to soften and disintegrate when cooked. Because no grades have been established for pasta, the cooked quality of various brands should be compared. Some forms of pasta are shown in Figure 9.5.

Because pasta is prepared from the endosperm of wheat, its nutritive value is very modest. With the increased emphasis on vegetable protein and reduction in meat consumption, nutritionists have been concerned about improving the nutrient content of some cereal products.

The processing of wheat to produce bulgur is similar to that of converted rice, except that the wheat is steamed in its husks and the husks and only a small part of the bran are removed after it is dried. Bulgur wheat has been produced for centuries in Mediterranean countries because it is more impervious to insect attack than unprocessed wheat. It has about the same nutritive value as whole wheat. Because bulgur wheat contains the germ with its high fat content, it is subject to rancidity and should be stored in a cool place. Use a porous container that permits the products of oxidation to evaporate, to protect its flavor. Bulgur wheat is available as whole grain groats or as cracked grains that cook in about 15 minutes.

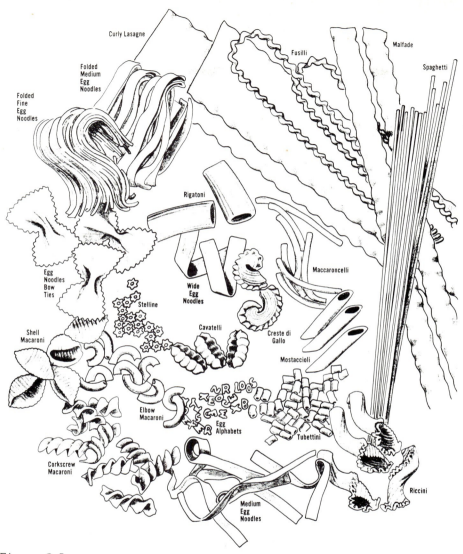

Curly Lasagne

Folded Medium Egg Noodles

Folded Fine Egg Noodles

Fusilli

Malfade

Spaghetti

Rigatoni

Maccaroncelli

Egg Noodles Bow Ties

Stelline

Wide Egg Noodles

Cavatelli

Creste di Gallo

Shell Macaroni

Mostaccioli

Elbow Macaroni

Egg Alphabets

Tubettini

Corkscrew Macaroni

Riccini

Medium Egg Noodles

Figure 9.5

Pasta is made in a variety of forms. *(National Macaroni Institute)*

Buckwheat   Buckwheat is neither a wheat nor even a cereal grain; it is a seed of several varieties of plants in the *Polygonaceae* family. Buckwheat has none of the cooking properties of true wheat, but it is ground and used for its unique flavor to replace part of the wheat flour in pancake mixes. It has more starch and less protein than wheat.

Cooking Cereal Grains

Cereal grains are cooked in water until they become hydrated, tender, and soft, a process of gelatinization.

BREAKFAST CEREALS

Most cooked breakfast cereals are coarse enough to be stirred into boiling water without lumping. Some, such as finely divided cornmeal, must be mixed with a small amount of cold water before being added to boiling water to prevent lumping. The proportion of water for cooking the cereals affects the consistency of the cooked product. A ratio of 1 cup of cereal, such as farina or oats, to 2 cups of water produces a cooked cereal of fluid consistency, that is, a thick gruel or porridge. To obtain a puddinglike consistency, use a smaller ratio of water.

RICE, BULGUR WHEAT, AND PASTAS

In many ways the preparation of these products is similar, but a few differences exist.

Washing Bulgur wheat and pastas never need to be washed before they are cooked. Most rice has been cleaned and does not require washing; enriched rice should never be washed. However, rice coated with talc must be washed to remove the talc, which is unhealthy to eat. If washing is necessary, it should be only enough to remove soil. Rice does not need to be washed until the wash water is clear, as has been the practice in the past. Such washing was intended to reduce the stickiness of rice, but this problem can be controlled in other ways. Excessive washing of rice prior to cooking increases solution loss of nutrients.

Toasting Occasionally, rice, bulgur wheat, and some pastas are toasted before they are cooked in water to produce a unique flavor. Such dry-heat treatment can destroy one half to two thirds of the thiamin and a large part of the protein of these grains. Toasting of grains should be minimal where they form a major part of the diet. If a wide variety of foods are eaten, however, so that thiamin and protein are provided by other sources, toasting cereal before steaming does not pose a nutritional problem.

Types of Liquid Water is the liquid most commonly used for cooking cereal grains, but other liquids can produce different flavors. Meat stock is often used in pilafs and casseroles. Milk may form part or all of the liquid. An acidic liquid, such as tomato juice or sauce, inhibits softening and gelatinization of the grain or pasta; they should be partially cooked before the acidic ingredient is added.

Proportion of Water Most types of rice and bulgur wheat that are cooked with 2 cups of water per cup of grain absorb all the water and become properly hydrated if they are cooked in a pot with a tightly fitting cover. If a large amount of water evaporates during cooking because of a loose cover, a larger ratio of water may be needed. Rice grown during a very dry season may require additional water to achieve full swelling and gelatinization. A larger proportion of water is also necessary if a soft-textured cooked grain is desired.

Rice and pastas are customarily cooked in a large excess of water that is later discarded, a practice that results in a greater loss of water-soluble nutrients, just as with vegetables. Both rice and pastas can be cooked only in the water that will be absorbed. Pastas and rice that are cooked in too much water tend to turn an off-white or yellow color, especially if the water is hard. The anthoxanthin pigments in cereal grains are the same as those in white vegetables. These pigments turn yellow in an alkaline medium but remain white in a neutral or acidic medium, as discussed in Chapter 7. The more water used to cook the cereal grains, the more alkaline ions are present to cause yellowing. When pastas and rice are cooked only in the water they absorb, no deleterious color changes occur even if the water is hard.

Noodles and spaghetti are not as easily measured in a cup as rice, which may be one reason why these products are less often cooked in only the amount of water that is absorbed during cooking. An alternative method, therefore, is to use the weight of the pasta, not the measure, to determine the proportion of water and pasta. Table 9.1 shows approximate ratios of water to pasta for cooking various weights of pasta. Greater amounts of pasta need proportionately less water because less evaporation occurs from a large amount of pasta and water than the same weight cooked separately in several smaller portions. This principle also applies in cooking rice. The type of pot also affects the proportion of water, as previously mentioned. If the pot has a loose cover, larger proportions of water may be needed than those in Table 9.1.

Cold Versus Boiling Water Pastas should always be added to boiling water. As the pieces of pasta contact the water, the starch on the outside of the pieces gelatinizes, causing it to adhere to the pasta. In Oriental rice cookery, rice is started to cook in cold water. The cold water dissolves the starch from the surface of the grain; the starch, when heated, forms a paste that causes the grains to stick together, a very desirable quality when rice is eaten with chopsticks. To obtain rice, pastas, or cereals with separate grains or pieces that do not adhere to each other, start the grain or pasta cooking in boiling water. For a gummy rice with grains that stick together, the rice should be started in cold water. Even though long-grain rice is supposed to produce a fluffier product than short-grain rice, even long-grain rice can become gummy if it is started to cook in cold water. A slightly higher ratio of water and increased cooking time also produces a soft, gummy texture. Pasta is best cooked until it is just tender—al dente.

Table 9.1
Approximate proportions of water and pasta for cooking

Water (cups)	Pasta (ounces)
1	2
1¾	4
2½	6
5	16

Cooking Time The cooking time for cereal grains and pastas depends on the size of the pieces and the grain or pasta itself. Rolled oats cook in a very few minutes in boiling water. If an electric surface unit is used, bring the water to a boil with a high heat setting, stir in the oats, cover the pan, and turn off the unit; the residual heat finishes the cooking. Whole wheat kernels must be cooked longer than broken or cracked kernels. Brown rice must be cooked longer than white rice because the bran layer on brown rice is slower to hydrate than the endosperm. One or two servings of cereal can be cooked in a microwave oven. Cooking small—but not large—amounts of cereals, grains, and pasta by microwave offers an advantage in time or energy saving.

Disodium phosphate is added to instant cereals to speed the gelatinization of the starch. Cooking cereals longer than the minimum time necessary for gelatinization changes the flavor of the cereal, a change that is preferred by some people. Excessively long cooking times should be avoided to prevent heat destruction of thiamin and other vitamins.

Cereal grains and pastas tend to boil over during cooking; a large enough pot should be used to allow for this. A small amount of fat added to the water during cooking also helps to reduce foaming; heat should be adjusted to maintain a slow boil.

Rinsing Cooked Grains and Pastas Cooked pastas and rice are traditionally rinsed to remove starch paste from the surface and to keep the pieces from sticking to each other. This procedure can cause considerable loss of nutrients, and it is not recommended.

Figure 9.6

Pilafs of barley (left) and bulgur wheat (right) provide protein and other nutrients that extend meat protein. Also shown are uncooked barley and whole wheat berries.

Correct cooking procedures reduce or eliminate stickiness. Good quality pastas also contain monoglycerides that help produce firm, nonsticky results, making washing after cooking unnecessary. A small amount of fat added during cooking also helps keep grains or pasta separate.

Oven and Pressure Cooking Both rice and pastas can be cooked in the oven, although baking takes longer than boiling. Containers should be large enough to allow for expansion and foaming. Boiling water should be used to start the pasta or rice to speed the cooking. There is not much point in cooking pasta in a pressure cooker, because most pastas cook in 15 to 20 minutes, as do some forms of rice. However, brown rice can be cooked in a pressure cooker to good advantage because brown rice requires about 45 minutes of cooking at atmospheric pressure. The pressure cooker should be filled no more than one-third full to allow room for expansion and foaming during cooking. Adding 1 tablespoon of fat to the pasta or rice cooked in the pressure cooker or oven helps reduce foaming.

Cereal grains, with the exception of rice and corn, are often limited to breakfast foods served with milk. Cereal grains can also be potato substitutes, as shown in Figures 9.6 and 9.7, where barley, bulgur wheat, and rice are used in pilafs. Figures 9.8 and 9.9 show spaghetti and macaroni served in place of potatoes in a meal. Grains served in this way also help extend the meat. Figure 9.10 shows rice used in a pudding for dessert.

Serving Cereal Grains

Figure 9.7
Rice pilaf makes a satisfactory substitute for potatoes in an American meal. *(Rice Council of America)*

Figure 9.8

Chicken cacciatore provides an interesting way to serve spaghetti. *(National Macaroni Institute)*

Figure 9.9

A savory lamb stew is delicious served on tender macaroni. *(National Macaroni Institute)*

Figure 9.10
Creamy rice pudding is served
with hard sauce as a dessert.
(Rice Council of America)

The nutrient composition of various grains is shown in Table 9.2. Grains are poor sources of calcium, vitamin A, and vitamin C. Their protein quality is not as good as foods from animal sources, both in amount and quality, for they lack the amino acids lysine and tryptophan. Whole grains have a higher nutrient content than their refined counterparts, as a comparison of brown and white rice demonstrates. Further refinement of grain to the endosperm alone decreases the nutrient content, as a comparison of corn grits with cornmeal, and farina with red wheat, shows.

Nutritional Value of Grains

Whole wheat contains *phytic acid,* a phosphorus compound that forms complex compounds with calcium, zinc, and iron in foods and in the digestive tract. The complex of phytic acid and mineral cannot be absorbed through the intestinal wall. How much of these minerals can be utilized by the body from whole grains is questionable. This does not mean that whole wheat should not be eaten, however. If adequate amounts of the minerals are obtained from other foods, and if cereal grains are not overly emphasized in the diet, then the phytic acid in whole wheat products does not present a problem. Some nutritionists

Table 9.2 Nutrient composition of cereal grains and refined cereals for 100-gram amounts, edible portion, uncooked

Food	Water (g)	Calories	Protein (g)	Fat (g)	Carbohydrate Total (g)	Carbohydrate Fiber (g)	Calcium (mg)	Phosphorous (mg)	Iron (mg)	Thiamin (mg)	Riboflavin (mg)	Niacin (mg)	Pantothenic acid (mg)	Pyridoxine (mg)
CEREAL GRAINS, WHOLE, DRY, UNCOOKED														
Pearl barley, light	11.1	349	8.2	1.0	78.8	0.5	16	189	2.0	0.12	0.05	3.1	0.503	0.224
Pearl barley, dark	10.8	348	9.6	1.1	77.2	0.9	34	290	2.7	0.21	0.07	3.7	—	—
Bulgur wheat	10.0	354	11.2	1.5	75.7	1.7	29	338	3.7	0.28	0.14	4.5	0.660	0.225
Cornmeal	12	355	9.2	3.9	73.7	1.6	20	256	2.4	0.38	0.11	2.0	0.580	0.250
Millet	11.8	327	9.9	2.9	72.9	3.2	20	311	6.8	0.73	0.38	2.3	—	—
Rolled oats	8.3	390	14.2	7.4	68.2	1.2	53	405	4.5	0.60	0.14	1.0	1.500	0.140
Brown rice	12.0	360	7.5	1.9	77.4	0.9	32	221	1.6	0.34	0.05	4.7	1.100	0.550
White rice	12.0	363	6.7	0.4	80.4	0.3	24	94	0.8	0.07	0.03	1.6	0.550	0.170
Converted rice	10.3	369	7.4	0.3	81.3	0.2	60	200	2.9	0.44	—	3.5	0.900	0.425
Rye	11.0	334	12.1	1.7	73.4	2.0	38	376	3.7	0.43	0.22	1.6	1.340	0.300
Sorghum	11.0	332	11.0	3.3	73.0	1.7	28	287	4.4	0.38	0.15	3.9	—	—
Hard red wheat	12.5	330	12.3	1.8	71.7	2.3	46	354	3.4	0.52	0.12	4.3	—	—
Soft red wheat	14.0	326	10.2	2.0	72.1	2.3	42	400	3.5	0.43	0.11	3.6	—	—
REFINED CEREALS UNCOOKED														
Corn grits	12	362	8.7	0.8	78.1	0.4	4	73	1.0	0.13	0.04	1.2	—	—
Farina	10.3	371	11.4	0.9	77.0	0.4	25	107	1.5	0.06	0.10	0.7	0.515	0.067

SOURCE: U.S. Department of Agriculture, *Composition of Foods; Pantothenic Acid, Vitamin B₆ and Vitamin B₁₂ in Foods.*

recommend the diet include both enriched refined and whole grain products in reasonable amounts, and that neither be emphasized over the other. Whole grains are excellent sources of fiber, some of the B vitamins, and trace minerals. Enriched cereal grains are nutritionally superior to nonenriched refined products. However, the fortification of refined, high-sugar, ready-to-eat cereals with a few vitamins and minerals is a practice that deceives the unwary by depriving them of the trace minerals, vitamins, and protein available in ordinary whole grain products. As a group, whole grain cereals that require cooking have a higher nutrient content than the ready-to-eat and instant cereals and grains.

Cereal products make up a major part of the human diet. As a whole, they are also the most economical source of calories. Unprocessed cereals are more economical than the processed products made from them, with a few exceptions, but whole wheat flour is often more expensive than white flour. Ready-to-eat cereals cost more than cereals that require cooking; instant oats are more expensive than regular rolled oats. Canned and frozen pasta and rice products cost more than if the dry products are cooked and seasoned.

Economy of Cereal Grains

Insect and rodent infestation of cereals and grains is a major problem in maintaining quality during the storage of cereals. Chapter 2 explains measures that will prevent infestation. Grains that have been parboiled before drying—such as bulgur wheat, converted rice, and some brown rice—are more resistant to insect infestation. Refined grains have a longer shelf life than whole grains. The germ of whole grains, with its high-fat content, is subject to rancidity. Dry cereals and grains should be stored in a cool, dry atmosphere in closed insect-proof containers for short-term storage. For longer periods, freezer or refrigerator storage are recommended.

Cooked cereal grains will keep for a few days in the refrigerator and indefinitely when frozen. A microwave oven is ideal for reheating refrigerated and frozen cereal products.

Storage Stability of Cereals

Study Questions

1. Name some cereal grains eaten in the United States.
2. Identify the bran, germ, and endosperm of a kernel of wheat.
3. How is wheat grain changed by milling?
4. Distinguish between whole grain and refined cereals, and indicate their relative nutritional contributions.
5. What are some reasons for milling cereal grains?

6. Explain the purpose of enriching cereals and name the added nutrients.
7. What is hominy?
8. How are oats processed to produce rolled oats? How do quick-cooking oats differ from regular rolled oats?
9. What is converted rice, and how does it compare nutritionally to white and brown rice?
10. What is triticale?

11. What is semolina, what is its source, and how is it used?
12. How is bulgur wheat produced?
13. What ratio of water to rice is required so that all water is absorbed when rice is properly hydrated and cooked?
14. Starting rice to cook in cold water affects its texture in what way? Why?
15. Starting rice to cook in boiling water affects its texture in what way? Why?
16. Explain the difference in cooking quality between long-grain and short-grain rice.
17. Why is it not advisable to cook rice and pasta in an excess of water that is later discarded?
18. Why do pastas and rice cooked in a large amount of water sometimes appear creamy white or yellow in color?
19. How does browning or toasting rice before steaming affect its nutrient content?
20. What procedure should be used for cooking rice when an acid food is to be added as an ingredient?
21. Why is the protein quality of cereal grains not equal to that of foods from animal sources?
22. Generally, how can the greatest economy be obtained in purchasing cereal products, including pasta and rice?

References

Charley, Helen. *Food Science*. New York: Ronald Press, 1970.

Clause, A. S. "Cereal Grains as Dietary Protein Sources," *Food Technology* 25 (1971): 821.

Davidson, Sir Stanley; Passmore, R.; and Brock, J. F. *Human Nutrition and Dietetics*, 5th ed. Baltimore, Md.: Williams & Wilkins, 1972.

Funk and Wagnalls' Standard Reference Encyclopedia, edited by J. L. Morse. New York: Standard Reference Works, 1963.

Griswold, Ruth. *The Experimental Study of Foods*. Boston: Houghton Mifflin, 1962.

Katz, S. H.; Hediger, M. L.; and Valleroy, L. A. "Traditional Maize Processing Techniques in the New World." *Science* 184 (1974): 765.

Mackey, Andrea C. "Cereals, the Staff of Life, Take on a New Importance in Today's World." In U.S. Department of Agriculture, *Food for Us All*, Yearbook of Agriculture. Washington, D.C.: Government Printing Office, 1969.

Matz, Samuel A. *Cereal Science*. Westport, Conn.: Avi Publishing, 1969.

Moore, A. C. *The Grasses: Earth's Green Wealth*. New York: Macmillan, 1960.

Reitz, L. P., and Barmore, M. A. "The Quality of Cereal Grains." In U.S. Department of Agriculture, *Food*, Yearbook of Agriculture. Washington, D.C.: Government Printing Office, 1959.

Starches and Starch Cookery

Cereal grains and some roots can be processed to yield pure starch. Starch is a common but important ingredient in food preparation.

Composition and Characteristics of Starch

The chemical and physical characteristics of starch determine the characteristics of products prepared from it. All starches are polysaccharides. A *polysaccharide* is composed of many molecules or units of monosaccharides linked together into chains; starch is composed of glucose units. Two major types of polysaccharide chains occur in starch; *amylose* and *amylopectin.*

Amylose is a straight chain with no branches. Amylopectin is a branched-chain polysaccharide. Typical structures of each are shown in Figure 10.1. The proportion of these two polysaccharides is the major factor influencing the characteristics of individual starches. A 5 percent dispersion of amylose heated in water gels when cooled; obtaining a gel with amylopectin requires a 30 percent dispersion. Gels result when bonds form between adjacent polysaccharide chains when starch is heated in water and then cooled. Water that is not absorbed by individual starch granules is trapped in the lattice structure of the gel. The straight chains of amylose form gels more readily because they are able to line up parallel to one another, close enough for bonds to form between them. The branches of amylopectin that project out from the chain prevent this close alignment; therefore, the dis-

Figure 10.1

Diagrams representing (a) a fragment of an amylose molecule and (b) a fragment of an amylopectin molecule.

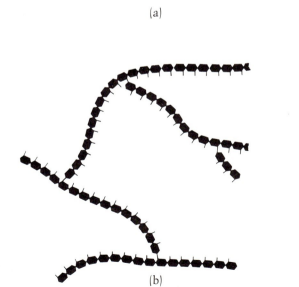

(a)

(b)

tances are too great for crossbonds to form unless a very high concentration of amylopectin exists to pack the chains closer together. When heated in water, amylopectin produces a thick, viscous fluid paste, or sol that is also mucilaginous or stringy.

Most starches, but not all, are composed of varying proportions of these two polysaccharides; a few have only one type of polysaccharide. Starches also differ in the length of their polysaccharide chains, that is, in the number of glucose units that make up the chain.

STARCH PASTES

When starch is mixed with cold water, starch granules gradually settle to the bottom and do not remain dispersed. If the starch and water mixture is heated, the starch granules swell and absorb water, a process called *gelatinization.* The watery starch mixture becomes thick, or viscous, when heated. This thickened starch mixture is called a *paste.* A fluid paste, or one that pours, is a *sol;* all hot pastes are sols. Some hot pastes when cooled form gels, as previously described. Not all pastes gel, however, when they are cooled, in which case they are still known as sols. Gels are rigid or solid pastes; sols are fluid. Long polysaccharide chains form more viscous sols and firmer gels than short polysaccharide chains. As gelatinization proceeds, the paste becomes more translucent. Individual starches differ in the temperature of maximum viscosity and in the degree of translucency.

RETROGRADATION AND SYNERESIS

The formation of a gel is the beginning of *retrogradation.* The longer a gel cools, the firmer it becomes, because more bonds are formed between the polysaccharide chains over a period of time. Thus, retrogradation increases. As more bonds form, the spaces in the lattice become increasingly smaller, causing the water held in the spaces to be squeezed out. This separation of liquid from the gel is known as *syneresis.* A starch paste must retrograde before syneresis can occur, but not all retrograded starches undergo syneresis. Pastes of amylopectin do not retrograde, that is, they do not form rigid gels. Pastes of amylose retrograde readily and often show syneresis.

Retrogradation is a particular problem in starch pastes that are canned and frozen. These products should contain starches that do not retrograde.

TYPES OF STARCHES

Starches differ in many ways. Some form more viscous sols than others, some do not form gels, some are mucilaginous, some are stable to freezing and others are not, and some form pastes that become thinner with extended heating or stirring. All starches are equally digestible, and cooking improves their digestibility.

Arrowroot Starch is obtained from the roots of the arrowroot plant, which is cultivated in the West Indies and Florida. This

Figure 10.2

Manioc or cassava root is used to make tapioca. *(Blue Goose, Inc.)*

starch is not widely used, however, perhaps because pastes made from it become thin if they are heated for too long. The starch also forms a mucilaginous, translucent, brownish-colored paste. Arrowroot forms a gel when it is cooled, and it retrogrades when it is frozen.

Cassava or Tapioca   The roots of the manioc or cassava plant, which is widely cultivated in South America and Africa (Figure 10.2), are grated and eaten as a staple food. Cassava juice is fermented and drunk as a beverage. The starch extracted from this plant is called Brazilian arrowroot, but is not the same as true arrowroot, although the two starches show similar characteristics. The cassava is also grown in Florida, where the whole root is ground and used.

Pearl tapioca is prepared from the starch of the cassava root. The starch is formed into a dough with water; the dough is then forced through a sieve to form pellets or pearls in a process similar to the shaping of pastas. The pellets are then dried at a high temperature. Pearl tapioca requires soaking and a long cooking period to gelatinize. The quick-cooking tapioca that is commonly eaten in the United States is processed by baking cassava dough in thin sheets until they are dry, and then pulverizing them into granules that hydrate readily and gelatinize quickly with heating. Quick-cooking tapioca is often called *minute tapioca.*

Cornstarch   Cornstarch is extracted from corn. Starches obtained from the variety of corn types differ slightly. Regular, but not waxy, cornstarch is sold in retail markets in this country; waxy cornstarch is widely used in the canning and frozen food industries. Regular cornstarch gels and retrogrades; waxy cornstarch does neither, probably because it is largely composed of amylopectin, with little or no amylose. Waxy cornstarch forms a mucilaginous sol that is more viscous than the same concentration of regular cornstarch.

Potato   Potato starch forms a very viscous sol that gels. This sol is not only mucilaginous but also ropy. In addition to the fact that potato starch has a high amylose content, the characteristics of this paste are thought to be related to the presence of phosphorous compounds in the potato that interfere with crossbonding between polysaccharide chains, as well as to the tendency of the amylose chains to fold back on themselves instead of remaining in straight or linear chains. Potato starch pastes are very translucent and retrograde when they are frozen.

Rice   Regular rice starch produces a not very viscous sol and a fragile, weak gel that is not translucent. Very little rice starch is used in the United States, because other starches seem to give more satisfactory results. Waxy rice starch and waxy rice flour were used for frozen products until the advent of modified starches.

Sago   The *pith,* or core, of the sago palm, which is widely grown in Malaya and Indonesia, is the source of sago starch. Starch is washed from the pith of the tree trunk after the tree has been felled and split. This starch is added to some processed foods; otherwise, it is little used in the United States.

Sorghum   Both regular and waxy sorghum starch are almost identical to cornstarch, except that sorghum pastes require heating to a higher temperature for complete gelatinization.

Wheat   The wheat flour that is used for baking in many parts of the world contains protein, starch, fat, pigments, and other substances. Wheat starch can be separated from the other components just as other starches are separated from their natural sources. Wheat flour, however, is more commonly used for thickening than wheat starch. Wheat starch produces a more viscous and a more translucent paste than wheat flour; the protein in the wheat flour contributes to its opacity when it is prepared into a paste. Both wheat starch and wheat flour form weak gels and retrograde readily.

Modified Food Starches   Modified food starches are natural starches whose molecular structure has been chemically altered to make them more satisfactory for particular purposes. A number of such treatments exist, including heating the starch in dilute acid solutions, oxidizing the starch to break it into smaller molecules, adding phosphorus and other compounds to the starch molecule to prevent crossbonding between the chains, and precooking the starch.

These starches do not retrograde; they are better for canning and freezing than waxy starches because they are not mucilaginous. Modified food starches are not sold at retail but are often used in institutional cooking as well as in manufactured foods. The modifications to the starches do not affect their nutritional value or their digestibility. The starches are designated safe for human consumption by the Food and Drug Administration.

Cooking Starch Mixtures

In cooking starch mixtures, a knowledge of ways to disperse the starch in water is necessary, as is a knowledge of the factors that affect the viscosity of starch mixtures.

DISPERSION OF STARCH

If dry starch is added to hot liquid, the starch lumps. Granules of starch on the outside of the lump absorb water and gelatinize, but granules in the center remain dry and ungelatinized. Three effective means of dispersing starch are:

1. Mix the starch with cool or warm, but not hot, liquid. In this method, the starch mixture must be stirred until the starch granules are gelatinized, to prevent clumping and lump formation on the bottom or sides of the pan while heating.
2. Mix the starch with sugar for foods with a high ratio of sugar, such as pudding and pie fillings. When the starch and sugar mixture is added to the liquid, the sugar dissolves and allows the water to surround completely each granule of starch, thus preventing lumping.
3. Mix the starch with fat before dispersing it in water. Fat coats the granules of starch and prevents clumping. Dispersion of starch in fat is called a *roux.* Meat drippings used for this purpose should not be hot if liquid or water is mixed in with the fat.

LIQUIDS USED IN STARCH PASTES

Water and milk are probably the most commonly used liquids in mixtures where starch is the thickening agent. Meat stock and fruit juices are also good liquid mediums. Various forms of milk may be used, from nonfat to thick cream, depending on the flavor desired. Nonfat dry milk can be used with water or meat stock instead of liquid milk. Milk makes starch mixtures opaque; water, stock, and juices produce more translucent pastes.

VISCOSITY OF STARCH PASTES

The viscosity of starch mixtures is affected by a number of factors. The type of starch has already been discussed, but concentration, prebrowning, presence of acid or sugar, speed of gelatinization, and amount of agitation of the starch paste are all factors that affect viscosity.

Concentration of Starch   The major cause of increased viscosity in starch pastes is the swelling of individual starch granules in water when they are heated. Obviously, the more starch granules present, the greater the viscosity will be, to a limit. Because water absorption is necessary to make the starch granules swell, a disproportionately large number of granules can exceed the amount of water available for absorption, thus limiting the extent of swelling by individual starch granules.

Effect of Sugar   Sugar needs water to dissolve in, and the water that dissolves the sugar cannot be absorbed by the starch granules. Thus, sugar competes with the starch granules for available water and causes a corresponding decrease in the viscosity of the starch paste. With very sweet starch pastes, withhold part or all of the sugar until after the starch is fully gelatinized. Even adding the sugar to the cooked starch paste results in some thinning of the paste.

Effect of Acid   Heating starch with acid causes the starch to hydrolyze to smaller polysaccharide molecules. Hydrolysis involves the addition of a molecule of water at a bond between two glucose units in the polysaccharide chain, causing shorter polysaccharide chains to form. The shorter chains have less thickening power than the long-chain polysaccharides. Where acids are combined with starch for flavor, as in a lemon meringue pie filling, the starch should be gelatinized with water first and the acid added after cooking is completed. A higher concentration of starch is often needed in these cases to obtain the desired viscosity.

Effect of Browning   Browning flour is a common practice in preparing gravy to obtain a rich brown color. When dry flour is heated to high temperatures, with or without fat, the polysaccharide molecules are *dextrinized,* that is, they are broken into smaller polysaccharide chains, just as with acid. If the flour or starch is browned before it is combined with liquid, a higher concentration is needed to obtain the desired viscosity; usually, the amount is doubled.

Speed of Heating   The more rapid the heating, the greater the viscosity of the starch paste will be. A starch paste prepared in a double boiler is thinner than the same concentration of starch and liquid cooked over high, direct heat. One reason for using a double boiler is that it prevents scorching of the starch mixture. Starch granules have a great tendency to settle to the bottom of the pan. If high heat is used for cooking starch mixtures, use a pan with a heavy bottom that heats evenly, and stir the mixture rapidly with a utensil that can scrape the starch granules from the bottom of the pan. (A coiled spring stirrer would be appropriate for this.)

Agitation   Although stirring is essential to keep the paste from scorching and lumping, once the starch is gelatinized, the swollen starch granules remain dispersed in the liquid with a lesser tendency to scorch. Gelatinized starch paste requires only occasional agitation. Too much stirring after gelatinization has occurred ruptures the swollen starch granules and causes the paste to thin. Agitating gelatinized potato or tapioca pastes increases their stringiness.

Heating after Gelatinization   Extended heating of a starch paste after the starch has gelatinized causes the swollen granules of starch to rupture and the paste to thin. Starch pastes should be brought to a boil and held at that temperature for 5 minutes or less to obtain maximum viscosity and a cooked flavor. It is better to cool a starch paste and reheat it than to try to keep it hot for long periods.

COMPARISON OF VARIOUS STARCHES   The substitution of one starch for another is possible and often necessary in cases of allergic reaction to a starch or its unavailability. In making substitutions, differences in thickening power, ability to form gels, opacity or translucency, and mucilaginous qualities are all characteristics to consider.

Natural starches have been ranked according to the viscosity of the sols they produce. In order of decreasing viscosity, they are: potato, waxy corn, waxy rice, waxy sorghum, tapioca, arrowroot, sorghum, corn, rice, sago, wheat starch, and wheat flour. In the United States, cornstarch and wheat flour are the most commonly used thickening agents. Wheat flour has the least thickening power of any of the starches. Table 8 in the appendix shows approximate substitutions for some of the starches listed. Generally, about twice as much wheat flour as cornstarch is required to obtain the same thickening power. Wheat flour is usually used for gravies, which characteristically have an opaque appearance. Cornstarch produces more translucent pastes.

PREPARATION OF STARCH PASTES   Preparing starch-thickened mixtures requires specific application of some of the principles of starch cookery previously discussed.

White Sauce   White sauce, probably the most commonly used starch-thickened mixture, is milk thickened with flour. White sauces of different viscosities have various uses in food preparation. Table 10.1 shows the proportions of wheat flour or cornstarch for sauces of varying viscosity, along with uses of the prepared sauces. Fat in a white sauce is optional and is added

Table 10.1 Ratio of starch to liquid for sauces of increasing viscosity and suggested uses

Sauces	Starch per cup of liquid		Use
	Cornstarch (Tbsp)	Wheat flour (Tbsp)	
Thin	½	1	Cream soups, thin gravies
Medium	1	2	Cream meats, vegetables, gravy
Thick	1 ½	3	Soufflés, puddings
Very thick	2	4	Croquettes, puddings

primarily for flavor. Because it contributes so many more calories, fat can easily be omitted where other ingredients, such as cheese, curry, meats, and fish flavor the sauce.

The flour or starch should be mixed well into the warm or cool milk until no lumps are present before heating begins (Figure 10.3). If fat is to be used in the sauce, a roux of fat and starch can be prepared and the hot or cold liquid stirred in. In a white sauce, fat remains better dispersed if it is mixed with the flour. A small amount of fat may be added to the cooked paste. The flour and milk mixture must be heated to the boiling point, however, for maximum gelatinization.

Nonfat dry milk can be stirred into water or other liquid along with dry starch in place of fluid milk. Use ⅓ cup of instant nonfat dry milk for every cup of liquid.

Hot Sauces and Gravies Gravies and hot sauces are prepared and cooked in the same way as white sauces, but milk is replaced partly or wholly by other liquids, such as meat stock, tomato

Figure 10.3

Starch or flour can be dispersed in cool or warm, not hot, liquids. Starch should be mixed into the liquid until no lumps remain before heating begins; an alternative method is to combine starch with a small amount of cool liquid in a cup or shake it with cool liquid in a jar before adding it to hot liquid.

purée or juice, fruit juices, wines, and fresh or sour cream. As with white sauces, fat is not a necessary ingredient in gravies and hot sauces, except for flavor in some instances. Gravy is usually prepared from the juices that drip from meat during roasting, broiling, and pan frying. These juices contain minerals, vitamins, and protein, as well as flavoring substances. Because juices are often encrusted in the pan, water should be added to dissolve and liquefy them (Figure 25.1). If time permits, the stock obtained from meat drippings can be chilled until the fat solidifies and can be lifted off.

Either browned or unbrowned flour may be used to thicken gravy. However, flour does not brown properly in the pan that contains the drippings; a clean pan must be used. Fat can be used to brown flour, although it is not necessary to do so. Heat the flour in a flat pan, stirring continuously over moderate heat until it reaches the desired brownness. If no fat has been added, cool liquid should be added to disperse the browned flour. Whenever a sauce or gravy is too thick, it can be thinned with additional liquid. If it is too thin, thicken it by mixing a small amount of flour with cold liquid before stirring the flour into the hot sauce or gravy. Pan drippings often contain coagulated lumps of meat juices that detract from the gravy's appearance. To break up these lumps, blend the gravy or liquified pan drippings in an electric blender or pass them through a strainer or follow both procedures.

Sauces and gravies can be varied with different liquids and seasonings, such as herbs, spices, onions, garlic, capers, chives, parsley, mushrooms, cheeses, and vegetables of various kinds. Sauces are a foundation of French cookery, and seasonings make them unique. The creative cook, who is familiar with the flavors of various seasonings, tastes sauces and adds seasonings as needed.

Wines add unique flavors to sauces, while adding only a negligible alcohol content. The alcohol in wine begins to evaporate when the sauce is heated to 180°F (82°C), or well below the boiling point. After cooking, little or no alcohol remains.

Dessert Sauces   Either milk or fruit juices usually serve as the liquid in sweetened dessert sauces. Dessert sauces can be thickened either with egg or starch or a combination of both. If acidic fruit juices are used, the starch and water should be cooked first and the acid juice and sugar stirred in afterward. Undiluted frozen concentrated orange juice, lemonade, and other juices are ideal for these sauces because of their rich, natural flavors.

Puddings   Puddings are essentially dessert sauces with a higher concentration of starch, and the method of their preparation is the same. Skin tends to form on the surface of puddings, custards, and sauces when they are cooled because of water loss from the top layer of protein and starch molecules. Prevent or reduce skin formation by covering the hot mixture tightly with plastic wrap after preparation and during chilling. As the mixture cools and evaporation occurs from the surface, moisture condenses on the cover and falls back onto the top surface of the pudding, thus replacing most of the lost water.

Puddings prepared with acidic fruit juices are more subject to syneresis than those prepared with milk. This effect can be reduced if the acidic pudding mixture is not prepared too far in advance of serving. Undercooking can also increase syneresis in starch paste.

Processed Starch Products

Puddings and sauces are available as dry mixes and canned products, and are often components of many frozen products. Regular dry pudding mixes contain starch, sugar, and flavoring ingredients premeasured; the mix is added to milk and cooked. Instant puddings contain pregelatinized starch—starch that has been cooked and then dried—along with sugar and flavoring. It is whipped into cold milk; no cooking is needed. Canned puddings utilize modified food starches that will not retrograde. Flavor and cost comparisons of these puddings with a comparable one made fresh from the basic ingredients often prove the fresh puddings to be superior on both counts.

Comparison of canned sauces and gravies with freshly prepared ones yields similar results. Skill in the preparation of canned products would limit the benefits of the convenience that leads many people to use them.

Storage of Starch and Starch Pastes

Pure starches, such as corn, arrowroot, and tapioca, have unlimited storage life and are stable in almost all climates and at all temperatures. These products are also not likely to become infested with insects. The stability of these products results from their negligible content of fat and protein.

Cooked pastes can be stored in the refrigerator for a few days. Puddings tend to become firmer and syneresis increases if they are made with regular cornstarch. Gravies and sauces form a gel, and heating with stirring returns them to their sol state. If they are frozen, gravies and sauces retrograde, but heating restores them to a sol.

Nutritional Quality of Starch Pastes

Table 10.2 shows the nutrient composition of cornstarch, tapioca, and wheat flour; other starches are similar in their nutrient content. Pure starch is almost entirely carbohydrate, with a small amount of water; its primary nutritional contribution is calories. The other foods and ingredients used in starch mixtures can contribute minerals, vitamins, and possible protein needed in the diet. Sauces and puddings can be empty-calorie foods unless the fat and sugar in these dishes is limited and ingredients rich in nutrients are added whenever possible.

Table 10.2 Nutrient composition of representative starches in 100-gram amounts, uncooked

Starches (uncooked)	Water (%)	Calories	Protein (g)	Fat (g)	Total carbohydrate (g)	Calcium (mg)	Phosphorous (mg)
Cornstarch	12	362	0.3	trace	87.6	0	0
Tapioca	12.6	352	0.6	0.2	86.4	10	18
Wheat flour, enriched	12	364	10.5	1.0	76.1	16	87

Starches (uncooked)	Iron (mg)	Sodium (mg)	Potassium (mg)	Thiamin (mg)	Vitamin B$_2$ (mg)	Niacin (mg)
Cornstarch	0	trace	trace	0	0	0
Tapioca	0.4	3	18	0	0	0
Wheat flour, enriched	2.9	2	95	0.44	0.26	3.5

SOURCE: U.S. Department of Agriculture, *Composition of Foods.*

Study Questions

1. What is starch?
2. Name the characteristics of, and the differences between, amylose and amylopectin.
3. What is a starch paste?
4. How is starch gelatinized? How does gelatinization affect starch?
5. What is syneresis? What causes syneresis?
6. How do waxy starches differ from regular starches?
7. What are modified food starches? Why are they preferred to waxy starches in frozen and canned products?
8. How do wheat flour and cornstarch differ in thickening power and in the translucency of pastes made from them?
9. Briefly describe three methods of dispersing starch to prevent lumping.
10. Explain how and why sugar affects the viscosity of starch paste.
11. Explain how and why acid affects the viscosity of starch pastes. When should acid ingredients be added in preparing starch pastes?
12. How is the viscosity of a starch paste affected when it is cooked in a double boiler? By direct heat on a surface unit?
13. Why should cooked starch pastes not be heated too long?
14. What is a roux? How it is used in preparing sauces and gravies?
15. Briefly distinguish between dessert sauces and puddings.
16. What causes skin formation on the surface of puddings and sauces? How can skin formation be prevented?

References

Davidson, Sir Stanley; Passmore, R.; and Brock, J. F. *Human Nutrition and Dietetics.* 7th ed. Baltimore, Md.: Williams & Wilkins, 1979.

Funk and Wagnalls' Standard Reference Encyclopedia, edited by J. L. Morse. New York: Standard Reference Works Publishing, 1963.

Osman, Elizabeth. "Starch and Other Polysaccharides." In *Food Theory and Applications,* edited by Pauline C. Paul and Helen H. Palmer. New York: Wiley, 1972.

Ingredients in Flour Mixtures

Figure 11.1
Gluten can be isolated from flour in the following way: mix flour and water to form a soft dough, then knead the dough until it becomes very elastic. Wash the starch from the dough by working the dough under a gentle stream of cool water until the water runs clear. The gluten appears in the form shown.

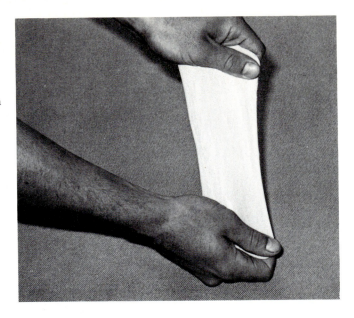

Flour is the basic ingredient of breads, cakes, cookies, and pastries. The type of flour, as well as the kinds and amounts of other ingredients, determines the characteristics of these baked products. In most baked products, ingredients such as sugar, fat, eggs, and liquids perform similar functions.

Wheat Flour

Wheat flour is the only flour that forms *gluten* when it is *hydrated*, or mixed with water. Various types of wheat flours are produced according to the type of wheat and the manner in which it is milled. Gluten results from the hydration of two proteins in wheat flour, *gliadin* and *glutenin* (Figure 11.1). Flour with a high-protein content yields more gluten than low-protein flour.

The variety of wheat influences its protein content. Hard wheat has a high-protein content and, therefore, a high-gluten potential of good quality and strength. Soft wheat flour yields small amounts of gluten of a weak quality.

MILLING WHEAT FLOUR

Both the structure of a wheat kernel and the milling that separates the bran and germ from the endosperm are discussed in Chapter 9. Milling wheat to produce flour is a complex process that can only be briefly described here.

The endosperm of a wheat grain is not uniform throughout; the outer layers have a high-protein content that decreases toward the center of the grain. Conversely, the starch content is highest in the center of the grain and decreases toward the outer layers. During milling, wheat grains are crushed between a series

Table 11.1   Composition of various types of wheat flour, classified according to their baking purpose

Flour	Protein (%)	Fat (%)	Carbohydrate (%)	Ash (%)
Whole wheat (hard)	13.3	2.0	71.0	1.7
Bread (hard)	11.8	1.2	74.5	0.46
All-purpose	10.5	1.0	76.1	0.43
Pastry (soft)	9.7	1.0	76.9	0.42
Cake (soft)	7.5	0.8	79.4	0.31

of steel rollers. They are then bolted, or sieved, to separate the coarse particles from the finer ones. The softer, starchy center of the endosperm crushes readily and becomes almost powdery; the outer portions of the endosperm with their high protein content resist crushing and form coarse particles. When the crushed product is sieved, the fine, powdery part passes through the sieve and the coarse particles remain. In this way, parts of the endosperm can be separated according to their protein content and gluten potential. The bran and germ of wheat, although they contain protein, do not have gluten potential.

TYPES OF FLOURS

Flours of specific fineness or coarseness with a specific protein content can be produced for specific purposes. Generally, flours are classified according to the product for which they are designed. The composition of different flours is shown in Table 11.1, and gluten balls from three different flours are shown in Figure 11.2.

Figure 11.2

Gluten isolated from three types of flour, both raw and baked.
Left to right: gluten from pastry flour, all-purpose flour, and bread flour.
(Wheat Flour Institute)

Bread Flour   Bread flour, prepared from hard wheat, is milled so that a large proportion of the high-protein outer layers of the endosperm remain in the flour. Yeast breads require a flour with a high gluten potential of good quality.

All-Purpose Flour   All-purpose flours have many different characteristics. As their name implies, these flours may be used to make any baked product. They are prepared either from soft wheat or from a mixture of hard and soft wheat and are milled so that neither the very center nor the extreme outer layers of the endosperm remain. Thus, these flours are intermediate in their protein content and gluten potential. Yeast breads made with all-purpose flour do not have the same qualities as those made with bread flour, but they are acceptable. Cakes prepared from all-purpose flour are likewise less desirable than those made from cake flour, but most are satisfactory. Because considerable variation exists in the gluten potential of all-purpose flours, different brands can be compared to find the one that best meets a specific baking requirement.

Pastry Flour   Pastry flour is prepared from soft wheat flour, and it includes the same portions of the endosperm as all-purpose flour. However, pastry flour has a slightly lower protein content and gluten quality than most all-purpose flours. As the name implies, it is intended for pastry where some gluten content is needed, but it can also be used for many quick breads.

Cake Flour   Cake flour is milled only from soft wheat and the center portion of the endosperm. It has a low-gluten content of weak quality. Cake flour is intended for very fine shortened and sponge cakes and is unsatisfactory for most other baked products.

Whole Wheat Flour   To be labeled "whole wheat," flour must contain all parts of the wheat kernel: bran, germ, and endosperm. The type of wheat from which the flour is milled determines its use in baking. Whole wheat bread flour is milled from hard wheat; whole wheat pastry flour is milled from soft wheat. A whole wheat all-purpose flour is milled from a blend of soft and hard wheat flours. Flours in which the bran is very finely ground are preferable for baking many products, because coarsely ground bran cuts gluten strands, weakening the structure and giving a coarse texture to breads.

AGING, OXIDATION, AND BLEACHING OF FLOURS

Freshly milled flour is not suitable for baking, because it produces baked products of very poor quality. *Aging*, or holding flour for several weeks or months, improves its baking quality, but this is a costly process. Today, most flours are treated with chemicals that accomplish the same results as aging. These chemicals have various names and slightly different effects. Flour improvers, or maturing agents, do not bleach the pigments in the flour but do improve the elasticity and strength of the flour's gluten potential. Bleaching, or oxidizing, agents oxidize the anthoxanthin pigments in flour so that they will be white rather than creamy white or yellow. Chemical aging of flour is more uniform and effective than natural aging. Some of these chemical agents destroy some vitamin E in flours, but not B vitamins. They are nontoxic and their use is permitted by the Food and Drug Administration.

PURPOSE OF FLOUR IN BAKED PRODUCTS

Flour is a structural ingredient in baked products. The elastic gluten in dough stretches to form the typical cell structure of most baked products; during baking, protein coagulates and starch gelatinizes to form the final stable structure.

USE OF FLOUR IN BAKED PRODUCTS

The ratios of starch and protein, the presence of bran and germ, and the fineness of division of flour particles affect the weight of flour necessary to fill a standard measuring cup. Table 11.2 lists the weights of 1 cup of various flours when it is filled with sifted flour or when the flour is stirred and spooned into the measure, as described in Chapter 3.

Other Ingredients in Baked Products

Although flours are the principal ingredient in baked products, other ingredients, such as eggs, sugar, fat, and liquid, serve a variety of functions in the final product. Different flours and grains add flavor and nutrients in these mixtures.

OTHER FLOURS AND GRAINS

Other types of flours and grains are used in many baked products for flavor and also for their nutritional contributions. All flours, with the exception of rye, lack the proteins to form gluten, and, therefore, cannot be used as the only flour in the product. Some of these flour substitutes include cornmeal, rice flour, soy flour, rolled oats, lima bean flour, buckwheat, peanut flour, rye flour, and wheat germ.

Table 11.2   Weight of 1 cup of various types of wheat flour

Type of flour	Grams per cup (237 ml)
Cake, sifted	96
Cake, spooned	111
Pastry, sifted	100
Bread, sifted	112
All-purpose, sifted	115
All-purpose, spooned	125
Whole wheat, stirred	132

Most substitute flours can be used in fair amounts in chemically leavened baked products with no deleterious effect on the quality of the product. Yeast breads lose quality if too much flour with no gluten potential is added, because gluten formation is essential for good volume and texture in yeast-leavened products. When substituted for part of the wheat flour, these flours dilute the amount of gluten available for structure, and some cause deterioration of the gluten supplied by the wheat flour.

Soy Flour   Soy flour is used primarily to improve the nutrient quality of baked products; it is a good source of *lysine,* the limiting amino acid of wheat. Soybean flour has a very high protein content, but the proteins lack elasticity and, additionally, reduce the elasticity of the gluten protein of wheat flour when the two are combined. This effect can be counteracted in yeast breads if soybean flour is added after the yeast dough has fermented. Coarsely ground soy flour is better for this purpose than finely ground flour. Replacing 1 to 3 percent of wheat flour with soy flour offers the following advantages: it inhibits staleness, its antioxidant effect inhibits rancidity, it provides improved crumb structure and texture, and it increases the nutritional quality of the baked product.

Rye Flour   Rye flour has the gliadin and glutenin proteins found in wheat, but it also contains some vegetable gums that seem to interfere with the formation of gluten from these proteins when the flour is hydrated. Yeast breads prepared only from rye flour are compact and heavy; most commercial rye breads have a large proportion of wheat flour. Doughs prepared from rye flour are plastic, but not elastic. Better rye breads result when a sourdough organism for producing leavening gas is substituted for the usual baker's yeast. Pumpernickel is a sourdough rye bread.

Triticale   A hybrid of wheat and rye, triticale flour has much less gluten potential than wheat flour, but the nutritional quality and quantity of protein in triticale exceeds that of either rye or wheat. Triticale is reported to improve the flavor and shelf life of baked products. It has been tested in most products with one part triticale to two parts wheat flour. In yeast breads, triticale works better if additional gluten flour is added to strengthen the deficient gluten potential of triticale.

Gluten Flour   Gluten flour finds its greatest use in yeast breads for adding to the gluten potential when flours with weak gluten potential are used.

Corn Flour and Meal   Corn flour and meal, which are lacking in gluten potential, are usually combined with wheat flour in baked products. Corn flour is more finely ground than the meal. Both add flavor to baked products; in addition, the meal adds texture.

Wheat Germ   Wheat germ is added primarily to improve the nutritional quality of baked products. Replacing more than 3 percent of wheat flour with wheat germ decreases quality in yeast breads, because wheat germ contains a substance that weakens the dough's gluten. Toasting the wheat germ before adding it to yeast bread dough offsets this effect.

Potato Flour   Potato flour or granules accelerate fermentation in yeast breads by supplying additional carbohydrate. Potato granules increase loaf volume, while potato flour decreases volume. Liquid in which potatoes have been cooked, or mashed potatoes, have been used in home baking for the same reasons.

The many functions of eggs in baked products include the **EGGS** following:

1. Their protein coagulates when heated, providing structure.
2. Both lecithin and protein in eggs serve as emulsifying agents.
3. Because they are 75 percent water, eggs are a source of liquid.
4. They foam readily and incorporate air to improve leavening.
5. They contribute flavor, color, and nutrients.

The functions of eggs in specific baked products are discussed in Chapter 19. Unless otherwise noted, most recipes are designed for large eggs. The substitution of larger or smaller eggs can cause unsatisfactory results. When the amount of egg is critical in a recipe, an exact measure should be used, for even eggs of the same size show some variation.

Egg substitutes, which are also described in Chapter 19, or egg whites can be used to replace whole eggs in all quick breads except cream puffs when low-cholesterol products are desired. Two egg whites or ¼ cup of egg substitute are equivalent to one whole egg.

Besides providing sweetness, sugar is a tenderizing ingredient in **SWEETENERS** baked products. It competes with gluten-forming proteins and starch for available water, preventing full hydration of these two components under certain circumstances. Because both gluten and starch are structure-forming components, inhibiting their development increases tenderness. Greater amounts of sugar also increase browning in baked products. Granulated sugar helps incorporate air into mixtures when it is creamed with fat and eggs, and is important in stabilizing egg-white foams. Yeast uses sugar to produce carbon dioxide gas for leavening yeast breads. Many baked products, however, do not contain sugar.

Honey produces more browning than sugar, because the fructose and glucose in honey brown more readily than sucrose does. Honey, syrup, and molasses can sometimes be used as sweeteners in baked products. Do not directly substitute these liquid sweeteners for table sugar, or sucrose, without adjusting the amount of liquid in the recipe, for they contain varying amounts of water.

Artificial sweeteners, such as saccharin and a mixture of saccharin and lactose, can be used in some baked products in place of part or all of the sugar when needed for medical or other reasons. Muffins and short bread made with an artificial sweetener are quite satisfactory. Yeast breads need enough sugar for yeast activity; additional sweetness can be provided by using an artificial sweetener. Other baked products would need to be tested to determine what proportion of the sugar could be replaced with an artificial sweetener.

FAT Fat is a more effective tenderizing agent than sugar. It inhibits the formation of gluten by coating flour particles and interfering with their hydration. Fats also produce crispness in some products as well as flavor.

Figure 11.3
Nonfat dry milk can be blended with the other dry ingredients in most baked products with water or juice used as the liquid. *(United Dairy Industry Association)*

Both liquid and solid fats may be used in baked products. Specific forms of fats and oils are preferred for specific products. Oil coats flour particles better than fat and inhibits gluten development almost completely. Some recipes call for melted solid fat; oil can often be used instead. A given measure of solid fat occupies a larger volume when it is melted, so it is important to note whether a recipe specifies "1 cup of butter, melted" or "1 cup of melted butter"; the former provides for slightly more fat than the latter.

LIQUIDS

The water in liquids in baked products is necessary for several reasons:

1. It hydrates the starch and gluten-forming proteins in flour.
2. It is a solvent for salts, leavening agents, and sugar.
3. It forms steam for leavening.

The most commonly used liquid in baked products is milk—fresh, canned, or dried; cream, whole, low fat, or nonfat; or cultured. Lactose and protein in milk increase the browning of baked products. Milk provides a softer crumb, which is less subject to going stale, than water. The most economical form of milk is nonfat dry milk, which does not need to be reconstituted but can be combined directly with the dry ingredients, with water substituted as the liquid (Figure 11.3). Many baked products tolerate additional nonfat dry milk for nutritional enrichment with no adverse effects on their eating quality.

Fruit juices can be added for flavor or to supply acid for freeing the carbon dioxide from baking soda. A few baked products contain water with no form of milk.

SALT

The only function of salt in most baked products is to provide flavor. In yeast breads, however, salt retards yeast activity. Salt-free yeast breads have a coarser texture than breads made from the same formula with added salt. Table fats contain salt; if they are used in place of other fats in products containing large proportions of fat, such as cream puffs and pie dough, the amount of salt may need to be correspondingly reduced.

Nutritional Value of Flours

The nutrients of some flours used in baked products are shown in Table 11.3. Some have a much higher protein, vitamin, and mineral content than wheat flour, but because these flours produce poor eating quality in most baked products, they can only be used to replace small amounts of wheat flour. Even this small replacement, however, improves the nutrient quality of the bread. Soybean flour is a particularly good addition to wheat, because it supplements and improves the protein quality of wheat breads.

Table 11.3 Nutrient composition of flours and meals
in baked products, 100-gram amounts

Flour or meal	Protein (g)	Fat (g)	Carbo-hydrate (g)	Calcium (mg)	Phosphorus (mg)	Iron (mg)	Thiamin (mg)	Ribo-flavin (mg)	Niacin (mg)	Pyri-doxine (mg)	Pantothenic acid (mg)
Buckwheat, light	6.4	1.2	79.5	11	88	1.0	0.08	0.04	0.4	—	—
Cornmeal, degerminated, enriched	7.9	1.2	78.4	6	99	2.9	0.44	0.26	3.5	0.250	0.580
Lima bean	21.5	1.4	63.0	—	—	—	—	—	—	—	—
Rolled oats	14.2	7.4	68.2	53	405	4.5	0.60	0.14	1.0	0.140	1.500
Peanut, defatted	47.9	9.2	31.5	104	720	3.5	0.75	0.22	27.8	—	—
Potato flour	8.0	0.8	79.9	33	178	17.2	0.42	0.14	3.4	0.008	0.720
Rye, light	9.4	1.0	77.9	22	185	1.1	0.15	0.07	0.6	0.090	2.220
Soy, defatted	47.0	0.9	38.1	265	655	11.1	1.09	0.34	2.6	0.724	1.100
Wheat, whole, hard	13.3	2.0	71.0	41	372	3.3	0.55	0.12	4.3	0.340	—
Wheat, all-purpose enriched	10.5	1.0	76.1	16	87	2.9	0.44	0.26	3.5	0.060	0.465
Wheat germ, crude	26.6	10.9	46.7	72	1118	9.4	2.01	0.68	4.2	1.150[a]	1.200[a]

SOURCE: In U.S. Department of Agriculture, *Composition of Foods; Pantothenic Acid, Vitamin B₆ and Vitamin B₁₂ in Foods.*
[a] Value for toasted wheat germ.

1. Why is wheat flour preferred for most baked products?
2. Distinguish between hard and soft wheat in gluten potential.
3. How does the milling of flour control its gluten content?
4. Rank the following flours according to gluten potential: cake, bread, all-purpose, and pastry. Indicate how each is used.
5. Why are bleaching, oxidizing, and flour-improving agents added to flours?
6. What are some advantages and disadvantages of soy flour as a replacement for some of the wheat flour in yeast bread?
7. Why is yeast bread that is prepared only from rye flour heavy and compact?
8. Why is it necessary to limit the amount of wheat germ in yeast bread?
9. What are some functions of eggs in baked products?
10. How does sugar act as a tenderizing agent in baked products?
11. How does fat act as a tenderizing agent in baked products?
12. What are some functions of liquids in baked products?

References

Campbell, Ada Marie. "Flour." In *Food Theory and Applications,* edited by Pauline C. Paul and Helen H. Palmer. New York: Wiley, 1971.
——, M. P. Penfield, and R. M. Griswold. *The Experimental Study of Foods.* Boston: Houghton Mifflin, 1979.
Lowe, Belle. *Experimental Cookery.* 4th ed. New York: Wiley, 1964.

Potter, Norman N. *Food Science.* 2nd ed. Westport, Conn.: Avi Publishing, 1973.
Pyler, E. J. *Baking Science and Technology,* vols. 1, 2. Chicago: Siebel Publishing, 1973.
Sweetman, M. D., and MacKellar, Ingeborg. *Food Selection and Preparation.* 4th ed. New York: Wiley, 1964.

Leavening Agents in Baked Products

A *leaven* is a substance that causes a dough or batter to become light and porous. Three gases leaven baked products: carbon dioxide (CO_2), air, and steam. Carbon dioxide gas may be produced by either a chemical or a biological leavening agent; air is trapped in batters and doughs in a number of ways; steam is formed from water in the mixtures when they are heated.

Air as a Leavening Gas

Air is trapped in batters and doughs when whole eggs, egg whites, or egg yolks are whipped into a foam that is combined with other ingredients to form a batter. Air in egg foams produces almost half the leavening of sponge cakes. A large amount of air can be incorporated into a creamed mixture when fat, sugar, and egg are beaten vigorously, especially if the fat or shortening contains an emulsifier. Shortened cakes depend on this creamed mixture for adequate leavening. Most hydrogenated shortenings contain about 12 percent air. Air can also be trapped on the face of sugar crystals in mixtures. Some air is incorporated into heavy batters and doughs by vigorous mixing alone.

Sifting flour before adding it to the other ingredients incorporates little or no air into batters and doughs. Air separates the granules of flour when it is sifted, temporarily preventing them from packing down, but the granules of flour cannot retain the air when they are combined in a liquid mixture. Thin batters, such as popover batter, are incapable of either trapping or holding air.

The main effect of incorporated air as a leavening gas is obtained when the batter or dough is heated. Heating causes the air to expand about one-third in volume. Air is never the only leavening gas in baked products; it is always present in combination with one or both of the other gases which expand the air cells or pockets even further.

Steam as a Leavening Gas

Steam is the only leaven in many baked products. The amount of leavening possible with steam depends on the ratio of flour to water in the batter or dough. In a thin batter, found in popovers, Yorkshire pudding, and cream puffs, a ratio of 1 cup of liquid per 1 cup of flour is used. These products expand considerably because the large amount of water produces a great deal of steam. Puff pastry and pie pastry are doughs with considerably less liquid; they produce much less steam, which separates the layers of the dough only slightly.

Some baked products, commonly called "unleavened" breads, are actually leavened by steam. These products include tortillas, chapaties, puris, and matzos. Steam from water in the eggs furnishes over half of the leavening gas in sponge cakes.

Water expands from 1,600 to 1,800 times its original volume when it is converted to steam. Because much of the steam produced in baked products is lost by evaporation, this amount of expansion does not occur in actual practice. Some steam leavening occurs in all baked products, however, because all baked products contain liquid.

Chemical Leavening Agents
BAKING SODA

Baking soda, also known as sodium bicarbonate ($NaHCO_3$), releases carbon dioxide gas in various ways from a number of different chemical leavening agents. To obtain the maximum yield of carbon dioxide gas from baking soda, an acid ingredient must be used with it. Some carbon dioxide gas can be obtained when baking soda is heated in the presence of water, but the chemicals formed from this chemical reaction produce bitter, soapy flavors and an alkaline medium in the baked product. The alkaline medium causes the anthoxanthin pigments in flour to turn yellowish, produces a coarse texture in the baked product, and increases the browning of the product. Because of these undesirable changes, avoid adding too much baking soda to baked products. Using sufficient acid with baking soda to release all the carbon dioxide gas produces an optimal leavening of the product during baking, and no undesirable chemicals form to affect adversely the flavor, color, or texture of the product.

Acid Ingredients Buttermilk or sour milk is a common acid ingredient to use with baking soda in leavening batters and doughs. One cup of either of these cultured milks contains enough acid to release the carbon dioxide from ½ teaspoon of baking soda. One cup of molasses or fruit, such as applesauce, also contains enough acid to release the CO_2 from ½ teaspoon of baking soda. Some recipes call for baking soda when honey, corn syrup, and brown sugar are the only sources of acid in the mixture. Because the acidity of these three sweeteners is variable and cannot be depended upon to supply sufficient acid to release all of the carbon dioxide in the baking soda, undesirable chemicals can be produced in the product. In such recipes, baking powder, rather than baking soda, should be the leavening agent.

BAKING POWDERS

Baking soda is also the source of carbon dioxide gas in baking powders, but baking powders include an acid or an acid-forming ingredient and starch, an inert ingredient. Baking powders are thus balanced to supply sufficient acid to release all carbon dioxide gas from the baking soda. Baking powder brands contain different types of acid-supplying ingredients. Some are soluble at room temperature and begin producing carbon dioxide as soon as water is added; others do not react with the baking soda to produce leavening gas until they are heated. Table 12.1 gives the acid ingredients of various brands of baking powder.

Standardization of Baking Powders Regardless of the acid-forming ingredient present, all baking powders are required by federal

Table 12.1   Acids and acid-forming ingredients found in various brands of baking powder

Retail brand[a]	Acid or acid-forming ingredient		Type of baking powder	Type of action
	Name	Chemical formula		
Calumet[b] Clabber Girl Crescent[c] Davis OK Hearth Club KC[c]	Sodium aluminum sulfate and monocalcium phosphate monohydrate	$Na_2SO_4 \cdot Al_2(SO_4)_3$ and $Ca(H_2PO_4)_2 \cdot H_2O$	SAS-phosphate	Double
Happy Family Jewel	Monocalcium phosphate anhydrous	$Ca(H_2PO_4)_2$	Anhydrous phosphate	Quick
Dr. Price Rumford	Monocalcium phosphate monohydrate	$Ca(H_2PO_4)_2 \cdot H_2O$	Phosphate	Quick
Royal Swansdown	Cream of tartar and tartaric acid	$KHC_4H_4O_6$ and $H_2C_4H_4O_6$	Tartrate	Quick

SOURCE: Vail, et al: *Foods*, 6th edition. Copyright © 1973 by Houghton Mifflin Company. Adapted by permission of the publisher.
[a]All the baking powders listed contain baking soda ($NaHCO_3$) as a source of carbon dioxide gas.
[b]Contains calcium sulfate.
[c]Contains calcium carbonate.

regulation to yield a minimum of 12 percent carbon dioxide. Most are formulated to yield 14 percent or more carbon dioxide, to provide for loss of activity during storage. The starch and calcium carbonate in baking powders are inert ingredients that fill out the volume so that a given measure of any baking powder provides the same amount of carbon dioxide. The inert ingredients also absorb moisture and separate the baking soda and acid ingredients so that they do not react.

Quick-Acting Baking Powders   Quick-acting baking powders contain acids or acid-forming ingredients that are readily soluble and, with the addition of liquid, react with baking soda at room temperature. These are the tartrate- and phosphate-containing powders shown in Table 12.1 (Baking soda combined with an acid ingredient, such as sour milk, is also a fast-acting leavening.) When quick-acting baking powders are used, the product must be quickly mixed and baked to prevent an excessive loss of leavening gas before baking. The gas must be available during baking to produce the product's desired porosity, before heat coagulates the protein and gelatinizes starch to solidify the structure. If too much gas is lost before baking begins, the product will not be sufficiently leavened during baking and it will become compact and heavy.

Double-Acting Baking Powders   Slow-acting, acid-forming salts are salts that do not react with baking soda until they are heated with liquid. Sodium aluminum sulfate is a slow-acting, acid-forming ingredient. No baking powder on the market uses this acid-forming salt as its only source of acid; instead, slow- and fast-acting ingredients are combined to produce "double-acting" baking powders, so called because sodium aluminum sulfate salt does not react until it is heated, and phosphate salt reacts at room temperature. Extended mixing time or allowing the product to sit before baking does not usually cause adverse effects in batters and doughs containing double-acting baking powders. A disadvantage of slow-acting, acid-forming ingredients, however, is that heat starts to set the structure of the product before the gas is fully evolved, an action that can cause the crust of the baked product to crack as the gas finally evolves. Double-acting leavenings leave a slightly bitter flavor in the products in which they are used.

Amount of Baking Powder   The amount of baking powder in a given product is determined by the amount of flour. The American Home Economics Association's *Handbook of Food Preparation* recommends 1¼ to 2 teaspoons of baking powder per cup of flour. Because of the ease with which gas is lost from quick-acting powders, it is generally recommended that the larger amount of quick-acting powders be used. Baked products containing egg need less chemical leavening because egg can incorporate some air into the mixture to provide part of the leavening.

Stability and Use of Baking Powders   Some acid ingredients in baking powders react at room temperature when they are combined with water. This reaction can also occur in a container of baking powder on the shelf if moisture from the air comes in contact with its contents. Baking powder containers must therefore be kept tightly closed to prevent loss of their leavening capacity. Lumps in baking powder indicate that moisture has been present and that some reaction of ingredients has occurred. Depending on the extent of the reaction, the powder may have lost some of its leavening activity and can no longer produce optimal leavening in baked products. Baking powder should be purchased in small amounts that can be used before it deteriorates. Containers of baking powder should be kept tightly closed to prolong storage life.

Baking powder and baking soda tend to pack down and should be stirred before measurements are made. Dip the measuring spoon into the leavening, fill it to overflowing, and level it off.

Always combine lump-free chemical leavenings with the other dry ingredients; never stir them into the liquid ingredients, because this results in an excessive loss of leavening gas.

One teaspoon of baking powder produces the same amount of carbon dioxide gas as ¼ teaspoon of baking soda. If a recipe requires 2 teaspoons of baking powder per cup of flour, then ½ teaspoon of baking soda will replace the baking powder if 1 cup of sour milk or acidic fruit is added to supply the acid. Substitution is usually called for in the other direction. For instance, a recipe calls for baking soda and sour milk, but only sweet milk is available. Sweet milk can be substituted in this case if baking powder is used instead of baking soda. If the recipe calls for 1 teaspoon of baking soda for 2 cups of flour, then 4 teaspoons of baking powder are necessary to provide the same amount of leavening gas.

Homemade baking powder can be prepared by combining 2 teaspoons of baking soda, 5 teaspoons of cream of tartar, and 1 teaspoon of cornstarch. One teaspoon of this mixture is equivalent to 1 teaspoon of any quick-acting baking powder.

SUBSTITUTIONS OF BAKING POWDER AND BAKING SODA

A baked product can be inadequately leavened because not enough baking powder or baking soda was added, or because carbon dioxide was lost from the product before baking began. Not enough leavening gas causes a compact low volume, a fine grain, and possibly a soggy texture in the baked product. The effects of too much leavening, however, depend partly on whether baking soda or baking powder was used. Some of the effects noted for baking soda with insufficient acid to release carbon dioxide gas can occur if baking soda is the leavening. Too much baking powder causes a coarse grain, bad flavor, excessive surface browning, and a less than white interior color in the baked product.

TOO MUCH OR TOO LITTLE CHEMICAL LEAVENING

Biological leavening agents are living organisms, such as yeast and bacteria, which contain enzymes that catalyze the chemical reactions that ferment glucose and produce carbon dioxide gas. Each organism individually influences the flavor and other characteristics of bread.

Biological Leavening Agents

The yeast used by bakers for leavening bread is *Saccharomyces cerevisiae.* A yeast cell is covered with a membrane that allows the passage of food and water into the cell and prevents the loss of cell constituents from the cell. The process by which yeast uses glucose to produce carbon dioxide and alcohol is called *fermentation* and, except that different kinds of yeast are used, is the same process employed for the production of alcoholic beverages. Fermentative spoilage of fruits occurs in a similar manner. Acids and other substances produced in minute amounts during fermentation contribute to the flavor of bread. Wild yeasts, which are plentiful in the air, produce undesirable flavors in breads.

BAKER'S YEAST

Even though yeasts utilize only glucose in fermentation, they contain enzymes that convert fructose to glucose and hydrolyze maltose and sucrose to their constituent monosaccharides. Yeast has no enzymes that can hydrolyze lactose, or milk sugar. Suitable sources of sugar for yeast fermentation include table sugar, honey, corn syrup, molasses, or any product that contains these sugars. The diastase enzyme in flour can convert some of its starch to maltose, but this is not an adequate source of sugar for yeast activity to leaven breads; some additional form of sugar, besides the maltose in flour, is needed.

FERMENTATION   During fermentation, yeast cells multiply using glucose as a source of food. The more active yeast cells become in a dough, the more rapidly carbon dioxide is produced for leavening the dough, under ideal conditions.

Temperature   Besides needing an adequate source of food, the yeast plant can grow and multiply only within a limited temperature range. At refrigerator and freezer temperatures, yeast multiplication is slowed or stopped; above 105°F (40.5°C), yeast organisms are destroyed at an increasing rate until complete destruction occurs at 140°F (60°C). Fermentation of yeast doughs around 85 to 90°F (30 to 32°C) yields the best flavored breads. Above this temperature, wild yeast and other undesirable organisms are more likely to thrive; lower temperatures take too long to achieve good results.

pH   Fermentation proceeds best at pH 4 to pH 6, although yeast can multiply to some extent between pH 2.7 to pH 7.4. A slightly acid dough is best for active fermentation. Some acid is produced by yeast during fermentation.

Other Requirements   To thrive, yeast also needs nutrients such as vitamins, minerals, and nitrogenous compounds. Too much salt or sugar exert an osmotic effect on yeast, causing the yeast cells to dehydrate or lose water and thus effectively inactivating them.

MARKET FORMS OF YEAST   Two forms of baking yeast are available: compressed cake yeast and active dry yeast. Both are suitable for yeast doughs.

Compressed Yeast   Cake yeast is more perishable than dry yeast and can be held for only a short time; it must be refrigerated or frozen. Mold grows readily on compressed yeast; if the yeast is badly contaminated with mold, it should be discarded. A small spot of mold on the outside of the cake, however, can be removed and the cake used with no bad effects.

A yeast cake weighs 14 grams, or ½ ounce; it measures 1 slightly rounded tablespoon when pressed into a spoon. Bakeries purchase cake yeast in bulk quantities of ½ pound or more. One cake of yeast ferments one to two loaves of bread. It should be dissolved in lukewarm liquid for use in a dough.

Active Dry Yeast   Active dry yeast is usually packaged in vacuum-sealed foil envelopes containing 7 grams, or about ¼ ounce, of granulated dried yeast cells, measuring 1 level tablespoon. Active dry yeast keeps several months at room temperature and several years in a freezer; it is also available in bulk amounts. Dry yeast must be rehydrated at temperatures between 105 to 115°F (40.5 to 46°C).

When yeast cells are dried, their outer membranes are altered. If the dried yeast cells are rehydrated in a cool to warm liquid, the membrane becomes porous, allowing the cell constituents to pass out of the cell. Glutathione, a tripeptide inside the cell, passes out of the cell and has a weakening effect on the gluten.

Rehydration of the dried yeast at 105 to 115°F (40.5 to 46°C) reduces the loss of glutathione from the yeast cell. Although the destruction of the less viable yeast cells does occur at this high a temperature, only a small percentage of the millions of cells present are destroyed in the short time required for their hydration. The addition of other ingredients—sugar, salt, fat, and flour—quickly lowers the temperature of the mixture to a safe level for the yeast cells.

Bacteria, along with yeast, produce carbon dioxide gas in sourdough and salt-rising breads. Rye flour furnishes the bacteria used for leavening sourdough bread; cornmeal furnishes the bacteria in salt-rising bread. The sourness in these breads results from the acetic and lactic acids produced by the bacteria. Flavor and character of the bread depends on the conditions and ingredients used in preparing the *starter*—a mixture of bacteria that causes fermentation—for the dough.

If they are mishandled, starters may become contaminated with putrefactive bacteria that cause spoilage and also with pathogenic bacteria that can cause disease. Clean ingredients and utensils must be used, and the starter should be covered loosely with a clean cloth so that air is available while the fermentative bacteria are being cultivated. Starter, dough, or bread should be discarded if bad odors or colors develop. Raw dough containing the starter, or the starter itself, should not be tasted or eaten. Novices preparing breads with these starters should include some baker's yeast in the dough. The use of starter packets that contain pure strains of desirable organisms instead of trying to culture wild organisms from the ingredients or the air is a recommended procedure.

BACTERIA AS A SOURCE OF CARBON DIOXIDE GAS

Study Questions

1. Name two biological sources and two chemical sources of carbon dioxide for leavening breads.
2. What are some ways that air is incorporated into flour mixtures for leavening?
3. Name some baked products that are leavened only by steam.
4. If baking soda is used in a baked product without an acid ingredient to release carbon dioxide gas, what effect does it have on the color, flavor, and texture of the baked product?
5. Name some ingredients capable of supplying sufficient acid for leavening with baking soda.
6. Name the ingredients in baking powder and the functions of each.
7. In what way do brands of baking powder differ from each other?
8. Distinguish between quick- and double-acting baking powders.
9. What is the recommended ratio of baking powder to flour for adequate leavening?
10. What amount of baking powder supplies the same amount of leavening gas as ½ teaspoon of baking soda?
11. Why should baking powder be stored in airtight containers?
12. What is fermentation?
13. What sugars can and cannot be utilized by yeast for leavening?
14. What is the best temperature for fermentation? Why?
15. Distinguish between compressed and active dry yeasts, their shelf life, storage conditions, and purpose.
16. What types of breads are leavened by carbon dioxide gas produced by bacteria?

References

Campbell, Ada Marie. "Flour Mixtures." In *Food Theory and Applications*, edited by Pauline C. Paul and Helen H. Palmer. New York: Wiley, 1971.

Charley, Helen. *Food Science.* New York: Ronald Press, 1970.

Handbook of Food Preparation. Washington, D.C.: American Home Economics Association, 7th ed., 1975.

Lowe, Belle. *Experimental Cookery.* 4th ed. New York: Wiley, 1964.

Potter, Norman N. *Food Science* 2d ed. Westport, Conn.: Avi Publishing, 1973.

Pyler, E. J. *Baking Science and Technology,* vols. 1, 2. Chicago: Siebel Publishing, 1973.

Sweetman, M. D., and MacKellar, Ingeborg. *Food Selection and Preparation.* 4th ed. New York: Wiley, 1964.

Quick Breads

Quick breads are breads that can be mixed and baked in a much shorter time than that required to mix and ferment yeast breads. Most quick breads are leavened with baking soda or baking powder. Other quick breads might be classified unleavened breads because they are leavened primarily by steam.

UNLEAVENED BREADS
Tortillas, chapaties, puris, and matzos are breads that are typically considered unleavened. All are prepared in the form of flat cakes cooked on a surface unit or in fat rather than in an oven. Figure 13.1 shows some unleavened breads.

Matzos Matzo is the unleavened bread eaten by Jews in the observance of Passover. Matzos are prepared from wheat flour according to traditional dietary laws.

Tortillas Tortillas, made from masa, are the most widely eaten bread in Mexico. Moist masa is shaped into a ball and patted between the palms of the hands to form a flat, round cake. The cake is cooked on a hot griddle like a pancake until it is set but not brown.

Chapaties and Puris Chapaties and puris are made from whole wheat flour passed through a coarse sieve to remove some of the coarse bran particles. This sieved whole wheat flour, called *atta,* is mixed with water and small amounts of salt and oil to form a dough. The dough is rolled into thin, round pieces. Chapaties are cooked in the same way as tortillas, while puris are fried in deep butter fat.

Figure 13.1

Unleavened breads are, center top and clockwise: tortillas, matzo, pappadam, chapaties, and puris.

The ingredients in most quick breads are the same; only their proportions differ. Table 13.1 shows the proportions of ingredients per cup of flour for various baked products. All the products require ¼ teaspoon of salt per cup of flour, unless a large amount of salted table fat is added, in which case the amount of salt should be correspondingly reduced. All-purpose flour serves for quick breads, although pastry flour, either whole wheat or refined, is also acceptable in some cases.

Triticale flour can be used as the only flour in muffins, waffles, and griddle cakes, and is quite satisfactory when used in equal amounts with wheat flour for biscuits. The use of oil or margarine instead of butter eliminates cholesterol and increases the polyunsaturated fatty acids. Either egg white or egg substitute can replace whole egg to eliminate cholesterol in all quick breads that use eggs except in cream puffs.

INGREDIENTS IN QUICK BREADS

As shown in Table 13.1, popovers contain equal amounts of liquid and flour. They are unleavened breads because they contain no source of carbon dioxide gas. Popovers are leavened by steam produced from the large amount of liquid.

POPOVERS AND YORKSHIRE PUDDING

Mixing Popovers Any method of mixing that produces a smooth batter without lumps is satisfactory for making popovers. The mixing can be done with a spoon, an egg beater, an electric mixer, or a blender. The ratio of liquid to flour produces a batter with gluten particles that are too widely dispersed to adhere to each other; consequently, neither over- nor underdevelopment of gluten is a problem in this product.

Table 13.1   *Proportions of ingredients per cup of flour for various quick breads*

Quick bread	Liquid		Fat		Eggs (large)	Sugar[a] (Tbsp)	SAS baking powder (tsp)
	Kind	Amount	Kind	Amount (Tbsp)			
Batters:							
French pancakes	Milk	2 cups	Oil	2	4	0	0
Popovers	Milk	1 cup	Oil	1–2	2–3	0	0
Cream puffs	Water	1 cup	Butter	8	4	0	0
Pancakes	Milk	¾–1 cup	Oil	1	½	0–1	1½
Waffles	Milk	¾–1 cup	Oil	3	1–2	0	1½
Muffins	Milk	½ cup	Oil	2–3	½	2	1½
Doughs:							
Biscuits	Milk	5–8 tbsp	Shortening	2–4	0	0	1½
Shortbread	Light cream	5–8 tbsp	Shortening	4	½	½	1½
Crackers	Milk	1 tbsp	Oil	4	1	0	0

[a]Artificial sweetener can replace sugar, if desired.

Effect of Egg on Volume   The volume of popovers is directly related to the egg content of the batter. Three eggs per cup of flour produce popovers with a greater volume than two eggs (Figure 13.2). Egg white appears to affect volume more than yolk and can be used in place of whole egg; egg substitute is satisfactory but results in a slightly reduced volume.

Baking Popovers   Containers for baking popovers should be several inches deep with fairly straight sides; 5-ounce glass custard cups are ideal. The containers must be greased so that the popovers can be removed in one piece after they have been baked. Pan sprays that prevent sticking are good for this purpose. Popover pans do not need to be preheated, but can be. Heated pans shorten cooking time, and heating can be accomplished while the oven is preheating. If the batter is placed in preheated pans, it should be baked immediately or else the popovers will not rise properly.

Bake popovers in a preheated oven at 425°F (218.5°C) so that the crust forms quickly to retain the steam that is also being rapidly produced. At this temperature, popovers reach their maximum volume in about 20 minutes. The oven should then be shut off, without being opened, to allow the structure of the popovers to set with residual heat for the next 20 minutes. This procedure prevents overbrowning, which popovers tend to do very easily because of their high content of egg and milk.

Desirable Characteristics of Popovers   Properly baked popovers are crisp, almost hollow shells, not too brown on the outside and slightly moist, but not soggy, on the inside (Figure 13.3). Popovers should not collapse when they are removed from the oven. Leave them in the baking pan for a few minutes for observation; if they show signs of collapsing, return them to the oven to finish baking.

Yorkshire Pudding   Yorkshire pudding is a kind of popover; it is made from the same batter and differs only in the manner in

Figure 13.2

The popovers on the left contain two eggs per cup of flour; the popovers on the right contain four eggs per cup of flour.

Figure 13.3
Almond popovers baked in an iron popover pan are lightly browned, crisp, hollow shells. Popovers may also be baked in deep custard cups. *(Wheat Flour Institute)*

which it is baked. True Yorkshire pudding is baked in meat drippings in the roasting pan after the meat has been removed. Because of the pan's large surface area, Yorkshire pudding has a more puddinglike texture, although it is also crisp. The fat drippings can also be spooned from the roast into the cups of the popover pan and the batter baked just as for popovers. This variation has the flavor or Yorkshire pudding but the texture and shape of popovers.

Cream puffs should not, perhaps, be classified as a bread, because they are strictly a dessert or pastry. However, cream puffs, like popovers, are hollow shells that contain a ratio of 1 cup of liquid per cup of flour. There the resemblance ends, as Table 13.1 shows; cream puffs are also mixed in an entirely different way than other quick breads.

CREAM PUFFS

Mixing Cream Puff Batter   To make cream puffs, water and fat are heated to the boiling point and flour is stirred in; the large amount of fat prevents lumping of the flour. Heating this mixture partially gelatinizes the flour and emulsifies the fat. The flour-water-fat mixture should be stirred and heated until the mixture forms a ball of dough (Figure 13.4). If the mixture is at all fluid at this point, the puffs will not rise properly. Eggs are then added one at a time with vigorous beating until the batter is smooth and homogeneous. The finished batter should be firm enough to remain where it is placed without flowing or losing its shape. Unbaked batter keeps well refrigerated.

Figure 13.4

Cream puff batter should form a ball and clear the sides of the pan before eggs are added.

Baking Cream Puff Batter Drop the batter by spoonfuls onto an ungreased baking sheet, or use a pastry bag to form it into desired shapes (Figure 13.5). The batter can be shaped into bite-sized puffs, large puffs several inches in diameter, or éclairs. All the puffs should be baked in an oven preheated to 400°F (204.5°C) until they have puffed and have started to brown, at which time the temperature should be reduced. If the puffs start to collapse after they are removed from the oven, return them to the oven to complete baking.

Figure 13.5

Cream puff batter should hold its shape on an ungreased baking sheet. Batter can be dropped by teaspoons or tablespoons, or shaped with a pastry bag and tip or with a cookie press into full-sized puffs, miniature puffs, or éclairs.

Figure 13.6

Figure 13.6

Cooled cream puffs or éclairs can be sliced open about one third of the way from the top. The moist membranes in the interior of the puff are removed before filling is added.

Moist membranes inside the puffs should be removed before the puffs are filled (Figure 13.6). Moist fillings make the puffs soggy if they are filled too far in advance of serving. Unfilled puff can be frozen. Unfilled puffs that lose their crispness can be freshened and crisped by heating on an open pan in a moderate oven.

Desirable Characteristics of Cream Puffs Cream puffs should have a good volume and be crisp, lightly browned hollow shells; they are more tender than popovers.

Problems in Making Cream Puffs Fat oozes from puffs during baking if the batter does not contain enough egg or water. Insufficient water can occur if the water and fat are allowed to boil too long before the flour is stirred in. Using small eggs instead of large eggs also reduces the water content. Too much fat also causes oozing during baking. In all three cases the fat is inadequately emulsified.

Gummy cream puffs of low volume result from too much water or egg or improper gelatinization of the flour. All these problems produce an excess of water in the batter. Eggs contain about 75 percent water; thus, using extra-large eggs instead of large eggs can increase the water content of a batter considerably.

GRIDDLE CAKES (PANCAKES)

This batter is poured onto a heated, oiled griddle to bake—hence its name. The ratio of ingredients for griddle cakes is shown in Table 13.1. Griddle cake batter is made by the muffin method of mixing: dry ingredients are measured and mixed together, then set aside. Egg and oil are mixed well, liquid is added, and the dry ingredient mixture is added to this mixture. This batter has a lower ratio of liquid than popovers. Mixing should therefore be limited only to that necessary for achieving a smooth batter. This limited mixing prevents the overdevelopment of the gluten, which would produce a less tender cake.

Baking Griddle Cakes Spray the griddle with pan spray to prevent sticking. Pour the desired amount of batter onto the griddle and cook it until bubbles form, but do not pop, on the top surface; then turn it over and cook it on the other side. The cake should be turned only once. After turning, do not press it down with the spatula, for this causes the structure to collapse and produces a heavy cake. If the cake is cooked on the first side until the bubbles pop, it overcooks, making the second side difficult to brown evenly.

Desirable Characteristics of Griddle Cakes The characteristics of finished cakes can be partly controlled by the ingredients in the batter. A thin batter with a high ratio of milk produces a thin cake; a thick batter with less milk produces a thicker, breadier cake. Ample fat as a frying medium produces crisp edges on the cake, but also increases the caloric content. Griddle cakes should be moist but not gummy, light, tender, and evenly browned.

A batter containing egg has a better flavor and texture than one without egg. Part of the flour can be replaced with other grains, or such ingredients as crisp fried bacon, ham, or fruit can be added to produce different flavors.

FRENCH PANCAKES The authentic name for French pancakes is *crepes.* This batter contains a higher ratio of liquid to flour than popovers but may be mixed in the same manner. Mixing the batter ahead of time and refrigerating it causes the flour to hydrate more completely, and is recommended.

Cooking French Pancakes Use a pan of the diameter desired for the finished cake, for only one cake at a time is cooked. Either a Teflon or heavy iron pan is suitable; both should be brushed lightly with butter or sprayed with pan spray. One person can usually keep two or three pans going at one time for faster preparation.

Pour only enough batter in the hot pan to barely coat the bottom. About 2 tablespoons of batter can be cooked at one time in a pan with a 5-inch diameter. Rotate the pan to spread the batter evenly over the bottom of the preheated pan. Cook the pancake on the first side until it is lightly brown, then turn it over to cook for a few seconds on the second side. A rubber scraper is excellent for turning French pancakes (Figure 13.7), because they are very

Figure 13.7

Choose a pan the same diameter as is desired for the finished crepe. The thin batter is retained by the sides of the pan. Wear a cotton glove and use a rubber scraper for turning the crepes. To make crepes Suzette, place a crepe in the hot, thin sauce, turn it over, fold it into quarters, and transfer it to a serving plate.

Figure 13.8

Blintzes are crepes filled with a mixture of cream cheese, cottage or ricotta cheese, and egg yolk, all slightly sweetened and seasoned with vanilla. Fold and roll the crepe as shown. Place rolled crepes in a baking dish, cover with foil, and bake. Like crepes Suzette, blintzes are served hot with a sweet sauce.

fragile and easily torn. Avoid overcooking, which will dry the cakes so that they will not fold or roll. The finished pancakes may be stacked as they are cooked.

Serving French Pancakes   Crepes are used in a variety of dishes, from entrées to desserts; they are most famous in crepes Suzette (Figure 13.7) and blintzes (Figure 13.8). Cooked crepes can be stored in the refrigerator for 2 or 3 days; they also freeze well.

Waffles are a variation of pancakes that are cooked on a gridded iron instead of a flat griddle. Waffles need more fat than pancakes to prevent the batter from sticking to the iron; the larger content of fat also provides a crisp texture. More egg is used in waffles than in pancakes to help emulsify the extra fat, and it also contributes color and flavor to the cooked waffle. Egg white foam added to the batter increases the lightness of the cooked waffle.

WAFFLES

Mixing Waffles Waffles are mixed in the same way as pancakes, except that the egg white foam is incorporated in the batter just before baking. Mix the batter only until it is smooth. Beat egg whites only to the soft peak stage so that they fold in easily without forming lumps.

Baking Waffles Preheat the waffle iron before baking the waffles. Pan spray on the grids should eliminate sticking. Most waffle irons take about 3 minutes to cook a waffle. Many have indicator lights or mechanisms to indicate both when the iron is hot and when the waffles are cooked. Usually, a waffle is ready when it stops steaming. A slightly extended cooking time produces a drier, crispier waffle.

The design of the waffle iron can affect the quality of the waffles. The top of the iron is hinged to the bottom of the iron with a spring that allows the top to rise with the expansion of gases in the batter. If the top is too heavy, or the spring mechanism too strong, too much pressure is placed on the waffle and it does not rise. A waffle baked in such an iron comes out heavy and compact. The design of the grid projections can also affect the texture of the waffle. Shallow projections spaced far apart produce a soft, cakelike waffle; projections that are spaced close together produce crisp waffles.

MUFFINS Muffins have a ratio of ingredients that is very similar to that of pancakes except that muffins contain less milk, as shown in Table 13.1. Muffins are more difficult to prepare than pancakes, because muffins tend to form tunnels and peaked tops, qualities that are considered undesirable.

Tunnel Formation in Muffins Both tunnels and peaks in muffins are caused by an excess of structure-forming ingredients (Figure 13.9). As mentioned in Chapter 11, eggs and flour contrib-

Figure 13.9

Too much gluten development in muffins produces the smooth crust, peaked top, and interior tunnels shown in the muffins at the right; at the left are properly baked muffins.

ute structure to a baked product. Flour with too much gluten potential along with too much gluten development contributes to tunnel formation. Gluten can be overdeveloped in several ways:

1. Too much liquid causes the gluten to overhydrate.
2. The batter is mixed too much.
3. Insufficient amounts of the tenderizing agents, fat and sugar, needed to interfere with gluten development, are present.

Mechanism of Tunnel and Peak Formation A high content of structure-forming ingredients offers resistance to the expansion of leavening gases when heating begins. Small amounts of gas are trapped in the batter until enough collects to exert pressure against the structural ingredients. By the time this occurs, the crust around the outer edges of the muffin has set so that the gas cannot penetrate in that direction. Because the center of the muffin is the last part to set, the large gas bubbles push up through the center, forming a tunnel. The bubbles push the soft dough ahead of them through the top of the muffin as they try to escape; the soft dough flows out with the gases and sets in a peak at the top of the muffin. Tunnels are formed by gases as they rise to the top.

Effect of Kinds and Ratios of Ingredients Muffins show less tendency to tunnel if a pastry or cake flour is used in place of all-purpose flour, but muffins made with these flours are more cakelike than breadlike. Flours and meals added to dilute the gluten in all-purpose flour—cornmeal, wheat germ, bran, and oats—are also effective in reducing tunneling. Muffins made from whole wheat pastry flour are least likely to have tunnels.

Along with less gluten, use only the minimal amount of egg. Increased amounts of fat and sugar also help prevent tunneling, but this, too, tends to produce a more cakelike product. Finally, use only the amount of liquid needed to moisten the dry ingredients and to dissolve the leavening agent, but not enough to cause the gluten to overhydrate. Muffin batter should not be fluid.

Effect of Mixing Method The muffin method described under Griddle Cakes is used to mix muffins. Sugar should be combined with the dry ingredients because it helps separate the flour granules so that the dry ingredients combine more readily with the liquid ingredients. When liquid and dry ingredients are combined, mixing should be limited to keep the gluten from overdeveloping. Use cutting and folding strokes to keep the gluten from stretching, an action that develops it.

Properly mixed muffin batter is lumpy, not smooth, and no pockets of unmoistened dry ingredients should be present (Figure 13.10).

Figure 13.10
Muffin batter should be lumpy, not smooth.

Figure 13.11
Properly baked muffins have slightly rounded tops, a thin, pebbled crust, and an even grain with thin-walled cells inside. *(Wheat Flour Institute)*

Baking Muffins   Bake muffin batter as soon as it is mixed. Muffin pans must be greased or sprayed with a pan spray. Teflon pans or muffin cup liners, or both, can be used. Muffin cups should be filled with a minimum of mixing. Preheat the oven to 425°F (218.5°C). After baking, leave the muffins in the pan a few minutes to allow the steam to soften the crust for easy removal.

Desirable Characteristics of Muffins   Muffins of good quality have a thin brown crust, and a slightly rounded top with a pebbled appearance (Figure 13.11). The interior of the muffin should be free of tunnels and tender, with an even grain, and thin cell walls.

BISCUITS   Two types of biscuits are popular in the United States, a breadlike biscuit in the South, and a flaky biscuit in many other parts of the country. The hot flaky biscuit separates into layers when the top is separated from the bottom. The interior texture of breadlike biscuits resembles that of muffins. The kinds and amounts of ingredients and the way they are combined determine the characteristics of a baked biscuit. Both types of biscuit should have a flat, lightly browned, crisp top and straight sides. The sides of a biscuit, unlike the top and bottom, do not become noticeably browned during baking (Figure 13.12).

Figure 13.12

Biscuits that have been mixed and baked
correctly have flat, lightly browned top
crusts, straight sides, and even,
thin-walled cells inside.
(Wheat Flour Institute)

Figure 13.13

The pastry method is used to make biscuits: solid fat is cut into dry
ingredients with a pastry blender before liquid is added.
(Wheat Flour Institute)

Figure 13.14

The correct ratio of milk to flour produces a soft dough that yields
a moist, superior biscuit. *(Wheat Flour Institute)*

Flaky Biscuits   Some gluten development is necessary for flaky
biscuits. Solid fat is needed to separate the gluten into layers. The
larger amount of fat shown in Table 13.1 is required for flaky
biscuits.

The pastry method is used to make flaky biscuits. In this procedure, the dry ingredients are combined, and solid fat is cut into
this mixture, part finely divided and part left in large pea-sized
lumps (Figure 13.13). The fat is divided in this way to ensure that
it coats some of the flour to prevent development of the gluten.
The remaining uncoated flour granules absorb water, forming
some gluten. The larger lumps of fat flatten out when the dough
is rolled to form layers of fat between layers of gluten.

After cutting the fat into the dry ingredients, add liquid to form a soft dough (Figure 13.14). A dry or firm dough with too little liquid produces dry, compact, heavy biscuits; too little water may also cause the top of the biscuit to freckle. Knead the dough 20 to 30 strokes to develop the gluten. (*Kneading* is flattening the dough with the palms of the hands and folding it over, which stretches the gluten and develops it [Figure 13.15].) Biscuits kneaded more than 30 strokes have a reduced volume and are less tender; underkneading similarly produces reduced volume and less flakiness.

Breadlike Biscuits   Breadlike biscuits differ from flaky biscuits in the following ways:

1. They contain the lower level of fat shown in Table 13.3.
2. All the fat is cut into the flour at once, finely dispersed.
3. The dough is kneaded less for less gluten development; about 10 strokes is adequate.
4. Flour for breadlike biscuits may contain a low level of protein; pastry flour or all-purpose flour prepared from soft wheat are suitable types.

In all other respects the preparation of the two kinds of biscuits is identical, and a soft dough here is also preferable to a dry, firm dough.

Rolling Out Biscuit Dough   Because a soft, moist dough produces the best biscuits, avoid using too much flour to roll out the dough. A pastry cloth on the bread board is a practical measure. Rub a small amount of flour into the cloth to prevent the dough from sticking.

Dough may be cut out with cutters or cut into squares or diamonds with a pizza or pastry wheel or a knife. Dough is less likely

Figure 13.15

Biscuit dough must be kneaded slightly to develop gluten for a flaky biscuit with good volume. The dough is folded and pressed during kneading. *(Wheat Flour Institute)*

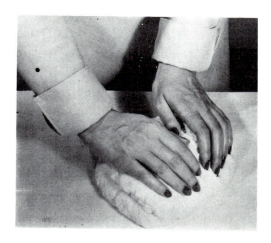

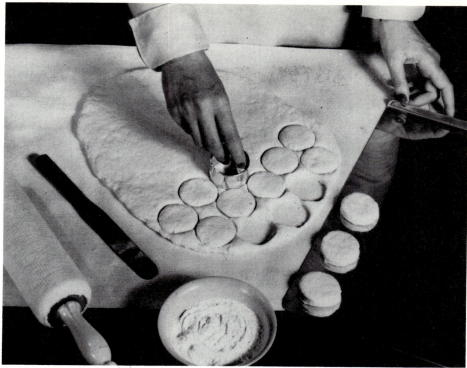

Figure 13.16
Biscuit dough is rolled to a thickness of ½ inch with minimal amounts of flour
on the board or pastry cloth. Leaving space between biscuits during baking
causes a thin crust, but no browning, to form on the sides of each biscuit.
(Wheat Flour Institute)

to stick to a cutting instrument that has been dipped in flour.
Place the biscuits on an ungreased baking sheet. If space is left
between them, they form a slight crust on the sides (Figure 13.16).
Brushing the biscuits with melted table fat before they are baked
produces a crispier top.

Baking Biscuits   Biscuits are baked in an oven preheated to 425°F
(218.5°C) for about 15 to 20 minutes, depending on the size of the
biscuits. Biscuits are done when they spring back after being
pressed lightly in the center.

During baking, both carbon dioxide from the chemical leavening and steam from the liquid expand and cause the biscuits to
increase to about double their original volume. The flattened
lumps of fat in flaky biscuit dough melt to form pockets for the
leavening gases, thereby producing layers of coagulated protein
and gelatinized starch.

Biscuits do not have to baked as soon as they are mixed. They may be held for a half hour or less at room temperature, or longer in the refrigerator. If refrigerated, they should be warmed to room temperature before baking.

Most baked biscuits have a crack on the side that is considered normal, especially if the biscuits have been leavened with a double-acting baking powder. Cracks are caused by the expansion of the leavening gases after the structure is set. The gas from the slow-acting component of baking powder does not form until the dough is heated, by which time the structure has already begun to set. The gas must thus escape by the route of least resistance, which happens to be the side of the biscuit. Cracks are less likely to occur in soft doughs.

Drop Biscuits   Drop biscuits need a larger amount of liquid than rolled biscuits and might best be classified as a thick batter rather than a dough. Drop biscuit batter is dropped by spoonfuls onto a greased baking sheet. This type of biscuit is muffinlike in texture and can also be used as dumplings or cooked in boiling stock or liquid.

SHORTBREAD AND SCONES   Shortbread, or shortcake, is a biscuit dough that contains a large amount of fat. Cream is often used as the liquid to increase the fat level and shortening effect. Scones resemble shortbread, except that they also contain egg, which means that less cream is added to balance the ratio of liquid. Cut into diamond or triangle shapes, scones are served as a quick bread or for afternoon tea. Shortbread is often served as a dessert with sweetened fresh, frozen, or canned fruit and whipped or light cream.

CORNBREAD   Cornbread resembles a muffin mixture both in its method of preparation and in its baked characteristics. A satisfactory bread cannot be made solely from cornmeal; some wheat flour is necessary to supply gluten for structure. Equal quantities of cornmeal and flour produce a very satisfactory product; for a lighter bread, one part of cornmeal for two parts of flour can be used.

Because cornmeal dilutes the gluten available in the flour, egg helps provide structure in cornbread. The mixing method is not critical and appears to have no effect on the product. Use the muffin method with oil as the fat.

Cornbread batter can be baked in any type of pan with an edge, such as muffin pans, cake pans, or cornstick pans. Pans should be greased well; ample fat helps give a crispy crust. In the South, the batter is cooked like pancakes and is called corn pone.

CRACKERS   Crackers prepared from the basic ingredients are not the same as those prepared commercially, but they are quite acceptable and are a good sugarless substitute for cookies. A low-gluten flour, such as enriched white or whole wheat pastry flour or triticale flour, should be used to make crackers. The dough is mixed by the muffin method just until the ingredients are combined to prevent overdevelopment of the gluten and a lack of tenderness in the baked crackers.

Variety can be achieved by the addition of grated cheese, sesame or caraway seeds, or other similar ingredients, which have been combined with the flour before the addition of the liquid mixture.

The dough should be rolled very thin. The rolled dough can be cut into strips or squares with a pastry wheel or cut with a cookie cutter. Rerolling leftover scraps of dough reduces the tenderness of the baked cracker. The pastry is baked at 350°F (176.7°C) so that the cracker dries out by the time it is lightly browned.

MICROWAVE BAKING

Muffins and biscuits can be baked in a microwave oven in a much shorter time than in a conventional oven, but some people consider products baked in a microwave oven unacceptable because they are not browned. Other disadvantages of microwave baking are the slightly lower volume and decreased tenderness of breads that are baked in a microwave oven. Popovers and cream puffs, which have a high egg content, become quite tough when they are baked in a microwave oven.

The microwave oven is ideal for reheating baked breads if minimum time is used to obtain the desired temperature. Excessive microwave heating causes a loss in tenderness and drying of the bread.

NUTRITIONAL VALUE OF BREADS

Two factors determine the nutritive value of breads: the type or types of flour and the kinds and amounts of other ingredients. Eggs, for example, contain more of the amino acid lysine than they need to balance the other amino acids present to form a complete protein. The extra lysine in eggs is an excellent supplement for cereal grains that are deficient in lysine. Eggs also supply vitamin A, which is lacking in many grains. Breads containing eggs thus have a higher nutritive value than those without eggs.

Higher levels of fat and sugar increase calories but do not add vitamins, minerals, or protein. Whole wheat flour, triticale flour, wheat germ, bran, and soy flour not only add variety in flavor but also increase the nutrients in the baked product. Ingredients such as cheese, raisins, nuts, and various fruits also add nutrients to the breads in which they are used.

The thiamin in bread mixtures is destroyed in small amounts by baking or heating; it is also destroyed by an alkaline medium. Therefore, do not overbrown or toast breads. Too much baking soda or baking soda with no acid to release carbon dioxide both produce an alkaline medium and should be avoided.

Study Questions

1. What is a quick bread?
2. What factor has the greatest influence on the volume of baked popovers?
3. Why is it advisable to reduce the oven temperature during the last part of baking popovers and cream puffs?
4. Describe the proper consistency of the fat-water-flour mixture of cream puffs before eggs are added.
5. What is the effect of too much or too little egg in a cream-puff batter?
6. When and how often should griddle cakes be turned?
7. How do waffles differ from pancakes in ingredients and mixing method?
8. In what ways do French pancakes differ from regular pancakes or griddle cakes?
9. Explain the causes of tunnel formation and peaked tops in muffins.
10. What kind and what amount of mixing is necessary to combine dry and liquid ingredients in muffins?
11. Describe the characteristics of a muffin of good quality.
12. Distinguish between the muffin method and the pastry method of mixing.
13. Describe how the type of flour, amount of fat, method of dividing the fat, and amount of kneading affect a biscuit's texture, making it either flaky or breadlike.
14. Describe how the division of fat contributes to flakiness in biscuits.
15. What is a drop biscuit and how is it baked?
16. What ingredients increase the nutrient content of baked products?
17. What ingredients increase the caloric content of baked products with no corresponding increase in vitamins, minerals, or protein?
18. Name the causes of thiamin loss in baked products and describe how these losses can be reduced.
19. What ingredients can be used in quick breads to reduce the cholesterol content?
20. Why are low-gluten flours and minimum mixing recommended in preparing crackers?

References

Campbell, Ada Marie. "Flour Mixtures." In *Food Theory and Applications*, edited by Pauline C. Paul and Helen H. Palmer. New York: Wiley, 1971.

Demus, T. A. "Baking Treats *ad Infinitum*: Breads and Tasty Pastry." In U.S. Department of Agriculture, *Food for Us All*, Yearbook of Agriculture. Washington, D.C.: Government Printing Office, 1969.

Pastry and Pies

A pie has two parts, the crust and the filling. Both the type of filling and the quality of the crust determine a pie's characteristics. Piecrust is most often prepared from pie dough, or pastry; it can also be made from graham cracker or cookie crumbs. Many kinds of fillings are used in pies.

Pie Pastry Many supposedly failproof methods exist for preparing pastry that cannot be described here; instead, a few representative methods are discussed. As a rule, any method that produces a desirable pastry is satisfactory.

CHARACTERISTICS OF GOOD PASTRY A good pastry should be both tender and flaky. A pastry that is too tender is mealy and crumbly; a pastry that is too flaky is tough. These two characteristics are antagonistic, for factors that produce tenderness inhibit flakiness, and vice versa. A balance in these characteristics is needed to achieve the best quality in pastry.

INGREDIENTS OF PIE DOUGH In theory, preparing pastry for pie should be a very simple procedure, for pie dough contains only four ingredients; flour, fat, water, and salt. Commercially prepared pastry sometimes includes nonfat dry milk and sugar.

Flour Most bakers use a soft wheat pastry flour for pastry, but all-purpose flour can also produce a satisfactory product. Pastry made from whole wheat flour is not satisfactory. Some gluten development is needed to produce flakiness in pastry; the flour must provide some gluten, but not too much.

Fat Several kinds of fat are suitable for pastry, but the amount of fat and the method of mixing must be adapted to each kind of fat to reach a balance between flakiness and tenderness. Fat coats some of the granules of flour and forms a barrier to prevent the absorption of water, and hence the formation of gluten. In this way, fat functions as a shortening agent; it shortens the strands of gluten and prevents their development, thus producing tenderness. Of the solid fats, lard is best because it is plastic at low temperatures and has good shortening characteristics. Hydrogenated shortening with no added emulsifiers is better than ones with emulsifiers. As discussed in Chapter 5, an emulsifier promotes the mixing of fat and water. A fat that contains an emulsifier is not a good shortening agent in pastry because it permits water to pass the fat barrier coating the flour granules. Emulsifiers in shortening increase flakiness but reduce tenderness, especially if the pastry is stored for a period of time.

Table fat contains water; therefore, adjustments are necessary to yield the desired amount of fat and water (Table 14.1). Oil has greater shortening power than any other fat, but the same amount

Table 14.1   *Volume measures and weights of various fats per cup of all-purpose flour (125 grams), with amount of water to be added, for pastry of good quality*

Kind of fat	Weight of fat per cup (g)	Fat			Water	
		Measure (cup)	(Tbsp)	Weight (g)	Measure (Tbsp)	Weight (g)
Lard	220	⅓	—	73	2	30
Hydrogenated shortening	188	⅓ +	1	75	2	30
Butter or margarine	224	⅓ +	1	89[a]	1	15 (+14)[a]
Oil	210	¼	—	52	2	30

[a] 89 grams of table fat yields 71 grams of fat and 14 grams of water; therefore, less water is added. Use 1 tablespoon of water for 1 cup of flour, providing a total of 29 grams of water (15 + 14).

of oil as lard would make the pastry extremely short and mealy. If oil is used, less is needed than solid fat. Additionally, the emulsion method of mixing produces a more desirable pastry with oil than the pastry method.

Water Water is the liquid usually used for pastry, although almost any kind of liquid could be substituted. Milk increases browning of the crust, which could become excessive if the pie requires a long baking time. Because the amount of liquid is so small, it has little effect on the flavor of the pastry.

Other Ingredients Salt contributes flavor to pastry; if salted table fat is used, reduce the amount of salt added to the mixture.

Nonfat dry milk in amounts equal to about 2 percent of the weight of the flour, or a small amount of dextrose, increases browning; the milk also increases sogginess in the crust.

PROPORTIONS OF INGREDIENTS IN PASTRY

The amount of fat in pie pastry is determined by the kind of flour and the kind of fat used. The usual proportion is ⅓ cup of lard per cup of all-purpose flour, which is measured by stirring and spooning into a cup, along with 2 tablespoons of water. Table 14.1 shows the measures and weight in grams of other fats that produce the same shortening effect with 1 cup (125 grams) of all-purpose flour.

MIXING PASTRY

Two mixing methods will be discussed. Regardless of the method used, best results are obtained when the ingredients and the room temperature are about 60°F (16°C). At a warmer room temperature, the ingredients, especially the fat and water, should be well chilled.

Pastry Method The pastry method was described in Chapter 13. The novice is more likely to achieve a balance between tenderness and flakiness in pastry by adding the solid fat in two parts. Cut half of the solid fat into the flour-salt mixture until it resembles coarse cornmeal. Cut the rest of the fat in so that some pieces remain the size of large peas.

Sprinkle the liquid over the flour-fat mixture all at once and work it in first with a fork, then with the fingers, to form a ball of dough. At this stage, beginners tend to add more water and to continue mixing with a fork or spoon. The result is a dough with too much gluten hydration, producing a tough pastry. It is almost impossible to form a dough with such a small amount of water while mixing with a fork or spoon. Working the dough with the fingers distributes the water more evenly.

If the first half of the fat is not properly dispersed, so that not enough flour granules are coated with fat, then more uncoated flour granules will be capable of absorbing water, and more water will be needed to form a dough. Inaccurate measurement of flour also alters the ratio of ingredients unfavorably. A ball of dough is not crumbly when it is properly prepared.

Crust should be prepared ahead of time and allowed to rest in the refrigerator for several hours or overnight before it is rolled out. Resting the dough equalizes the water throughout the mass; it hardens the fat and keeps the flour from being further coated by fat. The crust shrinks less during baking and is more tender, so long as the fat does not contain an emulsifier. If the fat does contain an emulsifier, opposite results are likely, for more gluten becomes hydrated during the rest period, decreasing tenderness. A dough that has been rested after mixing is easier to roll out.

Emulsion Method If oil is used as the fat in pastry, the emulsion method is the best mixing procedure to follow. Because of oil's great shortening power, the pastry method produces a very short, crumbly baked pie crust. The emulsion method permits the water and fat to act equally on the flour.

An emulsion of water and oil is obtained by combining them with a small amount of the flour to form a paste. This paste is mixed into the remaining flour to form the dough.

The dough should be kneaded about 10 strokes to develop the gluten and to increase flakiness. A rest period is recommended for the same reasons as for the pastry method.

FLAKINESS VERSUS TENDERNESS Flakiness in pastry results from gluten development in the dough. Gluten is developed when the flour is properly hydrated, when the dough is worked or kneaded, and when flour with a high protein content is used. Tenderness in pastry, on the other hand, requires the inhibition of gluten development. Gluten development is inhibited by preventing flour hydration and hence the formation of gluten, and by limiting the amount of mixing. Flour hydration is inhibited if the flour granules are coated with fat and if minimal amounts of water are used to form the dough.

Balancing these two opposing characteristics demands the proper proportion of ingredients, correctly measured and combined. Identifying the source of problems in baked pastry may thus help make a better product the next time.

Lack of Tenderness in Baked Pastry Lack of tenderness may result from one or more of the following conditions:

1. The dough did not contain enough fat.
2. The dough contained flour with too high a protein content.
3. The fat was not distributed finely enough in the flour.
4. The dough contained too much water.
5. The final dough was mixed or kneaded excessively.
6. The pastry was rolled out in too much flour.
7. The pastry was rolled two or more times.

Lack of Flakiness A mealy, crumbly pastry may result from one or more of the following conditions:

1. The dough contained too much fat.
2. The dough contained a low-protein pastry or cake flour.
3. The pastry method of mixing was used to add oil or a warm solid fat.
4. The fat was distributed too finely in the flour; not enough fat was left in larger pieces.
5. The dough did not contain enough water.
6. The final dough was not mixed or kneaded enough; this is an especially likely occurrence in a pastry that contains oil as the fat.

Assembling the Pie

A prepared crust must be rolled out and fitted into a pan. Either a top crust is placed over a filling, or else a bottom crust is baked alone with the filling or baked before the filling is placed in it, depending on the type of pie. Each of these steps and variations requires special techniques.

ROLLING OUT THE DOUGH

Avoid adding too much flour or handling and working the dough too much when rolling out dough; both practices decrease tenderness in baked pastry. Two methods can simplify the procedure of rolling out dough. The desired amount of dough can be shaped into a flattened ball and rolled out between two sheets of waxed or parchment paper, or the bread board can be covered with a pastry cloth. A small amount of flour rubbed into the cloth allows the dough to be rolled out without sticking. A cotton knit stocking on the rolling pin, or rolling the pin over the floured pastry cloth, keeps the dough from sticking to the rolling pin. If the dough tends to be sticky as it is rolled out, it may be turned over, although this procedure should not be done too frequently because it increases the amount of flour that is incorporated into the pastry dough.

With either method, the strokes of the rolling pin should all go in one direction until the dough is oblong in shape, with a length equal to the diameter of the pan. Then roll the dough in the cross-wise direction to form a circle that is 1 to 2 inches larger in diameter than the pie pan. Roll the rolling pin over the dough with moderate pressure and raise it from the outer edge to prevent excessive thinness around the circumference. Rolling strokes should shape the dough in as nearly a circular form as possible.

Refrigerated dough must be allowed to warm enough to be soft and pliable, but should not reach room temperature. If the dough splits at the edges during rolling, patch it by moistening the edges of the split with water and placing a patch from another area of the rolled-out dough over the split area.

PLACING THE CRUST IN THE PAN

Once the crust is rolled out, it is quite fragile and tears easily. If the pastry has been rolled out between sheets of waxed or parchment paper, peel the paper off both sides. Then handle the pastry in the same manner as for rolling it out on a pastry cloth; fold it in half and lay the fold across the center of the pie pan, and then unfold it (Figure 14.1). The pastry should then be eased into the pan for a snug fit. Push the dough into the pan with the tips of the fingers so that no air space is left between the pan and the dough. Do not stretch the dough while placing it in the pan, or it may shrink during baking. The manner of trimming the bottom crust depends on whether the pastry is intended for a two-crust pie or for a pie shell.

PIE SHELLS

When no top crust is added, enough of the bottom crust must be left on the pie to form a rim. Kitchen shears can be used to trim the crust so that it extends about 1 inch beyond the edge of the pan. This extra dough is folded under between the crust and the pan, and pinched to form a rim (Figure 14.2). As the dough is pinched, some of the points can be hooked over the edge of the pan to anchor the crust and help prevent shrinking during baking. If the pastry and the filling are baked together, as in custard pies, the filling is poured into the pastry at this point and baked.

Prebaked Pastry Shells If the pastry shell is baked before it is filled, it should be pricked repeatedly with a fork on the sides and bottom to allow steam to escape and to prevent the shape of the pastry from distorting during baking.

TWO-CRUST PIES

The bottom crust of a two-crust pie is trimmed so that it is even with the rim of the pie pan. Filling is then poured into the bottom

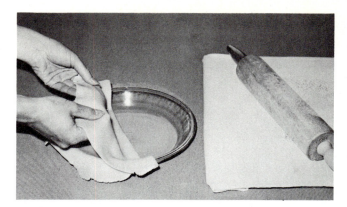

Figure 14.1

Rolled-out pie dough is folded in half with the fold laid across the center of the pie pan. The dough is unfolded and eased into the pan; it should not be stretched.

Figure 14.2

The crust of baked or unbaked pie shells is trimmed to leave a 1-inch overhang, which is folded under the crust and pinched to form a rim on the pan. Pastry shells that are baked before they are filled should be pricked repeatedly with a fork.

Figure 14.3

The juice of cooked fruit for a pie should be drained off and thickened with starch or tapioca. The drained fruit is placed in the pan and covered with the cooled, thickened juice, no more than two-thirds full.

crust (Figure 14.3). The juices or fruits in the filling should not be allowed to splash or drop on the rim of the crust, for this interferes with the formation of a good seal between the top and bottom crusts. The type of filling determines how much can be placed in a crust. If the filling is already cooked, the crust-lined pie pan should be filled only three-fourths to seven-eighths full to allow room for expansion with heating; otherwise, the filling may boil out.

The top crust is rolled out in the same way as the bottom crust, but with a diameter about 1 inch larger than the pan. Fold it in half or in quarters, and cut holes in it to allow steam to escape during baking. Artistic designs can be used, if desired. Moisten the rim of the bottom crust with water before placing the top crust over it, to improve the seal between the two crusts. Place the center fold of the top crust across the center of the filled pie, unfold the crust, and press it to the bottom crust around the rim (Figure 14.4). The top crust can be trimmed with kitchen shears so that it extends about ½ to 1 inch beyond the edge of the pan. Fold it over and under the bottom crust, between the crust and the pan. Crimp or pinch the edge, as for a pie shell (Figure 14.5). If desired, brush the top of the crust with melted table fat or a diluted mixture of egg and milk before baking to produce a rich golden crust color.

Figure 14.4

The rolled-out top crust of a pie is folded in half or in quarters, and holes for venting are cut in it. The folded crust is laid across the pie and unfolded from the center. To obtain a better seal between the two crusts, the rim of the lower crust should be moistened with water before the top crust is placed on it.

Figure 14.5

The top crust is trimmed to leave a 1-inch overhang, which is folded under the bottom crust between the crust and the pie pan. The two crusts are pinched together as for a single pastry shell.

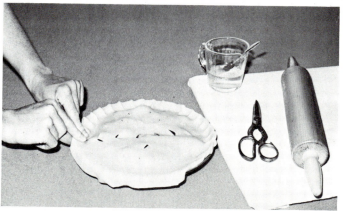

Table 14.2   Approximate times and suggested temperatures for baking various types of pies

Type of pie	Temperature		Time
	(°F)	(°C)	
Two-crust:			
Raw filling	440–450	227–232	35[a]
Cooked filling	450	232	30
Pastry shell:			
Custard filling	450	232	10, and then
	325	163	30
Unfilled	500	260	12

SOURCE: Calculated from M. J. Harder and H. W. Jabusch, ''Time and Temperature of Pie Baking,'' Bakers' Digest 20 (1946):101.
   [a]Uncooked apple needs 45–60 minutes of cooking time.

BAKING PIES AND SHELLS

The time a pie needs to bake depends on the pan, the filling, and the characteristics of the pastry. Table 14.2 shows average times and recommended temperatures for baking. As a rule, raw fillings take longer to bake than cooked fillings, and an empty pie shell bakes more quickly than pastry with filling.

With filled pies, proper cooking and browning of the crust must be reached by the time the filling is cooked. Since browning the bottom crust usually presents the greatest problem, the pie should be baked near the bottom of the oven, close to the heat source. Glass and dark-colored pans absorb more radiant energy and produce better browning than bright shiny pans. Lower temperatures than those shown in Table 14.2 may be used, but the baking time must be extended. A high oven temperature causes the steam that separates layers of gluten to expand rapidly, the protein to coagulate, and the starch to gelatinize in the crust so that it is less likely to become soaked by juices from the filling. A high temperature also melts the fat that forms pockets in which steam can form; the melted fat further coats the flour and inhibits soaking of the crust from water in the filling.

If the crust appears to be browning too much before the filling has cooked, reduce the oven temperature or place a sheet of aluminum foil loosely over the top of the pie to reflect some of the heat. The crust rim of custard pies often browns too much, an effect that can be prevented by folding a strip of aluminum foil over the rim of the pan and crust during baking.

SOGGY BOTTOM CRUSTS

Soggy bottom crusts are a common flaw in custard and fruit pies. Some measures that help reduce this effect include:

1. Use enough fat in the pastry dough to keep the flour from overhydrating.

2. Coat the unbaked bottom crust with raw egg white and partially bake it before pouring in the filling; the coagulated egg waterproofs the crust.
3. In custard pies, use a high ratio of eggs to milk to bind the water.
4. Partially or completely thicken the filling before placing it in the crust.
5. Make sure the filling is at room temperature; a cold filling takes too long to heat up and soaks the crust; a hot filling melts the fat in the pastry and destroys the flakiness of the crust.
6. Start baking the pie as soon as it is filled, in a preheated oven.
7. Bake the pie in a hot oven, at least during the first part of the baking period, to set the crust.

Crumb Crusts

Many kinds of crumb crusts can be made from graham crackers, ginger snaps, vanilla wafers, and melba toast crumbs. Crumbs may be easily ground in a blender or food processor and are then combined with soft or melted table fat. Sugar is often added to cracker and toasted crumb crusts. Variations include the substitution of peanut butter or melted chocolate for part of the fat, or the addition of chopped nuts or coconut.

Crumb crusts always require a precooked filling, and these fillings should be fairly dry. Juicy fillings cause sogginess in crusts made of crackers or toasted crumbs and dissolve the sugar in cookie-crumb crusts, making them watery or syrupy. Crumb crusts are ideal in the bottom of square and rectangular pans as a base for pie-type fillings. Some of the crumb mixture can be reserved to sprinkle over the top surface of the filling as a decorative effect.

Pie Fillings

Four basic pie fillings are considered here: fruit, meringue, custard, and chiffon. Each requires its own special preparation.

FRUIT PIES

Many kinds of fruits are used in pies, either singly or in combinations. Because fruits are juicy, some type of thickening agent must be added to them in pie fillings. Large fruits, such as apples and peaches, are usually thickened with cornstarch because it produces a thicker, more translucent sauce than flour. Small fruits, such as berries and cherries, are often thickened with quick-cooking minute tapioca.

Thickening should make the juices that surround the fruit viscous, but not gelled. Because the sugars added to sweeten the fruit and the fruit's natural acids both interfere with starch thickening, use only minimal amounts of sugar for sweetening. Canned and frozen fruits that are sweetened during processing may not need additional sugar. Too much sugar not only interferes with gelatinization of the starch but also causes diffusion of juices from the fruit, a reaction that shrivels and toughens the fruit and makes the sauce thin and watery.

Tapioca is sometimes slow to hydrate in acid juices. Softening tapioca in a small amount of cool water before adding it to the fruit may eliminate this problem. Either tapioca or cornstarch may be thickened with the fruit juice before the filling is placed in the crust or the uncooked starch and fruit can be gelatinized in the pie during baking. However, the filling must reach the boiling point to assure maximum thickening. The boiling point has been reached when the juices start to bubble through holes in the center of the pie.

Slices of raw fruit should be tossed with a mixture of starch, sugar, and spice to distribute the starch evenly throughout the pie and to prevent lumping. Large pieces of fruit placed in a pastry-lined pan with no arrangement leave air spaces. During cooking, the fruit shrinks and packs down, producing a very shallow filling. To avoid this problem, particularly with firm raw fruits such as apples, arrange the slices of fruit in layers in the pan, but do not stack the fruit too high or the crust will become excessively brown before heat can penetrate the thick layers of fruit. The raw fruit should be layered level with the top of the pan or slightly rounded above the top. When the pie appears to be done, pierce the fruit in the baked pie to be sure it is sufficiently cooked; do not depend solely on the brownness of the crust as an indication. If the fruit is not done, reduce the oven temperature while it finishes cooking so that the crust does not overbrown. A single-crust pie with a custard-pudding topping is shown in Figure 14.6.

Figure 14.6

Raw pears are placed in an unbaked pastry shell, covered with a custard-starch mixture, and baked. *(California Tree Fruit Agreement)*

MERINGUE PIES Meringue pies contain eggs as part of their thickening agent. The yolks are in the filling, and the whites are beaten into a foam with sugar for a topping. Meringue pies include the popular lemon and cream.

Lemon Meringue Cornstarch and egg yolk are the thickening agents for this pie. The lemon juice added for flavor is quite acidic and can cause the starch to hydrolyze and the filling to thin if it is cooked with the starch, as described in Chapter 10. Withhold the lemon juice and sugar until after the starch is gelatinized. The water, egg yolk, starch, and salt are cooked with constant stirring over direct heat until the mixture comes to a boil; then the lemon juice and sugar are stirred in.

Many recipes for lemon meringue pie call for more sugar than is actually necessary. Using less sugar permits greater thickening of the filling with less starch. Recipes often specify that the ingredients be cooked simultaneously and call for a higher concentration of starch to compensate for the consequent thinning, but such fillings are heavy and less flavorful.

Variations include lime, orange, or pineapple juice as flavoring. Limes can be directly substituted for lemons, but because the flavor of oranges and pineapples are weak when diluted with water, frozen concentrates of these juices produce a richer flavor than the fresh juices.

Lemon, lime, and orange meringue pies usually contain grated rind in the filling to enhance the flavor. Only the colored part of the rind should be used; the white albedo under the colored skin of citrus contributes undesirable bitterness. Grated rind can be stored in an airtight container in the freezer for use as needed.

Cream Pies Cream pies are thickened with egg yolk and cornstarch as in lemon meringue pies, but they contain some form of milk as the liquid rather than water and juice. Withholding the sugar for sweetening the mixture until after cooking is completed produces the best results. Minimal amounts of sugar should be added to these pies. The method of preparing these pies is the same as the method for preparing lemon meringue pie. Milk, starch, egg yolk, and salt are cooked over direct heat with constant stirring until the mixture starts to boil, when it is immediately removed from the heat and the sugar is stirred in. Because milk is present, these mixtures have a great tendency to scorch without rapid stirring that completely scrapes all areas of the bottom of the pot during cooking.

Cream pies can be made with nonfat milk, low-fat milk, regular milk, or light or heavy cream. The higher fat content of milk or cream adds to the richness and flavor of the filling, but it also increases calories and cost. Cream pies can also be varied by the addition of coconut, nuts, and fruit. Juicy fruits that may cause thinning when they are added to the cooked cream filling should be drained well, or more thickening should be added to the cream filling, to balance the extra liquid contributed by the fruit. Fruits, such as bananas, that tend to turn brown should be treated to inhibit browning before they are added to a filling, or they should be combined with the cooked filling only at the last minute. Some cream pies are topped with whipped cream instead of meringue, because whipped cream keeps better refrigerated than meringue. Cream pies are a major source of foodborne illness, as discussed in Chapter 2. Pay strict attention to good hygiene when preparing cream pies and refrigerate them as soon as they are cooked.

Soft Meringues   Soft meringues are egg white foams with added sugar for topping pies and other desserts. The preparation of egg white foams is described in Chapter 20. To make a meringue, beat the egg whites to the soft-peak stage, then add sugar—about 2 tablespoons per egg white—and beat the foam to the stiff-peak stage. Do not beat until it is rigid; the finished meringue should be pliable.

Pour the hot cooked filling thickened with starch and egg yolk into a baked pie shell. Place the meringue on top and spread it over the filling (Figure 14.7). Spread the meringue so that it adheres to the crust all the way around the circumference of the

Figure 14.7

To prevent shrinking, distribute the meringue evenly over the pie so that it adheres to the crust all the way around; swirl designs into the meringue before baking.

pie to anchor it and keep it from shrinking. Designs may be swirled into the meringue for a decorative effect. The meringue-topped pie is then baked in an oven at 425°F (218.3C) for 5 to 8 minutes to set the meringue, which should turn golden brown, not dark brown or burnt.

SYNERESIS AND BEADING IN MERINGUE PIES Two problems common to meringue pies are syneresis, which occurs between the filling and the meringue, and the formation of amber-colored beads over the surface of the meringue. Syneresis, a collection of liquids, can be caused by liquid lost both from the starch-egg filling and from the meringue. The loss of fluid from the filling is the result of normal retrogradation of the starch paste, as discussed in Chapter 10; high ratios of acid and sugar in a starch filling promote syneresis. The loss of fluid from the meringue, however, is caused by undercooking. If the meringue is not baked enough to set its structure, the foam gradually collapses and the egg foam reverts to its original fluid state. This is the reason why meringue is best placed on a hot filling, which helps cook the meringue adequately before it becomes too brown.

Amber beads that form on the surface of the meringue are caused by the overcoagulation of protein in the meringue. Adding cream of tartar to the meringue increases its tendency to form beads. Soft meringues should not contain cream of tartar. The meringue should also not be overcooked.

CUSTARD PIES Custard pies are custard mixtures, or milk thickened with egg; some also include gelatin. The preparation of custards is described in Chapter 19. Various kinds of milk, from nonfat to cream, may be used in custard pies. As with cream pies, high concentrations of fat produce richer flavor and more calories.

Custard mixtures for pies should contain a high ratio of egg, two large eggs per cup of milk, for example, to bind the water in the milk and keep the crust from becoming soaked. Too little egg, as might occur if small or medium eggs are substituted for large ones, extends the time required to set the custard. Too much sugar delays the coagulation of custard mixtures just as it does for cream fillings; therefore, use minimal amounts of sugar for sweetening. Custard mixtures are usually flavored with vanilla, but other flavors can be obtained by adding chocolate, coconut, or such nonacidic fruit purees as banana, pumpkin, sweet potato, and squash. (Acid curdles the milk in a custard mixture.)

To make a custard pie, mix the custard ingredients together, pour them into an unbaked pie shell, and bake the shell and filling together. In baking custard mixtures, it usually is necessary to place the custard container in a container of hot water to insulate the custard and prevent overheating. This procedure is not necessary with custard pies, however, because the crust of the pie serves as insulation.

Unbaked Custard Pies   Even though all precautions previously described may have been followed, a soggy crust is not unusual in custard pies. The only way to prevent sogginess in the crust is to bake the crust separately. One procedure is to bake the custard in a well-oiled pie pan of the same size as the pan in which the crust is baked. After the custard mixture has cooled and set well, slip it into the baked pastry. This process requires some practice and dexterity, but can be done without mishap.

An alternative to this method is to use a stirred custard that contains gelatin. Stirred custard is cooked on a surface unit, cooled until it starts to thicken, and poured into the baked pie shell. Coagulation comes not from the heat coagulation of the egg but rather from the gelatin it contains. This type of custard pie has a different, more translucent, appearance and a slightly different texture and flavor than a baked custard mixture. Figure 14.8 shows a gelatin-custard pie topped with fresh strawberries.

Figure 14.8

A gelatin-custard mixture prepared in a blender is partially thickened before being poured into a crumb crust. Ripe strawberry halves are arranged on the surface of the thickened gelatin mixture. *(Knox of Thomas J. Lipton, Inc.)*

CHIFFON PIES Chiffon pies are gelatin mixtures with a foam structure. The preparation of gelatin foams is described in Chapter 20. The egg yolk, gelatin, and liquid are heated on a surface unit until the mixture is steaming hot and the gelatin is completely dissolved. They should never be heated to the boiling point, for this curdles the egg. Sugar and fruit or other seasonings are added to the hot mixture, which is cooled until it begins to thicken. The meringue is folded in and the mixture is poured into a baked, cooled pie shell and chilled until set (Figure 14.9).

Chiffon pies come in several types. In one type, the gelatin mixture is whipped, with or without egg, into a foam. Another type contains a gelatin mixture with whipped cream or milk but no egg. A third calls for ice cream folded into the flavored gelatin mixture. In all these pies, juices, fruit purées, crushed or whole fruits, as well as chocolate, coconut, and nuts, provide a variety of flavors. As with other foods, sugar should be added in moderation according to the needs of the other ingredients. Less sugar is needed in ice cream pies or in combination with sweet fruits than with tart fruits or ingredients without added sugar. Too much sugar masks the natural flavors of the other ingredients besides increasing the calories.

Danish and Puff Pastries Danish pastry is a nonsweet yeast dough containing eggs and cardamon seasoning. Puff pastry is a mixture of flour, water, and a small amount of acid ingredient, such as lemon juice or cream of

Figure 14.9

Evaporated milk and frozen pink lemonade are used in this delectable chiffon pie. *(Knox of Thomas J. Lipton, Inc.)*

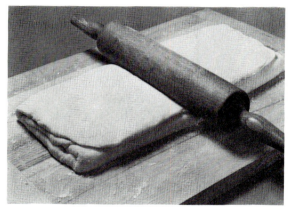

Figure 14.10

In Danish and puff pastries, solid fat is added to the finished dough. Cold table fat is rolled out between layers of waxed paper to form a solid sheet of fat. *(Fleischmann's Yeast)*

Figure 14.11

Dough for Danish and puff pastries is rolled out into a rectangle. Solid fat is layered over two thirds of the dough, which is folded into thirds around the solid fat. *(Fleischmann's Yeast)*

Figure 14.12

Dough for Danish and puff pastries is rolled out, folded into thirds, and chilled. This process is repeated two or more times. *(Fleischmann's Yeast)*

tartar. Both doughs are rolled out, and a large amount of a plastic fat, usually table fat, is spread or sliced evenly over the surface of the dough (Figures 14.10–14.12). The dough is folded into thirds with alternate layers of dough and fat, rolled out and folded again in thirds, and then refrigerated for a period of time that depends on the amount of dough.

Danish and puff pastry dough is chilled to solidify the fat and keep it from melting and soaking into the dough. Rolling, folding, and chilling are repeated from three to six times to develop the gluten into thin layers that are separated by layers of fat. Baked, the pastry is very flaky but not as tender as pie pastry. The acid ingredient in puff pastry promotes gluten hydration. Acid is not necessary in Danish pastry because it must be fermented before baking, and yeast cells produce sufficient acid in the dough during fermentation. Puff pastry may include egg, which gives it a richer flavor and color.

The more these doughs are rolled and folded, the more layered and flaky the baked pastry will be. During the final stage, the pastry dough may be rolled out and filled with fruit and nut fillings (Figure 14.13), which can either be baked or fried in deep fat. For tart shells, roll the pastry very thin or bake it in sheets that are cut into pieces of serving size. After baking, fill tart shells or layer flat pieces of pastry with a cooled, stirred custard mixture, fruit preserves, whipped cream, nuts, coconut, or combinations of these ingredients. Figures 14.14 and 14.15 show cockscomb and croissant pastries made from Danish or puff pastry dough.

Figure 14.13

Dough for Danish and puff pastries can be used to make cockscombs or bear claws. Roll out the dough and cut into strips. After placing filling on a strip of dough, fold it in half and cut into lengths desired; then slash each piece halfway into the fold several times and spread apart on a baking sheet to proof and bake.
(Fleischmann's Yeast)

Figure 14.14
Baked cockscomb pastries or bear claws are delicious for breakfast, brunch, or coffee breaks. *(Fleischmann's Yeast)*

Figure 14.15
Croissants also can be made from Danish and puff pastry dough. They are shaped in the same way as crescent yeast rolls, illustrated in Figure 16.14. *(Fleischmann's Yeast)*

Pie pastry is almost devoid of vitamins, minerals, and protein, but it is very high in calories because of its fat content. Any nutrients come from the ingredients in the filling. Those desserts that have a high content of milk, egg, and fruits and a low content of sugar and fat can be nutritious additions to the diet. Although pastry is emphasized in this chapter, the filling alone can provide a delightful dessert and decrease the calories by one half or more. The filling can be chilled in a pie plate or glass baking dish, with or without crumbs, such as those used for crumb crusts, thinly sprinkled on the bottom of the dish to make the contents easy to remove.

Nutritional Value of Pastry and Pies

Study Questions

1. Why must the mixing method for pastry be related to kinds of fat?
2. Name factors that cause flakiness in pastry.
3. Name factors that cause tenderness in pastry.
4. Why are flakiness and tenderness in pastry considered opposing characteristics, and how can a balance best be achieved between them?
5. Describe two methods for rolling out pastry where little or no additional flour is required. Why must additional flour not be

used to roll out pastry?

6. Why must pastry be pierced with a fork if it is baked without a filling.
7. Why are holes needed in the top crust of a two-crust pie?
8. Why is a high oven temperature desirable for baking pies, at least for the first part of the baking period?
9. What causes sogginess in the bottom crust of some pies, and how can this effect be reduced?
10. What are reasons for not adding excessive amounts of sugar to sweeten fruit pies?
11. Why is it advisable to withhold lemon juice and sugar until after cooking is completed when preparing a lemon pie filling?
12. What kind of pie shell is used for meringue pies?
13. What causes syneresis in meringue pies, and how can this effect be reduced?
14. What causes beading on the surface of meringue pies? How can beading be prevented?
15. What kind of pie shell is used for custard pies?
16. What is a chiffon pie?
17. In what ways can foam containing air be incorporated into chiffon pies?
18. Distinguish between Danish and puff pastries.

References

Bennion, Marion. "Fats as Cooking Media, Shortening Agents, and Components of Pastry." In *Food Theory and Applications,* edited by Pauline C. Paul and Helen H. Palmer. New York: Wiley, 1972.

Charley, Helen. *Food Science.* New York: Ronald Press, 1970.

Felt, S. A., Longree, K., and Briant, A. M. "Instability of Meringued Pies." *Journal of the American Dietetic Association* 32, no. 2 August 1956: 710.

Gillis, J. N., and Fitch, N. K. "Leakage of Baked Soft Meringue Topping." *Journal of Home Economics* 48, no. 9 November 1956: 703.

Hester, E. E., and Personius, C. J. "Factors Affecting Beading and Leakage of Soft Meringues." *Food Technology* 3, no. 7 July 1949: 236.

Lowe, Belle. *Experimental Cookery.* 4th ed. New York: Wiley, 1964.

Palmer, Helen H. "Eggs." In *Food Theory and Applications,* edited by Pauline C. Paul and Helen H. Palmer. New York: Wiley, 1972.

Pyler, E. J. *Baking Science and Technology,* vols. 1, 2. Chicago: Siebel Publishing, 1973.

Shortened Cakes and Cookies

Shortened cakes were once called butter cakes when butter was a preferred fat. Today, however, more specialized fats have been developed that yield products that are superior in volume and texture, but not necessarily in flavor, to cakes made with butter.

Desirable Characteristics of Shortened Cakes

A good shortened cake should have the following characteristics:

1. a good volume, not compact
2. an even grain with small, thin-walled cells
3. a soft, velvety crumb that is tender and moist
4. a flat or slightly rounded top with a smooth, dull, lightly browned surface
5. good flavor with adequate sweetness

Cake Ingredients

A good shortened cake must be made with the proper kinds and amounts of ingredients. The ingredients are the same found in other flour mixtures and perform the same functions described in Chapter 11.

KINDS OF INGREDIENTS AND THEIR FUNCTIONS

Flour Cake flour is best for shortened cakes and should be sifted before measuring. All-purpose flour can be substituted by using 2 tablespoons less flour per cup than specified for cake flour. Cakes made with all-purpose flour are less tender and light than those made with cake flour.

In recent years, there has been a new interest in the use of whole grain flours in cakes. About one third of the cake flour in a cake can be replaced by soybean flour with satisfactory results. Whole wheat pastry flour and triticale flour, if finely ground, are specially suited to special cakes, such as carrot cake, pumpkin cake, and applesauce cake. These flours usually are not available in regular retail food markets, but they can often be obtained from specialty food stores.

Fat Fat is probably one of the most important ingredients affecting the quality of shortened cakes. The type of fat determines the amount of air that can be incorporated into the batter, which, in turn, determines the volume and texture of the cake. The more air incorporated into a cake batter, the greater the volume and the better the texture of the baked cake will be.

Hydrogenated shortening with added emulsifier is the preferred fat for shortened cakes. Besides the emulsifier, the air in the shortening adds to the air incorporated in the cake batter. Most of the air in cake batters is incorporated when the fat, sugar, and eggs are creamed together. The fat must be sufficiently plastic and have other characteristics as well to aid the incorporation of air into the creamed mixture. Butter and margarine lack both emulsifiers and plasticity; they are too hard when cold and too soft at room temperature. A good shortening is neither hard nor soft, regardless of temperature; this characteristic is known as *plasticity.* Some shortenings have been specially developed for their creaming ability in shortened cakes; definite differences exist between brands, as Figure 15.1 demonstrates.

Fat interferes with the development of gluten in flour. Cakes can develop tunnels just as muffins do if the batter is mixed too much after the flour is added. Plain cakes with a low fat content develop tunnels more readily than rich cakes with a high fat content, because a plain cake contains less fat and sugar to interfere with gluten development.

Fat influences the quality of baked cakes because of its function in the batter during baking. As fat melts during baking, the batter becomes more fluid and permits greater expansion of gas cells, thus contributing to the volume of the baked cake. A plain cake has a less fluid batter, which offers resistance to the expansion of gas cells during baking and hence produces a lower baked volume.

Butter gives cakes a unique flavor, but their quality is less desirable than those made with a good shortening. A compromise is to use half butter and half shortening, or to add an artificial butter flavor to the cake batter. Commercial bakeries often add directly to the batter such emulsifiers as glyceryl monostearate, a monoglyceride, to increase the incorporation of air into the batter. Some types of coffee cakes contain oil instead of shortening.

Sugar   Sugar increases the tenderness of cakes by interfering with gluten development and by raising the temperature at which the coagulation of proteins and the gelatinization of starch occur. This function of sugar also keeps the batter more fluid during baking. Rich cakes, with their higher ratio of sugar and fat, are more tender than plain cakes.

Eggs   Eggs, along with flour, contribute structure to cakes. The yolk supplies an emulsifier that supplements, but cannot replace, the emulsifier in the shortening. Although egg white foams can

Figure 15.1

These cakes were made with the same proportions of ingredients. The cake on the left was made with a shortening containing no emulsifier; the cake on the right was made with a shortening containing adequate emulsifier.

increase the amount of air incorporated into a batter, this effect is of little value in a batter in which eggs, sugar, and fat have been creamed well, if a fat containing emulsifier is also present.

Eggs lower the temperature for the coagulation of protein in the batter during baking. Batters with a high egg content are less fluid and offer greater resistance to the expansion of gases, unless fat and sugar are increased proportionately to counteract the effect of the eggs.

Leavening Agents   Chemical leavenings are used in shortened cakes. Baking powder is the most commonly used leavening agent, but baking soda may be used if an acid ingredient is present to release carbon dioxide, as explained in Chapter 12. A slightly acidic batter is preferable because of the undesirable effects an alkaline batter produces on texture, color, and flavor. Because eggs increase the amount of air incorporated into the batter, more egg should be balanced with less chemical leavening. One egg replaces about ¼ teaspoon of baking powder. Both eggs and leavenings reduce the acidity of batters.

Liquid   Milk is the most commonly used liquid in cakes. Some specialty cakes depend on the water supplied by applesauce, fruit juices, and eggs. One of the main variations in shortened cakes is the substitution of other liquids for part or all of the milk to produce different flavors. Applesauce, pineapple, pumpkin, carrot, banana, orange, and lemon are frequently added for this purpose. Cakes that contain these ingredients are often moist in texture and not light, but are still of very good eating quality.

BALANCING INGREDIENTS IN CAKES   Wide variations in some ingredients in shortened cakes can still produce satisfactory results. However, the proportions of structural and tenderizing ingredients must always be balanced. Table 15.1 shows the proportions of ingredients in formulas for plain, standard, and rich cakes. Each cake is made with the same amount of flour, baking powder, and milk, but the plain cake has the least fat, sugar, and eggs, while the rich cake has the most (Figure 15.2).

Because of their high protein content, eggs produce a toughening effect in cakes; when the amount of egg is increased, therefore, the shortening and sugar must also be increased. The weight of the shortening should not exceed the weight of the eggs; the weight of the sugar should equal, or slightly exceed, the weight of the flour. Because shortenings with emulsifier are more effective tenderizing agents than shortenings without emulsifer, less shortening is needed; slightly less shortening than eggs provides excellent results if a shortening with emulsifier is used.

Adequate liquid is necessary in cake batter for good quality. Too little liquid produces a dry crumb and a harsh texture. Too

Table 15.1   Formulas for plain, standard, and rich shortened cakes

Ingredients	Plain cake		Standard cake		Rich cake	
	Volume	Weight (g)	Volume	Weight (g)	Volume	Weight (g)
Cake flour, sifted	1 cup	96	1 cup	96	1 cup	96
SAS baking powder	1 teaspoon	3.2	1 teaspoon	3.2	1 teaspoon	3.2
Salt	¼ teaspoon	1.5	¼ teaspoon	1.5	¼ teaspoon	1.5
Sugar	⅓ cup	67	½ cup	100	⅔ cup	133
Shorteningᵃ	2 tablespoons	24	¼ cup	47	⅜ cup	71
Eggs, large	½	24	1	48	1½	72
Milk	⅓ cup	81	⅓ cup	81	⅓ cup	81
Vanilla	½ teaspoon	2.5	½ teaspoon	2.5	½ teaspoon	2.5

ᵃShortening should contain emulsifier. Amounts shown are sufficient for one 9-inch layer, plain and standard formulas may also be baked in an 8-inch layer cake.

much liquid weakens the crumb structure, producing a low volume or even causing the cake to collapse in the oven. Both eggs and milk contribute to the total liquid of the cake.

Methods of Mixing Cakes

Cakes can be mixed many ways, but most are variations of three basic procedures; the conventional, muffin, and pastry methods. Even with the same basic formula of ingredients, widely different results can be obtained from these mixing methods.

CONVENTIONAL METHOD

In the conventional method of mixing, shortening, sugar, and eggs are beaten, or creamed, until the mixture resembles light, fluffy whipped cream (Figure 15.3). The dry ingredients, flour, salt, and leavening, are combined and added alternately to the creamed mixture with the milk and flavoring. The flour mixture is usually added in three parts, the milk in two parts. With each addition, mixing should be minimal to prevent overdevelopment of the gluten. After the last addition of flour, the batter should be mixed until it is smooth, or about 30 seconds.

Figure 15.2

These cakes were made from plain (top), standard (left), and rich (right) formulas, given in Table 15.1.

Figure 15.3

For best quality in a shortened cake, cream together the sugar, shortening, and egg until they form a light and fluffy mixture resembling whipped cream before adding the flour mixture and milk.

An electric mixer does a better job of creaming fat, sugar, and eggs than creaming them by hand, and it is quicker. The bowl must be scraped down regularly during mixing, however. Adding the liquid to the creamed mixture before the flour gives it a curdled appearance, but this does not affect the final quality of the cake. A rich cake tolerates more mixing than a plain cake, which tends to form tunnels more readily if it is overmixed.

Conventional Sponge This variation of the conventional method requires that the yolks and whites of the eggs be separated. The yolks are creamed with the fat and sugar, and the batter is mixed as described above. The egg whites are beaten into a foam, preferably with some sugar added to increase its stability, and this foam is folded into the finished batter. Egg white foams are of little advantage if a good shortening with enough emulsifier is used. Such foams, however, do improve the volume of cakes containing shortenings with no emulsifier.

MUFFIN METHOD The muffin method is a fast way to mix a cake. For cakes, the liquid ingredients—including melted fat or oil, egg, and milk—are mixed separately from the dry ingredients, and the two mixtures are then combined. Cakes made by this method are lower in volume, more compact, and not so tender as cakes made by the conventional method.

Forming a good emulsion with eggs and liquid fat helps produce a better cake, but it still does not permit the incorporation of very much air into the batter, which is why the muffin method produces lower-volume cakes. An egg white foam can help improve volume, but the additional effort required to separate the eggs, and to beat and fold in the foam, makes it as much work as the conventional method.

One-Bowl Method In this modification of the muffin method, all the dry ingredients are combined in a mixing bowl, all the liquid ingredients are added, and then they are mixed together all at once. With this method, as with the muffin method, all the dry ingredients, including sugar, must be mixed together well before the liquid ingredients are added so that the leavening agent is evenly dispersed.

In the pastry method, solid fat is very finely dispersed in the flour-salt-leavening mixture. This fine dispersion is necessary to coat the flour and to prevent the overdevelopment of the gluten. The sugar is stirred into the flour-fat mixture, and then the eggs and milk are added to form a smooth batter.

As in the muffin method, very little air is incorporated into the batter. Eggs can also be separated to make an egg white foam.

Function of Air in Shortened Cakes

The importance of shortening with an emulsifier and a mixing method that incorporates air into the batter has already been mentioned. A batter with a large amount of air produces a baked cake with a better volume and texture than a batter with less air for reasons related to the function of air bubbles in the batter.

Each air bubble has a surface film of water. When more air bubbles are present, more water is bound in the batter and the baked cake has a moister crumb. The air cells serve as nuclei for the leavening gases. As baking begins, carbon dioxide gas from the leavening agent and steam from the water in the batter expand these air cells. If many air cells are present, these leavening gases are able to disperse into many small cells and produce an even, fine-textured crumb in the baked cake. If only a few air cells are present, the leavening gases accumulate in large masses and tend to migrate to the top of the cake, where they produce tunnels, peaks and holes. Cake batter with little incorporated air has a coarser grain than one with many air cells.

Baking Shortened Cakes

Factors that can affect the characteristics of a baked cake include the structural material of the cake pan, the size of the pan, the temperature of the oven, and the position of the pans in the oven.

Pans with dark or dull surfaces that absorb heat are fast-baking pans; bright shiny pans that reflect heat are slow-baking pans. Fast-baking pans produce cakes of better texture and volume than slow-baking pans. However, cakes baked in slow-baking pans have a top that is flatter and less humped than those baked in fast-baking pans. Better texture and volume are obtained in cakes when heat penetration is rapid and uniform.

Cake pans should be the proper size for the amount of batter. Because they contain a large proportion of air, rich batters made by the conventional method should not fill the pan more than halfway so that they may expand completely during baking. For a plain cake or a cake made by the muffin or pastry method of mixing, the pan may be filled from one-half to two-thirds full. The ideal amount of batter in a pan is the amount that fills the pan completely when it is baked.

As a rule, a shallow pan with a wide diameter produces better volume and texture in a cake than a narrow deep pan, probably because the former promotes more rapid and uniform heat penetration. Batter baked in deep pans also tends to form peaks, probably for the same reasons as muffins.

Pans may be substituted for one another according to their surface area. The surface areas of pans of various dimensions are given in Table 15 in the appendix.

PREPARING THE BAKING PAN

Cake pans should be either greased and floured, or the bottom of the pan should be fitted with a liner made from waxed or parchment paper. Distribute the batter evenly in the pan by tilting it from side to side or by spreading the batter gently with a rubber scraper. A customary method is to tap the pan on the counter, or slap the bottom of the pan with the palm of the hand, to distribute the batter and get rid of large air pockets. These procedures are not recommended because they cause a sufficient loss of air in the batter to reduce the volume of the baked cake.

BAKING CAKES

Shortened cakes should be baked in a preheated oven to reach their best volume. A temperature of 365 to 375°F (185 to 190.5°C) produces a better volume and texture than lower temperatures, such as 325 to 350°F (163 to 177°C). Preheating and higher oven temperatures both produce more rapid heat penetration, the vital factor in achieving good volume and texture.

A baked cake will be lopsided if the oven is not level or if the heat is uneven. For this reason, cake layers should be baked as near the center of the oven as possible. Figure 3.5 shows the correct placement of layers for even baking.

Tests of doneness in cakes are similar to those for other baked products. Press the center of the cake gently with the ball of the finger. If the cake is done, the center springs back; if it is not completely cooked, an imprint of the finger remains. Pressure should be extremely light, for cakes are fragile and it is easy to leave a hole in the top. A second method is to insert a clean foodpick in the center of the cake. If the pick comes out clean, with no batter adhering to it, the cake is done. Often a cake pulls away from the sides of the pan when it is done, but this effect may not appear if the sides of the pan are ungreased.

A rich cake may take 5 to 10 minutes longer to bake than a plain cake. Presumably, the higher sugar content of the rich formula makes a higher temperature necessary to coagulate the protein and gelatinize the starch. Because of their higher sugar and protein content, rich cakes also brown more during baking than plain or standard cakes. Cakes containing honey should be baked at lower temperatures to minimize browning.

After a cake is baked, it should be cooled in its pan on a cake rack for 10 to 15 minutes. A tender, rich cake needs a longer cooling time for its structure to set. When the cake is sufficiently cool to handle, loosen it from the pan by running a table knife around the outer edge between the cake and the pan. Place a cake rack on top of the cake, then invert the cake and rack simultaneously and lift off the pan. If a cake is allowed to cool in the baking pan, it becomes moist and soggy. However, some coffee cakes are left in their baking pans so that they will be moist when they are served.

CARE OF BAKED CAKES

At elevations of less than 3,000 feet, recipes for baked products produce satisfactory results as given. Above this elevation, the ratios of ingredients, baking times, and temperatures must be altered. As a rule, the best practice is to use recipes specially developed for a particular altitude. Such recipes can often be obtained from state agriculture experiment stations.

High Altitude Baking

Because less pressure is exerted on the surface of liquids at higher altitudes, less heat is needed to volatilize water, which consequently boils at a lower temperature. This means that at higher altitudes more water is lost from a cake batter during baking than at sea level. Therefore, more liquid must be added to batters baked at higher elevations. Less leavening is needed, however, because less resistance is offered to the expansion of gas. The flour and egg content should be increased, and the sugar content decreased, to obtain satisfactory structure.

Even when a balanced recipe and exact mixing directions are faithfully followed, a baked cake sometimes turns out less than perfect or even unsatisfactory. Table 15.2 lists some of the problems that can occur in cake baking and their possible causes.

Problems in Making Shortened Cakes

Baker's chocolate is 53 percent fat, and cocoa powder can be from 8 to 24 percent fat, but is also about 15 percent starch. Recipes must be specially developed to incorporate either cocoa or chocolate. Chocolate must be melted before it can be added to the creamed mixture or combined with the fat. Cocoa powder is usually combined with the dry ingredients, although it can also be dispersed in the sugar, then creamed with the fat and eggs. The substitution of one form for the other is possible according to the ratios given in Table 8 in the appendix.

Chocolate Cakes

The color of chocolate cakes is influenced by the kinds and amounts of leavening. SAS-phosphate baking powders produce a brown color, and tartrate baking powders produce a reddish-brown color, in the baked chocolate cake. Chocolate cakes leav-

Table 15.2   Flaws in baked cakes and their possible causes

Flaw	Possible cause
Coarse crumb texture	Too much sugar or leavening
	Oven temperature too low
	Not enough mixing after addition of flour
Cake high on sides, low in center	Too much sugar, fat, leavening
	Not enough liquid
	Not enough mixing after addition of flour
	Too small a pan for amount of batter
	Oven temperature too low
	Cake was moved during baking
	Cake was not baked long enough
Heavy compact texture; low volume	Not enough leavening; gas lost before baking started
	Too much liquid, fat, or sugar
	Poor-quality shortening with no emulsifier
	Not enough air incorporated into creamed mixture
	Too much mixing after addition of flour
	Pan too small for amount of batter
	Oven temperature too low
Lack of tenderness; dryness	Not enough fat, sugar, or liquid
	Too much flour or egg
	Too much mixing after addition of flour
Sugary, crispy top	Too much sugar, fat, or leavening
Uneven shape of layers	Oven not level
	Paper liner in pan wrinkled
	Layer not centered in oven, uneven oven temperature
Humped, cracked top; tunnels	Not enough fat and/or sugar
	Too much mixing after addition of flour
	Too deep a cake pan used for baking
	Oven temperature too high

ened with baking soda and sour milk have a brown color if the batter is about pH 7. A more acidic pH makes the cake yellowish, a more alkaline pH makes it reddish brown. Too much baking soda, a common flaw of many recipes for chocolate cake, supplants the chocolate flavor with other, undesirable flavors. Additional information about chocolate is given in Chapter 31.

Care and Storage of Shortened Cakes

Shortened cakes with a high ratio of fat and sugar remain fresh longer than plain cakes. Shortened cakes are often iced, a condition that further delays drying. Cakes should be stored covered at room temperature to delay drying.

Baked cakes freeze well enclosed in plastic bags, cake boxes, or wrapped in foil or plastic. Since some types of frostings are not stable to freezing, the cake should be frozen uniced if possible. Furthermore, a cake is often easier to ice if it has been frozen first and it does not need to be thawed before the frosting is applied. Cake batters, however, do not hold up when they are frozen, because the emulsion in the batter breaks when it is thawed.

Fruit-Nut Breads

Fruit-nut breads contain the same ingredients as shortened cakes. However, these specialty breads contain less fat, sugar, and eggs than cakes and use all-purpose flour in place of cake flour. Some whole grain flours, such as triticale and whole wheat pastry flour, are especially suited for use in these loaves. The result of these alterations is a compact bread that can be thinly sliced without crumbling into pieces (Figure 15.4).

Fruit-nut breads may be mixed by any of the methods used for cakes. As a rule, fat, eggs, and sugar are creamed together, incorporating air so that the bread will have a fine, even grain. The flour mixture and liquid may be added and mixed in at the same time.

Many kinds of nuts and fruits—fresh, canned, frozen, or dried—may be added to these breads to add flavor and texture. Both nuts and fruits should be chopped very finely; large pieces are difficult to slice through and cause tearing and crumbling.

Bake the breads in regular-sized loaf pans (4½ inches by 8½ inches), in pup loaf pans (3¼ inches by 5¾ inches), or in fluted molds or empty cans. The baking container should be greased and floured; additionally, a piece of parchment paper or brown paper should be cut to fit the bottom of the container so that the bread may be easily removed. The pans should be about one-half full of batter. After they are baked, cool the breads in their pans for a

Figure 15.4
Fruit-nut breads are more compact and have a coarser texture than shortened cakes. *(Wheat Flour Institute)*

few minutes. When the loaves are cool, wrap them in aluminum foil or plastic wrap and store them in the refrigerator or freezer. Breads at least a day old slice more easily than fresh bread.

Loaves often have a crack on top, which results from their being baked in deep pans. The top forms a crust before the leavening gases in the center of the loaf have fully formed and expanded; these gases cause the top to crack when they finally escape. Loaves should be baked at moderate temperatures, about 350°F (177°C), so that they can cook in the center without becoming overly browned on top.

Fruit-nut breads can be served warm or cold, thinly sliced, spread with butter or cream cheese, for breakfast, luncheon, informal teas, and coffee breaks.

Cookies

Cookies, like fruit-nut breads, contain the same ingredients as shortened cakes, but many cookies contain more sugar and fat than cakes. Cookies also contain less liquid than cakes; eggs are often the only source of liquid in cookies.

MIXING COOKIE DOUGHS

Most cookie doughs use all-purpose flour and a modified conventional method of mixing. Whole grain flours, such as triticale, whole wheat pastry, and soybean flours are specially suited to cookies and are interchangeable with all-purpose flour in most recipes. Wheat germ and nutritional yeast can also be substituted for part of the flour to increase the nutrients in cookies.

A thorough creaming of the fat, sugar, and egg is necessary for a good texture. The flour and other dry ingredients should be mixed well. When they are added to the creamed mixture, the dough should be mixed only enough to become homogeneous. Too much mixing after the flour is added decreases the tenderness of the baked cookie. Refrigerating cookie dough for several hours before it is baked often makes it easier to handle.

The consistency of the cookie dough, and of the baked cookie, is determined by the kinds and amounts of ingredients. A chewy cookie has a high egg content, a crisp cookie has a high fat content, and cakelike cookies have a high liquid content. If cookies run together during cooking, the ratio of fat to flour may be too high. Cookies that are too hard after baking contain too much liquid and too little fat.

With a new recipe, bake a test cookie first to determine its characteristics. Add more flour, for example, to a dough that produces cookies that spread excessively. A test cookie can also provide information about spacing cookies on the pan, how much dough each cookie needs, and how long they must be baked.

BAKING COOKIES

Because of their high sugar and low water content, cookies have a greater tendency to burn than cakes. Using the correct pans and placing them properly in the oven can help prevent burning.

Bright, shiny pans are less likely to cause burning than dark-colored baking pans. Pans without edges permit cookies to brown evenly. The bottoms of cookies brown more when they are baked on the bottom shelf of the oven; the tops brown more when they are baked on the top shelf. Cookies should therefore be baked as near to the middle of the oven as possible. If several sheets of cookies are baked at the same time, bake them on the lower shelf for the first half of baking and shift them to the top shelf for the second half.

Cookie sheets should be placed in the oven in such a way that they allow for the circulation of hot air. Each baking sheet should be surrounded on all sides by about 2 inches of space. If one area seems to heat faster than another—the back of the oven more than the front, for example—it may be necessary to turn the sheets back to front about halfway through the baking period.

Baking time depends partly on the size of the pieces of dough. For this reason, cookies should be approximately the same size on any one sheet so that they will all bake in the same time. An even brown color is a good indication of doneness, unless the oven is too hot. Moreover, not all cookies are resilient when they are done, so that the finger pressure test may indicate that a cookie is not cooked when it actually is. An inserted food pick, however, should come out clean when a cookie is done. Overcooking is one of the biggest problems in cookie baking. Cookies must be checked for doneness, not overcooked just because the recipe calls for a specific amount of time for baking. The baking time given in recipes is not always dependable.

Seven main types of cookies are recognized, primarily according to the way they are shaped before or after baking. The shape a cookie can take is determined by the type of dough from which it is made.

TYPES OF COOKIES

Drop Cookies   Drop cookies are made from a fairly soft dough that is placed on the baking sheet by teaspoonfuls (Figure 15.5). The directions for mixing and baking most cookies apply here as well. Drop-cookie dough is sometimes rolled into balls the size of large walnuts before it is placed on the baking sheet, to obtain a more uniform shape. Whether a baking sheet needs greasing or not depends on the type of dough; if the fat content is high, the baking sheet need not be greased. Smears or spills of dough between cookies should be cleaned off before baking, for they burn on the sheet and make cleaning up more difficult.

Rolled Cookies   Dough for rolled cookies is stiffer and drier than dough for dropped cookies; it must be firm enough to be rolled out with a rolling pin. As with pie pastry, a minimal amount of flour for rolling out the dough produces a better-quality cookie.

Figure 15.5

For drop cookies, place teaspoons of dough on a baking sheet with space between to allow room for cookies to spread during baking. Use approximately the same amount of dough for each cookie so that all will bake evenly.

Figure 15.6

Rolled cookies can be cut with a variety of shapes of cookie cutters, or the rolled-out dough can be cut with a pastry wheel into diamonds or squares. A paper guide is used here to produce more even shapes.

Because cookie dough is usually stickier than pie pastry, a lightly floured pastry cloth on a bread board works best. Too much flour reduces crispness in cookies and makes them hard (Figure 15.6). Chilled dough is not so sticky and therefore is easier to roll out. Nuts and fruits are not usually added to rolled cookies because they interfere with rolling out the dough into a thin layer unless they are very finely chopped. Rolled dough can be cut into various shapes with cookie cutters or pastry wheels. These devices cut dough better if they are first dipped into flour.

Artificial flavors or chocolate may be added to the dough or it can be cut into a variety of shapes, iced, and decorated in many ways. Use paper patterns to cut the dough into desired shapes, such as gingerbread houses and dolls. The dough can be sprinkled with colored sugar crystals or candies before the shapes are cut out.

Bar Cookies   The batter for bar cookies is spread into a greased and floured pan, baked, and cut into squares, rectangles, diamonds, or other desired shapes. Many bar cookies are cakelike in texture, but some are chewy. Some types have two or more layers. Because they are not individually shaped, bar cookies are one of the fastest and easiest type of cookies to make. Nuts, dried fruits, or other ingredients make excellent additions to the batter.

Pressed Cookies   Pressed cookies are dough put through a cookie press to form interesting shapes. This dough has a high fat content and is fairly soft. Because the dough must be forced through templates with very small holes, nuts and fruits cannot be added unless they are finely ground.

One difficulty in making pressed cookies is getting the cookie dough to break away from the press and adhere to the baking sheet. To help this process, the cookie sheet should be clean, free of grease, and cold. A dough with a high fat content can produce the same problem, so adding a small amount of water or egg yolk to the dough can also make the dough adhere to the baking sheet. One cookie-press manufacturer has recommended not adding all the flour at once, but withholding some flour to determine the final consistency of the dough. The same manufacturer suggests resting the press against the baking sheet and turning or squeezing the handle until the desired amount of dough has been pressed through the template, and then lifting the press vertically to separate it from the dough.

Some templates are harder to work with than others. Changing the template can sometimes help the dough to stick to the baking sheet (Figure 15.7).

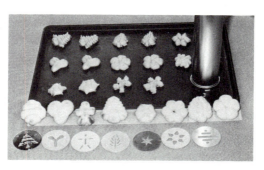

Figure 15.7

Change the template of a cookie press to produce a variety of cookie shapes.

Molded Cookies The dough for molded cookies should be soft but not sticky. Small pieces of dough are molded or rolled with the fingers, or between the palms, into such shapes as balls, sticks, crescents, vegetables, or fruits. Balls can be flattened with the tines of a fork or with the flat bottom of a glass to make a flat, round cookie, or indented with the thumb to form wells to hold filling after they are baked. Dough can also be shaped around a nut or piece of candy, or candies and nuts can be pressed into the top surface. Most molded cookie doughs have a high fat content that keeps the dough from being sticky and makes the cookies tender.

Refrigerator Cookies Refrigerator cookies require a fairly firm dough that is shaped into a roll, wrapped in plastic or foil, refrigerated for several hours, and then thinly sliced for baking.

Refrigerator cookie dough is difficult to slice if it is too soft or crumbly. Too much flour or too little liquid can cause crumbling, while too little flour or too much liquid causes oversoftness. Pieces of nut, fruit, or coconut added to the dough can also interfere with slicing or cause the dough to crumble. A very sharp knife or an electric knife and a well-chilled dough makes the easiest slicing. Dough is also easier to slice if its diameter is not too large. One way to ensure a small, even shape is to pack the dough firmly into 6-ounce juice cans (Figure 15.8).

Filled Cookies A filled cookie is a combination of a pie tart and a rolled sugar cookie. All of the rules that apply to rolled cookies apply to filled cookies. The dough can be a pie pastry, a puff pastry, a shortbread, or a rolled cookie dough, as long as it is of a consistency to be rolled out. The type of dough affects the flavor and texture of the cookie.

Figure 15.8

Dough for refrigerator cookies can be pressed into containers and chilled for easy slicing. Here, cardboard frozen orange juice containers were used; they are easily peeled off when the dough is ready to slice.

Figure 15.9

These filled cookies are made from leftover pie pastry and filled with a mixture of equal amounts of orange marmalade and shredded coconut. The outer circumference of the pastry was moistened with water before the edges were folded and sealed. Holes are pierced in the top of the filled cookie with a blunt fork to allow steam to escape during baking.

Regardless of the dough, the method of forming filled cookies is the same. The dough is rolled to a thickness of ⅛ to ¼ inch and is cut into circles 2 to 3 inches in diameter. Place the filling, often a fruit preserve, by teaspoonfuls into the center of the circle of dough and brush the outer edge with water to help form a seal (Figure 15.9). Then fold the circle in half or place another circle on top of the one with the filling. Seal the edges by pressing them down firmly with the tines of a fork. The dough can be cut into squares, rectangles, or triangles as well as in circles.

A slit must be made in the top of the filled pastry before it is baked so that steam can escape. A good seal around the edges also keeps the filling from running out during baking. The filling should be fairly thick, because thin fillings are more likely to leak out. A filling with too much water quickly makes the pastry soggy. After the cookie is baked, it can be sprinkled with powdered sugar or brushed with a flat icing.

CARE AND STORAGE OF COOKIES

All baked cookies except bar cookies should be removed from the baking sheet while they are still warm. Cool them on a cake rack or on a sheet of wax paper on a counter top. Warm cookies should never be stacked, for they will stick to each other and lose their shape. Store cake-like cookies in tightly sealed containers; store crisp or chewy cookies in containers with loose-fitting covers.

Cookie dough and baked cookies alike keep well when they are frozen; the dough occupies less space. Dough can be frozen in refrigerator containers, plastic bags, or empty, rustproof cans. Baked cookies also can be frozen in plastic bags, but they should be placed in such a way that they will not be broken or crushed. Baked cookies should be thawed in their wrapper to prevent a gain or loss of moisture. Stale cookies that have lost their crispness can be briefly reheated in an open pan in a moderate oven, about 300°F (149°C), but not long enough to brown again.

Nutritonal Value of Cakes and Cookies

Cakes and cookies mainly provide calories, not nutrients, and should only be served to make up the balance of caloric needs after obtaining adequate nutrients from other foods. Because they are considered desirable, cakes and cookies are often eaten in place of more nutritious foods, which contributes to problems both of nutrition and of obesity. The nutritional content of cakes and cookies can be increased by a careful choice of ingredients, as previously discussed.

Study Questions

1. Describe the characteristics of a good shortened cake.
2. What is the preferred fat for shortened cakes, and what characteristics make it desirable?
3. Name some functions of fat in a cake batter.
4. How do rich cake formulas differ from standard and plain cake formulas, and how does the formula affect the quality of the baked cake?
5. Briefly describe the three basic methods for mixing cakes. Indicate the advantages and disadvantages of each method.
6. What causes a cake batter to curdle? Does curdling affect the quality of the baked cake?
7. Why is it important that a large amount of air be incorporated into the batter of shortened cakes?
8. How is air incorporated into cake batters? What is the most important source of air in batter?
9. Why is rapid heat penetration important in baking shortened cakes? What are some ways used to obtain rapid heat penetration?
10. How is a shortened cake tested for doneness?

References

Campbell, Ada Marie. "Flour Mixtures." In *Food Theory and Applications*, edited by Pauline C. Paul and Helen H. Palmer. New York: Wiley, 1972.

——; Penfield, M. P.; and Griswold, R. M. *The Experimental Study of Food.* Boston: Houghton Mifflin, 1979.

Pyler, E. J. *Baking: Science and Technology*, vol. 2. Chicago: Siebel, 1973.

16

Yeast-Leavened Products

Yeast breads, as distinguished from quick breads, are leavened with carbon dioxide produced by yeast from glucose, a form of leavening that is a time-consuming process. The characteristics and quality of yeast-leavened baked products depend on the kinds and amounts of ingredients and the manner of mixing and baking used to make the product.

INGREDIENTS IN YEAST BREADS   The basic ingredients of yeast doughs are flour, liquid, and yeast. Sugar, fat, and salt are usually added to add flavor and improve the texture.

Flour   Bread flour is best in yeast breads because it has a high content of strong gluten. Widely used in commercial bread production, it is not available in most retail markets. All-purpose flour is the only available alternative, but brands vary considerably, with some having a better gluten potential than others. Yeast breads made from all-purpose flour do not achieve the volume and texture of those made from bread flour.

Satisfactory breads can also be made from whole wheat flours. Whole wheat flours made from hard wheat and finely ground are best. Bran in whole wheat flour is slow to hydrate; large, coarse bran particles cut and weaken the gluten strands in dough, producing a baked loaf with a smaller volume. Also, the germ in whole-wheat flour contains a tripeptide called *glutathione* that weakens the gluten and makes the dough sticky and hard to handle. The sulfhydryl (SH) groups of glutathione are responsible for this effect. Since heating changes the SH groups to disulfide bonds, toasted wheat germ can be used.

Triticale, soy, and rye flours all lack gluten potential and therefore are not satisfactory when used in yeast bread unless they are used with at least 60 percent good-quality bread flour or more of weaker gluten flours, such as all-purpose flour. Gluten can be isolated from wheat flour and is available as a flour. Gluten flour improves the quality of doughs containing those flours that lack gluten potential.

Liquids   Water hydrates the yeast and flour and dissolves the sugar and salt. The liquid that is most often used in yeast doughs is milk, although water and potato liquid are common alternatives. Fresh milk has a high content of sulfhydryl (SH) groups that have the same dough-softening effect as those in glutathione in wheat germ. Scalding the milk reduces the number of SH groups; the fresh milk should be heated to 190°F (88°C) for one minute—a microwave oven is useful for this purpose. Evaporated milk has been heat processed during canning and does not need to be scalded. Nonfat dry milk (NFDM) used by commercial bakeries is scalded before dehydration to reduce the number of SH groups, but this bakery-tested NFDM is not available in the retail market.

It is more economical and easier to use NFDM for home baking, even though it has not been heat treated. Some of the dough-softening effect of NFDM can be counteracted by use of the sponge method and the addition of the NFDM after the first fermentation with the remainder of the flour.

Milk improves the texture and volume of baked bread and delays staling. Doughs that contain milk need more mixing and kneading than doughs made with water. The lactose and protein of milk produce a darker crust in baked bread than is obtained in breads made of water. The milk protein is high in lysine, the limiting amino acid in wheat (Chapter 1), and supplements and improves the protein quality of the bread, as as well as contributing flavor.

The amount of liquid in a dough depends on how much water the flour can absorb. The higher the protein content of the flour, the more water is absorbed. At home, start with a given measure of liquid and add flour until the dough reaches the desired consistency. As a rule, from 2½ to 3 cups of flour absorb 1 cup of water.

Other Ingredients The requirements for yeast growth are discussed in Chapter 12. Yeast needs sugar to grow and to produce carbon dioxide gas. Enzymes in flour and yeast can convert starch in the flour to glucose, but this is a slow process. Dough ferments more rapidly if sugar is added. Salt inhibits yeast activity and prevents too much fermentation. Breads made without salt have a coarse texture. Salt also inhibits the dough-softening enzymes that make dough sticky and hard to handle. Proper amounts of fat in yeast doughs improve the volume, texture, grain, crust, and keeping quality of bread. Fat improves the tenderness of bread and makes dough more elastic. Plastic fat is more effective than oil. Egg adds structure and improves the elasticity of dough; it also contributes flavor and improves protein quality by adding extra lysine. Egg substitute or egg white can be used in place of whole egg.

MIXING AND KNEADING YEAST DOUGHS

Making a yeast bread of good quality requires a flour with high protein content and good gluten potential, properly hydrated. Moreover, gluten must be correctly developed by mixing and kneading. A good yeast dough should be both plastic and elastic. Elasticity allows the dough to stretch and entrap the leavening gases as they are formed; plasticity allows it to be molded into desired shapes for yeast loaves and rolls.

To make the dough elastic the gluten must be developed by stretching. Bakeries have mixers designed to pull and stretch the dough to develop gluten. At home, a different technique must be used. An ordinary twin-beater mixer cannot be used because the beaters chop up the gluten rather than develop it, although some mixers with hypocycloidal beating action have dough hook attachments for mixing yeast doughs. Most yeast breads made at home, however, are mixed and kneaded by hand. Two mixing procedures are effective, the straight dough method and the sponge method.

Straight Dough Method   In the straight dough method, all the ingredients are combined, mixed, and kneaded before fermentation begins. The yeast is dissolved in water or milk of the correct temperature as explained in Chapter 12, and the flour is added to the rest of the ingredients with enough mixing to develop the gluten properly (Figure 16.1). This method is quite satisfactory for regular doughs made from good quality bread flour or all-purpose flour.

Sponge Method   In the sponge method, the yeast is dissolved in the liquid. Salt, sugar, and fat are then added along with part of the flour. This fluid mixture is mixed well and allowed to ferment until it is light and bubbly. At the end of the first fermentation, the NFDM, if used, and the remaining flour are added. If extra sugar or low gluten potential ingredients—such as triticale, rye or soy flours, or wheat germ—are used, they are best added at this point. Sufficient wheat flour is added to produce a soft dough (Fig-

Figure 16.1

To form a yeast dough, combine liquid, yeast, sugar, salt, and fat; then add flour to form a soft dough. *(Wheat Flour Institute)*

ure 16.2). The sponge method is ideal for use with sweet doughs as it permits the addition of the extra sugar at the end of the first fermentation. Too much sugar initially can have a dehydrating osmotic effect on the yeast cells and reduce fermentation. The sponge method is also ideal for whole grain flours by allowing time for hydration of the bran, which takes time, and preventing formation of a stiff dough. Whole grain doughs must be soft so that there is sufficient water for bran hydration.

Mixing Techniques Using either method, the novice bread maker tends to add too much flour, producing a stiff dough, and to undermix the dough. For best results, add 1 cup of flour at a time and mix the batter or dough for several minutes, or 100 or more strokes, between each addition. Mixing strokes should either beat or stir around the bowl; both strokes help stretch the gluten. Thorough mixing between flour additions also prevents too much flour being added to the dough, by allowing time for hydration.

Kneading the Dough The more dough is mixed, the less kneading it requires, and vice versa. If the gluten is not developed by mixing, it must be developed by kneading. As with other doughs

Figure 16.2

Soft yeast dough is scraped out of the bowl onto a breadboard covered with a floured pastry cloth. *(Wheat Flour Institute)*

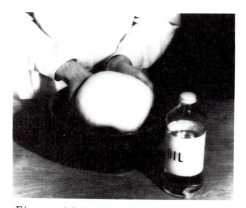

Figure 16.4
A well-kneaded ball of dough,
smooth and elastic, is placed
in an oiled bowl
for fermentation.
(Wheat Flour Institute)

Figure 16.3
Yeast doughs must be adequately kneaded to develop the gluten.
Fold and flatten the dough repeatedly; it should be soft
enough not to tear along the folded edge during kneading.
(Wheat Flour Institute)

described, do not add any more flour during kneading and shaping than is needed for easy handling. A bread board covered with a lightly floured pastry cloth is a helpful asset.

To knead the dough, flatten it with the heel of your hand and fold it over with the other hand. With each fold, turn the dough a quarter of a turn, repeating the pressing and folding operations (Figure 16.3). Folding is especially important in stretching and developing the gluten; punching and pressing is not enough. If the dough is soft, as it should be, it is easy to knead. If the dough contains too much flour, it is stiff and resists folding. Stiff dough also tears easily along the folded edge, further weakening the gluten.

Doughs prepared with soft wheat or all-purpose flour must be thoroughly mixed and kneaded to develop their full gluten potential (Figure 16.4). Soft wheat flour has a weak quality of gluten that may be damaged by overworking, but this does not usually happen. Most homemade breads tend to be kneaded too little rather than too much. Sweet doughs must be kneaded more thoroughly than ordinary breads because of the inhibiting effect of sugar on gluten development. Whole wheat breads and those that contain nongluten flours also benefit from ample kneading.

Insufficient kneading makes a baked loaf heavy and small in volume, with a compact grain and a coarse, irregular crumb texture.

FERMENTATION

The process of fermentation is described in Chapter 12. For the most part, yeast doughs are fermented until they double in size, and then are punched down. Doughs prepared from hard wheat flours benefit from a second fermentation period before the dough is shaped for baking. The stronger gluten of hard wheat flours requires longer fermentation to develop optimum elasticity and plasticity in the dough. The time required for the dough to double in volume depends on the number of yeast cells in the dough—that is, on the amount of yeast used. The more yeast cells present, the more carbon dioxide gas is produced in a given time. The fermentation time also depends on the amount of glucose available in the dough for fermentation by the yeast. Carbon dioxide gas cannot be produced by yeast cells if no glucose is present or if its supply is limited. The temperature of the dough also affects the fermentation time; the dough doubles its size more rapidly if it is held at 90°F (32°C) than if it is held at 80°F (27°C). A test of adequate fermentation is demonstrated in Figure 16.5.

Punching Down the Dough   When the dough doubles in volume, it must be punched down (Figure 16.6). Punching is accomplished by kneading the dough gently several times until the carbon diox-

Figure 16.5

Test for adequate fermentation of yeast dough by pressing fingers into the dough; if an indentation remains, the dough is ready to be punched or scaled.
(Wheat Flour Institute)

Figure 16.6

Punch down dough by kneading it gently in the bowl as shown or by kneading it on a breadboard. Handle dough gently at this stage to avoid damaging the gluten.
(Wheat Flour Institute)

Figure 16.7

Scale dough by dividing it into pieces for shaping into loaves and other yeast products. *(Wheat Flour Institute)*

ide gas is expelled. Other functions of punching the dough include incorporating additional oxygen needed by the yeast, redistributing yeast cells, and equalizing the temperature. Punching the dough also prevents the gluten from being overstretched by the gas and provides gas cells with tighter gluten walls.

Changes during Fermentation The production of carbon dioxide gas is only one of the beneficial effects of the fermentation process. Fermentation also increases the hydration of gluten and bran in whole wheat breads and improves the elasticity of the dough. Fermentation makes the dough more acidic, a condition that promotes hydration of the flour and its components. The dough is also less sticky and more easily kneaded after it is fermented, which is why the sponge method of mixing is often preferred for making bread. Also, substances are produced during fermentation that improve the flavor of the baked bread.

The bread-making process can be speeded up by increasing the amount of yeast, but this procedure sacrifices the desirable effects of fermentation on the dough. When the ordinary amount of yeast is used, the second fermentation usually takes about half as much time as the first fermentation, because the yeast has multiplied during fermentation to produce many more yeast cells.

SCALING, SHAPING, AND PROOFING DOUGHS After the dough has been fermented, it is divided into pieces according to the final form the pieces will take (Figure 16.7). In the baking industry, this process is known as *scaling*, because it requires weighing the pieces of dough. To make loaves, round the pieces of dough into smooth balls and allow them to rest for 10 to 15 minutes. Worked dough becomes resistant and loses its plasticity; the rest period improves plasticity so that the dough can be molded into desired shapes.

In large bakeries, the pieces of dough are *sheeted*, that is, they are passed through a set of steel rollers like the wringer on a washing machine, a process which flattens the dough into strips and presses out large gas bubbles that would, if allowed to remain, give the bread a coarse texture. These strips are then rolled up and placed in pans. At home, the piece of dough can be rolled into a rectangle with a rolling pin so that the width of the dough is about the same as the length of the pan in which the bread is to be baked (Figure 16.8). Moistening the surface of the dough with water helps the layers of dough stick to each other when they are rolled up and prevents large holes from forming between the layers. Figures 16.9 and 16.10 show how prepared dough is placed in loaf pans.

Figure 16.8

To shape a bread loaf, roll the dough into a rectangle as wide as the loaf pan is long. Moisten the surface of the rectangle lightly so that adjoining surfaces adhere to each other, then roll up the dough. *(Wheat Flour Institute)*

Figure 16.9

Pinch and seal the final edge to the roll of dough before placing the dough in the pan. *(Wheat Flour Institute)*

Figure 16.10

Place the roll of dough into an oiled bread pan, seam-side down. Leave the dough in the shape of a roll so that it will have a rounded top after baking; do not press into the pan. *(Wheat Flour Institute)*

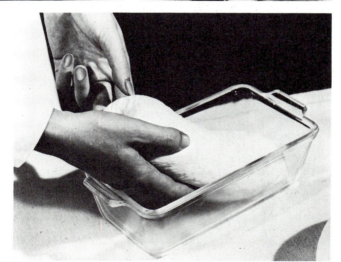

Proofing, the final fermentation period, takes place after the dough is shaped and before it is baked. The temperature for proofing should be the same as that for fermentation. If the dough has had only one fermentation, it may need a slightly longer proofing than a dough with two fermentations. During proofing, the dough expands sideways to fill the pan and also increases in height. Under these circumstances, it is sometimes difficult to judge when the volume of dough has doubled. With the proper proportion of dough in the pan, the dough will be slightly rounded above the top of the pan when proofing is complete.

If bread is fermented too long, the volume will be small and compact when baked. The crust will be light in color if the yeast has used all of the available glucose. If proofing alone was excessive, the bread has a flat top, a coarse texture, and a worm-eaten appearance on the sides and bottom. Too much proofing makes the gluten stretch too much; when baking begins, the cells collapse and are unable to retain the expanded gas. Too much proofing is more likely to happen in loaves with a poor gluten content that comes from either poor flour, insufficient hydration, or inadequate mixing or kneading of the dough.

Too little fermentation can also produce a baked loaf of small volume. Without enough fermentation, the gluten is less elastic and does not easily stretch with expanding gas. If not enough yeast cells are present because they had too little time to multiply, because not enough yeast was used initially, or because some of the yeast was destroyed by too high temperatures during fermentation, the baked volume is also small. The crust is dark, the top is slightly rounded and the sides and bottom are smooth, not worm-eaten in appearance.

BAKING YEAST BREAD

A full-sized loaf of yeast bread is baked at 425°F (218°C) for 25 to 30 minutes. Color is not an indication of doneness, for browning is always greater when milk, sugar, or egg is present in the dough. The top crust is usually too firm for doneness to be tested by finger pressure. When the bread appears to be done, remove it from the oven and gently empty it out of the pan on one side; then press the side of the loaf to see if it is done.

During baking, the dough often tears along one side, just above the level of the pan. An even shred is normal; uneven shredding indicates the underdevelopment of the gluten. The even shred shows where the gluten has been unable to stretch further with the expansion of gases during baking. Not all loaves show shreds, and a properly hydrated dough with good gluten development and proper fermentation will probably not shred during baking. Figure 16.11 shows a yeast loaf that has been correctly made and baked.

STALING OF BREAD

As soon as bread is baked, it begins to stale. Staling results from changes in the starch in the bread. As bread stales, the crust turns

Figure 16.11
A well-made loaf of yeast bread has a good volume with evenly distributed, thin-walled cells. *(Wheat Flour Institute)*

leathery, and the crumbs become firm and dry. Ingredients and storage temperature seem to be the most important factors in determining how fast a bread stales. Commercial bread contains monoglycerides that delay staling, and breads with a high content of fat, milk, egg, and sugar stale less rapidly than ordinary breads. French bread stales quickly because it contains no milk or egg and very little fat.

Staling occurs most rapidly at refrigerator temperatures, but can be delayed by freezing, providing the bread is frozen rapidly. Staling is slowed at warm room temperatures, but bread is also more likely to become moldy at this temperature. Large bakeries add calcium propionate to yeast dough to inhibit mold development. Breads baked from acidic doughs are less likely to become moldy. Stale bread can be freshened by warming; this may be one reason that bread is so commonly toasted.

Figure 16.12

Dough for yeast rolls is rolled out about ⅓-inch thick and cut into circles with a biscuit cutter. The circles of dough are folded in half with their open edges pressed together and their tops brushed lightly with melted butter to form Parkerhouse rolls. *(Wheat Flour Institute)*

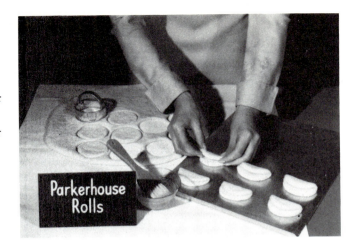

YEAST DOUGH PRODUCTS

A variety of baked products are produced from yeast doughs. The preparation methods are similar in all of these products, but individual products require specific changes.

Rye Breads Even though rye flour contains proteins capable of forming gluten, other components of rye flour prevent gluten formation. Certain vegetable gums in rye flour are thought to surround the protein and prevent its hydration. A dough made only of rye flour is plastic but not elastic; such breads are very heavy and compact. Most commercial rye breads contain varying amounts of wheat or gluten flour to lighten the loaf. Pumpernickel is a rye bread prepared by bacterial fermentation, a sour dough process in which the acids produced during fermentation counteract in part the adverse effects produced by the vegetable gums on the protein in the rye flour.

Dinner Rolls Regular yeast bread doughs can be shaped into dinner rolls; a richer dough containing egg and additional fat and sugar may also be used. Mixing, kneading, and fermentation procedures are the same as those used for preparing yeast bread. Figures 16.12 to 16.17 show a number of ways by which dough can be shaped to make dinner rolls. Figure 16.18 shows yeast dough used to make pizza.

Sweet Doughs Sweet doughs are yeast doughs with a large amount of added sugar, fat and eggs. They are a base for rolls, coffee cakes (Figure 16.19), and pastries that can be filled or studded with fruits, nuts, toppings, and glazes, which are often as beautiful to look at as they are to eat. Danish pastry, described in Chapter 14, is a type of sweet yeast dough in which solid fat is rolled into the dough after mixing.

Bowknots and Rosettes

Figure 16.13

To form strips, roll small pieces of yeast dough between the palm of the hand and the breadboard. To make a bowknot, form a loop in the strip and thread the other end through. To form a rosette, tuck both ends of the bowknot over and into the loop. Brush the rolls lightly with melted table fat before proofing. *(Wheat Flour Institute)*

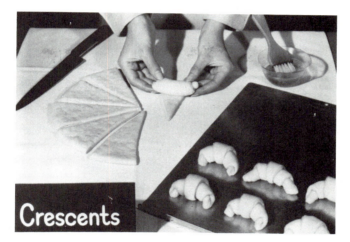

Crescents

Figure 16.14

To form crescent rolls, roll the yeast dough into a round circle with a rolling pin, then cut the circle of dough into wedges with a knife or kitchen shears dipped into flour. Lightly brush the surface of the dough, but not the points of the wedges, with melted table fat. Roll up starting with the wide end and rolling toward the point, which is pinched against the roll of dough and placed against the pan. Curve the roll into a crescent shape and brush lightly with melted table fat. *(Wheat Flour Institute)*

Cloverleaf Rolls

Figure 16.15

To form cloverleaf rolls, shape small pieces of dough into round balls. Place three balls in each cup of the muffin tin and brush the tops lightly with melted table fat. *(Wheat Flour Institute)*

Figure 16.16

To form fantans, roll dough into a very thin sheet and brush lightly with melted table fat; cut the sheet of dough into narrow strips. Stack six or seven strips evenly on top of one another, and cut the stack into pieces long enough to fit into muffin cups. *(Wheat Flour Institute)*

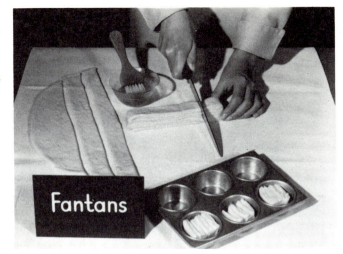

Figure 16.17

To form butterfly rolls, roll yeast dough into a rectangle with a rolling pin. Brush the surface lightly with melted table fat, roll it up, and seal the edge. Cut the roll of dough into lengths of about 1½ to 2 inches. Press the handle of a knife into the center of each roll, as shown, to form a butterfly shape. Crescent rolls can be pressed in the same way to form butterfly rolls. *(Wheat Flour Institute)*

Ordinary sweet dough is made in the same way as other yeast doughs except that it uses more of the ingredients previously mentioned. Better results are often obtained with sweet yeast doughs by using the sponge method and withholding most of the sugar until after the first fermentation. Sweet dough should be soft; the extra liquid is needed because sugar competes with gluten for the available water. Adequate kneading is required for the same reason.

Sweet doughs should be baked at a lower oven temperature than breads 350 to 400°F (177 to 204°C) because they become too brown at higher temperatures before cooking completely inside. When a microwave oven is available, sweet dough products can

Figure 16.18
A dough hook for mixing yeast doughs is shown at left; properly mixed dough should be elastic and should clear the bowl. Yeast dough is used to make pizzas, as shown: the dough is rolled out and flattened or stretched to fit the pan; a thin layer of tomato sauce or marinara sauce is spread over the dough. Many kinds of toppings can be used: a mixture of cooked, crumbled ground beef and sausage is shown on the pizza at the right; thinly sliced salami is shown on the pizza at the left. Thinly sliced or coarsely grated cheese may be placed on top of the pizza.

Figure 16.19
Many coffee cakes and sweet rolls can be made from sweet dough. Shown is a whole-wheat sweet dough shaped into a date-nut coffee cake. The dough is rolled into a rectangle, filling is spread evenly over it, and it is rolled up with the edge sealed against the roll. The seam side is placed down on an oiled baking sheet. The roll is cut almost all the way through into ½-inch slices, which are turned to alternate sides as they are cut.

be baked in a regular oven to the desired degree of brownness, and then transferred to the microwave oven to finish cooking, usually for 1 minute or less. This technique is also effective with breads that tend to brown too much before they are done, after removing the bread from the metal pan. (Metal pans should never be used in microwave ovens.)

Doughnuts   Yeast doughnuts are a sweet dough that is fried in deep fat instead of being baked. Like other yeast products, yeast doughnuts should be made from flour with a good gluten potential. The dough should be mixed and kneaded well and properly fermented. Roll out the doughnuts with a minimum amount of flour; use a pastry cloth on a bread board. Doughnuts must be proofed after they have been cut out and before they are fried (Figure 16.20).

Figure 16.20

Raised doughnuts made from yeast dough must be allowed to ferment before the dough is rolled out and cut, and the shaped dough must be proofed before it is fried. A clean cloth placed over the doughnuts during proofing reduces drying. *(Best Foods, Division of CPC International, Inc.)*

Cake doughnuts leavened with baking powder are satisfactory when they are made from all-purpose flour and can be mixed and fried immediately after they are rolled out and cut. As the name implies, cake doughnuts are cake-like in texture. Yeast doughnuts are large in size, with an open, airy interior structure. Because of their gluten development, they are less tender than cake doughnuts and also have a characteristic yeasty flavor. Both types of doughnuts should have a lightly browned, crisp crust and should show proper fat absorption.

When doughnuts are fried, they absorb some of the fat in which they are cooked. This effect is desirable so long as the amount of fat absorbed is not excessive. The proper amount of fat absorption imparts richness of flavor and texture and improves the keeping quality of doughnuts. Too little fat absorption gives a doughnut a pasty texture, whereas too much fat absorption makes it greasy and overly fat-flavored.

Fat absorption in doughnuts is affected by many of the factors described in Chapter 3. More fat is absorbed when doughs contain a high content of fat and sugar or are not mixed enough, although excessive mixing should be avoided because it reduces tenderness. Doughnuts made from a high-protein flour, as well as relatively dry doughs, absorb less fat.

When the dough is rolled out for cutting, its surface should be smooth. Ridges or wrinkles remain in the doughnut when it is fried and detract from its final appearance. The dough should not be rolled too thin. Thick doughnuts have less surface area, and, therefore, show less fat absorption than thin doughnuts. Dough at a warm room temperature (77°F or 25°C) absorbs less fat during frying than dough that is either chilled or very warm.

For best results, fry the doughnuts in fat at 360°F (182°C) for 3 minutes, or 1½ minutes on each side. The color of the doughnuts should not be too dark, because excessive browning detracts from the flavor (Figure 16.21). The time and temperature may need to be adjusted so that the doughnut reaches a light brown color by the time it has cooked on the inside; this factor depends partly on the thickness of the dough. Yeast doughnuts should be placed in fat so that their raised side, that is, the side that was up during proofing, is turned over and placed down in the fat to cook first.

Other Breads Bagels, English muffins, crumpets, and batter breads are also prepared from yeast doughs. Bagels are prepared from fermented yeast dough. The dough is shaped into strands about 6 inches long, and the ends of each strand are joined to form a doughnut shape. After a short proof, the bagels are lowered into boiling water and cooked about 5 minutes. The boiled bagels are then baked about 20 minutes until browned.

English muffins are prepared from fermented sour dough. The dough is rolled out and cut into 3-inch diameter rounds and

Figure 16.21

Fried doughnuts can be served plain; sugared with granulated, cinnamon, or powdered sugar; or dipped in glaze. *(Wheat Flour Institute)*

proofed. These are cooked about 9 minutes per side on a griddle at low heat—about 275°F (135°C). Most people like them best split crosswise and toasted.

Batter breads are made from a yeast batter rather than a dough, having a lower proportion of flour to liquid. The mixed batter is fermented and then well mixed again before baking. The batter is not proofed, and is baked in a round cake pan. With the lower flour ratio, the yeast batter does not have the structure to be baked in regular bread pans.

Crumpets are made from a batter and cooked like English muffins on a griddle. The batter is poured into a muffin ring placed on the hot, greased griddle to retain the batter.

CARE AND STORAGE OF YEAST PRODUCTS

Baked yeast products keep well for several days when wrapped in plastic or aluminum foil after they are cooled, to prevent drying, and stored at room temperature. Warm room temperatures promote molding and the development of *rope*, a fungus that destroys the interior of the loaf. Refrigeration increases the rate of staling but delays molding and rope. Baked products freeze well.

Yeast doughs can be refrigerated for a few days, but should be allowed to ferment again before they are shaped. Unbaked yeast doughs do not hold up well in frozen storage because some destruction of yeast occurs. If doughs are frozen, however, they should be thawed and fermented before being shaped. Commercially frozen doughs are specially formulated and processed to produce satisfactory baked loaves.

The ingredients of bread determine its nutritional quality. Egg, nonfat dry milk, wheat germ, and whole wheat, triticale, and soy flours improve the protein quality of yeast breads and add vitamins and minerals. Further, the fermentation process impedes the formation of the phytic acid mineral complexes mentioned in Chapter 9, thus increasing the availability of minerals in whole wheat.

NUTRITIONAL VALUE OF YEAST BREADS

Study Questions

1. What types of flours are preferred for yeast dough products? Why?
2. How and why is gluten developed in yeast breads?
3. What causes yeast doughs to tear when they are folded during kneading?
4. What are some factors that influence the time required for the fermentation of yeast doughs?
5. What are some changes that occur in yeast doughs during fermentation?
6. Why are yeast doughs punched down when they double in volume?
7. What are some reasons for preferring the sponge method of mixing yeast dough to the straight dough method?
8. What ingredients in yeast bread are effective in delaying staling?
9. How are sweet yeast doughs different from standard yeast dough in ingredients, preparation, and baking procedure?
10. What factors affect fat absorption in doughnuts?

References

Bennion, Marion. "Fats as Cooking Media, Shortening Agents, and Components of Pastry." In *Food Theory and Applications,* edited by Pauline C. Paul and Helen H. Palmer. New York: Wiley, 1971

Campbell, Ada Marie. "Flour Mixtures." In *Food Theory and Applications,* edited by Pauline C. Paul and Helen H. Palmer. New York: Wiley, 1971.

Gates, June C., and Kennedy, Barbara M. "Protein Quality of Bread and Bread Ingredients." *Journal of the American Dietetic Association* 44 (1964): 374.

Kinsella, J. E. "The Chemistry of Dairy Powders with Reference to Baking." *Advances in Food Research* 19 (1971): 148.

Pyler, E. J. Baking: *Science and Technology,* vols. 1, 2. Chicago: Siebel Publishing, 1973.

Sunset Cookbook of Breads. Menlo Park, Calif.: Lane Publishers, 1970.

U. S. Department of Agriculture. *Bread, Cakes, and Pies in Family Meals,* Home and Garden Bulletin No. 186. Washington, D.C.: Government Printing Office, 1971.

17

Gelatin

Gelatin is used in many prepared foods. A knowledge of gelatin and its preparation can increase its usefulness as a food.

Gelatin is extracted from the hides, skin, connective tissues, and bones of all types of animals. In the usual method of extraction, called *alkaline extraction*, these materials are soaked in lime or calcium hydroxide solution for a period of time and then are heated to dissolve the gelatin from the collagen tissues. A poorer quality gelatin can also be extracted with acids. Extracted gelatin is a pure protein.

The characteristics of gelatin depend on the method of extraction and the materials from which it was extracted. Both factors affect the strength and quality of gels obtained from the gelatin. Standard tests evaluate the strength of gels obtained from various extractions. A good gelatin produces a strong, yet tender, gel; poor gelatin produces a weak gel or one that develops a tough, leathery layer at the bottom.

Gelatin has no grades to help the consumer determine good quality. Manufacturers of gelatin maintain separate standards for their products by testing and combining extraction batches, but the consumer must compare available brands to locate the most satisfactory gelling qualities for the least cost.

Two major forms of gelatin are marketed, plain, unflavored granular gelatin and flavored, sweetened granular gelatin. Unflavored gelatin comes in envelopes containing 1 level tablespoon of granular gelatin. Flavored gelatin is available in 3- and 6-ounce packages that also contain sugar, citric acid, and artificial flavor and color; the 3-ounce package contains 1 level tablespoon of dry gelatin. Not only is it advisable to compare the gelling properties of the flavored products, but the flavors also should be examined. Some artificial flavors have bitter or chemical undertones that may be objectionable to a discriminating palate.

Dry gelatin dissolved in hot water absorbs water and forms a dispersion called a *sol*. Cooled, the gelatin sol becomes a *gel*. The proteins that compose gelatin are chains of amino acids. Chemical bonds form between these protein chains as the sol cools and trap water in the lattices between the chains, thus producing a gel. The sol and gel states of gelatin are reversible by a change of temperature: warming produces a sol; cooling, a gel. The sol can be changed to the gel and back again a number of times without its quality being affected, although in normal food preparation such frequent change should not be necessary.

As a rule, gelatin forms a gel more quickly the second and succeeding times it is cooled. The slow cooling of a sol produces a stronger gel that resists changing to the sol state at room temper-

SOURCE AND COMPOSITION OF GELATIN

MARKET FORMS OF GELATIN

GELATIN SOLS AND GELS

ature and holds its shape better when it is unmolded. However, a gel formation must sometimes be made quickly. The following techniques can speed up the gelling process:

1. The gelatin container can be placed in a larger container of ice water or a mixture of salt and ice.
2. The gelatin container can be placed in the freezer, where gelling occurs more rapidly than in the refrigerator.
3. The gelatin can be dissolved in only a part of the liquid; the remaining liquid can be partially or completely frozen, or replaced by ice if water is the liquid, and added to the dissolved gelatin.

Effect of Gelatin Concentration A gelatin gel can be strengthened by increasing the concentration of gelatin, which means that less liquid should be added for a given amount of gelatin. If gelatin must be cooled quickly, the weakening effects of fast cooling can be partially counteracted if the amount of water is reduced ¼ to ½ cup per tablespoon of unflavored dry gelatin. A higher concentration of gelatin may also be necessary if the gel is to be held at a warm room temperature for a long period of time, because the higher concentration reduces the gel's tendency to change to a sol. Too much gelatin produces a stiff, rubbery gel.

Effect of Acid Acid is often present in gelatin mixtures when acidic juices are the liquid medium. Because acid weakens the gel slightly, the concentration of gelatin should be increased.

Proteolytic Enzymes Proteolytic enzymes hydrolyze proteins either to amino acids or to shorter chains of amino acids. Hydrolysis of the protein chains in gelatin prevents gel formation. Four fruits contain proteolytic enzymes: pineapple (bromelin), papaya (papain), figs (ficin), and kiwi (actinidan). Papain is the enzyme used in meat tenderizers. Because enzymes are inactivated by heat, these enzymes present no problem in canned and cooked fruits. When these raw fruits, either fresh or frozen, are added to a gelatin mixture, however, no gel forms.

PREPARATION OF GELATIN MIXTURES The method of preparation of gelatin varies with its market form. Unflavored gelatin should be softened in cool or warm water, and then heated to be dissolved. Gelatin can be quickly dissolved in a liquid measure in a microwave oven. Because the gelatin granules in flavored gelatin mixes are dispersed in sugar, the mix can be added directly to boiling water. Either way, all the gelatin granules must be dissolved. Gelatin granules that stick to the sides of the pan or dish do not dissolve properly. If gelatin is not completely dissolved, the lower concentration of dissolved gelatin produces a weaker gel. Boiling is not necessary to dissolve gelatin; scalding temperatures, around 190°F (88°C), are adequate.

One tablespoon of unflavored gelatin usually forms a good gel with 2 cups of liquid. Less water is recommended for some uses.

Types of Liquids   Water is the most commonly used dissolving agent for flavored sweetened gelatin mixes. Unflavored gelatin can be dissolved in a number of other liquids to provide a variety of flavors as well as additional nutritional contributions. Milk produces a stronger gel than water. Almost any kind of fruit juice can be used; the syrup from canned fruits can be added as part of the sweetening when juices are used as the liquid. Canned fruits pureed in a blender are also suitable. Even lemonade, ginger ale, and other carbonated beverages have been used as liquids for dissolving gelatin. Aspics can be prepared from tomato juice or other vegetable juice combinations. Meat stock and whey provide good tasting bases for salads.

Unflavored gelatins combined with any of these liquids provide plenty of opportunity for creativity. Because flavored gelatins are already sweetened, however, liquids added to them should not be too sweet, or the gelatin mixture can become cloying.

Solid Foods in Gelatin Mixtures   Solid ingredients—chopped fruits, vegetables, or nuts—often either float or sink to the bottom when they are added to a gelatin sol. However, solid ingredients may be evenly dispersed throughout the mixture if the gelatin sol is chilled to the point where it begins to thicken, often described as "the consistency of thick, raw egg white." The solid ingredients can either be withheld until the gelatin starts to thicken, or they can be added to the sol and stirred as this stage is reached.

The liquid from canned vegetables and fruits should be completely drained off the solid ingredients before they are added to the gelatin mixture (Figure 17.1) so that the juices do not dilute

Figure 17.1

Canned fruits, such as the crushed pineapple shown here, should be drained well before they are stirred into slightly thickened gelatin.

Figure 17.2

A cheese gelatin mold garnished with asparagus and cherry tomatoes is a tasty luncheon dish. *(Knox of Thomas J. Lipton, Inc.)*

the gelatin and prevent it from gelling. Juices may be used as the dissolving medium for gelatin, but they must be properly measured to produce the correct ratio.

The presence of solid ingredients weakens the gel structure because they interrupt crossbonding between the protein chains. When solids are added to a gelatin mixture, a stronger concentration of gelatin should be used—that is, instead of 2 cups of liquid per tablespoon of unflavored gelatin, use only 1½ cups of liquid.

Gelatin Molds   Gelatin mixtures are often gelled in decorative molds. The molds may be small enough for an individual serving or large enough to hold several quarts (Figure 17.2). Gelatin is easier to remove from the mold if the mold has been previously oiled. Solid ingredients should be stirred into the slightly thickened gelatin before the mixture is transferred to the oiled mold. Gelatin can also be cut into slices and cubes.

To arrange slices or pieces of fruits or vegetables so that they are suspended around the sides or bottom of a mold, chill the empty mold in the freezer, then coat a small section with thickened, not gelled, gelatin, and arrange the fruit as desired. Chill this design in the freezer before the next section is arranged and proceed one section at a time until the mold is finished (Figures 17.3, 17.4).

Figure 17.3

A vegetable tomato aspic, attractively molded, is garnished with fresh mushroom slices and curly endive. *(Knox of Thomas J. Lipton, Inc.)*

Figure 17.4

A medley of fruits, attractively arranged in this gelatin mold, is garnished with sugared grapes and mint leaves. *(Knox of Thomas J. Lipton, Inc.)*

Layered Gelatins Different colors and flavors of gelatin can be layered into a mold. The first layer of gelatin should be completely gelled in the mold; the second and succeeding layers, partially thickened, are poured over the gelled layer. Solid ingredients may be arranged within the layers as previously described.

Unmolding Gelatin Mixtures The mold should be briefly dipped in a container of hot water, or wrapped with a hot wet towel, to soften the gelatin and loosen the gel from the mold. It is then inverted on a plate, as shown in Figure 17.5. Because a vacuum forms between the gel and the mold, it may be necessary to insert a knife between the mold and the gelatin to allow air to enter and break the vacuum. Avoid using too much heat to remove gelatin from molds because heat weakens the gel. If the gel appears soft after it is unmolded, it should be rechilled.

Dry gelatin becomes less soluble over a period of time, especially if it is stored at high temperatures. Old or improperly stored gelatin becomes difficult to disperse in water.

Gels made from gelatin, so long as they are properly cooled, become stronger and more rigid the longer they are held, up to 24

HOLDING AND STORAGE OF GELATIN AND GELATIN MIXTURES

Figure 17.5

To unmold gelatin, quickly dip the mold in warm water to loosen the gelatin. Insert a spatula or knife blade in one side to let in air. Place a plate over the top of the mold, invert the plate and mold together, then lift off the mold. *(Knox of Thomas J. Lipton, Inc.)*

hours. They should be served during this period for best quality and stability; after the first day, gels begin to show syneresis. Increased bond formation between the protein chains reduces the size of the spaces in the network or lattice; this causes water in the spaces to be squeezed out, producing syneresis. Gelatin mixtures may be rapidly cooled in a freezer, but the mixture should not be allowed to freeze, because considerable syneresis results when it is thawed.

NUTRITIONAL VALUE OF GELATIN MIXTURES

A common but erroneous belief is that because gelatin is extracted from animal tissues, it has the same protein quality as other proteins from animal sources. This is definitely not the case. Gelatin is not a complete protein; it is deficient in the amino acid trytophan. Gelatin is still a good food, however, and has a place in the diet. Because pure gelatin contains no vitamins and minerals, only protein, its nutritional contribution depends solely on the food ingredients added. Flavored, sweetened gelatin mixtures supply only calories and incomplete protein. An unflavored gelatin dispersed in fruit juice, or a fruit puree with added fruits or vegetables and minimal amounts of sugar, can provide far more nutrients for less calories.

The fad that promotes gelatin as a health aid for hair and nails has no scientific basis. The health of all parts of the body, including hair and nails, is best achieved by consuming a wide variety of foods to ensure a proper intake of all nutrients.

1. From what source is gelatin obtained?
2. Name the two market forms of gelatin and describe briefly the recommended method for dissolving each.
3. Distinguish between a gel and a sol.
4. How may the gel-sol state of gelatin mixtures be reversed?
5. Name several factors that affect the strength of a gel.
6. What are proteolytic enzymes, how do they affect gel formation, and how may this effect be counteracted?
7. At what stage of gelation should solid ingredients be added to gelatin mixtures? Why?
8. Is gelatin a good source of protein? Explain.

References

Bello, J., and Vinograd, J. R. "The Biuret Complex of Gelation and the Mechanism of Gelation." *Nature* 181, no. 4604 (January 25, 1958): 273–274.

Ferry, J. D. "Protein Gels." *Advances in Protein Chemistry* 4 (1948): 1–78.

Harrington, W., and von Hippel, P. "The Structure of Collagen and Gelatin." *Advances in Protein Chemistry* 16 (1961): 122.

Idson, B., and Braswell, E. "Gelatin." *Advances in Food Research* 7 (1957): 235–338.

Paul, Pauline C. "Proteins, Enzymes, Collagen, and Gelatin." Food Theory and Applications, edited by Pauline C. Paul and Helen H. Palmer. New York: Wiley, 1972.

Milk and Cheese in Food Preparation

Milk and its products have been used as foods for centuries. Consequently, many prepared foods contain milk or milk products. Most milk consumed in the United States is cow's milk, although milk from other animals is equally edible. Certain properties of milk affect its use in various food preparations.

Table 18.1   Composition of various market forms of milk and imitations

Type of milk product	Composition per 100 grams						Grams per 237-ml cup
	Water (g)	Energy (kcals)	Protein (g)	Fat (g)	Carbohydrate (g)	Ash (g)	
Fresh Fluid:							
Whole, 3.3% fat	87.99	61	3.29	3.34	4.66	0.72	244
Low fat, 2% fat	89.21	50	3.33	1.92	4.80	0.74	244
Low fat + NFDM	88.86	51	3.48	1.92	4.97	0.77	245
Nonfat (skim)	90.80	35	3.41	0.18	4.85	0.76	245
Concentrated (undiluted)	64.30	185	9.40	10.40	13.40	2.10	258
Filled milk	87.67	63	3.33	3.46	4.74	0.80	244
Imitation milk	88.18	61	1.75	3.41	6.16	0.50	244
Cultured:							
Buttermilk	90.13	40	3.31	0.88	4.79	0.89	245
Whey	93.12	27	0.85	0.36	5.14	0.53	246
Yogurt, low fat	85.07	63	5.25	1.55	7.04	1.09	227
Yogurt, regular	87.90	61	3.47	3.25	4.66	0.72	227
Sour half & half	80.14	135	2.94	12.00	4.26	0.66	240
Sour cream	70.95	214	3.16	20.96	4.27	0.66	230
Imitation sour cream	71.15	208	2.40	19.52	6.63	0.30	235
Fluid creams:							
Half-and-half	80.57	130	2.96	11.50	4.30	0.67	242
Light whipping	63.50	292	2.17	30.91	2.96	0.46	239
Heavy whipping	57.71	345	2.05	37.00	2.79	0.45	238
Pressurized cream topping	61.33	257	3.20	22.22	12.49	0.76	60
Coffee whitener	77.27	136	1.00	9.97	11.38	0.38	245
Dessert topping, imitation[a]	66.65	189	3.60	12.41	16.53	0.81	80
Canned, undiluted:							
Evaporated, nonfat	79.40	78	7.55	0.20	11.35	1.50	255
Evaporated, whole	74.04	134	6.81	7.56	10.04	1.55	252
Condensed	27.16	321	7.91	8.70	54.40	1.83	306
Dehydrated:							
Whole	2.47	496	26.32	26.71	38.42	6.08	105
Nonfat, regular	3.16	362	36.16	0.77	51.98	7.93	120
Nonfat, instant	3.96	358	35.10	0.72	52.19	8.03	68
Buttermilk	2.97	387	34.30	5.78	49.00	7.95	120
Whey	3.19	353	12.93	1.07	74.46	8.35	—
Coffee whitener	2.21	546	4.79	35.48	54.88	2.64	94

SOURCE: U.S. Department of Agriculture, *Composition of Foods—Dairy and Egg Products,* Agriculture Handbook 8-1, 1976.
    [a]Powdered product prepared with whole milk.

Composition of Milk

Milk contains water, protein, fat, carbohydrate, minerals, and vitamins. Many of these components vary with the method of processing, as indicated in Table 18.1. Milk fresh from the cow contains about 87 percent water; its only carbohydrate is lactose. Milk fat has a high content of saturated fatty acids, cholesterol, and phospholipids (see Chapter 1).

Milk is an excellent source of calcium, phosphorus, riboflavin, vitamin A, and complete protein, and contains small amounts of other vitamins and minerals as well. When fat is removed from milk, saturated fat, cholesterol, and vitamin A are also removed. Some nonfat milks, both fluid and dried, are fortified with vitamins A and D, as explained in Chapter 1.

Several kinds of proteins are found in milk. Casein makes up about 80 percent of milk protein; the whey proteins, lactalbumin and lactoglobulin, make up the other 20 percent. These proteins differ in the ways they are affected by acid, heat, and rennin, as shown in Table 18.2. They can be precipitated, or separated, from milk by these means. The precipitation of casein proteins is a part of cheese making.

The dispersion of casein *micelles,* or submicroscopic droplets, gives fluid milk its opaque white appearance. When casein is removed by precipitation to make cheese, the whey that remains is transparent and yellowish; the yellow color is partly the result of dissolved riboflavin in the whey.

*Table 18.2
Precipitation of
milk proteins*

Agent	Casein	Lactalbumin, lactoglobulin
Acid	Yes	No
Rennin	Yes	No
Heat	No	Yes

Milk Processing

Today milk is rarely sold just as it comes from the cow but is usually processed in one or more ways. Besides having its fat content adjusted to meet state standards, milk is usually pasteurized and is often homogenized. Concentrated, milk is sold fresh, frozen, or canned; it is cultured, dried, and converted into cheese. Milk fat is sold as cream and butter.

PASTEURIZED AND CERTIFIED MILK

Milk is pasteurized because it is an excellent food source for bacteria, and is easily contaminated by disease-carrying bacteria. Bacterial contamination of milk has been known to cause *brucellosis* (undulant fever), streptococcal infections, tuberculosis, typhoid, shigellosis, encephalitis, diphtheria, and many other infections. Pasteurization has greatly reduced or eliminated milk as a source of these diseases.

Milk is pasteurized when it is heated to 144°F (62°C) for 30 minutes, or to 162°F (72°C) for 15 seconds. Not all bacteria in milk are destroyed by pasteurization, but the numbers of bacteria are reduced sufficiently so that those remaining do not cause disease. Pasteurization is not destructive of any nutrients for which milk is a dependable source. Some thiamin and ascorbic acid is lost in pasteurization, but milk has very little of these nutrients to begin with; other foods in the diet are better, more dependable, sources.

The sale of unpasteurized, or raw, milk is not permitted in some states because of the likelihood of disease. Other states permit raw milk to be sold if it is certified, that is, when it is produced under controlled conditions of cleanliness in animal care and milk production. Dairies producing certified raw milk are inspected frequently to monitor the bacterial count of their milk. But even with these precautions, occasional outbreaks of some diseases still occur from raw certified milk. Milk from other animals, such as goats, can cause these diseases as well and should also be pasteurized.

Milk made into cheese should be pasteurized before the curd is precipitated. Unpasteurized cheese products can cause disease.

HOMOGENIZATION

Cream rises to the top of unhomogenized milk because fat globules are large and not as dense as the rest of the milk. Homogenization breaks up fat globules into very small particles that remain dispersed evenly throughout the milk. In this process, milk is forced under pressure through very small holes that divide the fat globules into small droplets. The nutritional value of homogenized milk is the same as that of unhomogenized milk. Homogenized milk is more viscous, whiter in appearance, more bland in flavor, less heat stable, foams more readily, and forms a softer curd than nonhomogenized milk. The homogenization process causes a mechanical denaturation of the protein causing unfolding or uncoiling of the protein chains. In addition, some of the casein is used to form films around the smaller, more numerous fat particles. Longer baking time is needed for baked custards containing homogenized milk, but the custards are firmer and show less syneresis. Homogenized milk has a greater tendency to curdle in acidic mixtures, produces a more viscous white sauce, and disperses the solids in cocoa and chocolate beverages better than nonhomogenized milk.

CONCENTRATION, DEHYDRATION, AND CANNING

The concentration and dehydration of milk involves the removal of water from milk in varying amounts. Water is removed by gravity separation, centrifugation, low-temperature vacuum dehydration, or combinations of several of these techniques. Concentrated and dried milks are reconstituted when water is added to produce a liquid milk of similar composition to fresh milk, but flavor is changed.

Fresh and Frozen Concentrated Milk   Concentrated milks have had two thirds of their water removed; thus 1 quart reconstituted milk yields 3 quarts of fresh whole milk. Milk sold in this form is usually sterilized for 3 seconds at a higher temperature (270°F, 132°C) than that used for pasteurization, causing greater bacterial destruction so that the milk keeps longer. In some areas of the United States, concentrated milk is sold fresh; in other areas, it is sold only as a frozen product.

Canned Evaporated Milk   Half the water of both whole and non-fat milk is removed to concentrate it; then they are canned and sterilized by heat. Half the water is also removed to make condensed milk; sugar is added, and the product is canned and processed. Canned evaporated milk needs a higher processing temperature than condensed milk because the sugar in the latter acts as a preservative. This higher processing temperature causes a slight browning in evaporated milk because the heat produces a reaction between lactose and some of the protein.

Dried Milks   Dried milks have had all but very small amounts of their water removed. Early methods of milk dehydration produced a powdered milk that was difficult to reconstitute. That type of milk is now called regular, or noninstant, dried milk. Processing techniques now produce instant dried milk with larger particles that dissolve more readily when they are mixed with water. As shown in Table 18.1, these two forms of nonfat dry milk show a different weight for the same volume. One and one-third cups of instant nonfat dry milk, or ¾ cup of regular nonfat dry milk make 1 quart of reconstituted nonfat milk.

Nonfat dry milk does not need to be reconstituted before it is used; the powder or crystals can be added dry to many products. Milk powder is often added to such foods as meat loaves, mashed potatoes, cream soups, cream sauces, casseroles, and many kinds of baked products to improve their nutritional quality.

Use in Cooking   Nonfat milk can be used in any recipe specifying liquid milk and is more economical and lower in calories than the other market varieties, especially in its dry form. Dry milk does not need to be reconstituted for some purposes, nor is it necessary to add fat to make up for the fat in whole milk. Canned and low-fat milks can be similarly substituted. For the most part, the differences in the characteristics of products prepared with different market forms of milk are minimal, and any form of milk can be used with comparable results.

CULTURED MILKS   Yogurt, sour half-and-half, sour cream, and buttermilk are milk products produced when fresh whole or nonfat milk or cream is cultured with bacteria that are capable of converting the lactose in the milk to lactic acid. Lactic acid produced by the bacteria causes the precipitation of casein in milk. If this process is allowed to proceed without stirring or disturbing the milk, a clot with a gellike character, as seen in yogurt and sour cream, is formed. If the clotted milk is stirred during or after the precipitation of the casein, the curd is broken into small particles, producing buttermilk or sour milk. Buttermilk has the same composition as nonfat milk except that it has a higher acid content. Buttermilk was formerly a by-product of butter making. The *clabbered* (coagulated or gelled) whole milk was stirred or churned, causing the cream to clump together to form butter. After the butter was removed, the remaining milk was called *buttermilk* and often had small flecks of butter floating in it.

Any type of milk containing lactose and casein may be cultured; the cultured milk will have the same composition as the milk from which it was made. The main difference between these cultured products is their fat content, which is itemized in Table 18.1. Different strains of bacteria, yielding slightly different flavors, can be used for culturing milk.

Sweet acidophilus milk is pasteurized milk to which the bacteria *Lactobacillus acidophilus* has been added. It has the same flavor and consistency as fresh sweet milk, and is purported to be of benefit to persons with lactase deficiency, described in Chapter 1, but this has not been proven.

CHEESE

Cheese production closely resembles the process used to make cultured milks. With a few exceptions, cheese is the precipitated casein of milk, commonly called *curds*. Casein can be precipitated either by acid produced by bacteria from lactose, or by acid added directly to milk. Casein can also be precipitated by the enzyme *rennin*, as indicated in Table 18.2. Rennin, a digestive enzyme, is isolated from the stomach of young calves. Because of the limited supply of rennin, mixtures of rennin and proteolytic (protein hydrolyzing) enzymes have been used. Also milk-clotting enzymes from bacteria and from plants are being used in production.

Rennin Precipitation of Casein As is true of most enzyme reactions, specific conditions must be met for the precipitation of casein by rennin. Rennin is most active at 104 to 108°F (40 to 42°C) and is inactivated at temperatures above 140°F (60°C). The optimal acidity for rennin activity is pH 5.8 to 6.4. Free calcium ions from the milk are required. Milk that has been heated to 149°F (65°C) or above no longer has free calcium ions because they are tied up in chemical bonds. Thus, canned milk cannot be clotted with rennin unless calcium chloride solution is added to supply free calcium ions.

Cheese Production Casein is precipitated both by acids and enzymes in the commercial production of cheese. In this process, pasteurized whole milk, nonfat milk, or mixtures of whole milk and cream are warmed and inoculated with lactic acid bacteria. After sufficient acid has been produced to yield a pH of 5.8, the milk is inoculated with rennin, which causes the milk to clot or gel. The gel is cut into pieces (Figure 18.1) and heated slightly to shrink the curd and expel the whey. Whey is separated from the curds (Figure 18.2).

Figure 18.1

This harplike instrument cuts coagulated milk into small pieces to help separate curds from whey. *(Switzerland Cheese Association)*

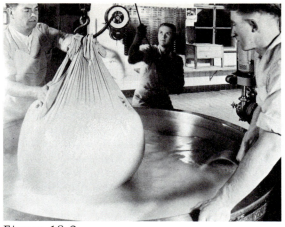

Figure 18.2

Curds are placed in large cloth bags to drain before being placed in molds where excess whey is pressed out. *(Switzerland Cheese Association)*

Table 18.3   Characteristics of some popular varieties of natural cheeses

Kind or name Place of origin	Kind of milk used in manufacture	Ripening or curing time	Flavor
SOFT, UNRIPENED VARIETIES			
Cottage, plain or creamed Unknown	Cow's milk skimmed; plain curd, or plain curd with cream added	Unripened	Mild, acid
Cream, plain U.S.A.	Cream from cow's milk	Unripened	Mild, acid
Neufchatel (Nû-shä-tĕl') France	Cow's milk	Unripened	
Ricotta (Rĭ-cŏ'-ta) Italy	Cow's milk, whole or partly skimmed, or whey from cow's milk with whole or skim milk added in Italy, whey from sheep's milk	Unripened	Sweet, nutlike
FIRM, UNRIPENED VARIETIES			
Gjetost[a] (Yĕt'ôst) Norway	Whey from goat's milk or a mixture of whey from goat's and cow's milk	Unripened	Sweetish, caramel

Whey   *Whey* is the watery, fluid part of the milk that remains after the curd, or casein precipitate, is removed; its composition is given in Table 18.1. Whey contains whey proteins, which are not precipitated either by acid or by rennin, along with most of the lactose and water-soluble vitamins and minerals. Whey is used primarily as animal feed, but some is also used in making special cheeses (Table 18.3). The use of whey in the production of alcohol and beer has been investigated in recent years. Because it has a mild, sweet flavor, whey can also serve as a liquid for gelatin desserts and salads.

Curd may be treated in a variety of ways to produce a great variety of cheeses, many of which are shown in Figure 18.3. Table 18.3 shows some of the factors that affect the flavor of cheese: the kind of milk, the length of its ripening period, and the final characteristics of some well-known cheeses.

TYPES OF CHEESES

Unripened Cheese   Unripened cheeses are made of curds produced as described previously, with no other treatment save for

Body and texture	Color	Retail packaging	Uses
Soft, curd particles of varying size	White to creamy white	Cup-shaped containers, tumblers, dishes	Salads, with fruits, vegetables, sandwiches, dips, cheesecake
Soft and smooth	White	3- to 8-oz packages	Salads, dips, sandwiches, snacks, cheesecake, desserts
Soft, smooth similar to cream cheese but lower in milkfat	White	4- to 8-oz packages	Salads, dips, sandwiches, snacks. Cheesecake, desserts
Soft, moist or dry	White	Pint and quart paper and plastic containers, 3-lb. metal cans	Appetizers, salads, snacks, lasagna, ravioli, noodles and other cooked dishes, grating, desserts
Firm, buttery consistency	Golden brown	Cubical and rectangular	Snacks, desserts, served with dark breads, crackers, biscuits or muffins.

Table 18.3 Continued

Kind or name Place of origin	Kind of milk used in manufacture	Ripening or curing time	Flavor
Mysost (Müs-ôst); also called Primost (Prēm-ôst) Norway	Whey from cow's milk	Unripened	Sweetish, caramel
Mozzarella (Mō-tsa-rel'la); also called Scarmorza Italy	Whole or partly skimmed cow's milk; in Italy, originally made from buffalo's milk	Unripened	Delicate, mild
SOFT, RIPENED VARIETIES			
Brie (Brē) France	Cow's milk	4 to 8 weeks	Mild to pungent
Camembert (Kàm'-ĕm-bâr) France	Cow's milk	4 to 8 weeks	Mild to pungent
Limburger Belgium	Cow's milk	4 to 8 weeks	Highly pungent, very strong
SEMISOFT, RIPENED VARIETIES			
Bel Paese (Bĕl Pǎ-ā'-zĕ) Italy	Cow's milk	6 to 8 weeks	Mild to moderately robust
Brick U.S.A.	Cow's milk	2 to 4 months	Mild to moderately robust
Monterey (Jack) U.S.A.	Cow's milk, whole	2 to 6 weeks	Mild
Muenster (Mün'stĕr) Germany	Cow's milk	1 to 8 weeks	Mild to mellow
Port du Salut (Por dü Sà-lü') France	Cow's milk	6 to 8 weeks	Mellow to robust

Body and texture	Color	Retail packaging	Uses
Firm, buttery consistency	Light brown	Cubical, cylindrical, pie-shaped wedges	Snacks, desserts, served with dark breads
Slightly firm, plastic	Creamy white	Small round or braided form, shredded, sliced	Snacks, toasted sandwiches, cheeseburgers, cooking, as in meat loaf, or topping for lasagna, pizza, and casseroles
Soft, smooth when ripened	Creamy yellow interior; edible thin brown and white crust	Circular, pie-shaped wedges	Appetizers, sandwiches, snacks, good with crackers and fruit, dessert
Soft, smooth; very soft when fully ripened	Creamy yellow interior; edible thin white, or gray-white crust	Small circular cakes and pie-shaped portions	Appetizers, sandwiches, snacks, good with crackers and fruit such as pears and apples, dessert
Soft, smooth when ripened; usually contains small irregular openings	Creamy white interior; reddish yellow surface	Cubical, rectangular	Appetizers, snacks, good with crackers, rye or other dark breads, dessert
Soft to medium firm, creamy	Creamy yellow interior; slightly gray or brownish surface sometimes covered with yellow wax coating	Small wheels, wedges, segments	Appetizers, good with crackers, snacks, sandwiches, dessert
Semisoft to medium firm, elastic, numerous small mechanical openings.	Creamy yellow	Loaf, brick, slices, cut portions	Appetizers, sandwiches, snacks, dessert
Smooth, open texture	Creamy white	Oblong pieces	As such in sandwiches, casseroles
Semisoft, numerous small mechanical openings; contains more moisture than brick	Creamy white interior; yellow tan surface	Circular cake, blocks, wedges, segments, slices	Appetizers, sandwiches, snacks, dessert
Semisoft, smooth, buttery, small openings	Creamy yellow	Wheels and wedges	Appetizers, snacks, served with raw fruit, dessert

Table 18.3   Continued

Kind or name Place of origin	Kind of milk used in manufacture	Ripening or curing time	Flavor
FIRM RIPENED VARIETIES			
Cheddar England	Cow's milk	1 to 12 months or more	Mild to very sharp
Colby U.S.A.	Cow's milk	1 to 3 months	Mild to mellow
Caciocavallo (Kä'chŏ-kä-val'lō) Italy	Cow's milk; in Italy, cow's milk or mixtures of sheep's, goat's, and cow's milk	3 to 12 months	Piquant, similar to Provolone but not smoked
Edam (Ē'dăm) Netherlands	Cow's milk, partly skimmed	2 to 3 months	Mellow, nutlike
Gouda (Gou'-dá) Netherlands	Cow's milk, whole or partly skimmed	2 to 6 months	Mellow, nutlike
Provolone (Prō-vō-lō'-nĕ); also smaller sizes and shapes called Provolette, Provoloncini Italy	Cow's milk	2 to 12 months or more	Mellow to sharp, smoky, salty
Swiss; also called Emmentaler Switzerland	Cow's milk	3 to 9 months	Sweet, nutlike
VERY HARD RIPENED VARIETIES			
Parmesan (Pär'mē-zăn'); also called Reggiano Italy	Partly skimmed cow's milk	14 months to 2 years	Sharp, piquant
Romano (Rŏ-mä'-nō); also called Sardo Romano, Pecorino Romano Italy	Cow's milk; in Italy, sheep's milk (Italian law)	5 to 12 months	Sharp, piquant

Body and texture	Color	Retail packaging	Uses
Firm, smooth, some mechanical openings	White to medium-yellow-orange	Circular, cylindrical loaf, pie-shaped wedges, oblongs, slices, cubes, shredded, grated	Appetizers, sandwiches, sauces, on vegetables, in hot dishes, toasted sandwiches, grating, cheeseburgers, dessert
Softer and more open than Cheddar	White to medium-yellow-orange	Cylindrical, pie-shaped wedges	Sandwiches, snacks, cheeseburgers
Firm, lower in milkfat and moisture than Provolone	Light or white interior; clay or tan colored surface	Spindle or tenpin shaped, bound with cord, cut pieces	Snacks, sandwiches, cooking, dessert; suitable for grating after prolonged curing
Semisoft to firm, smooth; small irregularly shaped or round holes; lower milkfat than Gouda	Creamy yellow or medium yellow-orange interior; surface coated with red wax	Cannon-ball shaped loaf, cut pieces, oblongs	Appetizers, snacks, salads, sandwiches, seafood sauces, dessert
Semisoft to firm, smooth; small irregularly shaped or round holes; higher milkfat than Edam	Creamy yellow or medium yellow-orange interior, may or may not have red wax coating	Ball-shaped with flattened top and bottom	Appetizers, snacks, salads, sandwiches, seafood sauces, dessert
Firm, smooth	Light, creamy interior; light brown or golden yellow surface	Pear-shaped, sausage and salami shaped, wedges, slices	Appetizers, sandwiches, snacks, souffle, macaroni and spaghetti dishes, pizza, suitable for grating when fully cured and dried
Firm, smooth with large round eyes	Light yellow	Segments, pieces, slices	Sandwiches, snacks, sauces, fondue, cheeseburgers
Very hard, granular, lower moisture and milkfat than Romano	Creamy white	Cylindrical, wedges, shredded, grated	Grated for seasoning in soups, or vegetables, spaghetti, ravioli, breads, popcorn, used extensively in pizza and lasagna
Very hard granular	Yellowish-white interior, greenish black surface	Round with flat ends, wedges, shredded, grated	Seasoning in soups, casserole dishes, ravioli, sauces, breads, suitable for grating when cured for about 1 year

Table 18.3   Continued

Kind or name Place of origin	Kind of milk used in manufacture	Ripening or curing time	Flavor
Sap Sago[a] (Săp'-sä-gō Switzerland	Skimmed cow's milk	5 months or more	Sharp, pungent cloverlike

BLUE-VEIN MOLD RIPENED VARIETIES

Kind or name Place of origin	Kind of milk used in manufacture	Ripening or curing time	Flavor
Blue; spelled ''Bleu'' on imported cheese France	Cow's milk	2 to 6 months	Tangy, peppery
Gorgonzola (Gôr-gŏn-zō'-là) Italy	Cow's milk. In Italy, cow's milk or goat's milk or mixtures of these	3 to 12 months	Tangy, peppery
Roquefort[a] (Rōk-fĕrt or Rôk-fôr') France	Sheep's milk	2 to 5 months or more	Sharp, slightly peppery
Stilton[a] England	Cow's milk	2 to 6 months	Piquant, milder than Gorgonzola or Roquefort

the addition of a small amount of salt and sometimes cream. Dry curd, baker's, or uncreamed cottage cheese all are names for the same product, untreated dry curd. Light cream is added to make partially creamed cottage cheese, and heavier cream is added to make regular creamed cottage cheese. The size of the curd in cottage cheese is determined by the size of pieces the clot is cut into. After the whey is drained off, the pieces of curd are pressed together in forms to produce wheels of cheese. At this point, depending on the type of cheese being prepared, additional water may be pressed from them. Table 18.4 shows the composition of some representative cheeses and indicates their various water contents.

Body and texture	Color	Retail packaging	Uses
Very hard	Light green by addition of dried, powdered clover leaves	Conical, shakers	Grated to flavor soups, meats, macaroni, spaghetti, hot vegetables; mixed with butter makes a good spread on crackers
Semisoft, pasty, sometimes crumbly	White interior, marbled or streaked with blue veins of mold	Cylindrical, wedges, oblongs, squares, cut portions	Appetizers, salads, dips, salad dressing, sandwich spreads, good with crackers, dessert
Semisoft, pasty, sometimes crumbly, lower moisture than Blue	Creamy white interior, mottled or streaked with blue-green veins of mold; clay-colored surface	Cylindrical, wedges, oblongs	Appetizers, snacks, salads, dips, sandwich spread, good with crackers, dessert
Semisoft, pasty, sometimes crumbly	White or creamy white interior, marbled or streaked with blue veins of mold	Cylindrical, wedges	Appetizers, snacks, salads dips, sandwich spreads, good with crackers, dessert
Semisoft, flaky; slightly more crumbly than Blue	Creamy white interior, marbled or streaked with blue-green veins of mold	Circular, wedges, oblongs	Appetizers, snacks, salads, dessert

SOURCE: U.S. Department of Agriculture, *How to Buy Cheese,* Home and Garden Bulletin No. 193 (Washington, D.C.: Government Printing Office, 1971).
ᵃImported only.

Ripened Cheese The process of ripening is also called *curing.* In this process, drained curds are inoculated with the specific strains of bacteria or mold that give a cheese its characteristic flavor and texture. Soft cheeses contain more water than hard cheeses. Fat content depends on the fat content of the milk used, for fat is trapped in the curd as it is formed. While most of the lactose present in milk goes into the whey, the small amount that remains clinging to the curd is converted to lactic acid by the bacteria that ripen the cheese, so that cured cheese contains very little lactose. The natural color of cheese is a creamy white such as that of Swiss cheese. Artificial color or carotene is added to the curd to produce orange-colored cheese.

Figure 18.3

Cheese comes in many shapes, sizes, and forms. The cheeses shown are: (1)cheddar, (2) Colby, (3) Monterey Jack, (4) pasteurized process, (5) cheese foods, (6) cheese spreads, (7) cold pack cheese food, (8) Gouda and Edam, (9) Camembert, (10) Muenster, (11) brick, (12) Swiss, (13) limburger, (14) blue, (15) Gorgonzola, (16) Provolone, (17) Romano, (18) Parmesan, (19) mozzarella, (20) cottage, (21) cream cheese. (*United Dairy Industry Association*)

Table 18.4   Composition of some common cheeses, 100-gram amounts

Type of cheese and name	Water (g)	Energy (kcals)	Protein (g)	Fat (g)	Carbohydrate (g)	Ash (g)
Unripened:						
Cottage, dry curd	79.8	85	17.3	0.4	1.8	0.7
Cottage, partially creamed	79.3	90	13.7	1.9	3.6	1.4
Cottage, creamed	79.0	103	12.5	4.5	2.7	1.4
Cream Cheese	53.7	349	7.6	34.9	2.7	1.2
Mozzarella	54.1	281	19.4	21.6	2.2	2.6
Neufchatel	62.2	260	10.0	23.4	2.9	1.5
Ricotta	74.4	138	11.4	7.9	5.1	1.2
Bacteria-ripened, soft:						
Limburger	48.4	327	20.0	27.2	0.5	3.8
Bacteria-ripened, semihard:						
Brick	41.1	371	23.2	29.7	2.8	3.2
Bacteria-ripened, hard:						
Cheddar	36.8	403	24.9	33.1	1.3	3.9
Parmesan	29.2	392	35.8	25.8	3.2	6.0
Swiss	37.2	376	28.4	27.4	3.4	3.5
Mold-ripened, soft:						
Camembert	51.8	300	19.8	24.3	0.5	3.7
Mold-ripened, semihard:						
Blue	42.4	353	21.4	28.7	2.3	5.1
Roquefort	39.4	369	21.5	30.6	2.0	6.4
Pasteurized processed:						
American	39.2	375	22.2	31.2	1.6	5.8
Cheese food	43.1	331	19.7	24.5	8.3	4.4
Cheese spread	47.6	290	16.4	21.2	8.7	6.0
Low-fat slices[a]	—	176	24.7	7.0	3.5	—

SOURCE: U.S. Department of Agriculture, *Composition of Foods—Dairy and Egg Products,* Agriculture Handbook 8-1, 1976.
   [a]Information from label.

Processed Cheese Processed cheese is prepared when natural cheese is heated to separate fat from protein. Emulsifiers and water are added, and the mixture is whipped to form a smooth, homogeneous product. Emulsifiers produce a better dispersion of fat and protein in the cheese. Processed cheese slices more smoothly without crumbling, and it melts into a smoother product than natural cheese, which tends to become grainy when it is melted. The evaporation of some of the flavoring compounds in natural cheeses when they are converted into processed cheese gives processed cheese a milder flavor.

Cheese food is a processed cheese with nonfat dry milk added and a higher water content than American processed cheese. Cheese spread contains even more water than cheese food. The composition of these products is shown in Table 18.4.

Imitation Dairy Products

Many products—including imitation and filled milks, imitation sour cream, coffee cream, whipped cream, and ice cream—have been developed to resemble and replace certain dairy products. Some imitation products contain some parts of milk, such as the proteins or nonfat milk solids; others are completely synthetic.

Filled milk is nonfat milk with a vegetable fat added to replace milk fat. Unfortunately, the fat that is most commonly used in filled milk is coconut oil, which has a very low content of essential fatty acids and consequently offers no nutritional advantage. Imitation milks may use casein or whey proteins and other constituents to produce a product that resembles milk; otherwise, soy may be the protein source. Soybean milks are intended for persons who have an intolerance or allergy to milk. These imitation milks vary considerably in their nutritional content; none is the nutritional equal of cow's milk. Imitation sour cream and ice cream and nondairy creams usually have the same calorie content as the products they imitate but lack the nutrients.

Economy of Dairy Products

As a rule, milk supplies a great deal of nutrition for its cost, but some forms of milk are more economical than others. Table 18.5 lists the price per quart of various forms of milk based on West Coast prices during 1979; prices for local areas should be substituted for purposes of comparison. The price differential varies from place to place and from time to time, possibly because of supply and demand or cost of production. Individual brands of milk also vary in price. The least expensive nonfat dry milk may not be the easiest to reconstitute, so that it might be more desirable to buy the product that is easier to mix; dry milk packaged in envelopes containing amounts for 1 quart are more expensive, but more convenient, than bulk packages. These are decisions each consumer must make.

Low-fat dried milk is less expensive than low-fat fresh milk,

Table 18.5 Comparative cost of various market forms of milk

Type of milk	Cost per quart ($)	Type of milk	Cost per quart ($)[a]
Fluid, fresh:		**Canned:**	
Whole	0.40	Evaporated, whole	0.53
Low-fat	0.39	Evaporated, low-fat	0.52
Nonfat	0.33	Evaporated, nonfat (skim)	0.51
Concentrated (diluted)			
	0.38	**Cultured:**	
Dried:		Buttermilk	0.37
Low-fat (Milkman)	0.33	Yogurt, low-fat	1.09
Nonfat (instant)	0.25	Acidophilus sweet	0.42

[a]Based on West Coast prices, spring 1979.

Figure 18.4

To economize on milk purchases, mix nonfat milk from powdered milk, using 1⅓ cups nonfat dry milk per quart of water, or mix whole milk from concentrated milk, using 1⅓ cups concentrated milk with 2⅔ cups water. Combine 1 quart of each mixture to yield 2 quarts of low-fat milk.

but even more economy is possible by mixing 1 quart of diluted concentrated milk with 1 quart of reconstituted nonfat milk prepared from dry milk. This mixture is a product similar to low-fat milk but costs much less (Figure 18.4).

As shown in Table 18.5, yogurt costs more than twice as much as the milk from which it is made. If yogurt is eaten in large amounts, learning to culture it rather than purchasing the ready-made product would make a considerable saving.

Unripened cheeses are usually more economical than cured cheese; the shorter the cure, the less costly is the cheese. Mild cheddar, for instance, is less expensive than sharp cheddar. Cheese with a high fat content costs more than cheese with a low fat content; thus, cream cheese is more expensive than cottage cheese. An exception is the new lot-fat American processed cheese slices, which are relatively expensive.

It is not always possible to buy the least expensive cheese, because a particular cheese may be needed for its unique flavor and texture. A salad dressing made with cream cheese does not have the same flavor as it does with blue or Roquefort cheese, nor would a cheese sauce be the same if cottage cheese were substituted for cheddar. However, blue cheese may be substituted for Roquefort, or mild cheddar for sharp, with slight differences in flavor and a small reduction in cost.

Storage and Sanitation of Milk Products

Milk, and foods containing or made from milk, are excellent media for bacteria. Avoid contamination with pathogenic bacteria by observing the rules of good hygiene. When reconstituting dry milk or diluting concentrated milks, thoroughly clean the containers in hot, soapy water; even scour them occasionally to remove residues that build up on the inside with continued use.

The storage life of milk products is limited and variable, depending on the type of product and its freshness when it was purchased. The lower the storage temperature, the longer the product may be stored. Not all milk products maintain their quality if they are frozen. Fluid milk does not freeze well because it becomes grainy when it is thawed; concentrated milk can be frozen, although some brands freeze better than others.

Thawed cottage cheese becomes powdery, so it should not be frozen. Cheddar and Jack cheeses can be frozen but may crumble and slice badly when they are thawed. Thawed hard cheese is less likely to crumble if it is frozen in blocks one inch thick at 0°F (−18°C) or below. Cheese can also be grated, packaged, and frozen. Processed cheese is satisfactory when frozen. Cream cheese freezes well.

Dried and canned milks have quite a long storage life under ideal conditions. Canned milk, even though it is sealed and sterilized, can suffer some loss in flavor and become darker in color if it is stored over a period of time at high room temperatures; otherwise, it keeps well for about 6 months. Once the can is opened, it should be refrigerated until it is used; its storage life after opening is the same as that for fresh milk.

Dried milks keep because they have a low moisture content; bacteria cannot grow without sufficient water. Nonfat dried milk keeps longer than dried milks containing fat, because fat gets ran-

Table 18.6   Sources of calcium from milk products and foods containing milk or milk products

Food	Average serving of food				Amount of food to yield about 291 mg of calcium	
	Measure	Grams	Kcals	Calcium (mg)	Measure	Kcals
Cheddar cheese	1 ounce	28	113	213	1⅓ ounces	150
Cocoa, with milk	1 cup	250	190	270	1¹⁄₁₀ cups	209
Cottage cheese, creamed	1 cup	225	239	212	1⅓ cups	299
Cream soup diluted with milk:						
Chicken	1 cup	245	179	172	1⅝ cups	292
Mushroom	1 cup	245	216	191	1½ cups	324
Custard	1 cup	265	305	297	1 cup	305
Ice cream, 10% fat	1 cup	133	257	194	1½ cups	385
Ice milk, 4.3% fat	1 cup	131	199	204	1⅖ cups	284
Macaroni and cheese	1 cup	200	430	362	⅘ cup	344
Oyster stew with milk	1 cup	240	233	274	1¹⁄₁₀ cups	256
Pizza with cheese	⅛ of 14″-diameter	65	153	144	¼ of 14″-diameter	306
Pudding, vanilla, cornstarch	1 cup	255	283	298	1 cup	283
Pudding, tapioca cream	1 cup	165	221	173	1⅔ cups	372
Yogurt, low-fat	1 cup	245	123	294	1 cup	123

SOURCE: Calculated from U.S. Department of Agriculture, *Nutritive Value of American Foods,* Agriculture Handbook No. 456, 1975.

Table 18.7   Food sources of calcium with no milk or milk products

Food	Average serving of food				Amount of food to yield about 291 mg of calcium	
	Measure	Grams	Kcals	Calcium (mg)	Measure	Kcals
Almonds, shelled	1 cup	142	849	332	9/10 cup	764
Legumes, cooked:						
Great Northern, Navy	1 cup	180	212	90	3¼ cups	689
Red, kidney	1 cup	185	218	70	4⅙ cups	908
Broccoli, cooked	1 cup	155	40	136	2⅛ cups	85
Cabbage, spoon, cooked	1 cup	170	24	252	1⅙ cups	28
Collard greens, cooked	1 cup	190	63	357	⅘ cup	50
Dandelion greens, cooked	1 cup	105	35	147	2 cups	70
Kale, cooked	1 cup	110	43	206	1⅖ cups	60
Mustard greens, cooked	1 cup	140	32	193	1½ cups	48
Turnip greens, cooked	1 cup	145	29	267	1 1/10 cups	32
Oysters, raw	1 cup	240	158	226	1¼ cups	198
Salmon, canned[a]	½ cup	110	155	215	1⅓ cups	207
Sardines, canned[a]	½ cup	106	330	375	⅘ cup	264

SOURCE: Calculated from U.S. Department of Agriculture, *Nutritive Value of American Foods*, Agriculture Handbook No. 456, 1975.

[a]Bones in these canned fish are the major source of calcium and should be eaten. If the bones are removed, the calcium content of the fish decreases significantly.

cid. Dried milks should be stored in closed containers or tightly closed plastic bags to prevent moisture absorption from the air, which causes lumping and affects the milk's usability. Nonfat dry milk may be stored in a cool place, but dried whole or low-fat milk keeps best if stored in the refrigerator or freezer in an airtight container.

Nutritional Value of Milk

Milk and most of its products are dependable sources of calcium, complete protein, riboflavin, and vitamin A. Fluid and dried milks are sometimes enriched with vitamin D, and nonfat milks with vitamin A, a fact that is listed on the label. If milk is not acceptable because of allergy, intolerance, or dislike, all these nutrients except calcium and riboflavin can easily be obtained from other foods or sources. Foods that supply calcium in the diet are limited. Table 18.6 gives foods containing milk and milk products that are acceptable substitutes for persons who do not like to drink milk. Table 18.7 gives alternative sources of calcium in the diet for persons with an intolerance or allergy to milk in any form. Both tables give the amount of food that supplies the same calcium found in 1 cup of milk, about 291 milligrams. Vitamin D is not found in other foods. Many of these food sources of calcium also are high in calories, especially when compared with the 88 calories of 1 cup of nonfat milk.

Despite claims to the contrary, yogurt contains the same nutrients as the milk from which it was made, except that some of the lactose has been converted to lactic acid.

Unfortunately, milk fat has a high content of saturated fat and cholesterol, a factor that has caused some people to stop using milk. Nonfat milk is free of fat and cholesterol, yet it still provides the high-quality protein, calcium, and other minerals and vitamins that make an important contribution to the diet. In food preparation, nonfat milk can be used in any recipe that requires milk.

Milk and Cheese in Food Preparation

Milk is used as a beverage, either by itself or combined with other ingredients, as described in Chapter 31. It is also part of many baked products, custards, puddings, sauces, soups, casseroles, and frozen desserts. Some of the ingredients combined with milk and cheese, as well as the heat to which the mixtures are subjected, exert adverse effects on milk or cheese unless they are properly controlled.

EFFECT OF HEAT ON MILK AND CHEESE

Heat causes precipitation of whey proteins, skin formation, and a change in flavor in milk; cheese can become stringy or grainy. Correct techniques help prevent these unfavorable changes.

Precipitation of Whey Proteins   When milk is heated, whey proteins settle to the bottom of the container along with calcium phosphate. Because these proteins adhere tenaciously to the bottom of the pan, they scorch easily and cause problems when milk mixtures are cooked. Scorching can be avoided with moderate heat or a double boiler. Using a pan with a heavy bottom that spreads heat evenly and constant stirring to scrape the precipitate off the bottom of the pan also help. With a double boiler, less stirring and more time is necessary than with direct heat. A microwave oven is ideal for scalding milk because the protein is not precipitated by the agitation of molecules.

Skin Formation   When milk is heated, water evaporates from the surface, causing the casein to concentrate at the surface and produce a skin. If the skin is left intact, steam cannot escape until it builds up sufficiently to cause the milk to boil up and, if the pan is small, out of the pan. Skin formation can be prevented by covering the pan during heating, if a double boiler is used and stirring is infrequent. On direct heat, continuous stirring is necessary to remove the whey proteins from the bottom of the pan. This stirring, especially if it produces a foam on the surface, prevents skin from forming.

Flavor   Milk develops a cooked flavor when it is heated. This change in flavor is thought to be related to a change in the structure of the protein chains. It is advisable to use the minimum amount of cooking in preparing products containing milk. Where possible, cooking should be completed before the milk is added. After the milk is added, the mixture can be heated to obtain the desired temperature or consistency. There should be no need to cook mixtures containing milk for long periods of time.

Stringiness and Graininess in Cheese When hard cheeses are heated, they soften first, because the fat in the cheese melts; the higher the fat content, the more readily the cheese liquefies. Continued heating or heating at high temperatures causes the cheese to lose moisture, shrink, and toughen. If cheese is heated dry, as it is in toasted cheese sandwiches, it becomes leathery and stringy with overheating. In such mixtures as cheese sauce, cheese curdles and gives the sauce a grainy texture if it is heated too long, at too high a temperature, or both. The water lost from the cheese thins the sauce as a further consequence. A smoother cheese sauce can be obtained if the milk and thickening agent are cooked together first and the grated cheese is withheld until just before the sauce is served.

Processed cheese is more stable to heat than natural cheese. The longer natural cheese is cured, the less likely it is to curdle or become stringy when it is heated. The emulsifiers in processed cheese improve its blending properties. Both processing and longer curing times make the cheese protein more soluble so that it is less likely to shrink when heated. Sauces prepared with processed cheese lack the flavor of those made with natural cheese, but they have a smoother texture.

As discussed, casein can be precipitated by acid. Small amounts of acid added to cold milk do not cause the casein to precipitate, but heating the acid-milk mixture does cause it to curdle. Milk that is not fresh or has started to sour curdles in some mixtures when it is heated. Precipitation of the curds is desirable in making cheese or yogurt, but not in such food mixtures as cream of tomato soup. Cheese becomes stringy or grainy when it is cooked in acidic mixtures. A smooth soup can be obtained by thickening the milk with starch, as in white sauce, then adding hot tomato juice or purée to the hot white sauce and serving the soup immediately with no further heating. In this method, the starch appears to have a protective effect on the casein and prevents its precipitation. Neutralizing the acid in tomato juice with baking soda is not recommended because the soda produces an alkaline medium that is destructive of the ascorbic acid in tomato juice.

EFFECTS OF ACIDS IN MILK AND CHEESE MIXTURES

High salt concentrations and tannins in vegetables also cause curdling in milk and cheese dishes. Dried beef, which is often used in creamed mixtures, has a high salt content; some of the salt can be removed by rinsing the dried beef in water before adding it to the white sauce.

OTHER FACTORS AFFECTING MILK AND CHEESE COOKERY

Tannins in vegetables, especially if the vegetables are puréed for use in soup, such as cream of asparagus soup, can cause curdling. This effect is prevented by preparing these soups in the same way as described for tomato soup. In a dish such as potatoes au gratin, the grated cheese can be added to a white sauce and then poured over the potatoes, or the potatoes can be cooked beforehand to reduce the effect of the tannins.

Study Questions

1. Several proteins occur in milk. Which is most plentiful? Which is precipitated by heat and which is precipitated by acid and enzyme?
2. Why is milk pasteurized?
3. Distinguish between certified and raw milk.
4. How and why is milk homogenized?
5. Give a brief description of concentrated, evaporated, condensed, and cultured milks.
6. What are the conditions required for the precipitation of casein by rennin?
7. What is whey? What are some components of whey?
8. How is cheese ripened or cured?
9. What determines the fat content of cheese?
10. What is the natural color of cheese? How are orange cheeses obtained?
11. How is processed cheese prepared? How do cheese food and cheese spread differ in composition from processed cheese?
12. Distinguish between filled and imitation milks.
13. What is the most economical market form of milk?
14. What are three factors that affect the cost of cheese?
15. Why does milk tend to scorch when it is heated?
16. What causes skin formation on the surface of milk mixtures when they are heated? How can this effect be prevented?
17. How does excessive heat affect cheese? What types of cheese are less affected by overheating?
18. What method can be used to reduce or eliminate curdling in milk mixtures that contain acidic ingredients?

References

Carr, Ruth E., and Trout, G. M. "Some Cooking Qualities of Homogenized Milk, 1. Baked and Soft Custard." *Food Research (Journal of Food Science)* 42, no. 5 (September–October 1942): 360–369.

Feeney, Robert E., and Hill, Robert M. "Protein Chemistry and Food Research." *Advances in Food Research* 10 (1960): 22–73.

Hollender, Herbert, and Weckel, K. G. "Stability of Homogenized Milk in Cookery Practice." *Food Research (Journal of Food Science)* 6, no. 4 (July–August 1941): 335–343.

King, N. "The Physical Structure of Dried Milk." *Dairy Science Abstracts* 27, no. 3 (March 1965): 91–104.

Newer Knowledge of Cheese 2d ed. Chicago: National Dairy Council, 1967.

Palumbo, Mary. "Milk and Milk Products." In *Food Theory and Applications*, edited by Pauline C. Paul and Helen H. Palmer. New York: Wiley, 1972.

Patton, Stuart. "The Review of Organic Chemical Effects of Heat on Milk." *Journal of Agriculture and Food Chemistry* 6, no. 2 (February 1958): 132–135.

Personius, C.; Boardman, E.; and Ausherman, A. R. "Some Factors Affecting the Behavior of Cheddar Cheese in Cooking." *Food Research* 9 (1944): 304.

Rose, Dyson. "Protein Stability Problems." *Journal of Dairy Science* 48, no. 1 (January 1965): 139–144.

Towson, Alice M., and Trout, G. M. "Some Cooking Qualities of Homogenized Milk, 2. White Sauces." *Food Research* 11, no. 3 (May–June 1946): 261–273.

U.S. Department of Agriculture. *How to Buy Cheese,* Home and Garden Bulletin No. 193. Washington, D.C.: Government Printing Office, 1972.

——. *How to Buy Dairy Products,* Home and Garden Bulletin No. 201, 1972.

——. *Composition of Foods—Dairy and Egg Products,* Agriculture Handbook No. 8-1, 1976.

——. *Cheese Varieties and Descriptions,* Agriculture Handbook No. 54, 1978.

Webb, Byron H.; Johnson, Arnold H.; and Alford, John A., *Fundamentals of Dairy Chemistry.* 2d ed. Westport, Conn.: AVI Publishing, 1978.

Wegner, Elizabeth S.; Jordan, Ruth, and Hollender, H. A. "Homogenized and Nonhomogenized Milk in the Preparation of Selected Food Products." *Journal of the American Home Economics Association* 45, no. 8 (October 1953): 589–591.

Eggs: Composition and Cookery

Eggs, like milk, are used in the preparation of many different kinds of dishes. Eggs can be cooked by boiling, baking, frying, scrambling, and poaching, and they are used in omelets, soufflés, fondues, custards, emulsions, cakes, cookies, breads, and many other foods. Their unique properties make eggs a versatile food.

Structure and Composition of Eggs
STRUCTURE OF EGGS

The structure of an egg is shown in Figure 19.1. The basic parts of the egg are the shell, the white, and the yolk. The shell, which is considered inedible, is discarded, making about 11 percent refuse of the total weight of the egg. Two membranes lie just inside the shell of the egg. One lines the shell and the other covers the egg contents, but both stick to the shell when the egg is broken out; only when the egg is hard-cooked are they apparent. As the raw egg ages, an air cell forms between the two membranes at one end of the egg. Another fragile membrane covers the yolk, separating it from the white. Attached to opposite sides of the yolk are threads of thick white, called *chalazae*, that help keep the yolk centered in the white inside the egg. Chalazae are egg white protein that are as edible as any other part of the egg, but for some purposes, as in custards, these thick threads form lumps and should be strained from the white before the egg is used. The shell of an egg is porous and permits passage of moisture and gases in and out.

COMPOSITION OF EGGS AND EGG SUBSTITUTES

Whole egg, egg white, and egg yolk vary in their chemical composition, which affects their use in food preparation. Table 19.1 shows the composition of a whole egg and its parts, along with the composition of low-cholesterol egg substitutes.

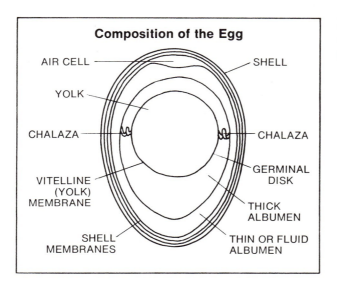

Composition of the Egg

AIR CELL — SHELL
YOLK
CHALAZA — CHALAZA
VITELLINE (YOLK) MEMBRANE
GERMINAL DISK
THICK ALBUMEN
SHELL MEMBRANES
THIN OR FLUID ALBUMEN

Figure 19.1

The principal parts of an egg. *(California Egg Program)*

Table 19.1 *Composition of whole egg, egg white, egg yolk, and egg substitutes, 100-gram amounts*

Egg product	Water (g)	Energy (kcals)	Protein (g)	Fat (g)	Polyunsaturated fatty acid (g)	Saturated fatty acid (g)
Egg white	88.1	49	10.1	Tr	0	0
Egg yolk	48.8	369	16.4	32.9	4.3	9.9
Egg, whole	74.6	158	12.1	11.2	1.4	3.4
Egg substitute:						
frozen	73.1	160	11.3	11.1	6.2	1.9
liquid	82.8	84	12.0	3.3	1.6	0.7

The proteins in egg are complete proteins. *Avidin,* a protein in egg white, combines when raw with *biotin,* a vitamin, forming a complex that cannot be absorbed with digestion. This complex is not formed if the egg is cooked. Many proteins in the yolk are combined with phosphorus to form *phosphoproteins,* which combine with fats to form *lipoproteins.* Lipoproteins cause the yolk to gel when it is frozen.

Most of the fat in an egg is found in the yolk; several of these fats, or *lipids,* have become very well known for their properties. The functions of cholesterol and its role as a possible cause of heart disease were discussed in Chapter 1; lecithin's emulsifying properties were mentioned in Chapter 5. The triglycerides in yolks contain mostly saturated fatty acids with very little polyunsaturated fatty acids. Eggs contain less than 1 percent carbohydrate.

The egg substitutes have similar protein content to the eggs they imitate. In some egg substitutes, egg white is the source of protein; some additionally contain sodium caseinate, a milk protein. The egg subtitutes have about the same iron content as whole egg; some are lower in fat and higher in polyunsaturated fatty acids, and all are almost free of cholesterol, which is their main advantage.

Grading Eggs

Three consumer grades exist for eggs sold in the shell: in order of highest to lowest quality, these are U.S. Grade AA, U.S. Grade A, and U.S. Grade B (Figure 19.2). Figure 19.3 shows how these three grades of eggs appear when they are broken out of the shell. The Grade AA egg is compact, with thick white and a yolk that is firm and high. The Grade A egg has a thinner white that spreads out when the egg is broken out of the shell, but the yolk is still firm and fairly high. In the Grade B egg, the white is even thinner and the yolk is flattened out. The two top grades are ideal for all purposes, but are especially suited for poaching and frying. Grade B

Cholesterol (mg)	Sodium (mg)	Iron (mg)	Vitamin A (RE)	(IU)	Pyridoxine (mg)	Vitamin B-12 (mcg)
0	152	—	0	0	0	0
1602	49	5.6	552	1839	0.31	3.8
548	138	2.1	156	520	0.12	1.5
2	199	2.0	135	1350	0.13	0
1	177	2.1	216	2160	—	0.3

SOURCE: U.S. Department of Agriculture, *Composition of Foods—Dairy and Egg Products,* Agriculture Handbook No. 8-1, 1976.

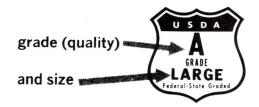

grade (quality)

and size

Figure 19.2

The official grade shield certifies that eggs have been graded for quality and size under federal and state supervision.

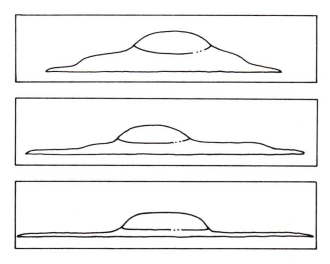

Figure 19.3

Three consumer grades of eggs spread differently when broken out of the shell. Top: U.S. Grade AA. Center: U.S. Grade A. Bottom: U.S. Grade B. *(California Egg Program)*

eggs are satisfactory for most cooking and baking purposes. Because the yolk membrane of Grade B eggs is more fragile, the yolk can be difficult to separate from the white.

The color of the eggshell does not in any way affect the grade, quality, or nutritional quality of the egg; the U.S. grades alone are indications of interior quality. Shell color is determined by the breed of chicken. Both brown and white shell eggs are available in all grades. Fertilized eggs have a good flavor but are not nutritionally superior to unfertilized eggs. They are considered poorer quality for food preparation and are therefore graded lower.

DETERIORATION OF EGGS

The interior quality of eggs is affected by age (time since the eggs were laid) and storage conditions. Once an egg is laid, changes gradually occur within it that lower its interior quality. These changes occur more rapidly at high temperatures, and more slowly with fast cooling and low temperature storage. The following changes occur within an egg over a period of time:

1. The size of the air cell increases.
2. Carbon dioxide is lost, making the egg more alkaline.
3. Increased alkalinity causes the white to thin.
4. The yolk enlarges, flattens, and stretches the yolk membrane, which becomes correspondingly more fragile.
5. With advanced aging, flavor as well as consistency deteriorates.

These changes are minimal in top-grade eggs. Evidence of the presence of these changes causes other eggs to be designated a lower grade. To ensure that eggs are of the quality indicated by the grade, purchase only those eggs that have been kept refrigerated. A few hours or a day without refrigeration can change a Grade A egg into a Grade B egg, depending on the temperature of the surroundings. Some markets handle eggs carelessly and allow them to remain at room temperature for long periods of time, which greatly reduces the quality of the egg.

Because an egg is covered by a shell, its interior quality is difficult to determine. Many years ago, eggs were held in front of a candle and their contents observed through the semitransparent shell, hence the name "candling." Today, large commercial operations use electronic equipment for mass scanning or flash candling of eggs, a process by which thousands of eggs per hour can

Figure 19.4

Different sizes of eggs must have the minimum weights per dozen, shell included. (*California Egg Program*)

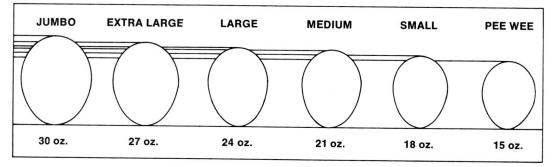

JUMBO	EXTRA LARGE	LARGE	MEDIUM	SMALL	PEE WEE
30 oz.	27 oz.	24 oz.	21 oz.	18 oz.	15 oz.

be examined. Additionally, random samples of eggs are broken so that their interior quality and characteristics may be observed.

Egg grading is not mandatory; the Department of Agriculture service is voluntary and must be requested and paid for by the producer or distributor. The official U.S.D.A. grade shield on a carton of eggs indicates that experienced federal or state egg graders have supervised the grading operations and have certified that the eggs are of the quality indicated by the grade label at the time of grading.

ECONOMY AND SIZE OF EGGS

Eggs are marketed by size, based on the minimum weight of a dozen eggs in the shell. Figure 19.4 shows the minimum weight per dozen of the different sizes of eggs. This standard does not indicate that each egg in a package is the same weight as every other egg in that package, but rather that the combined weight of the dozen eggs is at least as great as that specified for that size of egg. Constantly changing price differentials make it a problem to know which size to buy. One way to compare the prices of eggs is on the basis of cost per ounce, which is obtained by dividing the price per dozen by the minimum weight per dozen. A rule of thumb that involves no arithmetic states that if less than 7 cents difference exists between the prices of eggs of adjacent size, the larger size should be purchased.

Most recipes are developed for large eggs, and other sizes may not give satisfactory results. Thus, it might be false economy to buy a smaller size of eggs at a saving if they cannot be readily substituted in recipes. Table 19.2 shows the approximate number of yolks, whites, and whole eggs required to yield 1 cup. Many recipes would give more dependable results if a volume measure of egg, rather than a quantity, were given.

Sanitary Quality and Storage of Eggs

Eggs, like milk and cheese, are excellent media for the growth of pathogenic bacteria. The interior of an uncracked egg is sanitary, but the outside of the shell is usually contaminated with bacteria. When a raw egg is cracked out of the shell, it can easily pick up

Table 19.2   Minimum weight, per dozen, of eggs of various sizes

Size of eggs	Ounces per dozen (minimum)	Number of eggs to yield 1 cup		
		Whole	Egg white	Egg yolk
Jumbo	30	—	—	—
Extra large	27	4	6	12
Large	24	5	7	14
Medium	21	6	8	16
Small	18	7	10	18

bacteria, if not from the shell, then from the air, utensils, or people, as described in Chapter 2. Heating eggs at 180°F (82°C) for three minutes is necessary to destroy potential salmonella bacteria.

Cracked eggs are extremely likely to be contaminated with bacteria on the inside; therefore, they should only be used in dishes that will be properly cooked. Only uncracked eggs should be used in uncooked dishes. Eggs should be washed just before they are used; the dish should be prepared as close to the time it will be consumed as possible and should be kept cold. Eggs should not be washed and then stored in the refrigerator, for wetting increases the ability of bacteria to penetrate the shell.

Even when eggs are cooked, they are good media for bacterial growth. Cooked foods containing eggs should be prepared hygienically, and the temperature should be maintained either above 160°F (71°C) or below 50°F (10°C).

CONTROLLED
ATMOSPHERE STORAGE

Eggs can be stored for considerable time periods under conditions of controlled atmosphere and temperature. This is especially true if the eggs are thermostabilized by being dipped in hot mineral oil or coated in plastic; both methods reduce the loss of water and gases from the egg. A carbon dioxide atmosphere, with 90 percent humidity and a temperature of 30 to 40°F (−1 to 4.5°C), also helps reduce the loss of water and carbon dioxide from the egg. Such treatment and storage is not possible at home or in most institutions; in these situations, refrigeration is the only means of maintaining quality. Because the quality of eggs deteriorates even when they are refrigerated, purchase only the amount of eggs that will be used in a reasonable length of time.

Whole eggs out of the shell as well as egg whites can be stored for several days in the refrigerator; yolks tend to form a thick skin on the surface under these conditions. Unbroken yolks can be covered with a thin layer of water to prevent skin formation. All forms of eggs keep best when placed in tightly covered containers.

FROZEN AND
DEHYDRATED EGGS

All parts of the egg freeze well. Whites require no treatment; they need only be placed in a container that allows room for expansion. Whole eggs should be mixed until they are homogeneous. Both yolks and whole eggs tend to solidify when they freeze unless either salt or sugar is added to lower the freezing point; the intended use of the eggs after they are thawed determines whether salt or sugar is the more desirable additive. To each cup of yolk or whole egg, stir in either 1 tablespoon of sugar or ½ teaspoon of salt. The egg may be partially thawed in the refrigerator; remove the amount desired and refreeze the rest. Do not allow a frozen egg to warm up until it is time for it to be cooked, to prevent the growth of bacteria.

Eggs have many uses in food preparation, serving as:

1. a thickening agent in sauces and soft custards
2. a gelling agent in baked custards
3. a structural ingredient in baked products, particularly in sponge cakes and popovers
4. a leavening agent, incorporating air with their foams
5. a source of water in some cookie doughs and sponge cakes
6. an emulsifier in mayonnaise, hollandaise sauce, cake, and cream puffs
7. a binding agent in meat loaves, croquettes, and breading on meats

Eggs are also a part of many foods in which they have no particular function other than to provide nutrition, flavor, or texture.

COOKING EGGS

In many preparations, eggs require heating, which affects their protein. *Gelation* and *coagulation* are terms that describe the effect of heat on egg protein. Gelation is the formation of a gel structure by heat, as in baked custards, resembling the formation of a gel by gelatin in all but one respect: egg gels form in the hot mixture, while gelatin gels form during cooling. Coagulation is the change from liquid to solid state with no specific structure; it occurs in a stirred custard and in fried or boiled eggs. Egg white and egg yolk coagulate at different temperatures. Undiluted egg white coagulates between 140 and 149°F (60 and 65°C). Undiluted egg yolk coagulates between 149 and 158°F (65 and 70°C). If the egg protein is diluted, the temperature of coagulation increases; the greater the dilution, the higher is the temperature of coagulation. Stirred custards coagulate between 185 and 190°F (85 and 88°C), depending on the concentration of egg protein and other factors.

As is the case with milk and cheese, excessive heat is detrimental to egg protein. Cooking undiluted egg protein at too high a temperature for too long a time makes egg protein tough and rubbery. Overheating diluted egg, as in custards, causes curdling. Eggs and egg mixtures may be cooked over high heat if the time is shortened so that the temperature of the egg or the egg mixture does not exceed the critical temperature at which detrimental effects occur, about 185 to 190°F (85 to 88°C) in custard mixtures.

Eggs Cooked in the Shell   Eggs in the shell may be cooked until they are completely firm, or to lesser degrees of firmness (Figure 19.5). Eggs cooked in their shells are often known as boiled eggs. If eggs are cooked in boiling water, the whites become firmer and less tender than if they are cooked at temperatures of less than boiling. Firm whites in hard-cooked eggs are desirable if they are to be grated, sliced, or prepared as deviled eggs. If the egg white is too tender, the slices fall apart, the white does not hold together, and the egg itself is mushy and difficult to grate.

Figure 19.5

Eggs cooked in the shell are, center top and clockwise: a 3-minute soft-cooked egg with fluid yolk; a 6-minute egg with gelled, translucent yolk; an 8-minute egg with only slight translucency in the center of the yolk; a 10-minute egg with opaque yolk but no discoloration; and a 15-minute egg showing formation of iron sulfide on the surface of the yolk, a result of excessive heating.

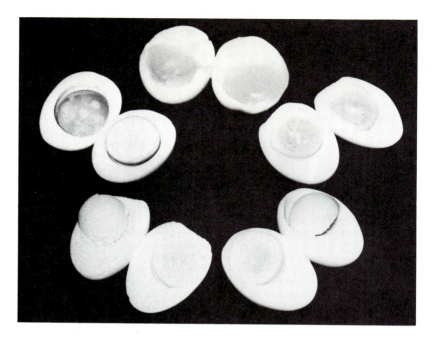

A hard-cooked egg should have a firm, not leathery, white; a firm mealy, opaque yolk; and no gray-green discoloration on the surface of the yolk next to the white. These characteristics are best obtained when large eggs are cooked for no longer than 10 minutes at simmering temperatures. The discoloration on the surface of the yolk occurs when eggs in the shell are overcooked, are not cooled quickly afterwards, or are not fresh enough. Discoloration is caused by iron and sulfur in the egg combining to form ferrous sulfide. Such discoloration is not harmful to eat, but it is not attractive in appearance. The alkalinity of older eggs promotes the formation of ferrous sulfide. Very fresh eggs are more difficult to shell after they have been hard-cooked than older eggs.

Soft-cooked eggs are more tender if the temperature of cooking is no higher than simmering. The length of time they are cooked depends on the actual temperature and the desired consistency of the yolk. The yolk may be either slightly fluid or partially solidified; the white should be opaque, not translucent.

Poached Eggs   To *poach* means to cook in simmering liquid. Eggs out of the shell can be poached in either milk or water; water is the more common medium. Eggs are poached in only a small amount of milk, which is usually consumed with the eggs. Eggs poached in milk can be cooked in the oven, with less chance of scorching, or on a surface unit.

Poaching eggs in water can be a difficult procedure because the water is not consumed with the egg. A considerable part of the egg can be lost in the water if it strings and spreads out excessively. Fresh eggs poach best, because their thick whites spread less than the whites of older eggs. Eggs broken out of the shell tend to spread, so they should not be broken until they are ready to be poached. Add the egg all at once to the boiling water; do not dribble it in, so that it will quickly coagulate in one mass. Then turn off the heat, cover the pan, and poach the egg for 3 or 4 minutes until it reaches the desired consistency.

One tablespoon of vinegar added to a pint of water used for poaching eggs is sometimes thought to reduce the egg's spreading by hastening its coagulation. Eggs poached in water containing vinegar, however, are vinegar-flavored, and the surface of the eggs are crinkly and less shiny than they would be if they were cooked in water without vinegar.

Fried Eggs Several methods of frying eggs are acceptable. If a Teflon pan or a pan spray is used, the equivalent of a fried egg can be produced without fat. As a rule, fried eggs are prepared either "sunny side up" or "easy over." "Sunny side up" eggs are cooked in a hot frying pan with enough fat to be spooned over the egg until it is coagulated to the desired consistency. As in soft-cooked and poached eggs, the white should be opaque and the yolk fluid or partially solidified, depending on preference. The longer cooking is continued, the firmer the egg becomes. Eggs fried at very high temperatures are less tender and frequently are browned and frizzled at the bottom and edges, an effect that is preferred by some but is not generally considered a desirable characteristic.

"Easy over" eggs can be cooked with less fat, although enough fat should be present to prevent the egg from sticking to the pan. The egg is cooked on the first side until nearly done; then it is turned carefully, so that the yolk does not break, and cooked briefly on the second side to achieve the desired degree of firmness.

To fry an egg without fat, use a Teflon pan or spray a regular pan lightly with pan spray. Heat the pan, add the egg along with several teaspoons of water, cover, and reduce or turn off the heat. Allow the egg to steam until the desired consistency is obtained.

The method of frying affects not only the flavor of an egg but also its caloric content. Where fat is spooned over the egg, the egg has the flavor of the fat—bacon, sausage, or table fat—but the fat also increases calories. One large egg cooked without fat is only 80 calories. When it is fried with 1 teaspoon of fat, the number of calories increases to 110.

Scrambled Eggs and Omelets Scrambled eggs and French omelets are prepared from the same mixture of beaten eggs, milk or cream, and seasoning. Both are cooked on a surface unit in a greased pan to prevent the egg from sticking. Scrambled eggs are stirred during cooking; the French omelet is not stirred. Scrambled egg mixtures may also be cooked in the oven or in the top of a double boiler.

These egg mixtures may turn green if they are cooked in an iron pan; free iron from the pan combines with sulfur in the eggs to form ferrous sulfide. This is especially likely if the eggs are not fresh, if the mixture is cooked too long, or if it is held in the pan after cooking is completed. Aluminum pans, and sometimes even stainless steel pans, contain mineral deposits from water or foods previously heated in them. They can contribute to the discoloration of egg mixtures, especially if the other contributory factors are also present. Discoloration can also occur if the egg mixture is tightly covered, because hydrogen sulfide gas formed from the eggs by cooking cannot volatilize.

Scrambled eggs are additionally subject to syneresis when they are held too long at warm temperatures after they are cooked. In this state, the protein shrinks and water trapped in the meshes of the coagulated protein is lost. Eggs that have undergone syneresis are dry and less tender than those that retain their fluid.

In making French omelets, too much egg should not be cooked in the pan at one time. One large egg in a pan with a 6-inch diameter or two large eggs in a pan with a 10-inch diameter produce a thin enough layer to coagulate without browning excessively and to be flexible enough for rolling or folding when properly cooked (Figure 19.6).

Yolks and whites are separated to make puffy omelets. Yolks and seasonings are folded into the egg white foam and cooked either on a surface unit or in the oven. Overbeating the egg whites is a major problem that is discussed in Chapter 20. The whites should be beaten only to the soft peak stage, so that the foam is pliable, and cooking should begin as soon as the foam is prepared and the yolk is combined with the foam.

Custards Custards are cooked mixtures of egg and milk. Sugar, flavorings, and other ingredients may be included. Custard mixtures are often used to thicken and bind together the ingredients in a casserole.

STRUCTURE OF CUSTARD MIXTURES Most of the thickening in a custard mixture is caused by egg protein. The major protein in milk, casein, is not coagulated by heat, and not enough heat-coagulable whey proteins are present to have much effect on viscosity. The egg and whey proteins form a kind of network with crossbonding between protein chains when they are heated. Water and the casein from the milk are trapped in its meshes. The casein provides body to the custard. Calcium ions are also important in forming the gel structure in baked custards. Excessive heating causes the protein to shrink, squeezing water

Figure 19.6

A properly cooked French omelet is not difficult to roll after the filling mixture has been placed on the egg. Here, sautéed mushrooms, chopped green onions, and cooked sausage are the filling. The finished omelet is served with a well-seasoned marinara sauce and sliced mushrooms.

from the meshes and producing syneresis. Both the time and temperature must be controlled to prevent syneresis and curdling when custards are cooked.

Baked custards are custard mixtures that are cooked undisturbed in the oven, forming a continuous gel structure. Soft or stirred custards are cooked directly on a surface unit or in a double boiler with constant stirring; these have a fluid consistency.

TYPES OF CUSTARDS AND THEIR PREPARATION

Scalded Milk   Recipes often recommend that milk be scalded for custards, but this procedure is not strictly necessary. Scalded milk shortens the baking time of baked custard mixtures because the mixture is at a higher temperature before it starts to cook.

Preheating the milk may also increase gel formation and thickening. Heating of proteins causes unfolding of the protein chains, which exposes chemical groups that are "hidden" in the folds and coils of the milk's natural protein structure. These exposed groups are more available for forming crossbonds between protein chains than they were in the coiled or folded protein. The more the protein is heated the more groups are available for crossbonding to form the network of protein that produces the gel in the baked custard or thickening in the stirred custard.

One cup of milk at room temperature can be scalded (heated to 190°F, 88°C) in a microwave oven in about 3 minutes. If milk is scalded on the surface unit of the range, it should be stirred continuously to prevent scorching of the whey proteins that collect on the bottom of the pan. If milk is scalded, stir a small amount into the beaten egg to dilute it; then stir the egg into the remaining hot milk.

Proportion of Ingredients   The usual proportions for custard are one large egg and 1 tablespoon of sugar per cup of milk. Increasing the amount of egg produces a firmer gel in baked custard or a thicker stirred custard and will also shorten the time required to gel or coagulate the custard. Decreasing or omitting sugar will also have these effects, for sugar inhibits the coagulation of protein. Conversely, increasing sugar or reducing egg produces less viscous custards and lengthens the cooking time.

Custards may be made from yolk, white, or whole egg. Because the protein of the egg produces thickening, more egg white is needed than whole egg or yolk to supply the same amount of protein, because egg white has a lower protein content than the yolk or whole egg (Table 19.1). Two yolks or two whites in place of one whole egg do not produce comparable custards. Equal amounts of protein from various parts of the egg, however, do yield custards of similar consistency and viscosity.

Stirred or Soft Custard A stirred custard should be smooth and creamy with no graininess. To achieve this texture, the milk and egg must be cooked together only to the coagulation point, which is indicated by the velvety coating of custard on the spoon (Figure 19.7). If heating continues after this point, it causes curdling and syneresis as previously described.

Custards are customarily cooked in a double boiler over simmering, not boiling, water. The top of the double boiler should not be submerged in water, and cooking should be terminated as soon as the custard thickens. Custard cooked in a double boiler can curdle if these precautions are not observed. Slow cooking provides a greater temperature differential between the thickening point and the curdling point of custard mixtures.

A custard may be cooked over direct heat, even high heat, so long as it is cooked in a pot with a heavy bottom and is rapidly stirred. Remove the pot from the heat to check the custard's spoon-coating properties. In this method, a thicker custard can be prepared much more rapidly, but because the temperature of curdling is closer to the thickening temperature, experience and skill are needed to remove the custard at the correct point.

Sugar and flavorings are often added to the custard mixture after it is thickened, because sugar raises the coagulation temperature and flavorings evaporate during cooking. Stirred custard is quite thin, about the consistency of gravy, when it has completed cooking. Stirred custard thickens with cooling but never gels; rather, it remains fluid and of sauce consistency. If curdling occurs, custard can sometimes be made smoother if it is immediately beaten rapidly in a blender or mixer before it is chilled.

Baked Custard Egg, milk, sugar, and flavoring are mixed until smooth with a blender or egg beater. The container holding the custard should be placed in another container and surrounded with water to a depth of 1 inch to insulate the custard from the

Figure 19.7

Properly cooked custard leaves a
velvety-smooth coating on a
spoon dipped into it.

oven heat and prevent overcooking. Boiling water shortens the
cooking time, and small containers of custard bake more rapidly
than large containers. Baking at 400°F (204°C) is faster than at
350°F (178°C), the customary temperature. One half cup of custard mixture prepared with scalded milk and surrounded with
boiling water gels in 10 to 13 minutes when baked at 400°F
(204°C). However, baking custards at the higher temperature is
more likely to result in overcooking. As with stirred custards,
rapid cooking leaves less differential between the gelation and
curdling temperatures.

Test a baked custard by inserting the tip of the blade of a clean
table knife in the custard just off center. If the blade comes out
clean, the custard is baked. Even though the center itself may not
be completely gelled, residual heat in the custard continues the
cooking even after the custard has been removed from the oven.

Other Ingredients in Custard Mixtures Cocoa powder or extra sugar for flavor can be stirred into the custard mixture before cooking begins. Cocoa solids tend to settle to the bottom of baked custards, but in a stirred custard they remain dispersed. Acid ingredients such as fruits can cause curdling, and they should be added after cooking is completed.

Egg and starch are often used together as thickening agents. The starch should be heated to the boiling point for maximum thickening, but the egg should not be boiled. Usually, the starch is boiled, then some of the cooked starch mixture is stirred into the beaten egg, and the egg mixture is then stirred back into the remaining hot starch mixture. The mixture is again heated so that the egg cooks. This technique is still advisable in preparing soufflés, because cooking the egg yolks with the starch mixture produces excessive thickening that interferes with the process of folding in the egg white foam.

For other mixtures, save time by cooking the egg with the starch mixture just to the boiling point. The starch appears to have a protective effect on the egg and prevents curdling so long as the mixture is not allowed to boil. Like other starch and custard mixtures, it should be rapidly stirred during cooking.

Egg Substitutes Egg substitutes can be used in soft custards in a high ratio, about ⅔ cup per cup of milk. Part of the protein in egg substitutes is supplied by casein, which is not coagulable by heat. The flavor is not the same as fresh egg, and some might prefer it masked by chocolate or some other ingredient. Egg substitute works best in bread or rice pudding where part of the thickening is obtained from rice or bread.

Use of Custard Mixtures Custard mixtures as a filling in pies are discussed in Chapter 14. Quiche Lorraine is an unsweetened custard pie that contains cheese; it can be baked without a crust, if desired.

Nutritional Value of Eggs

Not only are eggs a good source of complete protein, they are also excellent sources of vitamin A and iron, as well as other vitamins and minerals. Eggs contain almost twice as much riboflavin as milk and are a dependable source of this vitamin when milk is not consumed in the diet. The undesirable effects in the diet of cholesterol, of which eggs are a rich source, are discussed in Chapter 1.

Egg substitutes were developed to replace eggs in the diet of those on medically prescribed low-cholesterol diets. However, the substitutes are not nutritionally equal to eggs. In rat growth studies the substitutes have produced less growth than did dried whole egg.

1. Compare the differences between egg yolks and egg whites in water, protein, and fat content.
2. Name the changes that occur in the interior quality of eggs as they age.
3. How does the temperature at which eggs are stored affect their quality?
4. What is the basis for the size standards of eggs? Are all eggs in a package of eggs exactly the same size?
5. Why are cracked eggs unsafe in dishes in which they will not be cooked?
6. How is egg protein affected by heating? By excessive heat?
7. How does time and temperature affect the tenderness and consistency of an egg cooked in its shell?
8. What is the gray-green discoloration often seen on the outer surface of the yolk of hard-cooked eggs? What causes this color, and how can it be prevented?
9. What is a problem with poaching eggs in water, and how can this problem be reduced?
10. How does the cooking method used affect the flavor and caloric content of fried eggs?
11. Distinguish between French omelet, puffy omelet, and scrambled eggs.
12. What are possible causes of syneresis often seen in scrambled eggs? How does syneresis affect their eating quality?
13. What is a custard mixture?
14. The thickening of custard mixtures is caused mainly by what component of the mixture?
15. Why must both time and temperature be controlled in cooking custard mixtures?
16. What is the difference in ingredients, mixing method, cooking method, and method of testing for doneness, between soft and baked custards?
17. How do the concentrations of egg and sugar affect the firmness of baked custard and the time needed to bake it?
18. Although a double boiler is helpful in controlling temperature when custards are cooked, it is not essential. What precautions should be observed in cooking custard mixtures over direct heat?
19. What effect do acid ingredients have on custard mixtures? What is the best point at which to add the acidic ingredient to the custard mixture?
20. What are some of the principal nutrient contributions of eggs?

References

Baker, Robert C.; Darfler, June; and Lifshitz, Abraham. "Factors Affecting the Discoloration of Hard-cooked Egg Yolks." *Poultry Science* 46, (no. 3) (May 1967): 664–672.

Childs, M. T., and Ostrander, J. "Egg Substitutes: Chemical and Biological Evaluations." *Journal of the American Dietetic Association* 68, (no. 3) (March 1976): 229–234.

Everson, G. J., and Saunders, H. J. "Composition and Nutritional Importance of Eggs." *Journal of the American Dietetic Association* 33, (no. 6) (December 1957): 1244–1254.

Feeney, Robert, and Hall, Robert M. "Protein Chemistry and Food Research." *Advances in Food Research* 10 (1960): 22–73.

Feeney, R. E.; Silva, R. B.; and MacDonnell, L. R. "Chemistry of Shell Egg Deterioration." *Poultry Science* 30 (1951): 645–650.

——, ——, and ——. "Studies on the Deteriorative Mechanism of Egg White Thinning." *Poultry Science* 29 (1950): 757–758.

Fevold, H. L. "Egg Proteins." *Advances in Protein Chemistry* 6 (1951): 187–252.

Handy, Elizabeth, "Eggs—Nature's Prepackaged Masterpiece of Nutrition." In U.S. Department of Agriculture, *Food for Us All*, Yearbook of Agriculture. Washington, D.C.: Government Printing Office, 1969.

Hard, M. M.; Spencer, J. V.; Locke, R. S.; and George, M. H. "A Comparison of Different Methods of Preserving Shell Eggs. 2. Effect of Functional Properties." *Poultry Science* 42 (1963): 1085–1095.

Johnston, F. A. "Iron Content of Eggs." *Journal of the American Dietetic Association* 32 (1956): 664.

Korslund, H. J.; Marion, W. W., and Stadelman,

W. J. "Some Factors Affecting Quality Loss in Shell Eggs." *Poultry Science* 36 (1957): 338–341.

Miller, M. W.; Joukovsky, V., and Kraght, A. "Experiments Relating to the Spoilage of Washed Eggs." *Poultry Science* 29 (1950): 27–33.

Powrie, W. D.; Little, H., and Lopez, A. "Gelation of Yolk." *Journal of Food Science* 28 (1963): 38–46.

Solwin, H.; Block, I., and Mitchell, J. M. "Dehydration Stabilization of Egg: Importance and Determination of pH." *Food Technology* 7 (1953): 447–452.

Swanson, M. H. "Peeling Problems of Fresh and Shell-Treated Eggs When Hard-Cooked." *Poultry Science* 38 (1959): 1253–1254.

Tinkler, C. K., and Soar, M. C. "The Formation of Ferrous Sulphide in Eggs During Cooking." *Biochemical Journal* (London) 14, (no. 2) (April 1920): 114–119.

U.S. Department of Agriculture. *How to Buy Eggs,* Home and Garden Bulletin No. 144. Washington, D.C.: Government Printing Office, 1968.

——. *Composition of Foods—Dairy and Egg Products,* Agriculture Handbook No. 8-1, 1976.

Wooley, D. W., and Longsworth, L. G. "Isolation of an Antibiotin Factor from Egg White." *Journal of Biological Chemistry* 142 (1942): 285–290.

Food Foams

Foams are useful for the structure they contribute to food systems. In the absence of a foam structure, a soufflé would be scrambled eggs and whipped cream would be fluid cream. Angel and sponge cakes, Bavarian and Spanish creams, puffy omelets, and soft and hard meringues are just a few of the food systems that utilize foams. Cream, milk, egg, and gelatin are the principal foods that can be used for foam formation. The food industry also utilizes soy protein and vegetable gums to produce a foam structure.

Physical Properties of Foams

A foam is a gas (air) dispersed in a liquid. The liquid must have the characteristics required to retain the air that is incorporated by agitation of the liquid. The liquid in food foams is likely to be a protein dispersion such as that present in a gelatin sol, uncooked egg, cream, and some fluid milks. The protein is capable of forming a film around the air bubbles and stretching as the air bubbles increase in size.

Foams are often described as having stability or instability. An *unstable* foam tends to collapse soon after it is formed; a *stable* foam tends to retain the air in the foam structure for varying lengths of time. Water in a closed jar can be shaken, and bubbles of air will be trapped in the water, but the foam is unstable. The air bubbles are not retained once agitation ceases, for there is nothing in the water to stabilize the foam.

The stability of most foams can be improved by lowering the

Figure 20.1

Separating yolks and whites of eggs is a skill that takes practice. Using a heavy, sharp knife to crack the shell and break the membrane inside the shell makes it easier to pull the two halves of the shell apart. Hold the yolk in one half of the shell while draining off the white; use the other half of the shell to transfer the yolk back and forth, cutting away the thick white that clings to the yolk. In case of slips, use a separate dish for each egg white.

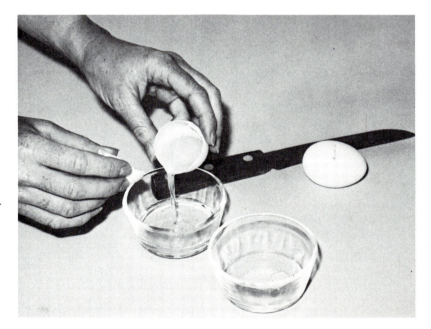

pH of the protein dispersion so that there are equal numbers of positive and negative charges on the protein molecules. This causes an attraction between the molecules, one for another, that makes them more insoluble and promotes better retention of the incorporated air. The pH of the dispersion can be lowered by the addition of an acid ingredient, such as lemon juice or cream of tartar, to the protein dispersion.

The viscosity of the protein dispersion also affects its stability. If the concentration of protein molecules in the liquid is too dilute, the foam is less stable. The addition of protein in the form of gelatin or milk solids increases the viscosity and stability of some systems. Freezing or partially freezing the protein dispersion binds part of the water in the form of ice crystals, thereby increasing the viscosity.

Some protein dispersions are too viscous and do not contain enough water for foam formation. Whole egg and egg yolk require the addition of water in order to form a foam of good volume.

Whipping aids are produced commercially by the enzymatic modification of soybean, wheat, and milk proteins for use in the food industry. These aids are used to improve the texture, consistency, and appearance of confections, meringues, icings, and marshmallows. Increased stability of the foam, decreased whipping time, and reduced energy usage are advantages gained by the industrial use of whipping aids.

Egg Foams

Whole eggs and egg yolks, like whites, can be formed into foams with proper techniques and the correct type of mixer. Whole egg and yolk foams, which are less versatile than egg white foams, are used in sponge cakes and puffy omelets. Figure 20.1 illustrates a technique for separating egg yolks from whites.

Whipped egg white traps air in bubbles with protein films, and water is held in the spaces between the bubbles. The more the egg white is whipped, the more air is incorporated into the foam. The foam's stability is its ability to retain this air without collapsing. Stability increases with the stiffness of the foam up to a point. A foam beaten past the stiff-peak stage collapses readily and is less stable.

STAGES OF BEATING EGG WHITE FOAMS

Recipes often specify that eggs be beaten to a particular stage or consistency. A description of these stages follows; the volume of a given amount of egg beaten to each stage is shown in Figure 20.2

Foamy   The egg white is lightly whipped and appears frothy and fluid; it does not hold a peak.

Soft Peak   The foam has small bubbles, flows in the bowl, and is moist and shiny. When the beaters are removed, peaks are formed, but their tips fold over.

Figure 20.2

Stages of beaten egg white are, left to right: foamy, soft peak, stiff peak, and dry foam. Note how volume increases with additional whipping; dry foam, the final stage, has a curdled appearance and is unsatisfactory for most purposes.

Stiff Peak   The foam does not flow in the bowl but is still shiny. When the beaters are removed, the tips of the peaks remain upright. A spatula cut through the foam leaves a "canyon" with straight sides. The stiff-peak stage of whipping yields a foam of maximum stability. For most purposes, it is not advisable to whip egg whites beyond this stage.

Dry Foam   The foam achieves maximum volume and appears dull, dry, and curdled. When the beaters are removed, the foam breaks instead of forming peaks. Foam beaten to this stage collapses readily and is lumpy when it is added to other mixtures.

FACTORS AFFECTING THE VOLUME AND STABILITY OF EGG WHITE FOAMS

A number of factors affect the stability and volume of egg white foams and the time it takes to whip them. Some factors include the characteristics of the egg white, the type of mixer or beater used, and the presence of acid, sugar, or fat.

Characteristics of Egg White   Because thin egg white beats into a foam more readily than thick egg white, older eggs and egg whites at room temperature are preferred for making foams. Both frozen and dehydrated egg whites have good foam-forming properties.

Type of Beater   An electric mixer with a wire beater produces a foam more readily than a blade beater, and any electric mixer is faster than a hand beater. Wire whips are the slowest tool for producing foams. Whether electric or hand operated, wire beaters produce foams with smaller air cells than blade beaters. An electric mixer is preferable for beating thick egg whites, but if the egg whites are thin, a hand whip or beater is less likely to produce overbeating.

Effect of Acid, Sugar, and Fat   Adding either sugar or acid, or both, increases the stability of foams. Both ingredients also delay foam formation, but the effect is greater with sugar. For the best volume in the least time, sugar should not be added until the foam reaches the soft peak stage. An egg white foam that contains sugar is more flexible and easier to fold into other mixtures than one without sugar. The common, most effective acid seems to be cream of tartar (potassium acid tartrate).

Fat inhibits foam formation. Beaters and bowls for egg white foams should be clean and free of all traces of grease. Plastic bowls should not be used because all traces of grease are difficult to remove from them. Careful separation of the eggs prevents egg yolk from getting into the whites, which would interfere with foam formation.

Several kinds of egg white foams have already been mentioned or discussed; their use in angel cake is discussed in Chapter 21. Egg white foams are also a base for soufflés, baked fondues, and soft and hard meringues.

EGG WHITE FOAMS IN FOOD SYSTEMS

Baked Soufflés and Fondues Baked soufflés and fondues are similar dishes with different types of thickening. A fondue is thickened with bread crumbs, a soufflé with a thick white sauce. Fondue is a little easier to prepare than a soufflé, because egg yolks are mixed with milk, cheese, seasonings, and bread crumbs; the egg white foam is folded in; and the mixture is baked. A white sauce must be prepared for a soufflé, and yolks, cheese, and other seasonings are added to the white sauce before the egg white foam is folded in (Figures 20.3, 20.4, 20.5).

Fresh bread crumbs, prepared by blending fresh bread in a blender, produce a light and tender baked fondue. The egg white foam should be beaten only to the soft-peak stage so that it is pliable and can be folded into the other mixture without forming lumps. Dessert soufflés contain sugar; at least part of the sugar should be beaten into the egg white foam to provide additional stability.

Figure 20.3

To make a soufflé, stir grated cheese into cooked white sauce after adding egg yolks. *(United Dairy Industry Association)*

Figure 20.4

White sauce with cheese added is folded into an egg white foam beaten to the soft peak stage. *(United Dairy Industry Association)*

Figure 20.5

Baked cheese soufflé should be lightly browned and show good volume. It is served immediately. *(United Dairy Industry Association)*

Bake soufflés and fondues like custards, surrounded by boiling water; test them for doneness in the same way. These dishes should be served immediately, because they start to collapse as soon as they are removed from the oven. An unusual use of a soufflé is in roulade (Figure 20.6).

Probably the most common mistake made in preparing soufflés and fondues is overbeating the egg white. Overbeating stretches the protein surrounding the air bubbles to its maximum. When heating begins and the gases further expand it, the protein can stretch no more and breaks, causing a loss of air and reducing the baked volume in the soufflé or fondue. Another common fault is overbaking, which causes curdling and syneresis in soufflés just as it does in custards. Soufflés containing acid ingredients, such as lemon, are particularly susceptible to overbaking. Acid should not be used in egg white foams for soufflés or puffy omelets for this reason.

Meringues   A meringue is an egg white foam containing sugar. Soft meringues are, as the name implies, soft; they have less sugar than hard meringues and bake quickly. Hard meringues have about twice as much sugar as soft meringues and are baked a long time at a low temperature so that they will dry out and become hard. Soft meringues top pies and baked Alaska and are added to a variety of dishes. Hard meringues are used for tortes, macaroons, and tart shells.

The preparation and serving of soft meringues has been described in Chapter 14. However, techniques suggested for preparing egg white foams should be observed to make both soft and hard meringues. Hard meringues contain ¼ cup of sugar per large egg white; ½ cup of egg white, or four large egg whites, requires 1 cup of sugar. The meringue should be prepared before the other ingredients, such as coconut or nuts, are added. Bake hard meringues at 250°F (121°C) for about 1 hour. A good practice is to leave hard meringues in the oven after it is turned off so that they cool gradually and dry out thoroughly. Hard meringues should be dry, crisp, tender, and lightly browned. They can be frozen in airtight containers.

WHOLE EGG AND YOLK FOAMS

To obtain a satisfactory foam from whole eggs and egg yolks, an electric mixer with hypocycloidal beating action and a wire whip attachment should be used. The addition of 1½ teaspoons of cream of tartar per cup of whole egg or yolk is essential. In addition, ¼ cup of water must be added to each cup of yolks because yolks have a much lower water content than whole eggs or egg whites. Adding water to whole eggs (2 tablespoons per cup) produces a larger volume of foam, but the foam is less stable for some purposes.

A longer beating time than for egg whites is necessary to obtain adequate foam formation from yolks and whole eggs; a stiff foam can never be obtained. If the proper mixer is available, beating whole eggs into a foam is a faster way to prepare a puffy omelet than the usual method that requires separating the eggs and fold-

Figure 20.6

Soufflé may be served in *roulade:* the soufflé mixture is baked in a paper-lined jelly roll pan and inverted after baking on paper sprinkled with bread crumbs. A mushroom-chicken filling is spread over the soufflé, which is then rolled up.

ing the yolk-cream mixture into the egg white foam. Both whole egg and yolk foam are used in sponge cakes, which are discussed in Chapter 21.

Whipped Cream and Milk Foams
WHIPPING CREAM

Cream with 22 percent fat can be satisfactorily whipped; heavy whipping cream contains as much as 38 percent fat. The greater the fat content of the cream, the more stable is the foam. When cream is whipped, air bubbles are enclosed in a thin layer of protein surrounded by clumps of fat that stabilize the foam by preventing the loss of air from the bubbles.

Heavy cream can become buttery and lumpy if it is over-whipped; a cream with 30 percent fat is sufficiently stable for most uses and is lower in calories and cost. High-fat cream is preferred for filling pastries, however, because the water in the lower-fat creams drains from the foam and causes sogginess.

Pasteurization of cream does reduce its whipping quality, but for reasons of health it is not advisable to use unpasteurized cream. Homogenized cream does not whip well, probably because the homogenization process keeps the fat globules from clumping around the air bubbles. Cream that has been frozen does not whip well because the fat separates when it is thawed.

Cream whips best when it is cold. Fat globules clump more readily in the solid state than in the liquid state (Figure 20.7). Also, cream is more viscous cold than warm, and increased viscosity improves foam formation. Sugar delays the incorporation of air bubbles in the cream, reduces the volume of whipped cream, and increases the beating time. Therefore, cream should be whipped to the desired stiffness and sugar stirred in without further beating. The addition of sugar also reduces the stiffness of whipped cream. Whipped cream can be flavored with almond or

Figure 20.7

The substance being whipped must be the correct temperature to produce good foam formation. *(Evaporated Milk Association)*

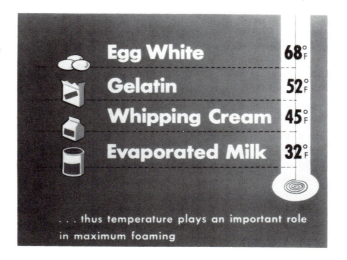

vanilla extracts and served as a topping or filling for pastries. Whipped, cream increases two to three times in volume, depending on the fat content of the cream.

Stabilizers added to cream reduce the foam's tendency to collapse. One teaspoon of 10 percent lime water (Calcium hydroxide) per cup of cream, or 2 level tablespoons of instant nonfat dry milk, improves the stability of the cream if it is added before whipping. Whipped cream is also more stable if it is kept cold. It can be frozen for later use if it has first been shaped according to its function. Form stiffly whipped cream into mounds of the desired shape and size (a pastry bag can be used) on a baking sheet covered with waxed paper. Freeze the mounds unwrapped and then transfer them to a closed container when frozen. Place the frozen mound of cream on top of the dessert or in the cream puff at serving time; thawing occurs in a very few minutes.

WHIPPED MILKS

Several forms of milk can be whipped into fairly stable foams and can thus replace whipped cream for some purposes. Whipped milks are lower in calories, have a higher nutrient content, and are more economical than whipping cream. They also take longer to whip, collapse more readily, and lack the characteristic texture and flavor of whipped cream, but for some uses whipped milk is quite acceptable. Table 20.1 shows the approximate yield of whipped milk from its unwhipped source and the approximate cost based on West Coast prices during 1980. Most of these milk foams are best used in mixtures in which other ingredients, such as chocolate or fruits, mask their flavor. They are often more stable when combined with a gelatin mixture, as in a Bavarian cream (Figure 20.8).

Preparing and Serving Milk Foams Slightly different techniques are needed to prepare foams from different forms of milk. Undi-

Table 20.1   Approximate yield, calories, and cost of whipped cream and whipped milk

Type of milk or cream	Volume (c)		Cost and size of market unit ($)[a]	One cup whipped product	
	Initial	Whipped		Cost ($)[a]	Kcals
Cream, light	1	2½	0.61/cup	0.25	287
Nonfat dry milk	½[b]	3	1.37/pound	0.04	42
Evaporated milk, whole	⅓	1	0.45/13 fluid ounces	0.09	115
Evaporated milk, skim	⅓	1	0.43/13 fluid ounces	0.09	65
Concentrated milk	⅓	1	1.29/quart	0.11	159

[a]Based on 1980 prices.
[b]Thirty-five grains of nonfat dry milk and ⅓ cup of water.

Figure 20.9

Evaporated milk whips best when it is partially frozen. *(Evaporated Milk Association)*

Figure 20.8

This is an orange-coconut Bavarian cream pie made with an evaporated milk foam. *(Evaporated Milk Association)*

luted concentrated and evaporated milk whip best if they are partially frozen (Figure 20.9); the crystallization of some of the water in the milk makes it more viscous. Dissolving a small amount of gelatin in the milk also increases the viscosity and contributes additional protein for surrounding the air bubbles (Figures 20.10, 20.11, 20.12). Concentrated milk whips better if it has been scalded because heat affects the protein so that the milk foams

Figure 20.10

Nonfat dry milk is measured in the same way as other dry ingredients, by filling and leveling a nested measuring cup. *(United Dairy Industry Association)*

Figure 20.11

Nonfat dry milk can be added to partially thickened gelatin mixtures and whipped into a foam. *(United Dairy Industry Association)*

Figure 20.12

Partially thickened gelatin can be added to a foam made from nonfat dry milk. *(United Dairy Industry Association)*

Figure 20.13

Adding a small amount of lemon juice to a foam made from evaporated or nonfat dry milk increases the stability of the foam. *(Evaporated Milk Association)*

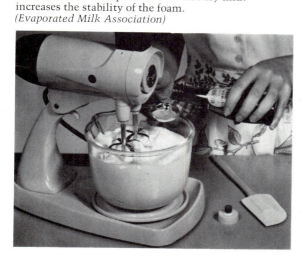

more readily. Finally, adding a small amount of lemon juice to milk alters the protein and increases viscosity, thereby producing a more stable foam (Figure 20.13).

Stabilizing milk foams with lemon juice would be objectionable in some cases, such as in a chocolate dish, because of the acidity. Furthermore, foams stabilized with gelatin have a gellike

Figure 20.14

One cup of undiluted
evaporated milk yields
approximately 3 cups of
whipped milk foam.
(Evaporated Milk Association)

consistency that is somewhat rigid. Because sugar reduces the stiffness of milk foams, minimal amounts should be folded into the whipped milk with as little stirring as possible. The foams should be whipped as close to serving time as possible because they do not remain stable for very long.

Foams made of nonfat dry milk are airy, light, lacking in body, but good in flavor. Foams made of concentrated milk more nearly resemble whipped cream in flavor and consistency. Evaporated milk foams have a decided flavor of canned milk, but they also have good body and texture (Figure 20.14) and are especially useful in dishes in which their flavor is masked by other ingredients.

If regular nonfat dry milk is used to prepare a foam, use equal amounts of milk powder and water. With instant nonfat dry milk, use a slightly larger volume of milk powder, about ½ cup of crystals per ⅓ cup of liquid (Figure 20.15).

Gelatin Foams

Because of their high concentration of protein, gelatin mixtures have the ability to form foams and retain air. Whipped gelatin is often called a "whip," but if raw egg white and gelatin are whipped together, the result is called a "sponge." To be whipped into a foam, the gelatin mixture must have the consistency of thick, raw egg white. Neither a sol nor a gel can be whipped into

Figure 20.15

One-half cup of nonfat dry milk
combined with ⅓ cup of water
produces about 2 cups of foam.

Figure 20.16

Warmed liquids can be mixed in a blender with gelatin to produce light, airy desserts. *(Knox of Thomas J. Lipton, Inc.)*

Figure 20.17

A slightly thickened strawberry gelatin–custard mixture is folded into an egg white foam to make a strawberry gelatin soufflé. *(Knox of Thomas J. Lipton, Inc.)*

Figure 20.18

This gelatin soufflé is garnished with fresh grapes, peach slices, and cantaloupe balls among leaves of endive. *(United Fresh Fruit and Vegetable Association)*

a foam. The easiest way to make a gelatin foam is to place the container of partially thickened gelatin in a bowl of ice water and whip it, preferably with an electric mixer, at high speed (Figures 20.16, 20.17).

Solid ingredients should not be added to whipped gelatin until after the foam is fully formed, at which point they should be folded in gently. Then chill the foam to set it. If the gelatin starts to set while the foam is being whipped and chilled in ice water, discontinue whipping. If it should gel prematurely, warm it slightly to complete the formation of the foam (Figure 20.18).

Study Questions

1. Define the term *foam* as used in food systems.
2. Differentiate between stable and unstable foams.
3. Explain how and why decreasing the pH of a protein dispersion affects the stability of foams formed from the protein dispersion.
4. Explain the effect of viscosity on foam stability.
5. Describe the characteristics of egg white foams beaten to the four different stages.
6. Explain the effect of sugar on egg white foam and state when it is best to add the sugar to the egg white foam and why.
7. Differentiate between baked soufflés and fondues with respect to their ingredients and method of preparation.
8. Explain how and why overbeating egg white is deleterious to the quality of the baked product.
9. Distinguish between hard and soft meringues; their ingredients, baking, and baked characteristics.
10. What are the essential procedures required to obtain good foam formation with whole eggs and egg yolks?
11. How does fat function in whipped cream?
12. How is the fat content of the cream related to the stability of the whipped cream?
13. What are some advantages and disadvantages of whipped milks compared to whipped cream?
14. Describe techniques that will improve the stability of the various whipped milks.
15. Describe the consistency of gelatin required for good foam formation.

References

Campbell, Ada Marie; Penfield, M. P.; and Griswold, R. M. *The Experimental Study of Foods.* Boston: Houghton Mifflin, 1979.

Charley, Helen. *Food Science.* New York: Ronald Press, 1970.

Idsen, B., and Broswell, E. "Gelatin." *Advances in Food Research* 7 (1957): 236.

Longree, Karla; White, J. C.; and Sison, B. Y. "Time-Temperature Relationships of Soufflés." *Journal of the American Dietetic Association* 41, (no. 2) (August 1962): 107.

Miller, E. L., and Vail, G. E. "Angel Food Cakes from Fresh and Frozen Egg Whites." *Cereal Chemistry* 20 (1943): 528.

Paul, Pauline C. "Proteins, Enzymes, Collagen, and Gelatin." In *Food Theory and Applications,* edited by Pauline C. Paul and Helen H. Palmer. New York: Wiley, 1972.

——. "Eggs." In *Food Theory and Applications.*

——. and H. H. Palmer. "Colloidal Systems and Emulsions." In *Food Theory and Applications.*

St. John, J. L., and Flor, I. H. "A Study of Whipping and Coagulation of Eggs of Varying Quality." *Poultry Science* 10 (1931): 71.

Sponge and Chiffon Cakes

Sponge cakes are made from egg foams. Cakes made from egg white foams are called angel cakes; cake made from yolk or whole egg foams are either yolk sponge cakes or whole egg sponge cakes. All are unique in that they contain no added fat, liquid, or chemical or biological leavening agents, although a yolk sponge needs extra water to make up for the low water content of yolks. Chiffon cakes are a hybrid of sponge and shortened cakes that contain an egg white foam along with fat, liquid, and chemical leavening. Three types of sponge cake are shown in Figure 21.1.

Sponge Cakes

The ingredients and the mixing methods for cakes prepared from egg white, egg yolk, and whole egg foams are mostly similar, but a few differences exist.

INGREDIENTS

The ingredients in sponge cakes are few: flour, sugar, salt, egg, and cream of tartar, plus water in whole egg and yolk sponge cakes.

Flour   Cake flour is the preferred flour for use in making sponge and chiffon cakes. Recent studies have indicated that angel cakes are most tender if one third of the cake flour is replaced with wheat starch. Angel cakes prepared from all-purpose flour have reduced volume and are less tender; they shrink excessively during the last part of baking and during cooling.

Egg   Egg furnishes the liquid for hydrating the flour and also supplies steam for leavening. Egg also supplies protein for structure, and the foam prepared from it provides both the cellular structure characteristic of these cakes and the air and steam for leavening.

Cream of Tartar   Cream of tartar, or potassium acid tartrate $(KHC_4H_4O_6)$, is an acid ingredient used in sponge cakes to stabi-

Figure 21.1

Three types of sponge cake are: chiffon (top), yolk sponge (left), and whole egg sponge (right). The yolk sponge becomes dark by the time the cake has baked enough to set the structure, as is indicated by its darker center.

lize the foam. Angel cakes use 1 teaspoon of cream of tartar per cup of egg whites; sponge cakes use 1½ teaspoons of cream of tartar per cup of whole eggs or yolks. Because eggs are slightly alkaline, and because the pigment in flour is creamy or yellowish in an alkaline medium, adding cream of tartar produces a whiter angel cake. The acidic medium also decreases the tendency of these high-protein cakes to become overly brown.

Cream of tartar reduces shrinkage during baking and produces a more tender cake with a softer, finer grain than a batter without cream of tartar.

Sugar   Sugar also stabilizes the foam structure, making it more elastic and pliable so that the air cells expand and retain the leavening gases during baking. Part of the sugar is combined with the flour to separate the flour granules and keep them from lumping when the mixture is folded into the foam. This procedure eliminates excessive mixing that would cause a loss of air from the foam and reduced volume. Sugar is used as a tenderizing agent in sponge cakes; higher levels of sugar increases the tenderness of the cake.

Ratio of Ingredients   The proper proportions of egg white, sugar, and flour are important to obtain a good balance of structural and tenderizing ingredients. Too much flour and egg make a dry, tough cake. Too much sugar increases the temperature at which egg protein coagulates. A baked cake that contains too much sugar may collapse and have a sugary crust. Table 21.1 shows three possible formulas for angel cake, all acceptable and all having approximately the same volume when baked. Their difference lies in their eating quality. Formula 1 is the most tender and moist, because it has the highest ratio of sugar and the lowest ratio of flour. Formula 3 ranks second. Both formulas 1 and 3

ANGEL CAKES

Table 21.1   Suggested formulas for angel cakes, based on 1½ cups of egg white (369 grams) with varying proportions of flour and sugar

Formula[a]	Ingredient	Volume (c)	Weight (g)	Grams of ingredient per gram of egg white	Grams of sugar per gram of flour
1	Flour, cake	⅞	84	0.228	
	Sugar	1⅞	375	1.016	4.46
2	Flour, cake	1	96	0.260	
	Sugar	1¾	350	0.948	3.65
3	Flour, cake	1	96	0.260	
	Sugar	2	400	1.084	4.16

[a]Formulas shown are adequate for a 10-inch cake, with the addition of 1½ teaspoons cream of tartar, ½ teaspoon salt, and 1 teaspoon flavoring.

Figure 21.2

The egg white–sugar foam should be beaten to the stiff peak stage before folding in the flour-sugar mixture in preparing angel cake.

require slightly longer baking times than formula 2 because the higher sugar content raises the temperature necessary to coagulate the egg white.

Mixing Angel Cakes   Flour should be sifted before measuring, if volume measures are used; sifting is not necessary if the flour is measured by weight. About one fourth to one third of the sugar should be thoroughly mixed with the flour and salt.

Beat the egg whites and cream of tartar to the soft peak stage, add the flavoring and two thirds to three fourths of the sugar, and beat the foam to the stiff-peak stage for 1 to 2 minutes, depending on the type of mixer used (Figure 21.2). The foam should be whipped enough to dissolve the added sugar, but it should not be beaten so much that it becomes rigid and inelastic. Fold the flour-sugar mixture into the meringue with a minimum of strokes to retain air and so that no lumps of flour remain. A French whip is ideal for this folding step, which should not be done with an electric mixer.

The mixing of an angel cake, once begun, must be carried to completion. Do not allow the meringue to stand before adding the flour; do not hold the batter before baking.

Baking Angel Cakes   Use a tube pan to bake sponge and chiffon cakes. The tube in the center provides a surface on which the foam can cling and rise and also permits heat penetration from the center for more rapid expansion of the foam. The pan should not be greased. A two-piece pan makes the cake easier to remove.

Sponge cakes have a better volume when baked at 400 to 425°F (204 to 218°C) than they do at 350 to 375°F (177 to 190°C). A 10-inch angel cake containing 1½ cups of egg whites bakes in 25 minutes at 425°F (218°C) and in 30 minutes at 400°F(204°C). Browning and overbaking are more likely at the higher temperature. Sponge cakes can be tested for doneness by the finger pressure test; if the cake springs back, it is done.

The baked cake is inverted and allowed to cool completely in the pan. Because its structure is not completely set until it is cool, the weight of the cake causes it to pack down if it is cooled in an upright position. The cake may be cooled more rapidly in a freezer or refrigerator, but it should be completely cool before it is removed from the pan.

Chocolate Angel Cake   Because the fat in chocolate has a foam-depressing effect, best results are obtained with the use of a low-fat cocoa powder in chocolate angel cakes. The cocoa should be dispersed well in the flour-sugar mixture, and the mixture folded into the foam as quickly as possible and baking started immediately, so that the effect of the fat on the foam can be minimized. A fairly satisfactory chocolate cake can be prepared, but it does not have quite as good a volume as white angel cakes.

Good volume in whole egg and yolk sponge cakes depends on good foam formation (Figure 21.3). Factors that influence the formation of foams from egg yolks and whole eggs are discussed in Chapter 20. After forming the foam, beat in the flavoring and half

WHOLE EGG AND YOLK SPONGE CAKES

Figure 21.3

A foam made with egg yolks (right) and a foam made with whole egg (left) were whipped in a mixer with a wire beater, using hypocycloidal action. Both foams were made from 1½ cups of yolks or whole eggs; ½ cup of water was added to the yolks.

of the sugar, then fold in the sugar-flour mixture, just as in angel cake batter. Whole egg and yolk sponge cake batters are extremely unstable and should be baked as soon as the batter is mixed and in the pan.

If a mixer with hypocycloidal action and a wire beater is not available, an alternate method for preparing a whole egg sponge cake is to separate the eggs, whip the whites and two thirds of the sugar into a meringue, and combine the yolks with a small amount of water and the other ingredients to form a batter, which is folded into the meringue.

These sponge cakes can be flavored with vanilla, almond, orange, or lemon extract. They are baked and cooled in the same manner as angel cakes.

Chiffon Cakes

Chiffon cakes are easy to make and have a light, moist texture. They resemble sponge cakes in appearance and are spongelike in texture because of their large proportion of egg white foam.

The muffin sponge method is used to mix chiffon cakes. Dry ingredients, including cake flour, baking powder, salt, and part of the sugar, are combined and added to a mixture of the liquid ingredients: yolks, oil, and milk or other liquid. This batter is folded into an egg white meringue and is baked and cooled in the same way as for angel and sponge cakes.

Variations in flavor are possible by the use of different liquids in place of milk, such as orange, lemon, lime, or pineapple juice, or purées of apricot or persimmon. Spices or cocoa may be added to the dry ingredients.

Cutting Angel, Sponge, and Chiffon Cakes

Because of their high egg content, these cakes stick to the knife when they are cut unless the knife is wet. Their structure is fragile, and they are easily compressed when they are divided into pieces for serving. The knife should be wet, not dripping, and free of adhering crumbs before cutting each slice. A thin, sharp blade used with a sawing motion without bearing down cuts best.

Table 21.2   Comparison of nutrient composition of cakes without icing, 100-gram amounts[a]

Type of cake	Calories	Protein (g)	Fat (g)	Carbo-hydrate (g)	Calcium (mg)	Iron (mg)	Vitamin A (I.U.)	Thiamin (mg)	Riboflavin (mg)
Angel	295	7	trace	67	7	trace	0	trace	0.16
Whole egg sponge	363	10	7	58	41	1.5	824	0.07	0.27
Yolk sponge	369	9	14	51	69	2.7	1582	0.11	0.21
Chiffon	373	6	14	48	44	0.6	308	0.03	0.15
Shortened cake, standard	460	6	21	64	56	0.6	232	0.04	0.12

[a]Nutrients were calculated from recipes and the cakes baked and weighed.

Most people who eat cakes probably never think about the nutrients in them, though they are likely to be aware of the many calories because of the fat and sugar content. Angel and sponge cakes have a lower calorie content and higher nutrient content than shortened cakes because of their ingredients. Table 21.2 compares the nutrient content of angel, sponge, and chiffon cakes with standard butter cake. The calorie-nutrient differential would be even greater for rich butter cake. Total nutrients are indicated for 100-gram amounts without frosting.

Nutritional Value of Sponge Cakes

Study Questions

1. What is the source and function of liquid in angel and sponge cakes?
2. What are the functions of cream of tartar in angel and sponge cakes?
3. How is sugar incorporated in angel and sponge cakes and why is it added in this way?
4. What ingredients in angel and sponge cakes increase the tenderness? What ingredients decrease tenderness?
5. How is flour incorporated in angel and sponge cakes?
6. Why does adding cocoa to angel cake cause a reduction in the volume of the baked cake?
7. What type of pan is preferred for baking angel, sponge, and chiffon cakes? Why?
8. How should these foam cakes be cooled? Why?
9. What ingredients are found in chiffon cakes that are not present in angel and sponge cakes?
10. In what ways can variety in flavor be obtained in chiffon cakes?
11. Compare the nutrient composition and caloric content of various types of cakes.

References

Campbell, Ada Marie; Penfield, M. P.; and Griswold, R. M. *The Experimental Study of Foods.* Boston: Houghton Mifflin, 1979.

Charley, Helen. *Food Science.* New York: Ronald Press, 1970.

Grewe, E., and Child, A. M. "The Effect of Potassium Acid Tartrate as An Ingredient in Angel Cake." *Cereal Chemistry* 7, (no. 3) (May 1930): 245.

Harns, J. Vivian; Sauter, E. A.; McLaren, B. A.; and Stadelman, W. J. "Relationship of Shell Egg Quality and Performance of Egg White in Angel Food Cakes." *Food Research* 18, (no. 5) (July–August 1953): 343.

Palmer, Helen H. "Eggs." In *Food Theory and Applications,* edited by Pauline C. Paul and Helen H. Palmer. New York: Wiley, 1972.

Pyke, W. E. "Factors the Baker Should Consider in Preparing Yellow Sponge Cake." *Cereal Chemistry* 18, (no. 1) (January 1941): 92.

Pyler, E. J. *Baking Science and Technology,* vol. 2. Chicago: Siebel Publishing, 1973.

22

Meats: Beef, Veal, Lamb, and Pork

Meat is one of the main sources of protein in the American diet. Because meat is so well liked, many persons probably consume more meat than they need to supply their protein needs. Any kind of animal is a good source of complete protein, but the animal meats that are most commonly eaten in this country are beef, veal, lamb, pork, fowl, fish of all kinds, and, less often, game animals. In recent years, shortages of animal foods combined with the high cost of their production have caused increased emphasis to be placed on supplementing animal protein by various means.

Meat Composition

The proportions of protein, carbohydrate, and fat in animals is extremely variable, depending on the type of animal and the particular cut of meat. In food preparation, most attention is given to the proportions of lean meat, fat, connective tissue, and bone. These components directly influence the edibility of the meat and, therefore, its proper method of preparation.

MUSCLE TISSUE

The muscle tissue of meat is commonly called the *lean* part. Muscle tissues consist of protein fibers enclosed in thin protein membranes of connective tissue. Bundles of these fibers combine to form larger muscles that are covered with a thicker membrane of connective tissue and attached to the bones.

CONNECTIVE TISSUE

The connective tissues bind together the meat fibers to form muscles, and then connect these muscles to each other and to the bones. There are two types of connective tissue, *collagen* and *elastin*. The membranes between muscle fibers and the gristle at the ends of the bones are made of collagen. Collagen is readily softened when it is cooked with moist heat, which converts the collagen into gelatin. Tendons are composed of elastin, which is not softened by cooking.

The more exercised parts of the animal, such as the legs, contain greater amounts of connective tissue than do the less exercised parts of the animal—along the backbone, for example. The more connective tissue a cut of meat contains, the less tender it is to eat. Older animals have larger amounts of elastin connective tissue than younger animals. Thus, lamb is more tender than mutton because lamb comes from a younger animal.

FATTY TISSUE

The *adipose* or fatty tissues of the animal are made up of connective tissues that contain large numbers of fat cells. The fat is usually deposited first under the skin and around the glandular organs in the living animal. As the animal continues to fatten, fat is deposited between and within the muscle tissues. Fat distributed in the lean tissues is called *marbling*. Well-marbled meat is often considered the choicest in eating quality, but meat with a minimal amount of marbling is better nutritionally.

BONE Bones are an aid in identifying retail and wholesale cuts of meat after an animal has been butchered. The long leg bones are hollow and contain yellow marrow. Other bones may be spongy inside and contain red marrow.

PIGMENTS *Myoglobin* is the name of the pigment in meat, and it is responsible for the red color of meat. The more myoglobin a meat contains, the darker red its color is. Beef contains more myoglobin than pork, and hence has a deeper red color. The amount of myoglobin increases with the age of the animal. Beef from a full-grown steer and mutton have more myoglobin than young veal or lamb, and thus their meat is a darker red in color.

Myoglobin in muscle is similar to hemoglobin in red blood cells. Both have the ability to carry oxygen and carbon dioxide, and both are bright red when they are carrying oxygen and bluish-red when they are not. For this reason, meat appears to change color when it is exposed to the air or when air is excluded. Several small steaks stacked on top of each other for a period of time will be bright red on the exposed surface, but the inside surfaces, where one steak touches the other, will be slightly bluish red in color. If these surfaces are then exposed to the air, they, too, will turn bright red. Such color change does not affect the flavor or quality of meat.

If raw meat is held for several days in the refrigerator, the myoglobin changes to a brownish-red color, indicating a loss of flavor and freshness. Heated, myoglobin changes to a grayish-brown color, a color change that indicates the doneness of meat. Meat cooked only to the rare stage retains a great deal of its original red color; well-done, it loses all its red and becomes completely gray-brown in color.

Cured meats, such as ham, bacon, corned beef, sandwich meats, wieners, and sausage, are meats treated with sodium or potassium nitrite or nitrate. The nitrate combines with myoglobin to form *nitrosomyoglobin*, which has a permanently pink color both raw and cooked. Nitrates, along with salt brines, help preserve meat to retard the growth of bacteria and provide a different flavor.

Grading Meat Meat grading is a voluntary action of the Agriculture Marketing Service that is provided for the consumer's benefit but paid for by the meat packer. A packer who chooses to use the grade names established by the government agency is required to have the grading performed by a trained government official according to established federal standards. The grade is stamped on the fatty outer covering of the wholesale cuts. When the meat is cut into retail cuts, however, the grade stamp may not be evident on individual cuts of meat.

Factors considered in meat grading were revised in 1976 so that the build of the animal is no longer the primary consideration. The amount, distribution, color, and texture of the lean muscle are used to assign grades. Grades have been established for beef, veal, mutton, and lamb. The shield bearing the grade is stamped on the surface of the carcass (Figure 22.1). For beef, the grades assigned are as follows:

U.S. Prime   Very tender meat, usually from well-fed steers. The meat is well-marbled and is the highest quality available. It is purchased by fine restaurants but is not available in most retail markets.

U.S. Choice   Very tender meat with some marbling, but not as high a quality as Prime grade. This is the top grade available in most retail markets.

U.S. Good   Less tender, less juicy, and showing less marbling than the Choice grade; this meat is available in some stores as the house brand, not under the U.S.D.A. grade name. Good is an economical grade that is just as nutritious as the higher grades.

U.S. Standard   A high proportion of lean meat and very little fat is found in this grade of meat because it is obtained from young animals. Standard is fairly tender, mild in flavor, and lacks marbling.

U.S. Commercial   Meat of this grade is obtained from older, mature animals. Although it is well-marbled, commercial tends also to be less tender and more flavorful because of the age of the animal it comes from. Together with the U.S. Canner grade, it is used for canned products, luncheon meats, and ground meat.

Animals are now being bred leaner with less fat. In the grading process, slightly leaner beef is being graded prime and choice than formerly. This is possible because more animals are reaching market at less than 2 years of age, and in animals this young, the fat marbling is not required as an indication of quality. In addition, grading standards have been made more stringent to provide more uniform characteristics and quality in meat that is graded Good.

As a rule, no grade of meat can guarantee tenderness because individual animals vary so greatly and because there is no way to know if a piece of meat is tender before it has been cooked. The eating quality of meat is influenced by an animal's genetic and environmental background and the way it is handled and processed before and after slaughter. Even within the same animal, the eating quality of meat varies from part to part.

U.S. QUALITY GRADES OF MEAT

Figure 22.1

This shield indicates quality grades of meat.

Lamb and mutton are graded U.S. Prime, Choice, Good, and Utility. These grades carry approximately the same standard of quality as comparable grades of beef. Mutton is rarely available in retail markets.

Pork is not federally graded. Grades have been established for pork, but they are not widely used and are based mainly on proportions of fat and lean meat. Some meat packers use brand names to identify different levels of quality in their pork and maintain these standards through their own quality control programs.

YIELD GRADES

Yield grading is important in purchasing wholesale cuts of meat. Meat animals are graded at the time of slaughter according to the amount of edible lean meat obtained from the animal, based on its fat content and the thickness and plumpness of the muscles. The government has established yield grades on a scale of 1 to 5, with grade 1 the leanest and highest yield and grade 5 the poorest yield (Figure 22.2).

When purchasing wholesale cuts of meat, be sure to compare prices according to yield grade. Table 22.1 shows the yield grades and the percent of fat trim, bone, and edible meat from each grade. A 150-pound beef quarter yields 123 pounds of edible meat if it is from a yield grade 1 animal, but only 95.4 pounds of edible meat if it is from a yield grade 5, a difference of about 28 pounds. The cost of the cut should therefore be calculated on the yield of edible meat. In making wholesale purchases, insist on seeing the yield grade stamped on the meat before it is butchered.

Yield grades are unrelated to quality grades. Choice grade ani-

Figure 22.2

The ratios of lean muscle tissue and fat from two yield grades of meat are different.

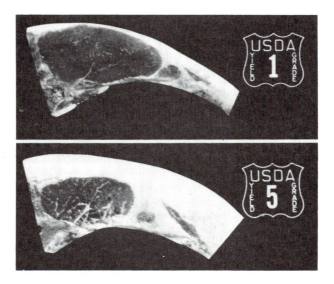

Table 22.1   Amounts of fat, bone, and edible meat in each yield grade of meat

Yield grade	Fat (%)	Bone (%)	Edible meat (%)
1	7.5	10.5	82.0
2	12.6	10.0	77.4
3	17.7	9.5	72.8
4	22.8	9.0	68.2
5	27.9	8.5	63.6

SOURCE: U.S. Department of Agriculture, *Food for Us All,* Yearbook of Agriculture. (Washington, D.C.: Government Printing Office, 1969.)

mals can vary in their yield of edible meat. Another change in the 1976 grading standards requires that all meat graded for quality must also be graded for yield.

Meat Inspection

Federal or state inspection of all meat for wholesomeness, freedom from disease, and sanitary handling is required by law. The Federal Wholesome Meat Act of 1967 required every state to provide by 1970 inspection of meat sold within its boundaries. Packers who do not comply with this mandate are subject to federal inspection. A law has also been in effect for some years that meat transported across state lines must be inspected. Thus, the consumer can expect national uniformity in meat standards and be assured of buying only wholesome, unadulterated, and uncontaminated meat.

Federal inspection of meat does not require that pork be free of *trichinae,* microscopic organisms that live in pork and can be transmitted to man, as discussed in Chapter 2. A federal regulation does state, however, that processed pork products that are likely to be eaten without cooking, such as wieners, ham, sandwich meats, and canned meats, must be processed at a temperature that causes the destruction of trichinae larvae. Several cases of trichinosis have been reported in recent years that may have been caused by the consumption of precooked hams with no further cooking. Because hams are large pieces of meat whose size slows down heat penetration to their center, it might be advisable to cook even precooked hams to an internal temperature of 140°F (60°C) to assure the destruction of this parasite.

The inspection stamp that indicates that a wholesale cut has passed federal inspection for wholesomeness (Figure 22.3) should not be confused with the stamps that designate grade (Figure 22.1). All meat must be inspected for cleanliness, but grading for quality and yield is not required.

Figure 22.3

Each wholesale cut of meat that passes U.S.D.A. standards for wholesomeness carries this inspection stamp.

Aging Meat   Several hours after an animal has been slaughtered, *rigor mortis* sets in. The muscle fibers swell with fluids and become taut and hard; the animal stiffens. After slaughter, enzymes in the tissues of animals are still active, but the circulatory system does not remove the products of enzymatic activity as it does in the living animal. Hence, these products accumulate. In fact, the accumulation of lactic acid and carbon dioxide in the muscles of the carcass are thought to contribute to the development of rigor by increasing acidity and causing the muscles to absorb water from the body fluids.

Lactic acid is formed by the oxidation of glycogen, which is a polysaccharide. In animals that have a low glycogen level at the time of slaughter, either because they have had exercise immediately before slaughter or because of a lack of food, less lactic acid is produced. The meat obtained from such animals develops a brownish-red color and a sticky, gummy texture. Beef in which this reaction occurs is called *dark-cutting* beef. Although dark-cutting beef has an altered appearance, its flavor and texture when cooked are unchanged. Most slaughterhouses today take precautionary measures to prevent glycogen depletion in animals before they are slaughtered.

The stiffening of rigor mortis makes meat less tender to eat. Meat is not usable immediately after slaughter, but must be held until the muscle becomes more flexible. This holding time is called *aging.* The longer meat is aged, the more tender it becomes. This increase in tenderness is thought to result from the breakdown of the collagen tissues by enzymes in the meat. Meat that has been aged also retains more water, and this characteristic is also thought to influence the tenderness and juiciness of the meat.

Because meat is an attractive medium for bacteria, the holding conditions during aging must be carefully controlled to prevent the growth of putrefactive bacteria. Ideal aging conditions include a temperature of 34 to 36°F (1 to 2°C), a carbon dioxide atmosphere, and 70 percent humidity for 3 to 6 weeks. Obviously, such storage for the length of time specified is expensive. Prime grade meat is usually aged in this way, which is one reason it is both high in quality and expensive. The long storage time is necessary because temperatures this low slow down enzymatic activity, causing the desired changes to take longer.

An alternate, less expensive, and more common method holds the meat at 70°F (21°C) at 85 to 90 percent humidity for 2 days. The meat is also exposed to ultraviolet light to inactivate bacteria. This procedure makes use of ordinary room temperature with a higher humidity to prevent the meat from drying. Meat is not portioned into retail cuts until after it is aged.

Beef is the most popular and widely eaten meat in the United States. Calf and veal are young beef animals. Veal, which comes from animals three months of age and younger, is prized for its delicate flavor. Veal has a grayish-pink lean portion that is velvety smooth in texture. It has very little fat but much connective tissue and is often served in jellied meat dishes. Slightly older animals, 3 to 8 months of age, are sold as calf meat. The lean portion of calves is grayish-red, the texture is fine and smooth, and the flavor is mild.

Grass-fed beef, as the name implies, are fed on grass for 12 to 24 months and are then sent to market. Grass-fed beef have less fat on their carcass and less marbling inside, although some marbling may be present in the rib and loin cuts. The fat present in the meat may be creamy in color, reflecting the high carotene content from grass. This low-fat meat is more flavorful when it is cooked only to the rare or medium-rare stage. There is no evidence to suggest that the eating quality of beef is adversely affected by a reduced fat content. The use of grass-fed beef reduces the cost of meat production and conserves grain. Furthermore, many nutritionists believe that grass-fed beef is a beneficial addition to the typical American diet, because it reduces the intake of saturated fats.

Most beef sold at retail comes from more mature animals of 15 to 30 months of age. Range-fed until they reach about 1 year of age, the animals are transferred to feed lots, where they are fed grain and concentrates for 4 to 7 months. The longer they are fed in the feed lot, the more fat is deposited on their carcasses and the more marbling of lean meat occurs. Older animals are usually not sold at retail. Instead, they are generally used for processed and canned meats.

Young sheep of less than 1 year of age are sold as lamb; older sheep are sold as mutton. Very little mutton is marketed in this country, because its flavor and texture make it less desirable than lamb. Because lamb is a young animal, much more of its carcass provides tender meat than beef does. Lamb is colored a lighter shade of red than beef. The castration of young males changes their hormonal balance, producing a milder-flavored, more acceptable meat. Yearling mutton comes from animals of 1 to 2 years of age; the gamey flavor of this older animal is sometimes preferred. Lamb, which is now available throughout the year, could formerly be purchased only in the spring.

Young pigs supply most of the pork marketed in this country. Good pork has a firm-textured, light-pink lean portion. Soft, watery, pale lean indicates poor quality. Pigs at the time of

Characteristics of Meat Animals
BEEF, CALF, AND VEAL

LAMB AND MUTTON

PORK

slaughter have a higher fat content in their total carcass than other meat animals, but the lean parts of all meat animals show a similar fat content.

Pork is processed by curing, smoking, cooking, and canning. Meat curing is described earlier in this chapter. When meats are cured, they absorb water. If the absorbed water is less than 10 percent of the weight of the meat, the meat must be labeled "water added." If the absorbed water is greater than 10 percent of the weight, the meat must be labeled "imitation." These water content standards apply only to pork, not to corned beef.

Pork products that have been exposed to smoke are labeled "smoked"; the use of artificial smoke flavoring must be indicated on the label. Smoking gives meat a unique flavor that many people find desirable. Pork may be both smoked and cured, and it may also be additionally cooked or canned. Because the ingredients in curing meats promote rancidity in the meat fat, cured meats should not be frozen for a long period of time, because their flavor deteriorates. Canned hams can be frozen, but the expansion of the liquids in the can may break the can seals. Frozen storage should be brief, and the hams should be used as soon as they have thawed to prevent bacterial growth.

Retail Cuts and Economy in Purchasing Meats
UNIFORM LABELING OF RETAIL MEAT CUTS

Identifying retail meat cuts has long been a problem for the consumer, especially those who must make purchases in different parts of the United States. The same cut of meat is known by several names in various regions of the country.

In 1974, the Uniform Retail Meat Identity Standards were instituted nationally, and their provisions should reduce guesswork in purchasing meat. The code specifies that a meat label must indicate three types of information: the type of meat (beef, veal, lamb, pork), the primal or wholesale cut (chuck, round, loin, rib), and the retail cut (T-bone, rib, spareribs). This ruling reduces names for retail cuts from more than 1,000 to about 300 standardizes names. If a retailer wishes to put a special name on a cut of meat (filet mignon, London broil), the name may be placed on the label after the required information. Unfortunately, adherence to this code is voluntary for retailers. The National Livestock and Meat Board, which developed the code, is promoting its use among meat retailers.

Some retailers can confuse the consumer with their labeling terms. A rib roast, for example, is a highly desirable tender cut of meat. Chuck is much less tender, needs special low-temperature roasting, and even then does not compare to rib roast. But it is common practice for chuck roasts, especially when they are boned and rolled, to be labeled cross-rib roasts. Often the word "chuck" does not even appear on the label. The uninformed consumer buys the "cross-rib roast" at a higher price than chuck, believing it to be true rib roast. The order of the words on the label is also important. A label that reads "cross-rib beef chuck" is incorrect; "crossrib" should be at the end, after "chuck," because it is the retailer's descriptive term and not a true indication of cut.

Primal (wholesale) and retail cuts for beef, veal, lamb, and pork are shown in Figures 22.4–22.8. Under the new labeling code, sirloin and short loin are combined into one primal cut, loin. The new labeling is shown only in the diagrams for beef (Figures 22.4, 22.5). Figure 22.5 shows the bone structure of beef in relation to the primal cuts and indicates the rib numbers. The bone structure of other animals is similar to that of beef.

GROUND MEAT

Ground beef labeling has also changed. Formerly, ground beef was called hamburger, ground chuck, and ground round, but these names carried no assurance that only meat from the round was included in ground round. The new code regulations specify that the percent of lean meat must be included on the label, which would thus read: "Not less than 70% lean," or "Not less than 80% lean." With this information, the customer can choose ground beef with a fat content that corresponds to specific cooking purposes.

Ground beef must be prepared from skeletal meat. Variety meats, such as heart, are not permitted in meat labeled "ground beef." A consumer can improve the nutrient content of ground beef by adding ground heart or liver, which can make a quite acceptable combination for some purposes.

VARIETY MEATS

Liver, heart, kidney, tongue, brains, sweetbreads, and tripe from various animals are classified as variety meats. Often these variety meats are less costly than muscle meats. Some—liver, heart, and kidney—have a higher vitamin and mineral content than muscle meats. Brains have an extremely high cholesterol content, and liver and kidney contain about three times the cholesterol found in muscle meats.

The membranes on liver, brains, and kidney should be removed before these meats are cooked. Tongue must be cooked in order to remove the skin covering it. Tongue, tripe, kidney, and beef heart require long, slow cooking for adequate tenderization. Liver and brains require very little cooking; overcooking of these meats is not uncommon. Properly cooked liver should remain slightly pink and should show pink juices when cut. Many people find liver objectionable because they have only eaten it overcooked.

SAUSAGE AND LUNCHEON MEATS

Sausages and luncheon meats are produced from ground meats—mostly from beef and pork in the past, but chicken and turkey are increasingly being used today. The use of fowl often results in products with a lower fat content. The products from beef and

Figure 22.4

The wholesale and retail cuts of beef. *(National Livestock and Meat Board)*

RETAIL CUTS OF BEEF

WHERE THEY COME FROM AND HOW TO COOK THEM

CHUCK
Braise, Cook in Liquid

Boneless Chuck Eye Roast* ②
Chuck Short Ribs ③ ④
Blade Roast or Steak ②
Arm Pot-Roast or Steak ③
Boneless Shoulder Pot-Roast or Steak ③
Cross Rib Pot-Roast ④
Beef for Stew ①
Ground Beef** ①

RIB
Roast, Broil, Panbroil, Panfry

Rib Roast ②
Rib Steak ②
Rib Steak, Boneless ②
Rib Eye (Delmonico) Roast or Steak

SHORT LOIN
Roast, Broil, Panbroil, Panfry

Top Loin Steak ① ② ③
T-Bone Steak ②
Porterhouse Steak ③
Boneless Top Loin Steak ① ② ③
Tenderloin (Filet Mignon) Steak or Roast (also from Sirloin 1a) ② ③

SIRLOIN
Broil, Panbroil, Panfry

Pin Bone Sirloin Steak ①
Flat Bone Sirloin Steak
Wedge Bone Sirloin Steak ③
Boneless Sirloin Steak ① ② ③

ROUND
Braise, Cook in Liquid

Round Steak ③
Heel of Round ④
Top Round Steak* ③
Boneless Rump Roast (Rolled)* ①
Bottom Round Roast or Steak* ③
Cubed Steak* ③
Eye of Round*
Ground Beef**

FORE SHANK
Braise, Cook in Liquid

Shank Cross Cuts ①
Beef for Stew (also from other cuts) ②

BRISKET
Braise, Cook in Liquid

Fresh Brisket ③
Corned Brisket ③

SHORT PLATE
Braise, Cook in Liquid

Short Ribs ①
Skirt Steak Rolls* ① ②
Beef for Stew (also from other cuts) ① ②
Ground Beef**

FLANK
Braise, Cook in Liquid

Ground Beef**
Flank Steak*
Beef Patties
Flank Steak Rolls* ①

TIP
Braise

Tip Steak* ④ ②
Tip Roast* ④ ②
Tip Kabobs* ④ ②

*May be Roasted, Broiled, Panbroiled or Panfried from high quality beef.
**May be Roasted, (Baked), Broiled, Panbroiled or Panfried.

This chart approved by
National Live Stock and Meat Board

© National Live Stock and Meat Board

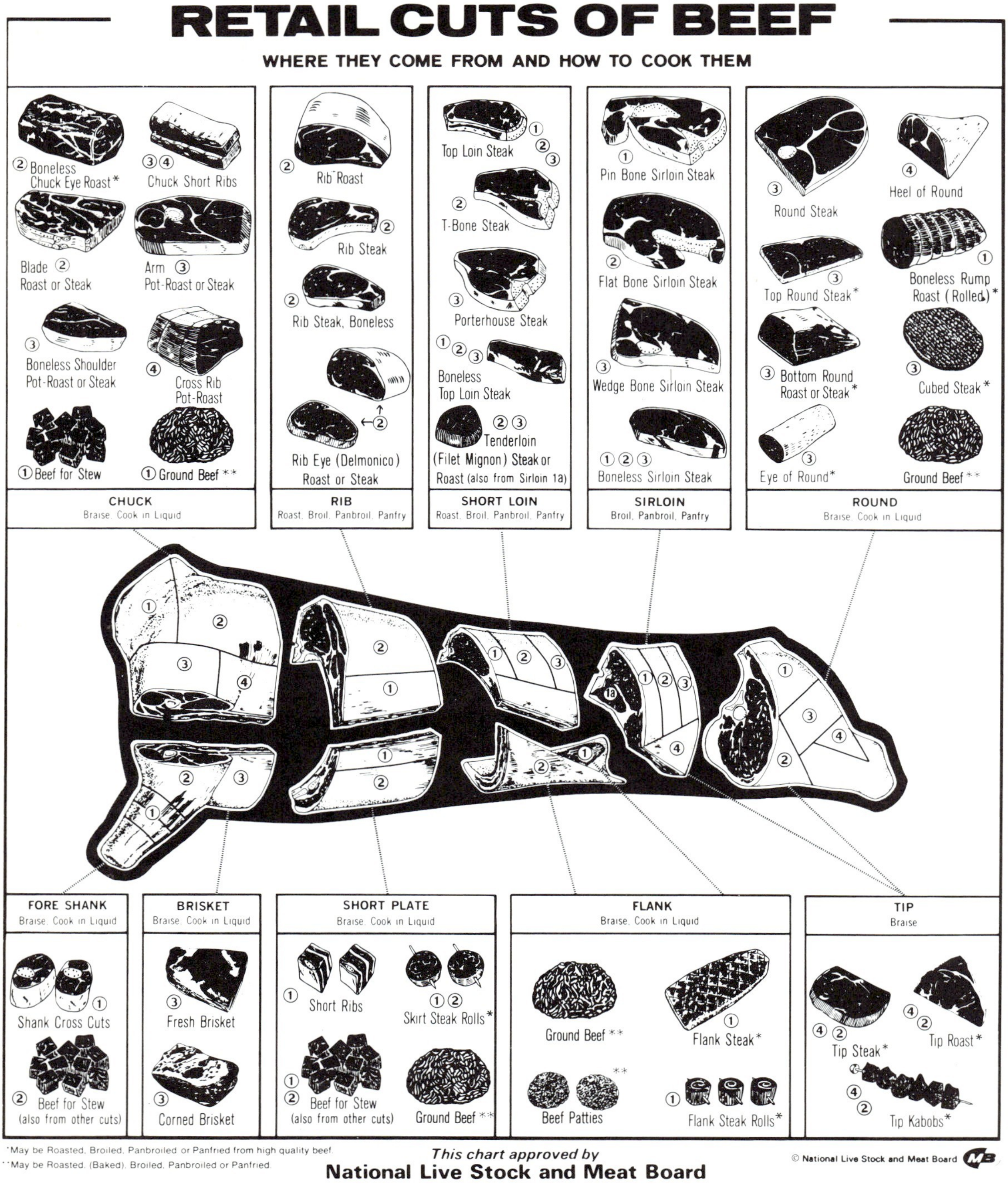

Figure 22.5

This diagram, which includes rib numbers, indicates which bones are found with various cuts of meat. *(National Livestock and Meat Board)*

PRIMAL (WHOLESALE) CUTS AND BONE STRUCTURE OF BEEF

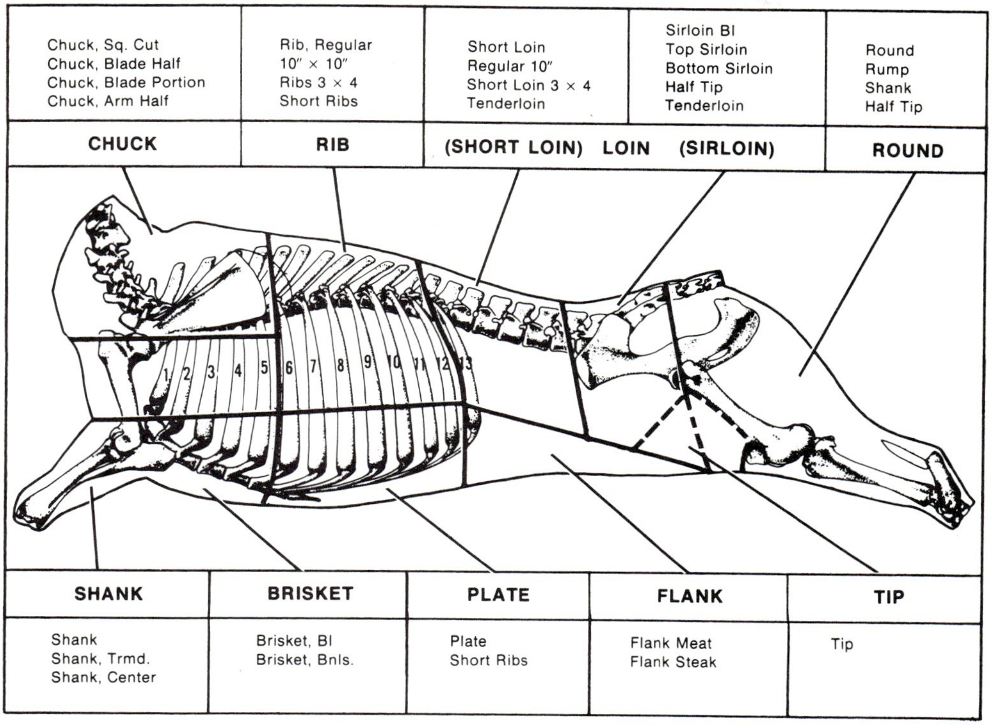

Chuck, Sq. Cut
Chuck, Blade Half
Chuck, Blade Portion
Chuck, Arm Half
Rib, Regular
10″ × 10″
Ribs 3 × 4
Short Ribs
Short Loin
Regular 10″
Short Loin 3 × 4
Tenderloin
Sirloin Bl
Top Sirloin
Bottom Sirloin
Half Tip
Tenderloin
Round
Rump
Shank
Half Tip
CHUCK
RIB
(SHORT LOIN) LOIN (SIRLOIN)
ROUND
1 2 3 4 5 6 7 8 9 10 11 12 13
SHANK
BRISKET
PLATE
FLANK
TIP
Shank
Shank, Trmd.
Shank, Center
Brisket, Bl
Brisket, Bnls.
Plate
Short Ribs
Flank Meat
Flank Steak
Tip

Figure 1

1 2 3 4 5 6 7 8 9 10 11 12

Figure 2

COUNTING RIBS IN A BEEF FOREQUARTER

The method used to count ribs in the beef forequarter (Fig. 2) is to start at the front (chuck) and count toward the rear (1 to 12). The primal chuck contains five ribs (1–5). The primal rib contains seven ribs (6–12).

Some retailers reverse the counting process in the primal rib. They number ribs 6–12 instead by starting at the loin end, and numbering 1–7 from rear to front.

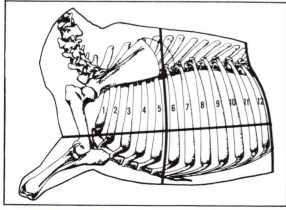

Figure 22.6

The wholesale and retail cuts of veal. *(National Livestock and Meat Board)*

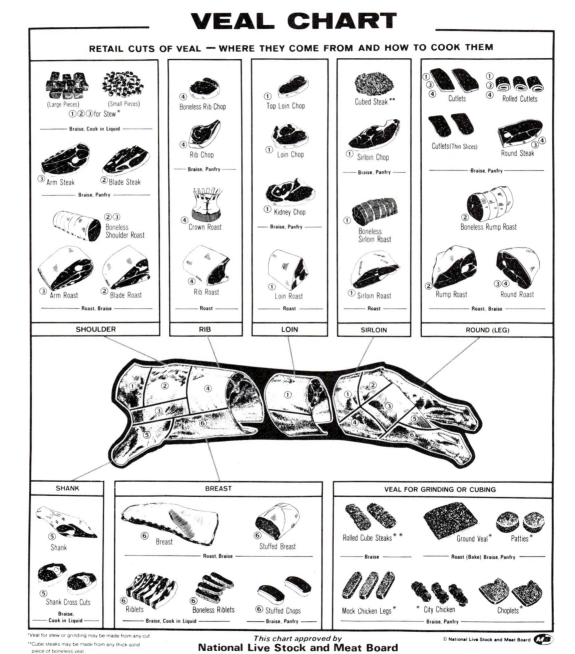

Figure 22.7

The wholesale and retail cuts of lamb. *(National Livestock and Meat Board)*

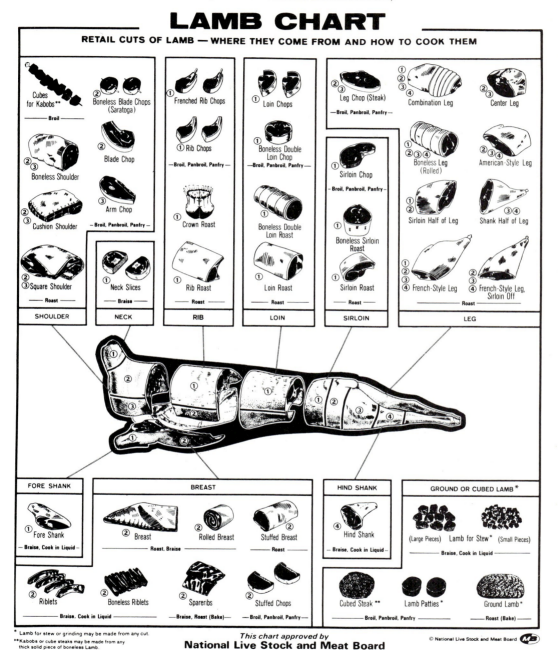

Figure 22.8
The wholesale and retail cuts of pork. *(National Livestock and Meat Board)*

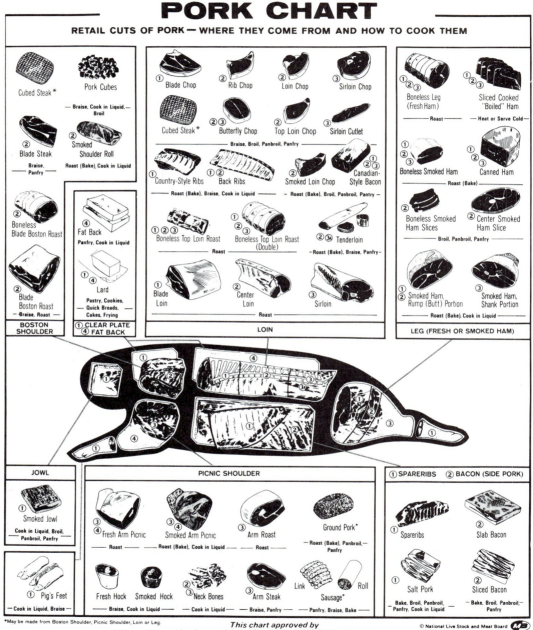

pork often contain about 30 percent fat. The ground meat is seasoned, nitrates are sometimes added, and the meat may or may not be smoked, or smoke flavoring may be used. Some meats are ready-to-eat, while others require cooking. The label must indicate all of this information. The nitrates inhibit bacterial growth, making these meats safer to use in sandwiches than fresh meats when refrigeration is not possible for several hours.

Tissue from ground bone (TFGB), formerly referred to as mechanically deboned meat (MDM), is permitted in these products. After a carcass is butchered, the bones are cut up and the meat is strained out under pressure. This process makes possible the recovery of an additional 15 pounds of meat from a beef carcass and about 3 pounds from a pork carcass. TGFB meat contains a small amount of ground bone and bone chips, but it is not considered harmful. The ground bone actually increases the calcium content of the meat. Products containing TFGB must be labeled accordingly.

ECONOMY IN PURCHASING MEAT

Even though prices vary for different cuts and grades of meat as well as in different geographical locations, some generalizations about economy in purchasing meat can be made. As a rule, higher grades of meat are more expensive, both in the price paid and in the edible lean meat obtained. Meat from the rib and loin primal cuts is usually more expensive than meats from the round and chuck primal cuts. Economizing by purchasing meats of lower grades and less expensive cuts may reduce eating quality to some extent. However, it is important to remember that the nutritional quality of lean meat is the same, regardless of cut or grade.

The proportion of lean meat to fat and bone in specific cuts of meat can affect the economy of the meat. A meat purchased at a low cost per pound, such as short ribs, may end up costing more per edible portion because of the high proportion of fat and bone than a more expensive cut with less refuse. Because meat varies so greatly, it is difficult to compare cuts of meat and to know for a fact which are the best buys at a given retail price. U.S.D.A. Agriculture Handbook No. 8, *Composition of Foods*, contains a table for nutrients in 1 pound of food as purchased that shows the percent of refuse and the amount of protein in meats and other foods. These figures were reached from a number of determinations, and so are average figures. Because an average serving of meat should contain about 20 grams of protein, it is possible to compare meats by determining how much meat one would have to buy to obtain 20 grams of protein for each serving.

Table 22.2 gives representative retail cuts of meat from beef, veal, lamb, pork, and fowl, showing the percent of refuse and the grams of fat and protein for a few cuts and grades, with and without bone. The factor shown, in either pounds or ounces, is the average amount needed to provide one serving of meat supplying

Table 22.2 *Protein, fat, and refuse content of 1 pound of various retail cuts of meat as purchased, with a factor for determining the amount and cost of amount of meat from each cut that supplies 20 grams of protein*

Type of animal	Retail cut	Grade	Bone	Refuse[a] (%)	Protein (g)	Fat (g)	Factor[b] (pound)	(ounces)
Beef	Chuck, entire	Choice	In	16	71.6	75.0	0.279	4.5
	Chuck, entire	Choice	Out	0	84.8	88.9	0.236	3.8
	Chuck, arm	Choice	In	11	78.8	62.9	0.254	4.1
	Chuck, arm	Choice	Out	0	88.0	70.3	0.227	3.6
	Chuck, arm	Good	Out	0	92.1	52.6	0.217	3.5
	Flank	Choice	Out	0	98.0	25.9	0.204	3.3
	Flank	Good	Out	0	98.9	23.1	0.202	3.2
	Shank, hind	Good	In	56	39.4	34.4	0.508	8.1
	Porterhouse	Choice	In	9	60.8	148.8	0.329	5.3
	T-bone	Choice	In	11	59.1	149.1	0.338	5.4
	Sirloin	Choice	In	7	71.1	112.3	0.281	4.5
	Plate ribs	Choice	In	11	59.7	150.6	0.335	5.4
	Plate ribs	Good	In	13	63.9	126.6	0.313	5.0
	Rib, entire	Choice	In	8	61.8	156.1	0.324	5.2
	Round, entire	Choice	In	3	88.5	53.9	0.226	3.6
	Round, entire	Choice	Out	0	91.6	55.8	0.218	3.5
	Rump	Choice	In	15	67.0	97.4	0.298	4.8
	Rump	Choice	Out	0	78.9	114.8	0.254	4.1
	Ground, lean, 10% fat		Out	0	93.9	45.4	0.213	3.4
	Ground, regular, 21% fat		Out	0	81.2	96.2	0.246	3.9
Lamb	Leg	Choice	In	16	67.7	61.7	0.295	4.7
	Leg	Choice	Out	0	80.7	73.5	0.248	4.0
	Loin	Choice	In	14	63.7	97.0	0.314	5.0
	Loin	Choice	Out	0	73.9	112.5	0.271	4.3
	Rib	Choice	In	20	54.7	110.2	0.366	5.9
	Rib	Choice	Out	0	68.5	137.9	0.292	4.7
	Shoulder	Choice	In	15	58.9	92.0	0.340	5.4
	Shoulder	Choice	Out	0	69.4	108.4	0.288	4.6
Pork	Shoulder	Medium-fat	In	15	48.9	148.1	0.409	6.5
	Fresh ham	Medium-fat	In	15	58.7	112.5	0.341	5.4
	Fresh ham	Medium-fat	Out	0	72.1	120.7	0.277	4.4
	Loin	Medium-fat	In	21	61.1	89.0	0.327	5.2
	Boston butt	Medium-fat	In	6	65.9	104.1	0.304	4.9
	Boston butt	Medium-fat	Out	0	70.3	111.1	0.284	4.5
	Spareribs	Medium-fat	In	40	39.2	89.7	0.510	8.2
Veal	Chuck	Medium-fat	In	20	70.4	36.0	0.284	4.5
	Round	Medium-fat	In	23	68.1	31.0	0.294	4.7
Chicken	Fryer, ready-to-cook		In	32	57.4	15.1	0.348	5.6
	Fryer, back		In	46	40.4	23.5	0.495	7.9
	Fryer, breast		In	21	74.5	8.6	0.268	4.3
	Fryer, drumstick		In	40	51.2	10.6	0.391	6.3
	Fryer, thigh		In	25	61.6	19.1	0.325	5.2
	Fryer, wing		In	51	41.1	16.5	0.487	7.8
	Hen, ready-to-eat		In	27	57.6	82.1	0.347	5.6
Turkey	Young, ready-to-cook (under 24 weeks)		In	27	70.9	19.9	0.282	4.5
	Mature (over 32 weeks)		In	27	60.9	97.0	0.328	5.3

[a]Refuse = bone.

[b]Factor = amount of meat in pounds that supplies 20 grams of protein. To determine amount of meat to buy, multiply the factor by the number of servings desired. Example: To serve spareribs to four people, multiply 4 times the factor for medium-fat spareribs, or 4 × 0.510 = 2.04 pounds, or approximately 2 pounds to provide enough meat for four servings supplying 20 grams of protein per serving. To serve beef chuck roast, choice grade to four people: 4 × 0.279 = 1.12, or approximately 1⅛ pounds. To compare costs, multiply the factor by the cost per pound of the meat: Spareribs: 0.510 × $.80 lb. = $0.41: Chuck roast: 0.279 × $1.50/lb = $0.42. Thus, chuck roast costs about $0.01 more per serving than spareribs at these prices and grades.

20 grams of protein. In pounds, it can be used to compare the costs of various retail cuts, such as chuck compared to round, or rib compared to sirloin. The factor can also determine the quantity of meat needed for a given number of people. Methods for making calculations are shown at the end of the table.

If larger servings are desired, the amount of meat to purchase for a given number of servings of that size can be determined by calculating another factor. Simply divide the amount of protein per pound by the grams of protein desired per serving.

Fat content is included to show the great variation in different retail cuts. The higher the fat content of the meat, the greater is the intake of calories and saturated fat.

Buying large pieces or wholesale cuts of meat that can be divided into serving portions is another economical practice (Figures 22.9–22.11).

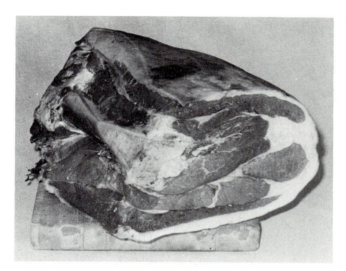

Figure 22.9

For a greater variety of meat dishes, buy the wholesale cut, such as this round, and trim off the fat, connective tissue, and bone, as shown in Figure 22.10.

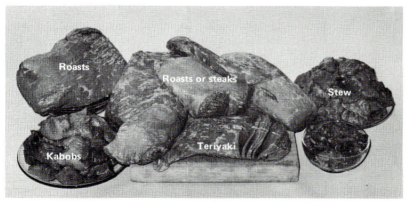

Figure 22.10

The trimmed meat from the wholesale round shown in Figure 22.9. Some pieces are large enough for roasts; smaller pieces can be either partially frozen to be sliced thin for teriyaki, or cut up in sizes suitable for kabobs, stew, soup, or Swiss and chicken-fried steaks.

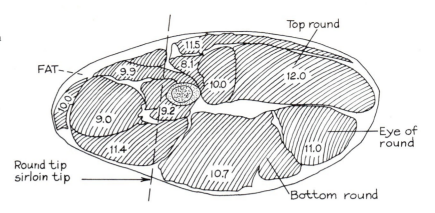

Figure 22.11

A diagram of a cross-section of a full-cut round steak, showing the average tenderness of various muscles when cooked, as determined by shear press; a low value indicates tenderness. (*After J. M. Ramsbottom and E. J. Strandine,* Food Research 13 *[1948]:322*)

Preparing Meat

The proper preparation of meat involves more than cooking. Trimming, cutting, and choosing a cooking method suitable for the cut of meat are also important parts of the process.

TRIMMING

Trimming is a frequently overlooked step in meat preparation. Proper trimming before cooking can make meat more tender by removing visible connective tissues, and it can reduce the caloric content by eliminating visible fat.

Many cuts of meat have membranes of connective tissue surrounding the outer portion that can be removed with a sharp knife. Even membranes within the muscle can often be removed without detracting from the appearance of the meat. With most of the connective tissue cut off, the meat may not need as much cooking to make it tender.

Many cuts of meat have thick layers of fat surrounding their outer surface. If meat is cooked with the fat left on, the fat melts and penetrates the lean portion, increasing both the saturated fat and caloric content of the lean, even if the fat itself is not eaten. When a roast that is one-fifth fat is cooked with the fat left on, a 2-ounce slice supplies about 14 grams of protein, 13 grams of fat, and 175 calories. A 2-ounce slice of the same roast cooked after the fat is trimmed off supplies 16 grams of protein, 3 grams of fat, and only 95 calories.

Fat left on meat smokes and spatters during cooking, making cleaning a more difficult process. It also melts into the drippings and increases the fat content of the gravy. Although many people like the flavor that fat gives meat, meat with no visible fat also has a good flavor and is superior nutritionally.

EFFECT OF HEAT ON MEAT

The most important reason to cook meat is to make it tender and edible by softening the collagen connective tissues. Excessive heating, however, can actually toughen meat because heat causes the muscle fibers in the lean tissues to shrink and lose water.

Meat becomes tough and dry with too much heat. Thus, heat can have opposite effects on muscle fibers and collagen and must be controlled to obtain a compromise that softens the collagen without toughening the muscle fibers.

To control heat in meat cooking, use a thermometer to measure the internal temperature of the meat or observe the interior color of meat when a thermometer is not practical, as with steaks and chops. Table 21.3 shows the relationship of internal temperature to the color of meat at different stages of doneness. Meat cooked rare is juicier than meat cooked well-done. Well-done meat is best served with a gravy or sauce to make up for its lack of juiciness.

Meat does not need to be cooked to an internal temperature above 170°F (76°C). Overcooking makes meat tough, rubbery, stringy, and dry. It causes excessive shrinkage of the protein with loss of water from the muscle fibers; collagen is converted to gelatin so that the fibers no longer adhere to each other, but separate into threads or strings if cooked by moist heat.

Proper cooking, besides making meat tender and contributing flavor, destroys pathogenic organisms and makes meat safer to eat, as discussed in Chapter 2. Bacteria grow on the outer surface of meat but not on the interior, unless the meat has been pierced. Cooking beef to the rare stage destroys bacteria on the surface; because no bacteria grow in the interior, the meat is safe to eat. This is not true of ground meats, however. Pork should be cooked to 140°F (60°C) or higher.

Methods of Cooking Meat

The amount of cooking a piece of meat needs to become tender and edible is the main factor in determining the method by which it should be cooked. The desired flavor is another factor. Tenderness in meat is determined by ease of chewing and cutting with the teeth or with a knife. Meats that must be thoroughly chewed or are difficult to cut with a knife are considered less tender than meats that are easily chewed and cut.

Tender cuts of meat can be cooked by dry heat methods, but cuts that are less tender require moist heat to be tenderized effectively. The rib and loin supply the tender cuts that are most suitable for dry heat cooking. The shank, brisket, and plate of all

Table 22.3   Internal temperature and color of meat at various stages of doneness

Stage of doneness	Temperature range		Color
	(°F)	(°C)	
Rare	140–150	60–65	Red or pinkish red
Medium	150–160	65–71	Pinkish brown
Well done	160–170	71–76	Tan or brown; no pink

animals are the least tender cuts and need moist heat cookery to become tender enough to eat. The rump, round, chuck, and flank of beef are medium-tender cuts, but are considered tender cuts in lamb and pork. Such medium-tender cuts from higher grades of beef may be cooked with dry heat methods so long as certain precautions are observed.

Any cut of meat that is ground is tender enough for dry heat cookery, because grinding cuts the meat fibers into very small pieces, making the meat tender.

DRY HEAT MEAT COOKERY

Methods of dry heat meat cookery include roasting, broiling, pan broiling, pan frying, and frying in deep fat. Deep-fat meat cookery is discussed in Chapter 4. In all of these methods except deep-fat cookery, heat is transferred by air and radiant energy; no water or liquid is added. Meat has a high content of water; meat wrapped in aluminum foil or cooked in a covered pan, either on a surface unit or in the oven, is cooked by its own moisture, not by dry heat. Dry heat gives meat a different flavor than moist heat.

Roasting Meat   Meat is roasted when it is cooked uncovered in an oven. Trimmed meat should be placed on a rack in the baking pan so that it does not cook in its own juices. Insert a thermometer in the meat so that the tip is in the center of the thickest part of the flesh or lean; it should not touch bone nor be in a large area of fat (Figure 22.12).

Both the internal temperature to which the meat is cooked and the oven temperature at which the meat is cooked affect the quality of roasted meat. Rib and loin roasts, which are naturally tender and flavorful, tolerate fairly high oven temperatures for roasting if they are not overcooked, because they do not have much connective tissue. Their internal temperature should not exceed 160 to 170°F (71 to 76°C).

Roasts from the rump, round, round tip, and chuck are less tender when cooked at high oven temperatures and less juicy cooked to internal temperatures above 160°F (71°C). These medium-tender cuts contain more connective tissue than tender cuts; therefore, a long, slow cooking period is necessary to soften the collagen. Desirable oven temperatures for slow cooking of medium-tender cuts of meat are 200 to 300°F (93 to 149°C). The lower the oven temperature, the longer is the time required to cook meat to a specified internal temperature.

The major disadvantage of lower oven temperatures for roasting meats is the absence of timetables as a guide. The time needed depends on the size of the roast and the oven temperature, but it can vary from 4 to 12 hours. As a rough estimate, small pieces cooked at the higher end of the temperature range take the shortest time, and larger pieces cooked at the lower end of the temperature range take the longest time. If the internal temperature of

Figure 22.12
Use a thermometer to roast meat properly. Place the tip of the thermometer in the center of the thickest part of the lean area; it should neither be placed in large areas of fat nor touch bone. *(National Livestock and Meat Board)*

the roast is still lower than desired when it is almost time to serve, increase the oven temperature. Conversely, if the internal temperature of the roast is reached too soon, reduce the oven temperature to 150°F (66°C) and hold the meat for about an hour or less, until serving time.

Searing roasts by cooking them in a very hot oven for a short time, or browning them in a small amount of fat in a pan on a surface unit, does not improve the retention of juices in the meat. Searing produces a browned meat flavor that many find desirable, but the high heat causes destruction of some of the thiamin in the meat. Roasting alone usually produces adequate browning. Lightly coating the surface of a well-trimmed roast with oil before cooking helps seal in moisture during roasting and produces a tender crust.

Meat continues to cook after it has been removed from the oven, especially if it has been cooked at a high oven temperature. It is advisable, therefore, to stop the cooking at a slightly lower internal temperature than desired and allow the meat to set for about 10 minutes before slicing it. Meat cooked at 200°F (93°C), however, does not show these effects.

Frozen roasts need not be thawed before cooking, but additional cooking time should be allowed. An additional one third to one half more of the normal time is necessary to cook a solidly frozen roast. The amount of extra time needed depends on the size of the roast and the temperature of the oven.

MICROWAVE COOKING   Microwave ovens do not produce satisfactory roasted meats. They cause meat to shrink excessively and dry out, and they toughen its fibers. Furthermore, the rapid cooking does not allow time for the collagen to soften, reducing the tenderness of the meat even more. Because the microwaves do not penetrate the roast deeply and uniformly, the outer portions are rapidly heated but conduction of heat to the interior takes much longer. The outer portions of the roast are thus overcooked by the time the center reaches the desired temperature. Meats cooked by this method do not brown unless the oven has a special browning unit, and they have the appearance and flavor characteristic of moist heat cookery.

Some microwave ovens have simmer cycles, or computer cycling, which slow cooking by spacing the cooking periods with rest periods to allow time for heat from the surface to be conducted to the interior. Even though this cycle cooking may lengthen the time sufficiently to cook tender roasts, it is not long enough to soften the collagen in medium-tender roasts. Also, meat shrinkage and the loss of juices are still apparent.

CARVING MEAT   Proper carving not only contributes to the attractiveness of a roast when it is served, but also makes the meat more tender and easier to eat. Some cuts of meat are more difficult to carve than others because of the shape and location of bones. Shoulder and chuck roasts are easier to carve if they are boned, rolled, and tied before cooking. The backbone should be cracked between the rib bones of loin and rib roasts before cooking for the same reason.

The way a roast is cooked can also affect ease of carving. Roasts cooked at high oven temperatures have thick crusts that are hard to slice; rare roasts lack firmness, which also makes slicing difficult. An overcooked braised roast may fall apart into stringy pieces when it is sliced.

A thin knife with a sharp blade or an electric knife are satisfactory tools for carving meat. A dull knife produces ragged, uneven slices and should not be used. The blade of the knife should be longer than the diameter of the roast. Because slicing meat on a hard surface dulls the cutting edge of the knife, place the meat on a cutting board for carving. The cutting board should be very clean so that the cooked meat does not become contaminated with bacteria. Hold the meat firmly with a meat fork or carver's helper and slice it across the grain. In this way, the meat fibers are cut into short lengths, making the meat easier to chew. For this reason, roasts from medium-tender cuts seem more tender if they are sliced very thin.

Broiling Meat   Smaller cuts of meat, such as steaks, chops, and meat patties, are suitable for broiling. Figure 22.13 shows kabobs broiling. Place the trimmed meat on a rack in a broiler pan. The

Figure 22.13
Because meat kabobs and
vegetables require different
broiling times, similar items
should be placed on separate
skewers, not alternated on a
single skewer. *(United Fresh
Fruit and Vegetable
Association)*

pan and rack are easier to clean if they have been sprayed with
pan spray; otherwise, aluminum foil can be placed in the bottom
of the pan under the rack. Radiant heat broils the meat.

The amount of browning and the stage of doneness are controlled by a combination of two factors, the distance of the meat
from the heat and the thickness of the meat. The closer the meat
is to the heat source, the faster browning takes place. Thin meat
or meat that is to be cooked rare but well-browned should be
placed close to the source of heat. Increase the distance of the
meat from the heat source for thick cuts, frozen meat, or meat
that is to be cooked well-done. Brown the meat on one side, then
turn it to brown on the other side. Tongs should be used to turn
the meat. If it is pierced with a fork, too much juice drains out. If
the meat is still too rare by the time if has browned on both sides,
turn off the broiler unit and leave the meat in the warm oven or
broiler with the door closed to finish cooking.

Meat may be brushed on each side with melted table fat or
with a barbecue sauce before broiling. Adding fat increases the
calories in meat, which can be broiled satisfactorily with no
added fat at all. Because most broiled meats are too thin for a
thermometer, they must be judged for doneness by their interior
color. Cut a small slit near the bone or in the thickest part of the
meat to make this test.

Because the broilers of different ranges vary considerably, the manufacturer's suggestions for using the broiler should be followed. Usually the door of an electric oven is left ajar, and the door of a gas oven closed, during broiling.

Pan Broiling Cooking meat in an uncovered pan on the surface unit of a range is pan broiling. The cuts of meat usually cooked by this method contain enough fat so that no additional fat is needed for the pan. However, the pan may be sprayed with a pan spray or oiled sparingly to keep the meat from sticking until some of its fat is rendered out. This method is suitable for cooking hamburger patties, tender pork, lamb chops, and breakfast beef steaks. Cook the meat at moderate heat until it is browned on one side, then turn it with a turner or tongs and brown it on the other side. Pan-broiled meats are customarily cooked well-done, but they should not be overcooked, or they will become too dry. Furthermore, the amount of heat under the pan should not be so high that the fat spatters or smokes. The meat may be turned more than once to control browning and adequately cook the interior. It does not need to be seared or browned initially.

If the meat has been properly trimmed of fat, very little fat will be rendered into the pan during cooking. Untrimmed meat and regular hamburger, on the other hand, lose considerable amounts of fat during cooking. This fat should be poured off as it accumulates; otherwise, the meat is fried instead of broiled, and its caloric content is greatly increased.

If meat is to be served with gravy, remove the cooked meat to a heated platter and keep it warm in an oven set at 160°F (71°C). Pour off and discard the excess fat. With the heat off, add water to the pan and scrape off and dissolve the juices (Figure 25.1) that have adhered to the pan. Add about 2 level tablespoons of flour for each cup of stock and mix until smooth and free of lumps. Heat the mixture to a boil, stirring constantly. If the gravy is not to be served with the meat, pour the dissolved juices into jars to use later as stock in gravies, soups, sauces, and other dishes. The stock can be frozen for longer storage.

Pan Frying Pan frying is the same as pan broiling, except that the meat is cooked in a small amount of fat. Meat can be fried uncoated, or it can be covered with seasoned flour, breaded, and then fried. Some less tender or medium-tender cuts of meat can be pan fried successfully if they are first pounded, scored, cubed, or tenderized, and then coated with flour or breading.

To pound meat, use a meat mallet made of aluminum, wood, or stainless steel that has small points on one side and grids or large points on the other side. Pounding causes meat fibers to separate and break, making the meat more tender. Meat may be scored instead of pounded by slashing the surface of the meat across the fibers at irregular intervals. This method is particularly appropriate for flank steaks, where the fibers run the length of the meat. Slashing meat cuts the fibers into shorter lengths, making the meat more tender. Meat can be cubed or tenderized if the butcher runs it through a scoring machine, which scores it more uniformly than hand scoring. Cubed meats are often floured or breaded before frying because cutting meat fibers causes greater losses of juices which the breading or flour coating absorb.

Meats should be seasoned before they are coated with flour or breading. Flour meats by rolling them in flour until all surfaces are covered. A meat to be breaded should first be floured, then dipped into a mixture of milk and egg, before it is covered with bread crumbs; this procedure makes the breading adhere to the meat. Allowing the breaded meat to set in the refrigerator for several hours before frying accomplishes the same purpose. Meat that is cooked uncoated may leave juice residues in the pan that can be reclaimed and used as stock.

Leave the pan uncovered to fry meat. The heat should be low enough so that the fat will not smoke or spatter. Turn the pieces of meat several times during frying to brown them evenly and cook the interior. Pan-fried meat is higher in calories than broiled, pan-broiled, or roasted meats.

MOIST HEAT MEAT COOKERY

Moist air and water are the media that cook meat in moist heat methods. Water itself, or liquids containing water, such as stock, juices, or milk, may be used to cook meats. The water may even be furnished by the meat itself. Ways of moist heat cooking include the use of a closed pan, a pressure cooker, an aluminum foil wrapping, a plastic baking bag, or steaming meat on a rack above water.

Cooking less tender meats with moist heat softens the collagen and helps make these meats with their high content of connective tissue tender enough to eat. Large pieces of meat cooked by moist heat are often called pot roasts and may be cooked by braising or pot roasting. Small pieces of meat cooked by moist heat are *stewed*.

Because meats that are usually cooked by moist heat come from the more exercised parts of the animal, they have a high content of meat extractives that provide added flavor. These cuts of meat are often preferred for their rich flavor, even though they may be less tender and require more effort to cook. If they are cooked in a large amount of the water, however, much of the flavoring-substance content is dissolved from the meat into the water. Both the flavor and the nutrient retention of the meat is greater if the meat is cooked in a minimum amount of water only long enough to make it tender.

A thermometer is not used when meat is cooked by moist heat methods; the meat is cooked until it appears tender when pierced with a fork. The time needed to achieve the desirable degree of tenderness depends on the quality, as well as the cut, of the meat. Meat should be cooked by moist heat until it is well-done, even beyond that point in some cases, to soften the collagen enough to make it edible.

Meat cooked by moist heat methods should be trimmed free of connective tissue and excess fat, just like meat cooked by dry heat, and may be browned in a small amount of fat before cooking to develop the flavor. If meat is started to cook while it is still frozen, it does not need to be browned at the beginning; the cooking liquid can be allowed to evaporate at the end of cooking to lightly brown the meat. Contrary to popular opinion, searing meat prior to braising does not seal in the juices. Recent studies have indicated that excessive searing of meats may result in production of possible carcinogens.

Adding liquid to meat that is stewed or braised on a surface unit is mandatory to prevent burning, but meat can be braised in the oven with no additional liquid if it is tightly covered. Meat also cooks in its own liquid wrapped in aluminum foil or enclosed in a plastic baking bag in the oven. A pressure cooker shortens cooking time, but the high temperature gelatinizes the collagen between the muscle fibers and shrinks the protein fibers, making the meat stringy and dry. Beef and lamb tongue, however, may be successfully cooked in a pressure cooker.

Most meats have a better texture when they are cooked at temperatures lower than the boiling point of water. Meats cooked by moist heat can be seasoned with herbs and vegetables. Onion, garlic, peppers, tomatoes, bay leaf, and other herbs add flavor and variety to braised and stewed meats. Figure 22.14 illustrates American-style chop suey, an example of meat cooked with vegetables.

COOKING GROUND MEAT

Ground meat sold retail has varying fat levels. Consumers should choose the fat content that meets their nutritional needs and cooking requirements. Meat for loaves and patties should be as lean as possible. However, if it is to be crumbled and cooked until brown, most of the fat can be rendered out during cooking, which makes the high-fat grade a more economical purchase. Fat should be poured off as soon as ground meat is cooked; the meat will reabsorb the fat if it is allowed to sit in the fat. After pouring off as much fat as possible, blot the meat with paper towels to absorb the fat still clinging to the meat and the pan.

Render the fat out of ground meat whenever possible before adding it to soups and casseroles, so that the fat content of these dishes may be reduced. However, the juices that accumulate in the bottom of the pan when ground meat is cooked are flavorful and nutritious and should be incorporated into sauce or other dishes in which the meat is used.

Figure 22.14
Oriental cookery uses stir-fry techniques to cook meat and vegetables together. This is an American version of chop suey, in which cubed pork is browned in the pan, then sliced celery, onions, and bean sprouts are added and cooked just until tender. Soy sauce, water, and cornstarch are added to form a sauce, and the mixture is served over hot rice.

In the past, medium-tender cuts of meat were cooked by moist heat methods to obtain adequate tenderness. Improved agricultural practices in meat production and a better understanding of the principles of meat cookery now make it possible to cook some of these meats by dry heat methods, especially if the meat is of good or choice grades.

MEDIUM-TENDER CUTS OF MEAT COOKED BY DRY HEAT METHODS

Holding meat between the time the animal is slaughtered and the development of rigor mortis at temperatures between 57 and 66°F (14 and 19°C) produces more tender meat than if the meat were held at temperatures below or above this range. It is thought that proper storage at this time is the most important factor in determining the tenderness of the meat.

The importance of trimming off visible connective tissues and slow roasting to increase tenderness has been mentioned. Freezer storage is also thought to improve the tenderness of these cuts of meat. The water in the cells of the meat expands when the meat is frozen, causing some of the cells to rupture, thereby breaking up the structure and fibers to some extent.

Proteolytic Enzymes *Proteolytic enzymes* hydrolyze protein tissue, an action that increases the tenderness of meat. A commercial meat tenderizer containing papain, an enzyme obtained from papaya, is described in Chapter 17. Papain is sprinkled on the surface of the meat, but acts only there unless the meat is pierced with a fork so that the enzyme can penetrate into the interior of the meat. This is obviously not an effective way to tenderize large pieces of meat, such as roasts.

The proteolytic enzyme is most active in the temperature range of 131 to 176°F (55 to 80°C), so that its action is greatest after cooking has begun. At 185° F (85°C), the enzyme is denatured and inactivated. Even when meat is cooked only to the rare stage, the heat on the surface easily exceeds 180°F (82°C). The enzyme is not capable of hydrolyzing stomach protein, as some have claimed, even if it is consumed uncooked. As protein, the enzyme is itself digested by acids and enzymes in the digestive tract. People eat raw papaya all of the time with no problems. Enzyme-treated meat can be broiled, pan-broiled, or pan-fried by methods previously described.

A problem with enzyme tenderization of meat is getting the enzyme into the tissues where it can be effective. Injection of the enzyme solution into the artery of the animal just prior to its slaughter allows the animal's circulatory system to carry the enzyme to all parts of the body and into all the tissues. In such animals, rigor mortis passes more quickly and the aging period is shortened. Meat treated in this way is labeled "ProTen." The presence of enzymes can give meat a mushy texture with too much exposure because the enzyme solution hydrolyzes the meat fibers as well as the collagen. Some packers have increased the tenderness of meat by injection of the enzyme solution into the carcass at a number of locations after the animal has been slaughtered.

Marinades A marinade is a flavorful mixture that imparts flavors to substances soaked in it; its function in flavoring fruits and vegetables has already been mentioned. The acids and alcohol used in meat marinades are thought to have a tenderizing effect on the meat by hydrolyzing the protein of connective tissues. Acids that are suitable for meat marinades include tomato juice, pineapple juice, lemon juice, and vinegar. Wine is the source of alcohol in most meat marinades; it also contributes some acid. Alcohol evaporates when the meat is cooked, as explained in Chapter 10.

Marinades are particularly effective for small pieces of meat, such as kabobs and steaks, that have been trimmed free of visible connective tissues and cut into pieces of the desired size. The meat should be refrigerated while it is marinating. If a concentrated marinade is used, the meat should be marinated for a shorter time. One procedure for marinating meat is to place the pieces of meat and the marinade in a freezer bag or container, and then freeze them until they are to be used. Leftover marinade also can be frozen and reused.

Marinated meat can be broiled, pan broiled, or pan fried. Enzyme tenderizer can be used in the marinade, if desired. With all methods of preparation, however, medium-tender cuts of meat should not be overcooked. Meat cooked rare or medium will be juicier and more tender than meat cooked well-done.

Both the enzymes that naturally occur in meat and the bacteria that contaminate its surface are active and produce changes in meat after the animal is slaughtered. The activity of enzymes and bacteria decreases at lowered temperatures. Meat can be refrigerated for short-term storage according to the type of meat, its freshness, and the temperature of the refrigerator. Fish, poultry, ground meats, and variety meats (liver, brain, heart, tongue) have a shorter storage life than muscle meats. The colder the refrigerator, the longer the meat can be kept in good condition. Even longer storage of meat is possible in the freezer.

Prepackaged meat can be stored for 2 days in the refrigerator or for up to 2 weeks in the freezer. For longer refrigerated storage, remove the prepackaging material and store the meat loosely wrapped. Some drying of the meat during refrigerator storage helps reduce the growth of bacteria on its surface. For longer storage in the freezer, cover the meat with freezer wrap. Trimming it first to remove excess fat and bones conserves freezer space. Complete trimming leaves meat ready to cook when it is thawed and saves last-minute preparation time.

When meat is thawed, some loss of juices from ruptured cells occurs. The meat should be placed in a container during thawing to catch these juices, which are flavorful and nutritious and can be added to soups and gravies. Leave the meat wrapped during thawing, a process that is best done in the refrigerator to prevent bacteria from multiplying. Occasionally thawed meat is not used. If such meat is not needed within a day or two, it should be refrozen for later use. No danger of foodborne illness exists if the meat has not been allowed to reach room temperature during thawing and if it is cooked sufficiently to destroy surface bacteria. Repeated freezing and thawing of meat causes a loss in eating quality, however, and is not recommended.

Raw meat kept in the refrigerator at too high a temperature or for too long develops bad odors and may become slightly slimy on the surface, as a result of spoilage by putrefactive bacteria. Such spoilage does not cause disease or lessen the nutritional or protein quality of the meat, but it does reduce eating quality. The meat can still be eaten if these changes are minimal and if it is washed under hot running water to remove as many of the bacteria and their products as possible, then immediately cooked until well-done, preferably by boiling or simmering. Such meat can be braised or used in soups and stews; seasoning with spices and herbs will make it more edible.

Cooked meat keeps for about a week, depending on the type of meat and storage conditions in the refrigerator. Cooked meat that is not to be used in 3 or 4 days should be frozen for safer storage. Cooked meat that has been kept as long as a week in the refrigerator, if it has no bad odors or sliminess, should be used in a soup or stew where it can be simmered for a half hour to destroy any bacteria that might have developed. Cooked meats that have been

Storage and Sanitary Quality of Meat

held in the refrigerator more than 3 or 4 days should not be used in sandwiches that will be carried to work or school and held at room temperature for more than 2 hours.

Nutritional Value of Meats

Meat is an excellent source of complete protein, a number of vitamins, and minerals, especially iron. Most meats, with the exception of liver and heart, are very poor sources of vitamin A, ascorbic acid, folic acid, and calcium. Meats are excellent sources of two trace elements that have recently been shown to be of great importance in human nutrition, zinc and chromium. Pork is recognized as an excellent source of thiamin.

The use of leaner cuts and grades of meat and the removal of all visible fat from meat before cooking can reduce both the saturated fat and the calorie intake often associated with meat consumption.

Study Questions

1. Name the two types of connective tissue of meats and indicate how each is affected by cooking.
2. How does the amount of connective tissue in meat affect its tenderness?
3. What is meant by marbling of meat?
4. What useful purposes do bones serve in retail cuts of meat?
5. What substance is responsible for the color of meat?
6. Explain why fresh raw meat may sometimes be bluish in color and other times bright red.
7. What effect does curing have on the flavor of meat and on the color of raw and cooked meat?
8. Who sets the grading standards for meat? Are all meats required to be graded?
9. What do quality grades attempt to measure in meats? What are the five quality grades for beef?
10. What are yield grades for meat, and how are they used?
11. What is the purpose of meat inspection? Is it mandatory?
12. Why is meat aged? What are two methods used to age meats?
13. What is the purpose of the Uniform Retail Meat Identity Standards? What information must be shown on meat labels, according to this code?

14. In what way is the price of meat related to its grade and cut?
15. In what way can a low-priced meat be more expensive than a meat that costs more per pound?
16. How can proper trimming make meat more tender and lower in calories than untrimmed meat?
17. Explain why heat has opposing effects on meat fibers and collagen.
18. Indicate the relationship of color and internal temperature to a meat's stage of doneness.
19. What effect does overcooking have on meat?
20. To what temperature should pork products be cooked? Why?
21. From what wholesale cuts are tender cuts of meat obtained? What is the preferred method of cooking for tender meats?
22. Name some less tender cuts of meat and indicate the cooking method that will make them tender enough to eat.
23. What wholesale cuts of meat are considered medium-tender?
24. Briefly describe the methods of dry heat cookery: roast, pan broil, broil, and pan fry.
25. How is the desired degree of doneness obtained in oven roasts?
26. How is the desired degree of doneness and the thickness of the cut of meat affected by

the meat's distance from the heat source during broiling?

27. What criteria determine the doneness of meat cooked by moist heat?

28. What factors influence the length of time a piece of meat must be cooked by moist heat to make it tender?

29. What is papain, and what is its effect on meat?

References

Bailey, A. J. "The Basis of Meat Texture." *Journal of Science, Food and Agriculture* 23 (1972): 995.

Beef Grading: What It Is, How It's Changed. Chicago: National Livestock and Meat Board, 1976. (May be ordered from the publisher, 36 South Wabash Avenue, Chicago, IL 60603.)

Bramblett, V. D.; Hostetler, R. L.; Vail, G. E.; and Draudt, H. N. "Qualities of Beef as Affected by Cooking at Very Low Temperatures for Long Periods of Time." *Food Technology* 13, no. 12 (December 1959): 707.

Carpenter, Z. L.; Abraham, H. C.; and King, G. T. "Tenderness and Cooking Loss of Beef and Pork. I. Relative Effects of Microwave Cooking, Deep-Fat Frying, and Oven Broiling." *Journal of the American Dietetic Association* 53, no. 4 (October 1968): 353.

Enloe, Cortez F., Jr. "The Red Owl's Wisdom." *Nutrition Today* 8, no. 2 (March –April 1973): 10.

Feeney, Robert E., and Hill, Robert M. "Protein Chemistry and Food Research." *Advances in Food Research* 10 (1960): 23.

Hiner, R. L.; Hankins, O. G.; Sloane, H. S.; Fellers, C. R.; and Anderson, E. E. "Fiber Diameter in Relation to Tenderness of Beef Muscle." *Food Research* 18, no. 4 (July – August 1953): 364.

Laakkonen, Eini. "Factors Affecting Tenderness During Heating of Meat." *Advances in Food Research* 20 (1973): 257.

Lessons on Meat. Chicago: National Livestock and Meat Board, 1978.

Lind, J. M.; Griswold, R. M.; and Bramblett, V. D. "Tenderizing Effect of Wine Vinegar Marinade on Beef Round." *Journal of the American Dietetic Association* 58, no. 2 (February 1971): 133.

Locker, R. H.; Davey, C. L.; Nottingham, P. M.;

Haughey, D. P.; and Low, N. H. "New Concepts in Meat Processing." *Advances in Food Research* 21 (1975): 157.

Marshall, N.; Wood, L.; and Patton, M. B. "Cooking Choice Grade, Top Round Beef Roasts. Effects of Internal Temperature on Yield and Cooking Time." *Journal of the American Dietetic Association* 36, no. 4 (April 1960): 341.

Office of Technology Assessment. *Perspectives on Federal Retail Food Grading.* Washington, D.C.: U.S. Government Printing Office, 1977.

Pearson, A. M.; Love, J. D.; and Shorland, F. B. "Warmed-over Flavor in Meat Poultry and Fish." *Advances in Food Research* 23 (1977): 2.

Penfield, M. P., and Meyer, B. H. "Changes in Tenderness and Collagen of Beef Semitendinosus Muscle Heated at two Rates." *Journal of Food Science* 40, no. 1 (January–February, 1975): 150.

Ream, E. E.; Wilcox, E. B.; Taylor, F. G.; and Bennett, J. A. "Tenderness of Beef Roasts." *Journal of the American Dietetic Association* 65, no. 2 (August 1974): 155.

Shaffer, T. A.; Harrison, D. L.; and Anderson, L. L. "Effects of End Point Temperatures on Beef Roasts Cooked in Oven Film Bags and Open Pans." *Journal of Food Science* 38, no. 7 (November–December 1973): 1025.

Szczesniak, A. S., and Torgeson, K. W. "Methods of Meat Texture Measurement Viewed from the Background of Factors Affecting Tenderness." *Advances in Food Research* 14 (1965): 33.

Tappel, A. L.; Miyada, D. S.; Sterling, C.; and Maier, V. P. "Meat Tenderization: Factors Affecting Tenderization of Beef by Papain." *Food Research* 21, no. 3 (May–June 1956): 375.

23

Poultry and Seafood

Poultry and seafood are sources of complete protein equivalent to the red meats discussed in the previous chapter. Although many of the principles discussed in that chapter apply equally to poultry and seafood, sufficient differences exist between them to merit specific consideration.

POULTRY

Turkey used to be reserved for Thanksgiving and Christmas dinners in the United States, and chicken was considered a treat for Sunday dinner. But with improved production techniques, these meats have become everyday fare and are often more economical than other meats. Because chicken and turkey have a lower fat content than other meats, they are, as a result, lower in calories as well.

Poultry is available fresh, frozen, canned, and dried, and each of these forms also comes in a variety of products. Poultry as a class includes chickens, turkey, geese, guineas, duck, and Rock Cornish game hens. As a rule, poultry is ranked according to age, because this factor more than any other affects its tenderness and the ways in which it can be prepared.

Market Forms of Poultry

Fresh Chicken Fully grown chickens are labeled mature chicken, old chicken, hen, stewing chicken, or fowl. Young chickens are labeled young chicken, broiler, fryer, roaster, capon, or Rock Cornish game hen. Most chicken today is marketed

CHICKEN

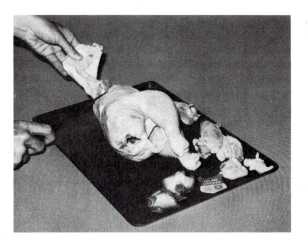

Figure 23.1
To disjoint a frying chicken, remove the giblets and neck from the body cavity and wash and dry all the parts. If desired, cut off the tail and wing tips and add them to the stock pot. Remove the wing by bending it up, away from the body, and cutting from the underside between the bones at the shoulder joint.

Figure 23.2

Remove chicken legs and thighs by bending the leg back away from the body; then slit the skin and cut through the flesh to expose the joint. Cut between the bones of the thigh and hip, then through the flesh close to the back.

Figure 23.3

Separate chicken thigh and leg bones by cutting through the flesh and skin on the inside of the joint to the bone; then bend the two bones away from each other to expose the joint, cutting through it and the remaining flesh and skin. Bone the thigh by cutting the meat away from the bone, starting from the inside of the thigh.

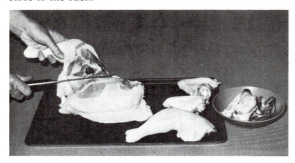

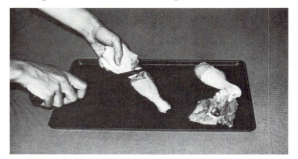

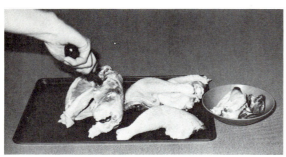

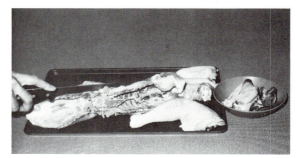

Figure 23.4

After separating the wings and legs from the body of the chicken, separate the back from the breast by cutting through the rib joints on each side, cutting from the hole formed just under the place where the wings were removed.

Figure 23.5

Bend apart the breast and back of the chicken and cut the bones apart at the shoulder by slicing through the joint with the knife held about parallel to the bones of the joint. Unlike the bones of all other joints, the bones of the shoulder joint cannot be separated by crosswise cutting.

"ready to eat," that is, the entrails have been removed (drawn or eviscerated). Whole-body or cup-up chickens as well as halves, quarters, or specific pieces can also be purchased.

As a rule, it is most economical to buy a whole chicken and cut it as desired. Figures 23.1 to 23.7 show how to cut up and bone chicken. If only the breasts and thighs are needed for a specific purpose, simmer the rest of the chicken until it is tender and remove the meat from the bones for curry, soup, casseroles, salads, and sandwiches. Both cooked meat and stock freeze well, but should be frozen in separate containers.

Figure 23.6

Cut the back and breast of the chicken into two pieces. Hold the back with the neck end in one hand, the tail end in the other, skin side up. Bend it down approximately in the middle to crack the backbone and cut the skin and flesh at that point to form two pieces of back. Cut the breast just above the keel bone, as shown; this method keeps the wishbone intact. The breast can also be split by cutting lengthwise through the keel bone.

Figure 23.7

Bone the breast by cutting through the flesh along the keel bone and the wishbone to remove a piece such as that shown in the center of the tray.

Processed Chicken   Frozen chicken can be purchased in many of the same forms as fresh chicken, plus additional forms—frozen precooked chicken rolls, barbecued chicken, fried chicken parts, stuffed chicken, and Rock Cornish game hens. Canned boned chicken and canned whole chicken are also available. Chicken is found in many canned soups and stews, frozen dinners, and entrées. Dried chicken is found in dried soup mixes and in dehydrated food for backpackers and campers. Chicken hot dogs and luncheon meats are also available.

TURKEY

Fully grown turkeys are labeled mature turkey, yearling turkey, or old turkey. Young turkeys are labeled young turkey, fryer-roaster, young hen, or young tom.

Fresh and Frozen Turkey   Most turkey is marketed frozen as whole, ready-to-eat birds. In some areas of the United States, halves, quarters, parts, steaks, and ground turkey meat are also available. Boneless frozen turkey rolls, as well as roasts of blended light and dark or all breast meat, are sold in many markets.

Other Turkey Products   Canned turkey products include boned turkey meat, turkey soups, and combination dishes. Frozen turkey pies, main-dish servings, and turkey dinners are also marketed. Turkey hot dogs and luncheon meats are also available.

DUCKS AND GEESE

About 90 percent of marketed ducks are sold frozen, whole, and ready to eat. Young ducks, the most popular, are labeled duckling, young duckling, broiler duckling, fryer duckling, or roaster duckling. Fully grown ducks, geese, and guineas are labeled mature or old.

Grading and Inspection of Poultry

All poultry must pass inspection for wholesomeness. The plants where poultry is processed must meet federal standards for sanitation. The inspection stamp is shown on the wing tag reproduced in Figure 23.8. In addition, the Department of Agriculture has established minimum requirements for many processed poultry products.

Grading of poultry, which is voluntary and paid for by the processor, defines the eating quality of poultry products; the grade is also shown on the wing tag, Figure 23.8. The grades are U.S. Grades A, B, and C. Grade A birds have good overall shape and appearance; they are meaty with a well-developed layer of fat in the skin and practically free of such defects as cuts and bruises. Grade B and Grade C birds differ only in degree, but they may have bone deformities, skin tears, bruises, and pinfeathers. These birds may be less fleshy or have a poor appearance. Birds below Grade A standards are usually sold in supermarkets without a grade mark. Grades are also given to processed and frozen poultry products.

Figure 23.8
The wing tag for graded chicken includes a round U.S.D.A. inspection mark for wholesomeness and a shield that shows the grade.

Economy in Purchasing Poultry

The prices of various poultry items vary at different seasons of the year and with supply and demand. Chicken and turkey are included in Table 22.2, which shows the factors to use for comparing prices between different forms of meats. Larger turkeys usually cost less per pound and have more meat in relation to bone. But the way the meat will be used must also be considered. It is no economy to buy a larger size if the meat is wasted or goes uneaten. The factors in Table 22.2 can also be used to calculate the quantity of meat to buy for a specific number of servings.

Sanitary Quality and Storage of Poultry

All poultry should be washed well inside and out, before it is cooked or frozen, to remove as many of the bacteria as possible. All knives, cutting boards, and counters should be cleaned and sanitized after the preparation of raw poultry as well as other raw meats, and hands should be washed with soap. Fresh poultry keeps refrigerated for several days and can be frozen for longer storage. Frozen poultry should be thawed in the refrigerator so that it does not warm to a temperature that permits bacterial growth before it is cooked. Table 23.1 provides a timetable for thawing poultry of various sizes. Faster thawing can be accomplished by submerging the poultry, tightly enclosed in a watertight plastic bag, in cold water that is changed at frequent intervals.

	Poultry weight	Time
Refrigerator:		
Chicken	Less than 4 pounds	12–16 hours
	4 pounds or over	1–1½ days
Ducks	3–7 pounds	1–1½ days
Geese	6–12 pounds	1–2 days
Turkeys	4–12 pounds	1–2 days
	12–20 pounds	2–3 days
	20–24 pounds	3–4 days
	Pieces: half, quarter	1–2 days
	Cut-up pieces	3–9 hours
	Boneless roasts	12–18 hours
Cold water:		
Chicken	3–4 pounds	1–2 hours
Turkeys	4–12 pounds	4–6 hours
	12–20 pounds	6–8 hours
	20–24 pounds	8–12 hours

SOURCE: U.S. Department of Agriculture, *Poultry in Family Meals*, Home and Garden Bulletin No. 110 (Washington, D.C.: Government Printing Office, 1971).

Stuffed poultry should neither be frozen nor stored in the refrigerator. Commercially frozen stuffed poultry has been produced under conditions that make freezer storage safe and should not be thawed before cooking. In all other cases, the bird and the stuffing should be frozen separately to prevent the growth of bacteria. After a stuffed bird has been cooked, all stuffing should be removed. Unused stuffing and poultry should be chilled or frozen separately. Freezing is an excellent way to hold leftover cooked poultry, which has many uses in other dishes.

Preparing Poultry

Most of the principles of meat cookery mentioned in Chapter 22 apply equally to poultry. Young poultry has a low content of connective tissue and can be cooked satisfactorily by dry heat methods. Mature birds require long, slow, moist heat cookery to make them tender. As with red meats, overcooking can cause dry, toughened, and stringy poultry meat. Many people tend to overcook poultry, which should be juicy for best eating quality. Poultry is safe to eat if the juices are slightly pink when they run out of the meat; a little redness around the joints is also not objectionable. The flesh should have lost its transparent appearance and be opaque. Oozing of blood from the joints of young chickens when cooked results from the expansion of the blood in the bone marrow. There is more blood in the marrow of young chickens than in older ones. This does not affect the flavor or quality of the meat and is indicative of young chickens.

Most types of poultry should be trimmed before they are cooked. Poultry skin is usually very fatty and can be removed for many methods of cookery to reduce the calories. Large areas of fat that appear in the cavities and at the end of joints when poultry is disjointed can also be removed to reduce the fat and caloric content. The wing tips and tails may be discarded or added with the skin to the stock pot.

ROASTING Poultry can be roasted with or without stuffing. Either way, the washed chicken is patted dry with paper towels and seasoned on the inside with poultry or other seasoning blends. The bird can be stuffed with a wide variety of stuffings, as a rule, about ½ cup of stuffing per pound of poultry. The stuffing should be placed loosely into the neck and body cavity to allow room for expansion during heating. The stuffing should not be placed in the bird until it is ready to cook. Fold the neck skin over the stuffing and fasten it with a skewer to the back. The legs can be slipped under a strip of skin at the bottom of the breast or tied together. Fold the wings back behind the back.

Like other roasts, the bird should be placed on a rack in an open pan, breast up. Roast at an oven temperature of 325 to 350°F (163 to 177°C); roasting young poultry at low temperatures has no particular benefits and, in any event, heat penetration at these temperatures is too slow to stop the growth of bacteria. Use a thermometer to determine when the bird is cooked. The thermometer should be placed in the thick part of the flesh on the inside of the thigh, but its tip should not touch the bone.

Poultry is roasted until the temperature of the bird reaches 160 to 170°F (71 to 77°C). The meat is juicier if it is cooked only to 160°F; at the higher temperature it tends to become dry. The temperature of the dressing in the center should register 165°F (74°C) to ensure adequate destruction of bacteria. If the dressing is hot when the bird is stuffed, it is more likely to reach this temperature. If its temperature is still too low when the bird has cooked, transfer the dressing to an oven dish and continue to cook it while the bird is being carved.

If the poultry appears to be browning too much before it has reached the desired temperature, place a piece of aluminum foil over the breast. When the poultry is half done, loosen the legs to allow the inside of the thigh meat to cook more evenly. Unstuffed poultry cooks more rapidly than stuffed poultry. Figure 23.9 shows a roast turkey.

BROILING Young broiler-fryer turkeys, ducklings, Rock Cornish game hens, and chickens may all be broiled, either in halves, quarters, or disjointed pieces. Season the meat as desired and place it in a single layer on the rack of the broiler pan. If the poultry is started to cook skin side down, the skin will turn crispier. Meats are cus-

Figure 23.9
Roasting is a popular way to cook turkey, especially during the holiday season. This roasted turkey, to be carved at the table, is embellished with scalloped orange cups filled with fresh fruits. *(Sunkist Growers, Inc.)*

tomarily brushed with melted table fat before broiling, but this step can be skipped for low-fat or low-calorie cooking. Chicken is especially satisfactory broiled without skin or added fat. However, it should be cooked only until it is just done, not overcooked. As with other meats, poultry is broiled on one side until it is brown, and then turned to brown on the second side. If thick pieces do not appear done when they are brown, leave the meat in the warm broiler or oven with the door closed to finish cooking. Turkey and duck pieces require a longer broiling time than chicken. Poultry can also be marinated in teriyaki sauce or other marinades before broiling.

Young chickens, capons, Rock Cornish game hens, and small turkeys and ducklings can be fried, preferably when they are cut into pieces of serving size. The meat can be fried in deep fat or shallow fat. To obtain a crisp crust on the bird, coat the meat with flour, breading, or batter. Fry the pieces in a small amount of fat at moderate heat and brown them on all sides. If desired, the skin may be removed before the pieces are coated. To oven fry chicken, cook the coated pieces of meat in a small amount of fat in a pan in the oven at 350 to 400°F (177 to 204°C); turn the pieces over halfway through to crisp and brown both sides.

FRYING

Mature, less tender poultry must be cooked by moist heat, and young birds can also be cooked by moist heat for some purposes. Either a whole bird, or one cut in pieces, can be braised in its own juices in a covered pan in a 325°F (163°C) oven. Poultry can be stewed in water if it is simmered on a surface unit. Remove meat

BRAISING AND STEWING

Figure 23.10

Chicken and turkey are both delicious served in a curry. Chicken curry is served over rice and topped with a choice of sliced green onions, pineapple tidbits, grated hard-cooked egg, chopped peanuts, and toasted coconut chips. Chutney is served with curry in the same way that cranberry sauce is served with roast turkey, as shown in the center left foreground.

from the bones of the braised or stewed mature birds and add it to soups, stews, gumbos, and similar dishes. Chicken fryers often cost less per pound than hens, cook more rapidly, and are less fat. However, young chicken is not as flavorful as a mature bird, although the meat of fryers is more tender and less stringy.

In many recipes that call for poultry, one kind of bird may be sutstituted for another, with some differences in flavor. Poultry in a curry is shown in Figure 23.10.

SEAFOOD

More than 240 different species of seafood are consumed in the United States. Seafoods may be divided into two general groups, fish and shellfish. Fish are aquatic animals with fins, found in fresh or salt water. Shellfish include crustaceans and mollusks.

Market Forms of Seafood
FISH

Whole fish are sold just as they are caught from the water. When they are scaled and eviscerated, with the head, tail, and fins removed, they are called "dressed" fish. Fresh whole fish should have a fresh, mild odor; bright, clear eyes; red gills free of slime; iridescent skin; firm, elastic flesh; and meat that does not separate from the bones. Dressed fish also should have a fresh, mild odor; the flesh should appear fresh with no traces of browning or drying. Frozen fish should be solidly frozen, and it should have little or no odor.

Market Forms of Fish   Dressed fish can be subdivided in several ways, as shown in Figure 23.11. The dressed fish may be purchased whole for baking or sliced crosswise into chunks or steaks for other cooking procedures. These pieces all come with a section of backbone. Fillets are obtained by slicing the sides of the fish off the backbone; these pieces are practically boneless and may or may not be skinned. Butterfly fillets are the two sides of the fish held together by the skin of the belly.

Crustaceans include crabs, lobster, and shrimp. Mollusks include abalone, clams, oysters, and scallops.

SHELLFISH

Crustaceans   Fresh crabs and lobsters should be alive and active when they are purchased; cooked crab and lobster should be bright red with a mild, fresh odor. Meat from cooked crab and lobster is available chilled, frozen, or canned.

Shrimp may range from greenish-gray to brownish-red in color when they are raw, but cooked they are always reddish white. Shrimp are usually sold with the heads removed. Two pounds of shrimp in the shell yields 1 pound of peeled, cleaned shrimp. Thus, it is more economical to buy peeled shrimp if the price per pound is double or less than that of shrimp in the shell, and labor is saved as well.

Mollusks   Oysters and clams in the shell should be alive when purchased, which is indicated by a tight closing of the shell when

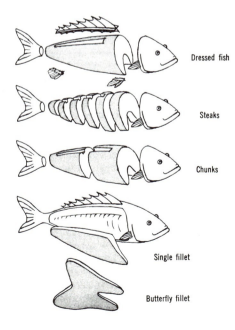

Dressed fish

Steaks

Chunks

Single fillet

Butterfly fillet

Figure 23.11

Market forms of fish. (*From Rose G. Kerr, "Savvy with Seafood," in U.S. Department of Agriculture,* Food for Us All, *Yearbook of Agriculture [Washington, D.C.: Government Printing Office, 1969]*)

it is tapped. These mollusks are sold in the shell by the dozen, but clams may also be sold in the shell by the pound. If meat is removed from the shell, it is called "shucked" clam or oyster. Clam meat is pale to deep orange with a fresh mild odor. Shucked oysters should be plump and possess a natural creamy color, clear liquid, and a fresh, mild odor.

Shucked scallops are sold by the pound. The meat may be creamy white, light tan, orange, or pinkish in color, and it should have a sweet odor. Abalone is sold as frozen, shucked meat shipped from Japan and Mexico.

PROCESSED SEAFOODS
Seafoods can be purchased frozen, canned, and cured. Frozen seafood products include raw or cooked meat as well as breaded items. The Department of the Interior (U.S.D.I.) has established standards for the minimum amount of meat in breaded seafoods according to type.

Canned tuna is packed from six species of tuna. Albacore has lighter meat than the others and is the only species that may be labeled "white meat" tuna. Tuna may be packed in oil or water in—in descending order of price—solid, chunk, flaked, and grated forms.

Canned salmon is packed from five species that differ in color, texture, and flavor. They are therefore sold by name, in descending order of price: red or sockeye; chinook or king; medium red, silver, or coho; pink; and chum or keta.

Some common cured fish on the market include pickled and spiced herring; salt cod and salmon; and smoked chubs, salmon, and whitefish.

Inspection and Grading of Seafoods
The Bureau of Commercial Fisheries of the U.S.D.I. is responsible for inspecting and grading seafood products. Inspection and grading are both voluntary procedures that are paid for by the processor. The inspection service requires adequate sanitation of plant facilities and operations and wholesome quality in the seafood. Only inspected seafoods can be graded (Figure 23.12). The quality grades for seafoods are U.S. Grades A, B, C, and substandard. Grade A products are most widely marketed in fresh and frozen form; the lower grades are often used in processed products in which reduced quality is not so noticeable.

Storing Seafoods
Seafoods are among the most perishable of all foods. Fresh raw or cooked seafoods, depending on their freshness and variety, can only be held in the refrigerator for a few days. Most seafoods freeze well when packaged in moisture-proof and vapor-proof packaging, if they are frozen rapidly and stored at 0°F (− 18°C) or below. Freezer space is conserved if waste is removed before freezing. Cooked seafood can be held for up to 3 months, and raw seafoods for up to 6 months, in frozen storage, after which the flavor deteriorates.

INSPECTION SHIELD

U.S. GRADE A SHIELD

Figure 23.12

Inspection and grade A shields for seafoods.

Canned seafoods can be stored for up to a year in a cool location, after which flavor deteriorates. Pickled, salted, smoked, and spiced seafoods should be refrigerated, and they keep for several weeks at such temperatures.

Thaw frozen seafoods in the refrigerator. Do not thaw frozen breaded seafoods before cooking them.

Preparing Seafoods

Seafoods are cooked to improve their sanitary quality and to develop flavor, texture, and tenderness. Because they have little or no connective tissue, very little cooking is necessary to produce tenderness. If seafoods are cooked at too high a temperature or for too long, they dry out and lose their tenderness and flavor. Raw seafoods have a watery, translucent coloring and turn opaque when they are cooked. Fish that is done flakes and separates from the bones when it is tested with a fork.

Seafoods can be cooked by any of the methods used for other meats. Deep-fat fried seafoods are widely eaten, as are pan-fried, broiled, and baked fish. Fish with a high fat content should be broiled or baked, although some are also frequently pan fried with very little added fat (Figures 23.13, 23.14). Fish with a high fat content include barracuda, catfish, herring, lake trout, mackerel, salmon, sturgeon, tuna, whitefish, and butterfish.

Figure 23.13

Salmon steaks can be broiled and seasoned with chopped parsley and fresh lemon. *(Sunkist Growers, Inc.)*

Figure 23.14

Thick halibut steaks can be baked with herbs and served with fresh lemon. *(Sunkist Growers, Inc.)*

Fish are fragile and are usually broiled only on one side without turning, unless the pieces are very thick. This prevents the fish from falling apart. Fish can be seasoned before broiling; brushing with fat is optional. It is probably advisable to thaw fish before baking or broiling. Cooked from the frozen state, the outer portions, which thaw first, overcook by the time the inner portions are thawed and cooked. The longer cooking time required for frozen fish also causes excessive drying and makes the fish less flavorful.

Crustaceans are usually cooked in simmering water for 2 or 3 minutes in the shell, and then cooled quickly in ice water. After it is removed from the shell, crustacean meat can be served in a variety of ways.

Fish do not normally require moist heat cookery to make them tender. Poached fish, however, are popular for their flavor and texture. To poach fish, place them in a single layer in a wide pan and barely cover them with a flavorful liquid, such as stock, milk, wine containing herbs and seasonings, or even simply water. Cover the pan and simmer the contents very gently on a surface unit (usually less than 5 minutes), or bake them in the oven, until the fish flakes easily when tested with a fork. Poached fish with a well-seasoned sauce makes a suitable entrée for a meal, or the meat can be served in salads, cocktails, casseroles, and soups. If it is not served with the fish, the liquid makes excellent stock for soups and sauces. Both liquid and fish can be frozen for later use.

Nutritional Quality of Poultry and Seafoods

Poultry and seafoods have become increasingly well known as meats that have low contents of cholesterol, saturated fat, and total fat. These meats have been emphasized in the U.S. Dietary Goals recommendations for these reasons. As a group, these meats are less satisfactory sources of iron than are beef and lamb, but the protein quality of all the meats is comparable.

Study Questions

1. Briefly describe some desirable characteristics of poultry and seafood that is "ready to eat" or "dressed."
2. Why should frozen poultry and seafoods be thawed in the refrigerator rather than at room temperature?
3. Why should poultry not be frozen or held in the refrigerator after being filled with stuffing?
4. What are ways to judge when poultry and seafoods are cooked? What are the effects of overcooking these meats?
5. Distinguish between the various market forms of finned fish and indicate which forms are less likely to contain bones.
6. What are the two types of shellfish? Give examples of each.
7. Why should fish not be broiled on both sides like other meats?
8. Why should fish be thawed before it is broiled or baked?

Crosby, Violet B., and Gulich, Ashley R. "Poultry: A Tasty Anytime Delight That's Popular Dozens of Ways." In U.S. Department of Agriculture, *Food for Us All*, Yearbook of Agriculture. Washington, D.C.: Government Printing Office, 1969.

Kerr, Rose G. "Savvy with Seafood in the Store and Kitchen for the Tang of the Deep." In U.S. Department of Agriculture, *Food for Us All*, Yearbook of Agriculture. Washington, D.C.: Government Printing Office, 1969.

National Marine Fisheries Service. *How to Eye and Buy Seafoods*. Washington, D.C.: Government Printing Office, 1973.

U.S. Department of Agriculture. *How to Buy Poultry*, Home and Garden Bulletin No. 157. Washington, D.C.: Government Printing Office, 1968.

——. *Poultry in Family Meals*, Home and Garden Bulletin No. 110, 1971.

24

Plant Proteins

During the last decade, there has been an increased emphasis on the use of plant proteins. The higher cost and reduced supply of animal protein, the economics of meat production, and the recognition that meat consumption is often accompanied with an increased intake of saturated fat are possible factors that have influenced this change in eating patterns. Many people in the United States probably consume more animal protein than they need for optimum nutrition.

Legumes (a name for dried beans and peas), nuts, and cereal grains are the major sources of plant proteins. The important nutrients in nuts, seeds, and legumes are listed in Table 24.1; the nutrients in cereals are listed in Table 9.2. The calories per gram of protein are given in Table 24.1; some of these protein sources are high in calories.

The characteristics and preparation of some of these plant proteins are described in this chapter. The use of soybean proteins in meat analogs, textured protein, and tofu is also examined. Cereals, discussed in Chapter 9, are not considered in this chapter.

Nuts and seeds contain about 50 percent fat, except for chestnuts, which contain only 4 percent. Most nuts and seeds are good sources of incomplete protein, essential fatty acids, some minerals, and B vitamins. Because of their high fat content, nuts and seeds become rancid readily. The shell does not protect a nut from becoming rancid. Commercial packages of shelled nuts may contain nitrogen or carbon dioxide gas instead of air or may be vacuum-packed to reduce oxidation. A longer shelf life is possible for both shelled and unshelled nuts in frozen storage.

Additionally, nuts and seeds are subject to insect infestation. Freezer storage also eliminates this problem. Insect larvae in nuts and seeds can be destroyed by freezer storage of at least a week.

Unshelled nuts can be difficult to shell. Some hard-shelled nuts become easier to crack after they are soaked overnight, or at least for several hours. This method also helps get the nutmeats out in one piece. Some nuts with thick skins covering their meats are preferred skinless. To remove skins from almonds, peanuts, and chestnuts, *blanch*, or scald, them in boiling water for several minutes. When the nuts have cooled, the skins should slip off easily; stubborn ones can be reheated. Filberts should not be blanched but baked in the oven at 300°F (149°C) for 10 to 15 minutes.

The flavor of many nuts is improved through roasting, which, however, should not be excessive, because dry heat causes destruction of thiamin and protein quality in nuts and seeds. Peanuts and chestnuts are often roasted in their shells, but chestnut shells should be slashed to allow steam to escape, thus preventing them from exploding. Shelled nuts can be dry-roasted

Importance of Plant Proteins

Nuts and Seeds

PREPARING NUTS

Table 24.1 *Nutrient composition of nuts, seeds, and legumes for 100-gram amounts, edible portion*

Foods	Water (g)	Calories (kcals)	Protein (g)	Fat (g)	Carbohydrate Total (g)	Carbohydrate Fiber (g)	Niacin (mg)	Riboflavin (mg)	Thiamin (mg)	Calcium (mg)	Iron (mg)	Phosphorous (mg)	Potassium (mg)	Kcals per gram protein
Nuts (fresh):														
Almonds	4.7	598	18.6	54.2	19.5	2.6	3.5	0.92	0.24	234	4.7	504	773	32
Brazil nuts	4.6	654	14.3	66.9	10.9	3.1	1.6	0.12	0.96	186	3.4	693	715	46
Cashews	5.2	561	17.2	45.7	29.3	1.4	1.8	0.25	0.43	38	3.8	373	464	33
Chestnuts	52.5	194	2.9	1.5	42.1	1.1	0.6	0.22	0.22	27	1.7	88	454	67
Coconuts	50.9	346	3.5	35.3	9.4	4.0	0.5	0.02	0.05	13	1.7	95	256	99
Filberts	5.8	634	12.6	62.4	16.7	3.0	0.9	—	0.46	209	3.4	237	704	50
Hickory nuts	3.3	673	13.2	68.7	12.8	1.9	—	—	—	66	1.4	254	—	51
Macadamia nuts	3.0	691	7.8	71.6	15.9	2.5	1.3	0.11	0.34	48	2.0	161	264	89
Peanuts	5.4	568	26.3	48.4	17.6	1.9	15.8	0.13	0.99	59	2.0	409	674	22
Pecans	3.4	687	9.2	71.2	14.6	2.3	0.9	0.13	0.86	73	2.4	289	603	75
Pine nuts (pinons)	3.1	635	13.0	60.5	20.5	1.1	4.5	0.23	1.28	12	5.2	604	—	49
Pistachio nuts	5.3	594	19.3	53.7	19.0	1.9	1.4	0.67	—	131	7.3	500	972	31
Walnuts, English	3.5	651	14.8	64.0	15.8	2.1	0.9	0.13	0.33	99	3.1	380	450	44
Seeds (raw):														
Pumpkin seeds	4.4	553	29.0	46.7	15.0	1.9	2.4	0.19	0.24	51	11.2	1144	—	19
Safflower seeds	5.0	615	19.1	59.5	12.4	—	—	—	—	—	—	—	—	32
Sesame seeds, hulled	5.5	582	18.2	53.4	17.6	2.4	5.4	0.13	0.18	110	2.4	592	—	32
Sunflower seeds	4.8	560	24.0	47.3	19.9	3.8	5.4	0.23	1.96	120	7.1	837	920	23
Legumes, cooked:														
Beans, white	69.0	118	7.8	0.6	21.2	1.5	0.7	0.07	0.14	50	2.7	148	416	15
Beans, red	69.0	118	7.8	0.5	21.4	1.5	0.7	0.06	0.11	38	2.4	140	340	15
Beans, lima	64.1	138	8.2	0.6	25.6	1.7	0.7	0.24	0.13	29	3.1	154	612	17
Cowpeas [blackeyed]	80.0	76	5.1	0.3	13.8	1.0	0.4	0.04	0.16	17	1.3	95	229	15
Lentils	72.0	106	7.8	Tr	19.3	1.2	0.6	0.06	0.07	25	2.1	119	249	14
Splitpeas	70.0	115	8.0	0.3	20.8	0.4	0.9	0.09	0.15	11	1.7	89	296	14
Soybeans, mature	71.0	130	11.0	5.7	10.8	1.6	0.6	0.09	0.21	73	2.7	179	540	12
Other:														
Soybean protein	8.2	322	74.9	0.1	15.1	0.4	—	—	—	120	—	674	180	4
Tofu (soybean curd)	85.4	72	7.8	4.2	2.4	0.1	0.1	0.03	0.06	128	1.9	126	42	9

SOURCE: U.S. Department of Agriculture, *Composition of Foods.* Agriculture Handbook No. 8. (Washington, D.C.: U.S. Government Printing Office, 1975).

without added fat, or a small amount of oil can be used. Nuts are usually roasted in a moderate oven or toasted in a pan on a surface unit.

Nuts are often eaten as snacks fresh from the shell, roasted, or candied. They also accent the flavor and texture of a wide variety of dishes. Most nuts except chestnuts can be used interchangeably, although they produce different flavors. In cooked dishes, such as vegetables and sauces, nuts should be added just before serving so that they remain crunchy. Nuts that become limp can often be made firm again when they are heated in a moderate oven for a few minutes. Substituting brown sugar for white in recipes and adding maple or almond flavor extracts where appropriate can enhance the flavor of nuts.

NUTS IN FOOD PREPARATION

Figure 24.1 shows many kinds of shelled and unshelled nuts.

KINDS OF NUTS

Almonds Almonds are closely related to peaches and plums. Shelled almonds can be purchased sliced, slivered, and whole. Canned almond paste is also available for confections, soups, sauces, and pastries. Check the ingredient listing on canned almond paste to make certain that the paste is not adulterated with apricot, peach, or plum pits.

Brazil Nuts Brazil nuts are easiest to shell after they have been soaked in warm water for several hours. These nutmeats are brittle and difficult to slice. For easier slicing, cover the nutmeats with cold water and simmer for about 5 minutes, drain, and slice.

Figure 24.1

Nuts shown are, center top and clockwise: shelled cashews, shelled and unshelled pistachios, shelled and unshelled pecans, shelled and unshelled pine nuts (piñons), shelled and unshelled English walnuts, shelled and unshelled Brazil nuts, shelled and unshelled almonds, shelled macadamia nuts, and shelled and unshelled filberts (hazelnuts).

Cashews Shelled cashew nuts are imported. They should never be eaten raw, because they contain a toxic substance that is destroyed by roasting or cooking.

Chestnuts Chestnuts are more like vegetables than nuts because they are low in fat and high in carbohydrate; they can be treated as either. Chestnuts are soft after roasting, not crunchy like other nuts. They are commonly used in stuffings for fowl or combined with brussels sprouts or red cabbage.

Coconuts Buy only fresh coconuts; shake the nut to make certain that it contains milk and check for cracks or punctures. Separate the coconut meat from its shell by freezing the whole, unpunctured coconut overnight, or bake it at 350°F (177°C) for 25 minutes. Drain the milk from the coconut by piercing the eyes, and then crack the coconut with a heavy hammer and pry the nutmeat from the shell.

The nutmeat's dark brown skin can be peeled off with a vegetable peeler. Coconut milk can be used in sauces, custards, and puddings, but because it is sensitive to high heat, either cook with low heat or add it near the end of the cooking period. Coconut milk should be refrigerated until it is ready to use and even when it is refrigerated it should be used within the day. Coconut meat is used in cookies, cakes, and a variety of desserts.

Filberts or Hazelnuts These nuts, grown in the south of England, are ready for harvesting on Saint Philbert's day, August 22, hence the name. The hazelnut, which in its cultivated form has been eaten for centuries, is a pleasantly sweet nutmeat.

Peanuts Another name for the peanut is "groundnut," because it develops underground; it is a pea and belongs to the legume family. Peanuts have a higher protein content and quality than any other nut, yet they are often the least expensive as well. The skin and germ of peanuts are good sources of thiamin. Commercially packed peanuts often come with the germ removed, because it is thought to contribute some bitterness to the taste, but the germ has a slightly higher nutrient content than the rest of the nut. Peanuts are available in many forms. Dry roasted peanuts are slightly lower in calories than peanuts roasted in oil. A lower-calorie, defatted peanut is also on the market; because part of its flavoring oils have been removed, it is milder in flavor than regular peanuts.

Peanut butter is prepared from ground roasted peanuts and a small amount of added oil, salt, and sometimes dextrose. The mixture is homogenized to prevent the oil from separating out. The U.S. Food and Drug Administration has limited the amount of oil that can be added to peanut butter; it must now contain at least 90 percent peanuts.

Pine Nuts (Piñons) Pine nuts were eaten as far back as biblical times. Many varieties fall under the broad classification of pignolias. The piñon, which is dainty in size, is often used as a decoration on confections and pastries.

Walnuts Walnuts are the most commonly used nut after peanuts. English walnuts are much easier to shell than black walnuts. The flavor of the two kinds of walnuts also differs; many people value the unique flavor of black walnuts.

Whether shelled or unshelled nuts make a better buy depends on the cost of each form and the time available for shelling. Table 24.2 shows the yield in ounces and the cups for 1 pound of nuts in the shell. It also shows the weight of 1 cup of shelled nuts or seeds in ounces and grams. If walnuts in the shell cost 3 pounds for $1.00, then 10.5 ounces of kernels (3 pounds times 3.5 ounces of kernels/pound) would cost $1.00. If shelled walnuts cost $1.50 per pound, then $1.00 would buy 10.7 ounces of shelled nuts (16 ounces divided by $1.50). In this case, the shelled nuts cost no more than the unshelled ones, and no labor is required.

ECONOMY IN PURCHASING NUTS

Table 24.2   Yield of nuts and seeds, with and without shells

Nuts and seeds	One pound in shells yields shelled kernels		Weight of kernels per cup	
	(c)	(oz)	(oz)	(g)
Almonds	1½	8.2	5.3	150
Brazil nuts	1⅔	7.7	4.6	130
Cashews	—	—	4.9	139
Chestnuts	2½	13.0	5.3	150
Coconut, fresh	1¾	8.3	4.6	130
Filberts (hazelnuts)	1½	7.4	4.7	133
Hickory nuts	—	5.6	—	—
Macadamia nuts	1+	5.0	4.7	133
Peanuts, roasted	2	10.7	4.9	139
Pecan halves	2¼	8.5	3.7	105
Pecan pieces	2	8.5	4.2	119
Pine nuts (piñons)	2	9.3	4.8	136
Pistachios	2	8.0	4.2	119
Walnuts, black: halves	¾	3.5	4.0	113
Walnuts, black: pieces	⅔	3.5	4.6	130
Walnuts, English: halves	2	7.2	3.6	102
Walnuts, English: pieces	1½	7.2	4.4	125
Pumpkin seeds	2½	11.8	4.5	128
Safflower seeds	—	8.2	—	—
Sesame seeds	3½	—	4.5	128
Sunflower seeds	2	8.6	4.6	130

SOURCE: U.S. Department of Agriculture, *Composition of Foods.*

Figure 24.2

Seeds often used as nuts include, center top and clockwise: shelled and unshelled pumpkin seeds, shelled and unshelled sunflower seeds, and sesame seeds.

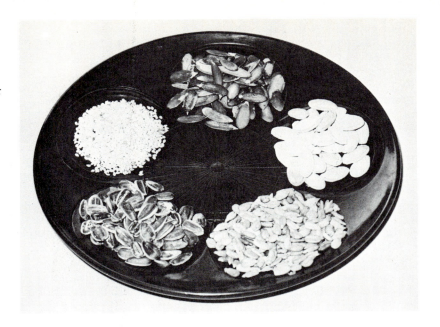

Purchasing unshelled nuts often entails some loss from nuts that have deteriorated. Shelled nuts are less expensive when purchased in pieces than in halves or whole.

SEEDS IN FOOD PREPARATION

Seeds have increased in popularity in the last decade. Not only are they used in cookies, cakes, and desserts, they also add texture and flavor to salads, breads, vegetables, casseroles, and many other foods. Sunflower seeds, sesame seeds, pumpkin seeds (Figure 24.2), and safflower seeds are most commonly used.

Legumes

Dried beans and peas are known as *legumes.* Table 24.1 which lists common varieties, shows that legumes are the best source of plant protein. A variety of legumes is shown in Figure 24.3.

One disadvantage in using legumes is the long preparation time. Canned beans are faster to cook but cost more than preparing the dried beans. A newer method of processing legumes has been developed that results in quick-cooking legumes. This method of processing involves soaking the legumes in a slightly alkaline (pH 9) saline (salt) solution that is later discarded. The method of processing is diagramed in Figure 24.4. The treatment speeds the rehydration and cooking of the legumes. It also has the beneficial side effect of reducing the "flatulence factor," or the substances in legumes that cause abdominal gas production when cooked legumes are eaten. Many legumes contain several undesirable substances that appear to be removed by this method of processing.

Figure 24.3

Dried beans and peas come in many varieties, including, center top and clockwise: lima beans, red beans, soybeans, red kidney beans, navy beans, split peas, blackeyed peas, great northern beans, chickpeas (garbanzos), and pinto beans; and in the center, lentils.

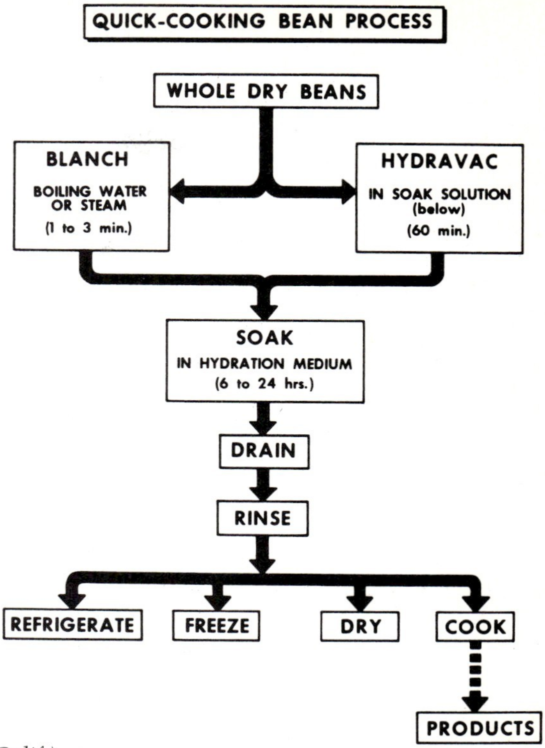

Figure 24.4

Legumes processed into quick-cooking beans are either blanched or held in a vacuum for a short time, after which they are soaked for a few hours in an alkaline saline solution. The processed legumes can then be dried, frozen, canned, or refrigerated for marketing. *(Courtesy of Louis B. Rockland, Chapman College, Orange, Calif.)*

QUICK-COOKING BEAN PROCESS

WHOLE DRY BEANS

BLANCH
BOILING WATER OR STEAM
(1 to 3 min.)

HYDRAVAC
IN SOAK SOLUTION (below)
(60 min.)

SOAK
IN HYDRATION MEDIUM
(6 to 24 hrs.)

DRAIN

RINSE

REFRIGERATE **FREEZE** **DRY** **COOK**

PRODUCTS

Although it is well known that soaking foods and discarding soaking solutions increase the solution losses of nutrients, quick-cooking legumes appear to have a vitamin content and protein efficiency ratio that is similar to regular cooked legumes, which undoubtedly suffer some loss in nutrient content from the longer cooking time required to tenderize them.

SELECTING AND STORING LEGUMES

Some legumes are sorted before they are packed so that the beans are of uniform size. Mixed sizes, even of the same variety of bean, cook unevenly; either the small beans overcook and become mushy, or the large ones remain undercooked and too firm. Choose legumes of a good color that have been sized and have a minimum amount of pebbles and decayed or broken beans. To check the quality of legumes, select only those sold in bulk, in cellophane or plastic packages, or in boxes with windows.

Only a few varieties of quick-cooking legumes are sold in some markets. None are presently available dried; they are sold only fresh as a refrigerated product in the vegetable section. Quick-cooking frozen beans will soon be available in retail markets. Both canned and frozen chili con carne products using quick-

Figure 24.5

Ground beef is combined with kidney beans to produce a spicy chili con carne. *(Courtesy of Louis B. Rockland, Chapman College, Orange, Calif.)*

cooking beans have been developed that contain meat and cheese in amounts providing a protein efficiency ratio equal to that of casein, the principal protein in milk. Recipes have been developed for quick-cooking beans in combination with other protein foods that also provide a balanced protein mixture (Figure 24.5). Frozen and refrigerated quick-cooking beans will be comparable in cost to other vegetables; dehydrated quick-cooking legumes are expected to cost more than regular dried beans because of their additional processing.

Store regular dried beans and peas in a cool, dry place. Legumes should be stored in airtight containers and kept dry. Improper storage can delay rehydration of the legumes when they are cooked. Cooked legumes may be frozen for later use.

PREPARING LEGUMES   Table 24.3 shows the yield of legumes when cooked, the ratio of legumes and water to use for pressure cooking, and approximate cooking times in a pressure cooker. Cooking time varies even for the same variety of legume; freshly dried legumes cook more quickly than older beans.

Sort the legumes to remove foreign matter and damaged beans, and then wash off surface soil. Measure the exact amounts of legumes, water, and salt into the saucepan and bring to a boil; boil for 2 minutes. Remove the beans from the heat and soak for 1 hour. Cook the legumes in the water in which they were soaked until they are tender. Legumes cooked on a surface unit at atmospheric pressure may require several hours of simmering to become tender; additional water may be needed to replace that lost by evaporation. The amount of evaporation depends on how tightly the lid fits the pot, how rapidly the beans are boiled, and how long they must be cooked to become tender.

Table 24.3   Preparation and yield of legumes

Legume	Yield (cups)		Cooking time (min) at 15 pounds pressure		Water per cup of dried legume (cups)
	Dried legume (cups/pound)	Cooked legume (cups/1 cup dried)	Soaked	Not soaked	
Beans:					
Kidney or red	2½	2¾	10	30	3
Large lima	2½	2½	10	30	3
Small lima	2⅓	2	8	25	3
Navy	2⅓	2½	10	30	2
Great northern	2½	2¾	7	20	2
Soybeans	2¼	2¾	10	35	2½
Peas:					
Chickpeas (garbanzo)	2½	2¾	10	30	3
Cowpeas (black-eyed)	2⅓	2½	3	10	3
Split	2	2⅔	3	10	2
Lentils	2	2⅔	3	10	2

Less salt should be added to the legumes during soaking and cooking if salt containing seasonings, such as soy sauce or salt pork, will be used; otherwise, add about 2 teaspoons of salt per pound of dried beans.

The "flatulence factor" appears to be water-soluble. Persons who are especially susceptible to this effect of cooked legumes may find some relief by discarding the soaking water and using fresh water for cooking, and by discarding the cooking liquid from the cooked beans. Nutrient retention is reduced, however, when the soaking and cooking liquids are discarded.

Shortening the Cooking Time   The preboil and short-soaking period described is a faster method than overnight soaking. Split peas and lentils can be cooked satisfactorily with no soaking, but other legumes take an excessive amount of time to rehydrate and soften during cooking if they are not soaked; the long cooking wastes energy, destroys nutrients, and produces cooked legumes with an unsatisfactory texture. Heating the legumes at the beginning of the soaking period hastens their hydration and shortens the cooking time.

Pressure Cooking   The advantages of the pressure cooker and techniques of pressure cooking were discussed in Chapter 3. A pressure cooker should not be filled more than one-third full of legumes and water at the beginning of cooking because the beans expand two or three times in volume when cooked (Figure 24.6). Like pastas and cereal, legumes foam during cooking. Beans can be soaked in the pressure cooker, and then cooked, thereby occu-

Figure 24.6

One cup of pinto beans soaked as described in the text and cooked in a pressure cooker yields almost 3 cups of cooked beans. Combined with meat and seasonings, 3 cups of cooked legumes make enough chili con carne for five or six people.

pying only one container. When legumes have been cooked for the suggested time, reduce the pressure quickly and test their tenderness. Legumes can be cooked longer, if necessary, either in the pressure cooker or at atmospheric pressure.

FACTORS AFFECTING THE TENDERNESS OF COOKED LEGUMES

An acidic medium and hard water can reduce the tenderness of cooked legumes. This effect is more pronounced in legumes than in any other cooked vegetable.

Effect of Acid   Acid interferes with the softening of legumes during cooking by inhibiting the solution of the pectic substances that cement the cells together and by delaying softening of the cellulose. If legumes are to be seasoned with an acid ingredient, such as tomatoes or a sweet-sour sauce, the acid should not be added until after the beans are tender.

Effect of Hard Water   Some of the minerals, or cations, in hard water can also interfere with the softening of legumes during cooking. Calcium combines with pectic substances in legumes to form calcium pectate, giving the cooked legumes a firm texture, regardless of how long they are cooked. This problem is usually greater when legumes are cooked at atmospheric pressure than when they are cooked in a pressure cooker, possibly because more water must be used for cooking at atmospheric pressure, and, therefore, more calcium is available for combining with the pectin. Magnesium in hard water can also have this effect.

About ⅛ teaspoon of baking soda per cup of dried beans can be added to counteract the effect of hard water. Excessive amounts of baking soda increase alkalinity and destroy thiamin, a vitamin that is plentiful in legumes. Cooking legumes in purified water (Chapter 3) is preferable to adding baking soda in any amount.

Soybeans have a higher vitamin and mineral content and better quality protein than any of the other legumes. One disadvantage of soybeans, however, is that they have a metallic aftertaste that many people find objectionable. Processing and purification of the soybean protein has produced a more acceptable flavor and a more usable product, but in the purification of the product, many of the nutrients are removed. In the purification of soy protein, the seed coat and fats are removed, and the bean is ground into a flour. Soluble carbohydrate is removed from the flour to produce soy concentrate. Further refining of the concentrate removes unwanted flavors and other components, and produces soy protein isolate. The three products—flour, concentrate, and isolate—are manufactured through various processes into textured protein or meat analogs.

The advantage of these products derives from the excellent protein quality of soybeans, which are closer to a complete protein than any other vegetable protein. Soy protein is deficient in the essential amino acid methionine, and is, therefore, an incomplete protein. It is possible to add the correct proportion of methionine to make soy protein comparable in quality to milk casein. Because soybeans are obviously less expensive to produce than livestock, they provide a less expensive source of protein in the diet. Textured protein and analogs now produced have not been enriched with methionine and therefore are not complete proteins. However, they are useful extenders and supplements to milk, eggs, and meat. Other nutritional deficiencies of soy protein are mentioned in Chapter 1.

Meat analogs are imitation meat products in which soy protein has been processed into a number of forms resembling specific meats, such as sausage, bacon, ham slices, chicken, and beef chunks (Figure 24.7). Some of these products have been fortified with vitamins and minerals that may or may not duplicate the nutrient content of the products they purport to simulate. Another proclaimed advantage of analogs is that they have little fat and no cholesterol, although some are equal to meat in fat content. However, meat analogs are expensive, although wider acceptance, with improved flavor and color, may eventually reduce the price. Meat analogs also have a very high salt content and therefore should not be used by those restricted to low-sodium diets.

Analogs are usually packaged frozen. Like other frozen foods, they should be kept frozen until used. Because of their much lower fat content, meat analogs cannot be cooked like the meats they represent. To cook sausages or ham analogs, for instance, place a small amount of oil in the pan and heat them without excessive browning, because such browning will toughen and dry analog products.

Soy Protein Products

MEAT ANALOGS

Figure 24.7

Some meat analogs available commercially in frozen form include imitation Canadian ham and sausage links (top) and bacon and sausage patties (bottom). *(Morningstar Farms, Grocery Products Division, Miles Laboratories, Inc.)*

TEXTURED PROTEIN

TVP, or textured vegetable protein, is soy protein shaped into large, ragged, porous granules that rehydrate rapidly (Figure 24.8). A cup of granules is rehydrated with ½ cup of water, or a liquid supplying water, such as stock, tomato juice, or milk. Textured protein can be used to extend almost any kind of meat that is added to dishes in small pieces, such as ground or chopped beef, lamb, chicken, turkey, or pork. Textured protein is available flavored and unflavored. Meat flavors and seasonings are needed with the unflavored TVP. It is most successful in such highly seasoned dishes as curries, tomato sauce for spaghetti, taco fillings, hamburger Stroganoff, lasagna (Figure 24.9) and chili.

Figure 24.8

Textured vegetable soy protein (TVP) granules are shown here, dry on the plates and reconstituted in the custard cups. The TVP on the left is natural-colored; the TVP on the right has been artificially colored with caramel.

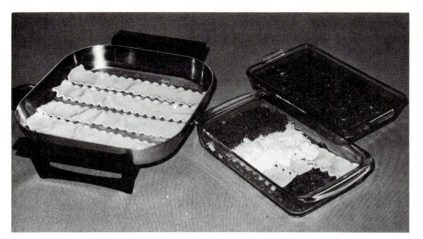

Figure 24.9
TVP can extend almost any dish containing ground beef. Here, TVP is used in a tomato sauce—ground beef mixture for lasagna. Lasagna noodles can be cooked in an electric fry pan and alternated in the baking dish with meat sauce, ricotta or cottage cheese, and grated Jack or cheddar cheese.

Even though textured protein is practically fat-free, it readily absorbs the fat rendered from the meat with which it is combined. If textured protein is combined with uncooked meat, such as ground beef, in meat loaf or patties, the meat should be lean to keep the cooked mixture at a minimal fat level. Ground beef with a high fat content can be used with soy protein if the fat is first rendered out of the meat and discarded, and the meat blotted with paper towels, before the textured protein is added. Textured protein absorbs juices from the meat and is a most satisfactory extender of meat protein. Dry TVP granules can be added directly to soup or used to thicken meat mixtures that are too thin, such as creamed tuna, chicken curry, or beef Stroganoff. Dry granules quickly absorb the excess liquid.

TVP comes in a natural-colored granule that blends well with fish and poultry in casseroles, soups, and other dishes. A caramel-colored granule is better to blend with ground beef mixtures. If meats are browned, the browning should be done before adding TVP, which burns easily.

TOFU PRODUCTS

Soybeans have been used in China and Japan for thousands of years to produce tofu, which has served as a major protein source in these Eastern cultures. Tofu is similar to a soft cheese or a firm cultured milk. It is the precipitated protein of soy milk. The flavor of tofu is bland, and it tends to pick up the flavor of the foods with which it is combined. It is used in many ways in oriental cookery and is adaptable for use in many Western foods. It has been used in egg dishes, casseroles, breads, and vegetable and meat dishes. Like other soybean products, tofu is an incomplete protein; its greatest value is in its ability to extend animal proteins.

Nutritional Value of Plant Proteins

Plant proteins make an important nutritional contribution to the diet, as discussed in Chapter 1. Plant proteins as a group are not only deficient in certain essential amino acids, but they are devoid of vitamin B-12 and are low in the essential minerals, zinc and chromium. Healthy adults can often exist on plants as the sole source of protein for many months, but for infants, children, and pregnant and lactating women, and during recovery from severe illness when extra protein is required for growth, the plant proteins may be inadequate to meet the protein needs of the body. The intake of other nutrients may be limited in a diet that depends solely on plants for protein. Iron is less well absorbed from plant than from animal foods, and less calcium is available from plants; milk and milk products are needed for adequate calcium intake.

The bulk and calories per gram of protein of plant foods (see Table 1.2) results in two other possible problems when only plant foods are consumed. Small children are unable to eat the quantity of plant foods to supply their protein needs. Adults who can eat the bulk risk obtaining an excessive caloric intake. If plants are to serve as the sole source of protein, the diet should be carefully planned and analyzed to make sure that adequate amounts and kinds of all of the amino acids, vitamins, and minerals will be obtained. The use of animal protein along with the plant proteins requires a little less care with these details.

Study Questions

1. What are legumes?
2. What is one disadvantage in preparing legumes?
3. Why is it preferable for legumes to be of uniform size for cooking?
4. What are quick-cooking legumes and what are the advantages and disadvantages of using them?
5. Name two ways to shorten the cooking time for legumes.
6. When cooking legumes, why should the pressure cooker not be filled more than one-third full?
7. Is the same amount of water needed to cook legumes at atmospheric pressure as in a pressure cooker? Explain why.
8. If legumes are to be seasoned with tomatoes, when should the tomatoes be added? Explain why.
9. What effect does hard water have on the texture of legumes cooked in it? Explain why.
10. Briefly describe the processing of soy beans to produce meat analogs and textured protein granules.
11. What are meat analogs?
12. What are the advantages and disadvantages in the use of textured protein?
13. Briefly describe the source and use of tofu.
14. What precautions should be observed in the use of plants as the only source of protein?

Adams, Russell S. "A Soil Scientist's View of Eating Meat." In *Contemporary Nutrition Controversies,* edited by T. P. Labuza and A. E. Sloan. New York: West Publishing, 1979.

Altschul, Aaron M. "The Revered Legume." *Nutrition Today* 8, no. 2 (March–April 1973): 22.

Cross, H. R.; Stanfield, M.S.; Green, E. C.; Heinemeyer, J. M.; and Hollick, A. B. "Effect of Fat and Textured Soy Protein Content on Consumer Acceptance of Ground Beef." *Journal of Food Science* 40, no. 6 (November–December 1975): 1331.

McGeary, B. K., and Smith, M. E. "Nuts, A Shell Game that Pays off in Good Eating." In U.S. Department of Agriculture, *Food for Us All,* Yearbook of Agriculture. Washington, D.C.: Government Printing Office, 1969.

Pimentel, D.; Dritschilo, W.; Krummel, J.; and Kutzman, J. "Energy and Land Constraints in Food Protein Production." *Science* 190 (November 21, 1975): 754.

Register, U. D., and Sonnenburg, L. M. "The Vegetarian Diet." *Journal of the American Dietetic Association,* 62, no. 3 (March 1973): 253.

Rockland, L. B., and Metzler, E. A. "Quick-cooking Lima and Other Dry Beans." *Food Technology* 21, no. 3 (March 1967): 26A.

Stephenson, M. G. "Textured Plant Protein Products: New Choices for Consumers." *FDA Consumer* 9, May 1975.

U.S. Department of Agriculture. *How To Buy Dry Beans, Peas, and Lentils,* Home and Garden Bulletin No. 177. Washington, D.C.: Government Printing Office, 1970.

Wagner, J. R.; Carson, J. F.; Becker, R.; Gumbmann, M. R.; and Donhof, I. E. "Comparative Flatulence Activity of Beans and Bean Fractions for Man and for the Rat." *Journal of Nutrition* 107, no. 4 (April 1977): 680.

25

Soups and Casseroles

Meats, legumes, vegetables, cereal grains, pastas, eggs, milk, and cheese have been studied individually. This chapter describes how to combine these foods in soups and casseroles. Economy, nutrient retention, and timesaving techniques in cooking are emphasized. Leftover foods can be added to these mixtures, and canned, frozen, and dehydrated products can speed preparation.

Stock

Stock is an extract of flavoring substances from meat or vegetables. A well-flavored stock is the base for many dishes, especially soups, sauces, and casseroles. Canned meat stocks are available as a time-saver, but stock is often more economically prepared from meat scraps and bones. The actual preparation time can be minimal; stock ingredients can be cooked while other meals are being prepared.

KINDS OF STOCK

The flavor of stock depends on its ingredients. As a rule, stocks are classified either brown or white, or by the type of meat extracted, such as fish stock. Meat mixtures are acceptable in some stocks, as in stock for vegetable soup. For other purposes, stock extracted from only one type of meat with no added vegetables is more suitable.

Brown Stock Brown stock has a brown color because it is extracted from the meat and bones of beef and lamb, which are browned before they are cooked in water. The meat and bones can be browned in a pan in a hot oven or in the dry soup pot in a small amount of fat or bone marrow.

White Stock White stock is prepared from the meat and bones of such light-colored meats as chicken, turkey, veal, and sometimes pork. These meats are not browned before they are cooked in water. Veal stock has very little flavor, but is rich in gelatin because the ends of the bones in the young animal contain a large amount of gristle, which is converted to gelatin by heating. Veal stock is excellent for aspics, but it may need to be combined with other meats and vegetables for flavor.

Fish Stock Fish stock is prepared from fish or fish parts, such as the head, bones, tail, skin, and trimmings. Fish stock can also be obtained from liquid in which the cleaned shells of crustaceans have simmered. Unlike other stocks, fish stock should be simmered only briefly, for an hour or less, because long cooking causes a loss in flavor. For the same reason, do not use fish stock in dishes that require long cooking. Fish stock is mostly limited to use in fish dishes. Such strong-flavored fish as skate, mullet, and mackerel are not used to make fish stock. Stock prepared from salmon, which is distinctively flavored, should be used only in salmon dishes.

Soup bones and meat, or chicken wings, necks, and feet, can be purchased to make stock. Economy is often overlooked when meats are trimmed and prepared. Trimmings left over from meat for a meal are frequently discarded, but even small amounts can be saved in a plastic bag in the freezer until enough are collected to make stock. Fatty tissue can be used for stock, because it contains some water-extractable substances that can contribute flavor. Bones and meat trimmings from dinner plates can also be used for stock if they are cooked in a pressure cooker for 30 minutes or more. Juices that cook out of fried and broiled meat are also suitable for stock.

PREPARING STOCK

Ingredients for making stock may need to be washed before they are cooked. Chicken feet, fish heads, and similar parts should always be washed. Other animal parts may or may not require washing, but they should be free of hair, sawdust, or other inedible substances. Long bones should be sawed or cracked into smaller pieces; thin bones, such as rib or chicken bones, should be crushed, because substances are present inside the bones that add both flavor and nutrients to stock. Scraps of meat are mostly used in preparing stock. Large pieces of meat should be cut into small pieces for the maximum extraction of flavor.

Meat and bones are browned to make brown stock. The importance of using a minimum amount of water for the best retention of flavor and nutrients has been emphasized in cooking vegetables and meat. This principle is reversed in stock making, where a large amount of water and a long cooking time is necessary to extract as much flavor as possible. A pressure cooker can speed extraction. It should not be more than half full; the stock ingredients cook at 15 pounds pressure for a half hour to 1 hour. To keep stock from boiling over when it is cooked at atmospheric pressure, use a large pot on heat only high enough to maintain a simmer. During a long cooking period, it may be necessary to add more water. Covering the pot reduces evaporation, but covered pots are more likely to boil over.

After extraction is completed, strain the stock to remove the bones and meat. The meat can be used in soups and casseroles; it still contains protein and some vitamins and minerals, although its flavor is greatly diluted. Chill the strained stock to solidify the fat, which rises to the top, and then lift it off and discard it (Figure 25.1).

Seasoning Stock Whether vegetables or herbs are cooked with the meat to make stock depends on the purpose of the stock. A strongly flavored herb in the stock might not be acceptable in a soup with a mild flavor, such as egg flower soup. When preparing stock for a future use that has not been determined, the best procedure is probably to emphasize only the meat flavor and not to

Figure 25.1

Save the juices left in a frying pan or broiler pan after cooking meat to use for stock by adding a small amount of water to the cooking pan to dissolve the juices, pouring the dissolved juices into containers, and chilling. The fat will rise to the top and can be removed before the stock is used.

add vegetables and herbs that might not be compatible with later needs. For the same reason, use a minimum of salt and pepper. Added to a mixture of ingredients with a high salt content, a well-salted stock could produce an excessively salty dish.

Reducing Stock   For a flavor that is more intense, stock is often concentrated or *reduced*. In this process, the stock is simmered uncovered to evaporate the water. If a recipe calls for stock to be reduced by half, let half the water evaporate so that the remaining stock has half the volume of the original stock. This is another reason for limiting salt, for the reduced stock can turn out far too salty if the original stock had a high salt content.

Clarifying Stock   For most purposes, stock can simply be strained through a coarse colander; for other purposes, it can be strained through a strainer with a fine mesh, or through a strainer lined with several layers of cheesecloth. A cloudy stock, however, can be clarified for special uses by being simmered with raw egg white and crushed eggshell for a half hour. The stock is then poured through several thicknesses of cheesecloth placed in a colander or funnel. Stock must be clarified in this way to make clear aspics and broths.

Freezing stock is an ideal way to preserve it for future use. Jars or freezer containers should be filled only three-quarters full to allow for expansion during freezing. Stock can also be canned, but it must be processed in a pressure cooker at 10-pounds pressure for 20 to 25 minutes, because stock is a nonacid food.

   Meat stock is an excellent nutrient broth for all kinds of bacteria. Stock should therefore be prepared and stored with the

STORAGE AND SANITARY QUALITY OF STOCK

same precautions that are taken for other protein foods. Do not hold stock at room temperature. Another good precaution is to boil stock that has been held in the freezer or refrigerator, as well as home-canned stock, before using it. Frozen stock should be thawed in the refrigerator or in cold water.

Soups

Soup is made by cooking meat, vegetables, fish, and other solid ingredients in a liquid medium. There are hundreds of soups and soup recipes. Not all include meat and vegetables; some are sweetened mixtures with fruits, suitable for desserts and snacks.

Soups and stews are not distinctly different foods. Many soups, like stews, are rich mixtures of hearty ingredients that make a one-dish meal. As always, however, the quality and good taste of a food are more important than its label.

KINDS OF SOUPS

There are three general types of soup: clear soups, cream soups, and chowders. These classifications are not clear-cut, for many soups have the characteristics of more than one, or none, of these types.

Clear Soups   Clear soups are known as consommé, broth, and bouillon, all of which are liquid in which meat has been cooked. Bouillon is sometimes called beef broth; consommé is sometimes called chicken broth. Broth or bouillon have been labeled "unclarified," and consommé, "clarified," meat stocks.

A rich, well-seasoned meat stock is preferable if clear soup is to be served alone with no flavor additions. Clear meat stock is the base for many Oriental soups, such as *won ton* (Figure 25.2) or egg flower soups. Stock for a clear soup often benefits from

Figure 25.2

Won ton soup is an example of a clear stock soup. Fold the purchased *won ton* wrappers as shown: the dark lines indicate points where the wrapper must be moistened with water before folding. Cook the filled, folded *won ton* in the stock like noodles, until they are opaque.

Figure 25.3

Add nonfat dry milk to meat stock or vegetable cooking liquids as a base for sauces and soups. *(United Dairy Industry Association)*

having vegetables cooked with the meat in preparing the stock. Minced parsley, watercress, chives, fresh herbs, or green onion tops floating on the surface of a clear soup add not just color but additional flavor.

Cream Soups Cream soups are made with a white sauce to which desired ingredients are added for flavor. White sauce can be made with any form of milk or cream, but milk with a higher fat content increases the caloric content of the soup. A good alternative is to use a well-flavored, fat-free meat stock as the liquid, with nonfat dry milk added as a milk equivalent. Use ⅓ cup of nonfat dry milk per cup of stock (Figure 25.3).

Most cream soups require a thin white sauce with 1 tablespoon of flour per cup of liquid. If the soup is to contain a starchy ingredient, however, such as split peas, potatoes, or corn, only ½ tablespoon of flour is needed per cup of liquid. Even though starchy vegetables have some thickening power, they remain more evenly distributed in the soup if the liquid has been thickened with a little flour or cornstarch.

Cream soups are likely to curdle if acid ingredients are added to the white sauce. Hot acid ingredients should therefore be mixed with the hot cooked white sauce immediately before they are served with no further heating or holding. Purées for cream soups can be prepared by blending cooked vegetables in a blender until they form a smooth liquid paste. If a blender is not available, press the vegetables through a food mill or a grinder and strain them.

A bisque is a cream soup containing shellfish. To make a bisque, cook the white sauce completely, then add the fish just before serving. Shellfish should be heated just to serving temperature, because further cooking makes them less tender. Some fish are poached before they are added to a soup; the poaching liquid can be incorporated into the white sauce.

Chowders Chowders are thick soups containing a large amount of solid ingredients, such as meats, vegetables, cereal grains, pastas, legumes, crackers, or bread. Originally, the term "chowder" was applied to thick soups containing seafood, particularly clams, but more recent usage includes thick soups with any type of meat or no meat at all, such as corn chowder. Thus, minestrone or thick vegetable-meat soups are now considered chowders (Figures 25.4, 25.5). The stock may be thickened with starch or left unthickened. Some chowders have such a high proportion of solid ingredients that they resemble stews, the only difference being that the ingredients are divided into smaller pieces in chowder than is customary in most stews. Chowders, like stews, are often used as the main and only dish for a light meal, along with bread and, perhaps, fruit for dessert.

Chowders traditionally have two types of bases. Manhattan chowder uses tomatoes and green peppers for flavor, while New England chowder has a milk or white sauce base and omits the tomatoes and green pepper.

Figure 25.4

German cabbage soup is a nutritious chowder that blends the flavors of apple, tomato, and onion with that of cabbage. *(United Fresh Fruit and Vegetable Association)*

Figure 25.5

Shrimp or chicken gumbo is a chowder that is often served spooned over steamed rice as the main dish of a meal; it blends the flavors of okra, tomato, green pepper, and onion with rich meat stock and available meat.

Chowders are fairly easy to prepare. Vegetables, cereal grains, pastas, and meat should be cooked in unthickened stock; the starch for thickening is added shortly before serving, because the thickened mixture has a greater tendency to scorch. Those ingredients that need the most cooking should be added to the stock first, those that need little or no cooking later. Nutrient retention is greater if all ingredients are cooked only until they are tender. Too much heating destroys some vitamins.

Soups are an ideal medium for leftovers. Thin leftover gravy for stock with water, milk, tomato juice, tomato sauce, or canned tomatoes. Leftover meat of any kind, even meat loaf, can be chopped into the soup, as can vegetables, legumes, rice or other grains, or pasta. Add sliced celery, leek, or onion for texture and flavor. If no leftover vegetables are available, a few frozen green peas, green beans, or lima beans, or other vegetables can be added in their place.

ECONOMY IN PREPARING SOUPS

Dehydrated onion soup makes a good stock for soup with vegetables and meat added. If little or no meat is available, the protein content of the soup can be improved with cheese. Cut the cheddar, Swiss, or jack cheese in cubes into the soup bowl and ladle the hot soup over it, or sprinkle grated Parmesan or Romano cheese over the top of the soup.

Preparing a soup only from food in the refrigerator or cupboard can be a creative experience. Soup can be made every day with no duplication of flavor. Curry powder, bay leaf, and other herbs and spices can produce an infinite variety of tastes. Such soup preparation need take no more than 20 to 30 minutes from the time it is begun until the time it is served.

Casseroles

Casseroles resemble soups in many ways; both are mixtures of similar kinds of ingredients. A casserole, however, is a much thicker mixture than even the thickest soup. Customarily, casseroles are baked and soups are cooked on a surface unit. Like some soups, casseroles often serve as the main and only dish for a meal.

A casserole usually contains the following ingredients:

1. a starchy food, such as cereal grain or pasta
2. a protein food, such as meat, cheese, egg, legume, fish, or poultry
3. a sauce of some kind to bind the ingredients, blend flavors, and add moisture
4. vegetables for flavor, color, texture, and nutritive value

Innumerable recipes for casseroles exist, but creating a casserole out of leftovers or other available ingredients is often the most economical procedure. Moreover, casseroles made from leftovers can use legumes and cereal grains to supplement and extend the protein from animal sources. For instance, ham from

Figure 25.6

Macaroni and cheese, an old favorite, is livened with sliced zucchini stirred into the cheese sauce with the cooked macaroni. *(National Macaroni Institute)*

one meal and chicken from another meal can be combined with rice to make a jambalaya. A bean casserole can be made from leftover ham or hamburger, or a combination of the two, with appropriate herbs and spices added to enhance the flavor.

PREPARING CASSEROLES

Casseroles can be assembled in two ways. The ingredients can either be mixed together all at once, poured into a baking dish, and baked (Figure 25.6), or they can be placed in a baking dish in alternating layers (Figure 25.7). Casserole ingredients may be raw or cooked, but they should be combined in such a way that some ingredients do not overcook before others are cooked through (Figures 25.8–25.10). Combine raw ingredients that require about the same cooking time, and use enough liquid for them to properly hydrate and cook. If all the ingredients in the casserole have been previously cooked, the casserole may only need to be heated to serving temperature. As with soups, excessive heating of casseroles should be avoided.

Milk, cheese, and egg mixtures curdle in casseroles if they are heated excessively or are combined with acid ingredients or ingredients with a high tannin content, as discussed in Chapter 18. Curdled potatoes au gratin or macaroni and cheese are often accepted, but they are not acceptable in good practice. If the eggs and grated cheese are stirred into a thin white sauce prepared from the milk before they are combined with potatoes or maca-

Figure 25.7

To make Gateau Florentine, alternate layers of crepes, spinach filling, and mushroom filling in a casserole and top with Mornay sauce and minced parsley.

Figure 25.8

Crumbled blue cheese is sprinkled over broccoli flowerets and chunks of cooked chicken in a casserole. *(United Dairy Industry Association)*

Figure 25.9

An uncooked custard mixture is poured over broccoli, chicken, and blue cheese in a casserole. *(United Dairy Industry Association)*

Figure 25.10

Serve the baked broccoli-chicken casserole with a tossed salad for a quick lunch or supper. *(United Dairy Industry Association)*

roni, a smoother, creamier casserole results. Starch in the white sauce helps stabilize the protein in the milk, eggs, and cheese, so that they are less likely to curdle when heated. Processed cheese—because it contains emulsifiers—and well-aged or sharp cheese are less likely to curdle when heated. Cooked potatoes, which have less tannin than raw ones, can also be used.

STORAGE AND SANITARY QUALITY OF CASSEROLES

Casseroles simplify meal preparation, because they can be prepared ahead of time and stored in the refrigerator or freezer until they are ready to serve, thus reducing last-minute preparation time. Frozen casseroles should be thawed in the refrigerator; whether they have been frozen or not, they should go directly from the refrigerator into a cold oven. (A cold casserole dish may crack in a hot oven.) Casseroles held in refrigerator or freezer storage are likely to have bacterial counts higher than a freshly prepared casserole, because bacteria can grow during the chilling period before the dish is completely cold. Casseroles should be heated to a high enough temperature to destroy any such bacteria.

Casseroles containing starch-thickened sauces do not freeze well. The sauce curdles and becomes watery when it is thawed, because the starch retrogrades, as discussed in Chapter 10. Commercially canned sauces and soups contain starches that tolerate freezing. Because these starches are not sold retail, such a canned soup or sauce can be used to advantage in casseroles that are meant to be frozen.

Economy here means conserving time in preparation and money in buying food. Because these two kinds of economy are often antagonistic, consumers must decide for themselves which factors predominate and where lines of compromise should be drawn. At one extreme, a casserole can be prepared with a minimum of time from canned or frozen soup, sauce, or stock; precooked meats, such as ham or turkey slices; pregrated cheese; and a preseasoned or instant rice or pasta product. However, only the briefest comparison of prices reveals that preseasoned or prepared products are far more expensive than the same product made from the basic ingredients; the rice in one preseasoned product has been calculated to cost over one dollar per pound of raw rice.

At the other end of the spectrum is a casserole that uses unprocessed or leftover ingredients but requires more time and effort at a saving in money. The time factor can often be reduced by adopting more efficient work habits. For instance, a double recipe takes a little longer, but not twice as long, to make, and half can be frozen for later use. This is a particularly practical procedure for small families.

ECONOMY IN PREPARING AND SERVING CASSEROLES

The nutrient content of soups and casseroles is directly related to their ingredients and procedures used to make them that promote maximum nutrient retention. Such mixtures can carry many more calories than they need to if the sources of the unnecessary calories are not recognized and eliminated. The procedures have been described, but they should be emphasized again: use fat-free stock; remove fat from meats; add minimal amounts of table fats, or omit them entirely; and replace high-fat milk products, such as cream and sour cream, with nonfat milk.

Many quick casserole recipes recommend undiluted canned condensed cream soups. The calories in a 10¾-ounce can of some undiluted cream soups are: asparagus, 154; celery, 193; chicken, 235; and mushroom, 338. One and a half cups of white sauce made with nonfat milk and no added fat provides 178 calories. The caloric contribution of such soups to a casserole must therefore be considered, and they should be used with discretion.

Nutritional Value of Soups and Casseroles

Study Questions

1. What is stock? Distinguish between brown, white, and fish stocks.
2. What are the advantages and disadvantages of seasoning stocks during extraction?
3. Distinguish between clear soups, cream soups, and chowders.
4. Why is it important not to overcook fish in soup?
5. Name some ways to reduce, or keep to a minimum, the caloric content of cream soups.
6. What are the basic ingredients of most casseroles?
7. What techniques prevent curdling of milk-cheese-egg mixtures in casseroles?
8. Discuss economies in preparing stock, casseroles, and soups.

Sandwiches, Canapés, and Hors D'Oeuvres

Sandwiches, canapés, and hors d'oeuvres are combined in one chapter for convenience. Canapés employ some of the same ingredients and techniques of preparation as sandwiches and are often served as hors d'oeuvres.

Sandwiches

Although sandwiches are a lunchbox mainstay, they are also appropriate for many other occasions. A *sandwich* is defined as a filling between two pieces of bread. Combining different types of breads and fillings makes possible an enormous variety of sandwiches.

The ingredients in sandwiches include bread, spread, fillings, and garnishes.

INGREDIENTS

Bread A wide variety of breads are available in most markets, including white, whole wheat, French, rye, cracked wheat, oatmeal, potato, cornmeal, raisin, nut, and many others. The flavor of the bread often strongly influences the flavor of the sandwich. Corned beef on rye tastes entirely different than corned beef on white bread. Rolls, such as English muffins, hard French rolls, or hamburger and hot dog buns, can be substituted for sliced bread.

The thickness of the bread also affects the flavor of the sandwich. Thickly sliced bread produces breadier sandwiches; thinly sliced bread places greater emphasis on the flavor of the filling. The thickness of the slices, as well as the size of the loaf, determines the number of slices of bread in a given loaf and the number of sandwiches that can be made from it. Table 26.1 shows the approximate number of slices in various types and sizes of commerically baked loaves.

The bread used in sandwiches may be toasted or not, as desired. Once toasted, however, the bread toughens if it becomes damp or moist; toasting also dries out bread. Toast only bread that is to be eaten immediately. Bread toasted for sandwiches should not be stacked; hold it for a few minutes only, spread in a single layer on a rack in a warm, not hot, oven. Toast bread on

Table 26.1   Average number of slices per loaf of bread

Type of loaf	Weight (lbs)	Number of slices
Enriched or whole wheat	1	16
Enriched or whole wheat	1¼	19
Enriched or whole wheat	1½	24
Sandwich loaf, thin-sliced	2	28
Sandwich loaf, thin-sliced	3	44
Rye	1	23
Rye	2	33

both sides at a time in a toaster or waffle iron; placing the slices in a single layer under the broiler unit or on a hot grill toasts them on one side at a time. Bread spread with table fat before it is toasted is crunchy on the edges and soft in the middle. Bread has the same caloric value toasted or untoasted, providing that no fat or spread has been placed on it.

Spreads Spreads are often put on sandwich breads before the filling is added to seal the bread and prevent moist fillings from soaking into it, to add flavor and moistness, and help hold the filling and bread together. Table fat—either butter or margarine—and mayonnaise or salad dressing are the most commonly used spreads for bread. All spreads must be cold to act as effective barriers to moisture, although table fat needs to be warm enough to be spread. Melted fat is not satisfactory because it soaks into bread; mayonnaise and salad dressing should not be used in sandwiches that are to be frozen. Season table fat and mayonnaise or salad dressing in various ways to produce different flavors in sandwiches. Some seasoning ingredients include garlic powder, orange or lemon rind, honey, curry powder, Roquefort or blue cheese, Parmesan cheese, horseradish, avocado, mustard, anchovy, or finely chopped dates. Any seasoning in the spread should be compatible in flavor with both the filling and the bread used for the sandwich.

Whipped cream cheese that has been softened makes a satisfactory spread for bread. Soften the cheese by warming it to room temperature and adding a small amount of milk. Peanut butter serves both as a spread and a filling; it can be placed directly on the bread with no other spread. Table fat spread on at least one slice of the bread in a peanut butter sandwich, however, provides a smoother combination than peanut butter alone.

All of these spreads have one problem: they are high in calories, averaging about 100 calories per tablespoon. A sandwich usually requires about 1 tablespoon of spread, or ½ tablespoon per slice of bread. Some spreads lower in calories that can be used for some types of sandwiches include prepared mustard and pickle relishes, such as hot dog or hamburger relish. These products do not seal the bread against moisture, however, so they are not satisfactory with moist fillings. Relishes are most suitable with sliced meat and cheese, because they add moistness and flavor while providing only 15 calories per tablespoon.

Fillings Popular fillings for sandwiches are sliced meats and cheeses of all kinds, including sandwich meats, such as bologna and salami, and sliced roast meats, such as beef and turkey. Sandwich meats are widely retailed and leftover roasts provide sliced roast meats. Many kinds of fillings can be prepared from chopped, ground, or grated cheese, hard-cooked eggs, and various cooked meats, as well as nuts, cooked legumes, and seeds, or combinations of these, which can be combined with mayonnaise, or pickle relishes can be used for fewer calories.

Garnishes Garnishes add flavor, texture, and color to sandwiches. Salad greens, such as various types of lettuce, watercress, shredded cabbage and parsley, and sliced tomatoes, cucumbers, onions, and green peppers can be used for this purpose. Sauerkraut, olives, relish, and pickles are also common garnishes for sandwiches.

Raw vegetable garnishes cannot be added to sandwiches that will be frozen, because, with the exception of onion, they become tough and stringy when thawed. Fresh leafy greens wilt readily and should not be placed in sandwiches too far ahead of time. Sliced tomato can make a sandwich soggy if it is added too far ahead of serving time. Sometimes garnishes are best served as a side dish so that they can be added to the sandwich as it is eaten. When sandwiches are carried to another location, keep the leafy green or sliced tomatoes in a separate plastic sandwich bag to maintain the best quality of both sandwich and garnish.

PREPARING SANDWICHES

Select pairs of bread slices from the loaf that match each other in shape and size. Lay out the slices so that the sides that will be the inside faces of the sandwich face up. Spread the two slices thinly with spread, unless the spread, such as peanut butter or cream cheese, is the main part of the filling, in which case use more. The spread should completely cover both bread slices. Place the filling on one slice, then the garnish, and, finally, invert the other slice on top.

Prepared sandwiches can be cut in halves or quarters with horizontal or diagonal cuts. If the sandwiches are not to be eaten immediately, they should be wrapped and refrigerated.

Efficiency in Preparing Sandwiches An assembly-line procedure can be used to good advantage if many sandwiches are to be prepared at one time (Figure 26.1). All the ingredients should be ready before the sandwiches are assembled; the meat and pickles should be sliced, the lettuce should be broken into pieces of the proper size, and the spread should have the correct consistency for spreading. Remove the bread slices from the loaf in pairs and open them up into rows so that the bottoms of each pair touch. Spoon the proper amount of spread onto each slice, then spread it on all the slices. Place the filling on one side of the pair for all the sandwiches, then place the garnish on the filling, and top with the second slice of bread. Stack several sandwiches and cut them at one time.

Figure 26.1

Figure 26.1
Use assembly-line techniques to make several sandwiches at a time: spread all the slices of bread with mayonnaise, put the meat on each piece of bread, and, finally, put the tomato slice on each slice of meat. *(Best Foods, Division of CPC International, Inc.)*

STORAGE AND SANITARY QUALITY OF SANDWICHES

Because sandwiches are often prepared in advance of eating and are often held at warm temperatures during this interval, they can be causes of foodborne illness. Foodborne illness has resulted from the use of unclean knives for cutting the sandwiches and from improperly cleaned blenders that grind cooked meat for a sandwich filling. Absolute cleanliness is essential in sandwich making because these foods are eaten with no further cooking. There is no opportunity to destroy bacteria that may have been present before the sandwich was eaten.

All ingredients in sandwiches should be kept well-chilled, especially the protein foods. If the meat is sliced and then must be held while other ingredients are being prepared, the meat should be refrigerated until it is ready to use. Prepared sandwiches should be chilled as quickly as possible. A well-chilled sandwich keeps for 3 to 4 hours after being removed from the refrigerator, after which time it is subject to spoilage. If the sandwich has been frozen, it can be held an hour or two longer at room temperature before spoilage occurs.

If it is not possible to freeze a sandwich that must be carried to another location, keep it cold longer by packing it next to a frozen can of juice or soft drink. Prepare sandwiches to be carried in a lunch the day or night before and freeze or chill them well. Do not use ingredients in sandwiches to be frozen that do not freeze well. Sandwiches may be wrapped in wax paper or plastic wrap; the latter is preferable for frozen storage and for moist sandwiches.

Club Sandwiches A club sandwich is a sandwich with three slices of bread and two sets of fillings that can be identical or different. In a Dagwood sandwich, a variation of the club sandwich, the two fillings—made from a great variety of meats, cheese, and garnishes—are each thicker than the bread. Bread for club sandwiches is often toasted, or is replaced by special buns, to offer greater strength than sliced bread.

Hero Sandwiches These oversized sandwiches, also known as big-boy sandwiches or submarines, are made with a French roll or loaf, depending on the size of sandwich desired. With this exception, the hero resembles the club or Dagwood sandwich. The roll or loaf is split in half lengthwise and spread with table fat, and then is filled with an assortment of sliced cheeses, ham, pastrami, or other sliced meats, and the usual assortment of garnishes. Some retail hero sandwiches are made with loaves that are 2 feet long; the finished loaf-sandwich is cut into pieces to serve several people.

Hot Sandwiches Many kinds of hot sandwiches are eaten in the United States; hamburgers and hot dogs lead the rest in popularity. Toasted sandwiches are prepared in the same way as cold sandwiches, except that salad greens, if they are used at all, are not added to the sandwich until after it has been toasted. The prepared sandwich is toasted on both sides in a frying pan, on a grill, in a waffle iron, or under a broiler. Spreading the outside of the sandwich with table fat before toasting is optional.

In another form of preparation, a cold sandwich is quickly submerged in a mixture of egg and a small amount of milk beaten together as for French toast. The dipped sandwich is cooked in a frying pan, on a griddle, or in a waffle iron; it can also be cooked in a wire basket in deep fat.

Hot roasted meat sandwiches are prepared open-faced. Split rolls, buns, or slices of bread are placed on a plate, layered with thin slices of roast meat, and covered with a hot flavorful meat gravy. Leftover roasted meat may be used in these sandwiches if it is warmed by steaming. Meat should be thinly sliced across the grain so that it will be easy to chew. Variations include creamed meats, such as tuna, chicken, turkey or dried beef, or cheese sauce. The bread may be toasted if desired. A Sloppy Joe sandwich is a hot meat mixture, with or without beans, in a tomato sauce, usually served on a hot hamburger bun. Figure 26.2 shows a pizza sandwich.

Sliced cheese can be placed on a slice of bread or split bun and toasted under the broiler unit until it melts. Alternately, hard cheese can be grated and combined with crisply fried bacon pieces and a small amount of mayonnaise, and then spread on bread or a bun and broiled until it is bubbly.

Figure 26.2

A long loaf of French bread sliced in half is the base for this chili-flavored pizza sandwich. The filling is made of textured vegetable protein combined with cooked, crumbled ground beef and topped with sliced tomatoes and grated cheese before baking. *(Thomas J. Lipton, Inc.)*

All hot sandwiches must be prepared immediately before they are served. If they are prepared too far ahead of time, they become soggy, tough, and cold. For heating sandwiches that do not require toasting, a microwave oven works very well. Wrapped in plastic wrap, the sandwiches heat in a microwave oven without drying out.

Pocket bread, or pita bread, is a thin, circular bread that is hollow in the center. It is increasingly popular for sandwiches.

Canapés

Canapés are small, open-faced, decorative sandwiches that can be eaten in one or two bites. They are usually served at tea parties, at cocktail parties, or as appetizers preceding a dinner.

INGREDIENTS   Like sandwiches, canapés are composed of several parts: base, spread, filling, and garnish.

Canapé Bases   Breads for canapés are often more unusual than those used for sandwiches. Nut breads, spicy loaves, herb breads, cheese breads, and breads made of special grains, such as corn, cracked wheat, oatmeal, rye, and potato, each contributes its own character as the base for a canapé. Breads for canapés should be firm, not crumbly; thin-sliced day-old bread is usually best for this purpose. Purchase an unsliced loaf and cut it lengthwise into slices about ⅓-inch thick for greatest economy.

Crackers and chips may also serve as canapé bases if they do not crumble too readily. Additionally, a crisp pastry made of dough seasoned with cheese, nuts, herbs, or small seeds can be baked into various shapes. A rosette iron can make small cups of thin crisp pastry. Tiny, bite-sized cream puff shells can also be used.

Spreads   Spreads for sandwiches can also be used for canapés. However, not all canapés need a spread in addition to the filling. A spread is desirable with a moist filling, to keep the canapé base from becoming soggy. Bread slices are easier to spread before they are cut into shapes.

Fillings or Toppings   Some type of protein food often serves as the topping for canapés. As with sandwich fillings, meat, cheese, or egg may be sliced or ground and combined with other ingredients. Canapé bases are often cut into irregular shapes that are difficult to spread evenly with ground meat or cheese mixtures. To avoid this problem, mound a small spoonful of the mixture on the center of the base instead of trying to spread it to all of the edges.

Garnishes   Because canapés are meant to be decorative, the garnish is a very important feature; it should blend in flavor, as well as in color and texture, with the other parts of the canapé. Table 26.2 provides some ideas for garnishes, illustrated in Figure 26.3.

Frequently, a large number of canapés must be prepared at one time. As in other forms of food preparation, the assembly-line technique is useful. Have all the ingredients ready, before assembling; then carry out one operation on all the canapés before proceeding to the next step. When trying a recipe for the first time, make one or two complete canapés before beginning the assembly-line procedure, to determine the best techniques and arrangement of fillings and garnishes.

PREPARING CANAPÉS

Table 26.2   Suggested garnishes for canapés

Slices, strips, or grated raw or cooked vegetables	carrots, radishes, cucumbers, green and red peppers, celery, parsley, watercress, mint, mushrooms, cherry tomatoes, chives, green onions
Slices or sections of fruit	Mandarin oranges; fresh or candied limes, lemons, or oranges; maraschino or candied cherries, grapes, melons, pineapples
Slices or wedges of condiments	pickles, olives, pimientos, cocktail onions, relishes
Slices, strips, or grated protein foods	hard-cooked eggs, cheeses, crisp fried bacon, salami, cocktail wieners
Small whole or pieces of fish	shrimp, sardines, anchovies

Figure 26.3

These canapés are garnished with strips of pimiento and green pepper and slices of radish, olive, and green onion. A cluster of raw cauliflower and parsley adds a decorative touch to the tray.

Bread cuts easily into various shapes if it has been chilled well or partially frozen and if sharp cutters or knives are used (Figure 26.4). Ragged edges can be trimmed smooth with kitchen shears. Bread bases can be cut in advance and stored in a tightly closed plastic bag in the refrigerator or freezer.

Bread bases for canapés should be toasted on at least one side, a process best that is done in a lightly oiled frying pan or griddle (Figure 26.5). If a bread base has been toasted only on one side, place the filling and spreads on the untoasted side. Crackers should be crisp when they are spread; do not use with moist fillings, which soak into the crackers. A cracker is least likely to become soggy if it is not spread with filling until immediately before serving time.

Figure 26.4

To prepare bread for canapés, cut the crusts from bread that has been sliced lengthwise, then flatten the slices with a rolling pin before cutting them into shapes.

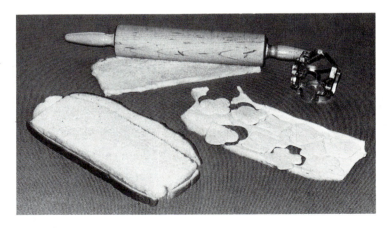

Toast the canapé bases on one side before spreading them with filling. Use a pastry bag with a suitable tip to distribute a seasoned mixture of softened cream cheese and mayonnaise on the untoasted side of the canapé base.

Rolled and ribbon sandwiches are not canapés but may be substituted or served together with canapés. Unlike canapés, rolled sandwiches use a very fresh, fine-grain, thin-sliced bread. Remove the crust from the bread slices, spread them with a soft filling, then roll them up like a jelly roll. Secure each roll with a food pick, wrap them in plastic wrap to prevent drying, and chill them for several hours to set the shape (Figures 26.6–26.9). Just before serving, cut the rolls into slices about ⅓-inch thick and garnish as desired. The bread can be well chilled or partially frozen for the spreading process, but it should be warm and flexible in order to roll easily.

ROLLED AND RIBBON SANDWICHES

Figure 26.6

Use bread sliced lengthwise to prepare rolled tea sandwiches. Trim off the crusts and flatten the bread with a rolling pin, as in making canapés, before placing the spread and filling on the slice. Place stuffed olives at the end at which rolling is to begin. *(Best Foods, Division of CPC International, Inc.)*

Figure 26.7

Roll the bread and filling tightly around the olives; wrap the roll in waxed paper or plastic wrap and chill well. *(Best Foods, Division of CPC International, Inc.)*

Figure 26.8

Slice chilled sandwich rolls with a sharp knife to form tea sandwiches. *(Best Foods, Division of CPC International, Inc.)*

Figure 26.9

Rolled tea sandwiches are an attractive treat served with punch. *(Best Foods, Division of CPC International, Inc.)*

Ribbon sandwiches are attractive when several kinds of bread, such as white and whole wheat, are combined. Ribbon sandwiches contain three slices of bread separated by two sections of filling, making a triple-decker sandwich. The prepared sandwich is wrapped, chilled, and sliced to form layered bars, squares, or triangular tea sandwiches.

Fillings for rolled and ribbon sandwiches are often made of seasoned cream cheese mixed with finely divided nuts, seeds, or crisp bacon bits for texture; or of grated tuna mixed with crisp celery bits.

SANDWICH LOAVES A sandwich loaf is prepared in the same way as a ribbon sandwich, with the following exception: it requires an unsliced loaf sliced lengthwise into six slices, thus providing enough bread for two sandwich loaves with three slices apiece. After the filling has been placed on the bread, the loaf is iced with softened, seasoned cream cheese, garnished, and served as it is. Alternatively, the loaf can be cut into individual portions that are iced separately. Either way, it should be chilled well and kept chilled until it is served. Sandwich loaves are more often served at luncheons than at teas.

STORING CANAPÉS Most canapés can be held in the refrigerator for several hours if they have been covered with plastic wrap to prevent drying; certain garnishes, however, are better withheld until serving time because they deteriorate quickly. Some canapés, depending on their ingredients, can be frozen and held for several weeks. Mayonnaise, hard-cooked eggs, raw vegetables, cream cheese, and cottage cheese do not freeze well, as previously mentioned. Additionally, loss of crispness may occur during freezing. Experiment with canapé combinations to determine which survives the freezing process most successfully. Some bases and fillings should be frozen separately, then combined just before they are served.

Hors d'Oeuvres

Appetizers are canapés and *hors d'oeuvres*. Hors d'oeuvres do not contain breadstuff, but bread may sometimes be eaten with one. Hors d'oeuvres include pickles, olives, nuts, chips, dips, fruit or vegetable tidbits, deviled eggs, stuffed celery, stuffed or pickled mushrooms, smoked, pickled, or barbecued tidbits of meat and fish, various cheeses, or any other small piece of seasoned food.

KABOBS

Kabobs are small pieces of food skewered on food picks or skewers. Foods suitable for kabobs include fruits, vegetables, meats, and cheese. They are often marinated before being skewered. Kabob foods may be cooked, may require no cooking, or may be cooked after being placed on skewers. A variety of foods—fruits and vegetables alternated with meats or cheeses, for example—are customarily skewered together. However, foods in these combinations should be ones that can be handled in the same way such as all being capable of being eaten raw, or all requiring broiling. Figure 26.10 shows fruit kabobs anchored in a large grapefruit.

Figure 26.10
These kabobs, anchored in a fresh grapefruit and garnished with fragrant jasmine, contain a variety of fresh fruits.

FONDUES   Cheese fondues, as described in Chapter 18, are cheese sauces that are kept warm, but not overheated, in a chafing dish. Various foods—bite-sized chunks of crusty French bread, flowerets of raw cauliflower or broccoli, or bite-sized chunks of raw zucchini— serve as dipper for the fondue.

Another fondue makes use of a fondue pot of hot oil in which each person cooks his or her own skewered tender beef. The cooked meat can be dipped in spicy sauces before eating (Figure 26.11). The oil in the fondue pot should be maintained at a temperature that will cook the meat in a reasonable period of time, as discussed in Chapter 4.

DIPS   Fondues are in fact a form of dip. *Dips* are mixtures into which other substances are immersed for flavor. Foods for dipping may include any of those mentioned for fondues, as well as all kinds of raw vegetables, fruits, crackers, and chips (Figure 26.12). Cooked chunks of meat or seafood can be dipped in a flavorful sauce. Cakes, cookies, and marshmallows can be used for dessert dips.

Dippers should be small enough to be eaten in one bite. Biting the dipped end of the dipper and then returning the dipper to the dip is not hygienic. The use of small dippers discourages this practice. Some dippers, such as the stems of broccoli or cauliflower flowerets, have natural handles. Others need to be pierced and lifted with a food pick or fondue fork, preferably the former;

Figure 26.11

Batter-dipped clams fried in a fondue pot make unusual dippers for spicy dill or mustard dips. *(Planters Peanut Oil)*

a clean food pick should be used for each piece of food dipped. For a unique serving method, insert food picks, with a dipper on one end, into a head of cabbage, a whole grapefruit, or a ball of cheese.

Dips are similar in many ways to canapé fillings. They need, however, to be fluid enough to allow for easy dipping, but not so fluid that they drip excessively. Sour cream and cream cheese, which are often used as a base for dips because of their firm texture, have a fairly high caloric content. Substitute sour half-and-half for sour cream; combine ricotta and cottage cheeses in a blender with a small amount of yogurt or sour half-and-half to reduce calories.

Seasoning ingredients in dips often need to be finely subdivided, a process that is easily accomplished in a blender. In this way tasty dips can be prepared from finely divided meats, seafoods, cheeses, nuts, and some fruits. Some ingredients should not be mixed in a blender because blending liquefies them excessively; this is true of yogurt, avocado, and pineapple.

Dips and dippers can be prepared ahead of time more easily than canapés. Raw vegetable dippers can be stored in plastic bags in the refrigerator; many can be prepared as much as a day ahead of use. Cooked meats also can be prepared in advance, but they should be kept clean and cold to prevent bacterial growth. Some fruits, such as fresh pineapple or melon, can be prepared in advance; those that tend to turn brown should be dipped in an acidic juice to inhibit enzymatic browning. Most dips can be stored in covered containers in the refrigerator. Fresh vegetables, such as minced watercress or sliced green onion tops, should be added to a dip immediately before serving time.

Serving Appetizers   The choice of appetizers depends on the occasion. Today the custom is to serve only two or three kinds of appetizers in ample amounts, a practice that greatly simplifies preparation in an era when labor is at a premium. Another popular method of serving provides a variety of ingredients for each guest to construct his or her own appetizers. Fruit, nuts, cheese, and crackers are always popular for appetizers and snacks (Figure 26.13).

For any occasion, appetizers should be attractive, easy to eat, and delicious. Appetizers served to people who are not seated at a table should be simple in form and arranged in such a way that they handle easily. Sturdy plates on which a beverage glass and a few appetizer selections can be placed are often a practical measure. Appetizers that are served as the first course of a seated meal can be more elaborate.

Appetizers can turn an ordinary meal into a special occasion. However, appetizers served before a meal should not detract from the meal but should stimulate the appetite. Appetizers therefore ought not be too rich in calories or too heavily seasoned. Foods served in the main part of the meal should not be used in the appetizers; chicken-filled canapés are inappropriate if chicken is to be the entrée.

Figure 26.13

Fresh fruits, cheese, and crackers are a delicious and nutritious snack that is easy to prepare. *(United Fresh Fruit and Vegetable Association)*

Like many other foods, the nutrients in sandwiches and appetizers will depend on the ingredients used to prepare them. One of the biggest problems with these foods is that they often carry excessive calories. Nutrients can be increased by using whole grain breads and crackers and by the ample use of fruits and vegetables. Calories can be reduced by the use of low-fat cheeses in place of the higher fat counterparts, by using spreads that are low in fat or that are fat-free, such as mustard, pickle relish, or catsup. An awareness of the caloric and nutrient contributions of the foods used can help immeasurably in providing good nutrition in sandwiches and appetizers.

Nutritional Value of Sandwiches and Appetizers

Study Questions

1. What is the purpose of spread on bread for sandwiches. What are some common spreads?
2. What is the fastest way to make many sandwiches at one time?
3. Name some different types of hot sandwiches.
4. What is a canapé?
5. What foods serve as bases for canapés?
6. Why should dippers for dips be small?
7. How should canapés be stored when they are prepared several hours in advance of serving?
8. How can the caloric content of dips prepared from sour cream and cream cheese be reduced?

References

West, Bessie B.; Shugart, G. S.; Wilson, M. F. *Food for Fifty.* 6th ed. New York: Wiley, 1979.

Sugar Solutions, Candy, and Frostings

The composition of sucrose and other sugars is discussed in Chapter 1. Sucrose is the sugar that is most often used in food preparation. Making candies and frostings requires some background knowledge of the function of sucrose and other sugars in these mixtures.

Sucrose, a disaccharide, can be hydrolyzed into the monosaccharides fructose and glucose if the acidic sucrose solution is heated. A molecule of water is added to the fructose and glucose molecules when the bond between these two sugars is broken. In chemistry, this process is known as *hydrolysis;* in candy making, the same process is known as *inversion.* When sucrose is hydrolyzed, or inverted, equal amounts of glucose and fructose are formed. This mixture of equal amounts of fructose and glucose is called *invert sugar.*

Dry sucrose heated to 320°F (160°C) becomes liquid or molten and in this form is called *barley sugar.* If it is heated to 338°F (170°C), the sucrose starts to decompose, gives off water, and forms other compounds including acids. The new mixture of compounds is known as *caramelized sugar;* the process of heating sucrose to this temperature is called *caramelization.* Caramelized sugar is brown in color and has a definite odor and flavor, with overtones of bitterness. The higher the temperature to which the sucrose is heated, the more extensive the caramelization becomes. Caramelization is inhibited in acidic media and promoted in alkaline media.

Other sugars that occur naturally in foods were listed in Table 1.3 together with their principal sources. Sugars vary in sweetness and solubility. In order of sweetest to least sweet, they are: fructose, sucrose, glucose, maltose, and lactose. Table 27.1 gives the amounts, as well as caloric values, of various sweeteners required

Sugars
HYDROLYSIS OF SUCROSE

CARAMELIZATION OF SUCROSE

OTHER SUGARS

Table 27.1   Sweetness equivalents and calorie content of sweeteners

Sweetener	Amount to yield equivalent sweetness	Calories
Table sugar (sucrose)	1 cup	751
Honey	¾ cup	770
Molasses	1½ cup	1050
Maple syrup	1½ cup	1050
Corn syrup	1½ cup	1250
Brown sugar	1⅛ cup	900
Fruit sugar (fructose)	9 tablespoons	430
Sorbitol	13 ounces	1230
Saccharin tablets (¼ grain)	48 tablets	0

to furnish the same amount of sweetening as a cup of sucrose. The solubility of the sugars closely parallels their sweetness; fructose is the most soluble, lactose the least soluble.

Solutions

A *solution* is a mixture of substances in which one substance is dissolved in the other to form a completely homogeneous mixture. Solutions have two parts, the *solvent* and *solute*. The solute is the substance dissolved; the solvent is the substance in which the solute is dissolved. In a sugar solution, sugar is the solute and water is the solvent. In many solutions it is impossible to distinguish between the solute and the solvent. Vinegar, which is 5 percent acetic acid mixed in water, is an example of a solution that shows this effect.

Not all mixtures of two or more liquids form solutions. Oil and water do not form a homogeneous mixture and therefore cannot form a solution. A solution can be formed between salt and water, but no solution can be formed between sand and water.

SOLUTES IN SOLUTIONS

The solute in solutions can exist either as molecules or ions, and solutions can be molecular solutions, ionic solutions, or combinations of these two, depending on the nature of the solute. Sucrose is a molecule and thus forms a molecular solution when it dissolves in water. Table salt, or sodium chloride (NaCl), *ionizes* when it is mixed in water; that is, it divides into sodium ions (Na^+) and chloride ions (Cl^-) and therefore forms ionic solutions. Tap water is an ionic solution because it contains ions of calcium (Ca^{++}), magnesium (Mg^+), chlorine (Cl^-), and others.

UNSATURATED, SATURATED, AND SUPERSATURATED SOLUTIONS

Solutes vary in their solubility in specific solvents. Sugar can be stirred into a given amount of water until it dissolves. If more sugar is added and stirred in, eventually the added sugar will not dissolve, but will settle to the bottom when the stirring stops. Heating this solution, however, dissolves the undissolved sugar. If lactose rather than sucrose were the solute, much less would dissolve. If alcohol in place of water were the solvent, practically none of either sugar would dissolve. Thus, the amount of solute that dissolves depends on the nature of the solute, the nature of the solvent, and the temperature. Generally, the higher the temperature is, the more solute can be dissolved in a given amount of solvent.

An *unsaturated solution* is one in which more solute is capable of being dissolved at a given temperature. A *saturated solution* is one in which no more solute can be dissolved at a given temperature. A *supersaturated solution* has more solute in solution than it would normally hold in solution at a given temperature. A supersaturated solution is unstable, because the amount of solute in excess of that needed to form a saturated solution is capable of crystallizing out of solution.

Formation of a supersaturated solution is an important process in candy making. The only way to form a supersaturated solution is by heating a saturated solution and allowing it to cool in such a way that the solute does not crystallize out. Ways of accomplishing this effect are discussed in the section on candies.

The boiling point of water is defined in Chapter 3. Water molecules have an attraction for each other that helps keep them in the liquid phase and inhibits their changing to vapor. Water molecules are also in constant motion. Heating increases the motion of the molecules and lessens the attraction between them, allowing more of the water molecules to change into vapor. Higher temperatures cause more molecules to change to vapor, increasing the vapor pressure in the water until the vapor rises and breaks through the top surface of the water. At this point, water is said to be *boiling,* and the bubbles that break through the top surface of the water are water vapor.

When solute is dissolved in water, water molecules show a greater attraction for the ions or molecules of solute than they show for each other. More heat is needed to overcome the attraction between solute and water molecules than is needed to overcome the attraction between water molecules alone. Thus, the boiling temperature of a solution is greater than the boiling temperature of water. The more solute present in the solution, the higher the boiling point of the solution becomes; thus the number of ions or molecules of solute dissolved in a given amount of solvent determines the boiling point.

It is impossible to count the number of molecules of sucrose in a cup of sugar or of any other substance. Sucrose is made up of atoms of carbon, hydrogen, and oxygen, and each atom has an atomic weight. By adding together the atomic weight of all of the atoms in sucrose, the weight of a molecule of sucrose, known as *molecular weight,* can be determined. By expressing molecular weight in grams it is possible to compare the number of molecules of one substance with another. A *mole* is the molecular weight of a substance expressed in grams. Thus, 1 mole of sucrose weighs 342 grams. Similarly, 1 mole of sodium chloride is the weight in grams of the atomic weights of sodium (23) and chlorine (35), or 58 grams.

The amount of solute in a solution can be calculated from the boiling point of the solution. More often, however, the boiling point of the solution is used to determine when the desired concentration of solute has been obtained, for the following reason: each mole of solute per liter of water raises the boiling point by 0.94°F (0.52°C). If 342 grams of sucrose are dissolved in 1 liter of water, the temperature of the boiling point of the solution will be 212.9°F (100.52°C). If 2 moles, or 684 grams, of sucrose are dissolved in 1 liter of water, the solution boils at 213.9°F (101.04°C).

EFFECT OF SOLUTES ON
THE BOILING POINTS
OF SOLUTIONS

Candies In most candy-making processes, sucrose solutions are boiled until enough water evaporates to give them the sugar concentration that yields a candy of the desired consistency. Other ingredients in candy mixtures influence its consistency as well as contribute flavor and color.

CONCENTRATION OF SUGAR SOLUTIONS Producing the concentration of sugar that gives a candy the desired consistency is often the biggest problem in making candies. Two accepted methods are used to determine the concentration of sugar syrup: the temperature of the syrup at its boiling point and the consistency of a small sample of syrup tested in cold water. Because both testing methods have advantages and disadvantages, they are often used together.

Temperature To obtain an accurate reading of the temperature of sugar syrup, the following precautions must be followed:

1. The syrup must be boiling when the temperature is measured.
2. The bulb of the thermometer should be submerged in the syrup, but should not touch the sides or bottom of the pan.
3. When making the reading, the eye should be level with the top of the mercury on the thermometer.

An accurate thermometer is a necessity: test it in boiling water.

Hydrolysis of the sucrose in the syrup can also affect its boiling point and cause a false determination of its concentration. One mole of sucrose, hydrolyzed, forms 2 moles of sugars, 1 mole of glucose and 1 mole of fructose. With no loss of water by evaporation, the temperature of the boiling point is increased by 0.94°F (0.52°C) simply by inversion of the sucrose. This change can affect the consistency of candy syrups if the mixture contains an ingredient that contributes acidity, such as cream of tartar, any type of fruit or fruit juice, brown sugar, honey, or molasses. The effect is greater if the concentration process is slow, that is, if the syrup is boiled over low heat so that excess water evaporates slowly: This difference can be demonstrated by preparing two identical batches of candy containing an acid ingredient, each cooked to exactly the same temperature, but one cooked over low heat and the other over high heat. The syrup that is cooked over low heat will be softer than the one cooked over high heat.

Consistency of Cooked Syrup Because inversion of sucrose can cause a misleading endpoint determination, the use of a cold-water test along with the measurement of temperature is often recommended. Table 27.2, which shows the relationship of boiling point temperature to syrup consistency when the syrup is tested in cold water, indicates the syrup consistency of specific candies.

Table 27.2   The relationship of boiling points of syrups to subjective tests for consistency

Boiling point range		Test characteristics	Use
(°F)	(°C)		
230–234	110–112	Syrup spins a 2-inch thread poured from a spoon; does not form a ball in ice water	Syrups
235–240	113–115	A portion of syrup tested in ice water forms a *soft ball*	Fudge, fondant, panocha
244–248	118–120	A portion of syrup tested in ice water forms a *firm ball*	Caramel
250–266	121–130	A portion of syrup tested in ice water forms a *hard ball* that is plastic	Nougat, taffy, divinity, popcorn balls
270–290	132–143	A portion of syrup tested in ice water separates into threads that are not brittle (also called *soft crack*)	Taffy, butterscotch
300–310	149–154	A portion of syrup tested in ice water separates into hard, brittle threads (also called *hard crack*)	Brittle, glacé
320	160	Melted sugar turns light amber in color (barley sugar)	
338	170	Melted sugar turns brown in color (caramelized sugar)	

To make a cold-water test, drop a few drops of syrup into a small amount of cold water and work them with a finger to form a ball or threads. There are, however, several problems with this test. Cold water can vary in temperature and therefore affect the consistency of the syrup; ice water is often called for because it is more likely to be approximately the same temperature with repeated tests. Moreover, one person's judgment of the consistency of the ball of syrup in cold water may be different from another's; what one person identifies as a soft ball, another may call a firm ball. Cold-water tests are also not specific for a single temperature, but apply over a range of temperatures that could make the difference between a soft or brittle fudge or fondant.

The cold-water test need not be used until the syrup is within 5°F of the endpoint temperature. When making the test, remove the syrup from the heat. If the test produces a ball softer than that desired, return the pan to the heat. If it produces too hard a ball, add 1 or 2 teaspoons of water, return the syrup to a boil, and retest; additional water can be added if it is needed. Avoid letting very concentrated syrups sit off the heat for too long a time while they are being tested, because they may solidify in the pan.

Crystalline candies contain sucrose crystals. Fondant, fudge, panocha, divinity, creams, and nougats are crystalline candies. The difference in size of crystals in candies is most readily distin-

CRYSTALLINE CANDIES

guished by the tongue. Desirable crystalline candies have extremely small, almost imperceptible crystals that quickly melt when a small amount is placed on the tongue.

Obtaining a crystalline candy with these characteristics requires that certain conditions be fulfilled: the sucrose must be completely dissolved, and the syrup must be cooked to the correct concentration and then supersaturated before being rapidly beaten to bring about crystallization.

Obtaining Complete Solution Sucrose must be completely dissolved in water so that no crystals remain to seed the cooked syrup and cause premature crystallization. Complete solution is achieved by covering the pot when heating first begins so that the steam formed will condense and wash down any crystals adhering to the sides of the pan.

Obtaining Desired Concentration Boil the sucrose solution as rapidly as possible in an open pan to evaporate excess water. If only sucrose and water are present, the syrup does not require stirring once the sugar is dissolved. If milk, chocolate, and other substances are in the mixture, however, stirring is necessary to prevent scorching; more moderate heat may also be needed. Syrup that spatters the sides of the pan can lose water and form crystals, which must be removed with a fork wrapped in damp, not wet, cheesecloth.

Placing a small pan on a large gas burner may permit the flames to extend up the sides of the pan and scorch the sugar solution on the sides of the pan. Reducing the flame, on the other hand, may result in slow cooking and excessive hydrolysis of the sucrose as previously mentioned. The temperature of the syrup must be checked and compared to the consistency of the syrup in ice water.

Obtaining a Supersaturated Solution A supersaturated syrup is necessary to produce small crystals in candy. As the syrup cools and becomes more supersaturated, it also becomes more viscous, an effect that favors formation of many small nuclei when crystallization finally begins. If crystallization begins in hot syrup, fewer and larger crystals are formed.

The hot syrup, which is a saturated solution at the time heating ends, must be allowed to cool with no formation of crystals. The process of supersaturation requires, first, that the syrup not be seeded either with crystals from the side of the pan or with dust or lint, and second, that the syrup not be agitated. All of these factors—crystals, lint, dust, and agitation—can trigger crystallization.

Interfering substances in the sugar solution also promote supersaturation by inhibiting the formation of crystals in several ways. Because they have a different crystalline structure than sucrose, foreign sugars interfere with sucrose crystals growing on each other. Foreign sugars commonly used in candy making include fructose, glucose, maltose, and lactose. Fructose and glucose may be incorporated in the sugar solution in the form of honey or invert sugar. Lactose is provided by any kind of milk, maltose and glucose from corn syrup. Inverting sucrose with an acid ingredient provides another source of fructose and glucose.

Fat and protein added to candy mixtures also inhibit crystallization by coating the crystal faces, thereby interfering with crystal growth. Butter, cream, milk, chocolate, and cocoa all contribute fat. Sources of protein in candy include milk, cream, egg white, and gelatin. Some of these ingredients also increase the viscosity of the syrup, promoting small crystal formation.

Fudge and panocha are usually allowed to cool in the pan in which they were cooked, but fondant should be poured from the pan onto a marble slab or a lightly greased plate to cool. The syrup should be cooled to 104 to 122°F (40 to 50°C) to obtain a sufficiently supersaturated solution for fine crystal formation.

Effect of Rapid Agitation   Once a supersaturated solution is obtained, the viscous syrup must be beaten rapidly to produce small crystals. Undisturbed cooling causes very large crystals to grow in the syrup. Rapid agitation, in contrast, causes many small crystal nuclei to form. Beating should be continuous until crystallization begins. Crystallization produces heat and causes the syrup to become soft and warm. At this point, the candy mixture should be poured into a container to harden undisturbed.

Beating continued past the point of crystallization turns such firm candies as fudge into a mass of lumps and crumbles as crystallization is completed. Premature crystallization can sometimes be reversed if the container of fudge is warmed enough to soften the fudge so that it can be remolded. Crumbling or lumping often occurs after cooking the fudge to too high a temperature, which causes the syrup to become overly concentrated.

After premature crystallization, the greatest problem in candy making is insufficient crystallization, which causes the syrup to remain soft, sticky, or even fluid. This effect is caused by a syrup that is not concentrated enough because it was not cooked to a high enough temperature. Excessive inversion of sucrose can also cause insufficient crystallization in candy mixtures that contain acidic ingredients.

Fondant   All the information previously given about crystalline candies also applies to fondant. The color of fondant depends on the type of water used, the presence of other ingredients, and the acidity of the mixture. Fondant made with hard water is cream-colored, but if it contains corn syrup, it turns gray. Fondant made

TYPES OF CRYSTALLINE CANDIES

with hard water is bright white if an acidic ingredient is also present. If corn syrup is the source of foreign sugar in a fondant mixture, distilled water should be used to prevent a gray color from developing. Tiny air bubbles incorporated into the fondant during agitation give it an opaque appearance; unbeaten fondant is translucent.

Fudge Brown sugar in fudge provides a small amount of acid that in turn produces a small amount of sucrose inversion to delay crystallization; white sugar may also be used, but no inversion occurs. Water, milk, or half-and-half are liquids used in making fudge. The fat and protein in milk and cream delay crystallization and improve the flavor of the fudge as well. Baker's chocolate or cocoa may be used in fudge; chocolate has a higher fat content that provides more interference with crystallization than cocoa. Syrup containing cocoa should be cooked to a slightly lower endpoint temperature than syrup containing baker's chocolate.

Panocha Panocha is very much like fudge, except that it contains no chocolate or cocoa and is always made with brown sugar and milk or half-and-half. The syrup for fudge and panocha alike should be cooked as rapidly as possible when brown sugar is present to prevent excessive inversion of the sucrose. Remember that milk or cream in these mixtures is more likely to scorch than the water in a fondant. Fudge and panocha should be stirred constantly during concentration; a flat wooden paddle that scrapes the bottom of the pan is best for this purpose.

Divinity Divinity syrup must be cooked to a higher temperature than fondant and fudge syrups to obtain the correct sugar concentration because it is diluted with water from egg white after it is cooked. Hot syrup is beaten into an egg white foam until the candy starts to crystallize. Because this candy is beaten hot, it would form large crystals except that the corn syrup used in the syrup and protein from the egg white prevent premature crystallization. The act of beating deposits the syrup into the films of liquid around the air bubbles in the egg white foam. The syrup crystallizes in these films, which provides the divinity with a solid, aerated texture. A whiter divinity is obtained if distilled water is used to make the syrup.

NONCRYSTALLINE CANDIES Noncrystalline candies are also known as *amorphous candies* because they do not contain crystals. Such candies either contain large amounts of interfering agents that inhibit crystallization, or they have been cooked until they reach such a high temperature that the concentrated syrup is too viscous for crystals to orient themselves.

Caramel Caramels contain brown sugar, a large amount of dark corn syrup, and a high concentration of milk solids, all of which inhibit crystallization. Thus, syrup for caramels is concentrated only a little more than syrups for crystalline candies. Because a caramel mixture has a great tendency to scorch and burn, it should be cooked with moderate heat and constant stirring. Some advantage is gained by adding only part of the milk at the beginning of cooking and the remainder later. Because of the acidity of the other ingredients, the milk curdles if it is added all at once at the beginning of cooking. Long, slow cooking helps develop the characteristic caramel flavor of the candy (Figure 27.1). Toffee is very much like caramel, except that its syrup is more concentrated to yield a firmer candy.

Taffy Taffy is pulled candy that usually contains an acid ingredient to invert sucrose and inhibit crystallization. Taffy syrup is cooked to a higher temperature than caramel syrup, but the endpoint temperature depends on the ingredients. If the cooking period is too long, excessive inversion of sucrose can make the taffy too soft to be pulled after it is cooked to the designated temperature. In the early stages of concentration, the syrup should be cooked with as high a heat as possible; in the later stages, the heat should be lowered to keep the syrup from scorching as it becomes more concentrated. If the cooled taffy is too sticky to pull, either because of excessive sucrose inversion or because it

Figure 27.1

Many kinds of candies can be prepared from a basic caramel recipe by rolling the pieces in chopped nuts, coconut, or chocolate candies. *(C and H Sugar Company)*

was not concentrated enough to begin with, it can be returned to the pan and cooked to a higher temperature. Use the ice water to test it for its pulling characteristics.

Brittles   Peanut brittle is the most common of the brittles. Its sugar syrup is cooked to a temperature that is high enough to cause the sucrose to caramelize. Baking soda (sodium bicarbonate), added to the cooked syrup as soon as the desired temperature has been reached, combines with the acid produced by caramelization of the sugar to form carbon dioxide gas, which aerates the candy and gives it a porous structure. Without the addition of baking soda, syrups cooked to such a high temperature would be glassy and hard.

Hard Candies   Hard candies are produced commercially by a vacuum process during the concentration of the syrup, making low temperatures possible for concentrating the syrup and thus preventing caramelization. Hard candies, consequently, can be flavored and colored in ways that are not possible with caramelized sugar.

Gum Candies, Jellies   Gum candies and jellies contain pectin or starch as thickening agents. Marshmallows, like divinity, contain a foam, but the foam is made from gelatin, not egg white. The sucrose in marshmallows does not crystallize as it does in divinity because the gelatin prevents crystallization. Noncrystalline candies that contain a large proportion of invert sugar to inhibit crystallization tend to turn sticky on standing, because fructose in the invert sugar absorbs moisture from the air. These candies should be stored in airtight containers.

Frostings and Fillings

The terms *frosting* and *icing* have the same meaning, a coating or covering spread on such baked products as cakes, sweet breads, and cookies. Frostings add flavor and sweetness, retain moisture, and enhance the appearance of the baked product.

FILLINGS

Fillings are spread between layers of cakes or pastry to add flavor and help retain moisture. Frosting itself can serve as a filling, as can fruit preserves or spreads of a custardlike consistency. However, the filling should not be so moist that it makes the pastry or cake soggy. The flavor of the filling should blend with the flavor of the cake and its frosting.

FROSTINGS

Frostings have a multitude of flavors and consistencies from simple to ornate, cooked to uncooked.

Uncooked Frostings   Most uncooked frostings contain powdered sugar, which tends to lump. Powdered sugar should be sifted before measuring to remove lumps, as described in Chapter 3. The simplest uncooked frosting is powdered sugar sifted over a paper lace doily on the top of a cake. When the doily is removed, its pattern in powdered sugar remains on the surface of the cake.

Ornamental icing is made by combining a large amount of powdered sugar with an egg white foam. Ornamental icing dries into a rigid structure that is good for making cake decorations. Because of the alkalinity of egg whites, this frosting has a grayish color that can be whitened by adding a small amount of blue coloring. However, blue coloring should not be used if the icing is to be tinted another color. Adding a few drops of lemon juice helps keep ornamental icing from becoming sugary by inverting some of the sucrose.

Butter-cream frosting is a mixture of solid fat, powdered sugar, cream, and flavoring. It does not always contain butter as the fat; it can also be made from margarine or hydrogenated shortening. The type of fat used and the ratio of fat to sugar can affect the color, flavor, and consistency of butter-cream frosting. Butter and margarine produce a pale yellow or creamy color that can only be tinted orange, yellow, or chartreuse. For a bright white icing or for an icing that is to be tinted other colors than those just mentioned, hydrogenated shortening must be used. Butter gives the frosting a buttery flavor; artificial butter flavoring can be added to icings made with shortening.

A high proportion of fat to sugar produces a soft, creamy icing that remains soft. A high ratio of sugar to fat produces a dry, firm icing. In warm areas, frosting with a high sugar content holds up better. Cream cheese can be substituted for part of the fat to provide a variation in flavor.

Baked yeast sweet breads and coffee cakes are iced with *flat icings.* To make these icings, mix powdered sugar into water, milk, or light cream to form a spreadable consistency so that the icing can be dribbled or ladled over the baked product. The icing can be heated slightly, if desired. These icings are often brittle, cracking and chipping off the baked product when they have dried. Cream instead of water and the addition of a small amount of honey helps keep the icing soft and prevents cracking.

Cooked Frostings The simplest cooked frosting is *broiled icing.* The frosting is cooked after being spread on the cake; a mixture of table fat, brown sugar, and cream is combined with nuts or coconut, spread on the cake, and broiled until bubbly. Other types of cooked frostings are cooked before they are spread on the cake.

Fudge and divinity cooked frostings call for a sugar syrup made with granulated sugar cooked to a temperature of 232 to 241°F (111 to 116°C). Hot syrup is beaten into an egg white foam to produce a soft, fluffy divinity frosting. Fudge frosting is made the same way as fudge is, except that it is soft for spreading. Both frostings contain corn syrup to inhibit crystallization. Divinity frosting does not form crystals, but fudge frosting does. If the fudge frosting is too thick to spread, thin it with a little cream; if it is too thin, thicken it by adding powdered sugar.

Seven-minute, or *double boiler, frosting* is prepared by combining egg whites, granulated sugar, water, and corn syrup in the top of a double boiler. The mixture is heated above boiling water while being beaten rapidly with a rotary or electric beater until peaks form. During the beating, the mixture should be scraped from the sides of the pan to equalize the temperature. Five to seven minutes of beating are needed to prepare this frosting (Figures 27.2, 27.3).

Another type of cooked frosting combines a thick white sauce with a high fat content together with powdered sugar to produce a smooth, creamy, noncrystalline icing.

Flavoring and Coloring Frostings These basic frostings, both cooked and uncooked, can be varied with artificial flavors, fruit juices or purées, chocolate or cocoa, nuts, coconut, peanut butter, cream cheese, candied fruits, marshmallows, brown sugar, coffee, and other ingredients. However, frostings with an egg foam base collapse if such high-fat content ingredients as chocolate are added to them.

To tint a frosting, first mix a small amount of the color with a spoonful of icing, then gradually add the colored icing to the rest of the icing to obtain the desired intensity of color. As a rule, pale, light colors are more attractive for cake frostings than are dark, intense colors.

Figure 27.2

The consistency of seven-minute or double boiler frosting is similar to that of whipped cream. The cake on the left has been given a crumb coating to bind crumbs before the final coating of frosting is applied.

Figure 27.3

Seven-minute frosting cannot be shaped into decorations. Here it is swirled and slices of unblanched almonds are placed around the sides of the cake for decorative effect.

ICING THE CAKE

To make an iced cake with an even top, layers can be leveled before icing, as shown in Figure 27.4. Keeping crumbs out of the icing is one of the most difficult tasks in frosting a cake. Several procedures can be used to lessen this problem: loose crumbs can be brushed off the cake before it is iced; the cake may be partially or completely frozen first; and, finally, a thin coating of icing can be applied to the cake, which is then chilled before the final coat of icing is applied. The thin coating helps bind loose crumbs and keeps them from getting into the final icing (Figure 27.5).

Figure 27.4

To obtain an iced cake with a flat top, level off the layers before putting them together. Use a long slicing knife or a string to cut the rounded top of the layer level with the sides of the pan.

Figure 27.5

The cake on the right is covered with a crumb coating of butter icing; the cake on the left is given the final coating of frosting, with shell borders added around the base and top edge of the cake.

Decorating the Cake After the cake is frosted, it can be decorated either with flowers and piping made of icing (Figures 27.6, 27.7) or with designs swirled into the icing. Use table knives, spatulas, or forks to form stripes, crisscross lines, circles, or swirls in the icing (Figure 27.8); to make a scalloped design, press the icing with the bowl of a spoon. Additionally, candies, coconut, nuts, candied fruits, or shaved chocolate can be sprinkled or arranged on the surface of the cake to produce a decorative effect. These decorations should be added to the cake as soon as it is iced, so that they will adhere to the frosting.

Figure 27.6

Roses for decorating a cake are shaped on a nail and easily transferred to the cake with a pair of scissors.

Figure 27.7

Steps in shaping a rose using two colors of icing are shown in the center. The rose is shaped on the nail at top left using the petal tube at the upper right. At the lower left is the tube that forms the shell borders; at the lower right is the tube that makes the drop flower to its left.

Figure 27.8

Use a teaspoon to make a pattern on this cake iced with an uncooked butter frosting by striping the spoon in adjacent stripes in one direction and leaving a space between the stripes in the other direction. Make a shell border around the base of the cake by twisting the top of the pastry bag containing icing as shown

Before decorating a cake with flowers or other ornaments made of icing, smooth the icing on the cake with a metal spatula that has been dipped in hot water. Excess water should be shaken off the spatula before the cake is smoothed, and only a small portion of the cake should be smoothed at one time. Avoid keeping the hot spatula too long in one area, or it may melt the frosting.

Either ornamental or butter-cream icings may be used to make flowers and other designs for decorating cakes. It is not necessary to decorate the cake with the same icing that frosted it. Ornamental icing is too stiff to use for frosting a cake; decorations made from it become hard on standing.

Icing for decorating is divided into portions according to the number of colors needed. The colors are mixed evenly into the icing, and each color is placed in a separate pastry bag with the desired tip. Disposable pastry bags or tubes can be made from parchment paper; if the bag becomes worn or a different tip is desired, squeeze the icing into a new bag. The top of the bag can be folded over like a tube of toothpaste to squeeze icing toward the tip; canvas and plastic bags can be twisted at the top to keep icing feeding through the tip. Allow one color of icing to dry a little before placing another color against it, so that the colors and designs do not run into each other.

Study Questions

1. What is a solution? In a sugar solution, what is the solute and what is the solvent?
2. How does temperature affect the solubility of a solute in a solvent?
3. Explain the effect of solute in water on the boiling point of the solution.
4. Discuss the advantages and disadvantages of a thermometer and a cold water test for determining the consistency of a sucrose syrup.
5. What is invert sugar? How is it obtained?
6. How does sucrose inversion affect the temperature of boiling syrup and its consistency when cooled?
7. What are sources of fructose and glucose?
8. Distinguish between a saturated and a supersaturated solution; describe briefly the procedure required to obtain a supersaturated solution.
9. Why must a supersaturated solution be obtained in making crystalline candies?
10. What is an interfering agent? Give some examples of interfering agents and explain how they function.
11. Why must a supersaturated solution be rapidly agitated in making crystalline candies?
12. What factors affect the color of fondants?
13. Name some typical crystalline and noncrystalline candies.
14. How does the type of fat present affect the color and flavor of butter frostings?
15. Why should powdered or confectioner's sugar be sifted before being used?
16. What are some ways to prevent crumbs from getting into the icing when frosting a cake?

References

Charley, Helen. *Food Science.* New York: Ronald Press, 1970.

Lowe, Belle. *Experimental Cookery.* 4th ed. New York: Wiley, 1964.

Mikesh, Verna A., and Nelson, Leona S. "Sugar, Sweets Play Roles in Food Texture and Flavoring." In U.S. Department of Agriculture, *Food for Us All*, Yearbook of Agriculture. Washington, D.C.: Government Printing Office, 1969.

Paul, Pauline C. "Basic Scientific Principles, Sugars, and Browning Reactions." In *Food Theory and Applications*, edited by Pauline C. Paul and Helen H. Palmer. New York: Wiley, 1972.

Pyler, E. J. *Baking: Science and Technology*, vol. 2. Chicago: Siebel Publishing, 1973.

Sweetman, M. D., and MacKellar, Ingeborg. *Food Selection and Preparation.* 4th ed. New York: Wiley, 1964.

28

Frozen Desserts

Frozen desserts are mixtures of ice crystals in a flavored liquid syrup. The most common frozen dessert is ice cream; sherbets, ices, and mousses are variants of ice cream. These frozen mixtures have a crystalline structure that resembles the structure of crystalline candies in many ways. The crystals in frozen desserts, however, are ice crystals. Frozen mixtures are most desirable when their crystals are small so that the mixture feels smooth on the tongue. Both the ingredients used and the method of freezing influence the characteristics of frozen desserts.

Effect of Solutes on the Freezing Point

The presence of solutes in water lowers its freezing point for the same reason that solutes heighten its boiling point. One mole of solute molecules or ions per liter of solution lowers the freezing point 3.35°F (1.86°C) below the freezing point of water (32°F, 0°C). Thus, a solution of 1 mole of sucrose (342 grams) in 1 liter of water would be expected to freeze at 28.65°F (−1.86°C). Because 1 mole of sodium chloride (58 grams) forms 1 mole of sodium ions and 1 mole of chloride ions in solution, it would lower the freezing point twice as much as the mole of sucrose. One mole of sodium chloride dissolved in a liter of water would be expected to freeze at 25.3°F (−3.72°C).

FROZEN DESSERT SOLUTIONS

Mixtures for frozen desserts are solutions. Sugar is added to milk, cream, fruit juices, or fruit purées, which are already solutions with freezing points below the freezing point of water. With the addition of sugar, the freezing point is lowered even further. As the mixture starts to freeze, sugars and other molecules and ions in the solution become more concentrated, so that the freezing point of the remaining unfrozen solution is lower than the initial solution; thus, the freezing point of the mixture decreases progressively.

A substance that lowers the freezing point of a solution must be soluble. As the temperature decreases, however, the solutes become less soluble. The amount of solute that can be added to a solution to decrease the freezing point is therefore limited. In frozen dessert mixtures, the amount of sugar needed to provide desirable sweetness is fully soluble at the freezing temperatures of the solution, except when excess lactose is present. Lactose is a disaccharide of limited solubility. If a high concentration of milk or milk solids is present in a frozen dessert mixture, lactose may precipitate out of solution and give the dessert a sandy or gritty texture. High concentrations of lactose are most likely to be caused by undiluted or partially diluted canned evaporated milk, concentrated fresh milk, or extra nonfat dry milk added to the dessert mixtures. It is not advisable to increase the milk solid content of frozen desserts too much if a smooth texture is desired.

Ices are frozen mixtures of fruit juice, water, and sugar; their sugar content is the highest of all frozen desserts. Sherbets are next highest in sugar; along with the ingredients found in ices, they also contain milk. Ice milk, made with milk, sugar, and added nonfat milk solids, contains slightly less sugar than sherbet. Ice cream contains milk, cream, sugar, and sometimes egg; its sugar content is less than that of ice milk.

In commercial production, special refrigeration systems are used to freeze dessert mixtures. At home, freezing is accomplished in an ice cream freezer, using salt and ice mixtures. Because they all have freezing points less than that of water, these mixtures cannot be frozen with ice alone.

The temperature of ice is lowered when a brine is formed. Rock salt mixed with the crushed ice in the freezer starts to dissolve in the melted ice, forming a brine with a temperature less than that of the ice. As more salt dissolves and more ice melts, the brine becomes more concentrated and the temperature lowers progressively. In freezing frozen dessert mixtures, therefore, you should always be sure to retain the brine in the ice-salt mixture; do not pour it off.

A suitable ratio of rock salt to ice for freezing desserts is 1 part of rock salt to 12 parts of ice by volume, or about ⅓ cup of salt per quart of ice. Rock salt is preferred because granulated salt dissolves too rapidly, cakes without dispersing evenly, and is more costly. If too much rock salt is present, the frozen mixture may harden before enough air has been incorporated into the mixture to produce a good texture. Too little salt either increases the freezing time unduly or never gets the mixture cold enough to freeze.

Ingredients in Frozen Desserts

The ingredients for frozen mixtures are simply water from some source and sugar. Optional ingredients include gelatin, eggs, milk solids, and other emulsifiers and stabilizers that produce frozen mixtures of a particular consistency, texture, and flavor.

WATER

Water is needed for the formation of ice crystals, which are necessary to change the liquid dessert mixture to a solid. Not all the water in frozen desserts is converted into crystals, however, because frozen desserts are mixtures of ice crystals in a flavored liquid syrup. The higher the proportion of crystals to liquid, the firmer the frozen dessert will be. Soft-serve ice cream, for instance, has a lower ratio of crystals to liquid than brick ice cream.

Ices are the only frozen dessert mixtures that use water alone as their liquid. In all other mixtures, water is added in the form of juices, fruit purées, milk, and cream; other substances in these ingredients besides water have specific functions in each frozen dessert. Fruits are often combined with milk or cream in preparing frozen desserts (Figure 28.1).

Figure 28.1

Many fresh fruits are delicious
in frozen desserts, either in
pieces or as purées in sherbets
and creams. *(United Dairy
Industry Association)*

SUGAR   Sugar adds sweetness to a frozen dessert. Because flavors are less
intense at lower temperatures, enough sugar must be added to
sweeten the frozen mixture adequately; the same mixture at
room temperature may taste excessively sweet. Because of the
acidity of fruits, fruit mixtures need more sugar to counteract
acidity. Ices, because they have the highest fruit content, have
the highest sugar content.

Sugar decreases the freezing point of frozen dessert mixtures,
thus interfering with water crystallization. This delay of crystallization causes smaller crystals to form, producing a smoother
texture in the final product. Excessive amounts of sugar, as are
sometimes found in sherbets, can surpass the limits of solubility;
in such cases the sugar crystallizes out of solution and hardens
the sherbet.

Sucrose is the preferred sugar in frozen desserts, but a substitution of 25 percent or less of the sucrose with honey or corn
syrup is also possible. Because of their high content of monosaccharides, both honey and corn syrup lower the freezing point of
the mixture more than sucrose, a circumstance that makes it difficult to obtain a stable frozen mixture.

Cream and milk provide the fat in frozen mixtures. The more fat a frozen dessert contains, the smoother it becomes. Fat interferes with crystal growth by coating ice crystals that are already formed, preventing other crystals from growing on them. Fat also coats the tongue when the dessert is eaten, which keeps the tongue from feeling or sensing the sharpness of the crystals. Fat occupies space that might otherwise be occupied by water, thus limiting the amount of water available for crystal formation. Fat, however, also increases the cost and caloric content of frozen desserts.

Homogenization makes fat more effective as an interfering substance. Commercial ice cream is homogenized, but this is not possible in noncommercial production of frozen desserts. For homemade desserts, homogenized products, such as homogenized cream, concentrated milk, canned evaporated milk, and whole milk, are preferred.

The fat content of commercial frozen desserts is highly variable. Premium quality ice cream has a fat content exceeding 15 percent of the mixture, standard ice cream has 10 to 12 percent fat, ice milk has 7 percent, sherbets have 1 percent, and ices have no fat. *Mellorine,* also known as imitation ice cream, contains the same amount of fat as regular ice cream, but a vegetable fat—usually coconut oil—is used in place of the butterfat; the same substitution is made in imitation ice milk.

FAT

All the other ingredients in frozen dessert mixtures are used to help emulsify the fat, to stabilize the mixture, and thus to improve the texture by keeping crystal size small. Ingredients are also added to give the frozen dessert body, so that it does not melt rapidly in the mouth, and to improve the flavor. Gelatin dissolved in a frozen dessert mixture absorbs or binds water, thus reducing the water available for crystal formation; it also provides body by delaying melting. Egg cooked with the milk or cream, as in a custard, also has these functions. Commercial frozen desserts use vegetable gums to bind water and provide body. Too much gelatin, however, produces a sticky, gummy texture. Egg improves flavor and color; nonfat milk solids bind water. Commercial frozen desserts usually contain emulsifiers, such as mono- and diglycerides. The proteins and lecithin of egg, used in noncommercial desserts, have some emulsifying properties.

STABILIZERS AND EMULSIFIERS

Overrun is the increase in volume of a frozen dessert mixture when it is frozen. Part of the increase in volume results from water expansion during freezing. Most of the overrun, however, results from incorporation of air in the mixture during freezing. Air is needed to make the mixture soft, light, and palatable. The

Overrun in Frozen Desserts

air cells produced in the mixture during freezing interfere with crystal growth. Without air, the mixture is soggy and heavy, with coarse crystals.

Both the ingredients and the agitation of the mixture during freezing are important factors in incorporating air into a frozen dessert. Nonfat milk solids and egg yolk improve air retention, but egg white does not, probably because of its inability to hold air in the presence of fat. Fat decreases air retention. Gelatin may promote air incorporation in nonfat mixtures, such as sherbets and ices.

A frozen dessert mixture is unable to hold air until it has cooled enough for crystal formation to begin. Agitation during the early period of freezing should be moderate or slow, sufficient to equalize the temperature throughout the mixture, but not enough to cause the fat to clump. Once crystallization begins, rapid agitation prevents crystal growth and promotes the development of many small crystals. Agitation should be rapid, vigorous, and continuous as soon as ice crystals begin to form.

Commercial ice creams often have an overrun of 100 percent; their volume doubles during freezing. Noncommercial mixtures usually have a 50 percent overrun; a container filled two-thirds full will be filled to the top when it is frozen. Commercial products are able to achieve greater overrun because of special equipment and techniques and controlled formulas that use stabilizers and emulsifiers. Excessive overrun is not desirable, because it would cause the product to lack body and be too frothy. The amount of overrun in commercial products is limited by law, which requires a specific minimum weight for particular products.

Preparing Frozen Desserts

Hand-cranked or motor-driven ice cream freezers that use mixtures of ice and rock salt may be used to freeze desserts (Figure 28.2). Motor-driven units that fit into the electric freezer storage space of a refrigerator or freezer are also available.

Ice cream is an excellent medium for bacterial growth, especially if it is held for some time after preparation. The container and the paddles should therefore be scalded before each use; only pasteurized milk and cream should be used; and eggs and gelatin should be heated to scalding temperatures. Contamination of the dessert with the ice-salt mixture should be avoided during and after freezing.

The freezing process can be speeded if the dessert mixture is chilled in the freezing container, along with the beaters, in the refrigerator or freezer. The freezing container should be only two-thirds full of the mixture. Place the mixture in the tub of the freezer and arrange the ice and rock salt around it; alternate 1

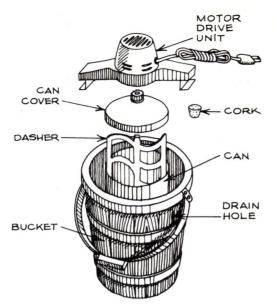

Figure 28.2
This diagram shows the parts of a motor-driven ice cream freezer. A hand-cranked freezer has a handle for turning the dasher.

MOTOR DRIVE UNIT

CAN COVER

CORK

DASHER

CAN

DRAIN HOLE

BUCKET

quart of ice with ⅓ cup of rock salt distributed evenly over the ice, until the ice reaches the top of the freezing container.

Crank the freezer slowly until cranking becomes more difficult, then crank it rapidly until the handle can no longer be turned. Most desserts frozen to this stage are too soft to serve; they must be packed in brine and ice until freezing is completed. Remove the paddles before packing the ice cream, because the paddles are difficult to remove once the dessert has hardened. Before removing the paddles, clean and dry the lid to prevent contamination. Cover the hole in the lid with plastic wrap or aluminum foil so that the dessert mixture does not become contaminated during the packing period. Place more ice and rock salt around the freezing container, ½ cup of rock salt per quart of ice lowers the temperature for faster freezing. Transferring the soft ice cream to a food-storage freezer to finish hardening is an alternate method.

Still-Frozen Desserts

Mousse, the typical still-frozen dessert, is a sweetened, flavored, whipped cream. The cream is whipped to incorporate air before it is frozen. Variations of mousses use whipped evaporated milk, whipped gelatin mixtures, and egg white foams to incorporate air. Some still-frozen desserts are whipped when they are partially frozen. This method is often used with mixtures containing evaporated milk and gelatin.

Table 28.1   Composition of commercial frozen dessert mixtures, 100-gram amounts

Dessert	Water (g)	Calories	Protein (g)	Fat (g)	Carbohydrate (g)	Calcium (g)	Vitamin A (I.U.)	Riboflavin (mg)	Weight per cup (g)
Ice cream:									
10% fat	63.2	193	4.5	10.6	20.8	146	440	0.21	133
12% fat	62.1	207	4.0	12.5	20.6	123	520	0.19	——
16% fat	62.8	222	2.6	16.1	18.0	78	660	0.11	148
Ice milk	66.7	152	4.8	5.1	22.4	156	210	0.22	131
Ices, fruit	66.9	78	0.4	trace	32.6	trace	0	trace	——
Sherbet	67.0	134	0.9	1.2	30.8	16	60	0.03	193

SOURCE: U.S. Department of Agriculture, *Composition of Foods.*

Still-frozen desserts are smoother if they are frozen rapidly, because quick freezing promotes the growth of small crystals. A high sugar content increases the freezing time and is a disadvantage in still-frozen desserts. Set the freezer at its lowest temperature and place the mixture in the coldest part to ensure rapid freezing.

The texture of still-frozen desserts is not as smooth as that of desserts that were agitated during freezing. Still-frozen desserts should be eaten soon after they are prepared because their crystals grow larger with continued storage.

Quality in Frozen Desserts

The quality of ice cream is best judged when it is not too cold; it should scoop readily, but not be mushy. The flavor of ice cream should be pleasantly sweet and natural, leaving a clean aftertaste. The texture should not be brittle or hard, crumbly, sticky, gummy, soggy, or fluffy. A spoonful taken into the mouth should melt smoothly with no undue sensations of cold or residual grittiness. Melted at room temperature, it should leave a smooth, uniform cream.

Nutritional Value of Frozen Desserts

The nutrient content of frozen desserts depends on their ingredients. Most nutrients in frozen desserts are contributed by milk. As Table 28.1 shows, a higher fat content means more calories and vitamin A and less riboflavin, calcium, and protein; the fat-soluble vitamin A is found in the cream portion of milk, while the water-soluble minerals, protein, and B vitamins are in the nonfat part of the milk, as discussed in Chapters 1 and 18. Thus, the presence of milk instead of cream in ice cream increases all nutrients except vitamin A and decreases calories. Eggs and fruit purées add nutrients; increased sugar, as indicated by carbohydrate content, adds no nutrients but does increase calories.

Study Questions

1. Explain how solutions of sugar or table salt dissolved in water affect its freezing point.
2. Distinguish between ice cream, ice milk, sherbet, and ices; how do imitation ice cream and ice milk differ from ice cream?
3. Why is rock salt combined with ice to freeze dessert mixtures?
4. How does the ratio of crystals to liquid affect the consistency of frozen desserts?
5. Briefly describe the functions of sugar and fat in frozen dessert mixtures.
6. Name some stabilizers in frozen dessert mixtures and describe how they function.
7. What is the cause of overrun in frozen dessert; why is it important?
8. How is air incorporated into frozen dessert mixtures?
9. Why must ice cream be packed after it has been frozen in a hand-cranked freezer?
10. What is a mousse?
11. How is air incorporated in still-frozen desserts?
12. How does the proportion of cream to milk affect the nutrient content of frozen desserts?

References

Arbuckle, W. S. *A Microscopic and Statistical Analysis of Texture and Structure of Ice Cream as Affected by Composition, Physical Properties, and Processing Methods.* Columbia, Mo.: University of Missouri, College of Agriculture, Agricultural Experiment Station, 1940.

Consumers Reports Buying Guide Issue, December 1965.

''Ice Cream: Quality Isn't What It Could Be,'' *Consumer Reports* 37 (1972): 495.

Lucas, P. S. ''Common Defects of Ice Cream, Their Causes and Control: A Review.'' *Journal of Dairy Science* 24 (1941): 339.

Palumbo, Mary S. ''Milk and Milk Products.'' In *Food Theory and Applications,* edited by Pauline C. Paul and Helen H. Palmer. New York: Wiley, 1972.

Potter, Norman N. *Food Science.* 2d ed. Westport, Conn.: Avi Publishing, 1973.

Sweetman, M. D., and MacKellar, Ingeborg. *Food Selection and Preparation.* 4th ed. New York: Wiley, 1964.

U.S. Department of Agriculture. *Federal and State Standards for the Composition of Milk Products,* Agricultural Handbook No. 51. Washington, D.C.: Government Printing Office, 1968.

29

Pectin Gels: Jams, Jellies, and Preserves

Gels studied in previous chapters included starch, gelatin, milk, and custard. In all of these, networks or meshes were formed by bonding between chains of molecules, with free water trapped in the meshes to form a solid gel. Each type of gel has slightly different requirements for gel formation; pectin, too, has specific requirements.

Pectin is a polysaccharide that is similar to starch and cellulose. However, the units in the pectin chain are composed of *galacturonic acid*, a derivative of galactose, instead of the glucose found in starch and cellulose chains. Pectin is present to some extent in the cell walls of most plants; many fruits are good sources of pectin.

Pectin exists in green fruits as *protopectin* and is changed by enzyme action to pectin as the fruits mature. Heating green fruits also changes protopectin to pectin. Another enzyme that is active in fruits changes pectin into pectic acid and alcohol. This change occurs as fruits become ripe; overly ripe fruit, therefore, may contain little or no pectin. Boiling fruit juices a long time can also change pectin to pectic acid. Pectic acid does not form gels.

Adequate pectin, sugar, and acid are the three requirements for gel formation. The amount and quality of pectin determines how much sugar the jelly can contain. Too much sugar for the amount of pectin present produces a weak gel or no gel at all; too little sugar makes the jelly rigid and tough. A finished jelly of good quality contains 0.5 to 1 percent pectin and about 65 percent sugar.

Jelly formation is possible only at pH 3.5 or below. The firmness of the gel increases with decreasing pH, but the best acidity for good jelly lies between pH 2.6 and 3.4. At a lower pH, syneresis is likely to occur. Acid in juices affects jelly making in two ways: it hydrolyzes the sucrose and thus inhibits crystallization of the sucrose in the finished jelly or jam during storage. But long boiling of pectin with acid degrades the pectin and weakens its gelling ability.

Acid is needed to neutralize the charges on the pectin molecules; sugar is needed as a dehydrating agent. Together, they cause the pectin molecules to aggregate or coalesce, forming the network in which liquid is trapped. Less sugar is needed to form pectin gels if the acid content is high (low pH); more sugar is required if the acid content is low (high pH).

All fruits contain pectin and acid, but in varying amounts. The quality of pectin from different fruits also varies. Pectin from citrus fruits produces more rigid, less elastic gels than apple pectin. Certain parts of a fruit have a higher pectin count than other parts. The *albedo* of citrus fruits is higher in pectin than the

Chemistry of Pectin and Pectin Gels

GEL FORMATION WITH PECTIN

Sources of Pectin and Acid

juice; the cores and skins of apples and quince are higher in pectin than the flesh. The albedo of citrus fruits is the white part just under the colored skin.

Table 29.1 divides fruits according to their levels of pectin and acid for gel formation. Fruits that are low in pectin and adequate in acid can sometimes be combined with other fruits that are adequate in pectin but low in acid, such as sweet apples with pomegranates or strawberries. Lemon juice can be added to fruits with adequate pectin that are low in acid.

Ripe fruits usually have the richest, fullest flavor, but they are also low both in pectin and acid. Immature fruit supplying pectin and acid can sometimes be mixed with fully ripe fruit for flavor.

COMMERCIAL SOURCES OF PECTIN

Commercial pectin is a by-product of the frozen and canned citrus juice and apple industries. The pulp of sugar beets may someday prove to be an equally good source of pectin. Pectin is available as a liquid and as a powder. Both forms have good gelling ability, although different brands of pectin do vary in their gelling properties.

Commercial pectins can be combined with fruits and fruit juices without concern for the pectin content of the fruit. Fully ripe, full-flavored fruit only needs to be boiled a few minutes if commercial pectin is added, and gels can be prepared from almost any kind of fruit.

Preparing Pectin Gels

Whether or not the gel is to be obtained from the pectin in the fruit itself or from commercial pectin, the fruit must be prepared according to the type of gel being produced. *Jellies* require

---

Table 29.1   Pectin and acid content of various fruits

Adequate pectin + adequate acid	Adequate pectin + low acid	Low pectin + adequate acid	Low pectin + low acid
Tart apples	Sweet apples	Ripe apricots	Ripe figs
Tart blackberries	Unripe bananas	European grapes	Peaches
Tart cherries	Sweet cherries	Huckleberries	Overripe fruit
Crab apples	Unripe figs	Pomegranates	
Cranberries	Pears	Rhubarb	
Currants	Sweet prunes	Strawberries	
Gooseberries	Ripe quince		
Eastern/wild grapes			
Tart guavas			
Lemons, limes			
Loganberries			
Tart oranges			
Tart plums			
Tart quince			
Black and red raspberries			

---

strained juice; *jams* contain pulp, and sometimes the skins, of fruits. *Preserves* contain some pulp and juice, but also include slices of large fruits or, if it is small, the whole fruit. Jellies form a rigid but elastic gel structure. Jams and preserves do not form gels, but are thickened mixtures of fruit or fruit pulp. Fully ripe, flavorful fruit should be used with commercial pectin. However, if only the pectin in the fruit is to provide the gel, then some fruit that is not fully ripe must be used.

All fruits should be washed well and trimmed free of bruises or decayed spots. The stem and flower ends of such fruits as apples, quince, and pears should be trimmed out and discarded, because dust and spray residues, which are likely to accumulate in these areas, are hard to clean out with washing.

PREPARING FRUIT

Extracting Juice for Jelly Coring or peeling fruit from which juice is to be extracted is not a necessary or a recommended procedure, nor must the pits be removed. Large fruits can be coarsely chopped; small fruits can be crushed. The juice of berries can be extracted without heating. Apples and similar fruits are cooked with added water, about 1 cup of water per pound of prepared fruit, for 20 to 25 minutes.

Pour the prepared fruit into a jelly bag or double thickness of cheesecloth in a colander over a bowl. Bring the edges of the cloth or bag together and twist them to squeeze out the juice (Figures 29.1, 29.2), pressing and working the bag with the bowl of a large spoon. When all possible juice has been extracted, discard the pulp remaining in the bag. If berries or grapes have been used with no extra water, add a small amount of water to the pulp, mix it well, and extract juice a second time. However, do not add too much water to extract juice, because it dilutes both the flavor and

Figure 29.1

Prepared fruit is placed in a jelly bag or in several layers of cheesecloth placed in a colander over a bowl to extract juice for making jelly. *(U.S. Department of Agriculture)*

Figure 29.2

The bag or cheesecloth is twisted and pressed with a spoon to extract the juice for jelly. *(U.S. Department of Agriculture)*

the pectin. The first extraction juice can be used for jelly; it will gel, but it will also lack clarity. To produce a clear, shimmering jelly, strain the extracted juice through another double thickness of dampened cheesecloth or through a clean jelly bag without squeezing it excessively. Starch present in immature fruits, such as apple, quince, and pears, produces cloudiness in the extracted juice. Tartaric acid in grapes is poorly soluble and tends to precipitate in the jelly during storage, producing grittiness. Chill the grape juice overnight, as near to the freezing point as possible, and filter off the precipitated crystals of tartaric acid before making jelly with the juice.

Preparing Fruit for Jam   Jam contains fruit pulp as well as juice. Several methods can be used to prepare the fruit, depending on the type of fruit and the equipment available. Soft berries can be crushed. Undesirable seeds and skins of grapes and berries can be removed by crushing the fruit through a food mill. Larger fruits, such as apricots, peaches, and apples, should be pitted or cored, but need not be peeled. Add ½ to 1 cup of water to each pound of fruit and simmer for about 20 minutes, then press the cooked fruit through a food mill. The peeled, cored or pitted fruit can also be mixed in a blender without cooking (Figure 29.3). Adding ascorbic acid prevents enzymatic browning and helps retain the natural colors of fruit, even during long storage.

Figure 29.3

Blend pitted cherries with 1 or 2 tablespoons of water and 1 teaspoon of ascorbic acid to prevent enzymatic browning. Use the blended fruit to make jam or strain the juice for jelly.

Figure 29.4
Mix fruit for preserves, either sliced or whole, with sugar and ascorbic acid powder dissolved in 1 tablespoon of water. Allow the sugar-fruit mixture to sit for several hours.

Preparing Fruit for Preserves   Pit or core and peel the fruit, then slice it in pieces of the desired size and dip them in ascorbic acid solution to prevent browning. To produce a rich flavor in preserves, some of the fruit is sometimes crushed and added to the larger pieces. Other fruits, such as berries and pitted cherries, are used whole (Figure 29.4).

Follow the directions included in the package of commercial pectin—for proportions of fruit, sugar, pectin, and acid and for combining and cooking the mixtures—to make gels with commercial pectin (Figures 29.5, 29.6). Do not increase or decrease these recipes, because such changes alter the amount of water that evaporates during cooking.

**OBTAINING
PECTIN GELS**

Figure 29.5
Add powdered pectin to the fruit pulp before adding the sugar; then cook the mixture for a short time.

Figure 29.6

Add liquid pectin to the sugar-fruit mixture just after boiling the mixture several minutes and just before pouring it into glasses or jars.

Figure 29.7

In the sheet test for jelling characteristics of syrup, two streams of syrup start to flow from a tilted spoon, and then combine to form a sheet.

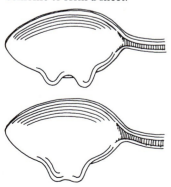

Preparing Jelly with Natural Fruit Pectin   To make jelly, cook only 3 to 4 cups of juice at a time; the amount of sugar needed depends on the pectin and acid content of the fruit. A ratio of 1 cup of sugar per cup of juice can be used with most crab apples, raspberries, currants, gooseberries, and wild grapes. Only ¾ cup of sugar should be used per cup of apples, cranberries, plums, and quinces. Blackberries and concord grapes may require either ratio.

Boil together with sugar and the juice to concentrate the pectin. Because a jelly mixture is a sugar solution, the temperature of the boiling syrup can indicate when the juice is sufficiently concentrated to form a gel. Cook the syrup until its temperature reaches about 8°F (4.4°C) above the boiling point of water, or 220°F (104°C) at sea level. Temperature is not always an accurate indicator, especially if the syrup was concentrated slowly and the juice was quite acid, because such circumstances cause sucrose to invert. The sheeting test can be used to verify the temperature reading. Remove the pan from the heat. With a metal spoon, lift a spoonful of the syrup about 1 foot above the kettle out of the steam. Tilt the spoon so that the syrup runs out the side. If two drops form and flow together, falling off the spoon in one sheet, the jelly is done (Figure 29.7). For another test, set the jelly off the heat and place a small amount on a cold plate in the freezer; if it gels, it is done.

Failure of the test portion to gel may indicate that not enough pectin or acid is present. Stir a small amount of lemon juice into the mixture and retest it. If a gel still fails to form, cook the syrup until the temperature is a few degrees higher; then retest it. If a syrup must be cooked to 224°F (106.5°C) or 12°F (6.6°C) above the boiling point of water to form a gel, too much sugar is present for the amount of pectin in the juice. Syrup that is cooked to higher temperatures than these is likely to cause sucrose to form crystals in the jam or jelly.

If no gel has formed by the time the temperature reaches 224°F (106.5°C), adding a small amount of liquid pectin may be advisable. Add two tablespoons of liquid pectin per quart of jelly to begin with; bring the syrup to a boil and boil for 30 seconds. Remove the syrup from the heat and test.

CONTAINERS FOR JAM AND JELLY

Jars for pectin gels should be clean, dry, and hot when they are filled; keep them hot in an oven set at 200°F (93°C). Jellies can be sealed with paraffin, but soft jams and preserves, which are more subject to mold and fermentation, should be sealed in canning jars.

After cooking the jam or jelly, skim off the foam before filling the jars. Pour jelly as soon as it is cooked; cool jams and preserves for about five minutes with occasional stirring to distribute the fruit and prevent it from floating before filling the jars (Figure 29.8).

Avoid spilling the gel mixture on the jars when filling them, and clean the rims of jars that have spills before sealing them with either lids or paraffin. Pour the hot paraffin over the gel in the jar to form a layer about ⅛ inch thick. Prick any air bubbles that appear in the paraffin, because these cause holes in the hardened paraffin and may prevent the formation of a good seal. Rotate the jars as soon as the paraffin has been poured to form a good seal around the edges. The jam or jelly does not have to be hot when the paraffin is applied. If a canning jar lid is used to seal the jam or jelly, the lid should be applied when the fruit is hot.

Figure 29.8

Skim the foam from the surface of cooked preserves before filling the glasses. Pour the preserves into the glasses with a wide-mouth funnel. After cleaning fruit from the rim of the filled glasses, pour the paraffin in a thin layer over the surface of the fruit. While the pectin is still fluid, rotate the glasses gently so that the paraffin forms a good seal with the jar.

Problems in Making
Pectin Gels

Some of the problems that occur in pectin gels are not always easily identifiable because of the many variables involved. Table 29.2 gives some of the problems that can occur, along with their possible causes.

Sugarless Jellies

Low-sugar pectins, known as *low-methoxyl pectins,* are commercial products for making sugarless jams and jellies. These pectins cannot be purchased on the retail market. Sugar is not needed to form a gel with them; instead, a divalent ion, such as calcium (Ca^{++}), forms bonds between the pectin chains. Commercial jellies containing low-sugar pectins are sweetened with an artificial, nonnutritive sweetener, such as saccharin, which produces a not entirely satisfactory flavor.

Fresh and frozen fruits can be puréed and sweetened to taste with sugar or artificial sweeteners and stored uncooked in the refrigerator or freezer. Adding a small amount of ascorbic acid to the mixture inhibits oxidation of the tannins, vitamins, flavors, and pigments and helps maintain good eating quality. Most fruits can be prepared in this way without cooking, although some are more stable, especially for long freezer storage, if they are first heated to boiling. Reduced amounts of sugar can be used if the fruit is not diluted with water and if fully ripe fruit is used. Fruit

Table 29.2   Problems in pectin gels and their possible causes

Problem	Possible causes
Syneresis	Too much acid
	Paraffin layer too thick
	Jelly stored at too high a temperature
	Fluctuation of temperature during storage
Weak gel, lack of gel	Not enough pectin, acid, or sugar
	Too much sugar
	Syrup not concentrated enough
Tough or very stiff gel	Too much pectin
	Fruit too green
	Syrup cooked too long
	Not enough sugar
Gummy texture	Syrup cooked too long
Fermentation (jelly)	Not enough sugar
	Improper seal
Molding (jelly)	Improper seal
Darkening on top (jelly)	Improper seal
	Stored at too high a temperature
Cloudy appearance (jelly)	Juice not strained properly to remove pulp
	Fruit too green
	Poured into glasses too slowly
	Allowed to set too fast
Fading or loss of color (jelly)	Stored at too high a temperature
	Stored for too long a time

purées made this way are excellent high-nutrient replacements for jams and jellies as well as for toppings for cake, ice cream, and puddings.

Jams and jellies are poor sources of nutrients because of their high sugar content. Additionally, the long heating necessary to make jelly without commercial pectin destroys the ascorbic acid in the fruit. However, much more sugar is needed in jellies made with commercial pectin than in ones made with natural pectin, further increasing calories and decreasing nutrients.

Nutritional Value of Pectin Gels

Study Questions

1. What substances are needed to form a pectin gel?
2. What are the commercial sources of pectin?
3. Distinguish between jelly, jam, and preserves.
4. If natural pectin in fruit is used to make jam or jelly, what tests can be made to determine if the fruit is properly concentrated to form a gel?
5. If a fruit jelly is cooked 8 to 12 degrees above the boiling point of water and still does not gel, what are some possible causes?
6. If too much sugar is added for the amount of pectin in the fruit, what effect will be observed in the finished gel?
7. How is low-methoxyl pectin used?
8. Even though jams and jellies are prepared with fruits, they are considered to be poor sources of nutrients. Why?

References

Gortner, Ross A.; Gortner, Ross A., Jr.; and Gortner, W. A. *Outlines of Biochemistry.* New York: Wiley, 1949.

Osman, Elizabeth. "Starch and Other Polysaccharides." In *Food Theory and Applications,* edited by Pauline C. Paul and Helen H. Palmer. New York: Wiley, 1972.

Sweetman, M. D., and MacKellar, Ingeborg. *Food Selection and Preparation.* 4th ed. New York: Wiley, 1964.

U.S. Department of Agriculture. *How to Make Jellies, Jams, and Preserves at Home,* Home and Garden Bulletin No. 56. Washington, D.C.: Government Printing Office, 1971.

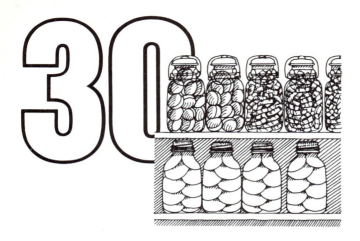

Preserving Foods: Canning, Freezing, and Drying

All foods have a natural tendency to deteriorate and spoil. Some foods spoil in a matter of hours; others keep for days, weeks, or months, depending on the nature of the food and its storage conditions. Food spoilage is caused by insects of many kinds; by microorganisms, such as bacteria, yeasts, and molds; and by physiochemical and biochemical changes caused by enzymes in the food itself. The purpose of food preservation is to treat foods in such a way as to delay spoilage.

Centuries ago, people learned to preserve some foods by such crude methods as underground storage, heating, drying, salting, fermenting, and heavy spicing. Many of these same techniques are today employed in more sophisticated ways. Modern technology has also provided mechanical refrigeration and freezing, ionizing radiation, and chemicals to prolong the life of foods. Not only are a wider variety of foods now available the year around, but many of the foods are packaged in a form that is more convenient than their natural state. Opening a can or a package of frozen peas is a far easier task than shelling fresh peas, and canned or frozen peas cook more quickly than fresh ones.

Some modes of food preservation, such as controlled atmosphere cold storage, ionizing radiation, freeze-drying, and dehydrofreezing are only possible on a commercial or industrial scale. Small-scale food preservation practical for home or farm includes dehydration, canning, freezing, and pickling. Only a small proportion of food eaten in the United States is processed at home, because commercial processing is often more economical and maintains a better quality. Processing foods at home is usually only practical and economical if the foods are home-grown or obtained at little or no cost.

Dehydration

Dehydration removes the water in foods that microorganisms need for growth; it also concentrates the acids and sugars in some foods, producing a medium that is unfavorable for growth of microorganisms. The amount of water that must be removed from the food to preserve it depends on the type of food. Plant seeds are a naturally occurring dried food. Sun-drying grains, fruits, nuts, and other foods has been a practice for many centuries, but because we cannot control the weather or climate, it is not always a feasible process.

COMMERCIAL DEHYDRATION

Modern technology has developed faster methods of dehydration as well as better quality than ever before possible. Both stationary cabinet and continuous belt tunnel dehydrators with special airflow systems are used in modern dehydration processing plants. Liquids are dried either by being sprayed into a warm atmosphere or by being coated in layers on a heated drum. In this process, known as drum-drying, the liquid or paste dries in a matter of minutes.

Many dehydration processes require heat in varying amounts to remove water from food. Heat produces changes in flavor, color, and texture that makes dehydrated foods less acceptable than the same foods processed by other methods. Low-temperature vacuum dehydration and freeze-drying have been developed as alternate methods to reduce undesirable changes. When foods are dried in a vacuum, the water can be removed at a much lower temperature than is necessary at atmospheric pressure. Freeze-dried foods are frozen and then dried; the water is removed by *sublimation*, that is, it changes from ice to steam without passing through the liquid phase. Freeze-drying, which is also performed in a vacuum, protects the structure of food; freeze-dried food rehydrates more readily then conventionally dried foods. Although freeze-dried and vacuum-dried foods tend to retain the flavors in foods, certain volatile flavors are lost during all methods of dehydration.

Oxidative Deterioration of Dried Foods   Dehydration does not prevent oxidative deterioration from enzyme-catalyzed changes in foods, although it slows down these reactions. Additional treatment is necessary to prevent enzymatic spoilage of dehydrated foods. Vegetables must be blanched, either by being dipped in boiling water or exposed to steam until the temperature of the vegetable is high enough to denature and inactivate the enzymes, as described in Chapter 3. Heating is not practical for fruits, however, because it softens their tissues and interferes with dehydration. Raw fruits, after being pitted or cored and sliced, are exposed to the fumes of burning sulfur or dipped into a sodium bisulfite solution. If oxidation is not prevented in fruits and vegetables, they become discolored and develop undesirable flavors.

Oxidation cannot occur in the absence of oxygen. Commercial dehydrated foods are sometimes vacuum-packed; or an inert gas, such as nitrogen or carbon dioxide, is introduced in place of the air that contains oxygen. An antioxidant is added to some dried foods to prevent oxidation.

ADVANTAGES OF FOOD DEHYDRATION

Not only does dehydration preserve food, but removing the water decreases its weight as well. Because they weigh less and do not require refrigeration, dehydrated foods are more economical to ship than foods in their natural state. A large market for dehydrated foods has developed in recent years for backpacking and camping.

STORING DEHYDRATED FOODS

Storing dehydrated fruits (Chapter 6) and vegetables (Chapter 7) has been discussed. Insect contamination of dried fruits is not visible until the larvae stage is reached. Some dehydrated fruits are already contaminated with insect eggs when they are purchased; these eggs later hatch out into small white worms or larvae. Sun-dried fruits are more likely to be contaminated than other forms of dried fruits because insect control is difficult in this process. Insect eggs can be destroyed if the dried fruit is frozen for 48 hours, after which time it can be held at room temperature in a closed container to prevent further infestation. Insect eggs can also be destroyed if the fruit is heated at 120 to 130°F (49–54°C) for 3 hours, or at 160°F (71°C) for 30 minutes. Fruit should be spread out in a single layer for heat treatment in the oven.

Dried fruits and vegetables darken if they are stored in the light or at too warm a temperature; to prevent this effect, store dried foods in lightproof containers in a cool location.

DEHYDRATING FRUITS AND VEGETABLES AT HOME

Preparing dried foods involves many of the same procedures as canning and freezing fruits and vegetables. Wash the foods and trim off defects; remove their pits and cores. Apricots, raisins, and prunes need not be peeled, although their skins may be pricked with a fork; apples, pears, and peaches should be peeled. Dry small fruits whole; cut large fruits into halves, quarters, or slices; slice or chop vegetables.

Blanching and Sulfuring Vegetables, with the exception of onions and green peppers, should be blanched in steam before drying for 5 to 30 minutes, depending on the size of the pieces and the type of vegetable. Fruits should be exposed to the fumes of burning sulfur for 1 to 5 hours, depending on the type of fruit. Figure 30.1 shows a diagram of the sulfuring process. Sulfuring should be done outdoors, because it produces obnoxious and irritating fumes.

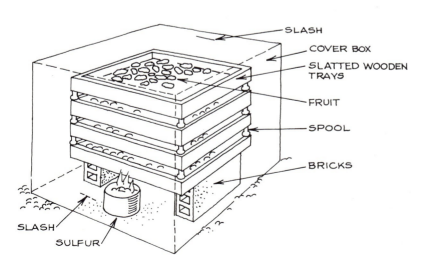

SLASH
COVER BOX
SLATTED WOODEN TRAYS
FRUIT
SPOOL
BRICKS
SLASH
SULFUR

Figure 30.1

A diagram showing trays of fruit to be sulfured in a vented box before they are dehydrated. (*From* Drying Fruits at Home [*HXT-80*]. *Berkeley, Calif.: Cooperative Extension, University of California, 1974*)

Dehydrating Fruits and Vegetables   In hot, dry climates, trays of fruits or vegetables are either spread out and exposed to the rays of the sun or stacked with space between each tray with a fan to blow hot, dry air over them. In humid climates, a warm air heater with a fan can supply the drying air indoors; otherwise, the fruit can be dried in an electric oven with the thermostat set at 140°F (60°C). In this procedure, the oven door should be left open; it is preferable as well to have a fan blowing on the fruit to circulate the air and speed drying. The room should be well ventilated to carry off sulfur fumes. Several kinds of small dehydrators are available in specialty food stores.

Trays of quarter-inch wooden slats can be constructed to hold the fruit. They should be built to fit into either the oven or the sulfuring box, or both. A layer of cheesecloth placed over the slats of the tray keeps fruit from sticking to the slats or falling between them.

Dehydration should continue until the fruit is leathery. Some water can be left in the fruit if it is to be stored in the freezer; a higher water content makes dried fruit more palatable if it is eaten without rehydrating or cooking. Sun-drying vegetables produces an inferior product; they are best dried in a dehydrator.

Canning   When foods are canned, they are sealed in tin or glass containers and processed by heat. Besides cooking the food, heat destroys microorganisms and inactivates enzymes that cause deterioration. Properly canned foods can be stored under a wide variety of conditions and temperatures; they are far more stable and have a longer shelf life than food preserved by any other method.

The heat needed to can foods causes deterioration in color, flavor, and texture, but most people find the eating quality of canned foods acceptable nonetheless. Canned fruits and vegetables lose their natural crisp texture. The chlorophyll in green vegetables is converted to pheophytin by the high heat, changing the color of the vegetables to olive green. The effect of heat on flavor varies according to food, but all fresh flavors are lost.

The acidity of a given food, its consistency, and the size of the container used for canning all determine the time and the temperature necessary to process canned foods by heat. Heating must be sufficient to destroy microorganisms that cause spoilage, as previously discussed.

PRINCIPLES OF HEAT PROCESSING   The nature and methods of heat transmission are discussed in Chapter 3. Heat conduction is more rapid in water and fluid substances than in air and solid substances. Thus, a given temperature is reached more quickly in the center of a can of tomato sauce than in a can of tomato paste. A solid-pack can of pumpkin takes longer to heat than a can of the same size of peas or green beans packed in water. A small can heats more rapidly than a large can. These principles of heat conduction are obvious, but they are factors that determine the processing time for canning foods.

Careful research studies over the years have developed time and temperature combinations necessary to process various foods in containers of different sizes. Reliable information can be obtained from the U.S. Department of Agriculture and university agricultural extension offices, some of which are listed in the references at the end of the chapter.

Both cans and jars are used to can foods at home. A properly adjusted can sealer must be used to obtain airtight seals. Three types of cans are used, each for a specific food. *C-enamel* cans are used for corn and hominy; *R-enamel* cans are used for red vegetables, fruits, pumpkin, and winter squash; and plain tin cans are used for all other fruits, vegetables, and meats. Cans should not have dents, especially around the sealing edges. Lids should be kept clean and dry. Do not wash lids in soapy water, for soap damages the sealing compound; wash cans and lids instead in clean hot water, drain the cans, and dry lids with a clean cloth.

Several jar closures are available for sealing jars (Figure 30.2). A two-piece lid is screwed tightly on the jar before processing. The two-piece lid includes a screw band and a lid with sealing compound. Screw bands can be used repeatedly as long as they are not dented or rusty and can still exert the proper pressure on the lid to seal it to the jar. Lids, however, should be used only once, with a fresh supply purchased each year, because the sealing com-

CONTAINERS FOR CANNING FOODS

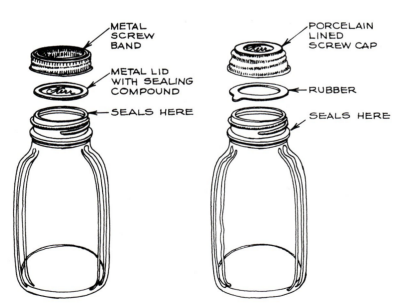

METAL SCREW BAND

METAL LID WITH SEALING COMPOUND

SEALS HERE

PORCELAIN LINED SCREW CAP

RUBBER

SEALS HERE

Figure 30.2

Two jar closures for canning jars and their method of assembly.

pound deteriorates with time; a year-old lid may not seal properly. The top, or sealing, edge of the jar should be smooth with no chips where air could enter the jar.

A second type of jar closure is a porcelain-lined zinc cap and rubber ring. The rubber rings should be clean, new, and unstretched before they are used. The ridge at the neck of the jar where the rubber ring fits is the sealing edge, and it, too, should be free of chips that allow air to leak. The rubber rings should be used only once; the lids may be reused. The zinc lid is screwed on tightly and then turned back a quarter of a turn before processing; after processing, the lid is tightened all the way.

Jars for canning should be free of cracks and washed in hot, soapy water, rinsed, and drained before being filled. After filling, the sealing edges should be cleaned of syrup or food particles; grease on the sealing edge prevents the sealing compound on the lid or the rubber ring from adhering to the jar.

PROCESSING EQUIPMENT

A pressure cooker must be used to can vegetables and meats because these low-acid foods require high temperatures for the destruction of bacteria that cause food spoilage. An accurate pressure gauge is important to achieve the temperatures required. County home demonstration agents, dealers, and manufacturers can often test the pressure gauge for accuracy. If a pressure saucepan is used instead of a canner, 20 minutes should be added to the processing time.

Figure 30.3

Place sealed jars in a pressure canner on a rack in 2 inches of water. Heat the canner with the lid in place and the vent open for 10 minutes to exhaust the air; then allow the pressure to rise to 10 pounds and hold it there with a minimum of fluctuation.

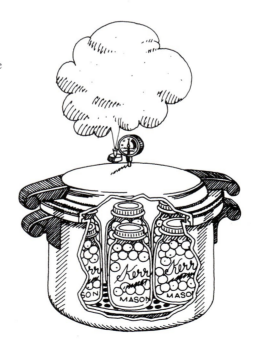

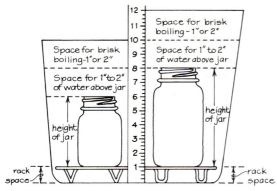

Figure 30.4

The requirements for processing containers in a boiling water bath vary according to the size of the container.

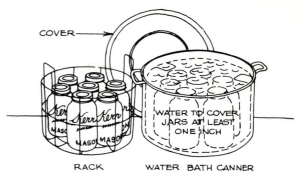

Figure 30.5

For processing by boiling water bath, place sealed jars of fruit on a rack in the canner and cover with boling water.

Filled and sealed jars or cans should be placed in the pressure canner on a rack in 2 inches of boiling water. Secure the lid and start heating with the vent open (Figure 30.3). The canner should be vented for 10 minutes to exhaust all the air it contains. If the vent is closed with air in the canner, the temperature inside will be less than that indicated by the gauge and foods will be under-processed. After letting out the air, close the vent and bring the pressure up to 10 pounds (240°F, 115.5°C) and start timing the operation. Adjust the heat under the canner to maintain the pressure with a minimum of fluctuation to prevent loss of liquid from the jars. After the required time has passed, remove the canner from the heat and allow it to cool gradually, if jars are being processed. Rapid cooling causes loss of liquid from jars. If cans are being processed, reduce the pressure quickly by opening the vent and allowing the steam to escape. Cans should be cooled quickly in cold water; jars should be cooled away from drafts in an upright position.

A hot-water bath is much simpler to use than a pressure cooker for canning acidic fruits. In this process, sealed jars are placed on a rack in a large kettle and covered with boiling water 1 to 2 inches above the top of the jar (Figures 30.4, 30.5). The canner is covered and timing begins when the water around the jars starts to boil. Remove the jars from the water bath as soon as the processing time is up. Both jars and cans are cooled in the same way as for pressure canner processing.

Oven and Open-Kettle Processing   Neither oven nor open-kettle processing is recommended for home canning. Sealed jars are likely to explode when they are processed in the oven. Moreover, oven air is a poor conductor of heat compared to water in a hot-water bath, and reaching the desired temperatures in the jars takes a long time. During this long, slow cooking, fruit in the jars is likely to darken excessively.

In the open-kettle method, fruit is cooked in syrup and then placed into hot, sterile jars, covered with more syrup, and sealed with no further processing. Such fruit can become contaminated with yeasts and molds while filling the jars, which may cause spoilage. This method is only recommended for very sweet preserves and jams.

CANNING ACID FRUITS   To achieve full flavor, the fruit used for canning should be ripe, but not overly ripe, because acidity is reduced in overly ripe fruits. Fruits should be washed well and trimmed of defects. Some fruits, such as plums, apricots, and cherries, are usually canned without peeling. Methods of peeling thin-skinned fruits, such as tomatoes and peaches, are described in Chapter 6. Less perfect fruit and slightly green fruit can be used for juices, jams, purées, jellies, and preserves. Fruits that are subject to enzymatic browning should be dipped in ascorbic acid solution as soon as they are peeled, and only small quantities should be peeled at a time.

Soft fruits are best packed into jars raw *(cold-pack method.)* Larger or firmer fruits may be partially cooked, or at least heated to a boil in the syrup *(hot-pack method)*, before being packed into jars. More fruit can be packed into a container if the fruit has been partially cooked. A larger proportion of syrup to fruit occurs in the cold-pack method than in the hot-pack method. With either method, the fruit is covered with boiling syrup (Figure 30.6), the sealing edge of the jar cleaned, and the jar sealed, as previously described.

Concentration of Sugar Syrup   Sugar is not an essential ingredient to preserve fruits by canning. Fruits can be canned in water, but flavor is lost into the surrounding medium. Sugar solutions help equalize the concentration of solutes inside and outside the cells of the fruit for better retention of flavor and shape. A thin syrup of 1 cup of sugar to 3 or 4 cups of water is more economical and lower in calories than more concentrated syrups; a decreased sugar intake, furthermore, is nutritionally advisable. Excessive sugar can detract from the natural flavors of fruits. A half teaspoon of ascorbic acid crystals per quart of syrup, or 250 milligrams of ascorbic acid per quart of fruit helps prevent darkening in fruit during storage.

Processing Fruits   Fruits with pH 4.4 or less are sufficiently acid for processing by a boiling water bath. Tomatoes have been included in this group in the past, but recently developed tomato varieties occasionally show a pH higher than 4.4, with the result that botulinum has been found in some tomatoes processed by a

Figure 30.6
Heat peeled peach halves in boiling syrup for several minutes, then pack them into hot clean jars, flat side down. Pour boiling syrup into the jar to cover the peaches, allowing ½ inch of space between the top of the jar and the syrup and peaches. *(U.S. Department of Agriculture)*

boiling water bath. Either add 1 tablespoon of lemon juice or process for a longer time, or both, to process less acid tomatoes. Processing time varies for different fruits and jars of different sizes. A more detailed publication, such as one published by the U.S. Department of Agriculture or local university agricultural extension offices, should be consulted. After processing, jars are handled as shown in Figure 30.7.

Figure 30.7
Remove the jars of fruit from the boiling water bath as soon as the processing time is completed, to prevent overcooking the fruit; cool the jars away from drafts. *(Kerr Glass Manufacturing Corporation)*

Figure 30.8

Leave head space in the top of all jars above the level of the food to allow room for expansion during processing. *(Kerr Glass Manufacturing Corporation)*

Figure 30.9

After covering food in the jar with liquid, remove air bubbles trapped between pieces of food with a knife or spatula. *(Kerr Glass Manufacturing Corporation)*

CANNING NONACID AND LOW-ACID FOODS

All vegetables and meats have pH 4.4 or higher and, therefore, are low in acid. Both meat and vegetables should be clean, fresh, and free of defects. Vegetables should not be overly mature. Young, freshly harvested vegetables are more tender and flavorful. Meat should be kept cold to reduce bacterial contamination prior to processing. Either a cold- or hot-pack method may be used.

The food is packed into the jars to levels indicated in Figure 30.8. Salt is not required but may be added for flavor. The meat or vegetable in the jars is covered with boiling water or stock and air pockets are eliminated as illustrated in Figure 30.9. Sealing surfaces are cleaned, and the jars are sealed and processed in a pressure canner, the time varying with the kind of food and size of container being processed.

TESTING JARS FOR PROPER SEAL

The day after food is canned, check the containers to be sure they are completely sealed. Jars with two-piece lids can be tested by the methods shown in Figure 30.10. Jars sealed with rubber rings and cans should be partially tilted and rotated to check for leakage of the contents. Imperfectly sealed containers can be processed again with new lids, but the quality of the food is less desirable the second time it is processed. Imperfectly sealed foods that are not processed again should be stored in the refrigerator and handled like any other cooked food; they can also be frozen for later use.

Figure 30.10

The day after canning foods, test jars for seal in one of three ways: (1) listen for the sound made by dome two-piece lids as they snap down to form a vacuum in the jar; (2) press the center of the lid, which should not move; or (3) tap the lid with a spoon. It should make a clear, ringing sound unless the food is touching the lid, in which case the sound should be dull but not hollow.

The danger of botulism poisoning from home-canned nonacid and low-acid vegetables and meats is very real. All such foods must be boiled for 10 to 15 minutes before they are served or even tasted. Canned food should be emptied into a saucepan, and the timing begun from the onset of boiling. Home-canned acid fruits do not require this treatment. However, do not taste or attempt to serve any product that shows signs of spoilage, such as foods that appear gassy, mushy, or moldy. A sour, rancid, or putrid odor can indicate spoilage, but poisonous food does not always contain such a clear warning. The odor of botulism may not be present in cold food, but bad odors become more evident during boiling. Botulinum has an odor of decomposition, usually somewhat cheesy, putrid, and rancid. Home-canned foods suspected of spoilage should be flushed down a toilet if they are sufficiently liquid; otherwise, they should be discarded where pets or humans cannot taste them accidentally. Jars and lids that contained spoiled foods should also be discarded.

BOTULISM IN CANNED FOODS

Whether in jars or cans, canned foods maintain a higher eating quality if they are stored at cool temperatures. Avoid storing them at freezing temperatures, however, because freezing causes the contents to expand, which can break glass containers and damage the seams of cans.

Foods left in opened cans may be refrigerated, but acid foods stored in this way are likely to develop a metallic flavor. They are not harmful to eat, but are not tasty, either. Discoloration that occurs on the insides of cans, which is caused by the reaction of acid and sulfur in foods with the metal in cans, is not harmful.

STORING CANNED FOODS

Freezing　　Preservation by freezing maintains the flavor, color, and texture of many foods to a greater extent than either canning or dehydration. However, not all foods retain their desirable qualities when frozen. The effect of freezing on hard-cooked eggs, mayonnaise, and starch-thickened sauces has already been mentioned. Vegetables meant to be eaten raw, such as lettuce, celery, or tomatoes, are not satisfactory to eat after they have been frozen.

ADVANTAGES AND DISADVANTAGES OF FREEZING FOODS　　Besides retaining the color, flavor, and texture of fresh food, most frozen products are convenience foods that require little or no additional preparation before they are served. Most foods can be frozen more quickly and easily than they can be canned or dehydrated. The cost of maintaining frozen storage, however, is greater than for canned and dehydrated foods, and freezer storage space may be limited. Although the texture of frozen foods is often more acceptable than that of canned and dehydrated foods, many foods show a definite loss in texture when they are frozen. Water in the cells of foods expands during freezing, often rupturing the cell walls, thereby causing a loss of texture in the foods. Some think that this phenomenon may have a tenderizing effect on meat, but it also increases the drip from meat during thawing.

Fast freezing limits the expansion of water in cells. This produces smaller ice crystals and less destruction of cell walls and thus protects the texture of foods.

PRINCIPLES OF FREEZING　　Extreme cold slows down enzyme activity and retards the growth of bacteria, two of the major causes of food spoilage. Oxidative deterioration can still occur in foods during frozen storage. Enzyme activity in vegetables is completely eliminated by blanching, as previously discussed. Fruits, which do not tolerate blanching, are packed with added ascorbic acid. Raw meat may be frozen without any treatment other than airtight packaging; enzyme activity is thought to be a factor contributing to improved tenderness of meats that have been frozen, and it does not have a negative effect on eating quality. Otherwise, oxidative deterioration during frozen storage of foods causes undesirable changes in color, flavor, and texture.

COMMERCIAL FREEZING　　A number of developments in commercial freezing of foods have resulted in improved quality and lower costs. In one method of fast freezing, food is placed on trays in single layers and subjected to a blast of air at 0° to −40°F (−18 to −40°C). In another method, small pieces of food, such as corn, peas, strawberries, or green beans, are spread in a single layer on a belt that moves through a freezing tunnel at −40°F (−40°C). Fluidized freezing is a modification of belt freezing; a current of cold air passed through a wire mesh belt lifts food off the belt and causes it to tumble and freeze.

Cryogenic freezing uses refrigerants, such as liquid nitrogen ($-320°$ F or $-196°C$) or solid carbon dioxide ($-109°F$ or $-78°C$) to freeze foods. During its early stages, cryogenic freezing was a costly process, but it is becoming more popular and more economical. Cryogenically frozen foods have a better texture and less drip when they are thawed, an effect that allows the freezing of delicate foods that were previously unacceptable when frozen.

Dehydrofreezing is a process that combines both dehydration and freezing of foods. Foods are dehydrated until they are about 50 percent of their original weight and volume and are then frozen. This amount of drying is less destructive of the quality of food than complete drying. The eating quality of dehydrofrozen foods is equal to that of regular frozen foods, but the cost is less because of the reduction in shipping weight and volume. Dehydrofrozen foods are not available in retail markets; they are marketed in bulk for use in the commercial production of soups and pies and in institutional cookery.

Home freezing of foods is becoming increasingly popular. Fruits, vegetables, and meats are the foods most commonly frozen at home, but prepared foods of all kinds can also be frozen. Freezing, like other food processing methods, does not improve the eating quality of foods. Foods of inferior quality that are frozen will still be inferior when thawed.

FREEZING FOODS AT HOME

Packaging   Foods to be frozen must be packaged in moisture-proof and vaporproof wrappings. Special plastic containers with tightly fitting lids are manufactured specifically for freezer storage; square containers conserve more space in a freezer than round containers. Frozen foods must be thawed before they can be removed from containers with narrow openings. Thus, straight sides and wide openings permit removal of the food while it is still frozen if desired. Canning jars may be used for frozen storage.

Plastic bags and plastic-coated freezer paper are also available for packaging foods to be frozen. Heavy-duty aluminum foil can be used, but lightweight foil tears too easily to be satisfactory. Waxed paper and waxed paper cartons are not satisfactory, nor are plastic cheese and margarine containers, because their lids do not fit tightly enough for long-term storage.

Foods should be packed into the containers with a minimum of space between pieces to reduce the amount of air present. As much air as possible should be excluded from foods packaged in bags or wrap. Head space of ½ to 1 inch, depending on the size of the container, should be left in rigid containers to allow for expansion of the product during freezing. Frozen food packages should be clearly labeled with the name of the product and the date of freezing.

Fruits and Vegetables Fruits and vegetables should be neither too ripe nor too green when they are frozen. Furthermore, not all varieties and kinds of fruits and vegetables freeze well. Information and specific details for freezing foods can be obtained from U.S. Department of Agriculture and university extension publications. When information is not available, the best policy is to freeze and thaw a test sample before investing time and money freezing large quanitites of a product that later turns out unsatisfactory.

The steps involved in preparing vegetables for freezing are illustrated in Figures 30.11 to 30.16 with green beans: the blanched vegetable is cooled quickly in ice water, drained, and packed in freezer containers.

Fruits subject to browning should either be dipped in an ascorbic acid solution or be packed in a syrup to which ascorbic acid has been added. Fruits may be packed in dry sugar (Figures 30.17–30.19), in sugar syrup (Figure 30.20), or without sugar.

Meats Meats should be trimmed of inedible parts, visible fat, and fatty skin to conserve space and reduce the development of rancidity, an effect that occurs readily during freezer storage of meats. Poultry should be washed inside and out and patted dry; other meats do not require washing. Poultry may be frozen whole, but should not be frozen with stuffing in it, as described in Chapter 23. Poultry cut into pieces occupies less freezer space. When

Figure 30.11

Wash vegetables in several changes of water until the water appears clear, then lift them out of the water and drain in a colander. *(U.S. Department of Agriculture)*

Figure 30.12

Cut off stem and flower ends of green beans; group together a dozen or so pods for cutting into 2-inch lengths. *(U.S. Department of Agriculture)*

Figure 30.13

Blanch vegetables before freezing by submerging them in boiling water for a specified time according to the type of vegetable and the size of the pieces. (*U.S. Department of Agriculture*)

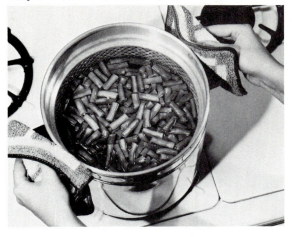

Figure 30.14

After blanching, quickly chill the vegetables by submerging them in ice water. (*U.S. Department of Agriculture*)

Figure 30.15

Vegetables can be packed into bags or other containers. A stand and funnel, as shown, make filling the bags an easy procedure. (*U.S. Department of Agriculture*)

Figure 30.16

Squeeze air from the bags, leaving ½ inch of head space in the top of the bag. Then twist the top and fold it over. Tie the bags with string, twists, or rubber bands. (*U.S. Department of Agriculture*)

Figure 30.17

Slice unpeeled nectarines and toss them in a mixture of sugar and ascorbic acid; then pack the slices into suitable containers for freezing. Dry sugar pack produces fresher and more flavorful thawed fruit than syrup pack. *(California Tree Fruit Agreement)*

Figure 30.18

Wash and hull strawberries for freezing. Use the tip of a floating-blade peeler for hulling; chill the fruit in ice water beforehand to lower its temperature for fast freezing. Work with small quantities of fruit at a time.
(C and H Sugar Company)

Figure 30.19

For a dry sugar pack, mix dry strawberries with sugar and ascorbic acid and pack into suitable containers. *(C and H Sugar Company)*

Figure 30.20

For a frozen syrup pack, fill containers with strawberries and cover with cooled syrup that contains ascorbic acid. *(C and H Sugar Company)*

uncooked young poultry is frozen, bloody marrow may leach through the joints of the legs, thighs, and wings during freezing and thawing, causing the meat to darken around the joints. This change does not affect the eating quality of the meat.

Fully trimming meat, cutting it into serving pieces, and packaging it in amounts required for single meals before freezing is an efficient and convenient way to freeze meat. For instance, pork can be cut into small cubes for chop suey and large cubes for sweet and sour pork. Beef can be cut for kabobs, Stroganoff, Swiss steak, stew, or teriyaki. Meats can also be dipped into a marinade, such as teriyaki, before freezing. When thawed, such meats are flavored for immediate preparation with no further marinating necessary.

Fast Freezing True fast freezing is not possible in home freezers. Although some models have fast-freezing compartments, they still take several hours to freeze foods. However, the freezing process can be speeded if the amount of food frozen at one time is limited to no more than 3 pounds per cubic foot of freezer space. Packages to be frozen should be distributed around the freezer, preferably positioned near the coils or in the coldest part of the freezer in single layers. Stacking unfrozen foods delays freezing in portions of the foods.

Foods should be frozen as soon as they are packaged, with the freezer temperature set as low as possible. Once foods are frozen, the freezer should maintain a temperature of 0°F (−18°C) or lower.

Not all foods and food mixtures can be frozen with their eating quality intact. Some problems that are encountered in freezing food and food mixtures are discussed here.

FREEZING FOOD MIXTURES

Gravies and Sauces Gravies and sauces that are thickened with cornstarch or flour retrograde, curdle, and show syneresis when they are frozen and thawed. Curdled sauce or gravy can be reblended if it is heated and stirred, but will be thinner than before it was frozen. If the sauce is part of a casserole, stirring to reblend may not be possible, making the thawed casserole watery instead of creamy. Adding ¼ teaspoon of dry, unflavored gelatin per cup of white sauce or gravy helps prevent curdling and syneresis of the sauce when it is thawed. Mixtures with no fat appear to be more stable than ones with large amounts of fat.

Eggs and Custards Uncooked egg whites freeze well and function as well in angel cakes and meringues as unfrozen egg whites. Information on freezing whole eggs and egg yolks is given in Chapter 19. Uncooked custard mixtures of milk and egg, with or without sugar, can be frozen, but the gel structure of cooked custard is disrupted by freezing, and it curdles and shows syneresis when it is thawed. Hard-cooked egg whites become tough and leathery when they are frozen, but hard-cooked egg yolks freeze well. Egg yolk sponge cakes develop rancid off flavors when they are frozen because of oxidation of the fat in the yolk; the same effect occurs in butter cakes with a large content of egg yolks. Adding an antioxidant to cakes that contain many egg yolks reduces the development of rancidity during frozen storage. Angel cakes freeze well.

Baked Products   Almost all baked products freeze satisfactorily if they are frozen after baking. Frozen cake batters show less volume after thawing and baking than the same cake baked before freezing. Uncooked yeast doughs do not produce satisfactory baked products when they are baked after freezing and thawing; freezing appears to destroy some yeast cells. Frozen unbaked doughs produce more satisfactory results if they are allowed to rise and double in volume after thawing before they are shaped for baking.

Fruit pies should be frozen unbaked. The lower crust of a frozen baked fruit pie tends to become soggy when the pie is reheated. Raw fruits subject to enzymatic browning should be protected by the addition of ascorbic acid before they are used in pies to be frozen. Pastry shells may be frozen either baked or unbaked, but must be stored carefully so that they will not be broken or crushed. Unbaked flat sheets of pastry can also be frozen and placed in the pie pan after thawing.

Most cookie doughs freeze well; cookies made from thawed dough are usually crispier than cookies that are frozen after baking. Macaroon cookies, baked or not, become tough when frozen.

Sandwiches   Because mayonnaise emulsions break and become oily when they are frozen, mayonnaise should not be used on the bread or in fillings of sandwiches to be frozen. Sliced meats are especially good for freezing, and it is a good way to use leftover roasts. Sandwich meats can be frozen for short periods of time; they become rancid quickly because of their high fat content. Peanut butter and hard cheese freeze well.

SERVING FROZEN FOODS   The time foods can be held in frozen storage varies with the type of food and the temperature of storage. If freezer temperature is higher than 0°F (−18°C), storage life is shortened proportionately. Holding foods in a freezer for longer times than those suggested does not cause illness, but reduces the eating quality. Table 30.1 gives the maximum frozen storage life of some common foods.

Some frozen foods, such as vegetables, are cooked without thawing. Other foods, such as fruits, require at least partial thawing before cooking or serving. Cooking frozen meats is discussed in Chapter 22. Baked products should be thawed before they are unwrapped to prevent drying. Frozen casseroles and soups can be cooked unthawed if they have been packaged in such a way that

Table 30.1	Storage times for foods frozen at 0°F (−18°C)
Maximum storage time	**Foods**
1 month	Sandwiches
3 months	Bacon, hamburger
6 months	Pork, fish, lamb, turkey, casseroles
9 months	Beef, veal, chicken, eggs
12 months	Baked breads, fruits, vegetables

the packaging material can be removed and the product placed in a container for cooking. Cooking frozen fish is discussed in Chapter 22.

Because freezing does not destroy bacteria, bacteria on food at the time it was frozen are still present when the food is thawed. For this reason, it is a good policy to thaw both raw and cooked meats, as well as all dishes containing protein and starch, in the refrigerator. These foods should not be allowed to stand at room temperature for very long and should be cooked to a temperature that is sufficient to destroy any bacteria that may be present. Thawing and refreezing foods is not advisable for the same reason. Meat or casseroles that have been frozen and thawed twice are likely to have twice the bacteria as the same food thawed only once.

Any food that appears slimy or has a peculiar odor or color when it is thawed should be discarded without being tasted.

SANITARY QUALITY OF FROZEN FOODS

Power Failure and Freezer Breakdown   In the event of a power failure or mechanical breakdown, the food in a fully loaded freezer may stay frozen for as long as 2 days, if the door of the freezer is not opened unnecessarily and if the outside temperature is not too warm. In a freezer that is less than half full, food may not stay frozen for more than a day. Dry ice can be placed inside the freezer to keep the temperature low; a 25-pound block of dry ice keeps a 10 cubic foot freezer below freezing for 2 or 3 days. Dry ice causes burns if it comes in direct contact with the skin, so it should be handled with gloves. The room or immediate area should be well-ventilated because dry ice is a source of carbon dioxide gas.

Some foods that thaw inadvertently can be refrozen, but their eating quality deteriorates. Twice-frozen and thawed fruits and vegetables are safe to eat if they have not reached room temperature and if, in the case of vegetables, they are cooked before being eaten. Twice-frozen and thawed meats and casseroles should be adequately cooked before they are eaten. Stewed meats, for instance, should be quite safe to eat.

Pickles and Relishes   Fermentation is used to process many different foods, a number of which have been studied or mentioned previously. The lactic acid bacterial fermentation of milk produces yogurt and cheese, the fermentation of glucose by yeast produces carbon dioxide for leavening yeast doughs and alcohol in alcoholic beverages, and the fermentation of carbohydrates by acetic acid bacteria produces vinegar. Fermentation is also necessary to produce coffee, cocoa, tea, vanilla, soy sauce, and citron. Lactic acid bacteria are also used to ferment the carbohydrates in some vegetables to produce acid; this method is used to produce cucumber pickles, green and ripe olives, and sauerkraut.

PRINCIPLES OF LACTIC ACID FERMENTATION   The fermentation process can be controlled by the kinds and amounts of ingredients, as well as by the temperature and conditions of fermentation, to produce pickles with the desired characteristics. Salt is added to inhibit the growth of undesirable microorganisms that cause food to putrefy and soften. A limited amount of salt does not inhibit the growth of lactic acid bacteria. In making sauerkraut from cabbage, a salt concentration of 2½ percent of the weight of raw cabbage is required. Two major types of pickles, *cured* and *fresh-pack,* are prepared from cucumbers. These types differ in flavor and texture because of the differences in their methods of preparation.

Cured Pickles   Pickles to be cured are cleaned and placed in vats of brine. Fermentation is controlled by temperature and the addition of salt; too much salt causes shriveling. The salt gradually penetrates the cucumbers in a process that takes from weeks to months. At the end of this period, the cucumbers are desalted and washed. The pickling process is completed in a vinegar solution with suitable seasonings. The fermentation process can produce many kinds of desirable flavors in pickles, which are usually crisp, dark green in color, and somewhat translucent. Fermented pickles, often called "genuine" pickles, are often sold in bulk in delicatessens.

Fresh-Pack Pickles   Fresh-pack pickles are not fermented in brine. In this method, raw cucumbers are either brined overnight or packed into jars without brining. A boiling pickling solution of vinegar, other sources of acid, salts, and seasonings is poured over the cucumbers in jars. The jars are sealed and heat-processed, as in canning. Pickles produced by this method have a fresher cucumber flavor than cured pickles, are a light green-yellow color, and have less acidity and salt than cured pickles.

Variety Pickles   Both the processes described can produce a variety of pickles with such special seasonings as dill. The label "kosher" indicates that such pickles have been prepared according to standards set up by Jewish dietary law. Kosher-style pickles are often highly spiced and have strong onion and garlic flavors.

Sour pickles are similar to dill pickles except that they are seasoned with spices and herbs other than dill. Sour pickles can be chopped to make sour relish or piccalilli, or they can be added to prepared mustard sauce to make hot dog relish. Sweet pickles are prepared from sour pickles by removing the vinegar and adding a sweet, spicy syrup to obtain desired sweetness and flavor. All these varieties of pickles are available in many forms, including relish, slices, chips, strips, and quarters, or whole, large, small, and midget. Many relishes, in which chopped, pickled cucumbers of various kinds are combined with other chopped, pickled vegetables, are produced commercially.

Cucumbers for pickling should be freshly picked and firm, with no soft spots or areas of decay, which, if present, could introduce undesirable microorganisms into the pickling solutions. They should not be waxed, for a wax coating interferes with the penetration of the brine into the cucumbers. Flowers should be removed because they contain enzymes that cause the cucumbers to soften during fermentation. Cucumbers should be carefully washed, for clinging soil holds bacteria that can cause problems during fermentation; they are best washed individually under running water.

PREPARING CUCUMBER PICKLES

Salt used for pickling should be granulated. It should not be iodized because this darkens the cucumbers; it should not contain anticaking compounds, which cloud the brine.

A good cider vinegar of 4 to 6 percent acidity should be used to pickle cucumbers. Cider vinegar produces a good blend of flavors in cucumbers but discolors white vegetables, such as onions and cauliflower. Use distilled vinegar of the same acidity for white vegetables and for cucumbers if cider vinegar is not available. Distilled vinegar gives pickles a sharp flavor of acetic acid. Always use the quantity of vinegar specified in recipes, because the full amount is needed for purposes of preservation. Sugar can be added to reduce sourness in pickles.

Utensils for heating pickling solutions, for brining, and for fermenting should not react with these solutions. Never use copper, brass, iron, or galvanized utensils for these purposes. Stainless steel, aluminum, glass, crockery, and unchipped enamelware utensils are suitable for pickling.

The proportions of ingredients and the fermentation time depend on the kind of pickle being produced. At all times follow only tested recipes; U.S. Department of Agriculture and university extension publications are excellent sources of reliable information.

Because of the air contained in their tissues, cucumbers tend to float during brining, but they must stay completely submerged

Figure 30.21

Submerge carefully cleaned cucumbers in brine with spices and herbs. Place a plate or glass lid on top and weight it with a jar of water to keep the cucumbers completely submerged. Formation of bubbles and scum indicates active fermentation; remove this scum daily. *(U.S. Department of Agriculture)*

Figure 30.22

After 3 weeks of fermentation, dills are ready for processing. Yeast development during fermentation causes cloudiness in the brine. Strain brine through several layers of cheesecloth before using it. *(U.S. Department of Agriculture)*

Figure 30.23

Pack the pickles into clean, hot jars with several pieces of dill and cover with boiling, strained brine to within ½ inch of the top. After sealing, process the pickles in a boiling water bath for 15 minutes. *(U.S. Department of Agriculture)*

in the brine under a weighted plate or cover. Scum that forms on the top of the brine should be removed every day; this is more easily accomplished if several layers of fresh cheesecloth are placed on top of the brine and removed and replaced each time.

After brining, pickles are packed into jars and covered with boiling pickling solution, as illustrated in Figures 30.21 to 30.23. Air bubbles should be worked out of the jar with a table knife. If air is left in the jar, the level of the liquid may leave the cucumbers exposed. The jars are sealed and processed in a boiling water bath.

Heat processing is essential to inactivate enzymes and destroy bacteria that could cause spoilage in pickles; as with other foods, open-kettle processing is not a desirable procedure. The processing time depends on whether the pickles are cured or fresh-pack.

After processing, pickles should be stored and handled in the same way as other canned foods. After the seal is broken, pickles stored for too long at room temperature may become moldy.

Problems in Making Pickles Because of the large number of variables involved in preparing pickles, problems may develop as a result of different factors or more than one factor. Table 30.2 lists some of the problems and their possible causes. Too much or too little salt, sugar, or acid can change the concentration of ions inside and outside the cells and, by osmosis in the uncooked pickle or diffusion in the processed pickle, affect its texture and appearance. Growth of lactic acid bacteria is desired in the preparation of pickles; all other organisms cause deterioration and poor quality.

Ionizing radiation, one of the newest forms of food preservation, appears to show promise, but also has definite limitations. Ionizing radiation is light of the shortest wavelengths, which are not visible to the eye. These light rays, also known as *X-rays, gamma rays, alpha rays, beta rays,* and *electron beams,* are produced by radioactive elements. The U.S. Food and Drug Administration has approved the use of gamma rays produced by cobalt-60 for research work in foods.

When gamma rays come in contact with matter, they can cause *ionizations,* that is the separation of electrons from the atoms in the matter. In this way, gamma rays can sterilize food by destroying microorganisms and even insects. Gamma rays seem to have greater potential than other light rays for preserving food because they penetrate further into food. They can also

Ionizing Radiation

Table 30.2   *Some flaws in pickles and their possible causes*

Problem	Possible causes
Shriveled	Too much salt, sugar, or acidity
	Overprocessing
Hollow	Poorly developed cucumbers
	Cucumbers held too long before processing
	Too fast fermentation at too high temperature
	Brine too weak or too concentrated
Soft, slippery	Too little salt or acid, permitting bacterial growth
	Cucumbers not submerged completely during brining
	Scum throughout brine
	Moldy garlic or spices that contaminate brine
	Cucumbers with soft or decayed spots that contaminate brine
Darkened	Iodized salt
	Overprocessing
	Hard water containing iron

destroy vital tissues in plants and animals and inactivate enzymes. Only moderate exposure to gamma rays is necessary to destroy microorganisms, but high exposure is necessary to inactivate enzymes. This is a decided disadvantage, because such high exposure also causes undesirable changes in food color, flavor, and odor. Irradiation with gamma rays does not make food radioactive.

The amount of irradiation emitted is measured in *rads*. Fewer than 100,000 rads are needed to prevent sprouting of potatoes or to destroy insects in nuts, grains, and spices. This amount of irradiation does not affect flavor, odor, or color. From 100,000 to 1,000,000 rads are needed to destroy many, but not all, microorganisms. Foods exposed to this amount of ionizing radiation are thus considered pasteurized, not sterilized. Meats, fish, and some other foods exposed to 1,000,000 or fewer rads can be kept in the refrigerator for a longer time than untreated foods.

Exposure of food to 1,000,000 rads causes a considerable loss in eating quality, with no inactivation of enzymes. Because heat readily inactivates enzymes but not many bacteria, ionizing radiation can possibly be combined with mild heating for effective food preservation. Research also continues to seek lower levels of irradiation, at reduced temperatures and in controlled oxygen environments.

At the present time, no food marketed for consumption has been exposed to ionizing radiation. Ionizing radiation appears to show the greatest promise in preventing potato sprouting, ridding grain and similar products of insects, extending the refrigerated shelf life of meats and some other protein foods, and destroying pathogenic bacteria in foods.

Nutritional Value of Processed Foods

The reduction of the nutrient content of foods has been a criticism against food processing. More than 40 years ago, a group of researchers explored this possibility by feeding a group of rats a balanced diet of canned foods over several generations. A control group of rats was fed the same kinds and amounts of foods fresh or uncanned. No distinguishable difference in growth, reproduction, or chemical analysis of the tissues of rats was seen in the two groups. Canning technology in the 1930s was far less sophisticated and controlled than it is today.

Many fruits and vegetables are now refrigerated in the fields as soon as they are harvested. Jet sprays of water wash foods to reduce solution losses of nutrients. Superheated steam for blanching also reduces both heat destruction and solution losses of nutrients. A high temperature of 285°F (140°C) is used for a few seconds to a few minutes to shorten processing time for canned foods and reduce heat destruction of nutrients. Oxidation of nutrients in foods is controlled by rapid processing and vacuum packing.

Treatment of fruits and vegetables with sulfur or sodium bisulfite to prevent enzymatic browning protects the carotene and vitamin C but is destructive of thiamin. Most foods that require the sulfur treatment are poor sources of thiamin. The natural acidity of some foods, such as orange juice, is protective of vitamin C, so that processed forms are as good sources of this vitamin as the fresh food.

As a rule, processing procedures that improve the eating quality of a food also improve its nutrient retention. Freezing preservation of foods produces better nutrient retention than either canning or drying. Part of the nutrient loss in canned foods is caused by leaching of nutrients from the food into the liquid, as discussed previously. The steril-vac process, discussed in Chapter 6, reduces these nutrient losses.

Most processed foods are not fully equal to their fresh, unprocessed counterparts either in eating quality or in nutrient retention, although many come close. However, processed foods are often available when the fresh food is not, and they are often more convenient and economical, depending on the food and the season of the year. Continuing research by government and industry can be expected to produce many improvements in commercially processed foods.

Study Questions

1. What factors cause spoilage of foods?
2. Why are freeze drying and vacuum drying more satisfactory procedures than heat drying for preserving foods?
3. How is enzyme activity controlled in fruits and vegetables that are to be dehydrated?
4. What factors affect heat transmission in canning foods?
5. What foods can safely be processed in a boiling water bath? Why?
6. Distinguish between cold-pack and hot-pack canning methods. Under what conditions is one more practical than the other?
7. Why are open kettle and oven-processing methods not recommended for canning?
8. What foods are nonacid or low-acid, what temperature should be used for processing them, and how are they processed?
9. Why should air from a pressure cooker be vented or exhausted before the pressure is built up to process canned foods?
10. How much water is needed to process canned foods in a pressure canner and hot water bath? What temperature of water should be used?
11. How is processing time measured when foods are processed in a pressure canner and boiling water bath?
12. What precautions should be observed in eating nonacid and low-acid home-canned foods? Why?
13. Why is freezing effective in preserving foods?
14. In what ways are oxidative enzymes inactivated when foods are prepared for freezing?
15. What procedures can achieve fairly fast freezing of foods in a home freezer?
16. Name some foods that have undergone fermentation during preparation or processing.
17. What is the function of salt in the lactic acid fermentation of foods?
18. Distinguish between cured and fresh-pack pickles.
19. Why should all pickles be heat processed?
20. Why is it preferable to promote growth of lactic acid bacteria and to repress growth of all other microorganisms in preparing pickles?

References

Boggs, Mildred M., and Rasmussen, Clyde L. "Modern Food Processing." In U.S. Department of Agriculture, *Food*, Yearbook of Agriculture. Washington, D.C.: Government Printing Office, 1959.

Clifcorn, L. E. "Factors Influencing the Vitamin Content of Canned Foods." In *Advances in Food Research*, edited by E. M. Mrak and George F. Stewart. 1:39. New York: Academic Press, 1948.

Miller, M. W.; Winter, F. H.; Groppe, C.; and Buslaff, C. *Drying Fruits at Home*. Berkeley: University of California, 1974.

Davidson, Sir Stanley; Passmore, R.; and Brock, J. F. *Human Nutrition and Dietetics*. 5th ed. Baltimore, Md.: Williams & Wilkins, 1972.

Gilpin, Gladys L. "Freezing Foods at Home"; "Canning Food at Home." In U.S. Department of Agriculture, *Food*, Yearbook of Agriculture. Washington, D.C.: Government Printing Office, 1959.

Klippstein, Ruth N. "The True Cost of Home Food Preservation." Ithaca, N.Y.: New York State College of Human Ecology, Cooperative Extension, 1979.

Michelbacher, A. E., and Ernst, F. H. *The Storage and Protection of Dried Food Products for Home Use*. Berkeley: University of California, Agricultural Extension, 1943.

Rasmussen, Clyde L.; Rogers, Robert O.; and Michener, H. David. "Processing—A Prime Protector." In U.S. Department of Agriculture, *Protecting Our Food*, Yearbook of Agriculture. Washington, D.C.: Government Printing Office, 1966.

Stewart, George F., and Amerine, Maynard A. *Introduction to Food Science and Technology*. New York: Academic Press, 1973.

Thompson, Edward R. "The Pedigreed Pickle Is Here: New Quality in Old Favorites." In U.S. Department of Agriculture, *Food for Us All*, Yearbook of Agriculture, Washington, D.C.: Government Printing Office, 1969.

U.S. Department of Agriculture. *Effect of Household Processing and Storage on Quality of Pickled Vegetables and Fruit*, Home Economics Research Report No. 28, by J. P. Sweeney, N. E. Liming, A. Beloian, and E. H. Dawson. Washington, D.C.: Government Printing Office, 1965.

—— *Making Pickles and Relishes At Home*, Home and Garden Bulletin No. 92. 1970.

—— *Home Canning of Fruits and Vegetables*, Home and Garden Bulletin No. 8. 1972.

—— *Home Canning of Meat and Poultry*, Home and Garden Bulletin No. 106. 1972.

Woodruff, J. G. "Frozen Foods—New Techniques." In U.S. Department of Agriculture, *Science for Better Living*, Yearbook of Agriculture. Washington, D.C.: Government Printing Office, 1968.

Beverages

Beverages are liquid foods that are consumed by drinking. Many liquids serve as beverages, including juices from fruits and vegetables served alone or in cocktail and punch mixtures; milk served alone or combined with other ingredients in chocolate drinks, milk shakes, eggnogs, and sodas; carbonated beverages served alone or in mixtures with other beverages; coffee; and tea.

Fruit and Vegetable Juices and Drinks

The juices and nectars of many fruits are used as beverages, but citrus juices are most commonly used in the United States. The introduction of the electric blender several decades ago increased the use of fruit purées. Many more commercially produced juices and juice drinks are now available in bottles and cans as well as in frozen and dried forms. Imitation products, which many people equate with the natural product, are nothing more than artificially flavored sweetened mixtures to which ascorbic acid has been added. Because of the proliferation of watered-down juices and juice substitutes, together with the nutritional claims made for them, the U.S. Food and Drug Administration has established standards to help consumers discern the contents of these products. Products for which standards have been set are given in Title 21 of the Code of Federal Regulations, summarized in Table 31.1. To be called a juice, a juice drink, a drink, an ade, or a nectar, a beverage must contain the minimum amount of single-strength fruit juice indicated.

NUTRIENTS IN FRUIT JUICES

Natural juices contain nutrients other than vitamin C. Because orange juice is an excellent source of vitamin C, people tend to overlook other nutrients, comparing beverages solely on their vitamin C content. Not all fruits or juices made from fruits are nutritionally equivalent. Table 31.2 shows the nutrients in many

---

Table 31.1   Federal standards for some fruit beverages

Name of beverage	Single-strength fruit juice (%)
Orange juice	Not less than 100
Orange juice drink	Not less than 50
Orangeade	Not less than 25
Orange drink	Not less than 10
Pineapple-grapefruit juice drink	Not less than 50
Fruit nectars	Not less than 40
Apricot nectar	Not less than 35
Papaya nectar	Not less than 33½

SOURCE: U.S. Government, *Code of Federal Regulations*, Title 21, section 27 (Washington, D.C.: Government Printing Office, n.d.).

Table 31.2

Table 31.2 Nutrient content of juices and beverages, 100-gram amounts

Juice or beverage	Water (g)	Kilocalories	Iron (mg)	Sodium (mg)	Potassium (mg)	Vitamin A (I.U.)	Ascorbic acid (mg)
Apple juice or cider, canned	87.8	47	0.6	1	101	—	1
Apricot nectar, 40% fruit	84.6	57	0.2	trace	151	950	3
Blackberry juice, canned, unsweetened	90.9	37	0.9	1	170	—	10
Cranberry juice cocktail, 30% fruit	83.2	65	0.3	1	10	trace	2[a]
Grapefruit juice, fresh, all varieties	90.0	39	0.2	1	162	80	38
Grapefruit juice, canned, unsweetened	89.2	41	0.4	1	162	10	34
Grapefruit juice-orange juice, canned, unsweetened	88.7	43	0.3	1	184	100	34
Grape juice, canned	82.9	66	0.3	2	116	—	trace
Grape juice drink, 30% fruit	86.0	54	0.1	1	35	—	16[b]
Lemon juice, fresh	91.0	25	0.2	1	141	20	46
Lime juice, fresh	90.3	26	0.2	1	104	10	32
Orange juice, fresh, all varieties	88.3	45	0.2	1	200	200	50
Peach nectar, canned, 40% fruit	87.2	48	0.2	1	78	430	trace
Pear nectar, canned, 40% fruit	86.2	52	0.1	1	39	trace	trace
Pineapple juice, canned	84.0	58	0.4	1	147	60	10
Pineapple-grapefruit juice drink, canned, 40% fruit	86.0	54	0.2	trace	62	10	16
Pineapple-orange juice drink, canned, 40% fruit	86.0	54	0.2	trace	70	50	16
Prune juice, canned	57.3	156	1.3	164	290	460	2
Sauerkraut juice, canned	94.6	10	1.1	787	—	—	18
Tangelo juice, fresh	89.4	41	—	—	—	—	—
Tangerine juice, fresh	88.9	43	0.2	1	178	420	31
Tomato juice, canned	93.6	19	0.9	200	227	800	16
Vegetable juice cocktail, canned	94.1	17	0.5	200	221	700	9

SOURCE: U.S. Department of Agriculture, *Composition of Foods.*

[a]Cranberry juice cocktail contains 2 milligrams of natural ascorbic acid per 100 grams but is usually fortified to supply 40 milligrams of vitamin C per 100 grams.

[b]Grape juice drink, with no naturally occurring ascorbic acid, is fortified with vitamin C.

juices and drinks for 100-gram amounts, or about 3½ ounces. Only a few of these fruit beverages have a high content of ascorbic acid; some are good sources of iron; some are high in potassium and low in sodium; some contain fair amounts of vitamin A; all are poor sources of B-complex vitamins, except for orange juice, which is a good source of folic acid, and bananas, which are rich in pyridoxine.

Drinking a variety of juices provides a wide assortment of nutrients in the diet. However, the nutrients shown for juice drinks vary according to the actual percentage of real juice in the drink and the level of ascorbic acid fortification. Imitation and watered down products are often no more economical than natural juice. Natural fruit juices, moreover, provide a greater range of nutrients other than ascorbic acid.

PIGMENTS IN FRUIT JUICES

Anthocyanin and anthoxanthin pigments are most likely to affect the color of fruit juice mixtures; chlorophyll pigment is not common in fruits, and carotenoid pigment is fairly stable and therefore causes no problems.

The red color contributed by anthocyanin pigment in an acidic medium is highly desirable in fruit punches. This pigment changes color reversibly with changes in pH. Anthocyanin is present in its red form in red raspberries, cranberries, pomegranates, and red cherries; it exists as a blue-purple pigment in its neutral form in black raspberries, blueberries, Concord grapes, blackberries, and boysenberries. Alkaline water mixed with any of these juices causes the pigment to change to a very definite blue or even green. The green color probably results from the simultaneous presence of some yellow anthoxanthin pigment in alkaline media, which combines with blue to produce green.

Anthocyanin pigment also combines with aluminum, tin, and iron ions dissolved from metal containers to form blue and blue-green colors. Adding lemon juice prevents the pigment from combining with iron by making the medium acidic, thereby producing a red color. Juices containing these pigments should not be mixed or stored in aluminum, tin, or iron containers.

PREPARING FRUIT PUNCH

Lemonade and tea are often used as bases for fruit punches. To these may be added one or more fruit juices to obtain desired flavors and colors. Carbonated beverages may be added to punches just before they are served for zest. The punch should not be diluted too much if ice is to be added, because melting ice will dilute the punch still further. The juices and syrups from canned fruits can be strained and added to punch and lemonade. Not only do they contribute sweetness, so that less sugar is needed, they also contribute the nutrients leached from canned fruit.

Decorative ice rings for a punch bowl, or ice cubes for a punch glass, can be prepared from the same punch mixture or a juice or

Figure 31.1

An ice ring can be floated in the punch bowl for decorative effect.

Figure 31.2

Curls of lemon peel can be frozen in ice cubes to flavor and decorate glasses of punch.
(Sunkist Growers, Inc.)

mixture of contrasting color and flavor (Figure 31.1). Colorful tidbits, such as marachino cherries, lemon or lime slices, or mint leaves, can be frozen in ice cubes or an ice ring for their decorative effect (Figure 31.2). Scoops of ice cream or sherbet, or slices of citrus fruit cut into shapes, can be floated in the punch bowl to enhance the flavor of the punch and make it attractive.

Hot Punches   Ice-cold punches are refreshing in hot weather; spicy hot punches are appropriate in winter. Tea and apple juice or cider, which are the same, are often used as the base for hot punch. Whole spices for seasoning should be tied in a piece of cheesecloth and heated in the punch long enough for the desired flavors to be extracted. Ground spices, which make punch cloudy and darken its color, should not be used.

Vegetable juices, either alone or in blends, are delightful appetizers and snacks. Tomato juice, either chilled with a twist of lemon or combined with other vegetable juices and seasonings, is a popular juice. Tomato juice is also tasty when seasoned with Worcestershire sauce, onion juice, bouillon, or clam juice. Juices can also be prepared from cabbage, carrots, or celery with a vegetable juicer, but a small amount of lemon juice or ascorbic acid should be

VEGETABLE JUICE COCKTAILS

added to prevent enzymatic browning. Because 1 pound of vegetable makes about 1 cup of juice, this is not an economical use of vegetables. Vegetable juices can be mixed with fruit juices, such as pineapple and orange juice.

Milk Beverages and Cocoa

The use of milk as a beverage is more common than its use for any other purpose, including making cheese. Milk is most often consumed with nothing added, but many delicious drinks can be prepared with milk.

FRUIT-MILK DRINKS

Many fruit juices and purées are compatible with milk (Figure 31.3). A mixture of half fruit purée or juice and half milk, sweetened, if needed, with a little sugar or honey, makes a good beverage. Milk can be whole, low-fat, nonfat, buttermilk, or yogurt. Most fruits can be liquefied in a blender, but those subject to enzymatic browning keep their fresh, natural color better if a small amount of pineapple or citrus juice is added for blending. Many such fruit and milk mixtures do not keep well and should be prepared just before they are consumed. Acidic juices precipitate the casein of fresh milk, which increases the viscosity of the mixture.

EGGNOGS

Eggnogs are mixtures of raw egg and milk, slightly sweetened with sugar or honey and flavored with vanilla and nutmeg or cardamom. A whole egg can be beaten into the milk with the sugar until the mixture is frothy, or the yolk and white can be separated, with the egg white foam folded into the yolk and milk mixture.

Figure 31.3

Refreshing milk drinks combine orange juice, banana, or peanut butter with milk and are easily prepared in a blender. *(United Dairy Industry Association)*

Figure 31.4

Chocolate milk or milk shakes are delicious and nutritious beverages for afternoon and bedtime snacks. *(United Dairy Industry Association)*

The formation of the biotin-avidin complex when raw eggs are consumed has been mentioned in Chapter 19. However, the occasional consumption of raw eggs does not normally cause nutritional problems. Another hazard of raw eggs is their sanitary quality, as discussed in Chapter 19. Cracked eggs should never be used in eggnogs; other eggs should be washed and dried before they are opened.

Eggnog mixtures can also be cooked like a stirred custard to scalding temperature (180°F, 82°C) to reduce the bacterial population. Combine the heated mixture with sugar and flavoring and mix it in a blender, then chill it before serving. Cooked eggnogs are preferable for children and invalids, who are more susceptible to illness than healthy adults. Fruits can be added to eggnogs to provide variety in flavor in the same way as they are used for fruit-milk drinks.

MILK SHAKES

Milk shakes are a combination of ice cream and milk. Ice cream parlors use a flavored syrup in addition, to sweeten and flavor the mixture. Delicious milk shakes can be prepared in a mixer (Figure 31.4) or blender. Part of the milk can be replaced with concentrated fruit juice, such as undiluted frozen orange juice, or with fruit purée, obtained by mixing such fruits as bananas or apricots in a blender before adding milk and ice cream. A sweet ice cream combined with naturally sweet fruit often requires no added sugar.

The ratio of ice cream to liquid determines the thickness of a milk shake. More ice cream produces a thicker milk shake, if the mixture is not blended too long. Blending for too long melts ice cream and thins the milk shake. Different ice cream flavors can be used to make a range of flavored milk shakes.

ICE CREAM SODAS An ice cream soda is made of carbonated beverage poured over scoops of ice cream in a tall glass. Various combinations and flavors of soda and ice cream can be used.

COCOA AND CHOCOLATE BEVERAGES Dried *cacao* beans, imported from Central and South America and Africa, are cleaned, roasted, and shelled by manufacturers to produce the *nibs,* the meat of the beans. Crushing the nibs causes them to liquefy, forming a chocolate liquor, which is about 54 percent fat. Part of the fat, or cocoa butter, is removed; the remainder is pressed into cakes, cooled, and ground into chocolate.

Baker's chocolate, packaged into 1-ounce, individually wrapped squares for cooking, contains about 50 percent fat. Cocoa powder labeled breakfast cocoa contains at least 22 percent fat. Products labeled cocoa are medium-fat powders with about 10 to 22 percent fat. Low-fat cocoa powders containing less than 10 percent fat are available for industrial use but not in retail markets. The substitution of cocoa for chocolate is listed in the table of substitutions (Table 8) in the appendix, but their flavors are not exactly equivalent.

Dutch Cocoa and Chocolate Alkaline processing of the nibs produces Dutch chocolate or cocoa. The nibs are boiled in a 2 percent solution of potassium carbonate or sodium carbonate, and then are dried, roasted, and processed as described previously. Alkaline treatment turns cocoa and chocolate a darker color and makes them more soluble, but also produces a milder flavor. Nibs that are not treated in this way are called *natural process* and have a fuller, richer flavor than Dutch-processed products.

Cocoa Beverage Mixes Cocoa powder combined with sugar forms a mix that need only be stirred into liquid milk; or cocoa powder, sugar, and nonfat dry milk mixes can be stirred into water to produce a chocolate beverage. Cocoa powder products can be distinguished by their ingredient listings.

Cocoa powders that contain sugar and nonfat dry milk cannot be substituted for plain cocoa powder in baking, because their cocoa flavor is too diluted and their added sugar or milk can upset the proper ratio of ingredients in the baked product.

Preparing Cocoa and Chocolate Beverages Chocolate contains about 8 percent starch, cocoa powder about 11 percent. Like any other starch mixed in cold liquid, the starch in the cocoa and chocolate settles to the bottom of the beverage, carrying with it the pigments and other solids in cocoa and chocolate. The starch is dispersed most evenly if the cocoa and chocolate beverages are heated to boiling, thus gelatinizing the starch. Because both chocolate and milk tend to scorch, do not heat the chocolate in the milk; instead, heat it in a small amount of water to the boiling point, and then add it to hot or cold milk. A microwave oven is useful for heating cocoa and chocolate mixtures and for melting baker's chocolate. Adding a small amount of vanilla to chocolate beverages gives them a balanced flavor.

Chocolate milk or cocoa held for a long time form a dark sediment; this effect cannot be avoided. The sediment can be stirred into the beverage just before it is served, or the milk can be decanted from the sediment and the sediment discarded. Skin formation can be prevented during preparation by constant stirring during heating. Covering the prepared hot cocoa prevents the formation of skin during holding. Skin formation can be prevented in drinking cups by pouring the hot chocolate over a marshmallow or by topping the beverage with whipped cream. Once the starch in the chocolate or cocoa has been boiled for complete gelatinization, the beverage needs no further cooking; to do so only causes a loss of volatile flavors. The beverage should be heated only to serving temperature.

A beverage made of chocolate and milk is called *chocolate milk*. If cocoa is combined with milk, the beverage is called "chocolate-flavored milk" or "cocoa." Occasionally, cocoa powder is mixed with water, but the resulting beverage cannot be called "chocolate-flavored milk" because it contains no milk; it is often called "cocoa," which is a misleading name. A liquid composed of half water and half milk is also sometimes called "cocoa."

Oxalic Acid in Chocolate Cacao beans contain oxalic acid, which combines with calcium and thus prevents the absorption of calcium in the human body. Occasional consumption of chocolate milk by young children is acceptable, but its habitual use should not be encouraged. Unlike spinach, which contains calcium, chocolate contains no calcium, so the oxalic acid binds some of the calcium in milk, making it unavailable for absorption.

Storing Chocolate Cocoa and chocolate can be stored for a limited time only, depending on storage conditions. The fat in these products can be oxidized, and volatile flavoring substances can be lost if they are kept for too long or stored at high temperatures. A white coating on the surface of squares of chocolate indicates that such changes have occurred; products made with such chocolate do not have as rich a chocolate flavor as products made with fresh chocolate.

Ground chocolate or cocoa has a shorter shelf life than solid chocolate because more surface area is exposed, from which losses can occur. A new, unopened can of cocoa can be held at room temperature for a year without noticeable deterioration. Once the can is opened, so that the cocoa powder comes in contact with air, the product has a shelf life of about 3 to 6 months, depending on the storage temperature. If such products are used only infrequently, either purchase the smaller-size can or store the container in the refrigerator or freezer.

Tea

Tea is an *infusion* of leaves or roots from a wide variety of aromatic shrubs and trees, prepared by extraction of substances in leaves or roots soaked in water. The flavor, odor, and color of tea depends on the leaves or roots extracted, their processing, and the method of preparing the infusion.

Most tea consumed in the United States is an infusion of the dried leaves from an evergreen shrub of the camellia family of plants. Many other herbs and roots, such as mint leaves and the bark of sassafras tree roots, also make tea infusions. This section discusses only those infusions prepared from the evergreen shrub of the camellia family. The two tip leaves and bud of each stem of the shrub are pinched off and processed to make the tea (Figure 31.5). These tender young leaves, designated by such names as *flowery pekoe, flowery orange pekoe, broken orange pekoe,* and

Figure 31.5

The three tender-tip leaves for making the best grades of tea. *(Tea Council of the U.S.A., Inc.)*

orange pekoe, are the highest grade of tea. The less desirable older and larger leaves further down the stem are used to make *pekoe* or *souchong* teas. Special blends of tea are available with added spices and flowers; jasmine tea, for instance, contains jasmine flowers.

What is commonly called a fermentation process that tea leaves undergo is not fermentation but rather an enzymatic oxidation of the tannins in the leaves. The oxidative enzymes become particularly active when the leaves are wilted and rolled. Green tea is not allowed to undergo oxidation. The leaves are steamed to inactivate the enzymes. The final step is drying the tea leaves by blowing hot air through the steamed green leaves or the oxidized black leaves.

FERMENTATION OF TEA LEAVES

A short fermentation or oxidation period produces *oolong tea;* a longer fermentation produces *black tea.* After fermentation, the leaves are dried. Oxidation of the tannins during fermentation causes the leaves to darken. Infusions are colored according to the fermentation of the leaves; that is, green leaves produce a pale infusion, black leaves produce a deep amber infusion, and oolong is intermediate in color. The flavor of the infusion, however, is the opposite of its color, for black tea produces the mildest infusion. Tannins, which are bitter and astringent, become less so after fermentation.

Most tea sold in the United States is black tea made from a mixture of orange pekoe and pekoe. Tea bags contain broken or crushed tea leaves, a smaller amount of which is necessary to produce a given amount of infusion than whole leaves, because crushed leaves expose more surface area, pack down more, and occupy less space. Many teas are available both in bulk and in tea bags.

MARKET FORMS OF TEA

Instant tea is a spray-dried or drum-dried tea infusion. Some instant teas have lemon added for flavor and maltodextrin to improve stability. Infusions for instant tea are usually made from black tea. Instant tea lacks the full flavor of tea leaves in a freshly prepared infusion.

Tea should be brewed in ceramic pots. Metal pots either react directly with the tannins in tea or contain metal oxides that react, forming a scum on the surface of the tea. If a metal pot is used to brew tea, it should be thoroughly scoured to remove the mineral deposits. Any pot used to brew tea should be preheated.

PREPARING TEA

Naturally soft water or distilled water are preferred for brewing tea. Hard water and artificially softened water both contain minerals that precipitate tannins and produce scum on the surface of the tea. Adding a small amount of acid, such as lemon juice, dissolves the precipitates and removes the scum, but may not be a practical measure for those who like milk or cream in their tea.

Water should be brought to a boil and poured immediately onto the leaves. Oxygen in water adds to the briskness and zest of tea; extended boiling causes water to lose oxygen. Tea leaves may be placed loose in the pot or in a tea ball, or tea bags can be used for easy removal. Tea leaves should be infused no longer than 3 to 4 minutes. This infusion time permits maximum extraction of desirable flavors and stimulants with minimal extraction of bitter components. Loose leaves should be strained out after this time.

Tea is called an infusion because the temperature of the water used for extraction is below that of boiling. The strength of tea is determined by the ratio of tea leaves to water. The usual ratio is 1 rounded teaspoonful per 8-ounce cup of water, or about $\frac{1}{3}$ ounce of leaves per pint of water. Tea bags use less than $\frac{1}{10}$ ounce of leaves per bag, with one bag recommended per cup of tea, although frequently a bag can be used to make two or three 6-ounce cups of tea.

Iced tea is often prepared simply by adding ice to hot tea. Because ice dilutes the tea, a double-strength infusion should be prepared with twice the normal amount of tea leaves, but the infusion time should still last not more than 4 minutes. Tea balls should be filled no more than half full of dry leaves to allow room for the leaves to expand; placing too many leaves in one tea ball causes incomplete extraction. More than one tea ball can be used if more tea leaves are required to prepare the desired strength of infusion. Iced tea can be prepared cold by placing loose tea leaves in a glass jar, covering them with cold water, placing a lid on the jar, and refrigerating for 24 hours.

Lemon lightens the color of tea because its acid bleaches the tannins. Cream or milk mellows the taste of tea; the casein protein in milk additionally makes the tannins insoluble.

Coffee

Coffee is an infusion of ground coffee beans. Beans are obtained from a variety of coffee trees indigenous to tropical regions. Harvested coffee beans are known either as berries or cherries (Figure 31.6), although, with a soft pulp covering a double pit, they more nearly resemble cherries. Pulp is removed from the coffee seed, or pit, by several methods. One common method is fermentation, which softens the pulp so that it can be easily washed off the seeds. Dried, these seeds are called green coffee beans. Most coffee is imported into the United States as green coffee beans.

MARKET FORMS OF COFFEE

Manufacturers of coffee products use several varieties of coffee beans to produce distinctive mixtures; each brand of coffee is a blend of coffee beans. Figure 31.7 shows how an experienced coffee taster roasts, grinds, and brews samples from each batch of imported coffee beans as a preliminary step to blending the amounts and kinds of beans desirable for a particular brand.

Figure 31.6

Because blossoms and ripe berries appear at the same time on coffee trees, coffee berries must be picked by hand. *(Pan American Coffee Bureau)*

Figure 31.7

An experienced coffee taster roasts, grinds, and brews coffee from each batch of coffee beans as they arrive, determining the proportions of each batch to blend together to achieve the characteristic flavor of a brand of coffee. *(Pan American Coffee Bureau)*

Green beans are roasted before they are ground. The amount of roasting affects the flavor of coffee brewed from the beans. Most Americans prefer a light roast; in Italy, a darker roast is preferred. Roasted beans are ground to different degrees of fineness or coarseness for particular methods of brewing coffee.

Instant coffee is a dehydrated coffee infusion obtained by drum-drying, spray-drying, or freeze-drying. The flavor of instant coffee is largely dependent on the blends it contains. Decaffeinated coffees are available in both instant and ground forms. The caffeine is removed from the green coffee beans by steaming the beans in water, which also removes flavoring components. The caffeine is then separated from the flavor components by extraction of the caffeine solution with methylene chloride. The caffeine-free solution is added back to the coffee beans, which are then dried, roasted, and ground.

In the preparation of coffee infusions, various acids are extracted that are irritating to the digestive tract of some people. Acid-free coffee is another form of processed coffee that is available both in instant and ground forms. The process used to produce acid-free coffee increases the potassium content.

STALENESS IN COFFEE

Coffee beans have a fairly high fat content. Once the bean is ground, the fat is subject to oxidation because of the greater surface area exposed. This oxidation is a type of rancidity that produces undesirable flavors and odors. The ground coffee is also subject to a greater loss of volatile flavoring compounds, which, along with the oxidation of fat, causes staling of the coffee. Because stale coffee produces poorly flavored infusions, ground coffee is frequently sold in vacuum-packed cans. Many markets in past years supplied a grinder so that the customer could purchase coffee freshly ground from beans. Freshly ground coffee or an opened vacuum tin of coffee that is allowed to sit at room temperature soon loses its fresh characteristics. Therefore, the exclusion of air and moisture is essential to maintain freshness in ground coffee. It can be stored in airtight containers in the refrigerator or freezer to maintain freshness.

COFFEE GRINDS

Grind refers to the size of particles produced from coffee beans. The more surface area exposed to water when an infusion is made—that is, the finer the grind—the more substances will be extracted from the ground coffee. Thus, the size of the grind must always be related to the method of making the infusion. If grounds are to be subject to very hot water for a long period of time, a coarse grind is recommended. Conversely, if they will be subjected to lower temperatures and shorter times, finer grinds can be used. The names of some grinds refer to the type of coffee maker suitable for that grind of coffee; the names of other grinds refer to the size of particles, coarse or fine.

Water for coffee infusions should be naturally soft or distilled and should contain oxygen. The material the pot is made of is of less importance for brewing coffee than for brewing tea. The pot must, however, be clean. Fats from coffee infusions that adhere to the inside of the pot build up if it is not washed with hot, soapy water after each use. These fats become rancid and produce off flavors in subsequent infusions. Special cleaners are available for some types of coffee pots, but cleaners and soap alike must be thoroughly rinsed from the pot so that they will not affect the flavor.

Regardless of the brewing method used, the coffee grounds should be removed as soon as brewing is completed, for the grounds tend to absorb aroma from the infusion. Infusions have the best flavor and aroma if they are prepared just before being served. Coffee infusions can be held at a serving temperature of 190 to 200°F (88 to 93°C), but should not be allowed to boil. Keeping coffee hot causes loss of volatile flavoring components. Iced coffee, like iced tea, requires a stronger brew using a higher ratio of coffee to water.

Time and temperature relationships for tea infusions also apply to coffee. To extract desirable flavors, not bitter components, from the coffee grounds, the water temperature should be between 190 and 200°F (88 and 93°C) and the brewing time should be limited. The method of brewing and the proportions of coffee to water, as well as the brand of coffee, determine the flavor and strength of a coffee infusion.

The more grounds that are present in relation to water, the stronger the infusion becomes; this is the preferred way to obtain strong coffee infusions. If brewing time is extended to obtain a stronger infusion, the infusion will contain a high proportion of undesirable flavors and bitterness; this procedure is not recommended. One, 2, or 3 level tablespoons of ground coffee should be used per 6-ounce cup of water to produce mild, average, or strong infusions, respectively. Because the average coffee or tea cup holds only 6 ounces, the marking on coffee pots and measurements for preparing coffee are based on this size. Thus, a 5-cup coffee pot holds 30 ounces, or slightly less than four 8-ounce measuring cups of coffee.

The brewing method used determines the temperature of water, which can be controlled in some methods of brewing, but not in others. Most automatic coffee makers have some built-in means of controlling brewing time.

Steeped Coffee   Ground coffee and water are heated to just below the boiling point and held for about 3 minutes. The grounds are then strained from the infusion; straining through cheesecloth helps remove most of the sediment. Any type of container can be used for brewing; this is a favorite method for use on camping

FACTORS AFFECTING THE QUALITY OF COFFEE INFUSIONS

BREWING COFFEE

trips in place of instant coffee. Regular grind coffee is recommended for brewing steeped coffee. High temperatures and excessive brewing times should be avoided to reduce bitterness in the infusion.

Percolated Coffee Heated water is forced up a tube in the center of a percolator and sprayed over the grounds held in a basket at the top of the pot. Water must be near the boiling point to be carried up the tube in the center of the pot. In the early part of brewing, this water is cooled by the grounds, but the temperature is close to the boiling point before percolation is completed. A diagram of the action in a percolator is shown in Figure 31.8. Five to 8 minutes of percolation provides a satisfactory infusion; nonelectric pots can be removed from the heat after this time. The control on an electric percolator is usually a lever that is used to select the strength of coffee brew desired. A mild brew percolates a shorter time than a strong brew. Regular grind coffee is used in nonelectric percolators; a special grind is available for electric percolators. Percolator infusions usually have some sediment.

Vacuum Coffee Makers Cold water is measured into the bottom part of a vacuum coffee maker, as shown in Figure 31.9. The filter is fitted into the top part of the coffee maker and the top is placed securely into the bottom section to form a good seal with the rubber gasket separating the two parts. Fine grind coffee is measured into the top, and the pot is placed over the heat. Because the water in the bottom of the pot is in a closed system, its steam exerts pressure on the hot water, forcing it up the funnel tip into the top part of the pot, where it comes in contact with the

Figure 31.8

A diagram showing the parts of a percolator coffee maker. (*From* Consumer Reports, *September 1974)*

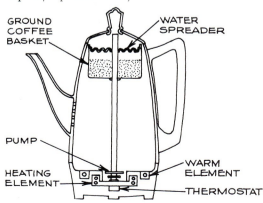

Figure 31.9

A diagram showing the action of a vacuum coffee maker.

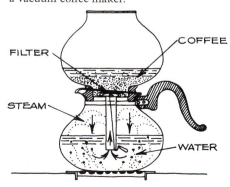

grounds. Heat is then reduced so that just enough remains to keep the water in the top of the pot for 1 to 4 minutes, when the pot is removed from the heat. As the pot cools a vacuum is produced in the bottom part, drawing the coffee infusion down.

If the seal between the top and bottom parts of the coffee maker is broken while the water is in the top section, the infusion does not return to the lower section. The two sections can be readjusted to form a seal and the bottom is again heated until steam forms. When the pot is removed from the heat, a vacuum will be present to draw the infusion into the bottom part of the coffee maker. If coffee grounds appear to be floating on the water in the top of the pot, the infusion may require stirring to wet them. Vacuum infusions usually have little or no sediment because of the type of filter used and have a good flavor if they are not brewed too long because the temperature remains below boiling.

Drip Coffee Makers Boiling water poured into a reservoir in the top section of the pot drips slowly through the grounds held in a basket in the center and into the bottom section of the coffee maker, as illustrated in Figure 31.10. The size of the holes in the top reservoir and in the basket determine how long the water remains in contact with the grounds. Filter paper can be used in the bottom of the basket before it is filled with ground coffee to reduce the amount of sediment in the infusion.

Drip grind coffee is used for drip coffee makers. Because artificially softened water does not readily pass through the tiny holes in the top reservoir of some drip coffee makers, it is not recom-

Figure 31.10

A diagram showing the action of a drip coffee maker.

Figure 31.11
Filtered coffee is prepared as shown.

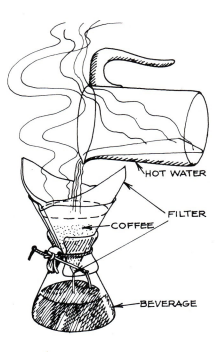

HOT WATER

FILTER

COFFEE

BEVERAGE

mended for this type of pot. Coffee infusions should not be poured through the grounds a second time. Sediment in the infusion may plug the holes in the reservoir and not drip through. If it does drip through, it may produce a bitter brew because of excessive extraction of the grounds.

Filter Coffee   Filter coffee is similar to drip coffee. A fine grind of coffee is placed in a funnel lined with filter paper over which boiling water is poured, as shown in Figure 31.11. The size of the holes in the filter paper determines the length of time the water remains in contact with the grounds. Filtered coffee is free of sediments and has a good flavor.

Automatic Drip-Filter Coffee Makers   Figure 31.12 shows an automatic drip-filter coffee maker; Figure 31.13 demonstrates its operation. Enough cold water is poured into the reservoir to make the desired amount of infusion. Water from the reservoir flows through the heating element and is heated instantaneously to the correct temperature for preparation of the infusion. The heated water is then sprayed over the finely ground coffee in a basket lined with filter paper, and the infusion drips into the carafe. An automatic drip-filter coffee maker produces a good infusion with no sediment in just a few minutes. The system can be used as a

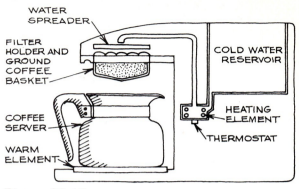

WATER SPREADER

FILTER HOLDER AND GROUND COFFEE BASKET

COLD WATER RESERVOIR

COFFEE SERVER

HEATING ELEMENT

THERMOSTAT

WARM ELEMENT

Figure 31.12

One type of automatic drip-filter coffee maker. *(Bunn-o-matic Corporation, Springfield, Illinois)*

Figure 31.13

A diagram representing the functioning of an automatic drip-filter coffee maker. (*From* Consumer Reports, *September 1974*)

source of hot water for tea, cocoa, or other purposes, and some models can be directly attached to a water source. Heating elements keep the infusions at serving temperature.

Coffee, tea, cocoa, chocolate, and carbonated cola drinks all contain *caffeine*, which is a stimulant. Cocoa and chocolate also contain *theobromine*, another stimulant. The amount of caffeine in beverages depends on the proportions of ground coffee, tea leaves, or chocolate used to prepare the beverage, and, in the case of coffee and tea, the method of brewing. Because it is soluble in water, most caffeine is extracted into infusions in the first 2 minutes of brewing. Table 31.3 shows approximate concentrations of caffeine in various beverages.

Caffeine has been credited with increasing the work output of people as well as decreasing the accuracy of the extra work done. Caffeine is indeed a cerebral stimulant; it also stimulates the flow of gastric juices, acts as a mild diuretic, and increases blood sugar.

In recent years, excessive intake of caffeine-containing beverages has been implicated as contributing to the development of heart disease, birth defects, bladder and lower urinary tract cancers, acceleration of aging, peptic ulcers, and nervous disorders.

Tea infusions contain catechin tannin, which has been implicated as a cause of esophageal tumors. However, if milk is used in the tea, the milk protein binds the tannin and prevents this effect. Some scientists have disagreed with these findings.

Pharmacological Effects of Some Beverages

Table 31.3 Caffeine content of beverages

Beverage	Caffeine/5-ounce cup (mg)
Decaffeinated coffee	2–6
Cola	19
Cocoa/chocolate	up to 50
Tea	70
Instant coffee	66–74
Drip or percolated coffee	90–120

SOURCE: *Journal of the American Medical Association* 229 (1974): 337.

Caffeine-containing beverages should be used in moderation by healthy adults. Children and pregnant and lactating women should limit their intake.

Study Questions

1. What standard is used to distinguish among juice products in the Code of Federal Regulations? What major factor determines the nutrient content of these products?
2. Why must pigments and pH of juices to be combined in punch mixtures be considered?
3. Why are whole spices preferred over ground spices in hot spiced punches?
4. What effect do acidic fruit juices and purées have on milk casein in milk-fruit drinks?
5. What method can be used to prepare a cooked eggnog?
6. Distinguish between cocoa and chocolate; and between chocolate milk and chocolate-flavored milk.
7. Describe briefly the process for preparing Dutch process cocoa and chocolate, and how this process affects the color and flavor of these products.
8. Why must cocoa and chocolate to be used in beverages be heated to the boiling point?
9. What names are applied to top-quality and lower grades of tea? What characteristic of tea leaves determines their grade?
10. What is the difference between green, oolong, and black teas in the amount of fermentation of the leaves and the color and flavor of infusions made from them?
11. What effect does hard or alkaline water have on tea infusions?
12. How long should hot water be left in contact with tea leaves when infusions are prepared? Why?
13. What procedure should be used to make a strong tea infusion?
14. Why should a tea ball not be filled full of dry leaves to prepare an infusion?
15. What effect does adding lemon juice have on a tea infusion?
16. Why do brands of coffee differ in flavor?
17. What causes staling of ground coffee? How does staling affect the flavor of infusions? How can staling be reduced?
18. What factors determine the best grind for brewing coffee?
19. Why must a coffee pot be cleaned after each use?
20. What are desirable and undesirable characteristics of coffee infusions?
21. What water temperature produces the best coffee infusion?
22. What size of cup is used to measure ground coffee and water for coffee infusions? Why?
23. Why do vacuum and drip methods of coffee brewing produce less bitterness than the percolator method?
24. What stimulants occur in some beverages? Which beverages?
25. What are some physiological effects of caffeine?

Davidson, Sir Stanley; Passmore, R.; and Brock, J. F. *Human Nutrition and Dietetics*. 5th ed. Baltimore, Md.: Williams & Wilkins, 1972.

Florey, Josephine. "Beverages." In U.S. Department of Agriculture, *Consumers All*, Yearbook of Agriculture. Washington, D.C.: Government Printing Office, 1965.

Mitchell, George F. "Heat Governs the Quality of Tea and Coffee." *Food Industries* 4 (1932): 166.

Morton, Julia F. "Tea with Milk." *Science* 204 (June 1979): 909.

Moses, Walter R., and Tennant, Margaret F. "Beverages: Milk, Coffee, Tea, Juices, Chocolate." In U.S. Department of Agriculture, *Food for Us All*, Yearbook of Agriculture. Washington, D.C.: Government Printing Office, 1969.

Prescott, Samuel C. *Report of an Investigation of Coffee*. National Coffee Roasters Association, 1927.

Punnett, P. W. "The Proof Is in the Drinking." *Food Industries* 5 (1933): 291.

——. "The Brewing Often Depends upon the Pot," *Food Industries* 5 (1933): 405.

Shuman, A. C., and Elder, L. W., Jr. "Staling Versus Rancidity in Roasted Coffee." *Industrial and Engineering Chemistry* 35 (1943): 778.

Stahl, William H. "The Chemistry of Tea and Tea Manufacturing." In *Advances in Food Research* 11:202. New York: Academic Press, 1962.

Wickremasinghe, Robert L. "Tea." *Advances in Food Research* 24 (1978): 229.

32

Planning, Preparing, and Serving Meals

Many factors must be considered in planning meals, from the needs and desires of people to the organization necessary to prepare several different dishes simultaneously.

People with their preferences, customs, and needs must be considered first in planning a meal. The interests, abilities, and time of those who must prepare the meal should be considered second. Finally, the cost of food and the equipment available must be taken into account.

Planning Meals

NUTRIENTS

Although eating as a social occasion should be a pleasurable experience, the food consumed must meet human physiological requirements. As discussed in Chapter 1, one day's supply of food should ideally contain the RDA of all nutrients, preferably from natural foods rather than from manufactured or imitation foods.

Because one third of all adults in the United States are obese, foods should be chosen and prepared to meet, but not exceed, caloric needs. This goal is sometimes difficult to achieve in the family unit, because adult females, adult males, and children all have different nutritional and caloric needs; physical activity also influences a person's caloric requirements. Individual differences can often, but not entirely be accommodated by size of serving. Women often need the same amount of vitamins and minerals, as well as more iron, as men do, but must obtain them with a lower caloric intake. Unless they are physically active, women may need to curtail empty calorie foods, that is, foods high in calories but containing few, if any, vitamins, minerals, or protein. Moreover, when caloric intake is greatly limited, each food consumed must contribute its full share of nutrients.

ESTHETICS OF MEAL PLANNING

The sensory qualities of foods—their appearance, odor, flavor, and texture—are very important. No matter how nutritious it may be, a food that looks unappetizing or smells bad is not likely to be eaten. Because a meal usually consists of more than one food, foods served together, either separately or in a mixed dish, should complement one another in flavor, color, texture, shape, method of preparation, and possibly temperature. Such factors taken together affect the esthetic impact of a meal.

Flavor Some foods have dominating flavors; others are mild or almost tasteless. The four taste sensations are discussed in Chapter 3. Besides these basic flavors, individual foods—garlic, onion, Brassica vegetables, fish, bananas, and cantaloupe, to name a few—have unique and unclassifiable flavors.

Food flavors in a meal should blend together with no single flavor being overemphasized. A meal consisting of a sweet gelatin salad, candied sweet potatoes, sweet and sour pork, and iced cake, for example, overemphasizes sweetness. A meal containing several foods seasoned with garlic is another example of too limited a flavor range. Similarly, a meal should not contain too many different strong flavors. Cooked cabbage with fish, especially if the cabbage is overcooked, is an undesirable combination of flavors that might produce undesirable odors as well. Too many bland flavors in a meal are also not advisable. For example, a meal consisting of a cheese soufflé served with creamed corn, buttered summer squash, cottage cheese salad, and a custard dessert is not only bland in flavor but also lacks color and texture contrasts. The same food should not appear in several forms in a meal; for example, pineapple should not be used in the dessert if it has already been used in the salad.

Color An attractive combination of colors in the foods used for a meal stimulates the flow of digestive juices and improves the appetite. The natural colors of most foods are red, purple, orange, yellow, white, green, and brown. Blue, an uncommon food color, is expected to be present in dishes containing blueberries but not in cooked red cabbage or grape juice. Monotonous or clashing colors should be avoided; red cabbage, beets, and tomato aspic would be unattractive served together. Lack of color or too many white or pale foods is also unappetizing. Color contrast variety within a single meal is a good indication that a variety of nutrients are present, because such colors as orange and green are associated with certain nutrients: for example, orange is associated with carotene and deep green with carotene and vitamin C.

Textures and Shapes Texture is the crispness, chewiness, crunchiness, or softness of a food. A meal containing several crisp or chewy foods can be tiresome to eat; too many soft foods in a meal is also objectionable.

A balance of soft and chewy foods must be maintained in each meal. The presence of a few raw foods, either in a salad or as relishes, adds texture to a meal, since most cooked foods tend to be soft. If a meat is served that requires a great deal of chewing, a salad of cooked vegetables or fruits balances the textures better than a raw carrot salad, which also requires chewing.

Variety in shapes is desirable in foods that are served together. The form of a food can often be altered by the way it is chopped or cut. Cubed beets, cubed carrots, and cubed meats are not as attractive on the same plate as shoestring beets and sliced carrots with cubed meat. Barely cooked spinach could likewise be served in place of beets, because of the similar textures of beets and carrots. Some mixed dishes, such as stew, succotash, and chop suey, are exceptions to this rule. In these dishes uniformity of shape is necessary to ensure that all the foods cook to the proper degree of doneness in the same period of time.

Preparation Methods   If all foods served in a meal are fried or are creamed, the meal would be not only high in calories, but also monotonous. As a rule, it is best to vary the methods of preparation for foods in a meal, but exceptions do occur. French-fried potatoes or onion rings often accompany fried meats, especially fish. Boiled, broiled, and baked dinners, moreover, save energy and time. In both these cases, variety can be introduced by means of seasonings, garnishes, and other such accompaniments.

SEASONAL AVAILABILITY OF FOODS

A food that is unavailable because it is out of season obviously cannot be served in a meal. However, many foods have become available for most of the year because of new technologies in food storage and processing. Nonetheless, certain foods are still associated with particular seasons: hot, warming foods with winter; cold, frosty foods with summer. Again, there are exceptions; many persons like cold drinks and ice cream all year long, and some like hot food at every meal, regardless of the season. Because a hot lunch contains no more nutritional benefit than a cold one, the primary consideration in preparing a meal hot or cold should be individual preference. The primary consideration in seasonal availability is the economic advantage of serving foods in season when they are more reasonably priced than at other times of the year.

FOOD PREFERENCES, CUSTOMS, AND ALLERGIES

Many foods, such as curries, tortillas, chappatis, or grits, are traditional to certain cultures. Some cultures greatly emphasize soups; other stress breads or cheeses. The most common foods are usually those that are locally available or can be prepared from available foodstuffs. Adequate meals that still observe custom and individual preference are possible with planning and some knowledge of the nutrient composition of foods. Meals for a person, particularly a child, who refuses to drink milk must be planned so that milk is present in cooked foods in enough quantity to provide sufficient calcium. Meals for a person who is allergic to a food, such as eggs, must be planned so that they do not contain eggs in any form. Such adjustments in meal plans require ingenuity and effort from the food preparer to meet the needs of persons with special problems.

SATIETY VALUE OF FOODS

Foods with satiety value delay feelings of hunger, an effect that is partly related to the speed at which foods leave the stomach. Sugars, which leave the stomach most quickly, have the lowest satiety value, although they are often credited with spoiling the appetite if they are eaten too closely before a meal. Starch remains in the stomach slightly longer than sugar, and protein remains slightly longer than starch. Fat stays in the stomach the longest time of any food.

The satiety value of a meal can be adjusted according to the ratios and amounts of these food components. If the time between meals is short, the first meal should be low in satiety value. If the next meal is to be eaten some hours away, however, the first meal should be high in satiety value. A breakfast of juice, toast, jam, and coffee has a low satiety value because it is high in starch and sugar and low in protein and fat. Egg, meat, or cheese would extend the satiety value of this meal by increasing its protein and fat content. Table fat on the toast, or an egg fried instead of poached, would further improve satiety value by increasing the fat content of the meal.

Fat consumption for purposes of satiety may need to be restricted when caloric or fat intake must be curtailed for health reasons. In such cases, protein should be the main provider of satiety; those who are trying to lose weight may have to tolerate a small degree of hunger.

ECONOMICS OF PLANNING MEALS

The cost of food materials is only one part of the cost of a meal. The cost of equipment and facilities for preparing foods is a factor, as is the time available for preparing foods.

Cost and Yield of Market Forms of Food   Several market forms of a food, such as fresh, frozen, and canned peas, are often available. Price comparisons are difficult because fresh peas have shells and canned peas have liquid occupying space in the can. The U.S. Department of Agriculture's Home Economics Research Report No. 37, *Family Food Buying,* indicates the edible portion of food from various market forms and provides a factor for determining the amount to buy per serving, as discussed in Chapter 7.

The market unit size of a food is often too much or too little for a given number of servings. A 1-pound can of peas, for example, contains 1¾ cups of peas, or not quite enough for four ½-cup servings; two cans, however, would be too much. A food may sometimes be too expensive in any of its market forms. Asparagus, which is about twice the price of many other vegetables either canned or frozen during most of the year, may have to be omitted from the menu in favor of a less expensive vegetable with a similar nutrient content. Not only the costs of foods but also their nutrient contributions should be considered so that substitutions can be made without sacrificing nutritional values. Previous chapters have provided information on unit pricing and cost comparison of market forms of milk, eggs, meat, and other products. Familiarity with these concepts is a necessity in intelligent food budgeting.

Convenience Foods   Convenience foods are foods that can be purchased in varying degrees of preparation. Frozen vegetables, for example, have been trimmed and washed and are ready to cook. Convenience foods are often more expensive than their raw form because of the cost of the extra labor required to produce them. Despite this fact, however, some convenience foods may be more economical than fresh, unprocessed food, particularly if the costs of edible portions are compared. Other convenience foods may be more expensive than the same food unprocessed, but the time needed to make the food may be prohibitive, and cost must be weighed against time. Moreover, the person preparing food may lack the skill needed to prepare certain foods. Most bread is purchased baked not only because of the time needed to make yeast breads but also because the art of bread making is not widely practiced at home. Some convenience foods may contain more calories or fewer nutrients than their counterparts prepared at home, a circumstance often found with canned soups, as discussed in Chapter 25. All these considerations must be weighed according to individual needs.

Equipment   Equipment may influence the kinds of foods prepared for a meal. The absence of electric mixers, blenders, and freezers can greatly limit both the variety and the quality of food that can be prepared. The absence of an oven or broiler is an even more limiting factor. Even a simple task like making bread crumbs can illustrate the necessity of having proper equipment. Without a blender or food grinder, bread could be dried until crisp and then crumbled with a grater or a rolling pin. Without either of these implements, the bread could be crumbled with the fingers, a slow and tedious process. Preparing food becomes an increasingly slow and complicated task as less sophisticated equipment comes into use.

INCREASING AND REDUCING RECIPES

Recipes must occasionally be altered to produce the desired number of servings, but such changes may not produce a result identical with that of the original recipe. As a rule, a tested recipe should be followed whenever possible with no alterations, at least until food preparation techniques become more familiar.

In some dishes, such as soups, casseroles, and stews, the amount of spices and herbs should not be doubled when the recipe is doubled; the foods should rather be seasoned to taste. In cooking rice, cereals, pastas, cream puffs, and candy, the amount of water should not be doubled when other ingredients are doubled. Because less evaporation occurs from a large mass than from a small mass, a smaller proportion of water is needed when the recipe is increased; additionally, the type of pan also influences evaporation. Similarly, reduced recipes may require the addition of extra water because of increased rates of evaporation from the smaller mass.

Alteration of recipes also affects cooking time. A cake may take longer to bake when the recipe is doubled, depending on the dimensions of the pan. A large mass of food cooked on a surface unit usually takes longer to reach the boiling point than a smaller mass. Some cooking occurs during the heating period, however, so that a long heating period accomplishes more cooking before boiling starts, reducing the time needed for cooking after boiling starts.

MENU PATTERNS Certain foods are often stereotyped for specific meals; some are thought of as suitable only for breakfast, others for lunch or dinner. This practice may differ widely from one cultural or ethnic group to another. Such typecasting of foods can become monotonous, because the time of day at which certain foods are eaten is of little nutritional importance. What does matter is that the foods chosen supply all the nutrients needed for the day.

Such guides as the Basic Four Food Groups or the Basic Seven Food Groups discussed in Chapter 1 are helpful in planning meals to meet daily nutritional needs. Table 32.1 shows some typical menu plans for breakfast, lunch, and dinner in three different patterns, representing simple, moderate, and elaborate plans. The more elaborate plans include foods that are likely to be higher both in calories and in cost than foods in the simplest plan.

The proportion of food and nutrients provided at each meal is

Table 32.1   Typical meal patterns, from simple to elaborate

Meal	Simple	Moderate	Elaborate
Breakfast	Fruit Cereal and/or breadstuff Beverage	Fruit Cereal and/or breadstuff Protein food[a] Beverage	Fruit Cereal Breadstuff Protein food[a] Beverage
Luncheon or supper	Soup[b] and/or salad[b] Breadstuff Dessert Beverage	Protein food[a] Salad and/or vegetable Breadstuff Beverage	Protein food[a] Salad and/or vegetable Breadstuff Dessert Beverage
Dinner	Meat Salad Vegetables Breadstuff Beverage	Meat Salad Vegetables Breadstuff Dessert Beverage	Appetizer: Soup and/or salad Meat Vegetables Breadstuff Dessert Beverage

[a]Protein foods can be soups, casseroles, salads or sandwiches that contain a serving of meat or other high-protein food.

[b]Soups and salads in the simple luncheon menu should supply a good source of protein.

solely a matter of personal convenience, preference, and need. The nutritional benefit is the same regardless of whether all the food is consumed at one meal or is divided into six separate meals. Some persons prefer three small meals, with snacks between meals and at bedtime. Desserts, for example, can be postponed for a between-meal or bedtime snack. Rich, sweet desserts are often unnecessary; fresh fruit can be refreshing, either after a large meal or between meals.

Meal plans should incorporate leftovers, preferably so that they are served differently the second time around. Leftover ham or other meat, for example, can be used in soufflés, omelets, sandwiches, casseroles, soup, and bean dishes, or baked in a loaf. Although reheated vegetables suffer loss of a few vitamins, enough nutrients remain to make them worthwhile. Leftover vegetables should be heated only to serving temperatures; they can often be used in salads with no further heating.

Except for staples, such as bread, milk, and eggs, the same foods should not be used too regularly. It is better not to use the same food twice in the same day, nor even every day. Not only does such a practice become monotonous, but it also limits nutrient intake. Even varying the type of bread is a good practice.

Breakfast Eggs are a commonly accepted breakfast food, as are pancakes, waffles, cereals, and toast (Figure 32.1). More diversified breakfasts, however, are becoming popular. Soups, cheese

Figure 32.1

Some popular breakfast foods include: breads, such as muffins and coffee cakes; eggs, scrambled or prepared as omelets; various kinds of cereals; and beverages, such as cocoa or other milk drinks. *(United Dairy Industry Association)*

toast, creamed meat or cheese sauce on toast, breakfast steaks, and similar foods that were formerly reserved for lunch now appear frequently on breakfast tables.

It is good practice to start breakfast with juice or fruit, because fruit is a good appetizer and may also have some slight laxative effect that helps maintain regularity. Some source of protein is also helpful for its satiety value. Other foods can be added for persons who need additional energy. Some adults like a stimulating beverage, such as tea or coffee; children may need milk to supply their daily quota.

Eliminating breakfast entirely can reduce efficiency later in the morning and should be avoided. On the other hand, breakfast should not be so rich and heavy that it carries unnecessary calories. Breakfast foods should contribute nutrients as well as calories; a breakfast of a sweet roll and coffee contains mostly empty calories.

Lunch, Supper, or Dinner "Dinner" is usually the name reserved for the principal meal of the day, which may be served at noon, in the evening, or at any time in between. If dinner is served in the late afternoon or evening, the meal at noon is called "lunch." If dinner is served at noon, the evening meal is called "supper." "Brunch," as the name implies, is a meal that combines breakfast and lunch and is usually served in the late morning.

Lunch or Supper As the lighter meals of the day, lunch and supper should consist of simpler foods than dinner, such as a sandwich, fruit, and beverage. These meals can resemble dinner except that fewer courses and lighter foods are eaten, or can be one-dish meals, such as a hearty soup served with cheese, bread, and a beverage, with fruit for dessert. Casseroles, entrée salads, soufflés, creamed meats or cheese sauce served on toast, rice, or noodles are common luncheon and supper foods (Figure 32.2). A thrifty person can find ingenious ways to use leftover foods in these meals.

Foods served at lunch and supper should help balance the nutrient intake for the day. If eggs were served at breakfast, they should not be served at lunch. If breakfast included only cereal protein, then some type of animal protein, such as cheese or meat, should be served for lunch or supper. If the fruit served at breakfast was low in vitamin C, a fruit or vegetable rich in vitamin C should be served at lunch or dinner.

Dinner Dinner is not only the largest meal of the day, it is also the social meal of the day. Dinner is usually more elaborate and requires more preparation time than lunch or supper. It may con-

Figure 32.2

Casseroles, hearty soups, and protein salads supplying meat or cheese, accompanied by a hot quick bread and a simple dessert, such as custard or fruit whip, are good choices for lunch or supper. *(United Dairy Industry Association)*

sist of several courses, such as soup, salad course, entrée, and dessert, with appetizers sometimes served before the meal itself.

Dinner is the best meal for serving vegetables, and as wide a variety as possible should be served from day to day. Only one starchy vegetable should be served at a meal, because they have more calories, and some have fewer nutrients than many of the nonstarchy vegetables. Vegetables high in starch or sugar include sweet potatoes, white potatoes, lima beans, peas, beets, corn, and carrots. Pastas or rice can replace starchy vegetables, but they should be served with a nonstarchy vegetable.

Besides those present in soups and salad, two kinds of vegetables are ideal for dinner. If only one vegetable is used, then a larger size serving should be planned. Most cooked vegetables other than starchy ones are low in calories and a good source of fiber. Ample vegetables at dinner helps keep the calorie content of the meal low, especially if the seasonings used are not high in calories. A leafy green vegetable should be served at dinner two or three times a week. Among the vegetables and fruits used in the soup and salad and as cooked vegetables should be ones that are good sources of vitamins A and C.

A dinner salad may be served either before, after, or with the entrée, either separately or on the dinner plate. The place of the salad in the meal often dictates the type of salad served. It is not practical to serve a gelatin salad on a hot dinner plate, for example, because the gelatin would melt before it could be eaten.

Figure 32.3

Such entrées as oven-fried
chicken or Swedish meatballs,
together with cooked
vegetables, salads, breads, and
desserts, are served in dinner
menus. *(United Dairy Industry
Association)*

The entrée of a family dinner does not need to be an expensive
cut of meat. Economy cuts, casseroles, and meat substitutes are
always acceptable (Figure 32.3). For those who must restrict their
caloric intake, fried foods and rich sauces with high fat content
should be limited.

**COMPUTING THE
NUTRITIONAL QUALITY
OF MEALS**

The nutrient composition of meals can be determined by listing
the nutrients in each food obtained from tables of nutrient composition and adding up the daily total. Because it is very time-
consuming, this process may be feasible only occasionally, as a
means of checking the nutrient intake of poor eaters. A quicker
way to assess dietary adequacy is to use a food group plan. Table
32.2 shows a menu for 1 day based on a moderate meal plan with
food groups tabulated for each item; Table 32.3 shows a menu
based on the same kind of meal plan but using meat extenders or
substitutes. The nutrient composition of the two menus is shown
in Tables 32.4 and 32.5, respectively.

As can be seen, although the menu in Table 32.2 provides the
recommended servings from each food group, it does not meet
the RDA for iron for women or the RDA for thiamin and niacin
for men. The menu in Table 32.3 contains about 250 fewer calories than the one in Table 32.2. It is short one serving from the
milk group, but it is adequate in calcium; however, it also lacks
adequate iron for women, and adequate thiamin and niacin for
men.

Table 32.2 *Menu based on moderate meal plan with food groups shown for each food item*

Menu items	Number of servings						
	Vitamin A fruit/vegetable	Vitamin C fruit/vegetable	Other fruit/vegetable	Milk	Meat or substitute	Bread or cereal	Fat
Breakfast:							
½ grapefruit		1					
½ cup oatmeal						1	
1 teaspoon sugar							
Cheese toast:							
1 slice whole wheat bread						1	
1 ounce processed cheese					⅓		
1 cup low-fat milk				1			
Lunch:							
Ham sandwich:							
2 slices enriched white bread						2	
1 tablespoon margarine							1
2 ounces sliced ham					⅔		
Lettuce-tomato salad:							
⅛ head lettuce			1				
1 small tomato		1					
1 tablespoon French dressing							1
1 cup fresh strawberries		1					
1 teaspoon sugar							
1 cup low-fat milk				1			
Dinner:							
3 ounces broiled chicken breast					1		
½ cup candied sweet potatoes	1						
½ cup dilled green beans			1				
½ cup apple-pineapple salad			1				
¾ cup pumpkin custard	1						
Tea or coffee							
Totals for day:	2	3	3	2	2	4	2
Recommended per day:	1	1	2	2	2	4	1

Table 32.3 *Menu based on moderate meal plan, using meat extenders, with food groups shown for each item*

Menu item	Number of servings						
	Vitamin A fruit/vegetable	Vitamin C fruit/vegetable	Other fruit/vegetable	Milk	Meat or substitute	Bread or cereal	Fat
Breakfast:							
1 cup tomato juice		1					
2 eggs, poached					2		
1 slice whole wheat toast						1	
1 teaspoon margarine							1/3
Coffee or tea:							
1 teaspoon sugar							
1 tablespoon half-and-half							
Lunch:							
1 cup chili beans with meat					1	1	
1/2 cup brown rice						1	
4 soda crackers							
Carrot sticks	1						
1 apple			1				
1 cup nonfat milk				1			
Dinner:							
1 cup spaghetti with meat					1/2	1	
1 cup broccoli with		1					
1/2 lemon wedge							
Lettuce with French dressing			1				1
1 slice French bread						1	
1 teaspoon margarine							1/3
1/4 cantaloupe	1						
Coffee or tea:							
1 teaspoon sugar							
1 tablespoon half-and-half							
Totals for day:	2	2	2	1	3 1/2	5	1 2/3
Recommended per day:	1	1	2	2	2	4	1

Table 32.4   Nutrient composition of menu shown in Table 32.2

Food	Amount	Calories	Protein (g)	Fat (g)	Calcium (mg)	Iron (mg)	Vitamin A (I.U.)	Thiamin (mg)	Riboflavin (mg)	Niacin (mg)	Vitamin C (mg)
Milk, low-fat	2 cups	290	20	10	704	0.2	400	0.2	1.04	0.4	4
Cheese, American process	1 ounce	105	7	9	198	0.3	350	0.01	0.12	—	0
Chicken, broiled	3 ounces	115	20	3	8	1.4	80	0.05	0.16	7.4	—
Ham, boiled, sliced	2 ounces	135	11	10	6	1.6	0	0.25	0.09	1.5	—
Beans, snap, cooked	½ cup	15	1	trace	31	0.4	340	0.04	0.05	0.3	7
Lettuce, head	⅛ head	7	—	—	11	0.3	187	0.03	0.03	0.2	4
Sweet potato, candied	½ cup	117	2	trace	27	0.8	8500	0.05	0.05	0.7	15
Tomato, fresh, small	1	20	1	trace	12	0.4	820	0.05	0.03	0.6	21
Apple, fresh	⅓	23	trace	trace	3	0.1	17	0.01	0.01	0.1	1
Grapefruit, fresh	½	45	1	trace	19	0.5	10	0.05	0.02	0.2	44
Pineapple, fresh	¼ cup	19	trace	trace	6	0.2	25	0.03	0.01	0.1	6
Strawberries, fresh	1 cup	55	1	trace	31	1.5	90	0.04	0.10	1.0	88
Pumpkin custard[a]	¾ cup	183	6	2	59	0.8	3986	0.07	0.15	0.4	13
Bread, white, enriched	2 slices	140	4	2	42	1.2	trace	0.12	0.1	1.2	—
Bread, whole wheat	1 slice	65	3	1	24	0.8	0	0.09	0.03	0.8	—
Oatmeal, cooked	½ cup	65	2	1	11	0.7	0	0.09	0.02	0.1	—
Mayonnaise	1 tablespoon	100	trace	11	3	0.1	40	trace	0.01	—	—
French dressing	1 tablespoon	65	trace	6	2	0.1	—	—	—	—	—
Sugar	1 tablespoon	40	—	—	—	—	—	—	—	—	—
Margarine	3 tablespoons	300	—	36	6	—	1410	—	—	—	—
Totals for day:		1904	79	91	1203	11.4	16255	1.18	2.02	14.9	203
Recommended Dietary Allowances[b]											
Adult male		2700	56	—	800	10	5000	1.4	1.6	18.0	60
Adult female		2000	44	—	800	18	4000	1.0	1.2	13.0	60

SOURCE: U.S. Department of Agriculture, *Nutritive Value of Foods.*
[a]Calculated from recipe.
[b]As of 1980.

Table 32.5 Nutrient composition of menu shown in Table 32.3

Food	Amount	Calories	Protein (g)	Fat (g)	Calcium (mg)	Iron (mg)	Vitamin A (I.U.)	Thiamin (mg)	Riboflavin (mg)	Niacin (mg)	Vitamin C (mg)
Milk, nonfat	1 cup	90	9	—	296	0.1	10	0.09	0.44	0.2	2
Half-and-half	2 tablespoons	40	2	4	32	—	140	—	0.04	—	—
Eggs, poached	2	154	12	11	52	2.2	1080	0.08	0.24	2.7	—
Chili beans with meat	1 cup	291	15	16	98	3.7	340	0.07	0.18	4.0	22
Spaghetti with meat	1 cup	330	19	12	124	3.7	1590	0.25	0.30	1.2	140
Broccoli, fresh, cooked	1 cup	40	5	1	136	1.2	3880	0.14	0.31	0.3	4
Carrot, raw	1	20	1	—	18	0.4	5500	0.03	0.03	0.2	8
Lettuce with French dressing	wedge	133	1	11	22	0.5	540	0.04	0.08	1.9	39
Tomato juice	1 cup	45	2	—	17	2.2	1940	0.12	0.07	0.1	3
Apple, fresh	1	70	—	—	8	0.4	50	0.04	0.02	0.6	31
Cantaloupe	¼	30	1	—	13	0.4	3270	0.04	0.03	—	6
Lemon wedge	⅙	3	—	—	3	0.1	3	0.01	—	0.7	—
Bread, French	1 slice	82	2	1	12	0.6	—	0.08	0.06	0.8	—
Bread, whole wheat	1 slice	65	3	1	24	0.8	—	0.09	0.03	0.8	—
Rice, brown, cooked	½ cup	68	1	—	7	0.4	—	0.06	0.01	0.1	—
Soda crackers	4	50	1	1	2	0.1	—	—	—	—	—
Margarine	1 tablespoon	100	—	12	3	—	470	—	—	—	—
Sugar	1 tablespoon	40	—	—	—	—	—	—	—	—	—
Totals for day:		1651	74	70	867	16.8	18813	1.13	1.84	13.6	255
Recommended Dietary Allowances:[a]											
Adult male		2700	56	—	800	10	5000	1.4	1.6	18.0	60
Adult female		2000	44	—	800	18	4000	1.0	1.2	13.0	60

SOURCE: U.S. Department of Agriculture, Nutritive Value of Foods.
[a] As of 1980.

Both menus are low in calories for some women and most men because fresh fruits were used for desserts instead of pie, cake, and rich pastries. Desserts that are high in fat and sugar would increase the calories and reduce the intake of vitamins, minerals, and possibly protein. If caloric intake must be reduced below the levels shown in these menus, substitute nonfat milk and use smaller servings. Ham could be used as the protein in a chef's salad with a low-calorie dressing instead of a sandwich.

Meal Service

Serving food is an art. Meal service includes both table setting and food service; one influences the other, and they should be coordinated. The arrangement of food, dishes, and eating utensils on the table should be both attractive and functional. Rules for serving meals are not rigid; there is no one right way, but rather a number of acceptable ways. Factors that affect serving include occasion, participants, facilities, and type of food served.

SETTING THE TABLE

Dishes and utensils for serving and eating a meal must be available at the table when they are needed during the meal and must also be placed in such a way that they are convenient to use. Equally important, the table should not be cluttered with unnecessary utensils and dishes.

The Cover   The term *cover*, or place setting, indicates all equipment required by any one diner, including the linens, dinnerware, flatware, and beverageware. The space allowed for a single cover can vary from 20 to 30 inches, depending on the space available and the type of meal served. A 2-foot space, which is acceptable for most meals, permits comfortable seating of the diners. The equipment in each cover should be placed so that it is clearly separated from adjoining covers. The depth of the cover should not exceed 15 inches, because a person cannot eat gracefully if required to reach a greater distance than this. Covers should be spaced around the table in such a way that the table has a balanced appearance and should be set up before the diners are seated.

Linens   The term *linen* includes both table cover and napkins. Table covers can be full-sized cloths that completely cover the table, place mats, or runners; they can be made of any material from linen and fine lace to gingham or paper. A "silence cloth" is often used under full-sized tablecloths to deaden the sound of dishes against the table and to protect the table top from being marred by hot dishes. For special occasions, creases in a tablecloth should be ironed out before the cloth is placed on the table. The cloth should be centered on the table with an overhang of 8 to 12 inches.

Place mats may be placed on a bare table or on a cloth. Rectangular place mats may be positioned flush with the edge of the table or from ½ or 1½ inches from the edge of the table; positioning depends on the size of both the place mats and the table. Oval and round place mats are positioned so that one edge is flush with the edge of the table; round ones can alternatively be positioned to overhang the edge of the table slightly.

Napkins vary in size from 10 to 18 inches square. Smaller napkins may be folded to form a square or triangle, but larger ones should be folded into rectangles or more compact shapes. A napkin may be placed in one of several acceptable positions. At formal dinners it is centered on the place plate. For other occasions the napkin may be placed to the left of the forks. If space is limited, the fork may be placed on top of the napkin or, conversely, the napkin may be placed in the center of the dinner plate or in the space between the forks and knife that will later be occupied by the dinner plate. The fold of the napkin may be placed either to the left or to the right, but the open edges of the napkin should always be nearest the edge of the table. Alternatively, the napkin can be folded into an attractive shape and placed at the top center of the cover.

Flatware All flatware needed for a meal, with the possible exception of dessert silver, should be placed at the cover. Forks are placed to the left of the plate, knives and spoons to the right. The cutting edge of knives should turn toward the plate, and the tines of forks and the bowls of spoons should face up. Spoons and forks are placed in order of use; they should be close together but not touching.

A seafood fork is placed to the right of the spoons, because it is used only in the right hand. A salad fork is placed to the right of the dinner fork if the salad is served after the main course and to the left of the dinner fork if the salad precedes the main course. When a salad is served along with the main course, either on the same plate or separately, the salad fork should be placed either to the right of the dinner fork or omitted entirely. Omitting the salad fork when the salad is served with the main course is probably the best practice, because changing forks during a single course can be confusing to the diner.

The dinner knife may be omitted for informal meals when it is not needed. It may also be used instead of a butter knife for buttering bread at informal meals. If butter spreaders are provided, they should be placed on the butter plate in one of the three positions illustrated in Figure 32.4.

Dessert silver may be included in the cover. If both dessert and salad forks are present, the dessert silver should be placed parallel to the edge of the table, above the dinner plate in the center of the

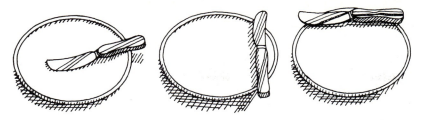

Figure 32.4

Three acceptable ways of placing a butter knife or spreader on a bread and butter plate.

cover. If a spoon is needed only for the beverage to be served with the dessert, the spoon may be placed on the saucer behind the cup when the beverage is served.

The ends of the handles of the flatware, the edge of the napkin, and the rim of the dinner plate should all form an imaginary line parallel to the edge of the table and about 1 inch from the edge. Flatware should be clean and free of spots and tarnish. Hands should not touch eating surfaces while placing flatware in the cover.

Dinnerware   A place plate, used only for formal dinners, is a decorative plate of a different pattern than the dinnerware itself and larger than the dinner plate. It sits in the center of the cover when diners are seated, and appetizer, soup, and salad courses are served on top of it in separate containers. The place plate is not removed until it is replaced by the dinner plate. Eating utensils and discarded food should never be left on the place plate.

An underliner plate is set beneath bowls of soup, appetizer, salad, or dessert when they are served as separate courses. The spoon or fork used with these dishes should not be left standing in the bowl, either during or after eating, but should always be placed on the underliner plate behind the bowl or sherbet glass. In a formal dinner, the underliner plate is placed on top of the place plate.

Each course is placed in the center of the cover as it is served. The bread and butter plate sits above the forks, toward the dinner plate; if salad is served on a separate plate with the main course, it is placed to the left of the forks and napkin. Salad is more difficult to eat in this position because the right hand must reach a long distance, making it easy for sleeves to drag across food on the dinner plate. An alternative practice is to omit the bread and butter plate and place the salad above the forks, or to serve the salad either as a separate course or on the dinner plate.

Dinnerware should be clean and free of water spots. Eating surfaces should not be touched while the dishes are being handled. All dishes used in a meal do not need to be of the same pattern, but all diners should preferably have the same pattern of any given dish. China dinner plates can be used at each cover, for example, but bread and butter plates can be glass or crystal. If more than one type of dinnerware is used, the patterns should blend attractively with one other.

Beverageware Water glasses should be placed at the tip of the knife or slightly to the right, within easy reach. Other glasses for milk or juice should be placed to the right of the water glass, closer to the diner. Iced tea or a similar beverage can either be placed to the right of the water glass or may replace the water glass. An underliner plate should be used under an iced tea glass to hold the iced tea spoon.

Coffee cups should be placed to the right of the spoons, 4 to 6 inches from the edge of the table, with the cup handle parallel to the edge of the table. They should not be placed in the cover if they are not to be used until the dessert course.

Beverageware should be clean and free of spots and lint. The rims of cups and glasses should never be touched; cups should be carried by the handles and glasses by their bases.

Serving Dishes Salt and pepper shakers are placed in line with the water glasses, parallel to the edge of the table, allowing one pair for two or three people. Serving dishes for country-style service should be easily reached by the diners and should not be too large, heavy, or hot for easy handling; serving utensils should be placed beside the serving dishes on the table.

Centerpiece A centerpiece of flowers, leaves, fruits, or small decorative plants adds to the colorfulness and attractiveness of the table. All parts of a centerpiece should be clean and free of garden soil and insects. The arrangements should be low enough that diners are able to see each other across the table. If lighted candles are used, the tapers should be low enough or high enough that the flame is not at the diners' eye level. Candles are not appropriate at breakfast or midday dinner, but they are festive for an evening dinner or supper.

TYPES OF MEAL SERVICE

Styles of service differ from highly formal to highly informal, but the goal of all meal service is to get the food to the diners with a minimum of confusion. In former times, the type of meal served and the manner of service was a means of displaying one's wealth and position; this function of meal service is less common today, at least in the United States. Few families have servants to prepare and serve meals; dining has become a much more informal and less pretentious experience. Nonetheless, formal service is still found in many fine restaurants.

Russian Service Russian service, the most formal of all meal services, is also known as European, Continental, or formal ser-

Figure 32.5

A formal, or Russian, cover. No bread and butter plate is used; no hot beverage is served until the dessert course. The first course is seafood cocktail, with the fork to the far right of the spoons; the second course is soup, with the spoon between the seafood fork and the knives; the third course is salad, with the salad fork to the far left and the salad knife closest to the soup spoon. These three courses are served on the place plate, which is then removed and replaced by the dinner plate. The dessert fork, used last, is closest to the place plate.

vice. It is intricate and distinctive and requires well-trained waiters or servants to carry out. A salad or appetizer may be on the place plate when the diners are seated. One waiter removes the first course dishes from the right and another waiter immediately places the soup course on the place plate from the left. At no time is the cover allowed to be without a plate. The waiters offer the main course meats and vegetables from serving dishes held to the left of each diner. No dishes of food are placed on the table other than fruit compotes or candies, which are present mainly for their decorative effect.

After the main course, all items of the cover are removed and the table is "crumbed" by the waiter, who brushes the crumbs with a folded napkin into his hand or a plate. The dessert plate and flatware are placed next; fingerbowls may be brought to the table with the dessert or after the dessert course is finished. Figure 32.5 shows a cover diagram of Russian service.

English Service In English service, the early courses are served by servants in the same way as Russian service. The main course is served by the host and hostess; the host carves and serves the meat, and the hostess serves the vegetables. A servant carries the plates from the host to the hostess and then to the guest. Serving dishes may remain on the table, and diners are served seconds if they desire. This service, only slightly less formal than Russian service, is not commonly used because it requires a servant. Figure 32.6 shows the host's and hostess' covers for serving the main course; individual covers at the beginning of the meal are the same as for Russian service.

Figure 32.6

The arrangement of the host's and hostess' covers for serving foods in
an English service. The host serves the meat on the plates and passes
them to the hostess for vegetable servings. The main course may have been
preceded by either a salad or a soup course, or both.
Dessert flatware is brought with the dessert.

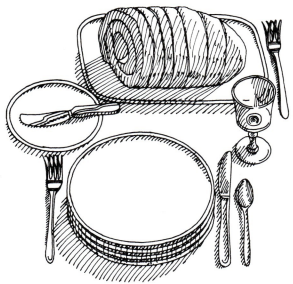

Host's cover

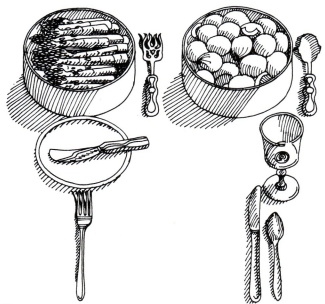

Hostess' cover

Family Service   Family service is often called "compromise" service as a modification of English service that requires no servants. Plates are served by the host and hostess, but filled plates are passed from one diner to the next until all are served. Both meat and vegetables are placed at the host's cover with a stack of dinner plates. The hostess may serve the salad from her cover, or the salads may be in place in the center of the cover or to the left of the forks when the diners are seated.

If salad or soup is served as a first course, one person from the table clears the covers and brings in the dinner plates and serving dishes for the main course. If dessert is served at the table, one person at the table must clear the main course and bring in the dessert and dessert plates for service by the hostess; flatware for the dessert course should already be in place at the cover. Coffee with the main course may be served by the hostess; coffee with the dessert course may be served by the host. Alternatively, the cups may be in place at the beginning of the meal to be filled by the person waiting on the table.

Both English and family service are best for small groups of six or eight people, because of the time required to serve each diner.

Country-Style Service   This service is sometimes called American service, but did not originate in the United States, even though it was probably the most common service when the country was young and remains the most common service today. Warmed dinner plates should be placed at the cover when the diners are seated. Serving dishes of food are placed on the table when the diners are seated and passed counterclockwise until all have served their own plates from each dish passed. Salad may be passed with the other dishes, to be served either on the dinner plate or on a separate plate. If salad is served as a separate course, one person from the table must remove the salad plates and serve the next course. Alternatively, the salad may be already served on separate plates or bowls above the forks, or to their left if a bread and butter plate is used.

Serving dishes should be removed before the covers are cleared. The water glass and coffee cup are left for the dessert course. The dessert may be portioned in the kitchen and served to each diner, or the serving dish of dessert may be passed at the table. If coffee is served with the main course, cups and saucers should be in the cover at the beginning of the meal.

Country-style service is practical for large groups. If more than 12 people are being served, more than one serving dish should be used for each food to speed service. Figure 32.7 shows a typical cover for country-style service.

Blue-Plate Service   Plates are served in the kitchen in blue-plate service, sometimes call "apartment service." In this service, salad

Figure 32.7

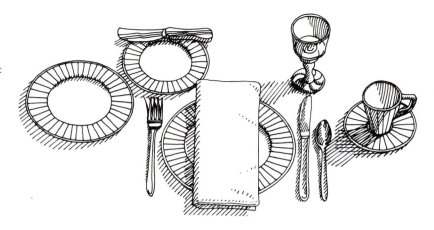

and dessert can be served as separate courses, but are also portioned in the kitchen.

Buffet Service Buffet service resembles country-style service because each person serves his or her own plate, but differs because diners fill their plates at a table reserved solely for holding food instead of passing dishes while they are seated at a dining table. Buffet service lends itself to informality and conviviality in large groups; the actual eating arrangements can vary considerably. Covers may be set at a dining table or small card tables like other types of service; otherwise trays may be provided to hold plates, flatware, and beverage.

Diners who are not eating at a table should be provided with large napkins to protect against spills. Foods served in this manner should not need to be cut with a knife, because balancing a plate of food on one's lap while manipulating a knife and fork is an impossible task. Foods should also not be soupy, because liquid is likely to spill off the plate or drip from the food while being lifted from plate to mouth. For diners seated at tables, foods served at a buffet dinner may be the same as those served at other types of meal service.

Foods on a buffet table can be kept hot on an electric tray. Otherwise, only small dishes of hot food should be placed on the table at one time, replenished at frequent intervals by food that has been kept hot in the oven. Cold foods should be placed in containers of chipped ice. If cold gelatins are to be served on the same plate with other foods, the dinner plates should be at room temperature, not heated, because gelatin melts on hot plates.

A buffet can be a simple combination of entrée, vegetables, and salad or an elaborate smorgasbord with several choices of entrée, vegetables, salads, and relish trays. The arrangement of dishes on a buffet table should allow for fast service and minimal waiting time. For a large group, arrange the buffet tables for two lines of service. Place the entrée dishes first, next to the dinner plates. Place the relishes, bread, and accompaniments at the end of the table with the forks, napkins, and beverage.

Forks should be placed close together in a single layer and napkins fanned out on the buffet table, if room permits; they may be stacked if necessary. Flatware, napkins, and beverageware do not need to be placed on the buffet table if table covers are set up. If space on the buffet table is limited, especially when a choice of beverages is offered, beverages may be served at another location. Figure 32.8 shows such a buffet table arrangement.

Because the buffet is a relatively new meal service, its forms are less standardized than those of other types of meal service. Foods served and details of service can be adapted to fit the needs of the situation. As always, however, careful organization and preparation make a successful meal.

Food is often served for other occasions than full meals. By custom, refreshments are provided at group meetings for both pleasure and business affairs. In such cases, the purpose of the gathering, whether it is a music recital, club meeting, or other group activity, is usually of primary importance; refreshments provide a break in activities or a time for informal socializing.

For such occasions, some form of beverage is a necessity. Most commonly, a choice of beverages, such as coffee, tea, cocoa, punch, or carbonated drinks, are provided. Foods at these gather-

TEAS AND RECEPTIONS

Figure 32.8

A buffet table arranged to serve a small group. All guests approach the table from the same direction; beverages are served elsewhere.

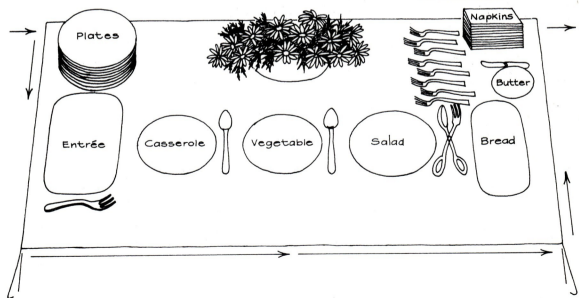

ings typically include cookies, thinly sliced fruit-nut breads, canapés, dips, hors d'oeuvres, doughnuts, pastries, crackers, chips, and cheeses. Alternatively, a simple dessert may be served with a beverage, in which case it is served on a dish with appropriate flatware.

The nature of the occasion, the number of people present, and the facilities for preparing and serving all influence the choice of foods. Obviously, the wedding reception would require a different form of service and food than an afternoon bridge club meeting. Some generalizations, however, apply to all such affairs. Guests should always be supplied with eating equipment appropriate to the food being served. A sticky cake must be served with a plate and a fork; guests should not be expected to eat it from a napkin with their fingers. If both a cup or glass and a food plate are supplied, guests must have a place to set either one or the other down, for they cannot eat with both hands full. If cups or glasses are meant to be set on the plate along with the food, place an absorbent coaster underneath to soak up spills and keep the drink from sliding on the plate. As a further device to prevent spills, do not fill beverage containers to the brim. Wherever possible, let the guests choose their own foods and serve themselves.

Service for teas and receptions varies widely. In one type of informal tea service, a tray or plate containing beverage, dessert, napkin, and flatware may be served from the kitchen. Another type of tea service simply provides a tray on the coffee table. If coffee and tea are served in either of these styles, a tray with

Figure 32.9

A tea table arranged so that guests can be served from opposite directions. The beverage cup is placed on the tea plate along with foods. Coffee is served at one end of the table, tea at the other.

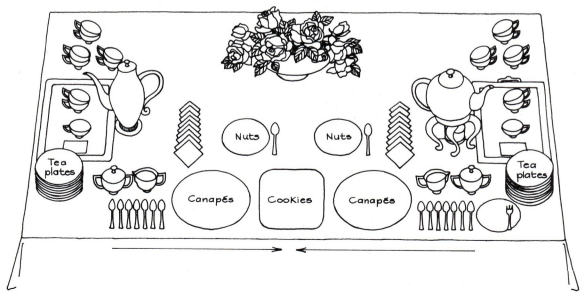

sugar, cream, and lemon must be passed from guest to guest. Additional foods, such as sandwiches, cookies, nuts, and candies, must also be passed to guests.

A formal tea service provides a tea table on which beverage service, food, dishes, flatware, and napkins are arranged in much the same way as for a buffet meal (Figure 32.9). In this arrangement, guests either may be served refreshments from the tea table by hostesses or they may serve themselves. A hostess typically pours the tea or coffee and ladles punch, and the guests choose their food.

Definite plans are necessary to organize a large tea served over a period of several hours. Specific duties must be assigned to helpers to replenish food, beverages, dishes, and flatware. Dishes and flatware that are washed and reused must be cleaned according to the rules of good hygiene. Foods must be properly refrigerated until they are ready to serve and should be handled with tongs, spatulas, or plastic gloves, not with bare hands.

Decorations contribute to the attractiveness of the table arrangement. Decorations may range from large floral displays to small individual flowers or objects of art.

Waiting on Tables

For either a simple family meal or a formal affair, serving food and removing dishes between courses and after the meal should be accomplished quietly and efficiently, with a minimum of disturbance. Just as patterns of table service have been adapted from traditional procedures to meet changing life-styles, so also have such changes altered procedures for waiting on tables to accomodate patterns of modern living.

SERVING AND REMOVING DISHES

The correct position of the waiter or waitress while serving and removing dishes from the cover is a matter of debate. Some authorities state that dishes should be served by a waiter from the left of the diner and removed from his right, a form that is necessary in Russian service, where at least two waiters are available to serve the table. Others believe that dishes may be both served and removed from the left, with only beverages served from the right, a less formal service that is certainly acceptable. Regardless of procedure, once a style has been adopted, it should be used throughout the meal so that the diners know what to expect.

The waiter or waitress should always face the diner whose cover is being served or cleared. Standing to the diner's left, the waiter or waitress serves and removes dishes with the left hand, and the right hand is used when serving from the right. Always place, refill, and remove glasses and cups from the diner's right; reaching in front of the diner to serve or remove dishes is never correct. Glasses always remain on the table for refilling; the waiter or waitress pours from a pitcher held in the right hand.

The cup and saucer, however, are picked up in the right hand and filled from the pot held in the left hand. The cup should not be refilled over the guest, in case the beverage spills. The spout of the pitcher or pot should not be allowed to touch the rim of the glass or cup, because this contact may transfer bacteria. The person pouring beverages should carry a small folded napkin, known as a "drip napkin," to catch spills and drips.

Salads served on separate plates with the main course, as well as bread and butter plates, are always served and removed from the diner's left. Because such plates are only used with informal service, the dinner plate may be conveniently served and removed from the left as well.

CLEARING THE COVERS

All serving dishes should be removed from the table before the covers are cleared. All dishes from one cover should be cleared before another cover is cleared. Clearing is accomplished in the following manner: remove the dinner plate with the left hand and pass it to the right hand, then remove the salad plate with the left hand and quietly place it on top of the dinner plate. Remove the bread and butter plate with the left hand and carry all dishes to the kitchen with the bread and butter plate held in the left hand and the dinner plate with the salad plate on top in the right hand. If only a bread and butter plate or a salad plate was used with the main course, do not place that plate on the dinner plate but carry it to the kitchen in the left hand.

After all the covers have been cleared, collect the salt and pepper shakers, unused flatware, and beverage glasses not needed for the next course on a small tray. The table should be crumbed if necessary.

DESSERT SERVICE

Refill all beverage glasses and cups before serving the dessert. Dessert is portioned in the kitchen in formal service. Flatware needed for the dessert course is placed on the plate behind the sherbet glass, and the dessert is served from the diner's left. For informal service, place the empty plates and flatware from the diner's left and pass the serving dish of dessert at the table for diners to serve themselves. Sauces or accompaniments for the dessert should also be passed. Alternatively, the hostess may serve the dessert, as described in English service. The dishes from the dessert course should remain on the table until the diners have left the table.

TABLE SERVICE BY THE HOSTESS

At meals with no waiters or waitresses, where the host or hostess prepares and serves the food with perhaps the help of one or more of the diners, table service should be simple and unpretentious. The host or hostess should choose foods that require minimum service so that he or she can spend as much time as possible with the guests. A serving cart for used dishes and for serving dessert can simplify service. Diners may pass used dishes to the host or hostess to place on the cart; the latter may also pass desserts to the diners in this manner.

Knowledge and practice of desirable table behavior imparts a feeling of confidence and security to a person dining in a group and makes the meal a pleasant experience for all. A common code of table conduct makes dining a natural procedure, allowing meals to proceed effortlessly. Consult the references at the end of the chapter for etiquette books that provide reliable guidelines for good table manners.

Table Manners

Preparing a meal is a skill that can be learned in the classroom, a situation that necessarily involves a different approach than preparing a meal at home. Unlike a home, where one or two people usually plan and prepare meals, meal preparation in a classroom may be carried out by two, four, or as many as 10 or 15 people, depending on the nature of the project.

Preparing Meals

Organization is the essential first step in preparing a meal. The menu should be planned according to concepts previously discussed: foods should not tax the abilities and time of those preparing the meal, and necessary equipment and utensils should be available. Meals at home are usually planned a week at a time. Classroom procedure may call for one meal at a time, or meals for a day or a week. Either way, the next step after initial organization is to order foods, calculate costs, and plan the preparation of the meal or meals.

ORGANIZATION

Grocery Orders   Making a grocery order for a class learning experience is a distinctly separate task from making a home grocery order, partly because the cost accounting in the two situations is different. When several groups and classes are preparing different foods, a bottle of catsup or a pound of margarine must be shared among groups; it would not be economical for each group that needed only a few tablespoons of margarine to buy a whole pound.

To accomplish this goal, forms such as those shown in Tables 32.6 and 32.7 are helpful. Table 32.6 lists the separate dishes of the menu in the first column and the ingredients needed for each dish in the second column. Table 32.7 is the market order that divides the foods into food groups, with all meats, staples, and produce listed in separate groups. If margarine or other foods are used in several dishes, the amounts are combined and listed as one item on the market order.

Table 32.7 lists the ingredients that must be purchased in the first column, the amount needed in the second, the size of the market unit in the third, the cost of the market unit in the fourth,

Table 32.6   Ingredients for dinner menu shown in Table 32.2, in amounts for four servings

Menu item	Ingredients	Amounts
Broiled chicken	Chicken breasts	1 pound, 1 ounce[a]
	Seasoning salt	1 to 2 teaspoons
Candied sweet potatoes	Canned yams, packed in syrup	1 16-ounce can[b]
	Margarine	2 tablespoons
Dilled green beans	Frozen green beans	3/5 of a 20-ounce bag (12 ounces)[c]
	Salt	1/2 teaspoon
	Margarine	1 tablespoon
	Dill weed	1/2 teaspoon
Apple-pineapple salad	Fresh red Delicious apples	3/4 pound[d]
	Fresh pineapple	1/4 of a whole pineapple[e]
	Mayonnaise	1/4 cup
Pumpkin custard	Canned pumpkin	1/2 16-ounce can
	Eggs	2 large
	Gelatin, unflavored	1 envelope
	Orange juice	1/3 cup
	Low-fat milk	1/3 cup
	Sugar, granulated	1/2 cup
	Salt	1/4 teaspoon
	Pumpkin pie spice	1/2 teaspoon
Tea	Tea bags	2 to 4 bags
	Lemon, fresh	1/2
	Sugar	1 to 2 tablespoons

[a]Use Table 22.2 to obtain the factor for one serving of chicken breasts, with bones, to supply 20 grams of protein, the amount in a 3-ounce serving. The factor of 0.268 per serving × 4 servings = 1.07 pounds, or 1 pound, 1 ounce.

[b]Can label specifies approximately four 1/2-cup servings per can.

[c]U.S. Department of Agriculture Home Economics Research Report No. 37 specifies 3 ounces of frozen green beans to provide 1/2 cup of cooked beans.

[d]U.S. Department of Agriculture Home Economics Research Report No. 37 specifies three apples, or 2.75 cups chopped apple, per pound; 3/4 pound would provide about 1/2 chopped apple per serving.

[e]U.S. Department of Agriculture Home Economics Research Report No. 37 specifies that a 2 1/2-pound fresh pineapple provides about 3.62 cups diced pineapple; a fourth of a fresh pineapple provides slightly less than 1 cup, and a third provides about 1 1/4 cups.

and the cost of the amount actually used in the fifth. To calculate the actual cost of the meal from this information, enter the cost of staples supplied from the stockroom, such as flour or sugar, at the bottom and calculate the costs in the same way. To calculate the cost per person of a recipe for a specified number of people, divide the total cost by the number of people being served.

Costs   Before either quantity or cost can be determined, the yield of various market forms of food, the amount of refuse, and the change in volume and weight that cooking produces in some foods must be established. Enough food must be purchased to provide the anticipated amount of edible portion after these factors have been considered.

Classroom costs are calculated on the basis of the amounts of food actually used. Home costs are more commonly calculated from a record of the total amount spent for food over a given

Table 32.7   *Market order for dinner menu shown in Table 32.2, with costs*

Foods	Amount in recipe	Market unit	Cost of market unit ($)	Cost of amount in recipe ($)
Dairy products:				
Milk, low-fat	⅓ cup	half gallon	0.88	0.04
Margarine	3 tablespoons	pound	0.69	0.06
Eggs	2 large	dozen	0.81	0.14
Meats:				
Chicken breasts	1 lb., 1 oz.	pound	1.25	1.33
Frozen foods:				
Orange juice	⅓ cup	6 ounce concentrate	0.28	0.03
Green beans	12 ounces	20-ounce package	0.80	0.48
Fresh fruits and vegetables:				
Apples, red Delicious	2 cups	pound	0.45	0.37
Pineapple, fresh	1 cup	each	1.10	0.28
Lemon	½	each	0.12	0.06
Canned foods:				
Yams in syrup	2 cups	1-pound can	0.48	0.48
Pumpkin	1 cup	1-pound can	0.45	0.23
Miscellaneous:				
Mayonnaise	¼	quart	1.75	0.11
From Storeroom:				
Sugar				0.08
Gelatin	⅝ cup	5 pounds	1.35	0.06
Tea bags	1 envelope	32 envelopes	1.92	0.13
Spices, salt, etc.	4 bags	48 bags	1.50	0.05
Total cost for four persons:				3.93
Cost per person				0.98

period of time, such as a week or a month, without detailed itemizing; costs are determined for the whole family, not for each person.

Preparing Food   The preparation of each item in the menu must be planned so that all dishes are ready at the designated time for eating. Obviously, some foods require more time and effort to prepare than others. At home, desserts, gelatin salads, and casseroles can be prepared ahead of time, and vegetables can be trimmed and washed or meat trimmed or marinated. In the classroom, advance preparation is often not possible, making a different type of planning necessary.

Timing Meal Preparation   A novice should begin planning the time required to prepare a meal by writing out the recipes for the foods and estimating the time needed to perform each step, taking into consideration the abilities and experience of those performing the tasks. A careful breakdown of the time needed helps pinpoint areas of time when one food is being cooked or chilled, allowing the preparation of another food to proceed. Table 32.8 shows the approximate times required to prepare the dinner menu shown in Table 32.2.

Table 32.8   Recipes and preparation times for foods in the dinner menu shown in Table 32.2

Menu item	Steps in preparation	Time (min.)
Broiled chicken	1. Wash and bone chicken breasts (boning is optional)	10
	2. Place breasts in single layer on broiler pan, skin side down; sprinkle with seasoned salt	3
	3. Place chicken about 5–6 inches below heat source and broil about 10 minutes or until brown	10
	4. Turn skin side up, sprinkle with seasoned salt and broil until brown	10
	5. Leave meat in oven with thermostat set at 160°F until ready to serve; let sit at least 10 minutes	
Candied sweet potatoes	1. Open can of yams and drain syrup into 1½-quart saucepan; add 2 tablespoons of margarine	3
	2. Place on moderately hot heat to evaporate half the liquid	9
	3. Add potatoes and heat to boiling	2
	4. Transfer potatoes to ovenproof serving dish and place in oven with chicken until time to serve	2
Dilled green beans	1. Place ⅓ cup of water in 2-quart saucepan; add 1 teaspoon salt; bring to boil; add 12 ounces frozen green beans	4
	2. Cover and reduce heat; simmer 8 minutes	8
	3. Drain off excess liquid; add margarine and dill weed	2
	4. Transfer green beans to ovenproof serving dish and keep warm in oven until time to serve	2
Apple-pineapple salad	1. Peel fresh pineapple and chop enough to yield 1 cup	20–30
	2. Wash and core ¾ pound of red apples	5
	3. Chop apples	5
	4. Combine chopped apple, pineapple, and ¼ cup mayonnaise	2
	5. Place in serving bowl and refrigerate until time to serve	1
Pumpkin custard	1. Separate eggs; place yolks in a 2-quart saucepan with a heavy bottom; place the whites in a small bowl	5
	2. Add to the yolks in the saucepan ⅓ cup milk and ⅓ cup orange juice and mix well with spring stirrer	4

Table 32.9 shows how one person at home can prepare the meal given in Table 32.2 by coordinating different jobs. At home, the pumpkin custard and the salad can be prepared in advance and refrigerated until serving time. Both keep well up to 24 hours. At least 45 minutes should be allowed to prepare the chicken; while the chicken cooks, the vegetables and tea can be prepared.

PREPARING MEALS AT HOME

Menu item	Steps in preparation	Time (min.)
	3. Add to saucepan: 1 envelope gelatin, ¼ cup sugar, ¼ teaspoon salt, and ½ teaspoon pumpkin pie spice; mix well	4
	4. Stir in 1 cup canned pumpkin and heat with stirring over moderately high heat until steaming hot, so that gelatin and sugar are dissolved and egg is cooked; set aside	5–10
	5. Whip egg white with rotary beater or electric mixer to soft peak stage	3
	6. Add ¼ cup sugar to egg white foam and beat to stiff peaks	3
	7. Fold cooked pumpkin mixture into egg white meringue using French whip	3
	8. Transfer to individual compote or sherbet glasses or to serving bowl	2
	9. Refrigerate until time to serve; allow at least one hour so that it becomes well-chilled	60
Tea	1. Place 1 quart of water in saucepan and bring to a boil	5
	2. Pour boiling water into teapot to heat pot	1
	3. Place another quart of water into saucepan and heat to boiling	5
	4. Drain water from teapot and place two tea bags in it so that strings are anchored and do not fall into the tea	1
	5. Pour boiling water over tea bags and allow to steep 3 minutes; remove bags	4
	6. Place teapot so that tea stays hot for serving	
Miscellaneous items	1. Wash lemon and cut into wedges; remove seeds and thick membranes	2
	2. Wash and prepare sprigs of parsley for garnishing plate	2
	3. Wash lettuce leaves for salad bowl or for individual plates	2
	4. Fill sugar bowl, salt and pepper shakers	2–4
	5. Set table	10–15

Table 32.9 Work schedule for one person preparing dinner menu shown in Table 32.2

Time (p.m.) start–end	Description of activity
5:00–5:13	Wash and bone chicken; place on broiler pan; sprinkle with seasoned salt; place pan under broiler; turn control to broil
5:13–5:23	Set table with service for four, to be served country style; fill sugar bowl and salt shakers and place on table
5:23–5:25	Turn chicken and sprinkle with seasoned salt; return to broiler
5:25–5:27	Open yams and drain syrup into saucepan; place on surface unit and turn on heat
5:27–5:28	Place water in pan for heating teapot
5:28–5:32	Place water and salt in saucepan and bring to a boil; add frozen green beans; cover, reduce heat
5:32–5:33	Add yams to boiling syrup, then margarine; continue heating; turn off broiler unit and leave chicken in oven
5:33–5:34	Pour boiling water into teapot; get out tea bags
5:34–5:35	Transfer yams to serving dish and place in closed oven with chicken
5:35–5:36	Place dinner plates in oven with chicken and yams
5:36–5:40	Prepare lemon wedges and parsley sprigs; start heating water for tea; place lemon wedges in dish and on table
5:40–5:42	Drain and season green beans; transfer to serving dish and place in oven with chicken and yams
5:43–5:45	Place lettuce leaves on salad plates and take up salads
5:45–5:47	Empty water from teapot, place tea bags in pot and add boiling water
5:47–5:50	Place salads on table; put ice cubes in water glasses and pour water
5:50–5:52	Remove tea bags from teapot; take up chicken on serving dish and garnish with parsley
5:52–5:55	Place dishes of yams, green beans, and chicken with serving utensils on table; distribute hot dinner plates to covers
5:55	Dinner is served

PREPARING MEALS IN THE CLASSROOM

In a classroom, several students often work together to produce a meal with a limited amount of time allotted for preparation, dining, and cleanup, requiring a different work schedule than in a home. One student in the group is usually appointed manager. His or her job is to plan the menu, write out the recipes, list the ingredients needed, make a grocery order and cost analysis, and prepare work schedules and job descriptions for each person in the group.

Work Schedule Table 32.8, which shows the recipes and time needed to prepare each menu item, can be used to plan the class work schedule and job allocations. Preparations can be divided into large and small tasks to be evenly distributed among the members of the group. Sometimes the preparation of a dish in a classroom situation can be speeded if more than one person works on it. Two people in the group could be assigned to prepare the dessert in the dinner menu in Table 32.2 so that it will be properly chilled by the time it is to be served.

Table 32.10 shows a possible work schedule for this menu in a classroom group of four people with a 2-hour laboratory period. Only brief descriptions of jobs are given on the manager's work schedule. More explicit directions are given in the job descriptions. The four members of the group are assigned numbers, from 1 to 4, with the manager as 1. Because he or she is expected to supervise, the manager should carry a smaller work load than other members of the group.

Table 32.10 Work schedule for classroom group of four persons preparing dinner menu shown in Table 32.2

Time (a.m.) start–end	Assigned jobs	Person responsible
10:30–10:41	Separate eggs; prepare meringue	1
–10:45	Wash, bone chicken breasts; broil	3
–10:50	Trim and chop pineapple	4
–10:50	Prepare pumpkin custard dessert	2
10:41–11:00	Set table	1
10:45–10:55	Cleanwork area; prepare parsley garnish and lemon wedges	3
10:50–11:15	Chop apple, mix salad; serve salad	4
–11:10	Prepare candied sweet potatoes	2
10:55–10:57	Turn and season chicken, continue broiling	3
10:57–11:05	Start preparing tea	3
11:00–11:05	Start cooking green beans	1
11:05–11:15	Fill sugar bowl, salt shakers	1
–11:15	Turn off broiler, place plates and serving dishes in oven to warm	3
11:10–11:20	Wash cooking utensils	2
11:15–11:20	Drain and season green beans	1
–11:25	Dry and put away cooking utensils	4
–11:20	Heat water for tea; fill water glasses	3
11:20–11:24	Brew tea	3
–11:25	Set out underliner plates for dessert	2
–11:25	Place chicken on serving plate	1
11:25–11:26	Distribute warm plates to cover	1
	Place meat, vegetables on table	2
	Pour tea	3
11:26	Dinner is served	1, 2, 3, 4
11:40	Remove serving dishes and clear covers	4
11:40	Fill water glasses, pour tea; serve dessert	2
11:50–12:10	Clear table; clean table, counters; rinse dishes after they are washed	3
	Wash dishes	4
	Dry dishes	2
	Put away dishes; check kitchen	1
12:10	Write evaluation of meal	1, 2, 3, 4

Job Descriptions   Each worker in the group, including the manager, must have a detailed job description that outlines all the activities necessary to prepare the meal. A common fault of job descriptions is vagueness, with too much being left unsaid. Steps of preparation not mentioned in the job descriptions require last-minute decisions by the manager and can lead to chaos. For example, the job description may fail to indicate how a food is to be served, in what container, and by whom. The manager must therefore think through the preparation of each food, from the beginning through the moment it is placed on the table to cleaning up, to be sure that the job description is exhaustive.

Table 32.11   Job descriptions for the work schedule shown in Table 32.10

Group member	Time (a.m.) start–end	Job description
1		Supervise other members of the group
	10:30–10:41	Separate yolks and whites of two eggs; give yolks to member 2 for pumpkin custard; beat egg whites in small bowl to soft peak; add ¼ cup sugar, beat to stiff peak; give meringue to member 2
	10:41–11:00	Set table according to cover and table diagrams; use place mats and centerpiece (see Figure 32.10)
	11:00–11:05	Start green beans cooking
	11:05–11:13	Fill sugar bowl; salt and pepper shakers; place on table with sugar spoon
	11:13–11:20	Drain and season green beans; place in serving bowl in warming oven
	11:20–11:25	Place cooked chicken on serving plate; place in warming oven; get parsley ready for garnishing chicken
	11:25–11:26	Distribute warm plates to covers
	11:26	Dinner is served
	11:50	Put away clean dishes; check all cupboards, equipment, for cleanliness and correct storage
2	10:30–10:50	Prepare pumpkin custard; obtain egg yolks and prepared meringue from member 1; portion custard into individual compote dishes and chill in freezer to speed setting; do not allow it to freeze
	10:50–11:10	Prepare yams; place in serving dish in warming oven
	11:10–11:20	Wash cooking utensils; wash broiler pan or start it soaking
	11:20–11:26	Set out underliner plates for dessert; place meat and vegetables on table
	11:26	Dinner is served
	11:40	Refill water glasses, pour tea; serve dessert (place compotes on underliner plate)
	11:50	Dry dishes

The job description should be written as though intended for someone with no knowledge of food preparation. It should include time allotments that agree with those on the work schedule as well as precautions that might not otherwise occur to the worker, such as recommending that a gelatin mixture be chilled in the freezer to set in time. The job description should list each duty in a separate paragraph, so that the worker can check off each task as it is completed. If possible, the manager should type job descriptions on large file cards, which are easier to handle in a kitchen area than a sheet of paper, and should attach a copy of appropriate recipes to each job description. Table 32.11 shows job

Group member	Time (a.m.) start–end	Job description
3	10:30–10:45	Prepare chicken and start it broiling
	10:45–10:55	Clean up counter and utensils; prepare parsley and lemon wedges; wash parsley and break off sprigs for garnishing meat; give parsley to member 1
	10:55–10:57	Turn chicken and continue broiling
	10:57–11:05	Heat water for warming teapot; set out pot and tea bags; wash lettuce; drain
	11:05–11:15	Turn off broiler, leave chicken in closed broiler; place dinner plates and platter for chicken in oven to warm; place serving utensils for meat and vegetables on table
	11:15–11:20	Start heating water for tea; place ice in glasses and pour water
	11:20–11:26	Empty water from teapot; place tea bags in pot and pour in boiling water; steep 3 minutes and remove tea bags; place teapot over very low heat to keep warm
	11:26	Dinner is served; pour tea
	11:50	Clear table after dessert course, rinse and stack dishes; rinse dishes after they are washed; wash tops of table and counters
4	10:30–10:50	Prepare fresh pineapple
	10:50–11:15	Prepare fruit salad; place lettuce leaves on salad plates and portion fruit salad on plates; clean up work area and put extra fruit and lettuce in the refrigerator; place plates of salad on table according to cover diagram
	11:15–11:26	Dry and put away cooking utensils
	11:26	Dinner is served
	11:50	Wash dishes; clean sink and stove

descriptions for four workers in a group and coordinates the jobs with the work schedule shown in Table 32.10.

Manager's Responsibilities The manager's duties in planning and preparing the meal have already been mentioned. As a supervisor, the manager must also make decisions. He or she may have underestimated the time required to complete a task, the group member performing a task may work more slowly than expected, or some other factor may arise to cause the manager to reassign jobs so that the meal may be served on schedule. By consulting the work schedule and observing the progress and duties of other workers, the manager can assign another group member to help, or the manager can lend assistance, if needed.

The manager should observe the work of other group members and suggest improvements when necessary. The manager can also offer encouragement by making approving comments on jobs that have been efficiently and properly completed. The manager must be aware of all cooking times in the meal, to check that cooking begins neither too early nor too late and to ensure that the food is being watched while it cooks.

The manager should include with the job description a cover diagram for serving the meal, even if the manager will be setting the table. Preparing such a diagram helps in thinking through the arrangement of flatware, beverageware, and dinnerware needed for the meal. Figure 32.10 is a cover diagram for the dinner menu given in Table 32.2 served country-style in two courses; the salad is served on a separate plate with the main course; no bread and butter plate is used. The manager can also prepare a diagram showing the placement of covers around the table and the location of salt and pepper shakers, sugar bowls, serving dishes, and so forth.

The manager should give group members their job assignments a day or more in advance so that they will have time to read and become familiar with their jobs, ask questions about assignments that are not clear, and practice ahead of time if they choose.

Responsibilities of Other Group Members It is as important to be a good follower as it is to be a good leader. Group members should be supportive of their manager and follow directions for the meal according to plan. If the manager needs to assign additional tasks during the actual preparation of the meal, group members should accept such assignments willingly and without resentment.

All members of the group need to think about their tasks and work out the most efficient way of accomplishing them. All ingredients and utensils should be assembled with as few steps and motions as possible, and one type of activity should be com-

Figure 32.10

The top cover diagram shows a single cover for country-style service at the beginning of a main course in which salad is served with the main course, on a separate plate; no bread and butter plate is provided. The cover does not include a salad fork because the dinner fork is used to eat both the salad and the food on the dinner plate. The dessert spoon is placed above the dinner plate with the handle to the right.

The lower diagram shows a single cover for country-style service at the beginning of the dessert course.

pleted before the next is started. For example, all apples should be washed and cored with cores discarded before they are chopped. Wastage of food should be held to a minimum; only inedible parts of meats, fruits, and vegetables should be discarded. Moreover, inedible parts should be discarded before additional work is done on the foods, to avoid mixing good food inadvertantly with scraps.

Evaluations   Planning and preparing meals in the classroom is a learning experience. A student improves through evaluation of his or her performance that points out areas where greater effort

---

Table 32.12   Form for evaluating meal manager

In the blank before the factor being evaluated, enter a number from 1 to 4. In the blank following the factor, comment about specific ways to improve the meal according to that factor.
1 = Poor   2 = Fair   3 = Very good   4 = Excellent

Score	Rating factors	Comments
	I. Choice of foods in menu	
_____	A. Compatible flavors	
_____	B. Variety in texture	
_____	C. Attractive color combinations	
_____	D. Variety in preparation methods	
	II. Organization and planning of meal	
_____	A. Equitable job assignments	
_____	B. Clearly written recipes	
_____	C. Explicit job descriptions	
	III. Service of meal	
_____	A. Attractive table setting	
_____	B. Service suitable for occasion	
	IV. Preparation of food (identify)	
_____	A. Properly cooked	
_____	B. Properly seasoned	
_____	C. Economical use of food	
_____	D. Efficiency in work habits	
_____	V. Adequate supervision of meal preparation	
	VI. Food service	
_____	A. Food ready on time	
_____	B. Correct service and removal of dishes	
_____	C. Quiet, efficient service of food	
	VII. Table manners	
_____	A. Correct use of flatware	
_____	B. General good manners	
	VIII. Cleanup	
_____	A. Responsibilities efficiently and properly completed	

and proficiency are needed. With successive meals, students should exhibit more skill and efficiency in organizing, planning, preparing, and serving meals.

Evaluations can be considered two ways: the meal manager must be evaluated on the basis of the menu and the organization, supervision, and service of the meal. The other members of the group must be evaluated on the basis of cooperativeness, efficiency, good working habits, and the quality of the meal they produce. Both the manager and other members of the group should evaluate themselves; additionally, each member of the group should evaluate the manager, and the manager should evaluate each of the other members. Tables 32.12 and 32.13 are forms that can be used for such evaluations. These forms are more practical then general criticisms, not only because they can be filled out quickly but also because they focus on major goals of the exercise. Evaluations are to be used constructively as a tool to point out weak areas that need improvement.

Evaluation forms can be altered to fit specific classroom situations. If one person must prepare more than one food for a meal, or if jobs must be done that do not involve preparing food, the form should be adapted to include these areas. Because all members of the group are not involved in serving food, all cannot be evaluated in this area.

Table 32.13   Form for evaluating other members of the group

In the blank before the factor being evaluated, enter a number from 1 to 4. In the blank following the factor, comment about specific ways to improve the meal according to that factor.
1 = Poor   2 = Fair   3 = Very good   4 = Excellent

Score	Rating factors	Comments
_____	I. Preparation of food (identify)_____	
_____	A. Properly cooked _____	
_____	B. Properly seasoned _____	
_____	C. Economical use of food _____	
_____	D. Efficiency in work habits _____	
_____	II. Cooperative and helpful in carrying out assignments _____	
	III. Food service _____	
_____	A. Food ready on time _____	
_____	B. Correct service and removal of dishes _____	
_____	C. Quiet, efficient service of food _____	
	IV. Table manners _____	
_____	A. Correct use of flatware _____	
_____	B. General good manners _____	
	V. Clean-up _____	
_____	A. Responsibilities efficiently and properly completed _____	

PREPARING MEALS AS A LEARNING EXPERIENCE

With so many convenience foods available today, many Americans tend to rely on prepackaged foods when they plan and prepare a meal, a procedure that takes little skill and ability. If a student is to become truly skillful in preparing food, he or she should depend as little as possible on the use of convenience foods in the classroom. They are sometimes necessary when other forms of a food are out of season or more expensive. As a rule, however, fresh fruits and vegetables rather than their frozen or canned forms should be emphasized for classroom use. Hot breads should be prepared, not purchased, as should desserts. Cake, bread, and pudding mixes should not be used. Classes should buy fresh, not canned, meats and dry, not canned beans. Students can learn to make stock rather than use canned stock. The old adage "practice makes perfect" is most applicable in preparing and serving food. To learn the various skills of food preparation, a beginner must repeat the techniques continually until they become automatic.

Study Questions

1. Briefly describe the esthetic and nutritional factors to be considered in planning meals.
2. What factor determines the satiety value of food?
3. What does the term *cover* mean?
4. What factors determine the choice of flatware and beverageware for a cover?
5. What factor determines the order of placement of pieces of flatware in the cover?
6. What is a place plate? When and how is it used?
7. What is an underliner plate? When and how is it used?
8. What are some names for formal dinner service? What are some distinguishing characteristics of formal service?
9. Distinguish between English and family service.
10. Briefly describe country-style service.
11. How should beverages be served, filled, and removed from the dinner table?
12. When may a dinner plate be removed from the left?
13. Indicate the order of clearing after the main course of a dinner served country-style.
14. What information is needed to prepare a grocery order for a meal?
15. What is the difference between a work schedule and a job description?
16. What are some responsibilities of the manager during actual meal preparation?
17. What is a cover diagram? A table diagram?

References

Baldridge, Letitia. *Amy Vanderbilt Complete Book of Etiquette.* Garden City, N.Y.: Doubleday, 1978.

Kinder, Faye, and Green, N. R. *Meal Management.* 5th ed. New York: Macmillan, 1978.

McLean, Beth Bailey. "Planning Meals for the Family." In U.S. Department of Agriculture, *Food,* Yearbook of Agriculture. Washington, D.C.: Government Printing Office, 1959.

Semrow, Ellen H. "Money-Stretching Ideas for Making Your Food Dollar Go Further." In U.S. Department of Agriculture, *Food for Us All,* Yearbook of Agriculture. Washington, D.C.: Government Printing Office, 1969.

Strow, Helen. "Exotic Food." In U.S. Department of Agriculture, *Consumers All,* Yearbook of Agriculture. Washington, D.C.: Government Printing Office, 1965.

Vanderbilt, Amy. *Everyday Etiquette.* New York: Bantam Books, 1974.

Appendix:

Reference Tables

Table 1 Interconversions of volumes and weights in the English system

To change	To	Operation	Number of	By	To get
Teaspoons	Tablespoons	Divide	Teaspoons	3	Tablespoons
Tablespoons	Teaspoons	Multiply	Tablespoons	3	Teaspoons
Tablespoons	Fluid ounces	Divide	Tablespoons	2	Fluid ounces
Fluid ounces	Tablespoons	Multiply	Fluid ounces	2	Tablespoons
Tablespoons	Cups	Divide	Tablespoons	16	Cups
Teaspoons	Cups	Divide	Teaspoons	48	Cups
Cups	Tablespoons	Multiply	Cups	16	Tablespoons
Cups	Teaspoons	Multiply	Cups	48	Teaspoons
Fluid ounces	Cups	Divide	Fluid ounces	8	Cups
Cups	Fluid ounces	Multiply	Cups	8	Fluid ounces
Fluid ounces	Pints	Divide	Fluid ounces	16	Pints
Pints	Fluid ounces	Multiply	Pints	16	Fluid ounces
Cups	Pints	Divide	Cups	2	Pints
Pints	Cups	Multiply	Pints	2	Cups
Pints	Quarts	Divide	Pints	2	Pints
Quarts	Pints	Multiply	Quarts	2	Pints
Cups	Quarts	Divide	Cups	4	Quarts
Quarts	Cups	Multiply	Quarts	4	Cups
Quarts	Gallons	Divide	Quarts	4	Gallons
Gallons	Quarts	Multiply	Gallons	4	Quarts
Pints	Gallons	Divide	Pints	8	Gallons
Gallons	Pints	Multiply	Gallons	8	Pints
Cups	Gallons	Divide	Cups	16	Gallons
Gallons	Cups	Multiply	Gallons	16	Cups
Avoirdupois ounces	Pounds	Divide	Ounces	16	Pounds
Pounds	Avoirdupois ounces	Multiply	Pounds	16	Avoirdupois ounces

Table 2 Interconversions of the English and metric systems of volumes and weights

To change	To	Operation	Number of	By	To get
Teaspoons	Milliliters	Multiply	Teaspoons	4.97	Milliliters
Tablespoons	Milliliters	Multiply	Tablespoons	14.8	Milliliters
Fluid ounces	Milliliters	Multiply	Fluid ounces	29.575	Milliliters
Cups	Milliliters	Multiply	Cups	236.6	Milliliters
Pints	Milliliters	Multiply	Pints	473.2	Milliliters
Quarts	Milliliters	Multiply	Quarts	946.4	Milliliters
Pints	Liters	Multiply	Pints	0.473	Liters
Quarts	Liters	Multiply	Quarts	0.946	Liters
Gallons	Liters	Multiply	Gallons	3.786	Liters
Milliliters	Teaspoons	Multiply	Milliliters	0.201	Teaspoons
Milliliters	Tablespoons	Multiply	Milliliters	0.068	Tablespoons
Milliliters	Fluid ounces	Multiply	Milliliters	0.034	Fluid ounces
Milliliters	Cups	Multiply	Milliliters	0.0042	Cups
Milliliters	Pints	Multiply	Milliliters	0.0021	Pints
Milliliters	Quarts	Multiply	Milliliters	0.00106	Quarts
Liters	Pints	Divide	Liters	2.1	Pints
Liters	Quarts	Divide	Liters	1.057	Quarts
Liters	Gallons	Multiply	Liters	0.246	Gallons
Avoirdupois ounce	Grams	Multiply	Ounces	28.35	Grams
Pounds	Grams	Multiply	Pounds	453.59	Grams
Pounds	Kilograms	Multiply	Pounds	0.453	Kilograms
Grams	Avoirdupois ounce	Multiply	Grams	0.035	Avoirdupois ounces
Grams	Pounds	Multiply	Grams	0.0022	Pounds
Kilograms	Pounds	Multiply	Kilograms	2.21	Pounds

Table 3 Interconversion of Celsius and Fahrenheit temperature scales

°C	°F	°C	°F	°C	°F	°C	°F
−20	−4.0	12	53.6	44	111.2	76	168.8
−19	−2.2	13	55.4	45	113.0	77	170.6
−18	−0.4	14	57.2	46	114.8	78	172.4
−17	+1.4	15	59.0	47	116.6	79	174.2
−16	3.2	16	60.8	48	118.4	80	176.0
−15	5.0	17	62.6	49	120.2	81	177.8
−14	6.8	18	64.4	50	122.0	82	179.6
−13	8.6	19	66.2	51	123.8	83	181.4
−12	10.4	20	68.0	52	125.6	84	183.2
−11	12.2	21	69.8	53	127.4	85	185.0
−10	14.0	22	71.6	54	129.2	86	186.8
− 9	15.8	23	73.4	55	131.0	87	188.6
− 8	17.6	24	75.2	56	132.8	88	190.4
− 7	19.4	25	77.0	57	134.6	89	192.2
− 6	21.2	26	78.8	58	136.4	90	194.0
− 5	23.0	27	80.6	59	138.2	91	195.8
− 4	24.8	28	82.4	60	140.0	92	197.6
− 3	26.6	29	84.2	61	141.8	93	199.4
− 2	28.4	30	86.0	62	143.6	94	201.2
− 1	30.2	31	87.8	63	145.4	95	203.0
0	32.0	32	89.6	64	147.2	96	204.8
+ 1	33.8	33	91.4	65	149.0	97	206.6
2	35.6	34	93.2	66	151.8	98	208.4
3	37.4	35	95.0	67	152.6	99	210.2
4	39.2	36	96.8	68	154.4	100	212.0
5	41.0	37	98.6	69	156.2	101	213.8
6	42.8	38	100.4	70	158.0	102	215.6
7	44.6	39	102.2	71	159.8	103	217.4
8	46.4	40	104.0	72	161.6	104	219.2
9	48.2	41	105.8	73	163.4	105	221.0
10	50.0	42	107.6	74	165.2	106	222.8
11	51.8	43	109.4	75	167.0	107	224.6

Table 4 Conversion formulas for temperatures and kilocalories–joules

$1°C = 1.8°F$ or $1°C = \frac{5}{9}$ of $1°F$ or $1°F = \frac{9}{5}$ of $1°C$

To convert Fahrenheit temperatures to Celsius:
$°C = \frac{5}{9} (°F - 32)$ or $°C = (°F - 32) \div 1.8$

To convert Celsius temperatures to Fahrenheit:
$°F = (\frac{9}{5} °C) + 32$ or $°F = (1.8 \times °C) + 32$

1 kilocalorie = 4.18 joules   1 joule = 0.24 kilocalorie

To convert kilocalories to joules: Joules = kilocalories × 4.18 joules

To convert joules to kilocalories: Kilocalories = joules × 0.24 kilocalorie

°C	°F	°C	°F	°C	°F	°C	°F
108	226.4	140	284.0	172	341.6	204	399.2
109	228.2	141	285.8	173	343.4	205	401.0
110	230.0	142	287.6	174	345.2	206	402.8
111	231.8	143	289.4	175	347.0	207	404.6
112	233.6	144	291.2	176	348.8	208	406.4
113	235.4	145	293.0	177	350.6	209	408.2
114	237.2	146	294.8	178	352.4	210	410.0
115	239.0	147	296.6	179	354.2	211	411.8
116	240.8	148	298.4	180	356.0	212	413.6
117	242.6	149	300.2	181	357.8	213	415.4
118	244.4	150	302.0	182	359.6	214	417.2
119	246.2	151	303.8	183	361.4	215	419.0
120	248.0	152	305.6	184	363.2	216	420.8
121	249.8	153	307.4	185	365.0	217	422.6
122	251.6	154	309.2	186	366.8	218	424.4
123	253.4	155	311.0	187	368.6	219	426.2
124	255.2	156	312.8	188	370.4	220	428.0
125	257.0	157	314.6	189	372.2	221	429.8
126	258.8	158	316.4	190	374.0	222	431.6
127	260.6	159	318.2	191	375.8	223	433.4
128	262.4	160	320.0	192	377.6	224	435.2
129	264.2	161	321.8	193	379.4	225	437.0
130	266.0	162	323.6	194	381.2	226	438.8
131	267.8	163	325.4	195	383.0	227	440.6
132	269.6	164	327.2	196	384.8	228	442.4
133	271.4	165	329.0	197	386.6	229	444.2
134	273.2	166	330.8	198	388.4	230	446.0
135	275.0	167	332.6	199	390.2	231	447.8
136	276.8	168	334.4	200	392.0		
137	278.6	169	336.2	201	393.8		
138	280.4	170	338.0	202	395.6		
139	282.2	171	339.8	203	397.4		

Table 5 Common can sizes

Industry term	Fluid ounces	Cups (approx.)	Principal products
6 ounces	6	2/3 – 3/4	Tomato paste, fruit and vegetable juices
8 ounces (Buffet)	8	1	Tomato sauce, fruits, vegetables
Picnic	9½	1¼	Condensed soups, fruits, vegetables, meat, fish, specialties[a]
12 ounce (Vacuum)	12	1½	Vacuum-packed corn
No. 300	13½	1¾	Pork and beans, beans, meat products, cranberry sauce and jelly, specialties[a]
No. 303	15	2	Fruits, vegetables, meats, ready-to-serve soups, specialties[a]
No. 2	18	2½	Juices, ready-to-serve soups, pie fruits and fillings, pineapple, specialties[a]
No. 2½	26	3½	Fruits, some vegetables
No. 3 Cylinder	46	5¾	Fruit and vegetable juices, pork and beans, condensed soups, vegetables
No. 10	96	12–13	Institutional size for fruits and vegetables

SOURCE: Information obtained from National Canners' Association.
[a]Specialties are usually a food combination, such as macaroni, spaghetti, ravioli, tomato aspic, Chinese or Mexican foods.

Table 6   Dipper sizes and equivalent measures

Dipper number[a]	Approximate measure	
	Tablespoons	Cups
6	10⅔	⅔
8	8	½
10	6⅖	⅜
12	5⅓	⅓
16	4	¼
20	3⅕	—
24	2⅔	—
30	2	⅛
40	1½	—
60	1	—

[a]The dipper number represents portion of a quart: No. 16 dipper is ¹⁄₁₆ of a quart. A quart contains 64 tablespoons; thus ⁶⁴⁄₁₆ = 4 tablespoons, the volume of a No. 16 dipper.

Table 7   Common abbreviations

Teaspoon	tsp
Tablespoon	Tbsp
Fluid ounce	fl oz
Cup	c
Pint	pt
Quart	qt
Gallon	gal
Milliliter	ml
Liter	l
Microgram	mcg
Milligram	mg
Gram	g
Kilogram	kg
Avoirdupois ounce	oz
Pound	lb
Degree Celsius	°C
Degree Fahrenheit	°F
Calorie	cal
Kilocalorie	Kcal
Edible portion	E.P.
As purchased	A.P.

Table 8   *Substitution of one ingredient for another*

In place of	Use
1 tablespoon cornstarch	2 tablespoons flour 1⅓ tablespoons minute tapioca 1 tablespoon potato, rice, or arrowroot starches
1 cup corn syrup	1 cup granulated sugar plus ¼ cup liquid
1 cup honey	1¼ cup sugar plus ¼ cup liquid
1 cup sugar	¾ cup honey minus 3 tablespoons liquid
1 ounce chocolate	3 tablespoons cocoa plus 1 tablespoon fat
1 cup butter	1 cup margarine ⅞ cup lard plus ½ teaspoon salt ⅞ to 1 cup hydrogenated shortening plus ½ teaspoons salt
1 cup milk	⅓ cup concentrated milk plus ⅔ cup water ½ cup evaporated milk plus ½ cup water ⅓ cup nonfat dry milk plus water to make 1 cup
1 cup sour milk or buttermilk	1 tablespoon lemon juice or vinegar plus milk to make 1 cup
1 teaspoon baking powder	¼ teaspoon baking soda plus ½ teaspoon cream of tartar ¼ teaspoon baking soda plus ½ fully soured milk ¼ teaspoon baking soda plus ¼ to ½ cup molasses
1 tablespoon dehydrated minced onion	¼ cup finely minced fresh onion
1 teaspoon onion powder	⅓ of a fresh onion
⅛ teaspoon garlic powder	1 clove of garlic
1 tablespoon dehydrated parsley flakes	2 tablespoons fresh minced parsley
1 whole egg	2⅔ tablespoons dried whole egg plus 2⅔ tablespoons water 2 egg whites, or 2 egg yolks; ¼ cup egg substitute
1 egg yolk	2 tablespoons dried egg yolk plus 2 teaspoons water
1 egg white	2 teaspoons dried egg white plus 2 tablespoons water

Table 9   Food yields and measures

Food product	Market unit	Pieces or measure per market unit	Yield	Weight per 237-milliliter cup (g)
Breads:				
Breads	Pound	18 slices, ½ inch	One ⅝-inch slice: fresh = 1 cup crumbs	46
			dry = ⅓ cup crumbs	102
Bread, sandwich	2 pounds	36–40 thin slices		
Bread crumbs, fresh	Pound	8 cups		
Bread crumbs, dry	Pound	4 cups		
Cereals:				
Barley, pearl	Pound	2 cups	1 cup uncooked = 3¾ cups cooked	227
Bulgur wheat	Pound	2¾ cups	1 cup uncooked = 3 cups cooked*	162
Bran, dry	Pound	8 cups		230 / 57
Cornmeal, yellow	Pound	3 cups	1 cup uncooked = 5½ cups cooked	152
Cream of wheat	Pound	2⅔ cups	1 cup uncooked = 4 cups cooked	238
Farina	Pound	3 cups	1 cup uncooked = 5 cups cooked	151
Hominy, whole	Pound	2½ cups		242
Hominy grits	Pound	3 cups	1 cup uncooked = 3⅓ cups cooked	182 / 156
Oats, regular	Pound	6¼ cups	1 cup uncooked = 1¼ cups cooked	236 / 72
Oats, quick	Pound	5⅔ cups	1 cup uncooked = cups 1¾ cups cooked	240 / 80
Rice	Pound	2¼ cups	1 cup uncooked = 3½ cups cooked	200
Tapioca, pearl	Pound	2¾ cups	1 cup uncooked = 2¾ cups cooked	169 / 165
Tapioca, minute	Pound	3 cups		152
Wheat germ	Pound	4 cups		113
Cheese:				
Cheddar, grated	Pound	4 cups		113
Cottage	Pint	2 cups	1 pint = 1 pound	226
Cream	Pound	2 cups	8-ounce package = 1 cup	230
Parmesan, grated, dry	Pound	5 cups	5 ounces = 1 cup	92

Food product	Market unit	Pieces or measure per market unit	Yield	Weight per 237-milliliter cup (g)
Chocolate/cocoa:				
Chocolate, bitter	Pound	16 squares		225
Chocolate, grated	Pound	3½ cups		
Chocolate, melted	Pound	2 cups		
Chocolate, semi-sweet bits, chips	Pound	2⅔ cups	6 ounces = 1 cup	
Cocoa	Pound	4½ cups	8 ounces make 50 cups of beverage	100
Cocoa mix	Pound	1⅔ cups	8 ounces make 28 cups of beverage	139
Coconut:				
Fresh, grated			1 cup = 3 ounces E.P.	80
Flaked	Pound	6 cups	1 cup = 2⅔ ounces	
Dry, shredded	Pound	6 to 7 cups		94
Canned, moist	Pound	5⅓ cups		90
Coffee:				
Coarse ground	Pound	5 to 5½ cups	1 pound makes 40 to 50 cups of infusion	85
Instant	6 ounces	4½ cups	1 ounce makes 10 to 15 cups of infusion	38
Condiments:				
Catsup	14 ounces	1½ cups		273
Chili sauce	14 ounces	1¼ cups, 22 tablespoons		247
Horseradish	1 ounce	2 tablespoons		
Mustard, prepared	1 ounce	4 tablespoons		
Tartar sauce	16 ounces	32 tablespoons		
Crackers:				
Graham	Pound	66 squares	15 squares = 1 cup	
crumbs	Pound	4⅓ cups		86
Snack	10 ounces	130, 1¼ inches square		
Soda	Pound	108, 2 inches square		
Soda	12 ounces	50, 2⅝ inches square		
Soda, crumbs	Pound	6½ cups		70
Cream:				
Half-and-half	Pint	2 cups		242
Whipping	½ pint	1 cup = 2 cups whipped		238
Sour	½ pint			230
Eggs:				
Fresh, whole, without shells:				248

(continued)

Table 9 (continued)

Food product	Market unit	Pieces or measure per market unit	Yield	Weight per 237-milliliter cup (g)
extra large	Dozen	3 cups	1 cup = 4 whole eggs	
large	Dozen	2⅓ cups	1 cup = 5 whole eggs	
medium	Dozen	2 cups	1 cup = 6 whole eggs	
small	Dozen	1¾ cups	1 cup = 7 whole eggs	
Frozen, whole	Pound	1⅞ cups	3 tablespoons + 1 teaspoon = 1 egg	248
Dehydrated, whole sifted	Pound	5¼ cups	2 tablespoons + 2 tea-spoons = 1 egg	86
Fresh, whites:				246
extra large	Dozen	1¾ cups	1 cup = 7 whites	
large	Dozen	1½ cups	1 cup = 8 whites	
medium	Dozen	1⅓ cups	1 cup = 9 whites	
small	Dozen	1¼ cups	1 cup = 10 whites	
Frozen, whites	Pound	1⅞ cups	2 teaspoons = 1 egg white	246
Dehydrated whites, sifted	Pound	5 cups	2 teaspoons = 1 egg white	89
Fresh, yolks:				233
extra large	Dozen	1 cup		
large	Dozen	⅞ cup	1 cup = 14 yolks	
medium	Dozen	¾ cup	1 cup = 16 yolks	
small	Dozen	⅔ cup	1 cup = 18 yolks	
Frozen yolks	Pound	2¼ cups	3½ teaspoons = 1 yolk	233
Dehydrated yolks, sifted	Pound	5½ cups	2 tablespoons = 1 yolk	80
Fats:				
Butter	Pound	2 cups	1 tablespoon = 14 grams	224
Hydrogenated shortening	Pound	2⅓ cups	1 tablespoon = 12 grams	200
Lard	Pound	2 cups	1 tablespoon = 14 grams	220
Margarine	Pound	2 cups	1 tablespoon = 14 grams	224
Oils: corn, cotton-seed, olive, peanut; safflower, soy	Quart	4 cups	1 tablespoon = 13 grams	218

Food product	Market unit	Pieces or measure per market unit	Yield	Weight per 237-milliliter cup (g)
Flours:				
Corn	Pound	4 cups		116
Rice:				
sifted	Pound	3½ cups		126
stirred, spooned	Pound	2⅞ cups		158
Rye:				
dark, sifted	Pound	3½ cups		127
light, sifted	Pound	5 cups		88
Soy:				
full-fat, sifted	Pound	7½ cups		60
low-fat	Pound	5½ cups		83
Wheat				
all-purpose			1 Tbsp = 7 g	
sifted	Pound	4 cups		115
stirred, spooned	Pound	3½ cups		125
instant	Pound	3⅝ cups		129
bread, sifted	Pound	4 cups		112
cake,				
sifted	Pound	4⅝ cups		96
stirred, spooned	Pound	4⅛ cups		111
gluten, sifted	Pound	3¼ cups		142
pastry, sifted	Pound	4½ cups		100
self-rising, sifted	Pound	4 cups		106
whole-wheat, stirred	Pound	3⅓ cups		132
Fruits:				
Apples, fresh	Pound	3 medium		
pared, sliced or diced	Pound	4 cups		109
Applesauce, canned	17 ounces	2 cups		259
Apples, pie-sliced, canned	20 ounces	2½ cups		204
Apples, sliced, frozen	20 ounces	2½ cups		205
Apples, sliced, dried	Pound	4½ cups	1 cup uncooked = 1¾ cups cooked	86
Apricots, fresh	Pound	8 to 12 whole		115
Apricots, canned,				
whole	Pound	8 to 12		225
halves	Pound	12 to 20 halves		217
Apricots, dried			1 cup = 17 halves	
halves	Pound	3 cups	1 cup uncooked = 2 cups cooked	150
Avocados, fresh	Pound	2 medium		
sliced, diced		2½ cups		142
Bananas, fresh	Pound	2 to 4		
sliced	Pound	2 cups		142
mashed	Pound	1⅓ cups		232
Bananas, dried	Pound	4½ cups		100
Blackberries, fresh	Pound	3 cups		146
Blackberries, canned				
canned, pie pack	15 ounces	1¾ cups		225
Blueberries, fresh	Pound	3 cups		146
Blueberries, canned	Pound	1¼ cups drained		170

(continued)

Table 9 *(continued)*

Food product	Market unit	Pieces or measure per market unit	Yield	Weight per 237-milliliter cup (g)
Blueberries, frozen	10 ounces	1¾ cups		161
Cantaloupes	18 ounces	1, 4½-inch diameter 2 cups diced melon		162
Cherries, fresh, red, pitted	Pound	2⅓ cups		154
Cherries, canned	Pound	1½ cups		177
Cherries, frozen	20 ounces	2½ cups		210
Cherries, glacé	Pound	100 to 150 whole	2¼ cups per pound	181
Citron, chopped	Pound	2½ cups		114
Cranberries, fresh	Pound	4 cups		114
Cranberries, canned sauce	Pound	1⅔ cups		278
Currants, dried	Pound	3¼ cups		140
Dates, dried whole	Pound	60 dates		
pitted, cut	Pound	2½ cups		178
Figs, fresh	Pound	12 medium		
Figs, canned	Pound	12 to 16 figs		230
Figs, dried, whole	Pound	44 figs		
cut fine	Pound	2⅔ cups		168
Fruit cocktail salad, canned	17 ounces	2 cups		230
Grapefruit, fresh	Pound	1 medium		
sections	Pound	1 cup		194
Grapefruit, canned sections	Pound	2 cups		241
Grapefruit, frozen sections	13½ ounces	1½ cups		219
Grapes, fresh seeded	Pound	2⅜ cups		184
seedless	Pound	2½ cups		171
Honeydew melon	Pound	⅔ of melon	= 1⅔ cups diced	168
Lemons, fresh	Pound	4 lemons	⅔ cup juice per pound	247
Lemons, fresh	Dozen	2¼ cup juice	1 dozen = 3 pounds	
Limes, fresh	Dozen	1½ cups juice		
Mangoes, fresh	Pound	1¾ cups diced		163
Nectarines	Pound	4 medium		
Oranges, fresh	Pound	2 large	= ⅔ cup juice per pound	247
	Dozen	6 pounds	= 2 cups sections per pound	214
Oranges, mandarin, canned	11 ounces	1¼ cups	with juice	247
Peaches, fresh	Pound	4 medium		
slices	Pound	2 cups		177
Peaches, canned: slices	Pound	2 cups		218
halves	Pound	6 to 10 halves		224
Peaches, dried	Pound	3 cups	1 cup uncooked = 2 cups cooked	160 240

Food product	Market unit	Pieces or measure per market unit	Yield	Weight per 237-milliliter cup (g)
Peaches, frozen				
halves	12 ounces	1⅓ cups		220
Pears, fresh	Pound	4 medium		
sliced	Pound	2 cups		158
Pears, canned	Pound	6 to 10 halves		227
Pineapple, fresh	Pound	½ medium	1½ cups diced fruit per pound	146
Pineapple, canned:				
chunks	20 ounces	1¾ cups		202
crushed	20 ounces	1¾ cups		254
sliced	20 ounces	10 slices		186
Pineapple, frozen				
chunks	13½ ounces	1⅛ cups		208
Plums, fresh	Pound	8 to 20 plums		
halves	Pound	2 cups		185
Plums, canned,				
whole	Pound	10 to 14 plums		223
Prunes, canned	Pound	10 to 14 prunes		196
Prunes, dried,				
whole	Pound	2½ cups	1 cup uncooked = 1¾ cup cooked	176
				229
Raisins, seeded	Pound	2¾ cups		143
Raisins, seedless	Pound	2⅞ cups		146
Raspberries, fresh	Pound	3⅜ cups		144
Rhubarb, raw	Pound	4 cups, 1-inch	1 pound raw =	122
cooked		pieces	2 cups cooked	242
Rhubarb, frozen				
sliced	12 ounces	1½ cups		168
Strawberries, fresh	Pint	2 cups		
whole	Pound	2⅔ cups	1 pint = ¾ pounds	144
sliced	Pound	2⅝ cups		148
Strawberries, frozen				
sliced	10 ounces	½ cup fruit		239
whole	Pound	1⅛ cups		204
Tangerines, fresh	Pound	4 tangerines		
sections	Pound	1¾ cups		193
Watermelon, fresh	Pound	1-inch slice, 6-inch diameter		
diced	Pound	1¼ cups		160
Gelatin:				
Flavored	3 ounces	7 tablespoons		179
Flavored	Pound	2⅓ cups		
Unflavored	Pound	3 cups	1 envelope = ¼ ounce = 1 tablespoon	150

Leavening agents:			grams/ tsp.	grams/ Tbsp.
Leavening agents:				
Baking powder			grams/ tsp.	grams/ Tbsp.
phosphate	12 ounces	1⅔ cups	4.1	12.7
SAS-phosphate	14 ounces	2½ cups	3.2	10.2
tartrate	6 ounces	1¼ cups	2.9	9.2

(continued)

Table 9   (continued)

Food product	Market unit	Pieces or measure per market unit	Yield		Weight per 237-milliliter cup (g)
Baking soda	Pound	2⅓ cups	4.0	12.2	
Cream of tartar	1¾ ounces	5¼ tablespoons	3.1	9.4	
Yeast					
active dry	0.28 ounces	1 tablespoon or envelope	2.5	7.5	
compressed	0.60 ounces	4 teaspoons (1 cake)	4.2	12.8	
Legumes:					
Chickpeas (garbanzos) dried	Pound	2¼ cups	1 cup uncooked = 2¾ cups cooked		200
Cowpeas (black-eyed) dried	Pound	2⅔ cups	1 cup uncooked = 2½ cups cooked		168
Great Northern dried	Pound	2½ cups	1 cup uncooked = 2¾ cups cooked		178 / 170
Kidney beans, dried	Pound	2½ cups	1 cup uncooked = 2¾ cups cooked		186 / 185
Kidney beans, canned	16 ounces	2 cups			180
Lentils, dried	Pound	2¼ cups	1 cup uncooked = 2¼ cups cooked		191 / 202
Lima beans, dried					
large	Pound	2½ cups	1 cup uncooked = 2½ cups cooked		177 / 180
baby	Pound	2⅓ cups	1 cup uncooked = 2 cups cooked		173 / 178
Navy beans, dried	Pound	2½ cups	1 cup uncooked = 2¼ cups cooked		181 / 180
Soybeans, dried	Pound	2¼ cups	1 cup uncooked = 2⅞ cups cooked		210
Split peas, dried	Pound	2¼ cups	1 cup uncooked = 2⅓ cups cooked		203 / 194
Meats (also see Table 22.2):					
Bacon	Pound	15 to 25 slices			
Beef, corned	Pound	9 ounces cooked meat			
Beef, dried	Pound	4 cups	1 cup = 4 ounces		
Beef heart	Pound	6 ounces cooked meat			
Beef liver	Pound	11 ounces cooked meat			
Beef oxtails	Pound	5½ ounces cooked meat			
Caviar, sturgeon:					
canned, granular	4 ounces	7 tablespoons			
canned, pressed	2 ounces	3½ tablespoons			

Food product	Market unit	Pieces or measure per market unit	Yield	Weight per 237-milliliter cup (g)
Chicken, dressed with bone	Pound	1 cup cooked chopped meat		
Clams, fresh shucked	Pound	7 ounces cooked meat		
Clams, canned minced	7½ ounces	1 cup		
Crabs, fresh, cooked in the shell:				
Blue	Pound	2 ounces cooked meat		
Dungeness	Pound	4 ounces cooked meat		
Crabmeat, canned	6½ ounces	5 ounces meat, drained		
Crabmeat, flaked	Pound	6 cups		
Fish, dressed	Pound	8 ounces cooked meat		
Fish fillets, steaks	Pound	10 ounces cooked meat		
Frankfurters	Pound	8 to 10 sausages		
Gelfilte fish, canned	16 ounces	9 ounces drained weight		
Ham, canned: boneless	Pound	12 ounces cooked meat		
with bone	Pound	10 ounces cooked meat		
Ham, picnic: boneless	Pound	12 ounces cooked meat		
with bone	Pound	7 ounces cooked meat		
Luncheon meats	Pound	16 slices	1 slice = 1 ounce	
Mackerel, canned	15 ounces	13 ounces, drained		
Meat, cooked, chopped	Pound	3 cups		
Oysters, fresh, shucked	Pound	7 ounces meat	1 quart = 40 large or 60 small	
Salmon, fresh or frozen steaks	Pound	9 ounces cooked meat		
Salmon, canned	Pound	2 cups		
Sardines, canned	Pound	48, 3 inches long	4 ounces = 12 sardines	
Sausage, links	Pound	14 to 16 small links		
Scallops, fresh, shucked	Pound	10 ounces cooked meat		
Shrimp, fresh, uncooked in shell	Pound	8 ounces cooked meat		

(continued)

Table 9   *(continued)*

Food product	Market unit	Pieces or measure per market unit	Yield	Weight per 237-milliliter cup (g)
Shrimp, small, cleaned	Pound	3¼ cups		
Tuna, cooked	Pound	2 cups		
Tuna, canned	6½ ounces		6 ounces, drained	
Turkey, dressed, with bone	14 pounds	11 to 12 cups chopped, cooked meat		141
Turkey, frozen, boneless	Pound	10 ounces cooked meat		
Milk:				
Fluid, fresh:				
whole, low-fat	Quart	4 cups		244
nonfat, buttermilk	Quart	4 cups		245
Canned, evaporated:				
whole	13 fluid ounces	1⅝ cups		252
skim	13 fluid ounces	1⅝ cups		255
condensed	11 fluid ounces	1⅓ cups		306
Dried:				
Buttermilk	Pound	3¾ cups		120
Nonfat, instant	Pound	6⅔ cups		68
Yogurt	½ Pint	1 cup		227
Nuts:				
Almonds, in shell	Pound	1½ cup meat		
shelled, whole	Pound	3 cups		150
chopped	Pound	3½ cups		127
Brazil nuts:				
in shell	Pound	1⅔ cups		
shelled	Pound	3½ cups		130
Cashews, shelled	Pound	3¼ cups		140
Chestnuts, in shell	Pound	2½ cups		
shelled	Pound	3 cups		150
Coconut, fresh:				
in shell	Pound	1¾ cups		
shelled	Pound	3½ cups		130
Filberts (Hazelnuts):				
in shell	Pound	1½ cups		
shelled	Pound	3⅓ cups		134
Hickory nuts:				
in shell	Pound	5.6 ounces meat		
Macadamia Nuts:				
in shell	Pound	1 cup +		
shelled	Pound	3⅓ cups		133
Peanuts, in shell	Pound	2 cups		
shelled, whole or chopped	Pound	3¼ cups		138
Pecan halves:				
in shell	Pound	2¼ cups		
shelled	Pound	4⅓ cups		105
Pecan pieces:				
in shell	Pound	2 cups		

Food product	Market unit	Pieces or measure per market unit	Yield	Weight per 237-milliliter cup (g)
shelled	Pound	3¾ cups		119
Pine nuts (Piñons):				
in shell	Pound	2 cups		
shelled	Pound	3⅓ cups		136
Pistachios:				
in shell	Pound	2 cups		
shelled	Pound	3¾ cups		119
Walnuts, black, halves:				
in shell	Pound	¾ cup		
shelled	Pound	4 cups		113
Walnuts, black, pieces:				
in shell	Pound	⅔ cup		
shelled	Pound	3½ cups		130
Walnuts, English or Persian, halves:				
in shell	Pound	2 cups		
shelled	Pound	4⅓ cups		102
Walnuts, English or Persian, pieces:				
in shell	Pound	1½ cups		
shelled	Pound	3⅔ cups		125
Pasta:				
Macaroni	Pound	4 cups	1 cup uncooked = 2⅛ cups cooked	123
				201
Noodles	Pound	6 cups	1 cup uncooked = 1½ cups cooked	76
				151
Spaghetti	Pound	4½ cups	1 cup uncooked = 2 cups cooked	71
				181
Pickles and relishes:				
Olives, green, small	Quart	109 to 116 olives		
Olives, ripe, small	Quart	150 olives		
Olives, ripe, large	9 ounces, drained			
sliced		1½ cups		
whole		54 olives		
Pickles, 3 inches long	Pound	3 cups or 36 halves		
Pickles, chopped	Pound	3 cups		148
Pimientos, chopped	Pound	2½ cups		
Pimientos, chopped	4 ounces	6¼ tablespoons	1 cup, chopped = 7 ounces	
Seasonings:				
Allspice	1 ounce	4½ tablespoons		
Celery seed	1 ounce	4 tablespoons		
Chili powder	1 ounce	4 tablespoons		
Cinnamon, ground	1 ounce	4 tablespoons		
Cinnamon, sticks	¾ ounce	4 sticks, 5 inches long		
Cloves, ground	1 ounce	5 tablespoons		
Cloves, whole	3 ounces	1 cup		
Curry powder	1 ounce	4 tablespoons		
Ginger, ground	1 ounce	5 tablespoons		

(continued)

Table 9   (continued)

Food product	Market unit	Pieces or measure per market unit	Yield	Weight per 237-milliliter cup (g)
Ginger, candied	1 ounce	1 piece, 2 inches × 2 inches × ⅜ inch		
Mustard, ground, dry	Pound	4½ cups		
Mustard seed	1 ounce	2½ tablespoons		
Nutmeg, ground	1 ounce	3½ tablespoons		
Paprika	1 ounce	4 tablespoons		
Pepper, ground	1 ounce	4 tablespoons		
Poppy seed	5 ounces	1 cup		
Sage, finely ground	1 ounce	½ cup		
Salt	1 ounce	1½ tablespoons		
Vanilla, extract	½ fluid ounces	1 tablespoon		
Seeds:				
Pumpkin, in husk	Pound	2½ cups seeds		128
husked	Pound	3½ cups		128
Safflower, in husk	Pound	8.2 ounce seeds		
Sesame	Pound	3½ cups	1 oz = 3 Tbsp	128
Sunflower, in husk	Pound	2 cups		
husked	Pound	3½ cups		130
Soups:				
Condensed, canned and frozen	10½ ounces		2½ cups prepared	
Ready-to-serve				
canned	8 ounces		1 cup prepared	
frozen	15 ounces		1½ to 2 cups prepared	
Dehydrated	2¾ ounces		3 cups prepared	
Starches:				
Arrowroot	Pound	4¼ cups		106
Corn, regular	Pound	3½ cups	1 Tbsp = 8.1g	128
Corn, waxy	Pound	3¾ cups	122 g/cup	
Potato	Pound	3¼ cups		142
Rice	Pound	4½ cups		107
Sugars and syrups:				
Corn syrup	Pint	16 fluid ounces	2 cups	328
Honey	Pound	1⅓ cups	22 tablespoons	332
Maple syrup	12 fluid ounces		1½ cups	312
Molasses	12 fluid ounces		1½ cups	309
Sorghum	Pound	1⅓ cups		330
Sugars:				
brown, packed	Pound	2¼ cups		200
granulated, white	Pound	2¼ cups	1 tablespoon = 11 grams	200
confectioner's, sifted	Pound	4½ cups		95
sugar cubes	Pound	76 cubes	1 cube = 1½ teaspoons sugar	

Food product	Market unit	Pieces or measure per market unit	Yield	Weight per 237-milliliter cup (g)
Tea:				
Tea leaves, loose	Pound	6¼ cups	1 cup leaves makes 50 cups infusion	72
Tea, instant	1½ ounces	1¼ cups powder	1 tablespoon powder makes 3 cups infusion	34
Vegetables:				
Asparagus, fresh:				
raw	Pound	16 to 20 spears		
cooked	Pound	2 cups of 1-inch pieces		187
Asparagus, canned	15 ounces	12 to 18 spears		215
Asparagus, frozen	10 ounces	12 to 15 spears		181
Bean sprouts, fresh	Pound	4 cups		113
Beans, green, fresh:				
raw	Pound	3 cups, cut		114
cooked	Pound	2½ cups		125
Beans, green, canned	15 ounces	1¾ cups		135
Beans, green, frozen	9 ounces	1¾ cups, cooked		161
Beets, no tops, fresh				
raw	Pound	6 small, 4 medium		145
cooked, chopped	Pound	2 cups		180
Beets, canned	16 ounces	2 cups		167
Broccoli, fresh				
raw	Pound	2 cups, cooked		164
Broccoli, frozen	10 ounces	1½ cups, cooked		188
Brussel sprouts, fresh:				
raw	Pound	4 cups		102
cooked	Pound	2½ cups		180
Brussel sprouts, frozen	10 ounces	1½ cups	18 to 24 sprouts	
Cabbage, green, red, fresh:				
raw	Pound	4 cups, shredded	½ small head	80
cooked	Pound	2 cups		146
Cabbage, Chinese, fresh:				
raw	Pound	4 cups, shredded	½ head	
cooked	Pound	2 cups		
Carrots, fresh:				
raw, strips	Pound	36 4-inch strips		
raw, sliced	Pound	3 cups		130
raw, diced	Pound	2¾ cups		125
raw, shredded	Pound	3 cups		109
raw, whole	Pound	6 small, 4 medium		
cooked	Pound	2¼ cups		160
Carrots, canned	16 ounces	2 cups		159
Carrots, frozen	10 ounces	1⅝ cups, cooked, drained		165

(continued)

Table 9   (continued)

Food product	Market unit	Pieces or measure per market unit	Yield	Weight per 237-milliliter cup (g)
Cauliflower, fresh:				
raw	Pound	1 small head	2 cups flowerets	104
cooked	Pound	1½ cups		125
Cauliflower,				
frozen	10 ounces	1½ cups, cooked		179
Celery, fresh:				
raw	Pound	1 bunch, medium	3 cups ½-inch pieces	119
raw, diced	Pound	4 cups		121
raw, sticks	Pound	32 4-inch sticks		
cooked, diced	Pound	3 cups		153
Chard, fresh	Pound	1⅜ cups, cooked		191
Collards, fresh	Pound	2⅛ cups, cooked		
Collards, canned	15 ounces	1⅜ cups		
Collards, frozen	10 ounces	1½ cups, cooked		170
Corn, canned:				
cream style	16 ounces	2 cups		249
whole kernel,				
vacuum pack	12 ounces	1½ cups		169
whole kernel,				
liquid pack	16 ounces	1¾ cups		173
Corn, frozen	10 ounces	1¾ cups, cooked		182
Eggplant, fresh:				
raw, diced	Pound	2½ cups		99
cooked	Pound	2½ cups		213
Endive, chicory,				
escarole, fresh,				
raw	Pound	1 large head	4¼ cups pieces	55
Kale, fresh	Pound	2⅝ cups, cooked		
Kale, canned	15 ounces	1⅜ cups		163
Kale, frozen	10 ounces	1⅛ cups, cooked		184
Kohlrabi, fresh	Pound	1¼ cups, cooked		
Lettuce, iceberg	Pound	1 medium head	6¼ cups pieces	70
Lettuce, leaf	Pound	25 leaves for salad garnish		
Lettuce, romaine	Pound	1 medium head	6¼ cups pieces	70
Mushrooms, fresh:				
raw	Pound	2½ cups slices		68
cooked	Pound	2 cups		175
Mushrooms, canned	4 ounces	⅔ cup		161
Mustard greens, fresh,				
trimmed				
cooked	Pound	1½ cups		221
Mustard greens,				
canned	15 ounces	1⅜ cups		
Mustard greens,				
frozen	10 ounces	1⅜ cups		214
Okra, fresh:				
raw	Pound	24 pods	3 cups, sliced	
cooked	Pound	2¼ cups		177
Okra, canned	15 ounces	1¾ cups		171
Okra, frozen	10 ounces	1¼ cups		150
Onions, green,				
fresh, sliced				99
Onions, mature:				
raw	Pound	3 large, 4 medium	2½ cups, chopped	173
			3¾ cups, sliced	113

Food product	Market unit	Pieces or measure per market unit	Yield	Weight per 237-milliliter cup (g)
cooked	Pound	1¾ cups		179
Onions, frozen, chopped	12 ounces	3 cups		
Onions, white pearl	Pound	24 onions	1⅞ cups, cooked	185
Parsley, fresh	1 ounce	½ bunch	5¾ tablespoons, chopped	
Parsnips, fresh	Pound	4 medium	2 cups, cooked	211
Peas, fresh, in pod	Pound	1 cup, shelled		138
Peas, fresh, shelled	Pound	2⅝ cups, cooked	(1 cup raw = 1 cup cooked)	163
Peas, canned	16 ounces	1¾ cups		172
Peas, frozen	10 ounces	1⅝ cups, cooked		167
Peas and carrots:				
canned	16 ounces	1¾ cups		160
frozen	10 ounces	1⅝ cups cooked		174
Peppers, green, fresh	Pound	3 to 6 pods		
raw, sliced	Pound	4 cups		82
raw, chopped	Pound	2⅜ cups		150
cooked	Pound	2⅝ cups		135
Potatoes, fresh	Pound	4 medium		
cooked, diced	Pound	2¼ cups		156
cooked, mashed	Pound	1¾ cups		207
cooked, sliced	Pound	2½ cups		159
Potatoes, canned whole	15 ounces	1½ cups	8 to 12 potatoes	179
Potatoes, dehydrated, flakes	7 ounces	4½ cups flakes		36
		10 cups, reconstituted		212
Potatoes, frozen French fries	9 ounces	1⅝ cups		
Pumpkin, fresh:				
raw	Pound	2½ cups		247
cooked	Pound	1¼ cups		244
Pumpkin, canned	16 ounces	1¾ cups		
Radishes, fresh	Pound	20 to 30 small		
	6 ounces	1 bunch: 10 to 15 radishes = 1¼ cups sliced		114
Rutabagas, fresh	Pound	1 large, 2 medium		
raw, diced	Pound	2½ cups		139
cooked, diced	Pound	2 cups		171
cooked, mashed	Pound	1½ cups		243
Salsify	Pound	1 or 2 bunches	8 salsify	
Sauerkraut, canned	16 ounces	2 cups		142
	27 ounces	3½ cups		
Spinach, fresh; raw, trimmed	Pound	4 to 5 cups leaves		50
cooked	Pound	1½ cups		156
Spinach, canned	15 ounces	1½ cups, drained		221
Spinach, frozen	10 ounces	1¼ cups, cooked, drained		190

(continued)

Table 9   *(continued)*

Food product	Market unit	Pieces or measure per market unit	Yield	Weight per 237-milliliter cup (g)
Sprouts, fresh:				
alfalfa	Pound	10⅓ cups		44
mung bean	Pound	7 cups, raw	7 cups raw = 2½ cups cooked	130
Sprouts, canned	16 ounces	1½ cups, drained		146
Squash, acorn	Pound	1 medium	1 cup, baked in skin	231
Squash, Hubbard:				
cooked, cubed	Pound	1⅛ cups		235
cooked, mashed	Pound	1 cup		244
Squash, summer, fresh:				
cooked, diced	Pound	1¾ cups		205
cooked, mashed	Pound	1⅝ cups		238
cooked, sliced	Pound	2 cups		176
Squash, summer, frozen	10 ounces	1⅜ cups, cooked		
Squash, winter, frozen	12 ounces	1¼ cups		241
Succotash, canned	16 ounces	1⅛ cups, drained		
Succotash, frozen	10 ounces	1⅛ cups, drained		192
Sweet potatoes, fresh	Pound	3 medium		
cooked, mashed	Pound	1½ cups		253
cooked, slices	Pound	1⅞ cups		159
Sweet potatoes, canned:				
syrup pack	29 ounces	2¾ cups		200
vacuum pack	18 ounces	2½ cups		
Sweet potatoes, frozen	12 ounces	3 to 4 potatoes		
Sweet potatoes, dehydrated, flakes	5 ounces			115
reconstituted	5 ounces	1⅝ cups		255
Tomatoes, fresh	Pound	4 small		
raw, diced, sliced	Pound	2¼ cups		181
cooked	Pound	1½ cups		162

Food product	Market unit	Pieces or measure per market unit	Yield	Weight per 237-milliliter cup (g)
Tomatoes, canned	16 ounces	1⅞ cups		238
	28 ounces	3⅜ cups		
Tomato paste	6 ounces	⅔ cup		255
Tomato sauce	8 ounces	1 cup		258
Turnip greens, fresh, partly trimmed	10 ounces	⅝ cups, cooked		
Turnip greens,				
canned	15 ounces	1⅜ cups, drained		159
frozen	10 ounces	1⅛ cups, cooked drained		163
Turnips, fresh	Pound	3 medium		
raw, diced	Pound	5½ cups		127
cooked, diced	Pound	1¾ cups		157
cooked, mashed	Pound	1⅜ cups		228
Watercress fresh	Pound	5 small bunches		
Miscellaneous foods:				
Ice cream	½ gallon	8 cups		133
Ice milk	½ gallon	8 cups		131
Jam	Pound	1⅓ cups		
Jelly	Pound	1½ cups		
Marshmallows	Pound	60 to 80 pieces	16 cut into ⅛ths	
		4 large/oz	= 1 cup	
Potato chips	Pound	5 quarts		
Sherbet	Quart	4 cups		193
Textured vegetable protein:				
fine granules	Pound	5¼ cups		86
coarse granules	Pound	4 cups		113

SOURCE: Calculated from: *Handbook of Food Preparation* (Washington, D.C.: American Home Economics Association, 1971); Kansas State University, Department of Foods and Nutrition, *Practical Cookery* (New York: Wiley, 1966); Bessie B. West, G. S. Shugart, and M. F. Wilson, *Food for Fifty* (New York: Wiley, 1967); U.S. Department of Agriculture, Agricultural Research Service, *Average Weight of a Measured Cup of Various Foods* (Washington, D.C.: Government Printing Office, 1969); U.S. Department of Agriculture, *Family Food Buying,* Home Economics Research Report No. 37 (Washington, D.C.: Government Printing Office, 1969); University of California, Agricultural Extension Service, *Food Yields and Measures* (Berkeley: University of California, 1969).

Table 10   Recommended Daily Dietary Allowances[a]

	Age (years)	Weight (kg)	Weight (lbs)	Height (cm)	Height (in)	Protein (g)	Fat soluble vitamins			Water soluble vitamins							Minerals					
							Vitamin A (μg R.E.)[b]	Vitamin D (μg)[c]	Vitamin E (mg α T.E.)[d]	Vitamin C (mg)	Thiamin (mg)	Riboflavin (mg)	Niacin (mg N.E.)[e]	Vitamin B6 (mg)	Folacin (μg)	Vitamin B12 (μg)	Calcium (mg)	Phosphorous (mg)	Magnesium (mg)	Iron (mg)	Zinc (mg)	Iodine (μg)
Infants	0.0–0.5	6	13	60	24	kg × 2.2	420	10	3	35	0.3	0.4	6	0.3	30	0.5[g]	360	240	50	10	3	40
	0.5–1.0	9	20	71	28	kg × 2.0	400	10	4	35	0.5	0.6	8	0.6	45	1.5	540	360	70	15	5	50
Children	1–3	13	29	90	35	23	400	10	5	45	0.7	0.8	9	0.9	100	2.0	800	800	150	15	10	70
	4–6	20	44	112	44	30	500	10	6	45	0.9	1.0	11	1.3	200	2.5	800	800	200	10	10	90
	7–10	28	62	132	52	34	700	10	7	45	1.2	1.4	16	1.6	300	3.0	800	800	250	10	10	120
Males	11–14	45	99	157	62	45	1000	10	8	50	1.4	1.6	18	1.8	400	3.0	1200	1200	350	18	15	150
	15–18	66	145	176	69	56	1000	10	10	60	1.4	1.7	18	2.0	400	3.0	1200	1200	400	18	15	150
	19–22	70	154	177	70	56	1000	7.5	10	60	1.5	1.7	19	2.2	400	3.0	800	800	350	10	15	150
	23–50	70	154	178	70	56	1000	5	10	60	1.4	1.6	18	2.2	400	3.0	800	800	350	10	15	150
	51 +	70	154	178	70	56	1000	5	10	60	1.2	1.4	16	2.2	400	3.0	800	800	350	10	15	150
Females	11–14	46	101	157	62	46	800	10	8	50	1.1	1.3	15	1.8	400	3.0	1200	1200	300	18	15	150
	15–18	55	120	163	64	46	800	10	8	60	1.1	1.3	14	2.0	400	3.0	1200	1200	300	18	15	150
	19–22	55	120	163	64	44	800	7.5	8	60	1.1	1.3	14	2.0	400	3.0	800	800	300	18	15	150
	23–50	55	120	163	64	44	800	5	8	60	1.0	1.2	13	2.0	400	3.0	800	800	300	18	15	150
	51 +	55	120	163	64	44	800	5	8	60	1.0	1.2	13	2.0	400	3.0	800	800	300	10	15	150
Pregnant						+ 30	+ 200	+5	+ 2	+ 20	+ 0.4	+ 0.3	+ 2	+ 0.6	+ 400	+ 1.0	+ 400	+ 400	+ 150	h	+ 5	+ 25
Lactating						+ 20	+ 400	+5	+ 3	+ 40	+ 0.5	+ 0.5	+ 5	+ 0.5	+ 100	+ 1.0	+ 400	+ 400	+ 150	h	+ 10	+ 50

SOURCE: Food and Nutrition Board, National Academy of Sciences, National Research Council. Revised 1980.

[a] The allowances are intended to provide for individual variations among most normal persons as they live in the United States under usual environmental stresses. Diets should be based on a variety of common foods in order to provide other nutrients for which human requirements have been less well defined.

[b] Retinol equivalents. 1 retinol equivalent = 1 μg retinol or 6 μg β-carotene.

[c] As cholecalciferol. 10 μg cholecalciferol = 400 I.U. vitamin D.

[d] α tocopherol equivalents. 1 mg d-α-tocopherol = 1 α T.E.

[e] 1 N.E. (niacin equivalent) is equal to 1 mg of niacin or 60 mg of dietary tryptophan.

[f] The folacin allowances refer to dietary sources as determined by Lactobacillus casei assay after treatment with enzymes ("conjugases[f]") to make polyglutamyl forms of the vitamin available to the test organism.

[g] The RDA for vitamin B12 in infants is based on average concentration of the vitamin in human milk. The allowances after weaning are based on energy intake (as recommended by the American Academy of Pediatrics) and consideration of other factors such as intestinal absorption.

[h] The increased requirement during pregnancy cannot be met by the iron content of habitual American diets nor by the existing iron stores of many women, therefore the use of 30–60 mg of supplemental iron is recommended. Iron needs during lactation are not substantially different from those of nonpregnant women, but continued supplementation of the mother for 2–3 months after parturition is advisable in order to replenish stores depleted by pregnancy.

Table 11 Estimated safe and adequate daily dietary intakes of additional selected vitamins and minerals[a]

	Age (years)	Vitamins			Trace elements[b]		
		Vitamin K (μg)	Biotin (μg)	Pantothenic acid (mg)	Copper (mg)	Manganese (mg)	Fluoride (mg)
Infants	0–0.5	12	35	2	0.5–0.7	0.5–0.7	0.1–0.5
	0.5–1	10–20	50		0.7–1.0	0.7–1.0	0.2–1.0
Children and adolescents	1–3	15–30	65	3	1.0–1.5	1.0–1.5	0.5–1.5
	4–6	20–40	85	3–4	1.5–2.0	1.5–2.0	1.0–2.5
	7–10	30–60	120	4–5	2.0–2.5	2.0–3.0	1.5–2.5
	11+	50–100	100–200	4–7	2.0–3.0	2.5–5.0	1.5–2.5
Adults		70–140	100–200	4–7	2.0–3.0	2.5–5.0	1.5–4.0

	Age (years)	Trace elements[b]			Electrolytes		
		Chromium (mg)	Selenium (mg)	Molybdenum (mg)	Sodium (mg)	Potassium (mg)	Chloride (mg)
Infants	0–0.5	0.01–0.04	0.01–0.04	0.03–0.06	115–350	350–925	275–700
	0.5–1	0.02–0.06	0.02–0.06	0.04–0.08	250–750	425–1275	400–1200
Children and adolescents	1–3	0.02–0.08	0.02–0.08	0.05–0.1	325–975	550–1650	500–1500
	4–6	0.03–0.12	0.03–0.12	0.06–0.15	450–1350	775–2325	700–2100
	7–10	0.05–0.2	0.05–0.2	0.1–0.3	600–1800	1000–3000	925–2775
	11+	0.05–0.2	0.05–0.2	0.15–0.5	900–2700	1525–4575	1400–4200
Adults		0.05–0.2	0.05–0.2	0.15–0.5	1100–3300	1875–5625	1700–5100

SOURCE: Food and Nutrition Board, National Academy of Sciences, National Research Council. Revised 1980.

[a]Because there is less information on which to base allowances, these figures are not given in Table 10 and are provided here in the form of ranges of recommended intakes.

[b]Since the toxic levels for many trace elements may be only several times usual intakes, the upper levels for the trace elements given in this table should not be habitually exceeded.

Table 12   U.S. Recommended Daily Allowances established by the Food and Drug Administration for nutrient labeling of processed foods[a]

Nutrient	Amount (adults and children)	Nutrient	Amount (adults and children)
Protein	65 g[a]	Vitamin B_6	
Vitamin A	5000 I.U.	(pyridoxine)	2 mg
Vitamin C	60 mg	Folacin	0.4 mg
Thiamin	1.5 mg	Vitamin B_{12}	6 mcg
Riboflavin	1.7 mg	Phosphorous	1 g
Niacin	20 mg	Iodine	150 mcg
Calcium	1 g	Magnesium	400 mg
Iron	18 mg	Zinc	15 mg
Vitamin D	400 I.U.	Copper	2 mg
Vitamin E	30 I.U.	Biotin	0.3 mg
		Pantothenic Acid	10 mg

SOURCE: U.S. Department of Health, Education and Welfare, *FDA Consumer Memo*, Publication No. (FDA) 74-2036 (Washington, D.C.: Government Printing Office, n.d.). May be ordered from: Food and Drug Administration, 5600 Fishers Lane, Rockville, MD 20852.
[a]If protein efficiency ratio of protein is equal to or better than that of casein, U.S. RDA is 45 g.

Table 13   Surface area and dimensions of common baking pans

Dimensions of pan		Surface area	
(in.)	(cm)	(sq in.)	(sq cm)
Round (diameter):			
8	20.3	50	323
9	22.9	64	413
10	25.4	79	510
Square:			
8	20.3	64	412
9	22.9	81	523
Rectangle:			
3 × 7	7.6 × 17.8	21	135
5 × 9	12.8 × 22.9	45	293
4.5 × 11	11.4 × 27.9	49.5	318
6 × 10	15.2 × 25.4	60	387
7 × 11	17.8 × 27.9	77	497
9 × 13	22.9 × 33.0	117	756
10 × 15	25.4 × 38.1	150	968
10.5 × 15.5	26.7 × 39.4	162.75	1052

Table 14   *The pH of some common foods and food ingredients*

pH	Foods
2.2	Lime juice
2.3	Lemon juice
2.8	Loganberries
2.9	Vinegar, plums
3.0	Apple juice, gooseberries
3.1	Apples, boysenberries, currant juice, grapefruit, prunes
3.2	Dill pickles, rhubarb
3.3	Apricots, blackberries
3.4	Strawberries
3.5	Orange juice, peaches
3.6	Raspberries, red sour cherries, sauerkraut
3.7	Blueberries
3.8	Sweet cherries
3.9	Pears
4.0	Grapes, yogurt
4.2	Tomatoes
4.4	Cottage cheese
4.5	Buttermilk or sour milk
5.0	Carrots, pumpkin
5.1	Cucumbers
5.2	Cabbage, molasses, squash, turnips
5.3	Beets, parsnips, snap beans
5.4	Bread, sweet potatoes
5.5	Active yeast, spinach
5.6	Asparagus, cauliflower
5.8	Aged meat, mushrooms
6.0	Flour, tuna
6.1	Evaporated milk, potatoes
6.2	Peas
6.3	Corn, dates, oysters
6.4	Egg yolks
6.6	Fresh milk
6.9	Shrimp
7.0	Baking powder, fresh slaughtered meat, purified water
7.3	Whole eggs
8.0	Baking soda, egg whites

[a]Average pH values; the pH of a given food shows an expected variation of several tenths of a unit from the average.

Table 15   Seasonings and their compatability with foods

Seasoning	Food
Spices:	
Allspice	Fruit cakes, pies, preserves, pickles, sauces and gravies, yellow squashes, tomatoes, stews, beverages
Cayenne pepper	Meats, sauces, eggs, fish, vegetables, Italian meat dishes, Mexican meat dishes
Cinnamon	Pickles, beverages, baked products, puddings, custards, meats, stewed fruits, sweet potatoes
Cloves	Beverages stewed fruit, pickles, cakes, cookies, pies, meat loaves, sauces, tomatoes, beets
Ginger	Cakes, cookies, pies, puddings, pot roast, meat marinades, pickles, meat sauces, carrots, onions
Mace	Cheese rarebit, stewed fruits, pickles, baked products, carrots, cauliflower, spinach, squash, trout
Nutmeg	Beverages, eggnog, baked products, puddings, meat balls, veal, creamed chicken, seafood, spinach
Paprika	Top of casseroles, appetizers, meat loaf, meat balls, salad dressings, cream sauces and gravy
Pepper, black, white	Meat dishes of all kinds, soups, casseroles, sauces, gravies, vegetables, salads
Turmeric	Cream sauces, eggs, marinades for meats, seafood salads, cream soups and chowders
Herbs:	
Basil	Tomato dishes, seafoods, spinach, soups, eggplant, squash, peas, onions, cheese sauces, eggs
Bay leaves	Soups, stews, pot roasts, carrots, custards
Chervil	Soufflés, eggs, lamb, veal, pork, seafood, sauces: verte, vinaigrette, remoulade, bernaise
Dill weed	Cream sauces, seafood, tomato dishes, pickles, green beans, squash, turnips, beets, meats, salads
Marjoram	Soups, sauces, seafood, eggs, mushrooms, carrots, peas, spinach, zucchini, meats, meat stuffings
Mint	Fruit salads, coleslaw, gelatin, beverages, sauces for lamb and veal, frostings, stewed fruits
Oregano	Tomato dishes, salads, zucchini, eggplant, meat loaves, stews, stuffings
Rosemary	Split pea and minestrone soups, salmon, cornbread, biscuits, dumplings, vegetables, poultry, meats, stews, stewed fruits
Saffron	Sweet breads, dumplings, seafood stews and soups, poultry, veal, meat sauces and gravies
Sage	Cream soups and chowders, poultry, sausage, seafood, lima beans, eggplant, onions, tomatoes, meats
Savory, summer	Seafood and lentil soups, salads, pork, poultry, peas, green beans, sauerkraut, rice, cauliflower, zucchini
Tarragon	Salads, seafood, sauces: tartar, egg, mushroom, fish; veal, lamb, poultry, sweetbreads
Thyme	Tomato dishes, clam dishes, seafoods, soups, salads, sauces, onions, carrots, beets
Aromatic seeds:	
Anise	Baked products, seafoods and sauces for seafood, picles, fruit and vegetable salads
Caraway	Cheese rarebits and wafers, meat marinades, coleslaw, tomato, potato or cucumber salads, cooked cabbage, carrots, sauerkraut, turnips, onions, noodles, rice
Cardamom	Beverages, pickles, marinades, pastries, cakes, puddings, stewed fruit, whipped cream, barbecue sauces

Seasoning	Food
Celery	Herb breads and rolls, canapés, meat loaves and patties, tomato aspic, salad dressings, sauces, casseroles
Coriander	Coffee, cake, pies, puddings, cookies, custards, frostings, egg dishes, stewed fruits, meat stuffings, sauces; lentil and bean soups, sweet pickles, sauerkraut
Cumin	Rye bread, sticks, crackers, meat marinades, chili, sausage, sweet pickles, tomato sauces, legumes, carrots, beets, potatoes, eggs, soups, stews
Dill	Cheese and ham canapés, soups and stews, pickles, green beans, cabbages, sauerkraut, squash, turnips
Fennel	Meatballs, meat loaves, pork marinades, pickles, macaroni, potato and crab salads, tomato sauces, lentils, legumes, artichokes
Mustard	Seafood dips, spiced meats, salad dressings, creamed vegetables, casseroles, vegetables
Poppy	Breads, cakes, cookies, cheese and egg dishes, salads, cooked noodles and rice, carrots, celery root, peas, spinach, turnips, cauliflower, potatoes
Sesame	Canapés, breads, chicken, fish, meat loaf and meat balls, cabbage, spinach, green beans, carrots, noodles, rice
Spice and herb blends:	
Apple pie spice	Pies, cookies, cakes, pudding, stewed apples
Barbecue spice	Vegetable-beef and cream soups, baked beans, eggs, meat loaf, meatballs, marinades for pork, poultry, seafood, barbecue sauce, sweet-sour sauce
Chili powder	Chili dishes, cheese and egg dishes, marinades, sauces, soups, corn, legumes, rice
Curry powder	Curries, eggs, cheese, marinades, creamed vegetables, tomato juice, dips, salted nuts, canapés, soups
Italian seasoning	Italian dishes, meat loaf, meatballs, stews, fish, poultry
Lamb seasoning	Lamb roasts, chops, loaves, patties, stews
Mixed herbs	Egg and cheese dishes, vegetables, meats, soups, sauces, gravy, salad dressing, marinades, casseroles
Pickling spice	Pickles of all kinds, relishes, cabbage, seafood, beef broth, stews, gravy
Poultry seasoning	Poultry soups, salads, stuffing for poultry, French fried onion rings, croquettes, baked, broiled, fried, and roast poultry
Pumpkin pie spice	Pies, cookies, cakes, gingerbread, sweet rolls, French fried pumpkin slices
Salad herbs	Fruit cup, vegetable and tomato juices, seafood cocktail, chicken broth, all types of salads, meatloaf, roast, stew, broiled fish
Seafood seasoning	All types of seafood dishes
Seasoned salt	Vegetable juices, soups, salads, meats, vegetables, salads, casseroles, sauces, gravy
Vegetable adjuncts:	
Garlic, powder, salt	Meats, soups, sauces, French, Italian, and Mexican dishes
Horseradish	Pickles, seafood cocktails, dips, spreads, salad dressings, relishes, barbecue sauce, salads
Lemon peel	Sweet breads, cookies, desserts, cakes, sauces, marinades
Mushrooms, dried	Soups, gravies, sauces, casseroles, meats, vegetables
Onion, salt, powdered, minced, flakes	In any dish that specifies fresh onion
Orange peel	Baked products, stewed fruit, puddings, marinades, stuffings for poultry and pork, candied sweet potatoes, glazed carrots, baked squash, rice pilaf
Parsley	Sauces, stuffings, marinades, salads, soups, vegetables
Vegetable flakes, dried	Soups, stews, casseroles

Index

Cholesterol
  implication in atherosclerosis 8
  in eggs and egg substitutes
    (Table 19.1) 336
Chowder 440–441
Clear soups 438–439
Clostridium botulinum 37–40
  in canned foods 509
Club sandwich 451
Coagulation
  of eggs 341
  of milk 315
Cocoa butter 532
Cocoa powder, breakfast 532. *See
  also* Chocolate
Coconuts 422
  composition of (Table 4.1) 81,
    (Table 24.1) 420
Coffee
  acid-free 538
  beans, processing of 538
  brewing of 539–543
  caffeine in 543, 544, (Table 31.3)
    544
  decaffeinated 538
  drip 541
  filtered 542
  grinds 538
  infusions 539
  instant 538
  market forms of 536, 538
  percolated 540
  staleness in 538
  steeped 539–540
  vacuum infusions 540–541
Coffee cake, yeast (Fig. 16.19) 297
Coffee makers
  automatic drip-filter 542–543
  drip 541–542
  filter 542
  percolator 540
  vacuum 540–541
Collagen
  changed to gelatin 391
  effect of heat on 373, 390
  softened by moist heat 397
Collard greens 138, 159, (Fig. 7.2) 129
  nutrients in (Table 7.1) 123
Components of foods 67–74,
    (Table 3.7) 68
Compote, fruit 102
Concentrated milk 313
  economy in use of 326–327,
    (Fig. 18.4) 327
  whipping of (Table 20.1) 359

Condensed milk 314
Condiments 71
Conduction 66
Confectioners sugar. *See* Powdered
  sugar
Connective tissue 373
  in medium tender cuts of meat
    392
  removal before cooking meat
    390
  in seafoods 415
  softened by cooking 390, 397
Consumer awareness 74–77
Controlled atmosphere storage of
  apples 105
  eggs 340
Convection 67
Convenience foods in meal
    planning 550–551
Conventional method of mixing
    cakes 269–270
Cookies 276–282
  baking of 276–277
  bar 279
  drop 277
  filled 280–281
  freezing preservation of 516
  mixing doughs for 276
  molded 280
  nutrients in 282
  pressed 279
  refrigerator 280
  rolled 277–279
  storage of 281–282
Cooking media 64–66. *See also*
    Air, Fat, Steam, Water
Cooking methods 64–66
  dry heat methods of 64, 392–
    397
    baking 64, 148
      at high altitudes 273
    broiling 64, 394–396, 410,
      415, 416
    frying
      deep fat 66, 86–90
      pan 66, 396–397, 411
  microwave oven 50, 67, 148–
    149, 296, 298, 345, 394
  moist heat methods 64–65, 397–
    398
    boiling 64, 146–147
    braising 64, 398, 411–412
    poaching 64, 342–343, 416
    pressure cooking 65, 148, 189,
      398, 427–428, 504–505

Cooking methods (*continued*)
  simmering 64, 398
  steaming 147–148
  stewing 65, 397, 411–412
  stir frying 148
  waterless cooking of vegetables
    148, (Figs. 7.13, 7.14) 149
Cooking of
  angel cakes 368–369
  cereals 186–189
  cheese 330–332
  cocoa 532–533
  coffee infusions 539
  cookies 276–277
  custards 345–348
  eggs 341–344
  fish 415–416
  fruit 103–104
  legumes 426–428
  meat 391–400
  milk 330–332
  pastas 186–189
  pastries 261–262
  pies 253
  poultry 410–412
  pudding 204–205
  quick breads
    biscuits 241
    cream puffs 232
    crepes 234–235
    griddle cakes 234
    muffins 238
    waffles 236
  rice 186–189
  sauces 202–205
  shellfish 415–416
  shortened cakes 271–273
  sponge cakes 368–369
  starch mixtures 200–205
  tea infusions 535–536
  vegetables 126–129, 145–149
  yeast breads 292
Copper
  as a nutrient 15
  as a toxicant 28
  use in cooking utensils 28, 54
Corn
  as a cereal 179–181
    nutrients in (Table 9.2) 192
  fresh, on the cob 137
    nutrients in (Table 7.1) 123
  pigments in 125
  for popping 181
Cornbread 242
Corn flour 212–213